Immigration, Poverty, and Socioeconomic Inequality

Immigration, Poverty, and Socioeconomic Inequality

David Card and Steven Raphael, Editors

The National Poverty Center Series on Poverty and Public Policy

Russell Sage Foundation ◆ New York

The Russell Sage Foundation

The Russell Sage Foundation, one of the oldest of America's general purpose foundations, was established in 1907 by Mrs. Margaret Olivia Sage for "the improvement of social and living conditions in the United States." The Foundation seeks to fulfill this mandate by fostering the development and dissemination of knowledge about the country's political, social, and economic problems. While the Foundation endeavors to assure the accuracy and objectivity of each book it publishes, the conclusions and interpretations in Russell Sage Foundation publications are those of the authors and not of the Foundation, its Trustees, or its staff. Publication by Russell Sage, therefore, does not imply Foundation endorsement.

Library of Congress Cataloging-in-Publication Data

Immigration, poverty, and socioeconomic inequality / David Card and Steven Raphael, editors.
    pages cm. — (National poverty series on poverty and public policy)
  Includes bibliographical references and index.
  ISBN 978-0-87154-498-8 (pbk. : alk. paper) — ISBN 978-1-61044-804-8
(ebook) 1 Immigrants—Social conditions. 2 Children of immigrants—Social conditions. 3 Emigration and immigration—Government policy. 4 Immigrants—Employment. 5 Immigrants—Cultural assimilation I. Card, David. II. Raphael, Steven.
  JV6225.I46 2013
    305.9'06912—dc23   2013008624

RUSSELL SAGE FOUNDATION
112 East 64th Street, New York, New York 10065
10 9 8 7 6 5 4 3 2 1

Contents

Contents

Tables and Figures

About the Authors

DAVID CARD is the Class of 1950 Professor of Economics at the University of California, Berkeley, and director of the Labor Studies Program at the National Bureau of Economic Research.

STEVEN RAPHAEL is professor of public policy at the Goldman School of Public Policy at the University of California, Berkeley.

MARIANNE P. BITLER is associate professor of economics at the University of California, Irvine.

IRENE BLOEMRAAD is associate professor of sociology and the Thomas Garden Barnes Chair of Canadian Studies at the University of California, Berkeley.

SARAH BOHN is research fellow at the Public Policy Institute of California.

CHRISTIAN DUSTMANN is professor of economics and director of the Centre for Research and Analysis of Migration at the University College London, U.K.

MARK ELLIS is professor of geography and director of the Center for Studies in Demography and Ecology at the University of Washington, Seattle.

CYBELLE FOX is assistant professor of sociology at the University California, Berkeley.

TOMMASO FRATTINI is assistant professor of economics at the University of Milan, Italy.

ROBERTO G. GONZALES is assistant professor of education at Harvard University.

HILARY W. HOYNES is professor of economics at the University of California, Davis.

CHRISTEL KESLER is assistant professor of sociology at Barnard College.

JENNIFER LEE is professor of sociology at the University of California, Irvine.

About the Authors

ETHAN LEWIS is an associate professor of economics in the Department of Economics at Dartmouth College.

MAGNUS LOFSTROM is research fellow at the Public Policy Institute of California.

RENEE REICHL LUTHRA is senior research officer in the Institute of Social and Economic Research at the University of Essex.

DOUGLAS S. MASSEY is the Henry G. Bryant Professor of Sociology and Public Affairs at Princeton University.

GIOVANNI PERI is professor of economics at the University of California, Davis.

MICHAEL A. STOLL is professor and chair of public policy at the University of California, Los Angeles, Luskin School of Public Affairs.

MATTHEW TOWNLEY is a Ph.D. student in geography at the University of Washington, Seattle.

ROGER WALDINGER is Distinguished Professor of Sociology at the University of California, Los Angeles.

RICHARD WRIGHT is Orvil Dryfoos Professor of Geography and Public Affairs at Dartmouth College.

MIN ZHOU is professor of sociology and Asian American studies and Walter and Shirley Wang Endowed Chair in U.S.-China Relations and Communications at the University of California, Los Angeles.

Chapter 1

Introduction

David Card and Steven Raphael

The rapid rise in the proportion of foreign-born residents in the United States since the mid-1960s is one of the most important demographic events of the past fifty years. As a consequence of this immigrant surge the country has become more diverse linguistically, culturally, socioeconomically, and perhaps politically. The increasing relative size of the immigrant population raises many key questions for understanding trends in U.S. poverty rates and inequality. To begin, immigration has altered the demographic composition of the nation, increasing the proportion foreign-born, the proportion of the resident population with extremely low levels of education, as well as the proportion with relatively high levels of educational attainment. These compositional effects alone have likely impacted overall U.S. poverty rates.

Second, immigrants supply new skills and compete for jobs in the U.S. labor market. The additional workers brought to the United States via immigration may impact the wages and employment levels of the native born, and in turn the likelihood that natives experience poverty through multiple channels. For natives most similar to immigrants in terms of their labor market skills, competition with immigrants may suppress wages and employment and increase poverty. Alternatively, natives whose skills are sufficiently different from those of immigrants may find their wages and employment rates enhanced by the presence of immigrants with skills that complement their own in the workplace. Immigrants may also bring investment capital to the United States either directly through personal savings and investment or indirectly through their very presence attracting international capital flows, a factor that would improve employment prospects and diminish poverty generally in the United States.

Third, new immigration flows may impact poverty rates among previous immigrants. Newly arrived immigrants and immigrants with some tenure in the United States are perhaps most likely to be in direct competition with one another in the U.S. labor market. Moreover, immigrant communities tend to geographically cluster in enclaves. To the extent that such geographic clustering provides ready social networks rich with information on negotiating U.S. institutions and finding work, the existence of enclaves may increase employment and reduce poverty among newer immigrants. On the other hand, such geographic clusters may inhibit English-language acquisition and perhaps make immigrants less willing to migrate internally for jobs in cities and states with smaller co-national populations.

Finally, over time immigration has and will continue to alter the demographic composition of the native born population, raising the fractions of people with Hispanic and Asian origin. The effects of these changes on overall poverty rates depend critically on the extent to which the children of immigrants climb the socioeconomic ladder. In general, the children of immigrants, especially immigrants from countries with low levels of educational attainment, tend to achieve educational attainment levels that greatly exceed those of their parents. Moreover, English-language acquisition in the 1.5 and second generation is nearly universal. However, there are important differences across national-origin groups in outcomes among the 1.5 and second generations, some of which may be culturally determined and others driven by specific policies that impact select groups within the United States.

This discussion highlights the complexities and subtleties of the relationship between recent U.S. immigration trends and the nation's poverty rate. In addition to the mediating role of economic forces operating through the channels of labor market competition and overall economic growth, the extent to which recent immigration trends enhance or diminish the nation's poverty rate depends on immigrant cultural practices brought to the United States, the cultural development of immigrant communities within the United States, as well as specific assimilation trajectories experienced by immigrants in different national-origin communities. Moreover, all of these avenues may be exacerbated or assuaged by policy governing antipoverty programs, education, the civil rights of the unauthorized, and immigration flows more generally.

The chapters in this volume are devoted to studying these various economic, social, and policy factors that may link immigration to poverty among immigrants themselves and among the native born. The contributors to this volume represent a multidisciplinary research team assembled with the specific aim of employing complementary methodological approaches to flesh out the relationship between immigration and poverty in the United States. In this volume, our authors employ microeconomic theoretical and empirical analysis, detailed demographic analysis of census data, ethnographic methods, historical policy analysis, as well as detailed investigations of the consequence of specific policy interventions with the aim of achieving a better understanding of the immigration/poverty nexus.

The research contributions can be grouped into four main categories: the impact of immigration on poverty operating through composition, labor market competition, and geographic segregation; immigration, poverty, and intergenerational mobility; public policy and poverty among the foreign born; and the relative socioeconomic status of immigrants in Europe. In the following sections, we provide a detailed summary of the various chapters, interwoven with some basic empirical analysis documenting recent trends in immigration and poverty in the United States.

COMPOSITION, COMPETITION, AND THE GEOGRAPHY OF IMMIGRANT POVERTY

Table 1.1 documents recent trends in the foreign-born share of the U.S. population, and the associated shifts in the composition of the population.[1] Between 1970 and 2009, the immigrant population increased from roughly 5 to 13 percent of the U.S. resident population. Classifying the foreign-born population into recent immigrants (those arriving within the last five years) and earlier immigrants, the fraction of recent arrivals rose from 18 to 24 percent between 1970 and 2000, but has fallen back in recent years as immigrant inflow rates have stabilized and declined. The table also reveals an important long-term effect of immigration: the changing ethnic composition of the native-born population. Specifically, the fraction of Hispanics among the native born increased from 3 to 12 percent between 1970 and 2010, and the proportion of Asians increased from 0.5 to 3 percent.

Focusing on the overall increase in the immigrant share masks large internal changes in the composition of the immigrant population over the past forty years. Latin American immigrants accounted for 19 percent of the foreign born in 1970 but 53 percent in 2009. We also observe a large increase over this period in the proportion of the immigrant population from Asian countries: approximately 7 percent in 1970 versus 26 percent in 2009. In contrast, the proportion of the immigrant population from European nations declined dramatically. Europeans made up 52 percent of immigrants in 1970, but only 10 percent in 2009.

The patterns documented in table 1.1 suggest two obvious pathways linking immigration to poverty in the United States. First, to the extent that immigrants are more likely to experience poverty than the native born, the higher proportion of foreign born will mechanically increase the national poverty rate. Second, to the extent that immigrants suppress the wages of the native born, immigration may elevate poverty rates among the native born and for the nation overall.

Regarding the first avenue, it is true that immigrants experience relatively high poverty rates. Figure 1.1 presents poverty rates for all U.S. residents and for the native born and foreign born separately from 1970 through 2009. Overall poverty rates declined modestly between 1970 and 2000 (from 14 percent to 12 percent), but increased sharply by 2009 (to 15.4 percent) with the onset of the recent recession. Poverty rates for the native-born population closely track the national averages, a fact that is not surprising given that natives still constitute 87 percent of the resident population at the end of the period. Among immigrants, poverty rates are distinctly higher each year. Moreover, relative immigrant poverty rates increased markedly between 1970 and 2000, and somewhat further over the past decade.

The increase in poverty among immigrants is driven mostly by the changing national-origin composition of the foreign born. This becomes evident when the

TABLE 1.1 / Distribution of the U.S. Resident Population

	1970	1980	1990	2000	2009
Foreign-born status of U.S. residents					
Native born	95.18	93.82	92.03	88.82	87.10
Immigrant	4.82	6.18	7.97	11.18	12.90
Immigrant arrival group					
Recent (≤five years)	17.54	23.85	24.85	24.37	17.37
Later (>five years)	82.46	76.15	75.15	75.63	82.54
Ethnicity of native–born					
Non-Hispanic white	84.50	81.61	81.52	76.67	70.31
Non-Hispanic black	11.43	11.94	10.50	11.71	13.72
Non-Hispanic Asian	0.50	0.69	1.07	2.11	3.01
Non-Hispanic other	0.42	0.74	0.99	1.39	1.11
Hispanic	3.15	5.02	5.91	8.10	11.84
Country of origin of immigrants					
Canada	9.60	6.13	4.12	2.90	2.07
Latin America					
Mexico	8.22	15.82	22.77	30.74	29.45
Central America	1.21	2.54	5.52	6.46	7.49
Caribbean	7.05	9.12	9.08	9.09	9.35
South America	2.71	4.08	5.18	5.93	6.87
Europe					
Western[a]	40.94	26.27	16.37	9.99	6.73
Eastern[b]	11.36	6.58	4.22	3.48	3.00
Russian Empire	6.09	3.51	1.99	2.79	2.82
Asia					
East	4.31	6.84	8.90	8.63	9.30
Southeast	1.74	6.60	10.13	9.89	9.47
India/SW	0.92	2.79	4.13	5.45	7.16
Middle East	1.33	2.02	1.95	1.71	1.85
Africa	0.63	1.35	1.54	2.50	3.92
Oceania	0.43	0.58	0.53	0.53	0.45
Other	3.45	5.77	3.57	0.00	0.06

Source: Authors' tabulations of microdata from the 1970, 1980, 1990, and 2010 One Percent Public Use Microdata Sample of the U.S. Census of Population and Housing and the 2000 American Community Survey.
[a]Excludes Warsaw Pact Countries plus the components of the former Yugoslavia.
[b]Includes former Warsaw Pact countries plus the components of the former Yugoslavia.

increase in poverty overall among the foreign born is contrasted with poverty rates for specific immigrants groups. Table 1.2 presents poverty rates for 1970 through 2009 for immigrant groups by region of origin. For the most part, poverty rates are fairly stable within each group after 1980, or even declining (for Southeast Asians in particular). Hence, an increase in poverty within specific national-origin

FIGURE 1.1 / U.S. Poverty Rates

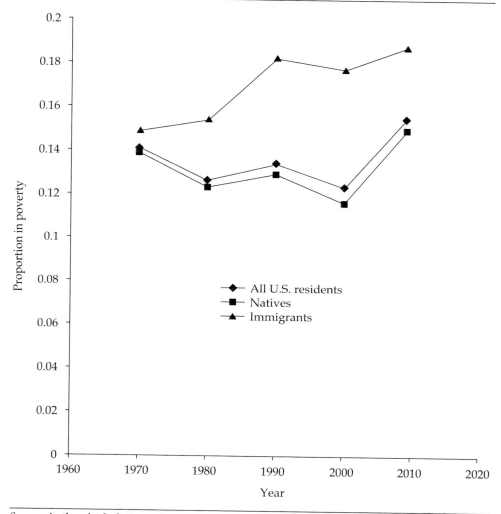

Source: Authors' tabulations of microdata from the 1970, 1980, 1990, and 2010 One Percent Public Use Microdata Sample of the U.S. Census of Population and Housing and the 2000 *American Community Survey.*

groups cannot explain the higher poverty rates among immigrants today relative to past decades. On the other hand, table 1.2 also reveals higher poverty rates among immigrant groups that have come to comprise larger proportions of the immigrant population (for example, immigrants from Mexico, Central America, and Asia) and lower poverty rates among immigrant groups whose relative share in the immigrant population is declining (for example, European immigrants).

TABLE 1.2 / Poverty Rates Among Immigrants

	1970	1980	1990	2000	2009
North America	0.090	0.080	0.081	0.076	0.091
Latin America					
Mexico	0.292	0.264	0.294	0.265	0.281
Central America	0.159	0.206	0.224	0.199	0.211
Caribbean	0.147	0.164	0.186	0.175	0.193
South America	0.145	0.153	0.146	0.155	0.129
Europe					
Western[a]	0.126	0.085	0.081	0.078	0.083
Eastern[b]	0.143	0.089	0.092	0.117	0.098
Russian Empire	0.161	0.149	0.197	0.196	0.157
Asia					
East	0.134	0.127	0.156	0.151	0.153
Southeast	0.162	0.198	0.184	0.122	0.117
India/SW	0.146	0.172	0.124	0.110	0.113
Middle East	0.143	0.201	0.195	0.183	0.261
Africa	0.125	0.204	0.149	0.176	0.213
Oceania	0.119	0.159	0.161	0.121	0.099
Other	0.208	0.231	0.247	—	0.364

Source: Authors' tabulations of microdata from the 1970, 1980, 1990, and 2010 One Percent Public Use Microdata Sample of the U.S. Census of Population and Housing and the 2000 American Community Survey.
[a]Excludes Warsaw Pact Countries plus the components of the former Yugoslavia.
[b]Includes former Warsaw Pact countries plus the components of the former Yugoslavia.

This suggests that the changing internal composition of the immigrant population is the likely driver of the immigrant poverty trends documented in figure 1.1.

To summarize the relative importance of changes in within-group poverty rates and changes in the internal composition of the U.S. resident population in driving national poverty trends, table 1.3 presents the results from various decompositions of the change in national poverty rates. The first set of results decomposes changes between various starting years and 2004, a relatively low-poverty year. The second decomposes changes from the same base years to 2009, in the midst of the Great Recession. For each interval, the entry in the first column shows the actual change in the national poverty rate. The second column shows the contribution of changing population shares to the poverty change (assuming that each group had constant poverty rates).[2] The third column presents the contribution of changes in the group-specific poverty rates between the base and end years.

Between 1970 and 2004, the overall poverty rate declined by roughly 1 percentage point. Behind this modest decline, changes in the composition of the population (defined by nativity, ethnicity, and country of origin) actually caused a 1.15 percentage point increase in poverty, which was offset by a decline in poverty rates for each group that averaged roughly 2.1 percentage points. Hence, the de-

TABLE 1.3 / Decomposition of Changes in National Poverty Rates

	National Poverty Rate	Population Shares	Group–Specific Poverty Rates
1970 to 2004	−0.94	1.15	−2.09
1980 to 2004	0.56	0.63	−0.07
1990 to 2004	−0.01	0.54	−0.56
2000 to 2004	0.90	−0.28	1.18
1970 to 2009	1.43	2.27	−0.84
1980 to 2009	2.94	1.70	1.24
1990 to 2009	2.36	1.61	0.75
2000 to 2009	3.28	0.84	2.44

Source: Authors' tabulations of microdata from the 1970, 1980, 1990, and 2010 One Percent Public Use Microdata Sample of the U.S. Census of Population and Housing and the 2000 and 2005 American Community Survey.

Notes: The decompositions above are calculated as follows. Let w_{it} be the proportion of the U.S. population at time t accounted for by group i, where the index i encompasses the native born and each of the country-of-origin groups listed in Tables 1.1 and 1.2. In addition, define *poverty*$_{it}$ as the corresponding poverty rate for group i in year t. The national poverty rate for 1970 and 2004 can be expressed as a weighted sum of the group-specific poverty rates:

$$poverty_{1970} = \sum_{i=1}^{I} w_{i1970} poverty_{i1970}, \quad poverty_{2004} = \sum_{i=1}^{I} w_{i2004} poverty_{i2004}.$$

The change in poverty rates can be expressed by

$$\Delta Poverty = \sum_{i=1}^{I} w_{i2004} poverty_{i2004} - \sum_{i=1}^{I} w_{i1970} poverty_{i1970}.$$

Adding and subtracting the term $\sum_{i=1}^{I} w_{i1970} poverty_{i2004}$ to equation (2) and factoring give the decomposition

$$\Delta Poverty = \sum_{i=1}^{I} (w_{i2004} - w_{i1970}) poverty_{i2004} + \sum_{i=1}^{I} w_{i1970} (poverty_{i2004} - poverty_{i1970}).$$

The first component on the right-hand side shows the contribution to the poverty change associated with the shift in population shares between 1970 and 2004. This component is reported in the second column of the table. The second component represents the contribution of changes in group-specific poverty rates between 1970 and 2004 holding the population shares constant at 1970 levels. This component is reported in the third column of the table.

composition suggests that if one were to roll back the demographic composition to 1970, the poverty rate in 2004 would have been an additional 1.15 percentage points lower. Relative to an overall poverty rate for 2004 of 13.8 percent, this suggests that eliminating the post-1970 wave of immigrants, and thereby stabilizing the various population groups' shares, would only reduce poverty by about 10 percent. The contributions of changes in the population composition using other base years are generally smaller, and between 2000 and 2004 are actually slightly negative.

Our decomposition results relative to 2009 show larger overall increases in poverty associated with the Great Recession, but again relatively small contributions of population composition changes. This is most clearly evident in the decomposition between 2000 and 2009. In this interval, changes in population composition increased poverty by 0.84 percent. Increases in poverty rates for each of the groups associated with the Great Recession contributed a much larger 2.44 percentage points to the rise in the national poverty rate.

Overall these decomposition results suggest that immigration does contribute modestly to U.S. poverty rates through compositional effects. Nevertheless, most poverty in the United States is not explained by immigration trends. Of course, this conclusion rests on the assumption that immigration has no general equilibrium effects on native poverty rates, operating through labor market competition between new immigrants and existing residents. This is the fundamental issue Giovanni Peri addresses in chapter 2.

At first blush, the basic proposition prompting Peri's analysis is relatively simple. To the extent that competition with immigrants suppresses the wages of native workers, immigration will reduce household income. This in turn should increase the likelihood that the native born, especially less educated native-born workers with income levels in the neighborhood of the federal poverty line, will fall into official poverty. Reality, however, is not so simple.

To start, the effects of labor market competition with immigrants on wages depends on a number of factors and can be either positive or negative. The direction of these effects for a particular native skill group will depend on the degree to which employers can substitute immigrants of various skill levels for native workers as well as possible complementarity or substitutability that may exist between workers of different skill levels. For example, the effect of an influx of immigrants with less than a high school diploma on the wages of comparatively educated natives would be large if such workers are perfect substitutes in production. Alternatively, the effects of such an inflow on less-educated natives may be negligible if employers cannot substitute such workers for natives because of poor English-language ability among the foreign born. Moreover, the effect of such an inflow will depend as well on the degree to which workers with less than a high school education can be substituted for those with a diploma. To the extent that this is true, the labor market shock associated with a concentrated increase in foreign-born workers with little education will be dissipated across a larger native labor pool and thus result in smaller wage declines.

Aside from substitution possibilities, high-skilled immigration into the United States may actually increase the demand for the low-skilled labor of the native born at greatest risk of experiencing poverty. Specifically, to the extent that high-skilled immigrants are complements for low-skilled workers in production, or demand goods and services produced by low-skilled natives, such immigration may—all else being equal—actually alleviate poverty among natives. In general, the skill distribution of immigration is a key factor in the overall and distributional effects of immigration on the native wage distribution. Balanced immigration flows (in terms of skill) should have little impact on the native wage distribution, whereas immigration flows biased toward a specific skill group will have disproportionately adverse effects on natives with comparable skills.

Peri simulates the effects of net migration during the 1990s and 2000s on the native wage distribution using a structural model of the economy and assuming parameter values characterizing the degree of substitutability between different skills groups that spans the existing literature on the wage effects of immigration. He then uses the simulated wage effects to construct a counterfactual native household income distribution that reverses net migration over the past two decades. A comparison of poverty rates using this distribution to actual poverty rates provides a gauge of the effect of competition with immigrants on native poverty.

The principal findings from the analysis are as follows. First, Peri documents a new stylized fact regarding the skill content of migration flows over the past two decades. Migration during the 1990s was heavily biased toward low-skilled immigrants, but the relative skill level of immigrants rose from 2000 to 2009. This is evident in both national data as well as state-specific and MSA-specific tabulations.

Second, Peri's simulations show relatively modest effects of immigration on native wages, even using relatively extreme values for the substitution parameters that would tend to yield the largest adverse effects of immigration on native wages. In fact, his analysis suggests that new migration inflows from 2000 to 2009 likely increased the wages of low-skilled natives, holding all else equal. Finally, in nearly all his model simulations, the labor market competition effects of immigration on native poverty rates are negligibly small, and suggest that immigration reduced native poverty from 2000 to 2009. When compared with actual changes in poverty for vulnerable native groups over the two decades analyzed, the contributions of immigration to poverty (or detractions as may be the case) are minuscule. This is true nationally as well as for key immigration destination states and metropolitan areas.

Although new immigrant inflows have negligible effects on native poverty, new low-skilled migration does appear to suppress the wages of previous low-skilled migrants, and by extension to raise poverty rates among the overall foreign-born population. This suggests that even within well-defined skills groups, defined by age, gender, and education, immigrants tend to work in labor markets that are somewhat segmented from those of native workers.

In chapter 3, Ethan Lewis assesses the degree to which limited English-language ability separates the foreign born in the United States into relatively isolated segments of the labor market. Lewis begins with a review of the large body of empirical research on labor market competition between the native born and the foreign born that establishes two stylized facts. First, immigration to the United States has had a relatively small impact on the average wages of native born Americans. Second, the limited impact of competition with immigrants is due in part to imperfect substitutability between native and immigrant workers in the U.S. economy. The inability of employers to perfectly substitute foreign-born workers for native-born workers shields the native born from immigrant competition, limiting the effect of immigration on wages and by extension, poverty among the native born. On the other hand, employers are better able to substitute new immigrants for previous immigrants. Hence, labor market pressures from new immigrant flows disproportionately affects immigrants already in the United States.

Lewis sets out to assess whether English-language ability is the key factor driving the imperfect substitutability between immigrants and natives. The chapter begins by documenting the large disparities in average earnings for immigrants and natives with similar levels of educational attainment and work experience. Lewis demonstrates that these earnings differential are almost entirely attributable to self-reported differences in English-language ability.

Lewis then turns to an analysis of substitutability between immigrants and natives. The principal results of this chapter derive from estimating a relatively simple empirical relationship. To be specific, if immigrants and natives are imperfect substitutes for one another, then an increase in the relative supply of immigrants, as measured by the ratio of immigrant hours worked to native hours worked in a given metropolitan area, should negatively affect the relative wages of immigrants. This follows from the fact that an increase in immigrant supply will have a larger effect on the wages of immigrants than those of natives, thus suppressing immigrant relative wages. On the other hand, if immigrants and natives are perfectly substitutable, an increase in the relative supply of immigrants will suppress the wages of both natives and immigrants equally. Under this scenario, no empirical relationship between relative wages and relative labor supply would exist.

Lewis uses this insight to assess whether immigrants with stronger English-language ability are more substitutable for otherwise similar natives than their counterparts are. He tests this proposition using several alternative gauges of English ability. First, he estimates the effect of relative immigrant supply and relative immigrant earnings for different groups of immigrants based on self-reported language ability, exploiting cross-metropolitan area and cross-time period variation in relative supply. These results show decisively that relative wages are much more responsive to relative supplies among immigrants with poor English relative to immigrants with strong English-language ability. Lewis also finds greater sensitivity of relative wages among immigrants with higher levels of educational attainment. This is a reasonable result, as one would expect language ability to be particularly important in jobs requiring greater skill.

Second, Lewis tests for differential substitutability between natives and different subgroups of immigrants, based on their age of arrival and time in the United States. The basic insight here is that immigrants who arrive at younger ages speak better English, as do immigrants who have been in the country for relatively longer periods. The results are as one would expect. The degree of substitutability between natives and the foreign born is greater when natives are compared with those who arrived at younger ages and who have been in the country longer than with those who arrived at older ages and have only recently arrived.

Finally, Lewis tests for imperfect substitution in a national context where immigrants and natives differ little in their ability to speak the principal language. Specifically, exploiting variation in relative supplies across groups defined by educational attainment and experience, he tests whether immigrants to Puerto Rico (most of whom are from Spanish-speaking Latin America) and native-born Puerto

Ricans are imperfect substitutes. Here, Lewis finds no relationship between relative supplies and relative wages. In parallel regression results estimated for the United States, the imperfect substitutability between immigrants and native emerges.

Overall, this chapter addresses and partially resolves a long-standing puzzle in the immigration literature. A key source of imperfect substitutability between native and foreign-born residents of the United States is differences in language ability. This limits the impact of immigration on the wages and poverty rates of native-born residents. However, it also implies that previous immigrants are indeed harmed through economic competition with more recent immigrants.

The relatively intense labor market competition between old and new immigrants suggests that immigrants may be harmed by their geographic concentration in specific states and metropolitan areas. Moreover, within metropolitan areas, immigrants tend to locate in older neighborhoods with a high fraction of black and Hispanic residents—a pattern that tends to alter the social geography of residential patterns within cities and suburbs across the country. In chapter 4, Michael Stoll studies the degree to which the foreign born are residentially segregated in U.S. metropolitan areas, and investigates several possible ramifications of segregation for both immigrants and natives.

The chapter begins with an analysis of segregation patterns using recent data from the American Community Survey. Although immigrants as a whole are fairly segregated from native-born whites, heterogeneity across groups is significant, with Southeast Asian and Latin American immigrants showing particularly high levels of residential segregation. One interesting finding in this chapter concerns the pattern of cross-metropolitan area heterogeneity in the degree of immigrant segregation. In particular, immigrants who migrate to U.S. cities with historically high levels of segregation between native-born whites and blacks tend to be more segregated from whites than those who migrate to areas with historically low levels of black-white segregation. Stoll speculates that this pattern reflects cross-area differences in what he calls "segregation infrastructure," referring to the collective effects of historical differences in land-use patterns, real estate practices, race relations, and other social and economic factors that have tended toward separating the spatial residential distributions of blacks and whites.

Building on this finding, Stoll explores whether greater immigrant segregation is associated with poor English-language skills among the foreign born, and whether any such association can be interpreted as a causal effect of segregation or simply self-selection of the linguistically isolated into ethnic enclaves. Indeed, the cross-metro area correlation is strong between the proportion of the foreign born with poor English skills and the degree of residential segregation between immigrants and whites. This relationship is particularly strong for Asian and Latin American immigrants and survives after controlling for observable metropolitan area physical and economic characteristics.

Moreover, Stoll presents evidence strongly suggesting a causal effect of segregation on linguistic isolation. Making use of the relationship between current immigrant-white segregation and historical measures of black-white segregation, Stoll estimates a series of IV models in which the key dependent variable is the proportion of immigrants with poor English skills, and the main explanatory variable is the dissimilarity segregation score between immigrants and native-born whites. The black-white dissimilarity score measured in 1990 (roughly a decade and a half before the period analyzed in this chapter) is used as an instrument for immigrant-native dissimilarity. The results from these models are nearly identical to the results from simple bivariate regressions.

In conjunction with Lewis's analysis in chapter 3, Stoll's research identifies a clear avenue through which spatial concentration may harm the labor market prospects of immigrants and isolate them from the broader national labor market. An alternative link between immigrants' locations and their labor market outcomes may arise through their choices of metropolitan areas. Although traditional destination cities offer new immigrants a denser social network and an instant community of compatriots, such destinations may have relatively poor labor market opportunities due to the intensified competition for jobs among linguistically isolated immigrant workers. New destination cities, by comparison, may offer superior employment opportunities at the expense of weaker social networks. In chapter 5, Mark Ellis, Richard Wright, and Matthew Townley analyze immigrants' location choices with an eye on the net contribution to immigrant poverty rates.

During the latter half of the twentieth century, most immigrants to the United States settled in a handful of metropolitan areas in California, Illinois, Florida, and the New York Consolidated Metropolitan Statistical Area (which includes parts of New Jersey and Connecticut). These traditional gateway cities remain important and still account for a disproportionate share of the nation's foreign born, but the array of geographic destinations has broadened. Over the past fifteen years, many areas that previously received few immigrants have become important destinations. These include smaller metropolitan areas as well as new areas of the country, such as the South.

An interesting empirical puzzle is that immigrants residing in these new destination cities earn higher wages and have lower poverty rates than their counterparts in traditional gateways. This pattern may reflect superior employment opportunities in these new destinations, selective in-migration of lower poverty immigrants, or some combination of both factors. Ellis, Wright, and Townley begin chapter 5 by documenting the large variation across metropolitan areas defined as either traditional-continuing gateway or emerging immigrant destinations in native and immigrant household poverty rates. They then go on to develop a decomposition method that allows them to distinguish what they call a "metropolitan context effect" from simple demographic composition effects. The metropolitan context effect essentially summarizes the net impact of the local economy on poverty among immigrants and natives, after taking account of the observable human capital and family structure characteristics of the local population. Comparing average metro-context effects across different metropolitan areas makes it possible to discern whether newer destination cities provide better opportunities to immigrants than traditional gateways.

The authors then use the metropolitan area composition results to characterize the sources of variation in immigrant and native poverty rates across all metropolitan areas. To be specific, cross-area difference in poverty rates can come from either difference in demographics, difference in metro-context effects, or the covariance between these two sets of determinants. Decomposition results are provided for both immigrants and natives for 2000 and 2007–2009 periods.

The authors reach several interesting conclusions. First, evidence is clear of more favorable metro-context effects for immigrants in the emerging destinations metropolitan areas, as well as of unfavorable metro-context effects in the traditional gateway areas. The cross-metropolitan area variability in these effects, however, narrows with the onset of the Great Recession. Second, for both immigrants and natives, metro-context effects provide the greatest contribution to cross-area variance in poverty rates, dwarfing the effects of variability in demographic characteristics in both years analyzed. Finally, the sorting of immigrants with more positive demographic characteristics (that is, those associated with higher income and lower poverty) to cities with higher metro-context effects increased substantially over the decade of the 2000s. As a result, when the Great Recession hit, the immigrant populations in many low-wage cities were particularly vulnerable to the risk of rising poverty. For natives, we observe the opposite pattern.

Taken together, the four chapters in this section suggest that immigration has had relatively small impacts on native poverty. However, residential crowding in specific metropolitan areas, linguistic isolation which in turn is reinforced by residential concentrations, and disproportion concentration of immigrants in traditional gateway cities have all contributed to the relatively high poverty rates experienced by immigrants themselves.

A key long-term outcome of concern that may also be impacted by these factors is the relative socioeconomic status of the children from these immigrant communities. One can imagine several avenues through which a dense social network of co-ethnics and pan-ethnics can serve to propel or retard socioeconomic mobility across generations. This is precisely the subject of the following three chapters.

INTERGENERATIONAL MOBILITY WITHIN IMMIGRANT COMMUNITIES

The long-term consequences of higher immigration for U.S. poverty levels depend on the degree to which immigrants rise out of poverty with time in the United States, and the likelihood that the children of immigrants experience poverty in adulthood. Regarding the relationship between poverty and time in the United States, the evidence in table 1.4 shows that poverty among immigrants tends to fall with time in the United States. The table presents poverty rates for specific immigrant arrival cohorts at different points in time—for example, the poverty rate for

TABLE 1.4 / Immigrant Poverty Rates by Census and Arrival Years

Year of first arrival	Census Year				
	1970	1980	1990	2000	2009
A: All immigrants					
1965–1970	0.180	0.123	0.108	0.103	0.103
1975–1980	–	0.279	0.163	0.131	0.126
1985–1990	–	–	0.303	0.179	0.158
1995–2000	–	–	–	0.278	0.166
2005–2009	–	–	–	–	0.280
B: Immigrants age 18 to 34 in census year immediately following arrival					
1965–1970	0.168	0.104	0.095	0.095	0.098
1975–1980	–	0.270	0.148	0.120	0.111
1985–1990	–	–	0.296	0.175	0.147
1995–2000	–	–	–	0.285	0.216
2005–2009	–	–	–	–	0.295
C: Natives age 18–34 in reference year					
1970	0.107	0.083	0.072	0.074	0.081
1980	–	0.114	0.089	0.071	0.094
1990	–	–	0.134	0.085	0.102
2000	–	–	–	0.138	0.121
2009	–	–	–	–	0.188

Source: Authors' tabulations of microdata from the 1970, 1980, 1990, and 2010 One Percent Public Use Microdata Sample of the U.S. Census of Population and Housing and the 2000 American Community Survey.

immigrants who arrived between 1965 and 1970 in the 1970, 1980, 1990, and 2000 censuses and the 2010 American Community Survey (ACS).[3] The data in the first panel pertain to all immigrants, in the second panel to those between eighteen and thirty-four in the survey year closest to their arrival date, and in the third panel to natives roughly the same age as the various younger arrival cohorts.

Table 1.4 reveals three notable patterns. First, immigrant poverty rates decline sharply within arrival cohorts across census years, greatly narrowing the poverty gaps between immigrants and comparably aged natives.[4] Second, the poverty rates of the newest arrivals are much higher today than in the past (for example, the most recent arrivals in the 1970 census had an 18 percent poverty rate, versus 28 percent in the 2010 census). This of course is consistent with the changing composition of immigrants documented in table 1.1. Third, even for the relatively recent arrival cohorts that start in the United States with historically high poverty rates, we observe large declines in poverty with time in the United States and convergence toward the lower poverty rates of natives from comparable birth cohorts.

Table 1.5 presents comparable tabulations for immigrants from specific national-origin groups. For Central American, South American, East Asian, and Southeast

TABLE 1.5 / Immigrant Poverty Rates by Region of Origin

Year of first arrival	Census Year				
	1970	1980	1990	2000	2009
A: Mexico					
1965–1970	0.292	0.209	0.222	0.163	0.151
1975–1980	—	0.298	0.272	0.264	0.178
1985–1990	—	—	0.350	0.264	0.231
1995–2000	—	—	—	0.325	0.336
2005–2010					0.362
B: Central America					
1965–1970	0.220	0.147	0.094	0.125	0.140
1975–1980	—	0.303	0.161	0.126	0.114
1985–1990	—	—	0.303	0.193	0.162
1995–2000	—	—	—	0.267	0.231
2005–2010	—	—	—	—	0.299
C: South America					
1965–1970	0.200	0.089	0.087	0.073	0.086
1975–1980	—	0.259	0.112	0.098	0.103
1985–1990	—	—	0.223	0.103	0.109
1995–2000	—	—	—	0.257	0.138
2005–2010	—	—	—	—	0.182
D: East Asia					
1965–1970	0.213	0.046	0.048	0.057	0.123
1975–1980	—	0.229	0.054	0.057	0.136
1985–1990	—	—	0.317	0.098	0.183
1995–2000	—	—	—	0.357	0.149
2005–2010					0.234
E: Southeast Asia					
1965–1970	0.157	0.037	0.024	0.056	0.070
1975–1980	—	0.284	0.078	0.075	0.102
1985–1990	—	—	0.264	0.106	0.108
1995–2000	—	—	—	0.215	0.119
2005–2010	—	—	—	—	0.302

Source: Authors' tabulations of microdata from the 1970, 1980, 1990, and 2010 One Percent Public Use Microdata Sample of the U.S. Census of Population and Housing and the 2000 American Community Survey.

Asian immigrants, we see patterns that are comparable to those for immigrants overall. Poverty drops sharply with time in the United States, even among the most recent arrivals who experience very high poverty rates upon arrival. The table does reveal a slower decline in poverty rates among Mexican immigrants, especially in the most recent decades. This may be driven in part by the high proportion unauthorized within the Mexican immigrant population.

The poverty rates of the offspring of immigrant families depend on the degree of intergenerational socioeconomic mobility experienced within immigrant communities, the chief determinant of which is the level of formal educational attainment among the children of immigrant households. In chapter 6, Renee Reichl Luthra and Roger Waldinger provide an empirical analysis of intergenerational mobility among the offspring of immigrants in Los Angeles. Analyzing data from the Immigration and Intergenerational Mobility in Metropolitan Los Angeles (IIM-MLA) Survey as well as data from various years of the March Current Population Survey, the authors document several stark patterns in educational and occupational mobility. First, in both the analysis of national data that compares members of given ethnic groups according to the first, 1.5, and second generation as well as the analysis of Los Angeles data that compares the outcomes for young 1.5- and second-generation adults with those of their parents, the authors find remarkable levels of mobility for all groups. It is true that the children of immigrants from groups with higher average education ultimately surpass other immigrant children, but at the same time the children of the least-educated immigrants also surpass their parents in both education and occupational status.

Second, the authors document large differences across groups in the degree to which parental advantage or disadvantage transfers from parent to child. The children of some ethnic groups perform uniformly better regardless of parental education or socioeconomic status. In particular, the children in Vietnamese, Korean, Chinese, and Salvadoran households exhibit fairly high levels of educational attainment and weak correlation between ultimate educational attainment and that of their parents. Intergenerational correlation in educational attainment within Mexican immigrant households is also remarkably low, indicative of a fair degree of intergenerational mobility in this group. For Mexicans, however, the low levels of average parental educational attainment often means that substantial intergenerational mobility coexists with relatively inferior within-generation education for Mexican youth relative to others.

Finally, the authors' results hints at a relatively novel pattern that is generally under-researched in the social science literature on economic assimilation. In particular, they characterize the degree to which immigrants from specific countries are positively selected along observable measures of human capital relative to their nonimmigrant co-nationals. In nearly all cases, immigrants are positively selected from their national-origin distributions in terms of educational attainment. One might argue that this is likely to carry over into other domains, such as motivation and entrepreneurial ability. More important for the question at hand, the degree to which immigrants are positively selected shows a fair degree of heterogeneity. For example, the degree of positive selection is particularly high among Asian immigrants and immigrants from the Caribbean and somewhat lower among Mexican immigrants. The intergenerational analysis suggests that the base level of second-generation educational attainment (the average component that appears to occur regardless of parental characteristics) is higher the more positively selected the immigrant group. Some evidence indicates that the intergenerational correlation in education and occupational status may be weaker among more positively immigrant groups.

In chapter 7, Jennifer Lee and Min Zhou present an in-depth qualitative analysis of social mobility pathways among 1.5- and second-generation Mexican, Chinese, and Vietnamese immigrants in the Los Angeles area that supplements and enriches the statistical analyses in chapter 6. Drawing on personal interviews with 140 study participants from the IIMMLA survey, Lee and Zhou shine a light on the role of inter-ethnic variation in culture in explaining differences in relative and absolute social mobility. From the outset, the authors establish the tremendous intergenerational mobility observed for the children of immigrants in all three ethnic groups, with even the least-educated study participants (those of Mexican descent) achieving levels of educational attainment and other markers of social mobility that far exceed those of their immigrant parents. However, the authors also establish sharp differences between the educational attainment of the adult children of Mexican immigrants relative to those of Vietnamese and Chinese immigrants. Through their qualitative interviews, the authors seek explanations for these disparities.

Lee and Zhou use the concept of *social frames* to explore the life courses of their study subjects. Defining a frame as a "way of understanding how the world works," the authors seek to understand systematic variation across ethnic groups in the frames within which decisions regarding education are made. Moreover, the authors shed light on how variation in the social resources available through co-ethnics and pan-ethnics reinforce differences in these frames and ultimately play a hand in determining educational attainment and social mobility.

The results of the interviews reveal sharp differences in frames, social networks, and ultimately outcomes. Among Vietnamese and Chinese immigrant families and their larger communities, graduation from high school with high marks is taken as given and college attendance is seen as an obligation. Several respondents echo the sentiment that the grade scale by which these individuals were judged as children is best described by "A is for average, and B is an Asian fail." Even those whose parents have little formal schooling were expected to excel academically.

Most important to their story is the reinforcing role of co-ethnics in bolstering and strengthening this particular frame. High average socioeconomic status, or at a minimum substantial numbers having the highest levels of formal education, expose young members of an ethnic group to role models and provide information about the keys to conventional success. Moreover, sharing information about which schools perform the best and how to ensure one's children are enrolled in Advanced Placement courses, along with a willingness to invest in supplemental educational services during summers and over the course of the school year, also reinforce and solidify the cultural ethic of academic achievement. The authors note that although performing well in school is sometimes derisively characterized as "acting white" by underrepresented minority youth, this particular frame carries no resonance among Chinese and Vietnamese youth in Los Angeles.

The frame revealed through the interviews with Mexican study participants is markedly different. High school graduation and minimal levels of postsecondary education are often seen as substantial achievements, given that such outcomes often exceed those of the parents. Parents see little distinction between colleges, and in some instances are not familiar with or do not understand the practice of moving from home to attend university. This difference in the framing of formal education appears to create particular barriers for young Mexican women, where cultural values regarding the living arrangements of unmarried daughters come into sharp conflict with relocation to further education.

Another sharp contrast concerns the availability of role models and the over-reliance on resources provided through public institutions (in particular, school guidance counselors) in charting out educational paths. Given the low level of education among Mexican immigrant parents and the low variance in education among co-ethnics, several participants found the concept of role models from within their community (as the concept pertains to education) to be an almost novel idea.

In chapter 8, Roberto Gonzales explores one barrier to socioeconomic mobility for a constrained set of 1.5-generation immigrants. He provides a qualitative analysis of the educational and post-education work experiences of 1.5-generation undocumented young adults in the Los Angeles area. An estimated 2.1 million unauthorized immigrants in the United States entered the country as children and attended U.S. public schools, have little or no experience with their country of birth, and are for all intents and purposes American youth. Their legal immigration status, however, is a substantial barrier to social mobility. Although all children have the right to K-12 education regardless of immigration status, access to higher education (including admission criteria as well as eligibility for financial aid and in-state tuition) varies from state to state. Furthermore, undocumented immigrants are categorically ineligible for federal student financial aid.

Perhaps most ominous is the lack of legal authorization to work. Jobs in the formal sector in the United States technically require proof of identity and legal authorization to work. Moreover, employers are increasingly checking the work eligibility of potential hires through the federal E-Verify system (the subject of chapter 10). Young undocumented immigrants clearly incorporate these limitations into their choices regarding whether to continue formal education at key junctures, in particular, whether to drop out of high school or to continue into higher education. In addition, undocumented youth who achieve bachelor's degrees and beyond often find that the available employment opportunities after graduation are painfully similar to those what would have been available had they dropped out of high school or not gone to college.

Gonzales describes the results of four years of fieldwork interviewing and documenting the lives of undocumented youth in the Los Angeles area. He presents separate narratives for youth who go on to postsecondary education and those who drop out of high school or stop at high school graduation. The analysis reveals some key differences between youth who continue onto college or leave early with those who continue attending smaller high schools and receiving considerably more attention from teachers and guidance counselors. Regardless, most youth ultimately find themselves working in very low-wage informal sector jobs, where there is no discernible return to formal education.

Collectively, the three chapters in this section provide reasons for optimism yet point to particular challenges for Latino youth. The chapters document substantial intergenerational mobility, especially for youth with the least educated parents. Culture certainly plays a role in generating inter-ethnic differences in average adult socioeconomic status among the children of immigrant households. However, even among Latino households with limited parental education, most children complete high school and many pursue postsecondary education. The chapters do reveal the importance of public institutions in furthering social mobility among such households: guidance counselors and teachers who go above and beyond the call of duty substituting for community social capital, for example, within the Chinese and Vietnamese communities. Most ominous are the prospects for unauthorized 1.5-generation immigrants trapped by their legal status.

PUBLIC POLICY AND POVERTY AMONG THE FOREIGN BORN

The material welfare and sense of security of immigrants in the United States depend on various domains of public policy. Just as the nation's policy choices have an impact on native well-being, policies governing redistribution, education, work eligibility, and legal status have an impact on the foreign born. Sometimes this occurs through eligibility standards applied to noncitizens. Sometimes it results from bodies of legislation targeted toward foreign-born noncitizens. These policy choices have an impact on immigrant poverty through employment, education, and benefits eligibility.

In chapter 9, Douglas Massey reviews U.S. immigration policy in the twentieth century with an eye on how this policy has affected Latinos. He argues that the various policy efforts to control undocumented immigration coupled with immigration reform intended to limit the eligibility of those with criminal convictions has effectively racialized U.S. Latinos, Mexican immigrants and Mexican Americans. Massey defines racialization as the "deliberate acts of psychological framing and social boundary definition undertaken to identify Latinos as a stigmatized out-group and to undermine their standing with respect to fundamental human attributes." He argues that policy choices driven by divisive politics catering to anti-immigrant sentiment are behind this racialization process and are creating a permanent underclass of U.S. residents with limited opportunities for social mobility and substandard civil rights.

The chapter documents the significant changes in the nature of immigration from Latin America over the twentieth century. At mid-century, most immigration involved temporary migration of Mexican men under the Bracero temporary worker program. The abrupt end of this program, coupled with the first imposition of numerical limits on annual immigration to the United States from Western Hemisphere countries, greatly shifted the composition of Latin American migrants. Under the Bracero program, most migrants to the United States were temporarily in the United States to perform agricultural work and were here legally. By contrast, migration after the end of the program was disproportionately unauthorized migrants. Moreover, the various efforts to strengthen security at the border greatly reduced the cyclical nature of Mexican migration, and in recent years also affected migration from Central American countries such as Guatemala, El Salvador, and Honduras. Undocumented migrants who manage to cross the increasingly militarized border without being apprehended have become reluctant to return home, given the enhanced difficulties and costs of border crossings. Hence, since the mid-1990s, the country has experienced a large increase in the size of the undocumented population with many settling away from the border states and settling into a more permanent existence in the United States.

To be sure, for most undocumented immigrants this permanent existence involves low-paying informal employment, the inability to engage in the most mundane activities legally (for example, driving), and not being able to engage the authorities when needed. Perhaps most distressing is the plight of the undocumented who arrive as children and are thus not able to fully participate in American society.

One sign of the drastic and punitive policy shift toward undocumented immigrants is the rise in state legislative activity intended to limit their work opportunities and, in general, make life as difficult as possible for them. The last few years have witnessed a turning point in the traditional relationship between federal and state governments when it comes to immigration policy. Although immigration policy is generally a federal responsibility, many states have now passed legislation intended to deter undocumented immigrants from settling within state borders. Arizona is at the forefront of this wave of legislation, having passed some of the most punitive and stringent state laws intended to limit the employment opportunities of undocumented workers and increase the ability of local police to find undocumented immigrants and turn them over to federal authorities.

In chapter 10, Sarah Bohn and Magnus Lofstrom evaluate the impacts of Arizona's legislative effort to prohibit unauthorized immigrants from finding employment. The authors focus on the effects of legislation on the employment outcomes of the unauthorized as well as on the employment outcomes of authorized workers most likely to compete in the labor market with undocumented immigrants. In 2007, Arizona passed the Legal Arizona Workers Act (LAWA), a law that mandated all employers to use the federal E-Verify system to establish the identity and work eligibility of all new hires beginning on January 1, 2008.

Because the E-Verify system queries social security records and immigration records maintained by the Department of Homeland Security, the new information verification requirement most certainly makes it more difficult for undocumented immigrants to find formal employment in Arizona.

Chapter 10 hypothesizes that LAWA should reduce demand for truly unauthorized workers and perhaps for authorized workers that may be easily misidentified as unauthorized (for example, naturalized Hispanics, or native-born Hispanics who speak accented English). Moreover, standard theory of labor demand suggests that an increase in the price of competing input may increase labor demand for other inputs via factor substitution.[5] In other words, a LAWA-induced decline in demand for unauthorized labor may increase demand for legal workers who are close substitutes in production for undocumented immigrants. To be sure, some employers may still be willing to risk hiring undocumented workers. Moreover, undocumented workers always have the option of seeking employment in the informal labor market, where the E-Verify mandate as well as other regulations governing labor exchange are likely to be ignored.

Employing the synthetic comparison method to generate a comparison group against which Arizona can be compared, the authors document several facts. First, the proportion of relatively less-educated noncitizen Hispanics employed in wage and salary jobs drops notably with the implementation of LAWA. The decline exceeds the trend for the comparison group, and is statistically significant. Second, there is no comparable decline in wage and salary employment among comparable naturalized Hispanic men, native-born Hispanic men, or native-born non-Hispanic white men. Taken together, these findings suggest that the reduction in demand in the wage and salary sector for unauthorized immigrants had little beneficial effect for less-skilled naturalized and native-born workers.

Aside from the decline in wage and salary employment, Bohn and Lofstrom also document a sizable increase (on the order of 8 percentage points) in the proportion of likely unauthorized workers self-identifying as self-employed. This change is larger than the trend observed in comparison states, is statistically significant, and is not observed for other groups of workers in Arizona. The authors interpret this finding as evidence of a shift into the informal labor market, and muster evidence that self-employment for less-educated Hispanic immigrants generally means lower earnings, a much lower probability of having health insurance and other benefits, and a discretely higher probability of having an income level below the federal poverty line. The authors speculate what these results mean for a national implementation of an E-Verify mandate, a policy choice now being debated in the U.S. Congress. Earlier research documents a sizable decline in the immigrant population of Arizona in response to LAWA, suggesting that the labor market impacts were dulled to a degree by out-migration and new migrants choosing alternative states. Such interstate migration would not be a viable option should the mandate be implemented nationwide, and thus the effects on wage and salary and informal employment are likely to be larger.

In chapter 11, Marianne Bitler and Hilary Hoynes analyze the role of the U.S. social safety net in reducing poverty among the nation's noncitizen foreign-born residents. The chapter begins with a comprehensive overview of the web of federal programs designed to mitigate negative income shocks and to more generally assure a universal minimum level of material well-being. The authors outline the eligibility criteria for major cash assistance programs, such as the Temporary Assistance to Needy Families (TANF), Supplemental Security Income (SSI), and the Earned Income Tax Credit program (EITC), as well as in-kind anti-poverty programs such as Food Stamps, school-based nutritional assistance programs, and subsidized health care programs for low-income children and adults, paying particular attention to eligibility criteria as they pertain to the foreign born. The 1990s were critical years of reform for these antipoverty programs. In addition to substantial expansions in the EITC and the introduction of public health benefits for near-poor children under the State Children's Health Insurance Program (SCHIP), cash assistance programs were fundamentally altered towards time-limited transitional assistance, with a heavy emphasis on work among recipients. While these reforms affected all households regardless of nativity, welfare reform had particularly transformative effects for immigrants.

Specifically, eligibility for several programs including cash assistance as well as Food Stamps was curtailed for legal permanent residents, with a new eligibility dividing line between those who arrived before welfare reform (that is, prior to 1996) and those who arrived after. In addition, for several programs (Food Stamps in particular) the federal government permitted states to reinstate immigrant eligibility at the state's expense. Notably, this is the first instance of state involvement in immigration policy, establishing a set of precedents that may become increasingly important in the future. Chapter 11 documents these changes in immigrant eligibility, the subsequent federal legislation that partially restored immigrant eligibility for certain groups of the foreign born and certain programs, as well state-by-state difference in program eligibility for antipoverty benefits for which states are afforded discretion by the federal government.

Chapter 11 goes on to contrast the trends in program participation among households with children headed by natives and by immigrants for the period from 1994 through 2009. These trends reveal several interesting patterns. First, when immigrants households are compared to like native households (in particular, households with pre-tax and transfer income below 200 percent of the poverty line), immigrant households are generally less likely to participate in programs than native households. This holds in most instances, though school-based nutritional programs provide a notable exception. Second, comparing program participation rates before welfare reform to those in recent years, the authors document sizable and statistically significant declines in program participation for foreign-born households relative to native households. Such relative declines are consistent with changes in eligibility criteria or a more general "chilling effect" of welfare reform on immigrant program participation.

Chapter 11 also explores whether immigrant children are more vulnerable to economic downturns relative to the children of the native born. Given the limited eligibility of immigrant households for various public safety net programs and the fact that labor earnings constitute a greater share of household income among the foreign-born poor, one might expect childhood poverty among immigrants to be particularly sensitive to the state of the economy. Chapter 11 shows that indeed a 1-percentage point increase in the unemployment rate during the Great Recession had a larger impact on childhood poverty among immigrant households than among native households. Most interestingly, this difference is largest when the authors analyze a new poverty measure that accounts for the implicit value of cash assistance and in-kind goods and services transferred through public assistance programs. In other words, although the safety net dampens the effect of unemployment on native child poverty rates, it is less effective at achieving the same result for children in immigrant-headed households.

In chapter 12, Cybelle Fox, Irene Bloemraad, and Christel Kesler investigate whether the nation has drifted toward less generous redistributive policies through taxes and transfer programs because of the increase in the proportion immigrant among the U.S. resident population. The authors hypothesize three possible causal channels. First, the fact that noncitizen immigrants cannot vote means that a sizable minority of adult U.S. residents is effectively disenfranchised. To the extent that policy preferences towards redistributive social policy differ among noncitizen adults relative to adult citizens, that the disenfranchised would exercise their voting rights if they were given the franchise, and that noncitizen are numerically important enough to shift electoral outcomes, such disenfranchisement might affect the degree of redistribution occurring through the state. The chapter presents evidence from California that indeed shows stronger preferences for redistributive social policy among noncitizen adults relative to the naturalized and to the native born. Some simple back of the envelope calculations for California (an admitted outlier given its high proportion of foreign-born residents) suggests that extending the franchise to immigrants may alter the balance of power over redistributive policy decisions using direct-democracy through the state's initiative process.

Second, the chapter hypothesizes that natives may simply feel threatened—for social, economic, cultural, or political reasons—by the increasing presence of the foreign born. Given the difference in income and human capital and that immigrants would be disproportionately represented among the beneficiaries of redistributive programs, such "group threat" may diminish support for redistribution among the nation's dominant groups. Such an argument is often implicit in worries over backlash against immigrants.

Finally, the chapter hypothesizes that immigration may increase the degree to which U.S. society has become fractionalized. To the extent that diversity—racial, ethnic, and otherwise—diminishes the sense of a common identity, general support for redistributive policy may in turn be diminished.

The chapter tests these three possible connections between a higher proportion of foreign-born residents and trends in state redistributive activity. Using state-level panel data, the chapter estimates a series of models in which the dependent variables are various gauges of redistributive activity measured at the state-year level (transfers per capita, state-determined AFDC/TANF benefit levels, a measure of benefit generosity pertaining specifically to immigrants). Support is mixed for the noncitizen disenfranchisement and group-threat hypotheses. However, evidence is fairly consistent that the more fractionalized a state's population, the less the state engages in redistributive social policy. This is particularly so in regard to race. The chapter reveals robust evidence of a negative impact of the proportion of black residents on the extent of redistributive policy within the state. Evidence in this regard is weaker with respect to the proportion of Asian and Latino residents.

IMMIGRANTS IN EUROPE

The primary focus of this volume is on immigration and poverty in the United States. Increasingly, however, immigration is a concern in other developed countries, including the those of Europe, which have experienced unprecedented increases in immigrant inflows over the past two decades. Many European immigrants are from Africa—a pattern of south to north migration that is similar to the flow from Latin America to the United States. However, specific historic events have also led to increased migration to western Europe since World War II. Of course, all of this occurs against an institutional back drop that differs markedly from that of the United States.

In chapter 13, Christian Dustmann and Tommaso Frattini provide an overview of the recent experiences of the foreign born in western European countries, provide a historical accounting of postwar migration throughout western Europe, and a thorough characterization of the relative socioeconomic status of international migrants from other European Union (EU) countries as well as migrants from non-EU nations. The historical overview details the major events driving population movements between European countries and from outside of Europe. In contrast to the United States, where economically motivated migration accounts for the lion's share of the foreign-born resident population, major contributing factors to the foreign-born population in Europe are often driven by political developments and institutional reform. For example, several European nations—including the United Kingdom, France, Spain, Portugal, and the Netherlands—experienced large in-migrations from former colonies, sometimes as a result of political turmoil leading up to and through formal independence. Countries such as Germany received economic migrants brought in to relieve labor shortages during the period of rapid growth in the 1960s. Other major internal migratory flows were unleashed by the fall of the Berlin wall, the collapse of the Soviet Union and the subsequent civil conflicts, as well as by the expansion of the European Union and the attendant granting of migration rights to new members.

The chapter distinguishes between the outcomes of immigrants from other EU nations, and the outcomes of non-EU immigrants. The authors document sizable differences in educational attainment between the foreign and native born in most nations, with immigrants generally considerably less educated than the native born, though there are some exceptions. Interestingly, both immigrants from other EU countries and those from non-EU countries have relatively low levels of education, though the difference are considerably larger for non-EU immigrants. The relative disadvantage of the foreign born is generally observed in other domains. The foreign born are occupationally segregated from the native born, in lower-paying, less prestigious occupational categories. They are also considerably less likely to be employed and considerably more likely to have earnings in the lower deciles of the earnings distribution of the host country. This is an interesting contrast with the United States. Although relatively less-educated immigrants in the United States certainly earn less than natives, employment rates among the foreign are quite high, especially when compared with natives with similar levels of education and work experience.

Chapter 12 also characterizes the relative well-being of children in immigrant-headed households. The higher fertility rate among the foreign born who live in western European countries translates into a higher proportional representation of children from immigrant households among all children than the comparable proportions among adults. Given the relatively poorer labor market outcomes for adult immigrants, it is not surprising that the children of immigrants are more likely to live in low-income households.

One of the most interesting findings documented in chapter 12 is that the relative disadvantage of the foreign born in Europe cannot be explained by observable difference in education, gender, and age. The lower employment rates of the foreign born, occupational segregation in less prestigious jobs, and lower position in the earnings distribution are observed both in unconditional comparisons of means as well as in regression-adjusted estimates that hold constant the effect of observable covariates. This may be determined in part by institutional rigidities within European labor markets and noncompetitive processes that ration employment opportunities along nonmeritocratic dimensions. The chapter presents some evidence that national economies with longer immigration histories tend to do a better job of integrating immigrants into the national economy. Moreover, some evidence also indicates that immigrants are occupationally segregated in economies with greater institutional rigidity, although there is no apparent connection to immigrants' relative employment.

SUMMARY

With the resurgence of immigration since the 1960s, issues of poverty and inequality are increasingly associated with nativity. Today about one-sixth of the U.S. population who are classified as poor were foreign born. Most of the traditional antipoverty programs and many other state and federal regulations now make explicit distinctions between immigrants and natives. Moreover, the intergenerational dynamics of the low-income population are more and more linked to the socioeconomic status of immigrants and their children.

The chapters in this book offer a multifaceted perspective on the linkages between immigration, socioeconomic inequality, and poverty, and provide answers to some of the key questions in the area. Given the increasing importance of immigrants and their children in the United States, we expect that nativity will become an increasingly salient dimension of coming policy debates about poverty, inequality, and program reforms. These chapters provide a wealth of ideas and hypotheses that we predict will influence the field for decades to come.

NOTES

1. The figures in the table use data from the 1970, 1980, 1990, and 2000 One Percent Public Use Microdata Samples of the U.S. Census of Population and Housing and 2010 American Community Survey. We restrict the sample to the noninstitutionalized resident population.
2. Note this also accounts for changes in the internal composition of the native-born population across the following race-ethnicity categories: non-Hispanic white, non-Hispanic black, non-Hispanic Asian, non-Hispanic other, and Hispanic. Hence, any impact on poverty operating through an effect on the internal composition of the native born is accounted for in these decompositions.
3. ACS data pertain to the calendar year prior. The 2010 ACS is therefore used to measure descriptive statistics for calendar year 2009.
4. Of course, this decline could be due to changing composition of arrival cohorts across census years. For example, if those most likely to be in poverty are more likely to return to their country of origin between census years, we would see a decline in poverty rates over time. Because we are presenting estimates for synthetic rather than actual cohorts, we cannot rule this out.
5. Of course, the negative scale effect on labor demand will temper the positive effects of factor substitution, and in some instances, may dominate leading to negative effects on labor demand for some authorized labor.

Part I

Composition, Competition, and the Geography of Immigrant Poverty

The first section of this volume is devoted to understanding the economic forces that link immigration to native poverty and that determine poverty rates within immigrant communities. The analysis in chapter 2 empirically assesses the role of immigrant-native competition in the labor market in explaining poverty rates among the native born. In a complementary analysis, chapter 3 investigates the degree to which poor English-language skills limits labor market competition between immigrants and natives and increases the intensity of labor market competition within immigrant communities between new arrivals and more established immigrants. Chapter 4 analyzes the spatial housing patterns of immigrants within metropolitan areas with a specific eye on how housing segregation impacts economic outcomes and English-language acquisition. Finally, chapter 5 assesses the degree to which new destination metropolitan areas located outside of the traditional gateway states such as California, Illinois, New York, and Florida provide superior employment opportunities for the foreign born.

Chapter 2

Immigration, Native Poverty, and the Labor Market

Giovanni Peri

T his chapter analyzes the effect of immigration on the proportion of American families falling below the poverty line, through the labor market effect that immigrants may have on native workers. Immigrants are a heterogeneous group of workers with different skills. Some compete with specific groups of native workers and complement other groups. Others compete and complement different groups of native workers. They may also increase or dilute the average level of schooling in the U.S. economy. Each of these effects has an impact on native wages that differs depending on the schooling, age, and location of natives. The first step is to analyze the impact of immigrants on wages of natives with different demographic characteristics. The second step is to map these wage effects into effects on the proportion of families falling below the poverty line. Poverty is defined in the conventional way, by considering before tax (transfers) total family income, relative to the federal poverty line, which is adjusted for inflation and for family size in each year. The mapping of the wage income effects onto changes in poverty rates, therefore, depends on the magnitude of the wage effects, on the importance of wages in total income and on the income distribution of families around the poverty line.

The effect of immigrants on wages of native workers is hard to measure and has been an object of debate among economists. First, the flow of international immigrants in a country or in a local economy depends itself on the wage paid there. Consequently, a positive correlation between immigrants and wages, driven by productivity growth in economically successful areas, may bias the estimates of a causal relation from immigration to wages. In regression approaches this issue is addressed using instrumental variable techniques.[1] Second, the supply of workers of a skill type affects the productivity and wages of workers of the same type (competition) and of different types (complementarity). Hence, a reduced-form estimation that does not account for these cross-skill interactions misses a large part of the effects of immigrants.[2] Third, especially at the local level, immigration may trigger other responses, particularly internal migration of natives, that may themselves attenuate its wage impact. By considering each area as an isolated unit of analysis we may underestimate the effects of immigrants on local labor markets.[3] In spite of these difficulties, a large body of empirical literature has tackled this issue. Each of these problems, however, contributes to make a reduced-form estimation approach of the wage effect of immigration problematic. Although solutions exist and have been adopted in the literature, I take a different approach in the present study.

Rather than estimating the wage impact of immigrants in a reduced-form regression I simulate this effect, using a labor market equilibrium model. The main difference is that an estimation approach would obtain from the data, for each skill group, a measure of the native wage response to immigration that is partial, in the sense that it accounts only for immigration in the same skill group. In particular, it would neglect general equilibrium effects of immigrants in other skill groups (through complementarity). To the contrary, a simulation effect relies on estimates of elasticities from the literature and on a specific model, but can calculate the total effect of immigration on native wages of each skill group accounting for the direct effects and for the indirect general equilibrium effects.

I adopt the aggregate production-general equilibrium framework, which is emerging as dominant in the national wage studies of immigration (see, for example, Borjas 2003; Manacorda, Manning, and Wadsworth 2012; Ottaviano and Peri 2012). This framework captures the relevant productive interactions between workers of different demographic characteristics (schooling, experience, and national origins), accounting for cross-skill effects on productivity but keeping the number of parameters needed for the simulation tractable. Besides these cross-skill complementarity effects, I include in the model the potential for *human capital externalities*. These are the positive effects on productivity through learning, technological adoption, and diffusion of ideas from a high concentration of educated people. Recent empirical studies relative to U.S. cities (Moretti 2004a, 2004b) and U.S. states (Iranzo and Peri 2009) have shown the existence of significant positive productivity effects from the concentration of college graduates. At the same time, the strength of these effects is debated among economists (for example, Acemoglu and Angrist 2001; Ciccone and Peri 2006) and hence we allow for different strength of such effects.[4]

I use such a model to simulate the wage effects of immigration flows in the decade from 2000 to 2009 (and, as a reference, also during the previous decade, 1990 to 1999). The same model is used, at different levels of aggregation, to represent the U.S. economy as a whole, U.S. states and U.S. metropolitan areas. Usually the approach is applied to evaluate national effects. However, one can use it to simulate the maximum wage effect of immigrants, in absence of offsetting migration of natives, for cities and states. The results of this model at the city and state level should be interpreted as an upper bound for the possible local wage effects of immigration if mobility of natives does not offsets them. The calculated national effects are the relevant ones in the more realistic scenario of long-run mobility of workers in the United States.

The simulated wage effects are then used to evaluate the impact on poverty. Specifically, I compute the proportion of families in each skill group whose total income was below the poverty line in 2009. I then recalculate that proportion after modifying the average wage of the skill group by "netting out" the effect of immigration during the 2000–2009 period. The difference between the two proportions is the increase in poverty rates caused by immigration. I perform this analysis for different groups (mainly different education, age and gender cells) and evaluate the aggregate effects for blacks and Hispanics. In the simulations, I use three different combinations of the relevant parameters: high, intermediate, and low. They span the range of the parameters estimates in the literature and are arranged according to their average wage impact on natives.

Three results from this exercise are worth emphasizing. First, at the national level, the impact of immigration on native poverty rates through wages effects is negligible for any of the chosen parameter configurations. The effects consist of extremely small reductions of poverty rates for all groups and decades, except for the group of individuals with a high school degree or less during the decade from 1990 to 1999. During that period, natives with no high school diploma experienced an increase in the poverty rate due to immigrants between 0.3 and 0.2 percent, when I use the low-parameter configuration. For the other configurations of parameters in the 1990–1999 period and for all configurations of parameters during the 2000 to 2009 period, I find immigration to have a poverty-reduction effect between 0 and 0.51 percent. This poverty-reduction effect is due to the fact that immigration to the United States has been very "college" intensive between 2000 and 2009 and hence wages of less-educated workers should have grown due to complementarity effects. Second, at the state level the model generally predicts insignificant effects of immigration on poverty. Interestingly, for the 2000 to 2009 period, the only sizeable effects predicted by the model, in states such as Arizona, California, Florida, and New Jersey are poverty percentage reductions for groups of workers with no diploma and with high school degree only. In the overwhelming majority of the top ten immigration states our model shows simulated effects of immigration smaller than 0.1 percent on native poverty rates of any group. Notice that, in both periods, the correlation between the native poverty changes and the simulated effects of immigration was essentially zero. In short, immigration drove a negligible fraction of poverty changes at the state level and often the simulated effects have a negligible correlation with the actual changes in poverty rates. Finally, the analysis at the metropolitan statistical area (MSA) level reveals that immigration had hardly anything to do with the evolution of native poverty even at the local level. Considering the twenty MSAs with the largest immigration rates, we learn that during the decade from 2000 through 2009 most of them experienced higher immigration rates among the college educated than among high school graduates. Hence, our model predicts mostly positive wage effects for the least educated natives. This produced a poverty-reduction effect of immigrants in most cases.

Overall, the imputed effect of immigration on poverty at the national and local level in the 2000s are smaller by one order of magnitude than the actual poverty changes. Moreover, usually the model predicts that immigration reduced poverty of less-educated natives while the actual rates increased. These are signs that immigration was not very relevant in affecting native poverty either at the national, state or local level.

MODEL

The framework used for the simulation follows Gianmarco Ottaviano and Giovanni Peri (2012). I assume that firms demand labor of different skill types up to the point in which wages are equated to the marginal productivity of each worker. Workers are heterogeneous and divided into groups according to their schooling and age. Each group competes in a separate labor market. Different workers types are combined and use physical capital to produce a homogeneous and perfectly tradable output. Workers supply a fixed amount of labor each, so that size of the population in working age for each skill group determines their supply. Physical capital adjusts to keep its return equal to the rate of inter-temporal preferences net of the discount rate. Immigration is a supply shock that adds a different number of workers to each skill group. The details of the model and the equations expressing the effects of immigration on wages are in shown in the appendix. Here it is enough to say that the effect of immigration on wage of each education-age group of natives depends on the measured inflow of immigrants in each education-age group and on the value of four key parameters that together determine the competition and complementarity of workers across and within skill groups. The first is σ_{HL}, the elasticity of substitution between more and less-educated workers and it regulates how relative wages of college educated change when the supply of college- and noncollege-educated vary. The second is σ_{IN}, the elasticity of substitution between natives and immigrants within an education and age group. It regulates the degree of competition or complementarity between native and immigrant workers. The third is λ, the intensity of the human capital externality. It captures whether the share of college graduates increases the productivity of other workers. For each of these parameters, I choose an estimate at the high end of the range estimated in the literature and one at the low end of the range and one that is close to the median. Table 2.1 shows the range for the parameter values. The fourth parameter needed for the simulation is σ_{YO} and it affects the relative substitutability between young and old workers. It is not the focus of our analysis. Hence I keep it fixed at 10, a value within the existing range of estimates (Welch 1979; Card and Lemieux 2001; Ottaviano and Peri 2012).

The parameter σ_H has a long history. It has been estimated in several studies beginning in the 1960s. Antonio Ciccone and Peri (2005) review some of the estimates and find most of them in the range between 1.5 (lower bound) and 2 (upper bound). I choose those as low and high values and 1.75 as the intermediate value.

TABLE 2.1 / Parameter Range in Simulations

Parameter Estimates	Most Pessimistic	Preferred Estimates	Most Favorable
σ_{HL}, Elasticity between more and less educated	1.5	1.75	2.0
σ_{IN}, Elasticity between immigrants and natives	infinity	20	12
λ, Strength of college externality	0.0	0.45	0.75

Source: Author's compilation based on estimates from the literature.
Note: The table summarizes the values of the parameters taken from the previous literature and used in our simulation of wage effects of immigrants and emigrants.

The estimates of the parameter σ_{IN} have been the focus of some recent papers. Potentially sensitive to the sample chosen and the method of estimation, the elasticity between immigrants and natives in the United States has been estimated at twenty by Ottaviano and Peri (2012) and at infinity by Borjas and colleagues (2012). Using data on California and a different methodology, Peri (2011) finds smaller values of σ_{IN} in the neighborhood of twelve. Estimates for the United Kingdom, provided by Marco Manacordao, Alan Manning, and Jonathan Wadsworth (2012) find even smaller values, around six. I consider only the estimates based on U.S. data for the range of our simulations. As for schooling externalities, I use the existing estimates that measure the elasticity of average wages (or total factor productivity) to the share of college educated workers. The existing studies estimate the parameter λ across cities or states in the United States. Enrico Moretti (2004a, 2004b) finds an elasticity around 0.75, which is at the high end of the range found in the literature. Daron Acemoglu and Joshua Angrist (2000) find a value close to zero; Susana Iranzo and Peri (2009) use a similar formulation and estimate a parameter value of 0.45. The reader should consider the full range of simulations to have a complete picture of the possible outcomes. In the interest of conciseness, however, I usually comment in greater detail the results obtained in the intermediate scenario.

IMMIGRATION AND POVERTY: TRENDS IN THE 1990S AND 2000S

The focus of this chapter is the analysis of immigration and its effect on native poverty in the last decade of available data, from 2000 to 2009. As a comparison, I also present some facts and the simulations for the period 1990 to 1999, a decade characterized by remarkable and steady economic growth. The present section describes some trends in immigration and poverty during those decades.

National Trends

Table 2.2 shows the net immigration rates at the national level for sixteen cells differentiated by schooling levels (no diploma, high school diploma, some college, and college graduates), age groups (young, with less than twenty years of potential working experience and old, with twenty years or more), and gender (male and female). In this and in all the following tables, we define *immigration rate* for a group as the net inflow of foreign born during the period, relative to the resident population (native + immigrants) in the group at the beginning of the period. During the 1990s, immigration rates show a well-known pattern: they are large at the extremes of the skill distribution (especially for college educated and individuals with no diploma) and low at intermediate levels (high school diplomas and some college). Overall, the net immigration rate for the decade was 5.8 percent, implying an inflow of immigrants equal to 0.58 percent of the initial resident population in each year. The immigration rate for the more educated group was 4.3 percent and for the less-educated 7.1 percent. Hence, during the nineties, immigration was more concentrated among the less educated than among the more educated. The opposite, however, is true for the 2000s. Relative to the 1990s, net immigration rates for the least educated dropped dramatically, but remained essentially stable for the college educated and college graduates. As a consequence, during the most recent decade, immigration rates were significantly larger among the more educated (4.1 percent) than among the less educated (2.4 percent), nationally. Two more tendencies became evident in the 2000s, relative to the 1990s. First, the drop in immigration rates among the less educated was particularly severe among young workers. Second, whereas among less-educated immigrants, men still represented larger shares; among the more educated, women showed larger immigration rates.

These dynamics are interesting. As the strongest wage competition derives from immigrants of similar demographic characteristics, the adverse competition effects from immigrants for young less-educated native women (the group at highest risk of poverty in the nation) should have dropped significantly in the 2000s. This should imply a benign effect of immigration on native poverty. Table 2.3 shows the percentage of individuals below the poverty line in each of the sixteen demographic groups. The poverty line is defined in terms of family income and depends on the age of the adults and on the number of children in the household. Table 2.A1 shows the value of family income denoting the poverty lines for different types of families in 2000. Those thresholds, adjusted by the change in consumption price index, were also applied in 2009.

As reported in table 2.3, the group with the highest poverty rates is that of young women with no diploma. Among them, 34.5 percent were below the poverty line in 2000 and a stunning 42.4 percent were in poverty after the recession in 2009. Even old women with no diploma had a poverty rate of more than 33 percent in 2009. At the opposite end, older college educated males have negligible poverty rates, of 2 to 3 percent. These data emphasize the higher vulnerability of women with low levels of schooling, usually in the lowest percentiles of the wage income

TABLE 2.2 / National Immigration Rates

Schooling Group	Age-Experience	Gender	Net Rates 1990–2000	Net Rates 2000–2009
No diploma	young	women	11.4%	–3.0%
	young	men	15.8	–2.4
	old	women	8.6	8.2
	old	men	10.3	11.2
High school graduate	young	women	6.6	–0.3
	young	men	8.0	1.3
	old	women	5.4	3.5
	old	men	7.7	4.8
Total less educated			7.1	2.4
Some college education	young	women	1.3	2.3
	young	men	0.8	2.7
	old	women	2.9	5.6
	old	men	3.3	5.2
College graduate or more	young	women	8.3	5.5
	young	men	6.5	3.8
	old	women	13.5	8.6
	old	men	9.5	7.1
Total more educated			4.3	4.1
Total			5.8	3.4

Source: Author's compilation based on the U.S. Census 1990 and 2000 and the 2009 American Community Survey.

Note: Net immigration rates for a group are measured as the net inflows of immigrants in the group during the period, relative to the population (natives + immigrants) in the group, at the beginning of the period. Young individuals are those with less than twenty years of potential experience in the labor market. Potential experience is (age-years of schooling−6). The population considered covers noninstitutionalized individuals in working age (sixteen to sixty-five).

distribution and likely to live as single mothers with children, and hence at very high risk of poverty. More interesting for our purposes, however, is the change of poverty rates in the considered decades. If the inflow of immigrants has affected wages differentially across demographic groups, then the cells with high immigration rates should show larger increase in poverty rates. Even a cursory look at the data in tables 2.2 and 2.3 reveals that during the 2000s the weakest groups—the less educated, the young, and women—experienced the largest increases in their poverty rates and had smaller immigration rates. On the other hand, the "stronger" groups of more educated and older individuals did not experience any increases in poverty rates, but did see relatively large immigration rates.

Figure 2.1 shows a simple scatterplot of changes in native poverty rates and immigration rates across the eighteen skill groups and across the two decades. While the figure is only meant to describe the data it shows a negative correlation, which

TABLE 2.3 / Adult Poverty Rates Among U.S. Born

Schooling Group	Age-Experience	Gender	Poverty Rates			
			2000	2009	Change 1990–2000	Change 2000–2009
No diploma	young	women	34.5	42.4	8.3	7.9
	young	men	20.0	26.1	4.9	6.1
	old	women	26.6	33.5	–6.9	6.9
	old	men	19.2	24.3	–9.5	5.1
High school graduate	young	women	17.0	23.9	–5.5	6.8
	young	men	9.5	13.1	–1.0	3.6
	old	women	8.9	11.7	–2.6	2.8
	old	men	7.2	9.4	–3.1	2.2
Total less educated			16.0	22.0	1.5	6.0
Some college education	young	women	11.0	16.5	–3.3	5.5
	young	men	7.9	11.3	–0.7	3.4
	old	women	5.6	7.9	–2.1	2.4
	old	men	4.4	6.5	–3.3	2.0
College graduate or more	young	women	3.5	4.6	3.7	1.0
	young	men	3.2	4.0	2.9	0.8
	old	women	2.5	3.3	2.8	0.8
	old	men	2.2	3.0	1.3	0.8
Total more educated			4.2	5.4	0.3	1.2
Total U.S. born			12	16	1.1	4

Source: Author's compilation based on the U.S. Census 1990 and 2000 and the 2009 American Community Survey.
Note: All numbers in percentages. Poverty rates are equal to the percentage of people in the group below the Federal Poverty line. The groups are defined as in table 2.1.

implies larger increase in poverty rates in cells with lower immigration rates. If wage competition of immigrants was an important driver of changes in poverty across skill groups, we should observe the opposite correlation. Obviously, many other factors affect poverty, and hence wages and incomes of natives — and in turn the wage competition effect of immigrants — even if important, may be completely masked by other factors in the scatterplot.

States and Metropolitan Areas

Within the general trends described in the previous section, individual states and MSAs experienced vastly different immigration rates and they also differed in the distribution of immigrants across skills. At the same time, poverty rates were quite different across U.S. states and cities. In this section I describe some of the notable characteristics of immigration in the top ten immigration states and in the top twenty immigration metropolitan areas (MSAs). The states with the highest im-

FIGURE 2.1 / Correlation Between Immigration and Poverty Rates

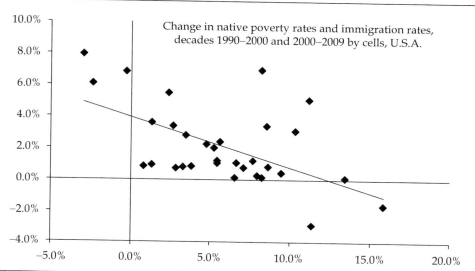

Source: Author's compilation based on the U.S. Census 1990 and 2000 and the 2009 American Community Survey.

migration rates for the last twenty years were, in decreasing order, Nevada, Arizona, Texas, Florida, California, Georgia, Utah, Colorado, and New Jersey. I add New York, which in spite of being only fourteenth in terms of immigration rates between 1990 and 2009, ranks second in the percentage of foreign born, 27 percent in 2009. Similarly, I consider sixteen of the top twenty MSAs in terms of their immigration rates over the last two decades. They include cities in Nevada, Georgia, Texas, Arizona, California, North Carolina, Connecticut, New Jersey, and Florida. I add Los Angeles, Miami, New York, and San Francisco, which are the largest MSAs with populations of more than 30 percent foreign born.

Table 2.A2 shows the immigration rates in four schooling groups by decade in the ten top states. Some tendencies are clear. First, the overall net immigration rates dropped dramatically from the 1990s to the 2000s. Nevada experienced a stunning immigration rate of 23 percent in the 1990s, which declined to 12 percent in the 2000s. Arizona saw a drop from 14.2 percent to 7.8 percent. Old immigration states, such as California and New York, had even larger declines in immigration rates, and in the 2000s saw rates of 4.2 percent and 2.1 percent, among the lowest in the group. Even more interesting is the composition of immigrants by skills. The states with largest immigration rates and the new immigration states, especially in the 1990s, had a tendency to attract disproportionately large fractions of immigrants among the least educated workers. Nevada and Arizona in the 1990s had immigration rates, among individuals with no diploma, of 61.6 percent and 38.8 percent, respectively. However, the immigration rates among the college educated for those two states were, respectively, "only" 19 percent and 10 percent. Similarly, new immigration states—such as Colorado, Georgia, and Utah—experienced much larger immigration rates among the least educated than among the most educated. On the other hand, states with older tradition of immigration— such as California, New York, and New Jersey—attracted a much more balanced inflow of immigrants during the 1990s, with immigration rates for college graduates as large as (or larger than) those of individuals with no diploma. During the 2000s, the very large drop in immigration at low levels of schooling, which was a national phenomenon, produced a substantial balancing of immigration rates across skills. This was true especially for states of more recent immigration, such as Arizona and Nevada. Meanwhile, older immigration states experienced immigration strongly biased in favor of the college educated. California and New York, for instance, had essentially no net immigration in the group with no diploma during the 2000s, but a 6 to 10 percent rate for the college educated.

The immigration rates by schooling group for the twenty MSAs considered are shown in table 2.A3. Some cities in Nevada, and Texas had massive immigration rates during the 1990s. Reno, Las Vegas, and McAllen, for instance, all had immigration rates of 30 percent with a distribution extremely skewed toward less-educated immigrants. Considering only less-educated workers, immigration increased the size of that group by 80 percent in Reno and by 70 percent in Las Vegas. Those rates dropped substantially in the 2000s. Rates in the 1990s were above 10 percent in all the top twenty cities, but in the 2000s in only seven. In terms of composition across education groups, the large cities of California, New York, and Florida— such as Los Angeles, San Francisco, New York City, and Miami—show much larger immigration rates among more educated groups, especially in the 2000s. The large cities of Nevada, Arizona, and Texas—such as Las Vegas, Phoenix, Austin, and Dallas—show much larger immigration rates among the less educated. However, even for these cities, magnets for less-educated immigrants during the 1990s, the composition across education groups was much more balanced in the 2000s. For instance, Las Vegas had an immigration rate of 78 percent among individuals with no diploma in the 1990s and one of only 27.4 percent among college graduates. The same city had immigration rates of 27 percent for no diploma and 22 percent for college graduates in the 2000s. Los Angeles had a net immigration of –10 percent among individuals with no diploma in the 2000s and of 10 percent among college graduates. Immigration contributed to substantially increase the numbers of college educated in that city.

Finally, changes in poverty rates by state and cities (not reported) also show large variation and differences. The largest positive changes in poverty rates are still for the group of no diploma or for high school educated during the 2000s, with alarmingly large increases in metropolitan areas such as Atlanta, Georgia; Fayetteville and Phoenix, Arizona; Raleigh-Durham, North Carolina; and Reno, Nevada. In each those places, poverty rates of least educated increased by more than 6 percent of the population in the group. Both for states and metro areas it is impossible to identify any correlation between immigration rates and evolution of poverty rates among the considered metropolitan areas. I analyze the relation between immigration and actual poverty rates in greater detail throughout the next section.

EFFECTS ON NATIVE WAGES AND ON POVERTY RATES: NATIONAL

Using the model described, I simulate the effect of immigrants on wages of natives in eight education-experience groups. Considering the total inflow of immigrants in each cell as a supply shock, I assume that in the long run (ten-year period) the adjustment takes place via wage adjustments. Hence, the change in marginal productivity of each type of native worker, in response to the supply shocks, measures the wage effect of immigrants on each of these groups. Considering the changes at the national level, I evaluate the average effect of immigrants on native wages, assuming perfect internal mobility of natives in the long run.

Effects of Immigration on Native Wages

Figure 2.2 shows the simulated effects of immigration on native wages (in percentages) for eight skill groups, nationally, during the period from 2000 to 2009. The groups are arrayed from young workers with no diploma to old workers with a college degree in increasing order of schooling. I connected the estimates to provide an easier reading of the relative wage effects across skills. The picture is quite positive in terms of wage effects for natives. For all parameter configurations, I obtain wage gains for native workers with no diploma or high school diploma between 0.7 percent and 1.6 percent. Only for the low-parameter estimates configuration, the group of old workers with no diploma has essentially no gains and no losses. In all other cases, the groups of less educated actually gain. As for the highly educated, they essentially have negligible positive wage effects in the intermediate and high-parameter configurations and small negative effects (around –0.3 percent) in the low-parameter-estimates scenario. Hence, the national effects of immigrants on native wages during the 2000s, simulated assuming a national integrated market, were mainly positive for the groups of the least educated individuals, at highest risk of poverty, and mostly negligible for the group of highly educated.

Effects on National Poverty Rates

I translate the estimated wage effects into effects on the poverty rates for different demographic groups as follows. Because the simulated wage effects vary by education and age, I consider the individuals from the American Community Survey in 2009 and I subtract the education-age specific effect of immigration during the 2000 to 2009 period from their wage income in 2009.[5] This produces the counterfactual wage for each individual in 2009, absent immigration during the decade. Then I aggregate the wage income with other sources of income within each family and apply the poverty thresholds (shown in table 2.A1) to the new counterfactual total family income.[6] Some native families will cross the poverty threshold

FIGURE 2.2 / Effect of Immigrants on Native Wages

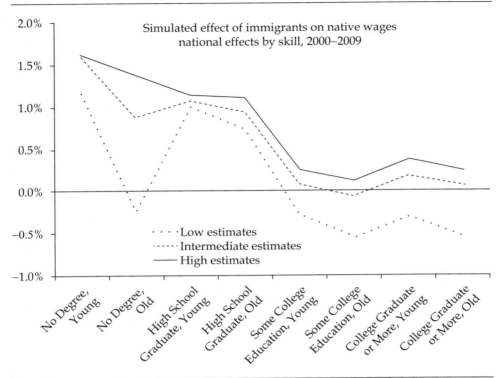

Source: Author's compilation based on the U.S. Census 2000, the 2009 American Community Survey, and the author's own calculations.
Note: The changes as a percentage of the native wage are calculated using the model in the chapter and three parameter combinations, as described in the table 2.1. The schooling groups are individuals with no degree, high school graduates, individuals with some college education, and college graduates. Each schooling group is divided into Young (individuals with less than twenty years of potential labor market experience) and Old (individuals with more than twenty years of potential labor market experience). We assumed that the national market is integrated in the run.

when considering the counterfactual relative to the actual wage. Those will generate differences in native poverty rates with or without immigration. Because groups of less-educated and young individuals are more concentrated in proximity of the poverty line, it is likely that a given wage change will cause larger effects on poverty for those groups. I document in table 2.2 that women were more susceptible of being in families below the poverty line relative to men. Hence, it is useful to show the effect of immigration on native poverty by education, age, and gender groups. Figure 2.3 and figure 2.4 show the simulated effect of immigration on native poverty rates across skill groups in the 1990 to 1999 and the 2000 to 2009 periods, respectively. The figures report the changes in poverty rates, as a percent-

FIGURE 2.3 / National Poverty Rate Change, 1990–2000

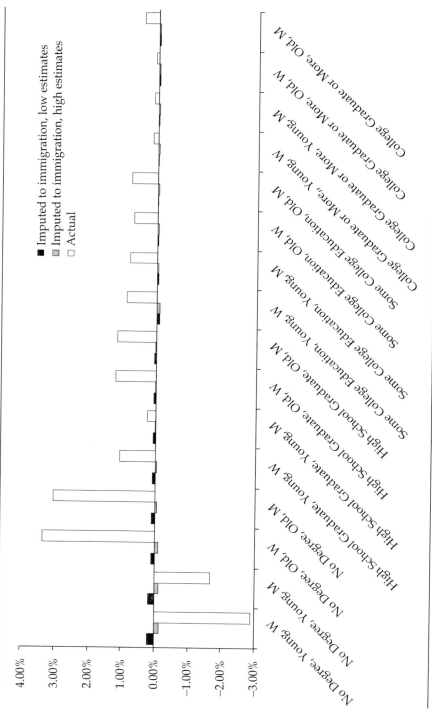

Source: Author's calculations based on the procedure described in the text.

FIGURE 2.4 / National Poverty Rate Change, 2000–2009

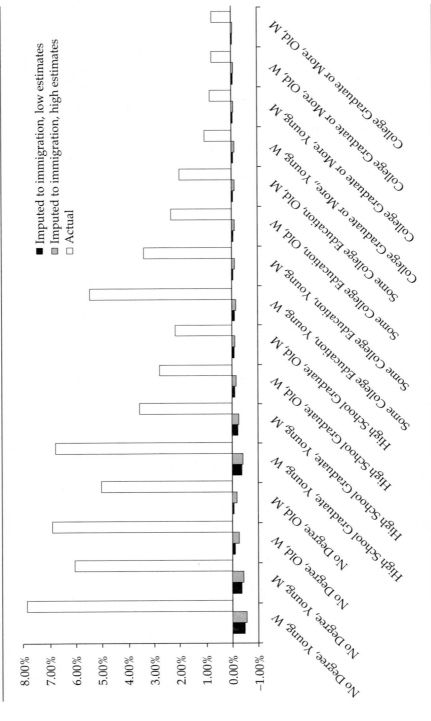

Source: Author's calculations based on the procedure described in the text.

age of the group population, imputed by using the high estimates (gray bars) and the low estimates (black bars). As a comparison, I also report the actual changes in poverty rates during the corresponding period for each group (light bars). The groups are arrayed from less educated to most educated, distinguishing within each education group between young and old and within each education-age group between women (W) and men (M).

Three main results emerge very clearly from these figures. First, consistent with the fact that the wage effects of immigration were rather small, the effect of immigration on native poverty are even smaller. When compared with actual poverty changes in the corresponding decade for any group, they are one order of magnitude smaller. Even in the case of the most pessimistic wage estimates, they cannot explain more than a very small fraction of actual poverty changes. Second, the largest imputed effects of immigration on native poverty are relative to the group of young women with no diploma. These imputed effects range between an increase in poverty of 0.20 percent, using the high estimate in the 1990s, to a poverty reduction of 0.50 percent, using the low estimates during the 2000s. In both cases, however, those are very small effects. They do not even approach explaining the evolution of poverty rates in that group, whose poverty rates dropped almost 3 percent in the 1990s and then stunningly increased by almost 8 percent in the 2000s. Third, consistently with the imputed wage effects, immigration during the 2000s had a percent poverty-reduction effect on all groups, albeit small. For the groups of less educated (of different age and gender), the effect ranged from 0.05 percent to 0.7 percent. Unfortunately, the actual poverty rates for these groups rose by between 3 percent and 8 percent. The most interesting fact is perhaps that the range of simulated effects of immigration on poverty rates, depending on the choice of parameters, is small and essentially irrelevant to explain actual changes in poverty rates. No matter what our preferred representation of the interactions across skills in the labor market is, as captured by the model's parameters, immigration at the national level does not explain a relevant fraction of the evolution of poverty rates.

To show the aggregate effects of immigration on native poverty rates, table 2.4 aggregates the skill groups and summarizes the effect on native poverty for all U.S. born, reporting men and women separately, and for two groups with particularly intense exposure to poverty: African American and Hispanic. Considering the evolution during the 2000s, the results shown in table 2.4 confirm that immigration had a poverty-reduction effect between 0.07 percent and 0.12 percent for U.S. natives overall, a bit larger for women (between 0.07 percent and 0.13 percent) than for men (between 0.08 and 0.09 percent). Immigration had also a poverty-reduction effect for African American up to 0.20 percent, and in particular black women might have experienced up to a 0.24 percent reduction in poverty rates due to immigration. The larger effects on black and women is due to their larger presence among young and less educated, the groups at highest risk of poverty. Immigration during the 2000s helped this group because it was relatively concentrated among the highly educated, relative to the young less educated. Finally, the simulated poverty reduction for the group of Hispanics born in the United States is between 0.15 and 0.20 percent. Interestingly, this is also the only group that actually

TABLE 2.4 / Imputed Effect of Immigrants on Poverty Rates and Actual Rate Changes

	1990–2000				2000–2009			
Skill Group	Imputed, High Estimates	Imputed, Intermediate Estimates	Imputed, Low Estimates	Actual	Imputed, High Estimates	Imputed, Intermediate Estimates	Imputed, Low Estimates	Actual
Overall, U.S. born	0.02	-0.02	-0.04	-0.38	-0.07	-0.10	-0.12	2.10
Male	0.02	-0.02	-0.04	-0.09	-0.08	-0.08	-0.09	2.04
Female	0.02	-0.02	-0.04	-0.65	-0.06	-0.11	-0.13	2.18
Overall black	0.04	-0.01	-0.06	-2.90	-0.13	-0.17	-0.20	1.52
Male	0.04	-0.01	-0.05	-1.39	-0.09	-0.12	-0.14	1.98
Female	0.04	-0.01	-0.07	-4.15	-0.15	-0.20	-0.24	1.23
Overall Hispanic	0.06	0.00	-0.06	-2.35	-0.15	-0.18	-0.21	-0.34
Male	0.05	-0.01	-0.06	-1.57	-0.15	-0.16	-0.18	-0.35
Female	0.07	0.00	-0.07	-3.11	-0.14	-0.20	-0.24	-0.16

Source: Author's compilation.
Note: The calculations are based on the imputed wage effects of immigrants, calculated based on the model in the text. The effect of immigration is calculated as the difference in poverty rates considering wage income with and without net immigration of the considered decade.

had a decrease in poverty rates, by 0.30 percent, during the 2000s. Native blacks and whites had an increase in poverty rates between 1.5 and 2 percent in the decade from 2000 to 2009. Immigration might have been a relevant factor in poverty-reduction for native Hispanics, concentrated among the less educated, in the 2000s.

The effects found in this section confirm the estimates for the period from 1970 to 1999 by Steven Raphael and Eugene Smolensky (2008). They found negligible effects of immigrants on native poverty, due to very small wage effects. Here I extend that analysis to the period from 2000 to 2009 and introduce combinations of parameters that span a larger set of models. I find that actually in the recent decade immigration had a small but consistently positive effect in poverty reduction. I turn now to local effects in States and Metropolitan areas.

SIMULATED EFFECTS ON NATIVE POVERTY IN STATES AND MSAS

Considering states and cities individually, and the specific immigration rates that they received, I simulate in this section the largest possible wage effect imputable to immigrants under the assumption that native workers were not mobile across states or cities. These effects are likely to be upper bounds of reasonable effects. In fact, if a large local influx of immigrants depresses (or raises) wages substantially, natives could flow in or out to attenuate these effects at least partially. Assuming that natives did not move in response to immigration, were the local inflows large enough and distributed appropriately across skills and geography to explain differences in the changes of native poverty rates across states and metro areas?

Top-Immigration States

I begin by considering the wage effect of immigrants on the usual eight skill groups of natives in the top immigration states, the trends of which were described earlier. Then I map these effects into effects on the corresponding poverty rates and show those in figures 2.5 and 2.6. These figures show the simulated poverty-rate effects of immigration for each of the four education groups (no diploma, high school graduates, some college, and college graduates) in the ten states, using the low (black), the intermediate (medium gray), and the high estimate (light gray) configuration. I also show the actual change in poverty rates for the education-by-state group in the decade as shaded bars. The education groups are always arrayed from the lowest to the highest one for each state. Figure 2.5 shows the effects in the 1990s. Only the low estimates for Arizona, Colorado, Nevada, and Texas produce a poverty increase for the least educated group of some significance, around 1 percent. For all other states, and for the other simulation scenarios, the poverty changes due to immigrants across top immigration states are less than 0.5 percent, even in the 1990s. Moreover in Arizona, Colorado, Nevada, and Texas, the actual poverty rates of the least educated during the 1990s dropped rather than

FIGURE 2.5 / State Poverty Rate Change, 1990–2000

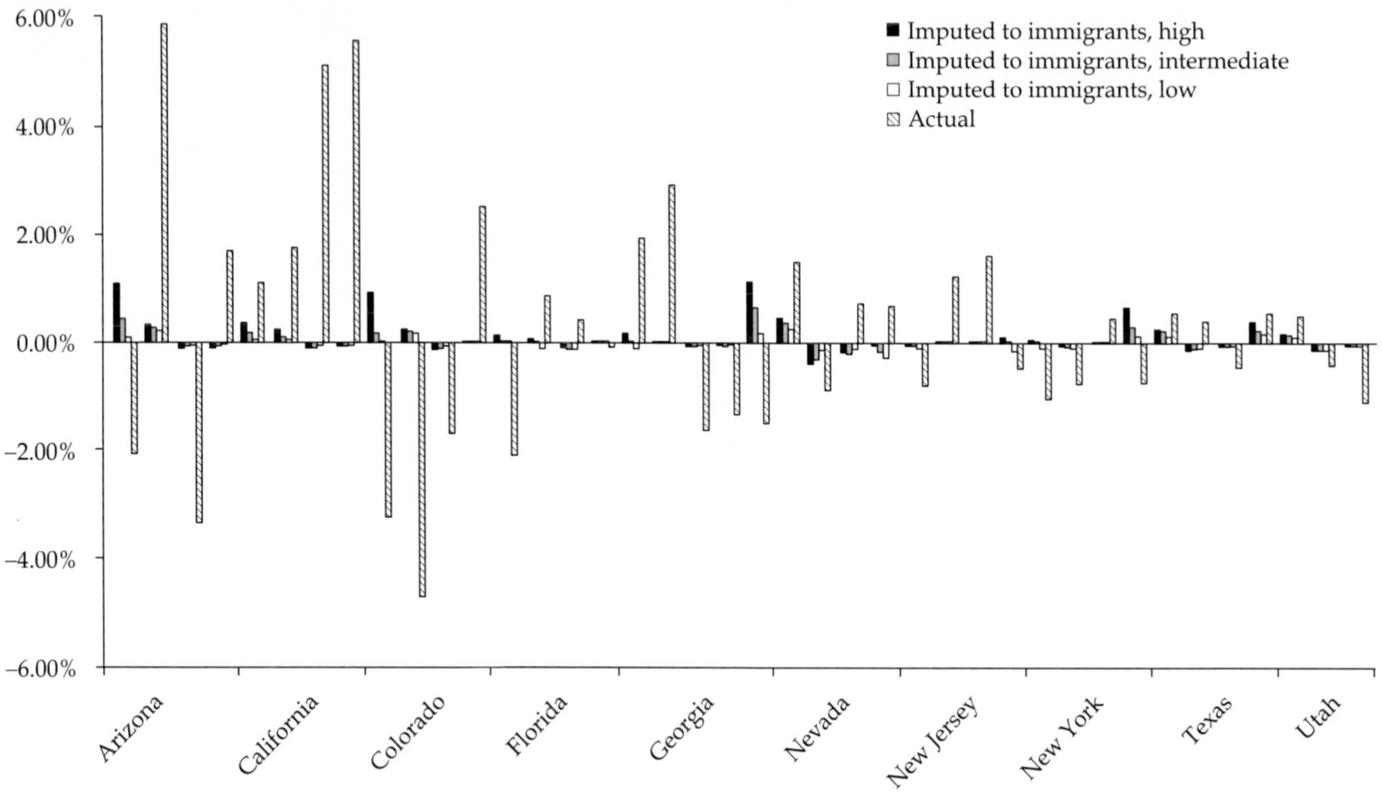

Source: Author's calculations, based on the procedure described in the text.

FIGURE 2.6 / State Poverty Rate Change, 2000–2009

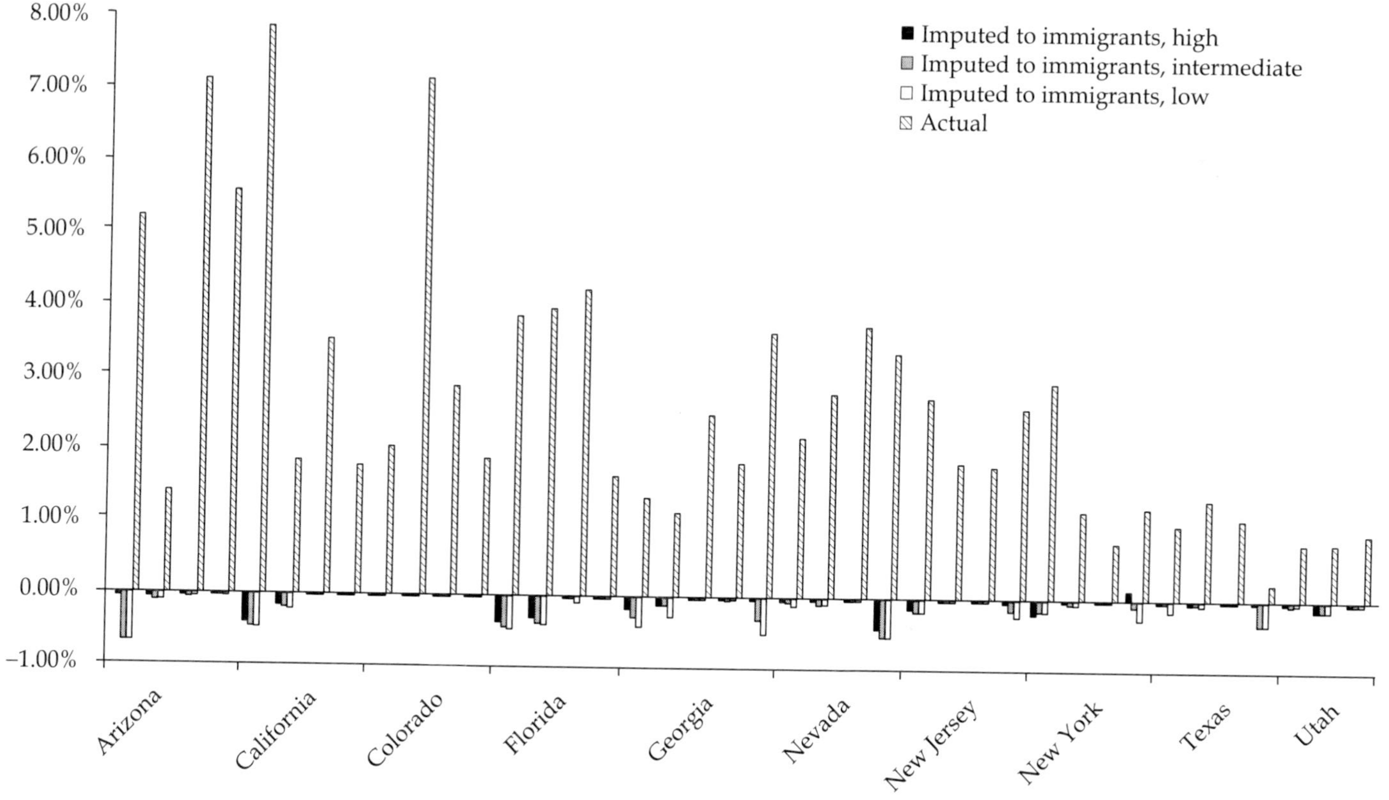

Source: Author's calculations, based on the procedure described in the text.

rose, as it would be if immigration were the main factor. Among natives with no diploma poverty rates dropped by 2 percent or more in Arizona and Colorado, and by almost 1 percent in Texas and Nevada.

The contrast between imputed and actual effects is even more striking in the 2000s. During the decade, immigrants had small poverty-reducing effects for the least educated natives, especially in states such as Arizona, California, Florida, and New Jersey. As mentioned, this was due to the schooling intensity of immigrants in those states. These groups, however, experienced an increase in poverty rates (shaded bars) in all states. Moreover, the magnitude of the actual increase in poverty rates was an order of magnitude larger than the reduction effect imputed to immigrants. The lack of explanatory power of the imputed effects, on the actual poverty changes across education groups by states is also revealed by the lack of any correlation between the two.

Top Immigration Metropolitan Areas

To complete the picture, I perform the same analysis considering the twenty top immigration metropolitan areas described in table 2.A3. Metropolitan areas are small enough that sometimes local immigration rates over a decade can be extremely high, and skewed toward some groups. This provides large cross-city variation in immigration and increases the potential explanatory power of this variable in terms of poverty effects. On the down side, however, the measurement error may be more severe at the MSA level in several variables and simulating the local wage effects under the scenario of no mobility of natives across metro areas is less plausible than for states and for the nation.

Focusing on the decade from 2000 to 2009, the wage effect of immigration by skill group in some cities was relatively large, at least compared with the national one. Hence in some cities and groups the wages of natives decreased as much as 4 to 5 percent due to immigration, according to our model. However, in the same cities, the wage of other groups increased by 6 to 10 percent due to immigrants. The most likely situation for the top twenty cities considered was that the wages of the less educated actually increased because of immigration. In cities such as McAllen, Texas; Yuma, Arizona; and Raleigh-Durham, North Carolina, for instance, our simulations (not reported) predict that immigration should have increased wages of less-educated individuals by 6 to 8 percent, provided that natives did not move during the 2000 to 2009 period. Similarly, assuming lack of mobility of natives and the low-estimate configuration, the least educated citizens in cities such as Reno, Las Vegas, and Austin should have experienced a 1.5 percent to 2 percent increase in poverty rates because of immigration during the 1990 to 1999 period. These are non-negligible values. Figures 2.7 and 2.8, however, put them into perspective by showing the actual changes in poverty rates (shaded columns) together with the imputed effects due to immigration (the bars in the gray scale) for the four schooling groups in the twenty MSAs considered. Although cities such as Houston, Las Vegas, and Reno had actual and imputed changes in poverty rates

FIGURE 2.7 / Metropolitan Statistical Area Poverty Rate Change, 1990–2000

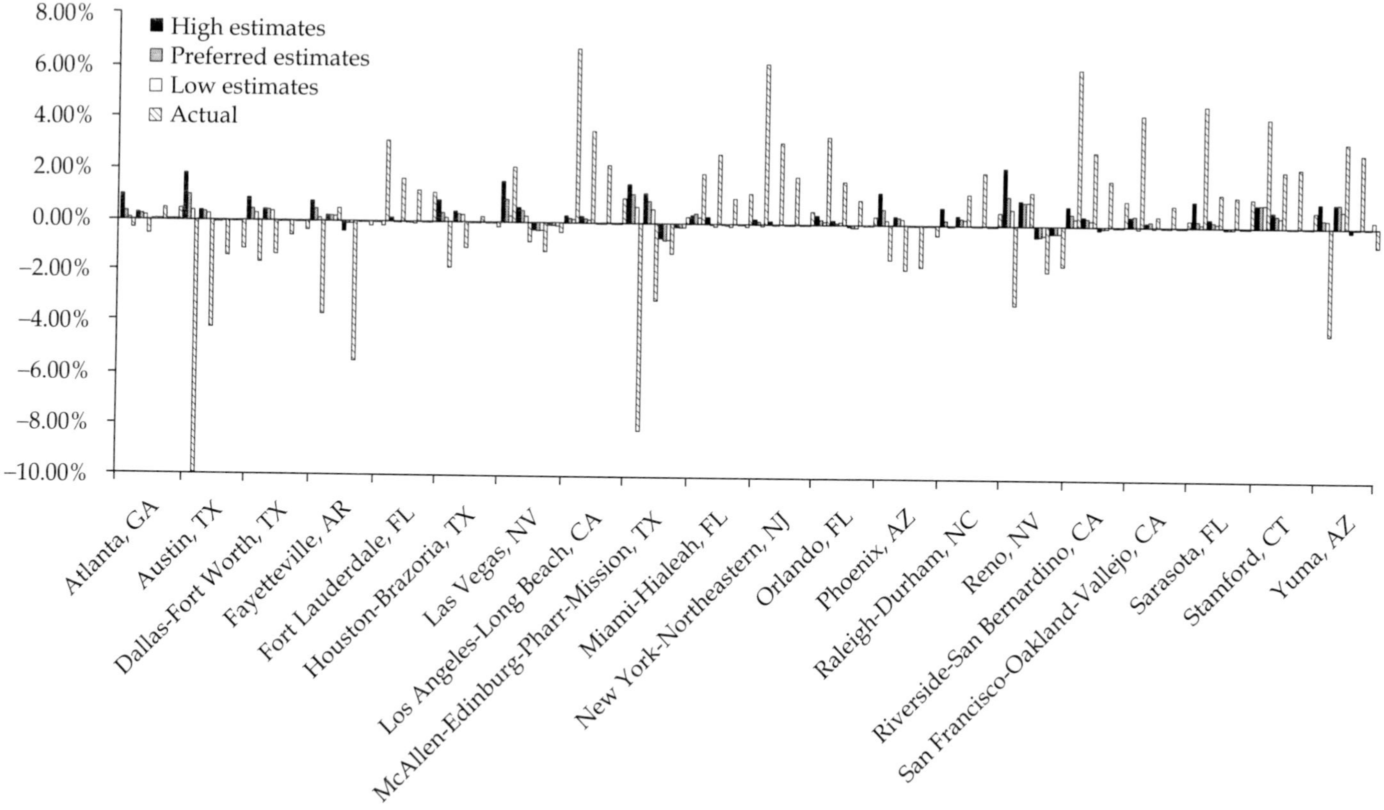

Legend:
- ■ High estimates
- ▨ Preferred estimates
- ☐ Low estimates
- ▨ Actual

Source: Author's calculations, based on the procedure described in the text.

FIGURE 2.8 / Metropolitan Statistical Area Poverty Rate Change, 2000–2010

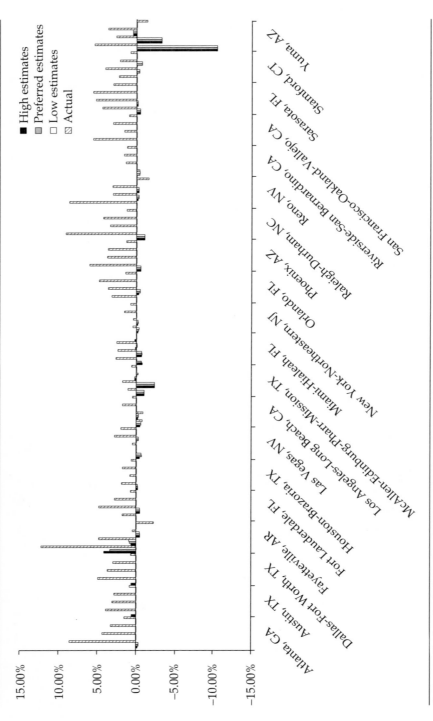

Source: Author's calculations, based on the procedure described in the text.

in the 1990s of comparable magnitude, the actual changes of poverty rates were usually much larger and much more variable than the imputed ones. For the changes in the 2000 to 2009 period, figure 2.8 shows that, except for Fayetteville, Arizona, in which immigration explains a non-negligible share of the actual increase in poverty, the simulations predict a reduction in poverty rates due to immigration for all the other cities. However, these MSAs experienced increases in poverty rates during between 2000 and 2009. Immigration's labor market impact cannot in any way explain the changes and variation in poverty rates, even at the metropolitan area level.

CONCLUSIONS

The most recent assessments of the wage impact of immigrants in the United States (Card 2009; Ottaviano and Peri 2012) agree that there is little evidence of a large wage competition effect on natives. In this study, I focus on a specific consequence of the wage competition of immigrants: the resulting increase in native poverty due to a negative income effect on individuals who are already near the poverty line. The poverty rate, though somewhat arbitrary, is a useful measure of the percentage of individuals in a weak and vulnerable situation and it is used as reference in several mean-tested welfare programs. Hence, the impact of immigration in increasing or decreasing native poverty is an interesting measure, possibly also affecting the size of welfare programs toward natives.

I assessed how the wage competition of immigrants, evaluated using a general equilibrium model of the labor market, affected native poverty rates. I find that immigration had essentially no effect on poverty at the national level during the entire period from 1990 to 2009. To be more specific, I am able to construct very small poverty-increasing effects of immigration during the 1990s by adopting rather extreme parameter values in the simulations. In the 2000s, even the simulations with parameter values most unfavorable to native workers deliver poverty-reduction effects of immigrants. This is because immigration in the 2000s has been quite skill-intensive with a much larger immigration rate among college educated than among any other group.

At the state and city level, a more nuanced picture confirms these findings. Even focusing on top immigration states and metropolitan areas, using the most reasonable parameter configuration, I only detect very small wage effects on natives. Considering immigration in the 2000s, these effects were actually positive for wages of less-educated individuals and, in general, poverty-reducing even across large immigration states and metropolitan areas. What is also striking is that the immigration-imputed effects (even with the most extreme assumptions of parameters and native mobility) do not explain the magnitude and the variance in poverty changes across education groups and states or cities. The impact of immigrants via wage competition is simply too small and not correlated enough to actual income to be a valid candidate to explain a significant part of poverty changes in the United States. Moreover, highly educated immigration may actually reduce native poverty rates.

APPENDIX

Details of the Model

Slightly adjusting the model used in Ottaviano and Peri (2012) and similarly to Docquier et al. (2010), the production function of the representative economy in year t is as follows:

$$Y_t = \tilde{A}_t K_t^{\alpha} Q_t^{1-\alpha} \qquad (1)$$

where Y_t is output, chosen as the numeraire, $\tilde{A}_t$ is total factor productivity K_t is physical capital, Q_t is a labor composite described below and α is the elasticity of output to capital. Assuming that physical capital is mobile across nations (or cities and states), the returns to physical capital are equalized across countries. If R^* denotes the international net rate of return to capital, the following arbitrage condition implicitly defines the equilibrium capital-to-labor ratio in the economy:

$$R^* = (1 - \alpha)\tilde{A}_t K_t^{\alpha} Q_t^{\alpha} \qquad (2)$$

In a small open economy the above condition holds in the short and in the long run. In a closed economy as in Frank Ramsey (1926) or Robert Solow (1951) condition (2) holds in the long run (balanced growth path), with R^* being a function of the inter-temporal discount rate of individuals (or of the savings rate).[7] Hence, in the long run we can substitute this arbitrage condition into (1) to obtain an expression of aggregate output as linear function of the aggregate labor Q_t:

$$Y_t = A_t Q_t \qquad (3)$$

where $A_t \equiv \tilde{A}_t^{1/\alpha}[(1 - \alpha)/R^*]^{(1-\alpha)/\alpha}$ is an increasing function of total factor productivity (TFP) and is referred to as modified TFP henceforth. Notice, as it is clear from expression (1), that with endogenous capital adjustment, output is a linear function of employment. Hence, an inflow of workers has no effect on average wages, which depend only on productivity. Moreover, an inflow of workers that is balanced across skill types will have no effect on any wage. In the long run (ten years), and for economies with free capital circulation (such as U.S. cities or states), endogenous capital response is a reasonable assumption.

The labor composite is defined as a nested CES (constant elasticity of substitution) aggregate of different types of workers as follows. First I distinguish between highly educated (Q_H) and less-educated (Q_L) workers who are combined in the following way:

$$Q_t = \left[\theta_H Q_{H,t}^{\frac{\sigma_{HL}-1}{\sigma_{HL}}} + (1-\theta_H) Q_{L,t}^{\frac{\sigma_{HL}-1}{\sigma_{HL}}} \right]^{\frac{\sigma_{HL}}{\sigma_{HL}-1}} \qquad (4)$$

In equation (4), the parameter σ_{HL} is the elasticity between highly and less educated and θ_H is the relative productivity of highly educated. In the empirical implementation highly educated are individuals with some college education or more,
and the less educated are high school graduates or less. In some studies (for example, Borjas 2003) the group of less-educated workers is further split into two
subgroups—high school graduates and those with no diploma—with an elasticity
of substitution of σ_{LL} between them. In most cases, however, the literature (for example, Katz and Murphy 1992; Goldin and Katz 2008) has used one homogeneous
group for less-educated workers. Then each group of workers with homogenous
schooling k is divided into two experience groups, young (Q_Y) and old (Q_O), also
combined in a CES fashion:

$$Q_{kt} = \left[\theta_Y Q_{Y,kt}^{\frac{\sigma_{YO}-1}{\sigma_{YO}}} + (1-\theta_Y) Q_{O,kt}^{\frac{\sigma_{YO}-1}{\sigma_{YO}}} \right]^{\frac{\sigma_{YO}}{\sigma_{YO}-1}} \tag{5}$$

In equation (5) the parameter σ_{YO} is the elasticity between young and old in the
schooling group and θ_Y the relative productivity of young workers. Finally within
an education-experience group employment of immigrants (I) and of natives (N)
are combined in a CES function.

$$Q_{kjt} = \left[\theta_I I_{kjt}^{\frac{\sigma_{IN}-1}{\sigma_{IN}}} + (1-\theta_I) N_{kjt}^{\frac{\sigma_{IN}-1}{\sigma_{IN}}} \right]^{\frac{\sigma_{IN}}{\sigma_{IN}-1}} \tag{6}$$

I assume that the marginal productivity of each type of workers equals its wage
and that the supply of each type of workers is given by a fixed proportion (proxied
by the employment rate) of the population of that group. Thus, we can write the
wage of native workers of skill k,j as a function of the total supply of labor aggregates, which depend on the total number of immigrants and vary with them.
Wages for native workers of skill k,j are given by:

$$w_{kj,t} = A_t \theta_k \theta_j (i-\theta_i) \left(\frac{Q_t}{Q_{k,t}} \right)^{\frac{1}{\sigma_{HL}}} \left(\frac{Q_{k,t}}{Q_{kj,t}} \right)^{\frac{1}{\sigma_{YO}}} \left(\frac{Q_{kj,t}}{N_{kj,t}} \right)^{\frac{1}{\sigma_{IN}}} \tag{7}$$

As the inflow of immigrants changes the relative supplies $Q_{k,t}/Q_t$, $Q_{kj,t}/Q_{k,t}$, and
$N_{kj,t}/Q_{kj,t}$ it will alter the wage of natives in different skill groups. I obtain the wage
effect of immigration by calculating the wages—including or excluding the new
immigrants (between 1990 and 2000 or between 2000 and 2009)—and taking their
difference as a percentage of the pre-migration wage.[8] These effects will be specific
to the education-age group and will depend on the whole distribution of new immigrants across cells.

Finally, as anticipated in the introduction, we consider that productivity may

TABLE 2.A1 / Federal Poverty Thresholds for Pre-Transfer Family Income, 1999

Number of People	Number of Related Children								
	None	One	Two	Three	Four	Five	Six	Seven	Eight +
One person under 65 years	8,667								
One person, 65 years or older	7,990								
Two people, RP under 65 years	11,156	11,483							
Two people, RP 65 years or older	10,070	11,440							
Three people	13,032	13,410	13,423						
Four people	17,184	17,465	16,895	16,954					
Five people	20,723	21,024	20,380	19,882	19,578				
Six people	23,835	23,930	23,436	22,964	22,261	21,845			
Seven people	27,425	27,596	27,006	26,595	25,828	24,934	23,953		
Eight people	30,673	30,944	30,387	29,899	29,206	28,327	27,412	27,180	
Nine or more people	36,897	37,076	36,583	36,169	35,489	34,554	33,708	33,499	32,208

Source: Author's compilation based on "Poverty Thresholds by Size of Family and Number of Children," U.S. Census Bureau (1999). Available at: http://www.census.gov/hhes/www/Poverty/data/threshld (accessed May 23, 2013).

Note: Poverty thresholds (yearly income) by size of family and number of children under 18 years. All numbers in 2000 dollars. To obtain those in 2009 multiply by 0.773. The poverty thresholds are the same for all parts of the country; they are not adjusted for regional, state, or local variations in the cost of living. For a detailed discussion of the poverty definition, see U.S. Census Bureau, Current Population Reports, Series P-60, No. 210, Poverty in the United States, 1999.

Table 2.A2 / Immigration Rates in Top Immigration States

State	1990–2009					2000–2009				
	No Degree	High School Graduate	Some College	College Graduate	Total 1990–2000	No Degree	High School Graduate	Some College	College Graduate	Total 2000–2009
Arizona	38.8	16.3	3.5	10.4	14.2	9.7	7.6	5.8	9.3	7.8
California	19.9	16.5	1.5	14.6	11.8	-1.2	3.2	5.3	9.8	4.6
Colorado	36.1	8.6	1.6	7.3	8.8	12.7	3.0	3.6	3.1	4.2
Florida	10.1	14.0	4.6	15.2	10.8	2.0	5.2	8.3	11.1	6.8
Georgia	15.2	7.3	3.5	10.1	8.5	7.9	4.0	4.7	7.5	5.6
Nevada	61.6	24.0	6.8	19.0	23.0	21.7	8.7	12.0	16.0	12.6
New Jersey	8.7	9.8	3.6	13.5	9.1	0.5	1.9	5.9	9.1	4.8
New York	8.9	10.7	2.2	11.1	8.3	0.6	-0.7	3.7	6.4	2.4
Texas	23.7	11.9	2.7	10.0	11.3	11.0	5.5	6.3	8.9	7.5
Utah	32.4	10.7	2.3	7.1	8.7	11.6	3.4	3.3	3.2	4.1

Source: Author's calculations based on the U.S. Census 1990 and 2000 and the 2009 American Community Survey.
Notes: All numbers in percentages. The top immigration states included in the table are the nine states with the highest immigration rate 1990–2006 and the six states with the highest share of foreign-born as of 2009.

TABLE 2.A3 / Immigration Rates in Top Immigration MSAs

State	1990–2009					2000–2009				
	No Degree	HS Graduate	Some College	College Graduate	Total 1990–2000	No Degree	HS Graduate	Some College	College Graduate	Total 2000–2009
Atlanta, GA	42.1	16.9	6.2	14.3	16.0	14.2	7.1	7.4	9.1	8.6
Austin, TX	61.6	19.9	4.1	14.2	17.6	32.6	8.7	4.7	9.7	10.9
Dallas-Fort Worth, TX	46.8	17.2	3.5	11.4	16.3	18.5	7.8	6.2	9.2	9.7
Fayetteville, AR	67.9	16.7	6.0	15.4	22.2	34.0	6.0	5.7	2.2	9.2
Fort Lauderdale-Hollywood, FL	20.2	29.5	16.5	32.1	24.7	4.8	7.5	11.6	19.6	11.3
Houston-Brazoria, TX	36.4	18.4	4.1	14.0	16.8	17.0	9.3	11.8	11.7	11.9
Las Vegas, NV	78.1	31.7	9.7	27.4	30.8	27.3	11.3	14.3	22.1	16.2
Los Angeles-Long Beach, CA	14.1	18.2	1.0	14.0	11.2	-10.8	0.6	6.3	10.3	1.7
McAllen-Edinburg, TX	33.4	35.1	11.5	29.4	29.5	8.6	12.0	22.2	28.6	14.1
Miami-Hialeah, FL	0.7	35.4	2.5	28.3	17.2	-18.5	2.3	13.9	17.0	4.0
New York-Northeastern NJ	12.5	16.2	4.3	15.9	12.6	-1.2	-0.7	5.9	8.4	3.4
Orlando, FL	21.5	17.3	7.5	15.6	14.4	10.1	8.5	12.2	10.7	10.2
Phoenix, AZ	60.6	20.4	3.9	12.3	18.1	13.3	10.2	6.9	11.1	10.0
Raleigh-Durham, NC	60.4	17.5	5.5	16.2	18.1	22.9	4.8	7.3	8.9	8.9
Reno, NV	89.5	34.8	8.7	19.6	29.7	13.5	4.7	7.5	4.9	6.6
Riverside-San Bernardino, CA	33.3	17.5	2.4	13.2	14.6	17.8	10.9	11.1	20.1	13.6
San Francisco-Oakland,CA	26.6	16.1	1.6	17.3	12.8	0.8	3.1	1.8	7.4	4.1
Sarasota, FL	44.5	17.5	8.0	15.9	17.5	5.0	5.7	6.6	11.7	7.2
Stamford, CT	97.0	63.0	24.9	56.5	55.3	4.0	0.5	9.6	5.2	4.7
Yuma, AZ	44.4	27.3	9.9	8.0	25.3	2.0	6.6	3.9	25.5	6.6

Source: Author's calculations based on based on the U.S. Census 1990 and 2000 and the 2009 American Community Survey.
Notes: All numbers in percentages. The top immigration metropolitan areas included in table 2.5 are the sixteen metro areas with the highest im-migration rate between 1990 and 2009 and the four largest metro areas with a share of foreign-born above 30 percent.

depend on a human capital externality. Using the formulation in Enrico Moretti (2004a, 2004b) we write:

$$A_t = A_0(\exp(h_t))^\lambda, \tag{8}$$

where A_0 captures the part of TFP independent of the human capital externality, and λ is the semi-elasticity of the modified TFP to the share of college educated in the economy, h_t, including natives and immigrants. Immigration may alter h_t if the immigrant distribution between college educated and noneducated is different than the one of natives. Moretti (2004a) and Iranzo and Peri (2009) use the formulation as in (8), emphasizing that the externalities depend on the share of college educated, rather than merely on average years of schooling.

Effects on Wages

I define the percentage change in the immigrant population in schooling group k age group j and in period t as $\Delta I_{kjt}/I_{kjt}$. I also call s_{Ikjt} the share of the total wage bill going to immigrants of schooling k and age j and similarly s_{kjt} is the wage share of workers (native and immigrants) with skills kj and s_{kt} the wage share of workers with schooling k. The overall percentage effect of the inflow of immigrants on the wage of native workers of education k and age kj is given by:

$$\left(\frac{\Delta w_{kjt}}{w_{kjt}}\right)^{Total} = \frac{1}{\sigma_{HL}} \sum_{k \in H,L} \sum_{j \in Y,O} \left(s_{Ikjt} \frac{\Delta I_{kjt}}{I_{kjt}}\right) + \left(\frac{1}{\sigma_{YO}} - \frac{1}{\sigma_{HL}}\right)\left(\frac{1}{s_{kt}}\right)\sum_{j \in Y,O}\left(s_{Ikjt}\frac{\Delta I_{kjt}}{I_{kjt}}\right)$$
$$+\left(\frac{1}{\sigma_{IN}} - \frac{1}{\sigma_{YO}}\right)\left(\frac{1}{s_{kjt}}\right)\left(s_{Ikjt}\frac{\Delta F_{bkjt}}{F_{bkjt}}\right) + \lambda\left(\frac{\Delta h_t}{h_t}\right)_{immigration} \tag{9}$$

The term $1/\sigma_{HL}\ \Sigma_{k \in H,L}\Sigma_{j,O}(s_{Ikjt}\ \Delta I_{kjt}/I_{kjt})$ captures the aggregate wage effect from immigration in all cells, the term $(1/\sigma_{YO} - 1/\sigma_{HL})(1/s_{kt})\Sigma_{j \in Y,O}(s_{Ikjt}\ \Delta I_{kjt}/I_{kjt})$ is the extra-competition effect due to immigration in the same education group and the term $(1/\sigma_{IN} - 1/\sigma_{YO})(1/s_{kjt})(s_{Ikjt}\ \Delta F_{bkjt}/F_{bkjt})$ is the further competition effect on native wages from immigrants in the same education and experience group. The term $(\Delta h_t/h_t)_{immigration}$ captures the change in the share of college educated individuals due to immigration and it contributes via the externality to the overall wage effect. This formula is used to obtain the simulated wage effects reported in the chapter.

NOTES

1. The set of instrumental variables that is currently most popular in the literature was first proposed by Daron Altonji and David Card (1991) and by Card (2001).
2. The difference between the partial effect and the overall effect of immigration on wages

of natives in different skill groups is pointed out and discussed in Ottaviano and Peri (2012).

3. This criticism to the area approach was raised in several studies beginning with that of George Borjas, Richard Freeman, and Larry Katz (1997).

4. Previous models that analyze the wage effect of immigrants usually do not consider the externality channel. However, we show that, especially following the increased college-intensity of immigration during the 2000 to 2009 period, this channel may be important when evaluating wage and productivity effects of immigrants.

5. In the counterfactual scenario, I consider only the wage impact of immigration. If labor supply of natives is not perfectly rigid there may also be effects of immigration on hours worked by natives. Those will amplify the impact of immigrants. However, as the elasticity of labor supply is usually estimated to be between 0 and 0.2 the effect would be quite small. This produces the counterfactual wage for each individual in 2009, absent immigration during the 2000 to 2009 period. Then I aggregate the wage income with other sources of income within each family and apply the poverty thresholds (shown in table 2.A1) to the new counterfactual total family income.

6. Notice that for families close to and below the poverty line wage income is a smaller share of total income, relative to the average U.S. family. This is because larger part of their income come from welfare programs. For instance in year 2000 for the average U.S. family 80 percent of total income was wage income, whereas for families below the poverty line only 54 percent was. This is an additional reason why the changes in wage income of natives has only small effects on poverty rates.

7. As long as immigration does not change the savings rate of an economy the pre- and post-migration $R*$ are identical.

8. The formulas to obtain the percentage wage effect of immigration, derived from equation (7), are in (9).

REFERENCES

Acemoglu, Daron, and Joshua Angrist. 2000. "How Large Are Human Capital Externalities? Evidence from Compulsory Schooling Laws." In *NBER Macroeconomic Annual 2000*, vol. 15, edited by Ben S. Bernanke & Kenneth Rogoff. Cambridge, Mass.: National Bureau of Economic Research.

Altonji, Joseph G., and David Card. 1991. "The Effects of Immigration on the Labor Market Outcomes of Less-skilled Natives." In *Immigration, Trade and the Labor Market*, edited by John Abowd and Richard Freeman. Cambridge, Mass.: National Bureau of Economic Research.

Borjas, George, Richard Freeman, and Larry Katz. 1997. "How Much Do Immigration and Trade Affect Labor Market Outcomes?" *Brookings Papers on Economic Activity* 28(1): 1–90.

Borjas, George, Jeffrey Grogger, and Gordon Hanson. 2012. "Imperfect Substitution Between Immigrants and Natives: A Reappraisal." *Journal of the European Economic Association* 10(1).

Card, David. 2001. "Immigrant Inflows, Native Outflows and the Local Labor Market Impacts of Higher Immigration." *Journal of Labor Economics* 19(1): 22–61.

———. 2009. "Immigration and Inequality." *American Economic Review* 99(2): 1–21.

Card, David, and Thomas Lemieux. 2001. "Can Falling Supply Explain the Rising Returns to College for Younger Men? A Cohort Based Analysis." *Quarterly Journal of Economics* 116(2): 705–46.

Ciccone Antonio, and Giovanni Peri. 2005. "Long-Run Substitutability Between More and Less Educated Workers: Evidence from U.S. States 1950–1990." *Review of Economics and Statistics* 87(4): 652–63.

———. 2006. "Identifying Human Capital Externalities: Theory with Applications." *Review of Economic Studies* 73(April): 381–412.

Docquier, Frederic, Caglar Ozden, and Giovanni Peri. 2010. "The Wage Effect of Immigration and Emigration." *NBER* working paper 16646. Cambridge, Mass.: National Bureau on Economic Research.

Goldin, Claudia, and Larry Katz. 2008. *The Race Between Education and Technology.* Cambridge, Mass.: Harvard University Press.

Iranzo, Susana, and Giovanni Peri. 2009. "Migration and Trade: Theory with an Application to the Eastern-Western European Integration." *CReAM* discussion paper 0905. London: Centre for Research and Analysis of Migration.

Katz, Larry, and Kevin Murphy. 1992. "Changes in Relative Wages 1963–1987: Supply and Demand Factors." *Quarterly Journal of Economics* 7(1): 35–78.

Manacorda, Marco, Alan Manning, and Jonathan Wadsworth. 2012. "The Impact of Immigration on the Structure of Wages: Theory and Evidence from Britain." *Journal of the European Economic Association* 10(1): 120–51.

Moretti, Enrico. 2004a. "Estimating the Social Return to Higher Education: Evidence from Longitudinal and Repeated Cross-Sectional Data." *Journal of Econometrics* 121(1): 175–212.

———. 2004b. "Workers' Education, Spillovers and Productivity: Evidence from Plant-Level Production Functions." *American Economic Review* 94(3): 656–690.

Ottaviano, Gianmarco I. P., and Giovanni Peri. 2012. "Rethinking the Effect of Immigration on Wages." *Journal of the European Economic Association* 10(1): 152–97.

Peri, Giovanni. 2011. "Rethinking the Area Approach: Immigrants and the Labor Market in California." *Journal of International Economics* 84(1): 1–14.

Raphael, Steven, and Eugene Smolensky. 2008. "Immigration and Poverty in the United States." UC Berkeley working paper. Berkeley: University of California

Ramsey, Frank. 1928. "A Mathematical Theory of Saving." *Economic Journal* 38(152): 543–59.

Solow, Robert. 1956. "A Contribution to the Theory of Economic Growth." *Quarterly Journal of Economics* 70(1): 65–94.

U.S. Census Bureau. 1991. "Poverty Thresholds by Size of Family and Number of Children." Available at: http://www.census.gov/hhes/www/poverty/data/threshld (accessed June 7, 2013).

Welch, Finis. 1979. "Effects of Cohort Size on Earnings: The Baby Boom Babies Financial Boost." *Journal of Political Economy* 87(5): 65–97.

Chapter 3

Immigrant-Native Substitutability and the Role of Language

Ethan Lewis

Studies have found that the massive flow of immigrants into the United States in the past few decades has had little negative impact on the average wages of native-born workers (reviews include Borjas 1994; Friedberg and Hunt 1995; Ottaviano and Peri 2012). However, many of these same studies tend to find that the new arrivals substantially depressed the wages of previous immigrant arrivals (Card 2001; Ottaviano and Peri 2012).[1] That immigrants seem, by this evidence, not to fully compete in the native labor market may contribute to the relatively high rates of poverty among immigrants, and understanding why they do not may inform policies aimed at reducing immigrant poverty.

A plausible explanation for why immigrants do not fully compete is that their limited English skills restrict them to occupations where English skills are less important. The ability to speak a country's native language is associated with higher wages (for example, Chiswick and Miller 1995, 2007; Carliner 1996; Dustmann and Fabbri 2003; Bleakely and Chin 2004; Ferrer, Green, and Riddell 2006). In addition, less-skilled immigrants in the United States appear to specialize in occupations that require relatively little communication (Peri and Sparber 2009), although factors besides immigrants' relative lack of English skills, such as a greater willingness to work in manual jobs, could also contribute to this.

In this chapter, I ask how immigrants' language skills affect how closely they compete with native-born workers. As described in the introduction to this volume, how closely two different groups of workers—in this case, immigrants and natives—compete in the labor market is revealed by how closely their wages move together in response to changes in the size of one group relative to the other. In economics jargon, two groups of workers are described as perfect substitutes if their wages move in sync in response to changes in relative numbers: from the labor market's perspective, they are identical. By contrast, two groups are considered imperfect substitutes if an increase in the size of one group relative to another lowers the wages of the first relative to the second. The more responsive relative wages are to relative supply, the less directly these two groups compete in the labor market. In the United States, immigrants and natives with similar education and experience are imperfect substitutes (Ottaviano and Peri 2012).

Put another way, this chapter asks whether immigrants with strong English-language skills are closer substitutes for natives than immigrants with poor English-language skills. Specifically, it asks whether the wages of immigrants who speak English well, relative to the wages of natives, respond more to changes in the relative total hours worked than do the relative wages of immigrants who speak English poorly. To estimate this relationship, I rely primarily on variation across metropolitan areas, using data from the 2000 U.S. Census of Population and American Community Surveys from 2007 to 2009 (Ruggles et al. 2010). All comparisons are made within broad education groups (high school or less, more than high school) that previous research has found represent distinct labor types (Card 2009; Goldin and Katz 2008). These data contain self-reports of English-language skills. Because language skills may be correlated with other factors, such as legal status, that affect substitutability with natives, I also make comparisons by age at arrival and time in the United States, exploiting the fact that immigrants who arrive in the United States as children tend to have far better English-language skills as adults (Bleakley and Chin 2004), and, similarly, that English skills tend to rise with time in the United States. The idea is that legal status and other confounding factors may have a weaker relationship with English skills across these groups.

This discussion is written as if all communication must take place in English. In some parts of the United States, however, Spanish is also an important language. The extreme case is Puerto Rico, where both immigrants—who include foreign-born from Latin American countries as well as U.S.-born ethnic Puerto Ricans—and natives speak Spanish. As a further test of the language hypothesis, I ask whether wage movements reveal Puerto Rican immigrants and natives to be perfect substitutes. Because Puerto Rico is usually considered a single labor market (see Borjas 2008), it is not possible to exploit geographic variation in the size of the immigrant population. Instead, this analysis relies on variation over time and across detailed education and experience groups in the relative size of the immigrant population, using Puerto Rican censuses from 1970 to 2000 along with the 2007–2009 Puerto Rican Community Surveys (Ruggles et al. 2010). I also perform a parallel aggregate analysis of the continental United States.

In less extreme cases, Spanish can be a dominant language, as in Miami and Los Angeles, or prevalent if not dominant, as in Chicago and San Francisco. I also consider whether the density of Spanish speakers affects how substitutable Spanish-speaking immigrants are for natives. Under what conditions does a parallel Spanish-speaking labor market develop in the area? A key hypothesis is that it requires not just a large number of Spanish speakers overall, but a sufficiently rich distribution of skills among Spanish speakers. This, for example, distinguishes Miami—where majority of both highly educated and less-educated workers speak Spanish—from Chicago—where Spanish speakers are disproportionately less educated.

Nearly all of the results are consistent with the view that language skills are an important source of imperfect substitutability between immigrants and natives. The estimates imply that the increase in the labor supplied by immigrants relative to natives since 1990 in the average metropolitan area is associated with about a 6 percent decline in the hourly wage of immigrants with poor English-language skills, but only a 2 percent decline in the wages of immigrants with strong English-language skills, each relative to natives with similar education and work experience. I also find that the wages of immigrants who arrived as young children and long ago are less sensitive to immigrant relative supply than those who arrived at older ages and recently. Also consistent with language driving imperfect substitutability, immigration is not associated in Puerto Rico with a decline in the wages of Puerto Rican immigrants relative to Puerto Rico–born workers.

Within the United States, several pieces of evidence suggest a parallel Spanish-speaking labor market emerges in areas where Spanish speakers are sufficiently numerous, and, in particular, where the skill distribution of Spanish speakers is sufficiently rich. First, for Spanish speakers, the wage premium for speaking English is small in markets with a heavy Spanish-speaking presence, particularly those with a well-educated Spanish-speaking presence. Second, an influx of less-educated Spanish speakers is associated with a larger decline in the wages of Spanish-speaking than non-Spanish-speaking, less-educated immigrants. Third, an influx of educated Spanish speakers is associated with an increase the wages of Spanish-speaking but not non-Spanish-speaking, less-educated immigrants. The reason this third fact is relevant is that in standard models (like the one used in chapter 2) an influx of more-educated workers is predicted to raise the wages of less-educated workers if they are in the same labor market. Thus, it also suggests that Spanish- and non-Spanish speakers operate in parallel labor markets in the same area.

The findings refine our understanding of the forces that affect immigrant poverty. Previous research already suggested that the wage effects of immigration were borne disproportionately by immigrants (Card 2001; Ottaviano and Peri 2012). These results indicate that the effects are borne particularly strongly by immigrants with poor English-language skills, who are among the poorest immigrants—in recent U.S. data, 29 percent of non-English-speaking immigrants were in poverty, versus 15 percent of immigrants overall—and by Spanish-speaking immigrants. The estimates here are consistent with the increase in immigration since 1990 contributing an additional 1 to 2 percentage points to the poverty rate of less-educated low-English immigrants, and an additional 2 to 4 percentage points to the poverty rates of less-educated Spanish-speaking immigrants. However, because poverty rates among these immigrant groups fell over this period, this finding is only that immigrant poverty rates would have fallen more quickly without additional immigration.[2]

MOTIVATION AND BACKGROUND

It is useful to begin with some basic facts about immigrants' and natives' language skills and wages. Table 3.1 shows average English skills for immigrants and na-

TABLE 3.1 / English-Speaking Ability

	All Working Age			Speaks Spanish at Home		
	All Education Levels	High School or Less	More than High School	All Education Levels	High School or Less	More than High School
Foreign-born, share speaks English . . .						
Only/very well	0.464	0.278	0.679	0.261	0.177	0.516
Well	0.221	0.227	0.214	0.234	0.227	0.257
Not well	0.211	0.318	0.088	0.317	0.365	0.173
Not at all	0.104	0.178	0.019	0.188	0.232	0.054
Native-born, share speaks English . . .						
Only/very well	0.983	0.971	0.990	0.820	0.764	0.879
Well	0.011	0.017	0.007	0.113	0.139	0.086
Not well	0.005	0.009	0.003	0.054	0.074	0.033
Not at all	0.001	0.003	0.000	0.013	0.023	0.002

Source: Author's compilation based on the 2007–2009 American Community Surveys (Ruggles et al. 2010), and the U.S. Bureau of the Census (2003).
Note: Sample limited to working-age population (age sixteen to sixty-five with positive years of potential work experience) living in 136 large metropolitan areas and not in group quarters. Sample weights used to construct shares.

tives. It was constructed by combining data from the 2007, 2008, and 2009 American Community Surveys (Ruggles et al. 2010) for the working-age residents of 136 high immigration metropolitan areas.[3] These areas are home to more than 80 percent of the immigrants living in the United States. Table 3.1 also shows separate means by whether the respondent has any college education. Throughout this chapter, those with a high school degree or less will be referred to as "less educated" and will be a focus of the analysis, because they make up a disproportionate share of those in poverty.

The first row of table 3.1 shows that only 46 percent of immigrants speak English "only" or "very well." In contrast, among the native born, this figure is over 98 percent. To a useful first approximation, U.S. natives are fluent in English, whereas only half of immigrants are. The latter rises to 68 percent if you include immigrants who say they speak English "well" but not "very well." By this broader measure, about half of immigrants without college are proficient in English, and 90 percent of immigrants with college education are proficient in English (columns 2 and 3).

Spanish speakers are also a focus of this study. Table 3.1 shows the English skills of just those immigrants and natives who report speaking Spanish at home. Spanish-speaking immigrants have below-average English skills, and only 26 percent are fluent in English; even within education category, their English skills are below average. This rating is mostly driven by Mexicans, who are the largest immigrant

FIGURE 3.1　/　Immigrants Speaking English, Years in United States

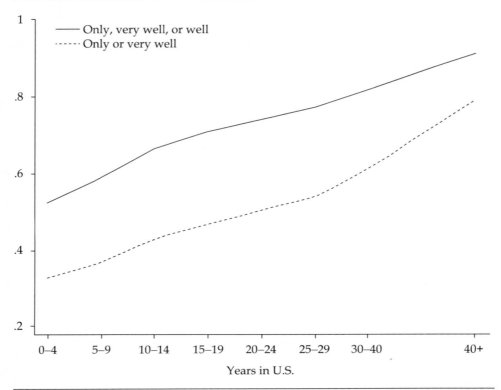

Source: Author's compilation based on the 2007–2009 American Community Surveys (Ruggles et al. 2010), and the U.S. Bureau of the Census (2003).
Note: Sample limited to working-age foreign-born living in 136 large metropolitan areas and not in group quarters.

group and as a group have poor English skills. (For example, 74 percent of Mexican immigrants in this sample report speaking English not well or not at all.) Among the U.S.-born Spanish speakers surveyed, who make up 7.7 percent of the working-age population, only 82 percent claim to be fluent in English, and almost 7 percent say they do not speak English well or at all.[4]

The following analysis also exploits variation in English skills by immigrants' age at arrival and time in the United States. Figures 3.1 and 3.2 show average language skills by these characteristics. The proportion who speak English well has a positive monotonic association with time in the United States, rising from half of those who arrived in the past five years to 90 percent of those who have been in the country at least forty years, a pattern that may partly reflect cohort differences in English skills. Figure 3.2 shows the sharp decline in English skills in adults in age at arrival: it is much higher among those who arrived before age ten than among

FIGURE 3.2 / Immigrants Speaking English, Age at Arrival

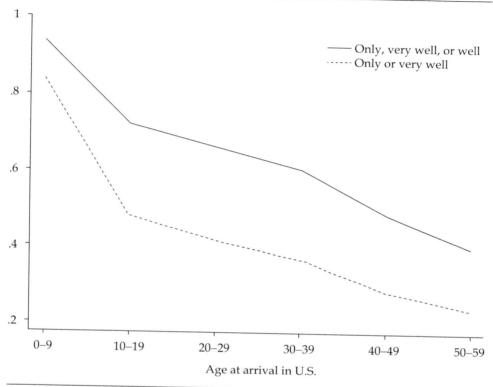

Source: Author's compilation based on the 2007–2009 American Community Surveys (Ruggles et al. 2010), and the U.S. Bureau of the Census (2003).
Note: Sample limited to working-age foreign-born living in 136 large metropolitan areas and not in group quarters.

those who arrived at older ages. This fact was exploited in Hoyt Bleakley and Aimee Chin (2004) to study the effect of language skills on wages. They argued that there is a "critical period" at young ages when children are able to easily learn English. I ask whether there is a similar kinked relationship in the substitutability of immigrants for natives by age at arrival.[5] Figures 3.3 and 3.4 show that this kinked relationship is mainly present among less-educated immigrants; among more educated immigrants, the relationship is smoother.[6]

Suggestive evidence that English skills are important for economic well-being is shown in table 3.2, which shows mean log hourly wages and poverty by nativity, education, and English- and Spanish-language skills. The first two rows of columns 1 through 3 show that even within education category, immigrants tend to earn less than natives. For example, less-educated immigrants earn on average 18

FIGURE 3.3 / Immigrants Speaking English, High School or Less

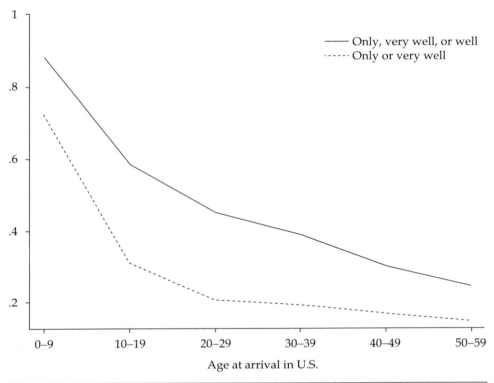

Source: Author's compilation based on the 2007–2009 American Community Surveys (Ruggles et al. 2010), and the U.S. Bureau of the Census (2003).
Note: Sample limited to working-age foreign-born living in 136 large metropolitan areas and not in group quarters.

log points (about 18 percent) less than less-educated natives. The next row shows, pertinent to the idea that language skills might matter for this wage gap, the wages of immigrants who are fluent in English are very similar to that of natives, including among less-educated immigrants and natives. Self-reported English skills show a steep wage gradient. These wage differences translate to differences in poverty as well, shown in columns 4 through 6. Whereas 30 percent of less-educated immigrants—and even 23 percent of those with college education—who do not speak English are in poverty, only 14 to 16 percent of less-educated immigrants who speak English well or very well are in poverty, similar to poverty rates among less-educated natives. Finally, the bottom rows of table 3.2 show that Spanish speakers are worse off than the typical immigrant, something their poor English skills (table 3.1) likely contributes to. Immigrants who speak only Spanish,

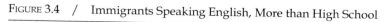

FIGURE 3.4 / Immigrants Speaking English, More than High School

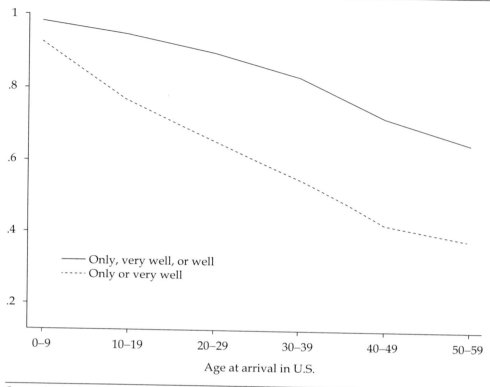

Age at arrival in U.S.

Source: Author's compilation based on the 2007–2009 American Community Surveys (Ruggles et al. 2010), and the U.S. Bureau of the Census (2003).
Note: Sample limited to working-age foreign-born living in 136 large metropolitan areas and not in group quarters.

shown in the bottom row of the table, have wages and poverty rates about the same as the typical non-English speaker.

The wage gap between less-educated immigrants and natives is analyzed directly in multivariate regressions in table 3.3. Column 1 repeats the finding in from column 2 of table 3.2, that less-educated natives earn about 18 percent less than less-educated natives. Column 2 of table 3.3 shows that a single control variable — a dummy for speaking English only or very well — can account for most of this gap. The coefficient on this control suggests that a 21 percent wage premium to speaking English fluently, a finding consistent with previous estimates of the returns to speaking English in the U.S. labor markets (see, for example, Chiswick and Miller 1995; Carliner 1996). This likely overstates the causal effect of English-speaking ability, however. Column 3 shows that the addition of simple demo-

TABLE 3.2 / Mean Wages and Poverty Rates

	Mean ln(hourly Wage), 1999$			Share of Group in Poverty		
	All Education Levels	High School or Less	More than High School	All Education Levels	High School or Less	More than High School
Native born						
All native born	2.25	1.94	2.39	0.10	0.16	0.06
Foreign born						
All foreign-born	2.05	1.76	2.35	0.15	0.20	0.08
Speaks English:						
Only/very well	2.31	1.91	2.46	0.09	0.14	0.06
Well	1.99	1.83	2.19	0.13	0.16	0.10
Not well	1.70	1.67	1.87	0.21	0.22	0.17
Not at all	1.55	1.54	1.71	0.29	0.30	0.23
Speaks Spanish at home						
All foreign-born Spanish speakers	1.80	1.70	2.07	0.19	0.22	0.11
Speaks no English	1.54	1.53	1.66	0.30	0.30	0.24

Source: Author's compilation based on the 2007–2009 American Community Surveys (Ruggles et al. 2010), and the U.S. Bureau of the Census (2003).

Note: Sample in columns 4 through 6 limited to working-age population (age sixteen to sixty-five with positive years of potential work experience) living in 136 large metropolitan areas and not in group quarters. Sample in columns 1 through 3 limited to respondents from columns 4 through 6 who are currently employed and had hours worked, positive wage and salary earnings, and zero self-employment and farm earnings in the past year. Wages are adjusted to 1999 dollars using the consumer price index, and wages exceeding $200 and less than $2 in 1999 dollars are replaced with these thresholds.

graphic and skill controls reduces the magnitude of this coefficient. Estimates in the Bleakley and Chin study exploiting age at arrival are, in fact, consistent with no causal effect of English-language skills on wages. They could account for wage gaps across immigrants with varying English-language skills entirely with education differences across these groups.

The last three columns of table 3.3 focus on the large minority of Americans — both immigrants and natives — who speak Spanish at home. Column 4 presents evidence of a somewhat smaller return to English fluency among Spanish speakers, and that, conditioning on English fluency, no immigrant-native wage gap exists. Might English skills matter less when large numbers of other Spanish speakers are in the same labor market? Column 5 presents an interaction between the English-fluency dummy and the proportion of the metro area's population who speak Spanish at home. The coefficient on this interaction is negative and significant, consistent with the idea that English skills become less valuable for Spanish speakers as the size of the Spanish-speaking population increases. Indeed, this control raises the coefficient on English-fluency dummy back to its level in the full sample; in other words, that Spanish speakers are geographically concentrated

TABLE 3.3 / Language Skills and Wage Gaps

	ln(Hourly Wage),					
	Workers with High School or Less			Spanish Speakers Only		
Immigrant	-0.186	-0.041	-0.021	0.000	-0.003	-0.004
	(0.009)	(0.007)	(0.007)	(0.013)	(0.013)	(0.013)
Speaks English						
Only or very well		0.209	0.168	0.149	0.208	0.174
		(0.008)	(0.009)	(0.008)	(0.021)	(0.019)
Only or very well × share of MSA who speak Spanish at home						
Among entire working-age population					-0.212	
					(0.081)	
Among those with high school or less						0.069
						(0.081)
Among those with more than high school						-0.306
						(0.165)
Sample size	724,737	724,737	724,737	173,590	173,590	173,590
R^2	0.019	0.028	0.189	0.016	0.018	0.018
Other controls?[a]	No	No	Yes	No	No	No

Source: Author's compilation based on Ruggles et al. (2010) and the 2007–2009 American Community Surveys.
Note: Sample limited to working-age population (age sixteen to sixty-five with positive years of potential work experience) who have twelve or fewer years of education, who live in 136 large metropolitan areas and not in group quarters, who are currently employed, and who had positive wage and salary earnings, and zero self-employment and farm earnings in the past year. Wages exceeding $200 and less than $2 in 1999 dollars are replaced with these thresholds. Standard errors, in parentheses, computed to be robust to arbitrary error correlation within metropolitan areas.

[a]Other controls are a quartic in potential work experience; years of education, years of interacted with education below nine years; born after 1950, and both; and dummies for education less than nine years, born after 1950, female, black, Hispanic, female black, and female Hispanic.

fully accounts for their lower average return to speaking English. Column 6 splits the Spanish-speaking share into shares among the more- and less-educated populations. Consistent with what was hypothesized in the introduction—that it requires a rich distribution of skills to create a Spanish-speaking labor market—it is only the Spanish-speaking share among more educated workers that is associated with a diminished importance of English-language skills among less-educated workers. To take an extreme example, in markets, like Miami, where a majority of college educated workers speak Spanish (see table 3.A1 for other examples) these estimates predict no premium to English fluency.[7] The following section defines an estimation framework and uses it to reassess how the relative wage of Spanish-speaking immigrants is affected by the density of Spanish and English speakers in the labor market.

THEORY AND DERIVATION OF AN ESTIMATION EQUATION

A starting point for a simple theory of how language skills matter in the U.S. labor market is the notion that among those with otherwise similar skills, those who cannot communicate in English well (hereafter, "speak" English) imperfectly substitute for workers who do; the former might not be very effective in occupations that require a great deal of communication, for example (Peri and Sparber 2009). For simplicity, imagine that workers can be sharply divided into those who can and cannot speak English, indexed with $j = 1$ and $j = 0$, respectively. If these two types are imperfectly substitutable, the wage premium to being able to speak English will decline in the relative number of workers who speak English and who do not, which is captured with the following relationship:

$$\ln(w_0 / w_1) = a - b \ln(L_0 / L_1) \tag{1}$$

L_j is the number of workers and w_j is the wage of language type j workers, and a and b are positive constants. The degree of imperfect substitutability is measured by b: it will be zero if those who can and cannot speak English are perfect substitutes.[8] In principle, equation (1) could be estimated using variation across labor markets and over time in the relative number of workers who speak English "only," "very well" or "well" as a proxy for L_1 and the remaining workers as a proxy for L_0. To be consistent with prior estimates of the impact of immigration on wages, however, it is useful to translate equation (1) into something that directly involves immigrants and natives.[9]

To do so, first recall that nearly all natives report speaking English fluently. The relative number of non-English speakers is driven almost entirely by immigration, and, in practice, moves almost one-for-one (in percentage terms) with the relative number of immigrants. Mathematically, $\ln(L_0/L_1) \approx c + \ln(L^F/L^N)$, where L^F and L^N are, respectively, the number of foreign-born and native-born workers. Imposing this linear approximation on equation (1), we have that:

$$\ln(w_0 / w_1) = a' - b \ln(L^F / L^N) \qquad (1')$$

To translate the left side of this equation into the wages of immigrants and natives, we can impose $w^N = w_1$, because all natives are assumed to speak English. (In practice, natives who report imperfect English will be dropped from the wage sample.) As for immigrants' wages, the analysis explores variation across groups of immigrants with varying English ability, in particular, the age-at-arrival and years-in-United-States categories shown in figures 3.1 and 3.2 in addition to the English-language skill categories shown in tables 3.1 and 3.2. So suppose g indexes these different categories of immigrants, and fraction φ_g of group g speaks English. The mean log wage of group g immigrants can be written as $\ln w^{Fg} = \varphi_g \ln w_1 + (1 - \varphi_g) \ln w_0 + \varepsilon_g$, where ε_g represents sources of immigrant-native wage gaps other than English skills (for example, ethnic discrimination or legal status). Translating this into a immigrant-native wage gap,

$$\begin{aligned}
\ln(w^{Fg} / w^N) &= [\varphi_g \ln w_1 + (1 - \varphi_g) \ln w_0 + \varepsilon_g] - \ln w_1 \\
&= (1 - \varphi_g)(\ln w_0 - \ln w_1) + \varepsilon_g \\
&= (1 - \varphi_g) \ln(w_0 / w_1) + \varepsilon_g
\end{aligned}$$

Substituting equation (1') into this produces

$$\ln(w^{Fg} / w^N) = a_g - (1 - \varphi_g) b \ln(L^F / L^N) + \varepsilon_g \qquad (2)$$

The intercept, a_g, is a combination of constants. Equation (2) implies that among otherwise similar immigrants and natives, the sensitivity of the relative wages of foreign workers to changes in foreign relative supply diminishes in the share of foreign workers who speak English. For example, immigrants who arrive as children tend to have better English skills than those who arrive as adults. Equation (2) thus implies that the relative wages of those who arrive as children should respond less to immigrant inflows than those who arrive as adults.

This simple model leaves out several factors. First, according to the model, immigrants with perfect English, $\varphi_g = 1$, are perfect substitutes for natives; their relative wages are insensitive to immigrant relative supply. An important simplification used to derive equation (2) was that other sources of immigrant-native wage gaps (ε_g) are unrelated to immigrant relative supply. If this is not the case, then even fluent immigrants' relative wages may be sensitive to the number of immigrants relative to natives. This may also bias the estimate of equation (2), an issue discussed further.

Second, this model assumes that English skills are equally important for all jobs—the slope "b" in equation (1) is a constant.[10] Because it is plausible that English skills are more important in high-skill jobs, the estimates that follow allow the effects to vary by the education level of the worker.

Finally, this simple model can also only partly accommodate the fact that in some parts of the United States, Spanish rather than English is the dominant language. In Puerto Rico, where both immigrants and natives speak Spanish, equation (2) applies, and implies that immigrants' relative wages should not respond to the relative number of immigrants. In markets with a mix of Spanish-speaking and English-speaking workers, it is not clear what will happen, but some theories are suggestive. According to Kevin Lang's (1986) theory of language discrimination, wages are lower for Spanish-speaking (or generally, non-English-speaking) immigrant laborers than natives because they bear the cost of training a bilingual supervisor. However, where Spanish is spoken by a majority of workers, as it is in some U.S. markets, the sign of wage gap with natives reverses. In a study by Giovanni Peri and Chad Sparber (2009), less-educated immigrants are segregated into manual occupations because of their inferior English communication skills. One might imagine, although this is not discussed in the study, that with a large enough density of fellow Spanish speakers, it might be possible for Spanish speakers to have access to a full range of occupations.[11] In both theories, having enough skilled (Lang's supervisors) or educated Spanish speakers would be important for a separate Spanish labor market to emerge, which is supported by preliminary evidence in table 3.3. This is evaluated by adding terms to equation (2) measuring the size of the Spanish-speaking labor pool by education.

ESTIMATION AND IDENTIFICATION

The main estimates of equation (2) use variation across skill groups and metropolitan areas in the relative aggregate hours worked of the immigrant population, as follows:

$$\ln(w_{ict}^{Fg} / w_{ict}^{N}) = \alpha_{git} + \beta_g \ln(H_{ict}^{F} / H_{ict}^{N}) + \varepsilon_{gict} \qquad (3)$$

where i indexes two education groups (high school or less, more than college) and c indexes metropolitan areas, and H represents the aggregate hours of the specified group. β_g is the estimate of $-(1-\varphi_g)b$ in equation (2). It is expected to be negative and to be smaller in magnitude for immigrants with stronger English-language skills. Equation (3) is estimated both jointly and separately by education group.

All estimates of equation (3) include time-varying education group controls, α_{git}, which, like the slope, will be allowed to vary across immigrant groups, g. These controls capture economy-wide changes in the wage structure. The dependent variable is computed as the difference in the mean log wages of immigrants in group g and natives with the same education, i, in the same metropolitan area, c, and year, t — or "cell ict" for short.[12] To reduce the influence of compositional differences between immigrants and natives on this estimated mean wage gap, natives' mean wages are computed using weights that give them, on average, the same education and experience as the immigrants in group g in cell ict.[13] (In practice, the raw wage gap produces similar results.) Equation (3) is estimated by ordinary least squares (that is, unweighted) and standard errors are computed to be robust to arbitrary error correlation across observations on the same metropolitan area.

The error term in equation (3) captures other determinants of immigrants' relative wages. There are two broad reasons to expect that it will be correlated with immigrants' relative hours, which will lead estimates of β_g to be biased. Areas with a high relative demand for some immigrant subgroup would tend to simultaneously have high relative wages and hours for the workers in this group, thereby generating a positive correlation between the error term and the explanatory variable and leading slope estimates to be less negative.[14] A standard way to address this is to use predictable variation in the size of immigrant inflows based on the labor markets in which immigrants from different parts of the world tend to cluster—Mexicans in Los Angeles, Russians in New York, and so on. This approach is described in the appendix. In practice, it tends to produce similar results to the ordinary least squares estimates presented later, suggesting that this type of bias may not be large. In addition, a later section presents estimates of equation (2) that rely only on aggregate variation—that is, across education × experience groups, similar to Ottaviano and Peri (2012)—rather than variation across labor markets. This also produces similar, if less precise, estimates.

Equation (3) is also likely to be biased because immigrants with poor English-language skills tend to be dissimilar from U.S. natives in other ways that affect their substitutability with natives. For example, Mexicans are the largest group of immigrants with poor English skills, and many live in the United States illegally. Their legal status may confine them to particular occupations, making it harder for them to compete head to head with natives. If so, immigrant relative hours may be more negatively correlated with low- than high-English immigrants' relative wages, but (at best) only partly because of the observed difference English skills. In the absence of a perfect way to identify immigrants who differ only in English skills (legal status in particular is not observable), I examine variation across immigrant subgroups, such as by age at arrival. Although the variation in English skills across these subgroups is also likely to also be correlated with differences in other factors that affect immigrant-native substitutability, the hope is that the relationship is not as strong or at least not as systematic across these other subgroups. For example, the hope is that age at arrival does not have a "kinked" relationship with legal status that it does with English skills (see figures 3.3 and 3.4). This approach is likely to be only partially successful, so the estimates are still likely to still be biased, probably toward finding that language skills are important.

Data

Data for the regression analysis come from the 2000 census of population and 2007, 2008, and 2009 community surveys. The latter three are combined into what

TABLE 3.4 / Regression Data Descriptive Statistics

	All Education Levels		High School or Less		More than High School	
	Mean	SD	Mean	SD	Mean	SD
ln(imm hours/nat hours)	–1.934	1.019	–1.581	1.113	–2.288	0.769
Immigrant-native wage gap						
All immigrants	–0.125	0.079	–0.156	0.072	–0.093	0.073
High English immigrants	–0.076	0.066	–0.088	0.064	–0.063	0.065
Low English immigrants	–0.360	0.201	–0.251	0.105	–0.469	0.215
Observations	544		272		272	

Source: Author's compilation based on the 2007–2009 American Community Surveys (Ruggles et al. 2010), and the U.S. Bureau of the Census (2003).

Note: Sample for constructing hours worked includes all those age sixteen to sixty-five who are old enough to be out of school (given normal progression) and live in 136 large metropolitan areas and not in group quarters. To be in the wage sample requires being in the hours worked sample plus being employed, with positive weeks and hours worked last year, nonzero wage and salary earnings, and zero self-employment and farm earnings; for natives it also requires speaking English only or very well. Hourly wages above $200 and below $2 in 1999 dollars are reset to these thresholds. Data have been aggregated to 136 metropolitan areas × two education groups × two years (2000 and "2008," combining the three ACSs). Table shows unweighted means and standard deviations (SD).

will be referred to as 2008 data (Ruggles et al. 2010). Information on hours worked and hourly wages were aggregated to the metropolitan area by year by broad education group. Included in the calculation of workers' hours were workers age sixteen to sixty-five, with positive potential experience (old enough to be out of school given a normal progression through school), living in one of the 136 metropolitan areas in the sample.[15] The wage sample is the subsample of these workers who are currently employed with positive wage and salary earnings and zero farm or business earnings in the past year.[16] Metropolitan areas were defined consistently using public use microdata areas (PUMAs) and 1990 metropolitan area boundaries.

Table 3.4 presents the unweighted means and standard deviations of these data. The relative log hours of immigrants in the average area are negative both overall and by education level, which indicates that immigrants are on average a minority of workers; in the mean education-metro-year observation, immigrants' hours represent about 14.4 percent (= $e^{-1.934} \times 100$) of natives' hours. The relative hours of immigrants shows considerable variation across these metro areas: the standard deviation is around 1, which will be useful for interpreting the magnitude of the regression estimates. The table also shows the immigrant-native wage gap is around 12.5 percent in the average metropolitan area, and is much larger for low-English immigrants, even the ones matched to natives with similar education and experience, as these gaps are calculated to do. There is also a great deal of variation in the immigrant-native wage gap across metro areas.

RESULTS

Table 3.5 presents estimates of equation (3). The first panel examines the relative wages of all immigrants. The –0.04 estimate in column 1 says that a one unit increase in immigrants' relative hours is associated with a 4 percent decline in the wages of immigrants relative to natives. Although a one unit increase in the independent variable means approximately tripling immigrants' labor supply, which sounds like a lot, it is actually a reasonable change to examine as it is both a standard deviation (table 3.4) and roughly equal to the increase in this variable since 1990 in the average metropolitan area.[17] In any case, the –0.04 response is similar in magnitude to previous estimates of this relationship (for example, Ottaviano and Peri 2012; Card 2009).

The second panel of table 3.5 produces separate estimates for the wages of immigrants who report strong English-language skills—immigrants who say they speak English "only," "very well," or "well"—and who report poor English-language skills—immigrants who say they speak English "not well" or "not at all." As expected, the relative wages of immigrants with poor English are more negatively associated the relative presence of immigrant labor: their wages decline 5.7 percent for a one unit increase in the independent variable, compared with a 2.2 percent decline for immigrants with stronger English. The difference between the two coefficients is statistically significant at the 1 percent level, shown as the p-value less than 0.01 in the row beneath these estimates.

Columns 2 and 3 show estimates separately by broad education. The first panel indicates that educated immigrants' wages are more responsive than less educated immigrants', despite the fact that educated immigrants tend to report substantially better English-language skills (table 3.1). This may not be inconsistent with the importance of English, however; it is plausible that language skills are more important in jobs that require college education, a view for which there is some evidence (Berman, Lang, and Siviner 2003). In addition, the difference in the wage responses of immigrants with poor and strong English are similar for more- and less-educated immigrants: the gap in coefficients is 3.6 (= 0.047–0.011) percentage points for less-educated and 3.3 (= 0.078–0.045) percentage points for more-educated immigrants.

The third panel of table 3.5 breaks out estimates by the more detailed English-language skills shown in tables 3.1 and 3.2. Going to this detail requires examining a smaller number of metro areas, 112, that are large enough to observe all immigrant subgroups. (In particular, wage-earning college graduates who report

TABLE 3.5 / Immigrant Relative Wage Response by English Skills

	All	High School or Less	More than High School
All immigrants	−0.040	−0.034	−0.054
	(0.003)	(0.004)	(0.006)
By broad English-language skills			
Speaks English only, very well, or well	−0.022	−0.011	−0.045
	(0.004)	(0.004)	(0.006)
Speaks English not well or not at all	−0.057	−0.047	−0.078
	(0.006)	(0.006)	(0.016)
P-value, equal coefficients	0.000	0.000	0.030
By detailed English-language skills (112 MSAs)			
Speaks English only or very well	−0.020	−0.012	−0.036
	(0.004)	(0.004)	(0.007)
Speaks English well	−0.028	−0.018	−0.047
	(0.005)	(0.006)	(0.011)
Speaks English not well	−0.049	−0.037	−0.071
	(0.006)	(0.007)	(0.013)
Speaks English not at all	−0.083	−0.050	−0.144
	(0.014)	(0.008)	(0.035)
P-value, equal coefficients	0.000	0.000	0.005

Source: Author's compilation based on the 2007–2009 American Community Surveys (Ruggles et al. 2010), and the U.S. Bureau of the Census (2003).
Note: Table shows coefficient estimates from regressions of the wage gap between specified immigrants and "similar" natives (see below) on the natural log of the ratio of aggregate hours worked of immigrants and natives, using variation across metropolitan areas, year (2000 or "2008"), and the two broad education of columns 2 and 3. All regressions control for year by education effects. Standard errors, in parentheses, computed to be robust to arbitrary error correlation within metropolitan area. Sample for constructing mean wages limited to working-age respondents (age sixteen to sixty-five and old enough to be out of school given normal progression), who reside in one of 136 large metropolitan areas and not in group quarters, who are currently employed, and who had positive hours and weeks worked, positive wage and salary earnings, and zero business and farm earnings in the past year; for natives, sample is further limited to those who report speaking English "only" or "very well." Hourly wages above $200 and below $2 in 1999 dollars were reset to these thresholds. The mean ln hourly wage of "similar" natives is computed by weighting natives to have the same distribution across potential experience (in five-year bands) × education (four groups: high school dropouts, high school, some college, and at least four years college) cells as the specified group of immigrants in the metropolitan area and year.

not speaking English at all are rare.) The wage response is monotonic in self-reported English-language skills, both overall and separately by education, and the differences across English categories are statistically significant. Interestingly, there is a significant negative response even in the top English category, what I referred to earlier as fluent. Although some of the workers in this category may not be truly fluent in English, a reasonable interpretation of this is that factors other than English skills make immigrants imperfectly substitutable with natives.

Figures 3.5 and 3.6 examine how the wage response varies, respectively, by age at arrival and time in the United States. The figures plot coefficient estimates (and confidence intervals) from estimates of equation (3) — that is, still using the same variation in immigrant relative labor by broad education, metropolitan area, and year — separately for immigrants in the age-at-arrival categories and years-in-United-States categories shown on the x-axis. Figure 3.5 shows that the response of wages by age at arrival follow the same "kinked" pattern that self-reported English-language skills did in figure 3.2. Although it is possible that other unobserved factors that affect immigrants' substitutability with natives follow this kinked pattern, this reinforces the direct evidence from English-language skills in table 3.5. On top of this, the kinked relationship in the response appears to be limited to the less-educated subsample where it was found (figures 3.3, 3.4, 3.7, and 3.8). There is also a monotonic relationship with time in the United States (figure 3.6).

FIGURE 3.5 / Immigrant Relative Wage Response, Age at Arrival

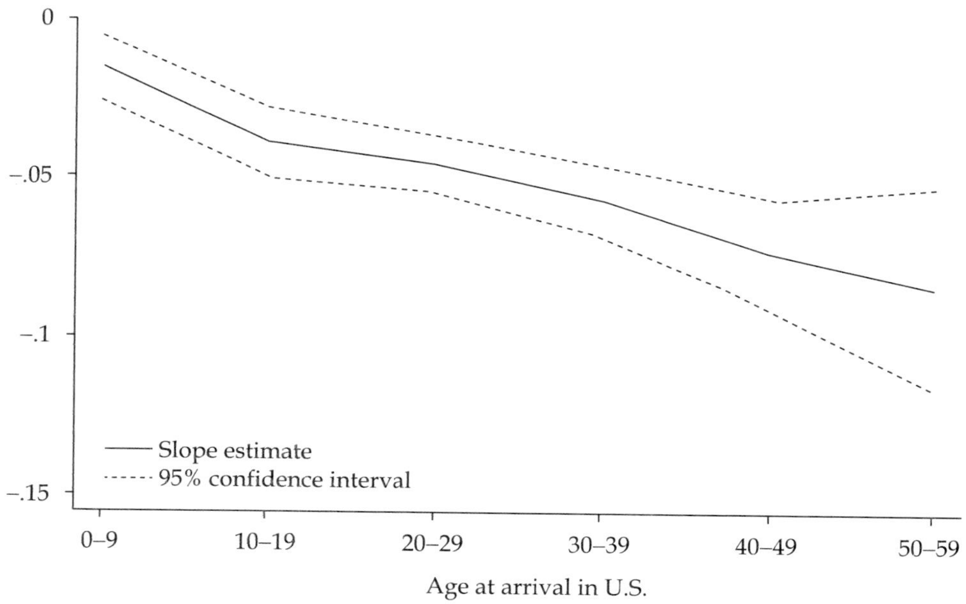

Source: Author's compilation based on the 2007–2009 American Community Surveys (Ruggles et al. 2010), and the U.S. Bureau of the Census (2003).

FIGURE 3.6 / Immigrant Relative Wage Response, Years in the United States

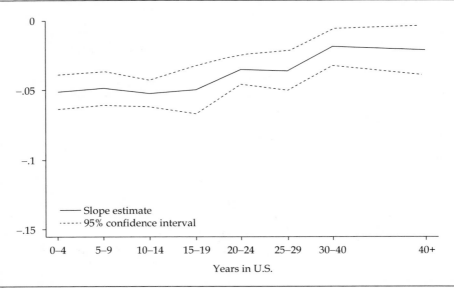

Source: Author's compilation based on the 2007–2009 American Community Surveys (Ruggles et al. 2010), and the U.S. Bureau of the Census (2003).

FIGURE 3.7 / Immigrant Relative Wage Response, High School or Less

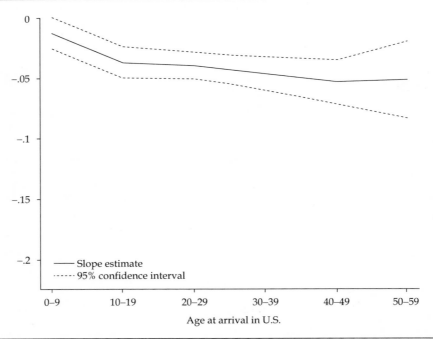

Source: Author's compilation based on the 2007–2009 American Community Surveys (Ruggles et al. 2010), and the U.S. Bureau of the Census (2003).

FIGURE 3.8 / Immigrant Relative Wage Response, More than High School

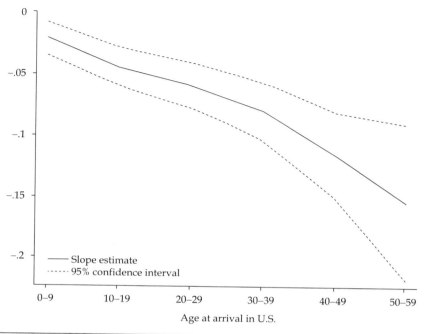

Source: Author's compilation based on the 2007–2009 American Community Surveys (Ruggles et al. 2010), and the U.S. Bureau of the Census (2003).

Effects of Language Supply

All of the regressions presented so far have used the same independent variable: the natural log of the ratio of immigrants' aggregate hours to natives' aggregate hours. This section instead uses direct measures of the supplies of language skills, including as the natural log of the aggregate hours of those who speak English not well or not at all (those with "poor English") to those who speak English only, very well, or well (those with "strong English"). In addition, to clarify what happens in markets with a large number of Spanish speakers, controls are included for the relative hours of workers who speak Spanish at home.

The results are presented in table 3.6. To keep things simple, the table examines only workers with a high school education or less. Column 1 repeats the estimate from the first panel of table 3.5: it says the overall immigrant-native log wage gap declines 3.4 percent for a 1 unit increase in immigrants' relative hours. Column 2 replaces this independent variable with the one measuring the relative hours of those with poor English relative to strong English. The coefficient is the same to two decimal places. This supports the argument made earlier that, as a practical

TABLE 3.6 / Immigrant Relative Wages and Language

	ln(Immigrant Wage/Native Wage), High School or Less				
	All		Spanish-Speaking		Other
ln(immigrant hours/ native-born hours)	-0.034 (0.004)				
ln(poor/strong English- speaking hours)		-0.034 (0.004)	-0.036 (0.007)	-0.033 (0.028)	-0.060 (0.018)
ln(Spanish-speaking hours/ strong English-speaking hours)					
Among workers with high school education or less				-0.045 (0.035)	0.052 (0.024)
Among workers with more than high school education				0.065 (0.017)	-0.015 (0.017)
Metro × year observations	272	272	272	272	272
R²	0.300	0.298	0.157	0.224	0.110

Source: Author's compilation based on the 2007–2009 American Community Surveys (Ruggles et al. 2010), and the U.S. Bureau of the Census (2003).

Note: Wage sample limited to working-age respondents (age sixteen to sixty-five and old enough to be out of school, given normal progression) that have twelve or fewer years of education (or a GED), that reside in one of 136 large metropolitan areas and not in group quarters, that are currently employed, and that had positive hours worked, positive wage and salary earnings, and zero self-employment earnings in the past year; for natives it also requires speaking English only or very well. The dependent variable is the difference in the mean ln hourly wage between the specified group of immigrants and similar natives, where the mean ln hourly wage of "similar" natives is computed by weighting natives to have the same distribution across potential experience (in five-year bands) × education (high school dropouts or completers) cells as the specified group of immigrants in the metropolitan area and year. Strong English-speaking hours worked is the sum of hours worked by those who report speaking English only, very well, or well. Poor English-speaking hours are the sum of hours worked reported by those who speak English not well or not at all among working-age respondents. Spanish-speakers are respondents who report speaking Spanish at home. All regressions are unweighted and control for year effects. Standard errors, in parentheses, computed to be robust to arbitrary error correlation within metropolitan area.

matter, the relative supply of English-language skills moves one-for-one with the relative supply of immigrants.

Column 3 of table 3.6 repeats the estimates of column 2 for the subgroup of immigrants who report speaking Spanish at home. The estimated wage response is nearly identical for this subgroup. To investigate whether the responses vary with the density of Spanish speakers in the market, column 4 adds controls for the aggregate hours of workers who speak Spanish at home relative to workers with strong English. This measure is entered separately for college and noncollege workers, following the results in table 3.3. Column 4 presents weak evidence of an additional depressing effect of having a large number of Spanish-speaking noncollege workers on the wages of noncollege Spanish speakers, in addition to the impact of a large number of non-English speakers. However, this is offset by the positive wage impact of greater density of college-educated Spanish-speaking immigrants.

A graphical version of the column 4 relationship is shown in figure 3.9. It plots Spanish-speaking relative hours among workers with more than a high school education versus those with a high school education or less—the two variables in the lower half of table 3.6—in 2008 data, and dotted lines indicate the median of each variable. The dashed line is not the fitted line, though it is very close; rather, it indicates the dividing line between areas with above- and below-average wages for less-educated Spanish-speaking immigrants relative to natives according to the estimate in column 4, ignoring the impact of the other variable, poor/strong English.[18] In areas above the dashed line, less-educated Spanish-speaking immigrants tend to have relatively high wages: this includes two Cuban enclaves, Miami and Jersey City, other areas in Florida, as well as areas on the Texas border (not labeled on the figure), and Riverside and Los Angeles. Interestingly, many new immigrant destinations (Singer 2004)—such as Atlanta, Charlotte, Denver, Greensboro, Portland, and Raleigh—are below the line, indicating the Mexican (or, really, any less-educated Spanish-speaking) immigrants there earn less than average wages. This is a reversal of these areas' position not so long ago—a similar graph for 1990 would show most of these new destinations above the line. In fact, the model in column 4 applied to 1990 census data predicts that Mexican immigrants would have earned a relative wage 7 percent higher in Singer's new destinations than in other large areas that were her historical immigrant gateways.[19] The relatively high wages may have been part of what attracted Mexicans to these areas beginning in the 1990s, although other research indicates faster employment growth was the primary draw (Card and Lewis 2007). Over the past twenty years, the wage advantage of these new areas for Mexicans has disappeared because the Spanish inflows have been disproportionately less skilled.[20]

The estimates in table 3.6 might additionally be interpreted as indicating that a rich enough skill distribution of Spanish speakers allows a parallel Spanish-speaking labor market to emerge within an area. As additional evidence for this, column 5 shows an estimate of the same relationship for non-Spanish-speaking immigrants who, in this view, should not be affected by the density of Spanish speakers. The wage boost from college-educated Spanish speakers is not present for them. Also in column 5 is a positive coefficient on the less-educated Spanish–English hours ratio that nearly offsets the coefficient on poor English–English hours, indicating that an inflow of less-educated Spanish speakers has little overall effect on the wages of non-Spanish-speaking immigrants. This is consistent with Spanish speakers working in a parallel labor market within the area.

Puerto Rico

Another reason to expect that a Spanish-speaking labor market emerges with a large enough density of Spanish speakers is that it must be where everyone speaks

FIGURE 3.9 / Natural Log of Spanish Relative Hours, 2008

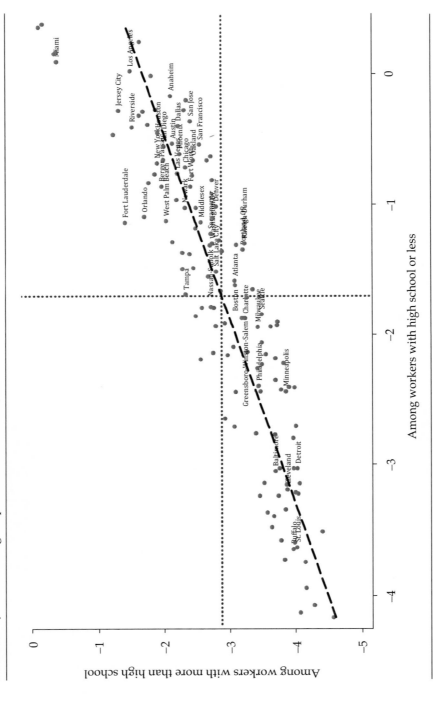

Source: Author's calculations based on Ruggles et al. (2010).
Note: Dotted lines are medians. Points above sloped line have above-average wages for Spanish-speaking immigrants, relative to natives according to estimates in table 2.6, column 4.

Spanish. In only one U.S. labor market—Puerto Rico—is this the case.[21] According to the view that language skills drive imperfect substitutability with natives, Puerto Rican immigrants should be perfect substitutes for Puerto Rican natives: their relative wages should not respond at all to immigrants' relative labor supply. The approach of examining a market where immigrants and natives share a language was used in a Costa Rica study (see Castillo, Gilless, and Raphael 2009).

Because Puerto Rico is a single labor market, the analysis cannot exploit geographic variation in the size of the immigrant population. Instead, I use variation over time and across education-experience cells in the size relative size of the immigrant workforce (see Castillo, Gilless, and Raphael 2009; Ottaviano and Peri 2012).

That immigration to Puerto Rico is significant may not be well known. Figure 3.10 shows the share of the working-age population born outside Puerto Rico—defined as immigrants for this analysis—between 1970 and 2009, broken out separately by the five education categories—four years of college, one to three years of college, high school diploma, one to three years of high school, and no high school—used in the analysis. It is based on data from Puerto Rican population censuses, which are taken in parallel to the U.S. Census, and the 2007–2009 Puerto Rican community surveys (Ruggles et al. 2010). Most of those born outside Puerto Rico are not truly immigrants but are other U.S. citizens, mostly of Puerto Rican heritage, who were born in the continental United States. Figure 3.10 shows that, until recently, about 15 percent of college-educated workers came from outside Puerto Rico. The less-educated immigrant share is lower but, until recently, had been rising.

The analysis will exploit variation across the cells in figure 3.10, and, within these, across years of potential experience, grouped into five-year cells up to forty. Usual weekly hours worked is not available in the 1970 census, so hourly wages and aggregate hours worked are replaced with weekly wages and weeks worked. In particular, the estimation equation is as follows:

$$\ln(w_{ikt}^{F} / w_{ikt}^{N}) = \alpha_{ik} + \gamma_{kt} + \delta_{it} + \beta \ln(WW_{ikt}^{F} / WW_{ikt}^{N}) + \varepsilon_{ikt} \qquad (4)$$

where $\ln(WW^{F}{}_{ikt}/WW^{N}{}_{ikt})$ represents the aggregate relative weeks worked last year by non-native workers in Puerto Rico with education i and potential work experience k. Estimates of equation (4) control for an exhaustive set of education × experience, experience × year, and education × year dummies.[22] For comparison, equation (4) is also estimated using data on the continental United States, which will also serve as an additional check on the cross-city results presented earlier.[23]

Results are presented in table 3.7. Column 4 shows a negative and marginally significant coefficient of –0.033 for the United States, which is surprisingly similar to the estimates in table 3.5 given the large difference in methodology. The estimate for Puerto Rico is not zero, but positive and significant. A likely explanation for this that changes in the weeks worked partly reflects labor demand, which moves weeks worked and weekly wages in the same direction. To address this, I

FIGURE 3.10 / Foreign-Born in Puerto Rico

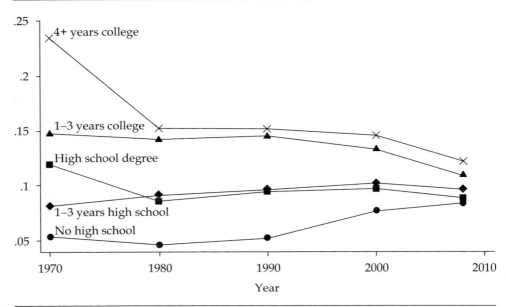

Source: Author's calculations based on Ruggles et al. (2010).
Note: Sample limited to population age sixteen to sixty-five, not living in group quarters, and old enough to be out of school with normal progression.

exploit the fact that much of the variation in the relative size of the immigrant workforce in Puerto Rico is driven by changes in the raw numbers of U.S.-born ethnic Puerto Ricans and Puerto Rican natives. As these reflect education and fertility decisions made long in the past, they are unlikely to be systematically related to present demand.[24]

The size of these two populations is computed using the combination of Puerto Rican and U.S. data, which is necessary because one-third of the Puerto Rican–born population lives in the United States. When relative weeks worked is replaced by the relative population size, in column 2, the coefficient is indeed nonpositive and is close to zero. Column 3 shows that this variable moves almost exactly one-for-one with the weeks worked variable, a highly significant relationship.[25]

The relationship in column 2 is unfortunately very noisy, and figure 3.11 shows why. It plots the relationship in column 2. The Puerto Rican wage estimates are much noisier than U.S. estimates, as shown by the large mean squared error (vertical variation around the line) in the Puerto Rican figure compared with the U.S. figure (see figure 3.12), owing to the much smaller number of observations in the Puerto Rican data.

TABLE 3.7 / Aggregate Estimates, 1970–2000

	Puerto Rico		Continental United States			
	$Y=\ln$ (foreign/native weekly wage)	$Y = \ln$ (foreign/native weeks)		Excluding 1970	Excluding 1970 Strong English	Excluding 1970 Poor English
ln(foreign-born weeks/native-born weeks)	0.150 (0.061)		-0.033 (0.017)	-0.021 (0.019)	-0.002 (0.020)	-0.031 (0.049)
ln(continental U.S. born ethnic Puerto Ricans/Puerto Rican-born)	-0.002 (0.126)	1.003 (0.126)				
Observations	224	224	180	144	144	144
R^2	0.489	0.919	0.935	0.942	0.913	0.976

Source: Author's compilation based on Ruggles et al. (2010).

Note: Sample for independent variable includes workers age sixteen to sixty-five who are old enough to be out of school given normal progression through school and not living in group quarters. The sample used to compute the dependent variable, weekly wages, is this sample with the additional requirement of being currently employed (U.S.) or reporting an occupation (Puerto Rico), not enrolled in school and without business or farm income. In U.S. data (columns 4–7), weekly wages exceeding $10,000 or below $10 in 1999 dollars were reset at these thresholds. In columns 5–7, native-born workers who did not report speaking English were excluded from the wage sample. Sample weights used to aggregate variables to the five-year experience × education cells used in the analysis (see text). Standard errors are calculated to be robust to arbitrary error correlation within education × experience cells.

FIGURE 3.11 / Immigrant Relative Wages and Supply, Puerto Rico

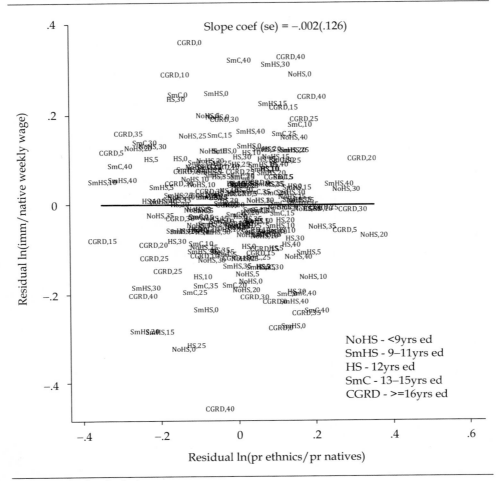

Source: Author's calculations.
Note: Labels identify education × five-year experiences cells. All variables are residuals from a regression on an exhaustive set of education × year, experience × year, and education × experience dummies. Raw data sources are Puerto Rican Population Censuses, Puerto Rican Community Surveys, and Ruggles et al. (2010).

The remaining columns of table 3.7 examine separately the relative wage response in the continental United States of immigrants with poor and strong English, measured in the same way as in the second panel of table 3.5.[26] This measure is not available until 1980, and so column 5 shows estimates excluding 1970, which are smaller in magnitude and less precise. Broken out separately by English skills, in columns 6 and 7, the negative response is limited to immigrants with poor English. Although these estimates are not precise, they are similar in magnitude to the

FIGURE 3.12 / Immigrant Relative Wages and Supply, United States

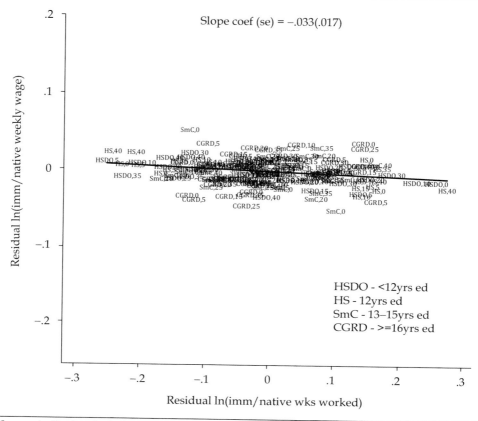

Source: Author's calculations.
Note: Labels identify education × five-year experiences cells. All variables are residuals from a regression on an exhaustive set of education × year, experience × year, and education × experience dummies. Raw data sources are U.S. Population Censuses, American Community Surveys, and Ruggles et al. (2010).

difference in response between high- and low-English immigrants that was found in table 3.5, around 3 percentage points.

IMPLICATIONS FOR POVERTY

What can we say about the effects of immigration on poverty in light of these estimates? A full answer requires estimates of the effect of immigration on a broader set of wage outcomes than were studied in this chapter, but are explored in other research (Raphael and Smolensky 2008, 2009). Chapter 2 explains this in greater detail but, to simplify, the main thing the present estimates omit is the effect immigration has on wages by shifting the ratio of noncollege to college labor. However, Card (2009) shows this is small, because the ratio is recently similar for recent immigrant and native workers. In addition to these previously estimated effects, the estimates in this chapter imply that immigration has a larger impact on the wages of immigrants with poor English-language skills, already a high poverty group (table 3.2) and, depending on immigrants' mix of language skills, on Spanish speakers.

Furthermore, the wage responses of these groups can be roughly translated into an effect on poverty rates, assuming that all immigrants' wages are shifted down by the amount implied by the estimates. The estimates in both table 3.7 and table 3.5 are consistent with a one unit increase in the relative supply of immigrant labor—again, roughly equal to the increase since 1990—lowering the wages of immigrant workers with poor English by 3 percentage points more than immigrants with strong English. The resulting 3 percent decline in wages, assuming all immigrants' income is from wages (which is close to true) would, without changing hours worked, be expected to drop the low-English immigrants between 100 and 103 percent of the poverty line into poverty. In 2008, this represented about 1 percent of low-English, less-educated immigrants. Given that the decline in wages might induce some immigrants to work less, a reasonable approximation is to double this estimate.[27] In short, the rise in immigration since 1990 might have added to 2 percentage points to the poverty rate of immigrants with poor English, versus those with strong English. Using the estimates in column 4 of table 3.6, the change in the supply of Spanish, English, and other hours between 1990 and 2008 is expected to have lowered the wages of Spanish-speaking immigrants by roughly 6 percent relative to natives, which translates similarly into an increase in their poverty rates of Spanish-speaking immigrants of roughly 2 to 4 percentage points.[28] In practice, poverty rates among less-educated immigrants declined since 1990: from 35 to 30 percent among non-English speakers and from 25 to 22 percent among Spanish speakers. These estimates are consistent with the large immigrant influx since 1990 attenuating this decline.

CONCLUSIONS

On balance, the estimates in this chapter suggest that though immigrants' imperfect English-language skills may not be the only reason that they are imperfect substitutes for native-born workers in the United States, they are a major reason. Across several approaches and samples, the wages of immigrants with poor English-language skills tend to respond more negatively to a greater presence of immigrants than the wages of immigrants with strong English-language skills do. At least among less-educated immigrants, then, immigration since 1990 might have pushed up the poverty rates of immigrants with poor English by 1 to 2 percentage points relative to immigrants with strong English and of Spanish-speaking immigrant by 2 to 4 percentage points relative to natives. These impacts are overwhelmed by a downward trend in immigrant poverty rates, and are smaller for Spanish-speaking immigrants in markets where Spanish is prevalent in the college-educated workforce. These impacts may also help account for the spread of Mexican immigrants to new destinations starting in the 1990s, because the lack of labor market competition from fellow Spanish speakers in those markets, compared with traditional Mexican destinations, would have made them a relatively attractive place to settle.[29]

I thank the editors, my colleagues at Dartmouth, and two anonymous referees for helpful comments and Chris Bachand-Parente for outstanding research assistance.

APPENDIX

To address the possibility that a high presence of immigrants in a market reflects high wages in those markets—which would tend to bias the coefficients in tables 3.5 and 3.6 toward zero, I use an instrumental variable for $\ln(H^F/H^N)$ from Card (2009), which measures the immigrant inflow rates predicted by the area's lagged origin mix of immigrants. In particular, it is

$$z_{jct} = \frac{\Sigma_o f_{oc,t-2} \Delta P^F_{ojt}}{P_{c,t-1}},$$

where $f_{oc,t-2}$ represents a two-decade lag in the fraction of U.S. immigrants from region o living in metropolitan area c, which apportions ΔP^F_{ojt}, the number of immigrants (nationally) arriving from o in skill group j in the past decade. (The regions are listed in table 3.A2, along with ΔP^F_{ojt} figures.) The numerator is thus the predicted number of immigrant arrivals in cell jc. This is converted to a predicted arrival rate by dividing by the area's beginning of decade population, $P_{c,t-1}$. The assumption behind this instrument is immigrants persist in locating in certain areas because they value being near similar immigrants, and not because these areas have persistently stronger wage for that type of immigrant.

This instrument is a strong predictor of immigrants' relative hours. F-statistics on the instrument in the first stage are in the 50 to 100 range. In addition, instrumental variables estimates using this instrument are similar to the ordinary least squares (OLS) estimates presented in table 3.5. This is shown in table 3.A3, which is identical in structure to table 3.5 but shows IV estimates. It shows the same pattern of coefficients, with greater (magnitude) wage responses for immigrants with worse English-language skills. The differences in coefficients across English-speaking categories are similar in magnitude to the OLS estimates, and are, as in OLS, statistically significant.

TABLE 3.A1 / Spanish-Speaking at Home

Area	High School or Less	More than High School	Area	High School or Less	More than High School
Anaheim, CA	0.543	0.118	McAllen, TX	0.928	0.789
Aurora, IL	0.502	0.097	Miami, FL	0.684	0.612
Bakersfield, CA	0.507	0.198	Oxnard-Ventura, CA	0.528	0.147
Brownsville, TX	0.816	0.670	Riverside, CA	0.505	0.213
El Paso, TX	0.846	0.678	Salinas, CA	0.673	0.193
Jersey City, NJ	0.526	0.270	San Antonio, TX	0.540	0.292
Laredo, TX	0.890	0.818	Santa Barbara, CA	0.589	0.151
Los Angeles, CA	0.633	0.216	Santa Cruz, CA	0.515	0.093

Source: Author's compilation based on Ruggles et al. (2010).
Note: Sample limited to working-age population (age sixteen to sixty-five and old enough to be out of school, given a normal progression), and not living in group quarters. Computed using ACS sample weights.

TABLE 3.A2 / National Immigrant Arrivals

	2000–2008		1990–2000	
	High School or Less	More than High School	High School or Less	More than High School
Mexican	1,944,656	292,542	2,618,328	296,963
Central American	517,066	105,261	493,669	92,671
South American	290,534	302,840	333,430	275,063
Caribbean (ex Cuban)	202,625	131,153	331,827	148,237
SE Asian (ex Filipino)	139,257	104,244	288,013	173,567
Chinese	135,836	220,608	158,375	302,729
Russian or E European	133,065	286,665	283,883	385,346
Sub-Saharan African	129,245	178,315	129,346	173,449
South Asian	123,072	497,999	148,698	430,311
Cuban	89,306	56,648	109,769	56,659
Middle Eastern (ex Israeli)	88,988	165,310	94,684	137,885
Filipino	56,810	229,456	91,406	219,320
Commonwealth	51,432	189,733	74,478	264,485
Korean or Japanese	50,217	220,028	84,669	248,958
Southern European	27,374	46,875	34,168	48,243
Northern European[a]	9,521	63,872	55,668	169,033

Source: Author's compilation based on Ruggles et al. (2010) and U.S. Bureau of the Census (2003).
Note: Sample limited to working-age population (age sixteen to sixty-five and old enough to be out of school, given a normal progression), and not living in group quarters.
[a]Includes Israelis.

TABLE 3.A3 / Instrumental Variables Estimates

	All	High School or Less	More than High School
All immigrants	−0.035	−0.030	−0.052
	(0.005)	(0.006)	(0.007)
By broad English-language skills			
Speaks English only, very well, or well	−0.018	−0.010	−0.044
	(0.005)	(0.005)	(0.006)
Speaks English not well or not at all	−0.043	−0.033	−0.074
	(0.009)	(0.009)	(0.016)
P-value, equal coefficients	0.000	0.001	0.060
By detailed English-language skills (112 MSAs)			
Speaks English only or very well	−0.022	−0.018	−0.036
	(0.005)	(0.005)	(0.007)
Speaks English well	−0.015	−0.005	−0.046
	(0.007)	(0.008)	(0.011)
Speaks English not well	−0.030	−0.017	−0.069
	(0.010)	(0.011)	(0.015)
Speaks English not at all	−0.057	−0.030	−0.137
	(0.014)	(0.013)	(0.029)
P-value, equal coefficients	0.000	0.009	0.001

Source: Author's compilation based on Ruggles et al. (2010), the 2007–2009 American Community Surveys, and the U.S. Bureau of the Census (2000).
Note: Table shows coefficient estimates from regressions of the wage gap between specified immigrants and "similar" natives (see below) on the natural log of the ratio of aggregate hours worked of immigrants and natives, using variation across metropolitan areas, year (2000 or "2008"), and the two broad education of columns 2 and 3. All regressions control for year by education effects and are estimated by instrumental variables using the lagged origin mix instrument described in the appendix. Standard errors, in parentheses, computed to be robust to arbitrary error correlation within metropolitan area. Sample for constructing mean wages limited to working-age respondents (age sixteen to sixty-five and old enough to be out of school given normal progression), who reside in one of 136 large metropolitan areas and not living in group quarters, who are currently employed, and who had positive hours and weeks worked, positive wage and salary earnings, and zero business and farm earnings in the past year; for natives, sample is further limited to those who report speaking English "only" or "very well." Hourly wages above $200 and below $2 in 1999 dollars were reset to these thresholds. The mean ln hourly wage of "similar" natives is computed by weighting natives to have the same distribution across potential experience (in five-year bands) × education (four groups: high school dropouts, high school, some college, and at least four years college) cells as the specified group of immigrants in the metropolitan area and year.

FIGURE 3.A1. Natural Log of Spanish Relative Hours, Residuals

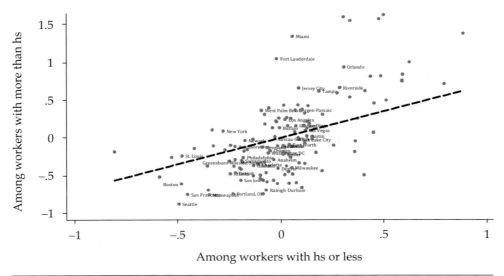

Source: Author's compilation based on Ruggles et al. (2010).
Note: Points are residuals of a regression of ln(Spanish/English hours) on ln(poor/strong English hours), separately by education (high school or less on the x-axis, more than on the y-axis). Points above sloped line have above-average wages for Spanish-speaking immigrants, relative to natives conditional on ln(poor/strong English hours), according to estimates in table 6, column 4.

NOTES

1. In Ottaviano's and Peri's preferred specification, for example, the largest estimated impact of immigration since 1990 they can find on the average wages of native-born high school dropouts is −0.1 percent, compared with −8.1 percent for immigrants. Much of the more recent literature (for example, Card 2001, 2009) does not examine impacts on average wages directly, but instead focuses on the wage gaps between groups of native workers. Even measured this way, however, the impact on less-skilled natives is generally found to be small.

2. Although poverty rates rose among immigrants overall during this period — see the introduction to this volume — poverty rates among less-educated non-English-speaking immigrants fell from 35 to 30 percent between 1990 and 2008, and among Spanish speakers from 25 to 22 percent.

3. *Working age* is defined as being between age sixteen and sixty-five and with at least one year of *potential work experience*, which means being old enough to have spent time outside of school given normal progression through school.

4. These numbers may understate native-born Spanish speakers' English skills if there is a tendency for undocumented Mexicans to claim native-born status.

5. Note that I am not fully implementing Bleakey's and Chin's methods here. A key thing I am not doing, but they did (2004), is differencing out age-at-arrival patterns among immigrants from English-speaking countries to account for other factors, besides language, associated with age-at-arrival. Wage response estimates for the small number of immigrants from English-speaking countries were too unreliable to exploit this approach.

6. Splitting the sample by age at arrival and education is somewhat problematic given the Bleakey and Chin finding that arriving as a young child tends to raise educational attainment (2004). The appropriate approach in light of this is to aggregate together more- and less-educated workers. Because the rest of the analysis is split by education, however, I will split it this way for the estimates by age at arrival.

7. Although this result is quite preliminary, it does provide some counterweight to the evidence that the tendency for immigrants to geographically cluster is bad for them (for example, Cutler, Glaeser, and Vigdor 2008). To be fair to those authors, though, their analysis is at the neighborhood, rather than market level. Immigrant segregation and language isolation are also analyzed in chapter 4 of this volume.

8. Equation (1) falls out of a capital-neutral single-good nested CES production function representation of the economy, where the innermost nest contains workers with and without English skills in this case, similar to the framework used in chapter 2. In this interpretation, the coefficient b represents an inverse "elasticity of substitution" between language types, and coefficient a represents a demand shifter which is a function of factor share and productivity parameters embedded in the production function. Other, more general, functional forms are possible, but this CES-derived approach is common (for example, Ottaviano and Peri 2012; Raphael and Smolensky 2008).

9. Another potential reason to do so is evidence that self-reported measures of language skills are not reliable (Dustman and van Soest 2001, 2002; Dustmann and Fabbri 2003). Despite this, the following results are similarly strong when using self-reported English skills directly, suggesting that they are at least reliable enough (at the aggregate level) to be useful.

10. This would be of great concern only if the variation in the wage response across immigrant groups were driven by variation in the importance of English rather than the English skills of the immigrants in the group — that is, variation in coefficient b not in φ_g.

11. In particular, one might assume the output of Peri and Sparber's production function made with Spanish-speaking workers was perfectly substitutable for the output made with English-speaking workers.

12. This uses the fact that $\ln\left(w_{ict}^{Fg}/w_{ict}^{N}\right) = \ln w_{ict}^{Fg} - \ln w_{ict}^{N}$.

13. In particular, those with high school or less are divided into high school completers and high school dropouts, and those with some college or more will be divided into those with and without four-year degrees. Within these cells, workers are further divided into five-year potential experience bands up to forty. The mean of native log wages are computed weighted by $p/(1-p)$, where p is the fraction of each detailed education $\times$

experience × metropolitan area × year cell that are group g immigrants, among group g immigrants and natives in that cell. (This weight is interacted with the ACS or Census sample weight.) Cells with no natives or no group g immigrants are dropped.

14. These estimates are also well identified only if the geographic units involved act as closed economies. U.S. evidence suggests that local labor markets behave like closed economies in the sense that immigrants do not appear to "displace" native-born workers with the same skills (for example, Card and DiNardo 2000) nor do they have much impact on industry mix (Lewis 2004).

15. Also, those living in group quarters were excluded from the analysis.

16. To be included in the wage sample, native-born workers also were required to report speaking English "only" or "very well." Hourly wages above $200 and below $2 in 1999 dollars were replaced with these thresholds.

17. In the average metro area-education cell in the sample, this variable rose from –2.69 to –1.75 between 1990 and 2008.

18. Specifically, it is a line with a slope of $0.7 = 0.045/0.065$ – the ratio of the two lower coefficients in column 4 – that goes through the sample median of the two variables, which are shown with the dotted lines in the figure. The residual scatter plot, conditioning out poor/strong English, is shown in figure 3.A1 and has the same qualitative patterns.

19. What I refer to as new immigrant destinations in the Audrey Singer (2004) typography include her three categories of emerging, re-emerging, and pre-emerging. The predicted values are computed using all three variables in column 4. Another major factor in the wage determination of less educated workers is the ratio of college to noncollege workers in a labor market (for example, Card 2009), but on this measure, new and old destinations were very similar in 1990. The actual average wage of Spanish-speaking immigrants was 13 percent higher in new than old destinations in 1990.

20. The patterns over time are similar for new relative to traditional Mexican destinations. I defined as *traditional* Mexican destinations the top twenty areas ranked on number of working age Mexicans in 1990. Drawing on Card and Lewis (2007), I defined fifteen new Mexican destinations with a large residual inflow rate of Mexicans between 1990 and 2008 over what is predicted from a linear regression on 1990 Mexican (working-age population) share, and which are not traditional Mexican destinations. The large areas among the latter are all new destinations according to the Singer (2004) typography. Estimates in table 3.6 imply that Mexicans would have earned 3.5 percent more in new than in traditional destinations in 1990, but by 2008 they would have earned 1 percent less.

21. Puerto Rico was not included in the earlier analysis. In 1990, which is the last year the question was asked, 97 percent of those born outside and 99 percent of those born in Puerto Rico indicated that they spoke Spanish. Note that this is a broader language measure than was used in the previous analysis, which only indicated whether the respondent spoke Spanish "at home."

22. All estimates of equation (4) are unweighted, with standard errors computed to be robust to arbitrary error correlation within education × experience cells. In the Puerto Rican data, weeks worked is computed for those age sixteen to sixty-five who are not living in group quarters and who are old enough to be out of school. The Puerto Rican

wage sample consists of those in the weeks sample with positive wage earnings, zero business and farm earnings, who are not currently enrolled in school and who report an occupation.

23. The U.S. samples are defined similarly to the Puerto Rican ones (see previous note), except for a few things. First, to be included in the wage sample, rather than reporting an occupation, workers need to report being currently employed. (This difference in methodology is due to the fact that employment rates are very low in Puerto Rico.) Also, weekly wages below 10 or above 10,000 in 1999 dollars were reset to these thresholds. Finally, the two lowest education groups are combined in U.S. estimates, owing to the very small number of high school drop-out natives in the United States.

24. Although demand conditions in Puerto Rico may influence the educational attainment of the Puerto Rican–born population, this influence may be limited because a substantial fraction (about one-third) of Puerto Ricans end up in the continental U.S. labor market.

25. This implies that an instrumental variables estimate of the effect of relative weeks works on relative weekly wages, using the population variable as an instrument, would have the same coefficient as appears in column 2.

26. These columns exclude native-born workers who do not report speaking English "only" or "very well."

27. This comes from assuming a labor supply elasticity of one (following Raphael and Smolensky 2009); that is to say, that a 3 percent decline in hourly wages is associated with a 3 percent decline in hours worked, for a total of a 6 percent reduction in annual labor income.

28. Between 1990 and 2008, ln(poor/strong English hours) rose 1.39, and ln(Spanish/English hours) among noncollege rose 1.16 and among college-educated workers rose 0.58, for a $-0.061 = -0.033*1.39 - 0.045*1.16 + 0.065*0.57$ change in the relative ln wage, using the coefficients from table 3.6.

29. Chapter 5 includes additional analysis of why poverty rates were lower in new immigrant destinations.

REFERENCES

Berman, Eli, Kevin Lang, and Erez Siniver. 2003. "Language-Skill Complementarity: Returns to Immigrant Language Acquisition." *Labour Economics* 10(3): 265–90.

Bleakley, Hoyt, and Aimee Chin. 2004. "Language Skills and Earnings: Evidence from Childhood Immigrants." *Review of Economics and Statistics* 86(2): 481–96.

Borjas, George J. 1994. "The Economics of Immigration." *Journal of Economic Literature* 32(4): 1667–717.

———. 2008. "Labor Outflows and Labor Inflows in Puerto Rico." *Journal of Human Capital* 2(1): 32–68.

Card, David. 2001. "Immigrant Inflows, Native Outflows, and the Local Labor Market Impacts of Higher Immigration." *Journal of Labor Economics* 19(1): 22–64.

———. 2009. "Immigration and Inequality." *American Economic Review* 99(2): 1–21.

Card, David, and John DiNardo. 2000. "Do Immigrant Inflows Lead to Native Outflows?" *The American Economic Review* 90(2): 360–67.

Card, David, and Ethan Lewis. 2007. "The Diffusion of Mexican Immigrants During the 1990s: Explanations and Impacts." In *Mexican Immigration to the United States*, edited by George J. Borjas. Chicago: University of Chicago Press.

Carliner, Geoffrey. 1996. "The Wages and Language Skills of U.S. Immigrants." *NBER* working paper 5763. Cambridge, Mass.: National Bureau of Economic Research.

Castillo, Federico, J. Keith Gilless, and Steven Raphael. 2009. "Comparing the Domestic Labor Market Impacts of a South-North and South-South Migration: The Cases of Costa Rica and the United States." Unpublished paper. Berkeley: University of California.

Chiswick, Barry R., and Paul W. Miller. 1995. "The Endogeneity between Language and Earnings: International Analyses." *Journal of Labor Economics* 13(2): 246–88.

———. 2007. "Occupational Language Requirements and the Value of English in the U.S. Labor Market." *IZA* discussion paper no. 2664. Bonn: Institute for the Study of Labor.

Cutler, David M., Edward L. Glaeser, and Jacob L. Vigdor. 2008. "When Are Ghettos Bad? Lessons from Immigrant Segregation in the United States." *Journal of Urban Economics* 63(3): 759–74.

Dustmann, Christian, and Francesca Fabbri. 2003. "Language Proficiency and Labour Market Performance of Immigrants in the UK." *Economic Journal* 113(489): 695–717.

Dustmann, Christian, and Arthur van Soest. 2001. "Language Fluency and Earnings: Estimation with Misclassified Language Indicators." *Review of Economics and Statistics* 83(4): 663–74.

———. 2002. "Language and the Earnings of Immigrants." *Industrial and Labor Relations Review* 55(3): 473–92.

Ferrer, Ana, David A. Green, and Craig W. Riddell. 2006. "The Effect of Literacy on Immigrant Earnings." *Journal of Human Resources* 41(2): 380–410.

Friedberg, Rachel, and Jennifer Hunt. 1995. "The Impact of Immigrants on Host Country Wages, Employment and Growth." *Journal of Economic Perspectives* 9(2): 23–44.

Goldin, Claudia, and Lawrence Katz. 2008. *The Race Between Education and Technology*, Cambridge, Mass.: Harvard University Press.

Lang, Kevin. 1986. "A Language Theory of Discrimination." *Quarterly Journal of Economics* 101(2): 363–82.

Lewis, Ethan. 2004. "How Do Local Labor Markets in the U.S. Adjust to Immigration?" Mimeo. Philadelphia: Federal Reserve Bank.

Ottaviano, Gianmarco I.P., and Giovanni Peri. 2012. "Rethinking the Effect of Immigration on Wages." *Journal of the European Economic Association* 10(1): 152–97.

Peri, Giovanni, and Chad Sparber. 2009. "Task Specialization, Comparative Advantages, and the Effects of Immigration on Wages." *American Economic Journal: Applied Economics* 1(3): 135–69.

Raphael, Steven, and Eugene Smolensky. 2008. "Immigration and Poverty in the United States." *Institute for Research on Poverty* discussion paper no. 1347–08. Madison: University of Wisconsin-Madison.

———. 2009. "Immigration and Poverty in the United States." *American Economic Review* 99(2): 41–44.

Ruggles, Steven, J. Trent Alexander, Katie Genadek, Ronald Goeken, Matthew B. Schroeder, and Matthew Sobek. 2010. Integrated Public Use Microdata Series: Version 5.0 [Machine-readable database]. Minneapolis: University of Minnesota.

Singer, Audrey. 2004. "The Rise of New Immigrant Gateways." Washington, D.C.: Brookings Institution Center on Urban and Metropolitan Policy.

U.S. Bureau of the Census. 2003. Public Use Microdata Sample, Census of Population and Housing. Washington, D.C.

Chapter 4

Immigration, Segregation, and Poverty

Michael A. Stoll

Immigration, especially from Latin America and Asia, has changed and contin- ues to change the demographic landscape in the United States. This chapter is concerned with factors that influence immigrant segregation as well as whether and how immigration affects a host of concerns including racial segregation, im- migrant poverty, and English-language proficiency. Although immigrants con- tinue to settle in established gateway areas, such as Los Angeles, New York City, and Chicago, many are dispersing to other geographic areas not previously char- acterized as immigrant destination centers (Park and Iceland 2011; Lichter et al. 2010; Singer 2004).

The dominant view, consistent with spatial assimilation theory, is that immi- grants tend to settle and concentrate in the oldest residential neighborhoods with the most dated housing. As they learn English and get better jobs, they eventually move to better housing and spatially assimilate to a greater degree with natives (Alba et al. 1999; Massey 1985). In this model, English-language proficiency and length of residence in the United States are expected to be the key determinants of immigrant residential concentration. This view, however, overlooks other impor- tant factors, such as the role of older black segregation that could influence their segregation beyond what we might. In areas where black segregation is persistent, immigrant segregation might be heightened as a result of spillover effects of such segregation.

On the other hand, immigrants could also influence the levels and patterns of segregation of the native born, in particular African Americans. This could occur through either the polarization or diffusion (White et al. 2002; White and Glick 1999). Polarization argues that immigrants, particularly those from diverse ori- gins, could heighten black-white segregation given whites' discriminatory views or practices toward African Americans. Immigrants would serve as a buffer be- tween them. This would increase such segregation. On the other hand, diffusion refers to the potential role of immigrants stirring the melting pot by helping dis- solve the color line in the United States and thereby reduce such segregation.

There is some reason to believe that immigration might influence segregation levels of these groups despite earlier evidence that immigrant representation in metropolitan areas has little to no influence on black-white segregation levels (White et al. 2002; White and Glick 1999). Over the past two decades, segregation levels especially between native-born blacks and whites have declined. For example, in 1980, the black-white index of dissimilarity (a commonly used measure of segregation) was 73.8, dropping nearly 9 points to 65.0 in 2000 (Iceland, Weinberg, and Steinmetz 2002; Logan 2003). During this period, immigration in the United States increased so that between 1990 and 2000 the foreign-born population increased by 57 percent (compared with an increase of 13 percent for the total U.S. population) with most (about 52 percent) migrating from Latin America, especially Mexico. Many immigrant households live in communities that were formerly highly segregated African American neighborhoods, characterized by high poverty rates and the many attendant social ills. Many immigrants, however, in particular Latinos, locate in distant suburbs close to higher income households yet often segregated in small enclaves (Singer 2004).[1] These temporal trends support the idea that increased immigration is influencing lower segregation levels, particularly among blacks.

Even if immigration proves to have little collateral consequence on native-born segregation patterns, it may lead to other concerns. To the extent that immigration leads to immigrant residential concentration, one might worry about whether such segregation influences immigrant poverty or delays English-language acquisition. This could occur through isolation or ethnic enclave influences. The isolation effect would be consistent, in the case of African Americans, with William Wilson's (1987) view of segregation, leading to heightened poverty as result of isolation from the middle class and limited presence or effectiveness of pro-social institutions. On the other hand, ethnic enclave effects could mitigate the effect of segregation on poverty through the formulation of social capital among immigrant groups. It could also serve as a mechanism for social incorporation, particularly for those who have difficulty speaking English well (Zhou 2004; Light and Bonacich 1991; Leiberson 1981). Little is known, however, about whether immigrant segregation influences poverty or English-language acquisition.

This chapter is intended to fill these voids and focuses on immigration, segregation and poverty. It explores the extent of residential segregation of immigrants, whether and the extent to which immigration influences racial and ethnic segregation in the United States, and whether and to what extent immigrant segregation influences poverty and English-language acquisition. Thus, the central questions follow:

How segregated are immigrants from natives, how does this vary across regions of the United States and across different immigrant groups, and what the broad determinants of this segregation?

Does immigration reduce the degree of residential homogeneity experienced by traditionally segregated native-born groups, in particular African Americans?

Does immigrant segregation aggravate poverty and linguistic isolation among the foreign born?

Pursuit of these questions is important not only to improve our understanding of these relationships, but also because the answers to them might prove useful for public policy. To the extent that segregation of vulnerable groups does influence important social and economic outcomes like poverty of English-language acquisition, and to the extent that either immigrants suffer high levels of segregation or influence high segregation levels of native-born racial minorities, we might be concerned about these potential costs to society of increased immigration. The results of this chapter, however, suggest that these potential concerns are not fully warranted. They indicate that very little evidence is found that immigrants influence segregation of other important groups, in particular African Americans, or that immigrant segregation is associated with social concerns such as poverty. They do, however, demonstrate that immigrant segregation is associated with exacerbating English-language acquisition that in turn could negatively influence immigrants' poverty outcomes.

DATA AND METHODS

To answer these central questions, I use data from 2005 to 2009 U.S. Census American Community Survey (ACS), which provide five-year averages of counts of the population and other relevant population characteristics at the metropolitan area and census tract levels. The 2005 to 2009 ACS also provides the most recent data available at geographic levels small enough to estimate reliable measures of segregation.[2]

The primary measure of residential segregation used in this study is the index of dissimilarity, and this measure is calculated for a number of pair-wise combination of groups for the 150 largest metropolitan areas in the United States.[3] Metropolitan areas are restricted to these areas (representing areas with populations greater than about 250,000) to generate enough population counts for specific groups, such as Asian immigrants, to reliably calculate measures of segregation. Each of the subgroups examined have at least 100 persons in the metropolitan area. The index of dissimilarity, a measure of evenness, is the most commonly used measure of segregation, but not the only one in the segregation literature. Others include the isolation, exposure, and entropy indexes, for example, and these measure different aspects of the scope or kind of segregation.

These alternative measures of segregation are well noted in the literature and their differences and consequences have been examined elsewhere (Massey and Denton 1988b). I alternately calculated segregation indices using the isolation index, a measure of exposure that indicates the probability that a group member would come into contact with a member of another group. The qualitative findings were very similar to those using the dissimilarity index, however, and thus their results are not reported. I focus on results using the dissimilarity index because it is a commonly used and well understood measure of segregation, and more importantly because its reliability as a measure is less sensitive to the relative size of groups being examined. This is important because some sub-immigrant groups analyzed in this chapter have smaller population counts in many metropolitan areas.[4]

The equation used to calculate the index of dissimilarity is quite straightforward. For example, define $immigrant_i$ as the immigrant population residing in census tract i (where $i = (1, \ldots, n)$ and indexes the tracts in a given metropolitan area), $white_i$ as the white (non-Hispanic, native-born) population residing in census tract i, $immigrant$ as the total immigrant population in the metropolitan area, and $white$ as the total number of whites in the metropolitan area. The dissimilarity score between immigrants and whites is given by

$$D = \frac{1}{2} \sum_i \left| \frac{immigrant_i}{immigrant} - \frac{white_i}{white} \right|. \tag{1}$$

As written, the dissimilarity index ranges between 0 (perfect balance) and 1 (perfect imbalance). Hence, the index value between immigrants and whites for metropolitan areas in the sample describes the extent to which the areas (measured as census tracts) where immigrants tend to reside in are different from the areas in which whites are located. The results from this equation are multiplied by 100 to allow one to interpret the index values as the percentage, rather than the proportion, of either of the populations that would have to move to yield perfect balance.

The potential problems of using a dissimilarity index to measure segregation are well documented. For example, the dissimilarity index does not actually measure the physical distance between the average member of a given population. The index measures the imbalance across geographic subunits of the metropolitan area, such as census tracts, between members of populations. To take an extreme example, suppose that all immigrant residents lived in one zip code of a city and all whites in another. Whether these two tracts are one mile or twenty miles apart will not influence the dissimilarity measure. In both instances, the dissimilarity index will be equal to 100. Yet, the geographic distance could influence the likelihood of social contact of individuals across tracts. Nonetheless, as a summary measure, the dissimilarity measure does allow comparisons across geographic areas.

Despite this, the dissimilarity index has a number of strengths as well. First, it allows segregation to be measured in a uniform way across metropolitan areas. Second, the actual numerical value of the index of dissimilarity has a convenient interpretation. Specifically, the index can be interpreted as the percentage of either the immigrant or white population that would have to relocate to different areas to completely eliminate any geographic imbalance. For example, as figure 4.1 indicates, the 2005 to 2009 index value describing the imbalance between the residen-

FIGURE 4.1 / Index of Dissimilarity by Country of Origin

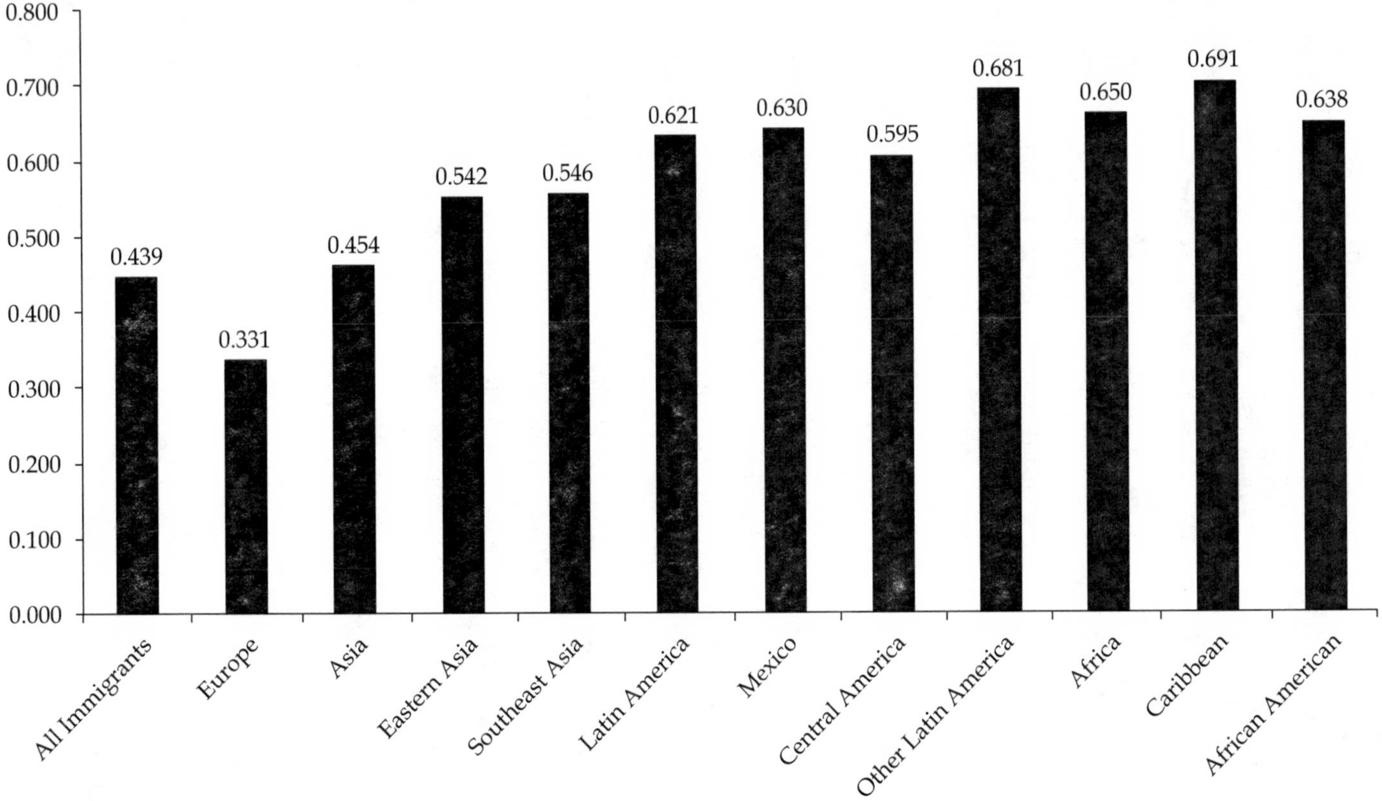

Source: Author's compilation.
Note: Weighted by respective immigrant group.

tial distributions of immigrants and whites is 43.9 for the metropolitan areas in the sample.[5] This indicates that in the 2005 to 2009 period, about 44 percent of immigrants would have had to relocate within metropolitan areas to be spatially distributed in perfect proportion with the geographic residential distribution of whites (native-born, non-Hispanic).

Immigrant Segregation Levels

Figure 4.1 demonstrates the tremendous variation in immigrant segregation depending on immigrants' area of origin.[6] Immigrants from Europe have the lowest levels of segregation from whites, followed by those from Asia, Latin America, Africa, and the Caribbean.[7] These results and their magnitudes are largely consistent with previous research in this area using census data from 2000 (Park and Iceland 2011). However, segregation levels of those from Asia and Latin America also vary by the areas of origin within these large sending regions. For example, within Latin America, the levels of segregation from whites varies somewhat for immigrants from Mexico, other parts of Central America, and the rest of Latin America, the latter having higher segregation scores. Also, the index of dissimilarity of immigrants from East Asia (including China, Japan, and Korea) is 54.2 and that for those from Southeast Asia (including Vietnam, Philippines, and Cambodia) is 54.6, much higher than that for those from Asia as a whole.[8]

A key question is whether these immigrant segregation levels should be considered high or low. One way to think about this is to compare these segregation levels with domestic groups with persistently high segregation scores such as African Americans. Figure 4.1 also provides their segregation score, 63.8 in 2005 through 2009. Thus, relative to black segregation in the United States, the segregation levels of those from the Caribbean, Africa, Mexico, and other parts of Latin American are comparable.

Another way is to consider the literature on racial segregation in housing. It has developed a typology of segregation levels based on the following categories: low, moderate, and high segregation levels according to the following cutoffs: 0–40, 40 to 60, and over 60. The literature describe indexes of dissimilarity of over 60 as being high (with 80 + indicating hyper levels) of segregation, with that between 40 to 60 as moderate, and below 40 as low (Massey and Denton 1993). According to these conventions, immigrant segregation from Europe is considered low, and that from Asia is considered moderate. Segregation levels of those from the Caribbean, Africa, Mexico, and other parts of Latin American are considered high.

Do immigrant segregation levels vary by region in the United States? This is an important question because, in the postwar period, segregation levels of minority groups of concern have been higher in the Midwest and Northeast than in the West or South. Table 4.1 provides data on segregation levels by region for broad subcategorizations of immigrants. Interestingly, the variation in segregation levels for immigrants from Europe and Asia by region is not statistically significant.

This is not the case for immigrants from Latin American, Africa, or the Carib-

TABLE 4.1 / Dissimilarity, Immigrants and Whites, Region

	Northeast	Midwest	South	West
All Immigrants	0.463	0.415	0.428	0.438*
Europe	0.335	0.382	0.321	0.291
Asia	0.486	0.482	0.441	0.436
Latin America	0.676	0.624	0.538	0.598*
Mexico	0.787	0.677	0.593	0.628*
Africa	0.679	0.693	0.623	0.619*
Caribbean	0.769	0.783	0.609	0.657*
African American	0.737	0.728	0.573	0.578*

Source: Author's calculations.
*Indicates F-test of null hypothesis of equal means across region is statistically significant at at least the 5 percent level.

bean. For these groups, segregation levels are lower in the South and West than in the Midwest or Northeast, following regional patterns of segregation experienced by African Americans. In particular, segregation levels of immigrants from Latin America and Mexico are highest in the Northeast and lowest in the South. Immigrants from African and the Caribbean experience higher levels of segregation in the Midwest, but the lowest levels of segregation differ for each group: slightly lower for Africans in the West, and lower for those from the Caribbean in the South.

The reasons for these regional variations are likely many, but could include a few noteworthy factors. Segregation levels are on average higher for more recent immigrants than those with a longer vintage (Park and Iceland 2011). Consequently, the higher levels of segregation in the Northeast for those immigrants from Latin American and in particular Mexico could reflect their relatively new presence in these areas.[9] On the other hand, the lower levels of segregation in the South and West could reflect trends consistent with notions of a new South characterized by more openness as displayed lower levels of segregation over the past decades despite the residue of Jim Crow.

Factors Influencing Immigrant Segregation

The preceding evidence reveals rather high segregation levels for many immigrant groups, a few nearly equal to the levels of segregation experienced by African Americans. A key question is the factors that drive immigrant segregation levels. This section examines whether historic segregation, English-language difficulty, or age of dwelling influence these outcomes. Of course, these are not the only factors likely to influence immigrant segregation levels. Among other factors, studies have shown that levels of income, homeownership, and recency of arrival play significant roles in this regard, with higher income, homeownership, and longer tenures in the United States associated with lower segregation levels (Iceland and Scopilliti 2008).

Segregation Infrastructure

Other factors that have driven African American segregation could also influence immigrant segregation. These include, among others, current or past suburban housing discrimination including steering by agents, discrimination in renting by landlords or in home mortgage lending by banks and other lending institutions (Yinger 1997; Ondrich, Ross, and Yinger 2001; Ondrich, Sticker, and Yinger 1999; Goering and Wienk 1996; Massey and Denton 1993), and asymmetric racial-ethnic preferences for integrated neighborhoods (Charles 2005).

Spatial assimilation theory suggests and recent empirical work shows that immigrant segregation levels fall with average tenure in the United States. What has been overlooked, however, is that these potential segregation infrastructures could influence immigrant segregation levels from the start in and across metropolitan areas. That is, cities with an existing segregation infrastructure may tend to systematically segregate immigrants more, above and beyond the role of other relevant factors duly noted in the literature. This infrastructure could be influenced by a variety of factors, including the historical residue of racial housing covenants, racial attitudes or race relations, or intensity of historic or current racially discriminatory practices in housing markets, among many other factors. Such infrastructure could play a role in shaping immigrant residential patterns as well.

One way to examine this potential relationship is to explore the relationship between current segregation levels of immigrants and African American segregation from an earlier period. African American segregation reflects deeply rooted, historical segregation patterns in the United States that could influences segregation patterns of other groups, especially immigrants. To do this, I calculate indices of segregation between blacks and whites in 1990 for the same metropolitan areas in the sample.[10]

Figure 4.2 first presents a scatterplot of the segregation index for all immigrants between 2005 and 2009 plotted on the y-axis, against 1990 segregation scores between blacks and whites plotted on the x-axis. A linear regression line is fitted to the data and is shown in the right side of the figure. The data in the figure demonstrate that segregation levels of immigrants from whites are statistically significantly higher in metropolitan areas with higher levels of black-white segregation in 1990. The regression equation indicates that a 10 percentage point increase in segregation levels in 1990 between blacks and whites is associated with a 1.5 point increase in the segregation levels of immigrants from whites between 2005 and 2009.

Figure 4.2 also includes results from a linear regression that is weighted by the

FIGURE 4.2 / Scatterplot of Dissimilarities

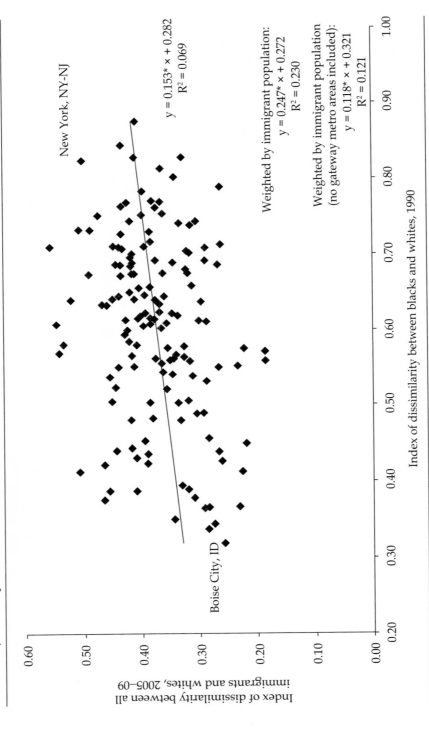

Weighted by immigrant population:
$y = 0.247^* \times + 0.272$
$R^2 = 0.230$

Weighted by immigrant population
(no gateway metro areas included):
$y = 0.118^* \times + 0.321$
$R^2 = 0.121$

$y = 0.153^* \times + 0.282$
$R^2 = 0.069$

New York, NY-NJ

Boise City, ID

Index of dissimilarity between all
immigrants and whites, 2005–09

Index of dissimilarity between blacks and whites, 1990

Source: Author's compilation.
$^*p < .05$

number of immigrants in metropolitan areas. This technique allows metropolitan areas with larger numbers of immigrants to have more influence in estimating the relationship, so that it (perhaps appropriately) reflects the segregation experience of the typical immigrant rather than that of the typical metro area. When the data are weighted in this manner, the results show a stronger and still statistically significant relationship between current immigrant segregation and older black-white segregation—a 10 percentage point increase in black-white segregation levels in 1990 is associated with a 2.5 point increase in the segregation levels of immigrants from whites in 2005–09. This indicates that the typical immigrant group member lives in metropolitan areas with a stronger relationship between immigrant segregation and historic black segregation than across average metropolitan areas in the sample.

A concern in weighting in this way, however, is that metropolitan areas that have larger numbers of immigrants in the sample, such as New York, Los Angeles, Miami, Chicago, San Francisco, and Houston, are also established immigrant gateways that could reflect different immigrant experiences than those in nongateway metro areas (Park and Iceland 2011; Litcher et al. 2010). Furthermore, these established gateway metro areas are also likely to be systematically different than other metro areas in a variety of characteristics, including higher overall black segregation levels. However, though not shown, when the two biggest established gateway metro areas, New York and Los Angeles, are excluded from the calculation, the weighted bivariate regression result is unaffected. When all traditional gateway metro areas are excluded, as shown in figure 4.2, the strength of the relationship between older black segregation levels and current immigrant segregation levels is reduced by nearly half, as shown in the lower panel of the figure, suggesting that much (but not all) of the influence of black segregation on immigrant segregation comes from established gateway metro areas. Still, the coefficient on older black segregation remains statistically significant and close in magnitude to the unweighted results using the full sample.[11]

Nevertheless, inferences based on these bivariate relationships could be misleading, particularly if they are confounded further by other metropolitan area characteristics. For example, even after weighting for immigrant group size, larger metropolitan areas are more likely to have higher levels of racial-ethnic segregation and higher percentages of immigrant representation, and thus the relationship between immigrant segregation and older black segregation could be spurious through, say, metropolitan area size.

To address this and other related issues, I control for a set of observable metropolitan area characteristics through the following model:

$$immseg_i = blackseg1990_i \beta_{11} + \beta'_{12} X_i + \varepsilon_{1i} \qquad (2)$$

where i indexes metropolitan areas, $immseg_i$ is the dissimilarity index (from whites) for the respective immigrant group, $blackseg1990_i$ is the 1990 black-white segregation index, and X_i is a variety of metropolitan area characteristics variables, and ε_{1i} is a mean-zero, randomly distributed disturbance term. Obvious metropolitan area characteristics that may covary with immigrant segregation and mediate the relationship between immigrant segregation and older black segregation include physical characteristics such as region, population size, and the age of the oldest, main central city of the metropolitan area. They also include socioeconomic and political characteristics such as the percentage of the metro area that is black, Latino, aged over sixty-five, with college degrees, or impoverished, the structure of the economy (shares of employment in either retail, manufacturing, or service), its labor market strength (employment rate), and the number of political jurisdictions.[12] Finally, they also include important immigrant characteristics including the length of residence (average number of years) in the United States and English-language ability.[13]

Figure 4.3 provides coefficients for the black-white segregation in 1990 variable from a series of regressions specified in equation (2) for the respective immigrant groups. These regressions are weighted by the respective immigrant groups and of course control for the listed observables. The first two bars from the left indicate that controlling for these observable metro variables moderates the influence of older black segregation on immigrant segregation for the full sample, but increases the point estimate of its influence on immigrant segregation in nongateway metro areas. Most of this influence operates through metropolitan size and the average number of years in the United States: immigrants tend to be in larger metro areas and have been in the country less time in nongateway metro areas.

Thus, after controlling for all of these factors, the coefficients for older black segregation are more comparable between the full sample of metro areas and those without gateway metro areas (than when no controls are included). Though not shown, this pattern is largely consistent for all sub-immigrant groups analyzed here. This demonstrates that the role of established gateways in influencing these results is not as large as originally indicated.

Figure 4.3 also provides estimates of the older black segregation coefficient for the respective sub-immigrant group regressions. The results show for every case except for European and Caribbean immigrants, a fairly strong, positive, and statistically significant relationship between older black segregation and current immigrant segregation. In particular, this relationship is strongest for immigrants from Mexico, and Latin America more generally, as well as for those immigrants from Southeast Asia. Taken together, the evidence suggests that the segregation of these immigrant groups is heighted by the negative collateral consequences of historic black segregation in the United States, and that this remains true even after controlling for important factors such as length of residence in the United States and English-language ability.

Nevertheless, none of the coefficients from these regressions compare in magnitude with the relationship between older black segregation and current black segregation. Still, the latter coefficient does not equal one suggesting that segregation levels have weakened in metropolitan areas at varying paces over the past fifteen or so years. What is also noteworthy is that, compared with other immigrant groups, African and Caribbean segregation levels are significantly less correlated with native-born black segregation from an earlier period (even though their mean

FIGURE 4.3 / Immigrant and Black Segregation

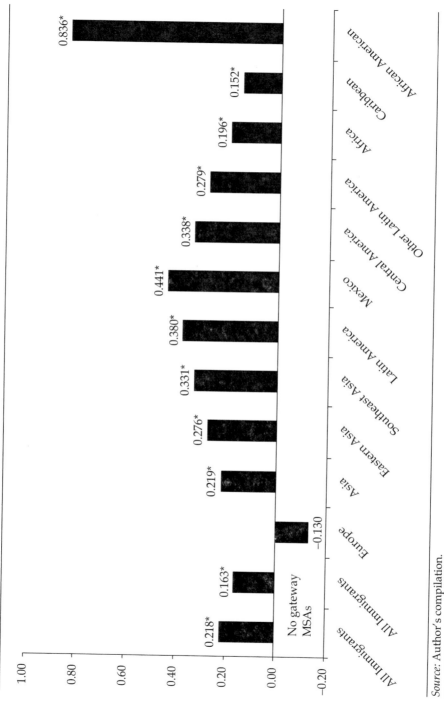

Source: Author's compilation.
Note: Weighted by respective immigrant group. All MSAs included except where noted.
* p < .05

segregation levels are relatively high), indicating that they tend to either move to or live in metropolitan areas less characterized by existing segregation infrastructures, or are less segregated from whites in these areas.

English-Language Difficulty

The spatial assimilation literature predicts and shows quite clearly that ethnic assimilation processes include the role and limitation of English-language difficulty in influencing immigrants' locational choices, especially for newer than older immigrants (Park and Iceland 2011; Burr and Mutchler 2003; Leiberson 1981). Immigrants with limited English-language ability are more likely to choose neighborhoods where other co-ethnics with similar languages are predominant in order to limit the costs of transition and transactions. As immigrants gain skills in the English language, and as familiarity with the dominant culture and customs improve, immigrants tend to move to more diverse neighborhoods (Light 1991).

This implies that those immigrant group members with limited English ability are likely to be more segregated than those without. The data in figure 4.4 are presented to address this question. It provides coefficients from a series of regressions of the respective immigrant groups as a function of the percentage of each of these groups that indicate that they have difficulty speaking in English, controlling for the observable metro variables listed earlier. Except where noted, these regressions are also weighted by the respective immigrant groups and are estimated using the full sample of metro areas. In the sample as a whole, about 27 percent of all immigrants indicate English-language difficulty, ranging from a high of 49 percent for Mexican immigrants to lows of 7 to 10 percent for immigrants from Europe, Africa and the Caribbean (see table 4.A1).

The results from figure 4.4 are entirely consistent with this expectation and with previous results (Iceland and Scopilliti 2008; South, Crowder, and Chavez 2005a, 2005b; Massey and Denton 1988a).[14] They show that across immigrants as a whole and for all sub-immigrant groups where English is likely a second language, those with English-language difficulty are more likely to be segregated from whites than those without. In the farthest left column, the results indicate that for all immigrant groups across all metro areas, those with limited English have on average a segregation score that is about 47 points higher than those with less difficulty.

When the regression is weighted by the number of immigrants in metro areas, that estimated difference in scores between these two groups decreases to 40 points, taking into account the disproportionate influence of metro size on this estimate and variation in the average number of years in the United States for immigrants across metro areas. Omitting established gateway metro areas from the equation reduces the coefficient by about 20 percent. However, it still remains fairly large in magnitude and statistically significant, indicating that nongateway metro areas are not immune from the influence of English-language difficulty on segregation. The remaining coefficients indicate that this relationship is observable

FIGURE 4.4 / Segregation and English-Language Difficulty

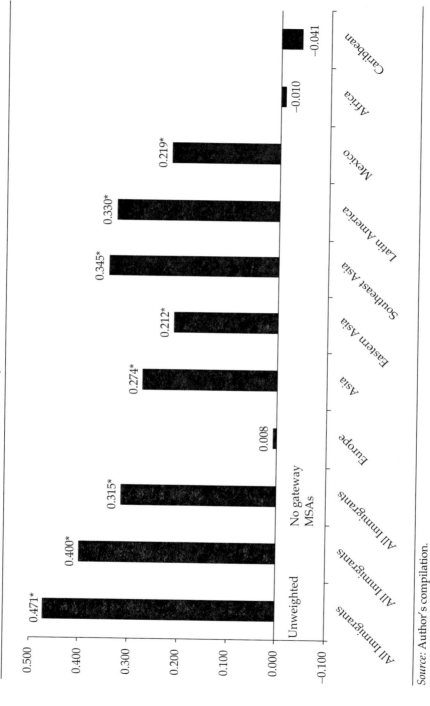

Source: Author's compilation.
Note: Weighted by respective immigrant group. All regressions include control variables listed in respective place in text.
*p < .05

for those from Asia and Latin America, a result that likely highlights the strength of these ethnic enclaves in influencing this result.

Housing Stock Age

The age of housing stock, which is highly correlated with age of the oldest main central city, across metro areas is another potential factor that could influence immigrant segregation. The spatial assimilation literature suggests that immigrants settle in the oldest residential neighborhoods where the housing stock is more dated (Massey 1985). The average age of housing is important because it is highly correlated with quality and affordability, older housing stock on average being more correlated with lower housing quality and therefore with more affordability. Given the disproportionate lower average incomes of immigrants, and in particular of many sub-immigrant groups such as those from Mexico, variation in the age of housing stock across metro areas could influence immigrant segregation levels.

This expectation is also supported by housing filtering theories. In this model of urban housing markets, durable dwelling units filter though a quality hierarchy. The supply of housing of a given quality is determined by several factors including the age of the stock of housing, where older housing stocks are more likely to filter to low-income housing (O'Sullivan 2011). To the extent that older housing stock is more likely to be low income, and that the average income of immigrant groups are disproportionately lower income, we should expect immigrant segregation levels to be higher in metro areas with older housing stock.[15]

The data in figure 4.5 are presented to examine this question. It shows the average immigrant segregation score for all metropolitan areas, as well as the segregation scores for immigrants in metropolitan areas where the average housing stock is at the 10th and 25th percentile of the distribution, from oldest to youngest housing stock. The data presented do not support this theoretical expectation and show that the average immigrant segregation scores are not statistically significantly different across metropolitan areas with some of the oldest housing stock and for the average metropolitan area.

Because of the variation in spatial location of immigrant groups, the results for all immigrants could mask important associations between the age of housing stock and segregation for sub-immigrant groups. Table 4.2 is provided to examine these relationships. The results indicate that despite no relationship between these factors for immigrants as a whole, the association between age of housing stock and immigrant segregation is statically significant for those immigrants from Latin American and the Caribbean.

Indeed, the largest difference in segregation scores between all metropolitan areas and for those with the oldest housing stock is for immigrants from Central America and Mexico. For these groups, the difference in segregation scores between all metro areas and those at the 10th percentile of the housing stock age distribution ranges from 13 to 15 points, results that are consistent with immigrant spatial assimilation and housing filtering contributing to immigrant segregation

FIGURE 4.5 / Dissimilarity, Immigrants and Whites, Age of Housing

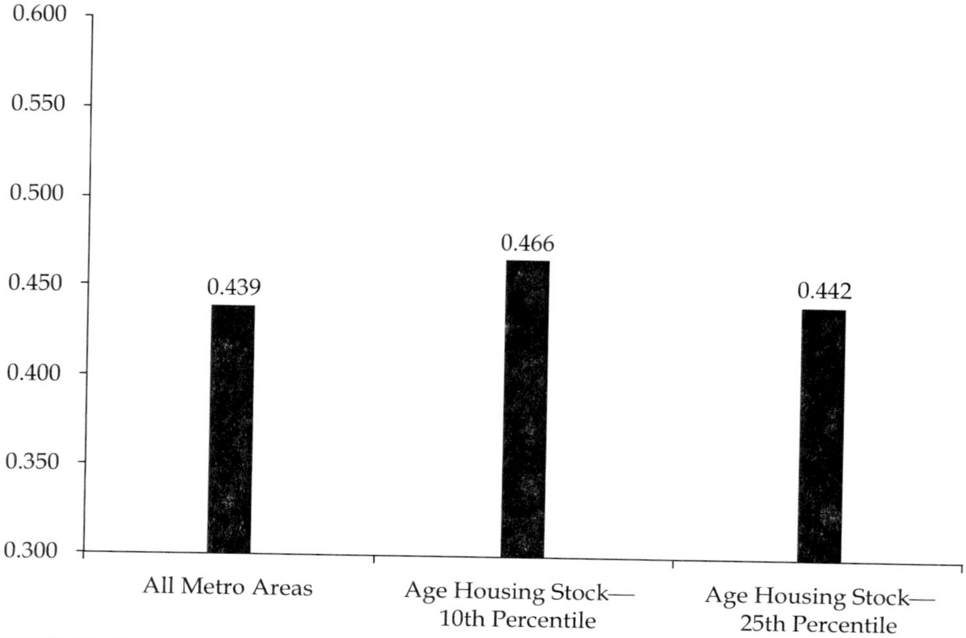

Source: Author's compilation.

TABLE 4.2 / Dissimilarity, Immigrants and Whites, Age of Housing

	All Metro Areas	Age Housing Stock—10th Percentile	Age Housing Stock—25th Percentile
Europe	0.331	0.337	0.339
Asia	0.454	0.482	0.469
Eastern Asia	0.542	0.582	0.564
Southeast Asia	0.546	0.577	0.561
Latin America	0.621	0.676	0.642*
Mexico	0.630	0.784	0.709*
Central America	0.595	0.730	0.695*
Other Latin America	0.681	0.681	0.655
Africa	0.650	0.674	0.656
Caribbean	0.691	0.770	0.761*
African American	0.638	0.713	0.659*

Source: Author's calculations.
*Indicates F-test of null hypothesis of equal means across region is statistically significant at at least the 5 percent level.

levels. Further probing of the data indicates that these results are likely driven by the greater spatial distribution across metropolitan areas of Central Americans and Mexicans than, say those from Asia, and these groups are also more represented in older metropolitan areas than most other sub-immigrant groups.

Racial Segregation and Immigration

This section turns to address whether immigrants influence segregation levels of particularly those groups such as African Americans who experience relatively high levels of segregation. The expected effect of whether and how immigrants might influence black segregation is an empirical matter, however. A priori, the influence of immigrants could lead to either increases or decreases in segregation levels of native-born African Americans.

On the one hand, to the extent that immigrants face less discrimination in either rental or owner-occupied housing markets or are preferred by whites as neighbors over blacks, immigrants are likely to out-compete blacks in competition for housing—particularly in areas outside predominantly black neighborhoods—thereby driving upward blacks' segregation levels. This process would also be consistent with polarization. On the other hand, consistent with diffusion models, to the extent that blacks face less discrimination in housing markets and tend to move out of black neighborhoods either because of choice, through conventional neighborhood sorting mechanisms, or because they prefer not to live near immigrants, black segregation levels could decline as immigrants move to areas where blacks predominate.

I address this question in two ways. One includes examining simple differences in segregation scores among three mutually exclusive groups. The other estimates regressions of relevant black segregation scores as a function of the percentage of immigrants in the metropolitan area.

In the first approach, I define three mutually exclusive groups in metropolitan areas: native-born blacks, native-born nonblacks, and the foreign born. I then calculate four segregation indices including between native-born blacks and the combination of native-born nonblacks and the foreign born (a measure of native-born black segregation from all others), between native-born blacks and the foreign born, and between native-born blacks and native-born nonblacks. Finally, I calculate a segregation score of the final pair-wise combination between native-born nonblacks and the foreign born. Differences across these scores, and the direction of the difference, should provide important information regarding the potential direction of the influence of immigrants on black segregation. The finding that native-born blacks are less segregated from immigrants than others, especially native-born nonblacks, would be consistent with the idea that immigrants are less likely to influence further segregation of African Americans.

Figure 4.6 provides the average segregation scores for each of these mutually exclusive pair-wise combinations. The data indicate that segregation scores between native-born blacks and the foreign born are statistically significantly lower

FIGURE 4.6 / Index of Dissimilarity for Blacks

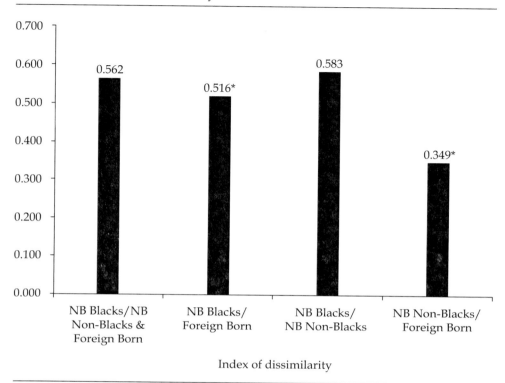

Source: Author's compilation.
Note: NB = Native Born
*$p < .05$, between the foreign born and native-born blacks or native-born nonblacks

(by about 5 points) than those between native-born blacks and native-born non-blacks, and between native-born blacks and others (native-born nonblacks + the foreign born). This implies that among these groups, native-born blacks are less segregated from immigrants than others, suggesting that the greater the share the immigrant population, the less segregated blacks should be in metropolitan areas, (relative to segregation from native-born nonblacks). The data also reveal that native-born nonblacks are also less segregated from immigrants than from native-born blacks, suggesting that that growing immigration could mediate the segregation of native-born blacks from native-born nonblacks as well.

How does this pattern unfold across major regions in the United States? Table 4.3 provides the segregation scores for these pair-wise combinations of mutually exclusive groups by region. The data show that patterns across regions are similar to that for metropolitan areas as a whole: native-born blacks are less segregated from immigrants than from native-born nonblacks, and that immigrants are less

T𝐀𝐁𝐋𝐄 4.3   /   Dissimilarity, Mutually Exclusive Groups, Region

Region	NBª Blacks/NBª Nonblacks and Foreign Born	NBª Blacks/ Foreign Born	NBª Blacks/ NBª Nonblacks	NBª Nonblacks/ Foreign Born
	Index of Dissimilarity			
Northeast	0.617*	0.520*	0.654*	0.381
Midwest	0.673	0.623	0.682	0.386
South	0.521	0.490	0.542	0.346
West	0.479	0.463	0.497	0.297

Source: Author's calculations.
*Indicates F-test of null hypothesis of equal means across region is statistically significant at at least the 5 percent level.
ªNB = native born.

segregated from native-born nonblacks than blacks. However, the gaps in segregation scores across these groups are much larger in the Northeast and smallest in the West, where segregation scores in general are the lowest across regions. Note also that, consistent with data in table 4.1, segregation scores are uniformly higher in the Midwest where overall segregation scores are highest across regions.

What immigrant subgroups appear most likely to integrate with native-born blacks? To help answer this question, table 4.4 presents segregation scores of immigrant subgroups to native-born blacks for all metropolitan areas and by region. The data indicate that the lower segregation scores are driven by lower segregation levels between native-born blacks and immigrants from Africa, the Caribbean, and Latin America, especially those from South America. Given the relatively smaller immigration flows of those from African and the Caribbean, immigrants from Latin America likely make up the bulk of this influence. These patterns largely hold across regions as well, along with the usual caveats consistent with earlier results that these segregation scores are highest in the Midwest and Northeast and lowest in the West.

The second approach entails estimating the influence of immigrants on measures of black segregation directly through regressions of the pair-wise combinations of mutually exclusive groups as a function of the percentage of the metropolitan area population that is immigrants. I do so by conducting a series of regressions that estimate the influence of immigration on segregation given the following equation:

$$seg_i = imm_i \beta_{11} + \beta'_{12} X_i + \varepsilon_{1i} \tag{3}$$

where i indexes metropolitan areas, seg_i is the dissimilarity index for the relevant mutually exclusive pair-wise group, imm_i is the percentage of the metropolitan area that is foreign born (and area of origin of the foreign born), and X_i is a variety

TABLE 4.4 / Dissimilarity, Immigrants and Blacks, Region

		Northeast	Midwest	South	West
All Immigrants	0.515	0.521	0.660	0.502	0.482*
Europe	0.686	0.716	0.775	0.635	0.605
Asia	0.630	0.715	0.724	0.614	0.568*
Eastern Asia	0.726	0.801	0.800	0.711	0.669*
Southeast Asia	0.603	0.713	0.701	0.619	0.554*
Latin America	0.517	0.441	0.699	0.520	0.516*
Mexico	0.580	0.743	0.742	0.566	0.542*
Central America	0.602	0.625	0.778	0.616	0.553*
Other Latin America	0.494	0.430	0.676	0.529	0.512*
Africa	0.512	0.483	0.547	0.502	0.549
Caribbean	0.466	0.393	0.718	0.515	0.658*

Source: Author's calculations.
*Indicates F-test of null hypothesis of equal means across region is statistically significant at at least the 5 percent level.

of basic metropolitan area characteristics variables previously discussed, and ε_{1i} is a mean-zero, randomly distributed disturbance term.

Table 4.5 provides a series of coefficients from these regressions predicting segregation between these pair-wise mutually exclusive groups as a function of immigrant representation in metropolitan areas, for all immigrants and by their area of origin. Each cell shows the coefficient for immigrant representation and therefore each cell represent a separate regression. For each of these groups, three regression models are estimated that include sequentially only a measure of immigrant representation, include controls for metropolitan area characteristics, and exclude the established gateway metro areas from the sample.[16] The first column of estimates are for all immigrants combined, and the next set of columns are for the sub-immigrant groups. A positive coefficient on immigrant representation indicates that the measure of segregation for the relevant group increases with the percentage of immigrants in the metro area.

Table 4.5 shows in the first column these results of black segregation measures as a function of immigrant representation in the metro area for all immigrants. The first measure of black segregation, panel 1, is native-born blacks from all others (native-born nonblacks and the foreign born), a measure of native-born blacks' total isolation. For all model specifications, the results show virtually no influence of immigrant representation on this measure of black segregation. In the next panel, the second measures of segregation is native-born blacks' segregation from the foreign born. The positive and statistically significant coefficient of immigrant representation on this measure of black segregation disappears after the full set of controls are entered into the equation (mostly from metro size); excluding established gateway metro areas from the sample has no impact on the estimated coefficient.

TABLE 4.5 / Immigrant and Black Segregation

		% of Metro-Population Immigrants from:						
Index of Dissimilarity	All Immigrants	Europe	Asia	Latin America	Mexico	Africa	Caribbean
1. NB blacks/(NB nonblacks and FB)							
No controls	0.065	2.846***	-0.190	-0.005	-0.225	0.278	0.129
Metro P + SE controls	0.114	0.935	-0.158	0.052	0.091	-0.385	-0.209
Metro P + SE controls, no gateway MSAs	0.118	1.452***	-0.167	0.159	0.072	-0.493	-0.287
2. NB blacks/FB							
No controls	0.145*	1.149**	-0.191	0.285**	0.235*	0.131	0.313**
Metro P + SE controls	-0.071	1.632*	-0.262	0.080	0.115	-0.256	-0.240
Metro P + SE controls, no gateway MSAs	0.060	1.746	-0.311	0.064	0.096	-0.350	-0.331
3. NB blacks/NB nonblacks							
No controls	0.141*	2.764***	-0.132	-0.020	-0.348**	0.305	0.191**
Metro P + SE controls	0.122	1.883**	-0.199	0.103	0.118	-0.301	0.115
Metro P + SE controls, no gateway MSAs	0.111	1.930**	-0.197	0.072	0.181	0.411	0.218
4. (NB blacks/NB nonblacks), (NB blacks/FB)							
No controls	-0.003	-0.428*	-0.054	-0.327**	-0.044	2.701***	-0.139
Metro P + SE controls	0.132	0.990**	0.106	0.212	0.026	-1.030	-0.306
Metro P + SE controls, no gateway MSAs	0.119	1.481**	0.294	-0517	-0.072	0.800	0.322

Source: Author's calculations.
Note: NB = native born; P = metro physical controls; SE = metro socioeconomic controls.
$*p < 0.10; **p < 0.05; ***p < 0.01$

Panel 3 shows the third measure of black segregation; native-born blacks' segregation from native-born nonblacks. The results are similar to those results earlier: the positive and statistically significant coefficient of immigrant representation on black segregation from the foreign born disappears after the full set of controls are entered into the equation (again, mostly from metro size). Excluding established gateway metro areas from the sample also has no impact.

Finally, in panel 4, the last measure of segregation shows the difference between the segregation scores of native-born blacks and nonblacks and the scores for native-born blacks and the foreign born. Consistent with the previous results, the coefficients are never statistically significant in any of the model specifications.[17]

The sub-immigrant results shown in columns to the right indicate similar results as to those for all immigrants combined, except for immigrants from Europe. The results for this group show that greater immigrant representation is associated with greater black segregation for all measures of black segregation, depending on whether gateway metro areas are included in the sample.

The coefficient results from black segregation measures, panel 4, is particularly interesting. This measure of segregation is the difference between the segregation scores of native-born blacks and nonblacks and the scores for native-born blacks and the European foreign born. The coefficients in panel 4 thus indicate whether the increase in blacks' segregation from native-born nonblacks associated with an increase in European immigrant representation in the metro area is being driven by more rapid increases in native-born blacks' segregation from native-born nonblacks (an expected positive coefficient) or from the European foreign born (an expected negative coefficient). This results is positive and statically significant after controlling for the set of observables. This indicates that the higher European immigrant representation associated with increases in blacks' segregation from native-born nonblacks operates more through blacks' segregation from native-born nonblacks than from European immigrants, and that this pattern is stronger is nongateway metro areas.

These results are instructive, but immigrants from Europe are a smaller share of the total and thus these results do not represent the average or the bulk of the immigrant effect on black segregation.[18] Taken together, the results from both approaches indicate very little influence of immigrants on racial segregation patterns of native-born blacks, a finding that is consistent with the previous literature (White, Bueker, and Glick 2002; White and Glick 1999) .

IMMIGRANT SEGREGATION AND ENGLISH-LANGUAGE DIFFICULTY

Much of the literature on immigrant segregation has focused on its causes, but less emphasis has been put on its potential consequences. English-language difficulty could be both a cause and consequence of immigrant segregation. It could be a cause in the ways described earlier, which is consistent with spatial assimilation theory. On the other hand, segregation could also influence language proficiency.

This could occur a variety of ways, including peer influence, institutions, or spatial influences, among others. Interactions with peers, especially those in segregated neighborhoods where English is not the primary language, could delay or stunt increasing English-language proficiency (Leiberson 1981). So too could interactions with leaders in or personnel of important community or employment institutions who have similar English-language limitations. These interactions would serve to reinforce use of the foreign borns' primary non-English language. To the extent that those in these segregated neighborhoods do not venture outside of them in any significant way, that is, that segregation may influence the duration or time spent in these areas relative to others, immigrants in segregated areas will have difficulty enhancing proficiency with English.

I test for the potential influence of immigrant segregation on English-language difficulty through the following model:

$$eld_i = immseg_i\beta_{21} + \beta'_{22} X_i + \varepsilon_{2i} \tag{4}$$

where i indexes metropolitan areas, eld_i is whether the relevant immigrant group has difficulty speaking English, seg_i is the dissimilarity index for the relevant immigrant group, and X_i is vector of metropolitan area characteristics variables previously discussed, and ε_{2i} is a mean-zero, randomly distributed disturbance term.

Figure 4.7 reports the coefficients for immigrant segregation on immigrants' English-language difficulty. The results from the bivariate regression results in model 1 provide initial evidence that immigrant segregation is positively associated with English-language difficulty. The point estimate indicates that a 10 point increase in the dissimilarity scores between immigrants and whites is associated with about a 7.6 percentage point increase in the fraction of immigrants indicating that they have limited English-language ability.

Models 2, 3, and 4 address potential concerns of whether this relationship is driven by problems of spurious relationships and reverse causation. Models 2 and 3 include, consecutively, controls for metropolitan area physical and socioeconomic characteristics. The statistical significance of the point estimate largely survives after the inclusion of this full set of metro controls, but its magnitude is reduced by nearly half. Metro size and average years in the United States account for much of this decline as immigrants with more English-language difficulty are also more likely to live in larger metro areas with higher levels of immigrant segregation.

Model 4 addresses the potential problem of reverse causation that immigrants with limited English-language ability self-segregate to reduce transition costs of integration, thereby potentially upwardly biasing ordinary least squares (OLS) estimates of the causal effect of segregation on English-language difficulty. Model 4 instruments the 2005 to 2009 immigrant segregation scores with the 1990 blacks-whites segregation scores.[19] The coefficient on immigrant segregation remains statistically significant and directly comparable in magnitude to that for the OLS regressions with only physical metro controls.

Thus, undoing part of the reverse causation between these variables highlights

FIGURE 4.7   /   Immigrant English-Language Difficulty and Segregation

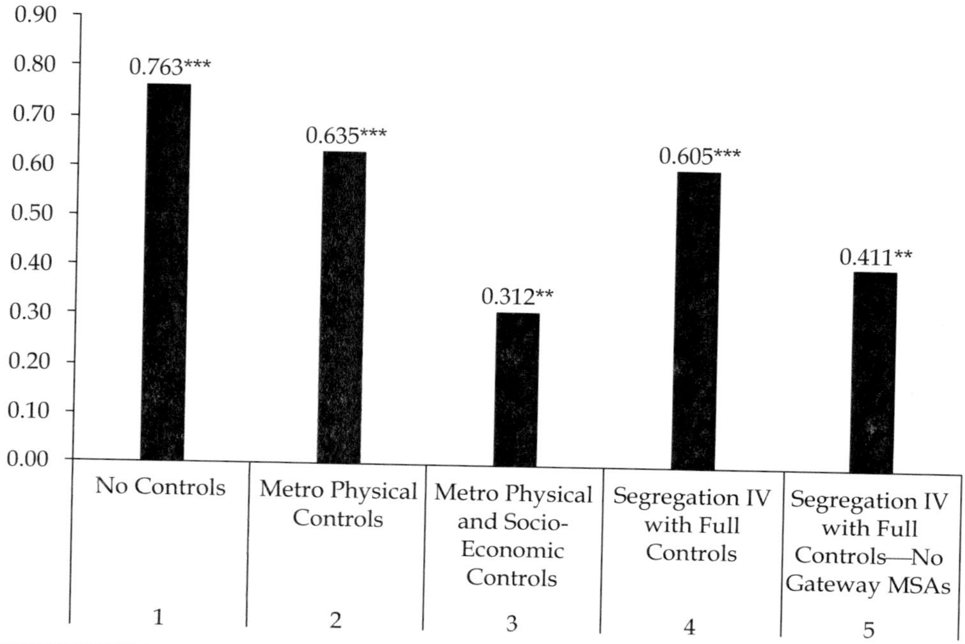

Source: Author's calculations.
*p < .10; **p < .05; ***p < .01

a stronger potentially casual impact of immigrant segregation limiting English-language acquisition. Model 5 excludes the established gateway metro areas from the sample. The estimate using the IV approach is smaller in magnitude than that for the full sample, but still remains statistically significant. Taken together, the results of these exercises provide strong evidence that immigrant segregation also limits immigrants' English-language acquisition and that this effect is stronger in the established gateway metro areas, though the exact mechanism or mechanisms by which this might occur remains unknown.

Table 4.6 provides coefficients for similar exercises examining the influence of sub-immigrant segregation on English-language difficulty. Three main findings are worth noting. First, the results indicate that the significant positive relationships between immigrant segregation and English proficiency are being driven by those from Asia, including Southeast Asians, and from Latin America, especially South America. Second, the significant, positive relationship between immigrant segregation and English-language difficulty shown for these groups does not appear to be driven by differences in metropolitan observable characteristics or by reverse causation. Finally, the effect of immigrant segregation on English-language

TABLE 4.6 / English-Language Difficulty and Immigrant Segregation

	Index of Dissimilarity from NB Whites									
	All Immigrants	Europe	Asia	East Asia	Southeast Asia	Latin America	Mexico	Other Latin America	Africa	Caribbean
No controls	0.763***	-0.055	0.170**	-0.038	0.347***	0.111	0.203**	0.187*	0.005	-0.046
Metro physical and socioeconomic controls	0.312***	0.025	0.133	0.170	0.252**	0.165*	0.133	0.066	0.093	-0.177
Segregation IV with full controls	0.605***	0.893	0.504*	0.089	0.302*	0.849**	0.371	1.286**	-1.309	-0.288
Segregation IV with full controls, no gateways MSAs	0.411**	-0.083	0.499*	0.030	0.266**	0.467**	0.322	0.558**	0.209	0.170

Source: Author's calculations.
Note: Segregation IV = IV regressions (without further controls) using 1990 black/white Index of dissimilarity as instrument for respective immigrant segregation indices. Immigrant English-Language Difficulty is a function of immigrant segregation from whites for each respective immigrant group.
*p < 0.10; **p < 0.05; ***p < 0.01

difficulty for those from Asia and Latin America is stronger in the established gateway than nongateway metro areas.

Immigrant Segregation and Poverty

Another major concern of immigrant segregation could be its potential influence on immigrant poverty. The direction of this influence is theoretically ambiguous, however. On the one hand, such segregation could negatively influence poverty in the ways predicted by the role of isolation or concentration. For example, in the case of African American segregation, William Wilson (1987) and others theorized about the negative consequence of high levels of segregation on black poverty as a result of isolation from the middle class and limited presence or effectiveness of pro-social institutions. This could also result from the breakdown of social capital that serves as the glue for overall community health, or in the emergence of "concentration" effects wherein the high levels of negative social outcomes such as crime, joblessness, etc., become community norms that are expected (Wilson 1987; Cutler and Glaeser 1997).

On the other hand, immigrant segregation could have limited influence or in fact lower poverty. This could occur if immigrant segregation overlaps or is synonymous with "ethnic enclave" communities. Such communities may help formulate social capital among immigrant groups and could serve as a mechanism for social incorporation, particularly for those who have difficulty speaking English well (Zhou 2004; Edin, Fredriksson, and Aslund 2003; Light and Bonacich 1991; Leiberson 1981).

I test for the potential influence of immigrant segregation on poverty by conducting a series of regressions of the kind

$$pov_i = immseg_i\beta_{31} + eld_i\beta_{32} + \beta'_{33} X_i + \varepsilon_{3i} \tag{5}$$

where i indexes metropolitan areas, pov_i is the poverty rate for relevant immigrant group, eld_i is whether the relevant immigrant group has difficulty speaking English, seg_i is the dissimilarity index for the relevant immigrant group, and X_i is vector of metropolitan area characteristics variables described earlier, and ε_{3i} is a mean-zero, randomly distributed disturbance term.

The measure of poverty is based on the federal definition of the poverty rate for individuals, and the data is gathered from combining the 2005 to 2009 IPUMS census. The poverty rate is measured at the individual level for all relevant groups at the metropolitan area, and the summary statistics are presented in the appendix (table 4A.1).[20]

Figure 4.8 reports the coefficients for immigrant segregation on immigrant poverty for immigrants as a whole. Model 1 includes only immigrant segregation and the results show some evidence that such segregation is associated with higher levels of poverty. The point estimate indicates that 10 point increase in the dissimilarity scores between immigrants and whites is associated with an approxi-

FIGURE 4.8 / Immigrant Poverty and Segregation

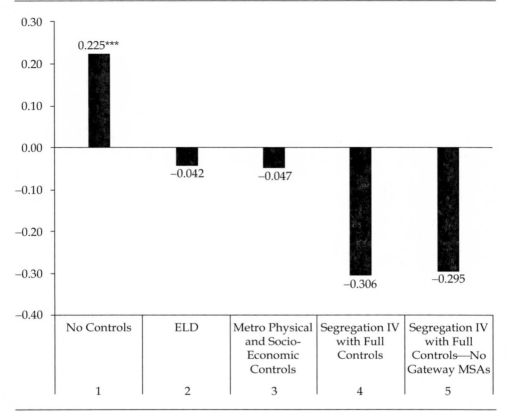

Source: Author's calculations.
Note: ELD = English-language difficulty.
*p < 0.10; **p < 0.05; ***p < 0.01

mate 2.3 point increase in immigrant poverty rates. Of course, it is difficult to interpret this results as being causal because of problems of spurious relationships, reverse causation and omitted variables.

Model 2 includes the measure for English-language difficulty and this simple inclusion knocks out the significance of segregation on poverty, indicating that language is an important intermediating factor between segregation and poverty. That is, language may drive location decisions to live in or near co-ethnic communities, and influences immigrants' poverty outcomes such as through limiting employment or lowering wages as demonstrated in chapter 3. Model 3 adds the full set of controls and the coefficient result is not affected.

Another problem in estimating the effect of segregation on poverty concerns the direction of causation. Segregation could affect poverty in ways implied or understood from previous literature on segregation and the underclass. Alternatively, the residential choices of the poor or immigrant groups could be influenced by other factors such as the geographic distribution of low-income housing or preferences to live near each other for all the reasons described by the ethnic enclave literature. This would imply that poverty could cause segregation, likely upwardly biasing OLS estimates of the causal effect of segregation on poverty. Model 4 address this problem by instrumenting the 2005 to 2009 immigrant segregation scores with the 1990 black-white segregation scores.[21] The IV regressions are not significant, though the coefficient magnitudes get larger, that is, more negative. Finally, model 5 excludes the established gateway metro areas and the results are unaffected by this exclusion.

Table 4.7 provides coefficients for similar exercises examining the influence of sub-immigrant segregation on sub-immigrant poverty. For comparison, results for African American segregation are provided as well. The results indicate a significant relationship for Southeast Asians and those from other parts of Latin America (a negative relationship). As before, however, these significant relationships are explained away by controls for English-language difficulty alone. Note, however, that the positive statistically significant relationship between African American segregation and poverty remains statistically significant in all cases, consistent with the view of the unique negative effects of isolation for this group (Wilson 1996; Massey and Denton 1993). Taken together, the results of these exercises provide strong evidence that immigrant segregation has very little direct influence on immigrant poverty, except through its influence in limiting English-language acquisition, which in turn influences poverty.

CONCLUSION

This chapter sought to explore the relationship among immigration, segregation, and poverty. It did so by tabulating segregation scores for immigrants using the most recent census data, and to compare these scores by the area of origin of the foreign born, as well as to those native-born groups, such as African Americans whose segregation scores have been extremely high historically. The chapter also explores some potential reasons for immigrant segregation, and in turn whether the relative presence of immigrants across metro areas influences racial/ethnic segregation. Finally, the chapter also examines whether immigrant segregation plays a part in raising immigrant poverty.

The findings indicate that while immigrant segregation levels are moderately high for immigrants as whole, they vary by the area of origins, with those from Europe displaying the lowest segregation scores and those from Latin America, Caribbean and Africa the highest. Immigrants from Asia have segregation scores in between these poles. Still, English-language difficulty partly drives these segregation levels as does immigrant settlement in areas with older housing stock, thus concentrating them in ways consistent with the spatial assimilation literature. This implies that as immigrant gain additional language skills and perhaps better jobs

TABLE 4.7 / Immigrant Poverty and Segregation

Metro Poverty Rate for:	All Immigrants	Europe	Asia	Eastern Asia	Southeast Asia	Latin America	Mexico	Other Latin America	Africa	Caribbean	African American
No controls	0.225***	0.040	0.105	-0.041	0.198**	-0.040	-0.135	-0.147**	0.173	0.073	0.202***
ELD	-0.042	0.047	0.091	-0.034	0.156*	-0.076	-0.081	-0.117*	0.172	0.088	0.205***
Metro P + SE controls	-0.047	-0.092	-0.142	-0.062	0.005	-0.121	0.003	-0.156	0.161	-0.033	0.143**
Segregation IV with full controls	-0.306	-0.198	0.141	0.131	-0.177	0.181	-0.045	-0.109	0.101	0.166	0.111*
Segregation IV with full controls + no gateway MSAs	-0.295	0.133	0.282	-0.253	0.195	0.126	-0.134	-0.109	0.152	-0.071	0.092

Source: Author's calculations.

Note: Segregation IV = IV regressions (without further controls) using 1990 black/white Index of dissimilarity as instrument for respective immigrant segregation indices. Immigrant poverty is a function of immigrant segregation from whites for each respective immigrant group. African American poverty is a function of African American segregation from whites. ELD = English-language difficulty; P = metro physical controls; SE = metro socio-economic controls.

*$p < 0.10$; **$p < 0.05$; ***$p < 0.01$

they move to better housing and increase their spatial assimilation with native-born whites.

However, what is less known is that immigrants segregation levels are heightened above and beyond what English-language difficulty and length of residence in the United States would predict as a result of existing segregation. The evidence indicates that immigrant segregation is influenced by historic black-white segregation across metropolitan areas such that immigrant segregation levels are higher in metropolitan areas that have higher older black segregation scores, and that this is especially true in established gateway metropolitan areas and for immigrant from Latino American and Southeast Asia. This is of social concern because the influence of this segregation infrastructure could stunt immigrant spatial assimilation and limit the extent to which they make material gains absolutely and relative to the native born.

The consequences of increased immigration and immigrant segregation, however, are more mixed. The evidence in this chapter is consistent with previous research in this area, that increased immigration has little influence on black segregation levels in the United States. However, immigrant segregation itself could have deleterious effects on English-language proficiency. Thus, the evidence strongly suggests that English-language difficulty is both cause and negative consequence of immigrant segregation, especially in more established gateway metropolitan areas and for those from Latin America and Southeast Asia. This finding is all the more important in light of other findings in the chapter relating to immigrant segregation and poverty. The positive association between immigrant poverty and immigrant segregation is completely accounted for by English-language difficulty. This strongly suggests that English-language challenges are driving some immigrant groups to segregate partly because of the reduced transition and transaction costs of living near others who speak similar languages, but such segregation provides perhaps disincentives to gain English-language skills and in turn limits labor market opportunities and economic mobility more generally.

APPENDIX

TABLE 4A.1 / Means for MSA Independent Variables

	(1) Unweighted	(2) Weighted by Metro Population Size
Population Size (Log)	13.571 (0.924)	14.785 (1.189)
Northeast	0.145 (0.353)	0.204 (0.379)
Midwest	0.243 (0.441)	0.212 (0.430)
South	0.401 (0.489)	0.328 (0.475)

TABLE 4A.1 / (Continued)

	(1) Unweighted	(2) Weighted by Metro Population Size
West	0. 211	0.256
	(0.409)	(0.429)
City age (log)	5.169	5.228
	(0.322)	(0.393)
Percent Black	0.121	0.135
	(0.106)	(0.088)
Percent Latino	0.127	0.173
	(0.161)	(0.153)
Percent over sixty-five years old	0.122	0.112
	(0.026)	(0.028)
Percent with college degree or more	0.270	0.299
	(0.072)	(0.063)
Percent in poverty	0.133	0.125
	(0.042)	(0.036)
White male employment-to-population rate	0.805	0.821
	(0.047)	(0.033)
Share of employment in manufacturing	0.115	0.106
	(0.067)	(0.042)
Share of employment in retail trade	0.118	0.114
	(0.014)	(0.099)
Share of employment in service	0.449	0.455
	(0.050)	(0.038)
Number of political jurisdictions (log)	3.319	3.943
	(1.152)	(1.115)
Average years in U.S. foreign born (FB)	19.2	18.8
	(2.985)	(2.502)
Average years in U.S. Europe FB	27.8	26.6
	(4.646)	(3.761)
Average years in U.S. Asia FB	17.4	17.3
	(2.652)	(1.931)
Average years in U.S. East Asia FB	19.0	18.3
	(4.358)	(2.921)
Average years in U.S. Southeast Asia FB	19.1	18.9
	(2.926)	(1.971)
Average years in U.S. Latin America FB	15.2	15.7
	(3.482)	(3.157)
Average years in U.S. Mexico FB	13.9	13.9
	(4.913)	(3.997)
Average years in U.S. other Latin America FB	16.9	16.6
	(3.615)	(2.907)
Average years in U.S. Caribbean FB	21.6	22.4
	(7.892)	(7.063)
Average years in U.S. Africa FB	15.3	15.7
	(7.069)	(6.697)

Table 4A.1 / (Continued)

	(1) Unweighted	(2) Weighted by Metro Population Size
English-language difficulty foreign born (FB)	0.236 (0.101)	0.267 (0.091)
English-language difficulty Europe FB	0.072 (0.066)	0.101 (0.065)
English-language difficulty Asia FB	0.176 (0.070)	0.201 (0.069)
English-language difficulty East Asia FB	0.184 (0.101)	0.244 (0.115)
English-language difficulty Southeast Asia FB	0.207 (0.113)	0.203 (0.088)
English-language difficulty Latin America FB	0.399 (0.112)	0.429 (0.092)
English-language difficulty Mexico FB	0.462 (0.145)	0.486 (0.109)
English-language difficulty other Latin America FB	0.248 (0.139)	0.301 (0.114)
English-language difficulty Caribbean FB	0.063 (0.072)	0.068 (0.071)
English-language difficulty Africa FB	0.072 (0.084)	0.079 (0.060)
Poverty rate foreign born (FB)	0.174 (0.058)	0.166 (0.044)
Poverty rate Europe FB	0.104 (0.055)	0.098 (0.039)
Poverty rate Asia FB	0.132 (0.067)	0.127 (0.048)
Poverty rate East Asia FB	0.132 (0.118)	0.132 (0.072)
Poverty rate Southeast Asia FB	0.111 (0.088)	0.103 (0.058)
Poverty rate Latin America FB	0.234 (0.092)	0.221 (0.067)
Poverty rate Mexico FB	0.272 (0.135)	0.253 (0.093)
Poverty rate other Latin America FB	0.157 (0.087)	0.156 (0.064)
Poverty rate Caribbean FB	0.175 (0.160)	0.157 (0.106)
Poverty rate Africa FB	0.184 (0.183)	0.183 (0.129)
N	150	150

Source: Author's calculations.
Note: Standard errors in parentheses. FB = foreign born.

NOTES

1. Evidence regarding segregation indices among different racial-ethnic groups offer some additional clues that immigrants might influence racial-ethnic segregation levels, especially those for blacks. In 2000, for example, the black-white segregation index was 65, and the black-Latino index was 51. Moreover, during the 1990s, racial segregation between blacks and Hispanics declined more dramatically than between blacks and whites: the index of dissimilarity between blacks and whites declined by 3.8 points from 1990 to 2000; the equivalent decline between blacks and Hispanics was 6.1 percentage points (Stoll 2008). To the extent that many Latinos are foreign born, this would imply that increased immigration, especially from Latin America, should be correlated with decreased black segregation.

2. The one-year ACS data are collected annually during the interceding census years but are not collected at lower levels of geography (typically below 50,000) to generate reliable estimates.

3. The metropolitan areas used in the analysis are metropolitan statistical Areas (MSAs) and primary metropolitan statistical areas (PMSAs) as defined by the Office of Management and Budget (OMB) in 1999 for Census 2000. Consolidated metropolitan statistical areas (CMSAs), which are usually much larger than MSAs or PMSAs, were not included among these metropolitan areas.

4. The dissimilarity index provides information on how geographically evenly distributed members of a certain group are relative to members of another group, and thus the population size of that group does not affect the calculation of the index. In contrast, the isolation index, is much more sensitive to the size of groups being examined because, all else equal, the larger the group being examined, the higher will be the isolation index. This is because a larger group will more likely share neighborhoods with other members of that same group, and thus would be more isolated according to the index calculation.

5. In these and subsequent segregation scores, the index of dissimilarity results are weighted by the respective populations in each metro area. For example, the immigrant/white dissimilarity score is weighted by the number of immigrants in the metro area. Weighting in this way permits us to interpret the scores as the average degree of segregation by the typical member of the respective group. Also, weighting in this way tends to place more weight on metropolitan areas with larger populations since members of respective groups tend to be larger in larger metropolitan areas. This also puts more emphasis on traditional immigrant gateway metropolitan areas, which tend to be larger in population size. Given the consequence of weighting in this way, I examine in the chapter whether and how these immigrant gateway metropolitan areas influence the results.

6. Throughout the chapter, whites and blacks (or African Americans) refer to those that are native born.

7. Latin American immigrants do not include immigrants from Spanish speaking islands in the Caribbean; only those from Mexico, Central and South America. Caribbean immigrants do not include those from Puerto Rico (because of their American citizenship

they are migrants rather than immigrants) and do include immigrants from Spanish-, French-, and Dutch-speaking islands. Excluding Puerto Ricans from the Caribbean category did not alter the basic findings reported here for immigrants from the Caribbean (or from Latin America if they are included in that group) .

8. Obviously, the lower index of dissimilarity score for Asians as a whole relative to that of Southeastern and Eastern Asians is driven by lower segregation scores of those from Central Asia (including India, Afghanistan, and so on) whose separate scores are not reported.

9. Though not shown, the data are consistent with this potential explanation. In the Northeast, Mexican immigrants have the lowest average years (11.9) in the United States compared with other immigrant groups, ranging from between fifteen and twenty-eight years. The average number of years in the United States is also lowest for Mexican immigrants in the Northeast than any other region, beating out the South, however, by only half a year.

10. I also calculated segregation indices between blacks and whites for 2000, and found similar results to that reported here. I chose to report the results using the 1990 data because a better case can be made that segregation levels during that period should be more independent of immigrants' locational decisions in the current period.

11. Traditional immigrant gateway metropolitan areas are defined using Park and Iceland's (2011) definitions, which further categorizes these borrowing from both Hall et al. (2009) and Singer (2004). These include twenty-six metro areas including Boston, Massachusetts; Brownsville, Texas; Chicago; Dutchess County, New York; El Paso, Texas; Miami-Fort Lauderdale; Fresno, California; Hartford, Connecticut; Honolulu; Houston; Los Angeles; McAllen, Texas; New Haven; New York; Newburgh, New York; Providence, Rhode Island; Riverside, California; Salinas, California; San Antonio; San Diego; San Francisco; Springfield, Massachusetts; Tacoma, Washington; Tampa, Florida; and Trenton, New Jersey. I also categorized new destination metro areas according to Julie Park and John Iceland's (2011) and Audrey Singer's (2004) definitions as well, and excluded these from the full sample (with and without the established gateway metro areas included), and found very little impact of these areas in estimating the relationship between immigrant segregation and older black segregation.

12. Table 4.A1 shows the means of all independent variables, both with and without weights for the metropolitan area's population size, mostly collected from the 2005 to 2009 ACS. However, data on the age of the main central city and the number of municipalities in the metropolitan area are from the U.S. Census of Governments Organization file (provided to me by Jordon Rappaport from the Kansas City Federal Reserve Bank).

13. This English-language ability variable is derived from a question in the 2005 to 2009 ACS that asks whether the respondent speaks English very well, well, not well, or not at all. Those with English-language difficulty are defined as those who responded that they either speak English not well or not at all.

14. Again, the magnitude and strength of these coefficients survive even after controls for the physical and socioeconomic characteristics of metropolitan areas are included in the regressions, though not shown here.

15. To be sure, there are other factors that influence the geography of lower income hous-

ing both within and across metro areas (that may ultimately influence immigrant segregation levels) than the age of the housing stock. Housing development regulations such as zoning requirements for multi- or single-family housing and the existence and levels of development impact fees could also have this affect as well (Evans-Cowley, Forgey, and Rutherford 2005; McDonald and McMillen 2004).

16. As before, I test for and find no evidence of potential nonlinear influences of immigrant representation on racial segregation.

17. In separate analysis not shown here, I test for potential nonlinearities in these relationships by splitting the percentage of the metro population that are immigrants into quintiles (and alternatively by squaring the proportion immigrant term) and regressing these segregation scores against these quintiles (and squared term). I find no evidence of nonlinear influences of immigrant representation on black segregation levels as the point estimates of quintiles.

18. The data from the 2005 to 2009 ACS indicate that 12 percent of all immigrants are from Europe.

19. Of course, the result of the first stage regression of 1990 black-white segregation predicting 2005 to 2009 immigrant segregation is presented in figure 4.3.

20. One concern is that the results of this analysis could be sensitive to the poverty level used. In response, I experimented with alternative poverty rates calculated at 150 and 200 percent of the poverty line and found very (qualitatively) similar results, though not shown. Similarly, I calculated poverty rates for adults, those between eighteen to sixty-five years of age, as well as those for different age based demographic groups, and at the household level. Again, I found similar qualitatively results to those shown here, indicating that the results of the influence of immigrant segregation on poverty does not appear sensitive to the poverty level used, or to the demographic categories used.

21. Again, figure 4.2 displays the result of the first stage regression of 1990 black-white segregation predicting 2005 to 2009 immigrant segregation.

REFERENCES

Alba, Richard D., John R. Logan, Brian J. Stults, Gilbert Marzan, and Wenquan Zhang. 1999. "Immigrant Groups in the Suburbs: A Reexamination of Suburbanization and Spatial Assimilation." *American Sociological Review* 64(3): 446–60.

Burr, Jeffrey, and Jan E. Mutchler. 2003. "English Language Skills, Ethnic Concentration, and Household Composition: Older Mexican Immigrants." *Journal of Gerontology: Behavioral and Psychological Science and Social Science* 58(2): S83-92.

Charles, Camille Zubrinsky. 2005. "Can we Live Together? Racial Preferences and Neighborhood Outcomes." In *The Geography of Opportunity*, edited by Xavier de Souza Briggs. Washington, D.C.: The Brookings Institution.

Cutler, David M., and Edward L. Glaeser. 1997. "Are Ghettos Good or Bad?" *Quarterly Journal of Economics* 112(3): 827–72.

Edin, Per-Anders, Peter Fredriksson, and Olof Aslund. 2003. "Ethnic Enclaves and the Economic Success of Immigrants-Evidence from a Natural Experiment." *Quarterly Journal of Economics* 118(1): 329–57.

Evans-Cowley, Jennifer S., Fred A. Forgey, and Ronald C. Rutherford. 2005. "The Effect of Impact Fees on the Price of Housing and Land: A Literature Review." *Journal of Planning Literature* 17(3): 351–59.

Goering, John, and Ron Wienk, eds. 1996. *Mortgage Lending, Racial Discrimination, and Federal Policy*. Washington, D.C.: Urban Institute Press.

Hall, Matthew, Deborah Roempke Graefe, Gordon F. De Jong, and Shelley K. Irving. 2009. "The Geographic Inequality of Immigrant Human Capital: A Skills Typology of Old and New Metropolitan Destinations." Population Research Institute of the Pennsylvania State University Working Paper Series.

Iceland, John, and Melissa Scopilliti. 2008. "Immigrant Residential Segregation in U.S. Metropolitan Areas, 1990–2000." *Demography* 45(1): 79–94.

Iceland, John, Daniel H. Weinberg, and Erika Steinmetz. 2002. *Racial and Ethnic Residential Segregation in the United States: 1980–2000*. Census Bureau, Series CENSR-3. Washington: U.S. Department of Commerce.

Leiberson, Stanley. 1981. *Language Diversity and Language Contact*. Palo Alto, Calif.: Stanford University Press.

Lichter, Daniel T., Domenico Parisi, Michael C. Taquino, and Steven Michael Grice. 2010. "Residential Segregation in New Hispanic Destinations: Cities, Suburbs, and Rural Communities Compared." *Social Science Research* 39: 215–30.

Light, Ivan, and Edna Bonacich. 1991. *Immigrant Entrepreneurs: Koreans in Los Angeles, 1965–1982*. Berkeley: University of California Press.

Logan, John R. 2003. "Ethnic Diversity Grows, Neighborhood Integration Lags." In *Redefining Urban & Suburban America: Evidence from Census 2000*, edited by Bruce Katz and Robert E. Lang. Washington, D.C.: The Brookings Institution.

Massey, Douglas, S. 1985. "Ethnic Residential Segregation: A Theoretical Synthesis and Empirical Review." *Sociology and Social Research* 69(3): 315–50.

Massey, Douglas S., and Nancy A. Denton. 1988a. "The Dimensions of Residential Segregation." *Social Forces* 67(2): 281–315.

———. 1988b. "Suburbanization and Segregation in U.S. Metropolitan Areas." *American Journal of Sociology* 94(3): 592–626.

———. 1993. *American Apartheid: Segregation and the Making of the Underclass*. Cambridge, Mass.: Harvard University Press.

Massey, Douglas S., and Mary J. Fischer. 2000. "How Segregation Concentrates Poverty." *Ethnic and Racial Studies* 23(4): 670–91.

McDonald, John F., and Daniel P. McMillen. 2004. "Determinants of Suburban Development Controls: A Fishel Expedition." *Urban Studies* 41(2): 341–61.

Ondrich, Jan, Alex Stricker, and John Yinger. 1999. "Do Landlords Discriminate? The Incidence and Causes of Racial Discrimination in Rental Housing Markets," *Journal of Housing Economics* 8(3): 185–20.

Ondrich, Jan, Stephen L. Ross, and John Yinger. 2001. "Geography of Housing Discrimination," *Journal of Housing Research* 2(2): 217–38.

O'Sullivan, Arthur. 2011. *Urban Economics*. New York: McGraw-Hill/Irwin.

Park, Julie, and John Iceland. 2011. "Residential Segregation in Metropolitan Established Immigrant Gateways and New Destinations, 1990–2000." *Social Science Research* 40(3): 811–21.

Singer, Audrey. 2004. *The Rise of New Immigrant Gateways*. Washington, D.C.: The Brookings Institution.

South, Scott J., Kyle Crowder, and Eric Chavez. 2005a. "Migration and Spatial Assimilation Among U.S. Latinos: Classic Versus Segmented Trajectories." *Demography* 42(3): 497–521.

———. 2005b. "Geographic Mobility and Spatial Assimilation Among U.S. Latino Immigrants." *International Migration Review* 39(3): 577–607.

Stoll, Michael A. 2008. "Race, Place, and Poverty Revisited." In *The Colors of Poverty: Why Racial and Ethnic Disparities Persist,* edited by Ann Chih Lin and David R. Harris. New York: Russell Sage Foundation.

White, Michael J., and Jennifer E. Glick. 1999. "The Impact of Immigration on Residential Segregation." In *Immigration and Opportunity: Race, Ethnicity, and Employment in the United States,* edited by Frank D. Bean and Stephanie Bell-Rose. New York: Russell Sage Foundation.

White, Michael J., Catherine Bucker, and Jennifer E. Glick. 2002. "The Impact of Immigration on Residential Segregation Revisited." Paper presented to the American Sociological Association Annual Meetings, Chicago (August 2002).

Wilson, William J. 1987. *The Truly Disadvantaged: The Inner City, the Underclass, and Public Policy*. Chicago: University of Chicago Press.

Yinger, John. 1997. "Cash in Your Face: The Cost of Racial and Ethnic Discrimination in Housing." *Journal of Urban Economics* 42(3): 339–65.

Zhou, Min. 2004. "Revisiting Ethnic Entrepreneurship: Convergences, Controversies, and Conceptual Advancements." *International Migration Review* 38(3): 1040–74.

Chapter 5

"New Destinations" and Immigrant Poverty

Mark Ellis, Richard Wright, and Matthew Townley

The 1990s and 2000s saw the spatial diversification of immigration to new destination states away from the Southwest, West, and Northeast to the Plains, the South, and East. Some states recorded a doubling and tripling of populations; some counties grew at even higher rates (for example, Li 2009; Massey 2008; Light 2006; Zúñiga and Hernández-León 2006). Dispersion to suburbs and rural areas was an allied dimension of these new immigrant geographies (Singer et al. 2008; Jones 2008).

Martha Crowley and her colleagues (2006) report that immigrants, including Mexicans, who lived in these new destination areas in 2000 had lower rates of poverty than immigrants in traditional gateway regions.[1] This could be because the economies of new destinations were more vibrant than traditional gateways; immigrants who lived in new destinations had characteristics that enabled them to escape poverty more readily; or a combination of these two factors. Crowley and colleagues' analysis suggests that new destination economies rather than immigrant characteristics are the cause of this new destination advantage. Thus, relocation to new destinations in the 1990s likely had a poverty-reducing effect for immigrants.

In this chapter, we investigate what happened to the geography of immigrant poverty in the 2000s. One possibility is that the differences between traditional gateway and new destination immigrant poverty rates remained as they were in 2000. Alternatively, the new destination advantage could have grown, perhaps because immigrants in new destination economies weathered the 2007 to 2009 economic recession better than immigrants in traditional gateways. Or perhaps the slow economic growth of the early 2000s and the subsequent recession reduced or reversed the new destination advantage and compressed the variation in immigrant poverty rates across space.

Whatever the geographical changes were in the 2000s, they unfolded against a backdrop of diverging trends in immigrant versus native poverty rates. In the 2007 to 2009 period, the national immigrant poverty rate stood at 16.4 percent, a 1.5 percentage point decline since 2000. The national native-born poverty rate rose by 1.5 percentage points to 13.3 percent over the same period.[2] Thus, although the poverty rate remained higher for immigrants than the U.S. born, their rates began to converge in the 2000s. In raw numbers, the percentages correspond to 6,164,679 immigrants in poverty in 2007 to 2009, an increase of 10.9 percent from 2000; and 34,280,367 native-born persons in poverty, an increase of 16.5 percent. So, while the deteriorating economy pushed more people into poverty, immigrants appear to have weathered the storm better than the U.S. born, especially when one factors in the faster growth of the foreign-born population during the 2000s—something we do explicitly later in the chapter.

Other chapters in this volume discuss explanations for these differential national trends in immigrant and U.S.-born poverty, such as the changing national-origin composition of the immigrant population (chapter 1), changing skills of immigrant arrivals (chapter 2), and changes in immigrant household composition, possibly in response to welfare reform (chapter 11). In this chapter, we turn our attention to changes in the geography of immigrant and U.S.-born poverty in the 2000s, paying particular attention to the evolution of new destination versus traditional gateway differences as distinct from a more general analysis of state and metropolitan area trends (compare chapter 2). Three interlinked questions drive the analysis:

Does the pattern of lower poverty rates in new destinations in the 1990s persist into the 2000s?

Why do immigrant poverty rates vary geographically? Specifically, does this variation stem mostly from local area economy effects or from geographical variations in immigrant characteristics, such as education, that affect the likelihood of being poor?

Between 2000 and the most recent period for which we have data, how have local area economy effects and the spatial variation in immigrant characteristics changed the geography of immigrant poverty?

BACKGROUND

As discussed in chapter 1, immigrants are more likely to be poor than the U.S. born. For example, in 2000, 17.9 percent of foreign-born persons lived below the federal poverty line versus 11.8 percent of U.S.-born persons. The higher poverty rate for immigrants derives mainly from their disadvantageous sociodemographic characteristics (human capital) and the types of jobs they hold. A simple comparison with the U.S. born on mean years of education reveals that today's immigrants on average are less educated than the native born (Borjas 1999). This difference occurs in part because a disproportionately large share of immigrant adults, especially from Mexico, lack the equivalent of a high school degree. This educational disadvantage plus poor English-language skills (for an extended discussion of language issues, see chapter 3) places a large fraction of the contemporary immigrant workforce at risk of low-wage employment regardless of the sector in which they work. In addition, and partly because of their poor qualifications, many immigrants work in highly competitive employment sectors, such as agriculture, nondurable manufacturing, and personal service work, where wages are especially low and prospects for advancement minimal (Waldinger and Lichter 2003).

Poverty among immigrant groups varies considerably (Iceland 2006). Latino immigrants, who are mostly Mexican, tend to have higher rates of poverty than immigrants from Asia do. On average, the poverty rate for Asian immigrants is quite similar to that for the native born. Some Asian immigrant groups, however, have above-average poverty rates, such as refugees from Cambodia and Vietnam. Over time, as immigrants increase their human capital, their poverty rates tend to fall in line with assimilation theory's expectations. Despite these gains, some immigrant groups remain at greater risk of falling below the poverty line in a pattern that mirrors the native-born groups they most closely resemble.

Because immigrants tend to be poorer than the native born, and because of concerns that recent immigrants are even more disadvantaged in human capital relative to the U.S. born, some commentators see the growing presence of foreign-born populations in the country as elevating overall U.S. poverty rates (Borjas 1990). On initial inspection, data from the most recent decade hint at an association between rising poverty and immigration. Between 2000 and 2007 to 2009, the overall U.S. poverty rate increased from 12.5 percent to 13.7 percent and the foreign-born share of the population grew from 11.1 percent to 12.6 percent. Some trends in the 2000s, however, suggest that factors other than a growing foreign-born population are more significant drivers of poverty dynamics. In the 2000s, the immigrant poverty rate declined from 17.9 percent to 16.4 percent, which reduced the share of immigrants in the poverty population from 16.1 percent to 15.2 percent. Thus immigrants were a disproportionately large share of the poor population at the end of the 2000s, as they were at the start of the decade, but that fraction had declined. Rising U.S.-born poverty rates—11.8 percent in 2000 to 13.3 percent in 2007 to 2009—rather than increased numbers of immigrants is the major cause of increased overall poverty since 2000.

This finding becomes even clearer from a simple counterfactual. If we apply to the entire U.S. population a technique similar to that in chapter 1, we can assess the effect of the rising share of the immigrant population on national poverty rates. If we roll back the foreign-born percentage of the population to that found in 2000—effectively making the assumption that the immigrant population did not grow faster than the native-born population after that date—and assumed 2007–2009 poverty rates for the native- and foreign-born populations, the overall U.S. poverty rate in 2007–2009 would have been 13.6 percent.[3] Thus, without any increase in immigration in the 2000s, the U.S. poverty rate would have only been a tenth of a percentage point lower in 2007–2009 than the actual rate—a marginal difference. Of course, this simple procedure does not take into account changes in the characteristics of immigrant and native populations that may affect their odds of being poor; nor does it account for shifts in the geography of these populations that may alter their exposure to poverty-generating local economic conditions. We factor in the effects of these changes later in the chapter.

The Geography of Poverty

The odds of being poor vary considerably across the country, a variation observable at several spatial scales. In some counties in the South, poverty rates exceed 30 percent in 2008 (for example, Perry County, Alabama). In Connecticut, in the same year, poverty rates were at or below 10 percent in all its counties.[4] In general, poverty rates tend to be higher in rural and small metropolitan areas than in the larger metropolitan areas, and cutting across these urban hierarchy differences, they tend to be higher in the South (Glasmeier et al. 2008). Within large metropolitan areas, lower overall poverty rates disguise clusters of high poverty neighborhoods in central city and suburban locations (Cooke and Marchant 2006). These areas of concentrated poverty have generated considerable interest over the last three decades because of the ways in which the clustering of poverty exacerbates poor people's disadvantages (Jargowsky 1997). Spatially concentrated poverty declined in the 1990s as overall poverty rates fell, but rose in the 2000s in line with increases in overall poverty rates (Kneebone and Berube 2008).

Neighborhood concentrations of poverty within cities arise because of the segregating effects of income disparities combined with structural racism. At broader scales, such as counties and metropolitan areas, spatial variations in poverty rates reflect a combination of unfolding local economic circumstances — sectoral (by industry and occupation) employment mix, exposure to the forces of global competition, and economic restructuring more broadly — and the sociodemographic characteristics of residents, including their race, nativity, education, age, and family structure. As one might expect, these people and place effects are not independent; workers who are able to do so will adjust to unfavorable local labor market circumstances by migrating; capital will respond by redistributing resources to locations where human capital is more favorable. In any event, the map of poverty is not a cartography of "lassitude," as Janet Kodras (1997) pointed out in reaction to Reagan administration claims that poverty stemmed from laziness and ignorance, rather than from the social and economic marginalization people face in their communities. Geographies of poverty arise from the conjunction of economic conditions and population structures in particular places (Lawson, Jarosz, and Bonds 2010).

New Destinations

Social networks are the conventional explanation for why immigrants to the United States tend to cluster in relatively few locations — or at least did until the last two decades. Networks channel information from immigrants to prospective migrants in the home country (Boyd 1989; Massey 1990). Those who elect to move to the United States use this information to follow in the footsteps of family and friends. Pioneering immigrants who move in response to economic opportunity or recruitment by employers establish the outlines of an immigrant enclave; those who follow may also be responding to those economic pulls, but the cumulative causation process of migration works to channelize later arriving newcomers to the enclave well after the initial economic forces that attracted the initial arrivals have weakened. Consequently, U.S. immigration in the last half century has been experienced mostly in a handful of states—California, New York, Texas, Florida, and Illinois—and within those states disproportionately in the largest metropolitan areas. In this geography, late twentieth-century immigration differed in regional orientation from the last great inflow in the early twentieth century (more southern and western now; more northeastern and midwestern then) but resembles that wave again by being a largely big-city phenomenon.

Over the course of the last two decades, this concentration in a handful of states and their major metropolitan areas has weakened as the foreign born started to settle in multiple locations across the country (Singer 2004). Explanations for this dispersal group into four categories. First, shifts in labor and housing market conditions made older gateways less attractive relative to new destinations (Card and Lewis 2005). For example, the 1990s saw a waning labor demand and higher-than-average housing costs in places like southern California. In contrast, new destination regions had lower living costs and growing economies. Ivan Light (2006) argues that these conditions were part of an emerging regulatory environment in southern California that was unfriendly to continued immigration. Second, initial settlers in new destinations laid the foundations for others to join them in emergent enclaves via networks. Growing immigrant populations in new destinations increased enclave vitality in these places, which in turn attracted more immigrants (Leach and Bean 2008). Three, by the 1990s a maturing immigrant population had sufficient socioeconomic and cultural experience in the United States for some to leave gateway enclaves to seek opportunities elsewhere—a process that operated both within and between cities (Ellis and Goodwin-White 2006). And, fourth, the growth of border and immigration enforcement in the southwest in the 1990s encouraged new arrivals to go elsewhere (Massey and Capoferro 2008).

Despite the rural orientation of some new immigrant settlement in the United States, this dispersal has mostly been associated with large metropolitan areas. For example, between 2000 and 2009, metropolitan areas that were over a million people by 2000 and not traditional gateways saw their share of the U.S. foreign-born population rise by 13.8 percent.[5] In comparison, over the same period, the share of immigrants in smaller metropolitan (under 1 million) and nonmetropolitan areas grew by 5.6 percent. As immigrant settlement moves down the urban hierarchy, it is unquestionably transforming the social and economic landscapes of small towns and rural areas (Kandel et al. 2011; Marrow 2011). Nevertheless, it appears that the shift to new destinations has so far generally sustained the large urban area bias of new immigrant settlement: in 2009, three-quarters of the immigrant population compared to just under half of the native-born lived in metropolitan areas of 1 million or more. Accordingly, in our analysis of new destinations and immigrant poverty, we note the rise in immigration to small towns and rural areas but pay particular attention to categories of large metropolitan areas; these are the places where most immigrants live or choose as destinations when they migrate.

Specifically, we categorize large metropolitan areas by immigrant gateway type using Singer's (2004) destination typology. Her taxonomy identifies six classes of gateways: three older types (former, continuous, post–World War II) and three new types (emerging, re-emerging, pre-emerging). Using this typology, we assess whether immigrants are better off — less likely to be in poverty — in new destinations than traditional gateways. The schema allows us to make comparisons between groups of new and traditional destinations; it also allows us to see whether the poverty rate trajectories of immigrants differ in subcategories of traditional and new destinations defined by vintage. For example, we can compare immigrant poverty rates in new destinations where foreign-born communities are more established (for example, emerging) to the situation in pre-emerging destinations where, presumably, such communities are likely to be more precarious.

Table 5.1 describes criteria for membership in each gateway category and lists metropolitan areas in these types. The set of metropolitan areas we use is almost identical to that used by Singer but differs in one respect. We consolidated the constituent metropolitan areas of New York classified as continuous gateways (for example, Bergen-Passaic) into the aggregate New York consolidated metropolitan statistical area (CMSA). And because not all metropolitan areas of greater than 1 million are immigrant gateways, we add a seventh residual category for these.

As one might expect, the share of immigrants in each gateway type is changing. Continuous and post–World War II gateways — the two most important traditional gateway types — were home to 51.3 percent of immigrants in 2000, dropping to 46.5 percent in 2009 (see table 5.2). Collectively, the three new destination gateway types increased their share of the foreign-born population from 18.2 percent in 2000 to 21 percent in 2009. There are indications that this growth stalled for emerging and re-emerging destinations in the 2007 to 2009 period, however. Other large metropolitan areas registered small increases in immigrant percentage share in the 2000s, but accounted for only 3.8 percent of all immigrants in 2009. Smaller metropolitan areas (fewer than 1 million) and rural areas gain a relatively minor share in the 2000s: combined, they account for 23.3 percent of immigrants in 2000 and 24.6 percent in 2009. To put this proportion in perspective, their share is roughly the same as that held by the four continuous gateway metropolitan areas of New York, Boston, San Francisco, and Chicago.

Table 5.2 also lists native-born population share in the same categories. The biggest differences between them and the foreign born are in the top and bottom two rows of the table. Much smaller fractions of the native born live in continuous and post–World War II metropolitan areas than immigrants do. In contrast, small metropolitan and rural areas have much higher shares of the native born relative to the foreign born.

The lower panel of table 5.2 illustrates the concentration of the foreign- and native-born populations in another way using location quotients (LQ): that is, the

TABLE 5.1   /   Gateway Classification

Gateway Type	Metro Area	Total Pop. 2000	% Foreign-Born
Continuous	Boston, MA-NH	3,951,557	14.64
	Chicago, IL	8,804,453	16.53
	New York-Northeastern NJ	18,372,239	26.33
	San Francisco-Oakland-Vallejo, CA	4,645,830	26.33
Post–WWII	Fort Lauderdale-Hollywood-Pompano Beach, FL	1,624,272	25.22
	Houston-Brazoria, TX	4,413,414	19.66
	Los Angeles-Long Beach, CA	12,368,516	34.86
	Miami-Hialeah, FL	2,327,072	49.67
	Riverside-San Bernardino, CA	3,253,263	18.73
	San Diego, CA	2,807,873	21.53
Emerging	Atlanta, GA	3,987,990	10.45
	Dallas-Fort Worth, TX	5,043,876	15.45
	Las Vegas, NV	1,375,174	18.01
	Orlando, FL	1,652,742	11.85
	Washington, DC/MD/VA	4,733,359	17.41
	West Palm Beach-Boca Raton-Delray Beach, FL	1,133,519	17.35
Pre-emerging	Austin, TX	1,167,216	12.76
	Charlotte-Gastonia-Rock Hill, NC-SC	1,499,677	6.75
	Greensboro-Winston Salem-High Point, NC	1,252,554	5.52
	Raleigh-Durham, NC	1,182,869	9.21
	Salt Lake City-Ogden, UT	1,331,833	8.53
Re-emerging	Denver-Boulder, CO	2,412,400	10.84
	Minneapolis-St. Paul, MN	2,856,295	7.22
	Phoenix, AZ	3,070,331	14.47
	Portland, OR-WA	1,789,019	11.25
	Sacramento, CA	1,632,863	13.94
	San Jose, CA	1,688,089	34.09
	Seattle-Everett, WA	2,332,682	13.99
	Tampa-St. Petersburg-Clearwater, FL	2,386,781	9.83
Former	Baltimore, MD	2,513,661	5.82
	Buffalo-Niagara Falls, NY	1,175,089	4.36
	Cleveland, OH	2,255,480	5.04
	Detroit, MI	4,430,477	7.49
	Milwaukee, WI	1,499,015	5.12
	Philadelphia, PA/NJ	5,082,137	6.99
	Pittsburgh, PA	2,500,497	2.50
	St. Louis, MO-IL	2,602,448	3.14

TABLE 5.1 / *(Continued)*

Gateway Type	Metro Area	Total Pop. 2000	% Foreign-Born
	Cincinnati-Hamilton, OH/KY/IN	1,473,012	2.75
	Columbus, OH	1,443,293	4.99
	Indianapolis, IN	1,603,021	3.22
	Jacksonville, FL	1,101,766	5.42
	Kansas City, MO-KS	1,682,053	4.88
	Nashville, TN	1,234,004	4.70
Other >1m	New Orleans, LA	1,381,841	4.72
	Norfolk-VA Beach-Newport News, VA	1,553,838	4.45
	Oklahoma City, OK	1,157,773	5.38
	Providence-Fall River-Pawtucket, MA/RI	1,025,944	12.89
	Rochester, NY	1,030,303	5.89
	San Antonio, TX	1,551,396	10.61

Source: Authors' compilation based on U.S. Census Bureau Decennial Census (2003).
Note: Continuous, Post–World War II, Emerging, and Re-Emerging gateways have foreign-born populations greater than 200,000 and either foreign-born shares higher than the 2000 national average (11.1 percent) or foreign-born growth rates higher than the national average (57.4 percent), or both. Former gateways are determined through historical trends (see below). Pre-Emerging gateways have smaller foreign-born populations but very high growth rates in the 1990s. The gateway definitions and selection are also based on the historical presence (in percentage terms) of the foreign-born in their central cities:
  Former: Above national average in percentage foreign-born 1900–1930, followed by percentages below the national average in every decade through 2000
  Continuous: Above-average percentage foreign-born for every decade, 1900–2000
  Post–World War II: Low percentage foreign-born until after 1950, followed by percentages higher than the national average for remainder of century
  Emerging: Very low percentage foreign-born until 1970, followed by a high proportions in the post-1980 period
  Re-emerging: Similar pattern to continuous gateways: Foreign-born percentage exceeds national average 1900–1930, lags it after 1930, then increases rapidly after 1980
  Pre-emerging: Very low percentages of foreign-born for the entire twentieth century.

share of the FB(NB) population in a particular metropolitan category at time t divided by the share of the total population in that category at time t. If the foreign born were distributed across the country in proportion to the total population in each location, location quotients everywhere would equal one. The location quotients for the foreign born show high concentrations of immigrants (double or more of that expected) in continuous and post–World War II gateways. Emerging and re-emerging gateways location quotients are smaller but still greater than one. All other gateway metros show relative concentrations of immigrants less than one, though in all these cases, the location quotients increased over the course of the decade. The variation of location quotient values for the foreign born is much greater than those for the native born. Most LQ scores for the native born are

TABLE 5.2 / Distribution of Populations

	Foreign Born				Native Born			
	2000	2007	2008	2009	2000	2007	2008	2009
Population share								
Metro > 1m								
Continuous	25.7%	23.4%	23.6%	23.0%	10.6%	10.1%	10.2%	10.2%
Post-WWII	25.6%	23.6%	23.3%	23.5%	7.5%	7.8%	7.8%	7.8%
Emerging	8.5%	10.0%	10.3%	10.2%	6.1%	6.6%	6.7%	6.8%
Pre-emerging	1.7%	2.1%	2.2%	2.3%	2.4%	2.6%	2.7%	2.7%
Re-emerging	8.0%	8.8%	8.7%	8.5%	6.3%	6.6%	6.6%	6.7%
Former	3.9%	4.0%	4.0%	4.1%	8.3%	7.9%	7.8%	7.8%
Other metro > 1m	3.3%	3.6%	3.6%	3.8%	6.5%	6.5%	6.5%	6.6%
Metro < 1m	15.9%	16.8%	16.7%	16.9%	25.9%	26.1%	26.1%	26.1%
Nonmetro	7.4%	7.6%	7.6%	7.7%	26.3%	25.8%	25.7%	25.5%
TOTAL	100.0%	100.0%	100.0%	100.0%	100.0%	100.0%	100.0%	100.0%
Location quotient								
Metro > 1m								
Continuous	2.09	1.98	1.99	1.95	2.09	1.98	1.99	1.95
Post-WWII	2.68	2.42	2.40	2.41	2.68	2.42	2.40	2.41
Emerging	1.34	1.41	1.44	1.42	1.34	1.41	1.44	1.42
Pre-emerging	0.76	0.83	0.85	0.86	0.76	0.83	0.85	0.86
Re-emerging	1.23	1.28	1.26	1.24	1.23	1.28	1.26	1.24
Former	0.50	0.54	0.54	0.56	0.50	0.54	0.54	0.56
Other metro > 1m	0.53	0.59	0.58	0.61	0.53	0.59	0.58	0.61
Metro < 1m	0.64	0.68	0.67	0.68	0.64	0.68	0.67	0.68
Nonmetro	0.31	0.32	0.32	0.33	0.31	0.32	0.32	0.33

Source: Authors' compilation based on U.S. Census Bureau (2003, 2010).

within 10 percent of the expected value of 1.0. The native-born distribution is out of this range only in continuous and post–World War II gateways, signifying that the number of natives is less than expected in these places.

GEOGRAPHICAL CONTOURS OF IMMIGRANT POVERTY

Figure 5.1 plots overall poverty rates in 2000 and 2007–2009 using these metropolitan categories. To capture variability in poverty rates outside large metropolitan areas this chart and all subsequent analysis subdivides the broad categories of small metropolitan areas and rural areas — the last two rows of both panels in table 5.2 — by the four major census regions. The lighter shaded portion of each bar is the fraction of the native-born population in poverty; the darker shaded portion represents the foreign-born fraction.

Starting from the left, the bars are ordered by gateway category as in table 5.2. The first two sets of bars are the traditional gateway metropolitan area categories; the next three are new (for example, emerging) destination gateway categories; then come the residual gateway types for large metros. Finally, the four sets of small metropolitan area and rural area categories appear, grouped by census region. U.S. poverty rates are plotted for comparison purposes in the rightmost set of bars.

Figure 5.1 shows two main things. First, following the national trend, poverty rates increased everywhere between 2000 and 2007–2009 with one exception: post–World War II gateways. Second, increases in the native-born share of the poverty population is driving overall increases in poverty in several location types, a tendency most notable in new destination gateways and in small metropolitan and rural areas in the Midwest. In post–World War II gateways, the drop in poverty appears to derive mostly from a decline in the foreign-born share of the poverty population.

In addition, figure 5.1 illustrates that poverty rates are highest in small metropolitan and rural areas in the South and West, which confirms prior findings about the geography of rural and small urban area poverty (Lichter and Crowley 2002). Furthermore, new destination metropolitan areas had lower poverty rates than traditional destination metropolitan areas (continuous and post–World War II gateways) in 2000. However, poverty rates rose rapidly in all three new destination gateway types between 2000 and 2007–2009. In 2007–2009, their poverty rates were above those in continuous gateways and much closer to the higher rate in post–World War II gateways.

Table 5.3 confirms these impressions in two ways. First, it documents that the foreign-born share of the population in poverty — the middle columns of the 2000 and 2007–2009 panels — declined in continuous, post–World War II gateways, and re-emerging gateways. It nudged up in emerging and pre-emerging gateways and in several other locations as well. Even in locations where the foreign-born share of the population in poverty increased, however, the change is dwarfed by the increased share of the overall foreign-born population. To see this effect, the third

FIGURE 5.1 / Poverty Rates

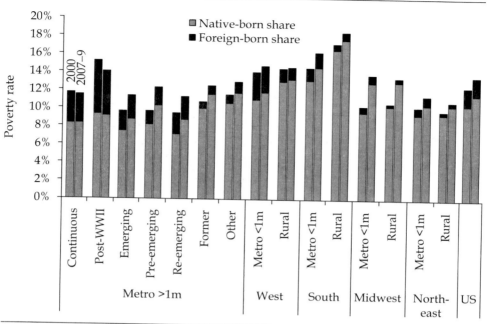

Source: Authors' compilation based on U.S. Census Bureau (2003, 2010).

column in each panel divide the percentage of the immigrant poor population by the percentage of the foreign-born population—the second column by the first column in each panel. In all locations these ratios dropped between 2000 and 2009. Thus, across the country, regardless of location type, the disproportionate concentration of the foreign-born among the ranks of the poor continued through the 2000s but became less pronounced by decade's end.

Building on this share perspective, we next explore how the rates of being poor changed for immigrants and the native born. Table 5.4 lists poverty rates by nativity in each period and the percentage difference between them. Nationally, the poverty rate differential between immigrants and natives halved during the 2000s, a trend replicated more or less in all locations. This occurred largely because of substantial percentage increases in native-born poverty rates—see figure 5.2. In some gateway types, this convergence is accelerated because of declining rates of poverty among the foreign born (for example, continuous, post–World War II, and re-emerging gateways, plus small metropolitan and rural areas in the West). In others, it occurred because the rise in native-born poverty is much greater than the rise in foreign-born poverty (for example, pre-emerging gateway, rural and small metropolitan areas in the Midwest). In the remainder, it occurred because native-born rates increased and foreign-born rates virtually did not change.

Foreign-born poverty rates are higher than native-born in all locations in both

TABLE 5.3 / Foreign-Born Share of Poor Population

	2000			2007–2009		
	% pop FB	% poor pop FB	% poor pop FB / % pop FB	% pop FB	% poor pop FB	% poor pop FB / % pop FB
Metro > 1m						
Continuous gateway	22.94	29.04	1.27	24.56	28.13	1.15
Post-WWII gateway	30.12	39.09	1.30	30.53	35.39	1.16
Emerging gateway	15.03	22.91	1.52	18.04	23.21	1.29
Pre-emerging gateway	8.55	15.92	1.86	10.73	16.69	1.56
Re-emerging gateway	13.88	25.14	1.81	16.06	23.31	1.45
Former gateway	5.64	7.08	1.26	6.99	7.94	1.14
Other metro > 1m	5.81	8.63	1.48	7.37	9.97	1.35
West						
Metro < 1m	13.69	22.48	1.64	14.55	20.27	1.39
Rural	6.66	10.09	1.51	7.13	9.52	1.34
South						
Metro < 1m	5.93	9.99	1.69	7.41	10.68	1.44
Rural	2.95	4.28	1.45	3.74	4.97	1.33
Midwest						
Metro < 1m	3.88	6.48	1.67	4.76	6.44	1.35
Rural	1.93	3.35	1.74	2.25	3.41	1.51
Northeast						
Metro < 1m	6.67	8.73	1.31	8.29	9.47	1.14
Rural	3.56	3.95	1.11	4.21	4.26	1.01
US	11.24	16.09	1.43	12.68	15.24	1.20

Source: Authors' compilation based on U.S. Census Bureau (2003, 2010).

TABLE 5.4 / Native- and Foreign-Born Poverty Rates

	2000			2007–2009		
	Native-Born	Foreign-Born	Difference	Native Born	Foreign-Born	Difference
Metro > 1m						
Continuous gateway	10.79	14.83	37.46	10.99	13.21	20.23
Post-WWII gateway	13.31	19.82	48.93	13.13	16.37	24.65
Emerging gateway	8.76	14.71	67.98	10.66	14.64	37.31
Pre-emerging gateway	8.92	18.06	102.33	11.50	19.17	66.72
Re-emerging gateway	8.26	17.22	108.37	10.36	16.46	58.90
Former gateway	10.57	13.48	27.54	12.40	14.23	14.75
Other metro > 1m	11.21	17.17	53.07	12.65	17.58	39.05
West						
Metro < 1m	12.71	23.23	82.79	13.80	20.60	49.28
Rural	13.95	21.93	57.18	14.28	19.60	37.21
South						
Metro < 1m	13.98	24.63	76.10	15.76	23.55	49.39
Rural	17.07	25.10	47.07	18.35	24.68	34.54
Midwest						
Metro < 1m	10.02	17.20	71.68	13.56	18.66	37.60
Rural	10.54	18.56	76.09	13.30	20.37	53.15
Northeast						
Metro < 1m	10.05	13.46	33.97	11.42	13.21	15.72
Rural	9.80	10.91	11.32	10.86	11.01	1.36
US	11.79	17.85	51.43	13.26	16.43	23.85

Source: Authors' compilation based on U.S. Census Bureau (2003, 2010).
Note: All numbers in percentages.

Figure 5.2 / Native- and Foreign-Born Changes in Poverty Rates

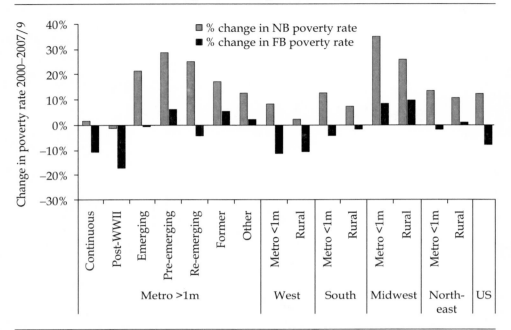

Source: Authors' compilation based on U.S. Census Bureau (2003, 2010).

periods but the gaps are uneven. In traditional gateway metropolitan areas, such as continuous and post–World War II gateway types, the difference between immigrant and native-born poverty at the start of the decade was below the national average. It was considerably above that average in new destination gateway types, especially in pre-emerging and re-emerging gateways. This difference perhaps reflects the presence in traditional gateways of diverse native-born populations many of whom are second-generation descendants of Asian and Latino immigrants. These people, who may contribute to elevated native-born poverty rates, will be much smaller fractions of pre-emerging and re-emerging gateway populations.

THE GEOGRAPHY OF IMMIGRANT POVERTY: A DECOMPOSITION APPROACH

What factors cause immigrant poverty rates to vary across gateway types—to be lower, for instance, in continuous than in post–World War II gateways, or to be higher in pre-emerging than in emerging gateways? One possible reason is that immigrants do not have the same personal-household characteristics in each location. In some places, they might be less likely to have the skills necessary to get a decent job and more likely to be in household types (for example, single parent) prone to economic marginality. Locations with greater concentrations of the foreign born with these characteristics would tend to have higher immigrant poverty rates than locations with smaller concentrations. Spatial variation in key personal or household characteristics, however, is unlikely to explain all of the spatial variation in immigrant poverty. Those with the same human capital and family structure may face different risks of being poor depending on their local economic conditions. Broadly speaking, the geography of poverty is attributable to both people and place effects and one way to measure their relative importance is to follow the decomposition procedure outlined in a John Odland and Mark Ellis study (1998). Comparisons of these two effects at different periods — 2000 versus 2007–2009 — will reveal the changing relative importance of demographic characteristics and local economic circumstances (which we label metro context) in generating the geography of poverty.

We decompose immigrant poverty rates, and for comparison purposes native-born poverty rates, as follows. Let f_{ij} be the proportion of a particular group (immigrants or the native born) in area j who are in category i (which indexes personal, family, and human capital characteristics), and q_{ij} is the poverty rate for these same households then the overall poverty rate p_j for area j is equal to:

$$p_j = \Sigma_i f_{ij} q_{ij} \tag{1}$$

This in turn can be re-written in deviation form as:

$$\Sigma_i f_{ij} q_{ij} - \Sigma_i f_i q_i = \Sigma_i q_i (f_{ij} - f_i) + \Sigma_i f_i (q_{ij} - q_i) + \Sigma_i (q_{ij} - q_i)(f_{ij} - f_i) \tag{2}$$

where f_i is the mean proportion in category i and q_i is the mean poverty rate in category i — both calculated across the set of local areas. Thus $\Sigma_i f_i q_i$ is the mean poverty rate over all j areas for the group in question. The first term on the right-hand side, $\Sigma_i q_i (f_{ij} - f_i)$, measures the effect of variation in the composition of local populations calculated at mean immigrant poverty rates for each category. We call this the demographic structure effect. The second term, $\Sigma_i f_i (q_{ij} - q_i)$, measures the effect of deviations of local poverty rates from the mean poverty rate, calculated at mean proportions of the population in category i. We label this the metro context effect. The final term, $\Sigma_i (q_{ij} - q_i)(f_{ij} - f_i)$, is necessary to account for any interaction between poverty rates and the distribution of the group population over the i categories.

The relative importance of the demographic and metro context effects in specific gateway types over time is of primary interest. We can extend the analysis to measure how much of the variance in p_j is due to variations in metro context and demographic structure effects. The variance of p_j is the sum of the variances of the three terms of equation (2) plus relevant covariances. Although it is possible for these covariances to be large, we expect from previous research that the most important terms will be the variances for the metro context effect and the demographic structure effect. The former will be the largest component of the variance when local conditions explain variations in immigrant poverty across the country; the latter will be the largest component when geographical variation in group characteristics explains the geography of group poverty. The magnitude of the covariation between the metro context and demographic structure effects is poten-

FIGURE 5.3 / Poverty Rate Variation, Native Born

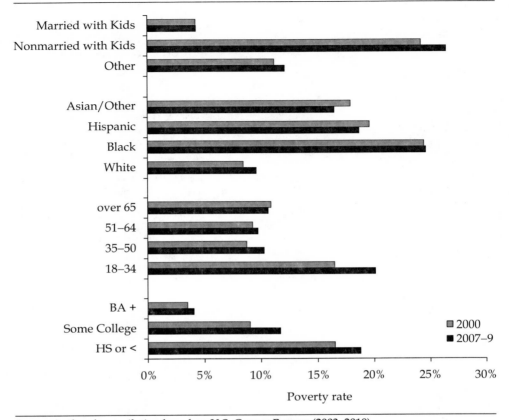

Source: Authors' compilation based on U.S. Census Bureau (2003, 2010).

tially interesting; it is a measure of how well we can separate these two influences. If this covariation is positive then subgroups that are disproportionately poor tend to cluster in locations that are unfavorable for escaping poverty and vice versa. The covariances involving the interaction effect—the final term in equation (2)—are likely to be very small.

Householders age eighteen and older are the demographic units in the decomposition. We switch the unit of analysis because some of the key determinants of poverty vary by household type (single, married, presence of children) rather than by individual; or they are most logically associated with an adult member of the household (for example, education), typically the householder. The mixture of immigrants and native-born individuals in the same household, typically native-born children of immigrant parents, further complicates analysis at the individual scale. For example, the native-born children of immigrants will likely experience risks of poverty based on their parent's characteristics. In our household scale analysis, such children are members of a foreign-born headed household.

FIGURE 5.4 / Poverty Rate Variation, Foreign Born

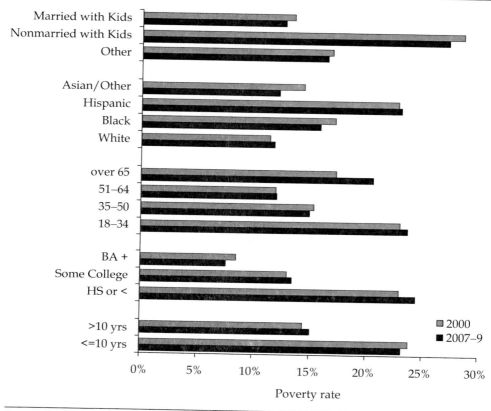

Source: Authors' compilation based on U.S. Census Bureau (2003, 2010).

Figures 5.3 (native-born) and 5.4 (foreign-born) chart household poverty rates by categories of key sociodemographic variables used in the decomposition: race, education, age, family type, and duration of U.S. residence (foreign-born households only). Poverty rates vary in broadly similar ways for the native and the foreign born. Married households with children have the lowest rates of poverty; unmarried households with children have the highest. Whites have the lowest poverty rates in both native- and foreign-born households. Blacks have the highest native-born poverty rate whereas Hispanics do among the foreign born. More education reduces the chances of being poor for both the native and the foreign born. At all grades, however, equivalent levels of education translate into lower poverty rates for the native born than the foreign born. For immigrants, more time in the country corresponds to substantially lower household poverty rates.

We acknowledge that finer categorizations of these variables might capture more subtle effects and that other characteristics, for example region of origin of the foreign-born householder, might affect the odds of being poor. The categoriza-

FIGURE 5.5 / Geographic Variation, Native-Born Poverty, Metro

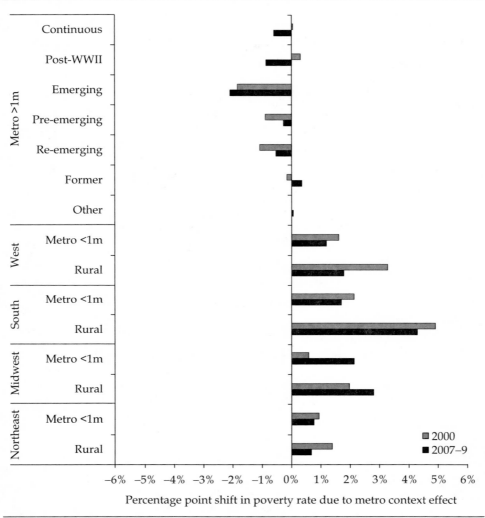

Source: Authors' compilation based on U.S. Census Bureau (2003, 2010).

tions of variables presented in figures 5.3 and 5.4, however, are enough to explain national variation in household poverty rates. Log-linear models successfully predict household poverty as a function of the main effects and the two-way interaction of education with other main effects.[6]

The decomposition procedure actually uses the full interaction of these variables, which strengthens our conclusion that the variable categorizations in these figures are fully capable of capturing the effects of subnational differences in demographic structure on the geography of poverty. In the native-born case (figure

FIGURE 5.6 / Geographic Variation, Native-Born Poverty, Demographic

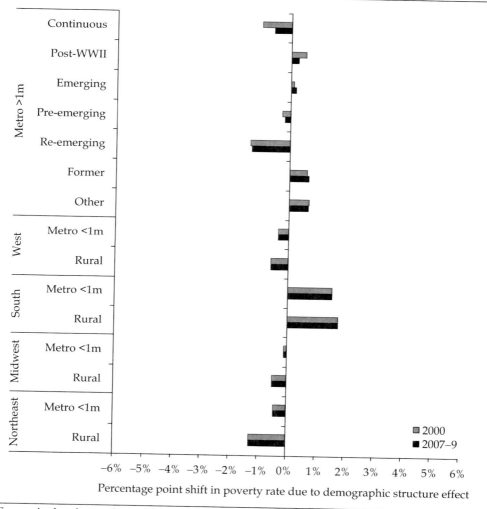

Source: Authors' compilation based on U.S. Census Bureau (2003, 2010).

5.3), the procedure subdivides households in each gateway location *j* into 144 demographic categories *i*: 4 (race) × 4 (age) × 3 (education) × 3 (family). It subdivides foreign-born households (figure 5.4) into 288 levels of *i* (double the native-born number because of the binary category of years in the United States). Applying the decomposition technique in equation (2) to these data yields the distribution of demographic and metro context effects by gateway type displayed in figures 5.5 and 5.6 (native born) and figures 5.7 and 5.8 (foreign born). Because the decomposition explains the poverty rate, any positive direction (rightward) on the figures raises poverty and is thus, descriptively, disadvantageous. By extension, leftward trending

FIGURE 5.7 / Geographic Variation, Foreign-Born Poverty, Metro

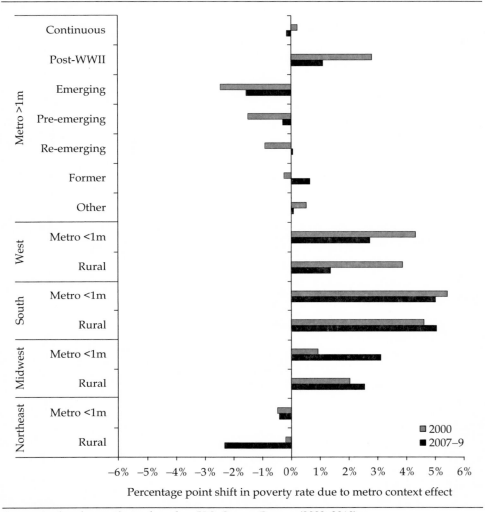

Source: Authors' compilation based on U.S. Census Bureau (2003, 2010).

bars are advantageous or favorable, indicating conditions or characteristics that reduce poverty.

Native-Born Decomposition

As shown in figures 5.5 and 5.6, metro context effects for the native born in the top fifty metro areas are generally leftward in orientation, meaning that they reduce

FIGURE 5.8   /   Geographic Variation, Foreign-Born Poverty, Demographic

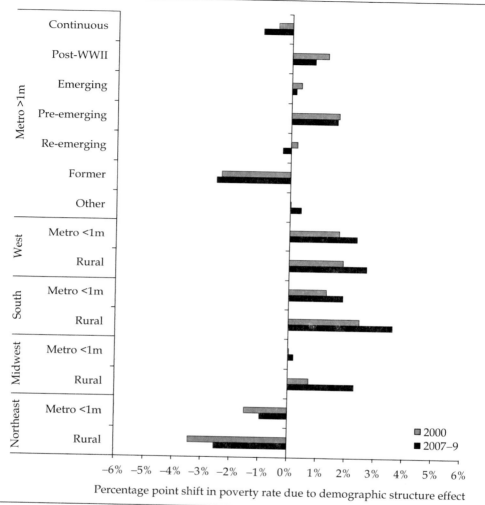

Percentage point shift in poverty rate due to demographic structure effect

Source: Authors' compilation based on U.S. Census Bureau (2003, 2010).

poverty. At the same time, they are substantially positive or rightward trending, meaning unfavorable, in rural and small metro areas. Trends over time suggest that local economies have become relatively more favorable for poverty reduction (that is, the bars have shifted more to the left) in continuous, post–World War II and emerging gateways and in small metro and rural areas of the South and West. The trend from 2000 to 2000–2009 also suggests an attenuating of the advantageous metro context effect in pre-emerging, re-emerging, and former gateways and especially in the Midwest. The Midwest region was hit especially hard by the Great Recession, so its distinctiveness in these findings is not surprising.

Demographic structure effects do not correlate strongly with metro structure effects for the native born. The native-born population structures of continuous and re-emerging gateways and the rural northeast are favorable for reducing poverty (leftward trending bars); the rural and small town native population in the South has characteristics that tend to elevate poverty (rightward trending bars). Not much changed in these demographic structure effects in the 2000s. In continuous gateways, however, demographic structure shifted to the right, indicating disproportionate growth in subpopulations at risk of being poor by the 2007 to 2009 period. This perhaps signals the rising importance of households headed by second-generation immigrants — a subpopulation of the native born more likely to be poor than households headed by third- or higher-generation natives.

Foreign-Born Decomposition

The pattern of foreign-born metro context effects plotted in figures 5.7 and 5.8 shows some broad similarities with these effects for the native born. Small metro and rural areas are powerfully disadvantageous — except, notably, in the Northeast. Like those for the native born, metro context effects are generally advantageous in most large metro areas except in post–World War II gateways where, in 2000, the effect elevates the foreign-born poverty rate almost as much it does in the rural and small metro West. In the same year, the three new destination gateway types (emerging, pre-emerging, re-emerging), had metro contexts favorable to poverty reduction among immigrants. Hence, in line with Crowley and colleagues' (2006) findings, the dispersion of foreign-born populations from post–World War II gateways to the largest new metropolitan destination types probably had a poverty reducing effect at the national level in the period leading up to 2000.

In 2007–2009, however, metro context effects converged: the new destination gateway advantage declined (bars shifted to the right), and the disadvantage in post–World War II gateways diminished (bars shifted to the left). The place disadvantage associated with the rural and small metropolitan area West also diminished over this period whereas it hardly changed in the South. Just as for the native born, place effects turned increasingly unfavorable for immigrants in the Midwest, especially so in small metropolitan areas. If avoidance of the local conditions that elevate the odds of being poor was a motivating factor for shifts in immigrant geography away from post–World War II gateways — and the western United States in general — to new destinations, metropolitan or otherwise, in the 1990s, then the underlying conditions for that movement appear to have weakened during the 2000s.

Comparing the pattern of these metropolitan context effects with that for immigrant demographic structure effects — figures 5.7 and 5.8, respectively — reveals some interesting contrasts. In both 2000 and 2007–2009, immigrants in post–World War II gateways faced an unfavorable local environment and have characteristics that made and make them more prone to poverty, although these disadvantages diminished over the decade. This contrasts with the situation in emerging and pre-emerging gateways. As mentioned, these places have favorable metro contexts for avoiding poverty, though this advantage weakened by 2007–2009, but also have immigrants populations with characteristics more likely to make them poor. In other words, a large subset of new destination metropolitan areas are relatively good places to be as an immigrant—they are locales with labor market conditions that reduce the odds of being poor—but the immigrant populations in these places have elevated poverty rates because of their unfavorable demographic characteristics. This is probably because the immigrant population of new destinations are mostly Hispanics and mostly from Mexico (Singer 2004; Massey and Cappoferro 2008).

Elsewhere, with the exception of former gateways, which have neutral metropolitan context effects but strongly favorable (that is, poverty reducing) immigrant demographic structure effects, the correlation between local conditions and population structure is positive. That is, locations where immigrant populations disproportionately possess characteristics which make them poverty prone are also places with local conditions that elevate the general risk of poverty, and vice versa.

A comparison between the geographic pattern of immigrant and native demographic structure effects reveals interesting similarities and differences by type of place. Demographic structure effects are large and disadvantageous in rural and small metropolitan areas of the South for both immigrants and the native born. In other words, these places have characteristics that elevate the odds of being poor regardless of nativity. The opposite is true in continuous gateways; there both native- and foreign-born populations have characteristics that alleviate the likelihood of being poor. Immigrant and native populations in the small metropolitan and rural areas of the Northeast both have favorable demographic characteristics; but these poverty-reducing demographic structure effects appear to be markedly stronger for the foreign born, especially in rural areas of that region. But elsewhere, demographic structure effects for immigrants and natives diverge. For example, in all three pre-emerging gateways—rural and small metropolitan areas of the West and the rural Midwest—immigrants have characteristics that increase their poverty rate whereas the opposite is true—albeit only slightly—for natives. In former gateways, immigrants have characteristics that reduce their poverty substantially but the native-born have the opposite—their characteristics increase their poverty rates in these places. In sum, immigrant and native populations coincide in their greater or lesser risk for poverty in some gateway types but not in others. Places where immigrants have characteristics that elevate their poverty risk but the native born do not may be locations with enhanced political and cultural sensitivity to the growth in the foreign-born population.

A close inspection of the pattern of bars in figures 5.7 and 5.8 suggests a possible increasing positive association over time between people and place effects for immigrants; places with conditions likely to elevate poverty are also places with immigrants who have characteristics likely to render them poor. A partition of the variance in poverty rates across the fifty-seven locations—forty-nine metropolitan areas with a million or more people and the eight rural and small metropolitan

FIGURE 5.9 / Sources of Variation

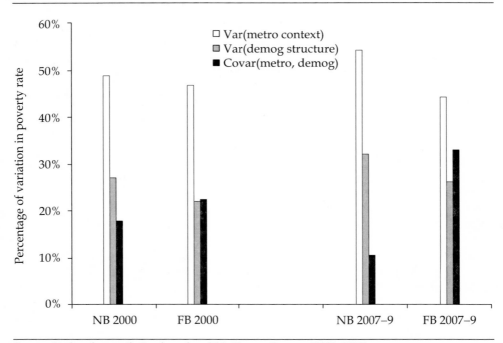

Source: Authors' compilation based on U.S. Census Bureau (2003, 2010).

location categories—by the components on the right side of equation (2) confirms this impression (see figure 5.9).[7]

Before we turn to a lengthier discussion of this covariation, we offer some insights on the trends in the other major components of the variance decomposition. The first is that for both groups in both years variations in metropolitan context effects explains most of the geography of poverty. This means place effects account for more of the variance in poverty rates than variation in the characteristics of local populations does. Metropolitan context effects account for more of the variations in native-born than immigrant poverty in both 2000 and 2007–2009 and these effects become markedly more important for the native born at decade's end. The growing importance of place for native poverty during the 2000s accords with the notion that this group has been substantially harmed by the recession and that the geographic unevenness of the effects of the economic downturn is increasingly driving spatial variability in native-born poverty rates. The opposite appears to be true for the foreign born; difference in context effects became a little less important source of the variance in immigrant poverty.

The reasons for this divergence become clear on inspection of the trends in variance attributable to demographic structure and, especially, its covariation with metropolitan context. Demographic structure effects are more important sources of variation in native- than foreign-born poverty in both 2000 and 2007–2009, and they rise in importance for both groups during the decade at roughly equal rates. This suggests that who lives where has become a more important predictor of the geography of poverty for both natives and immigrants.

The most dramatic change, however, and the biggest divergent trend in source of variation between the native and foreign born, is the covariation between people and place effects. Recall that this effect measures the extent to which the geography of population subgroups has adjusted to the spatial distribution of local economic conditions. If it is positive, places with buoyant labor markets that are poverty reducing are populated with people with characteristics that lower their odds of becoming poor, and vice versa. If it is negative, people with characteristics that elevate their chances of becoming poor have the good fortune, on average, to live in places where local conditions are poverty reducing, or people with characteristics that reduce poverty tend to live in less prosperous places.

The covariance terms for both groups in both years are positive, meaning that people with favorable (unfavorable) characteristics tend to cluster in favorable (unfavorable) places. But the trends in this covariance term are markedly different. It declines—almost by 50 percent—for the native born over the period in question, suggesting that the positive association between people and place effects has considerably weakened for this group. One possible explanation is that the Great Recession has disproportionately affected parts of the country previously immune from economic trouble, places where the populations have previously had relatively few people at risk of being poor because of their demographic characteristics. Consequently, these locations will register a weakening or reversal of their favorable metropolitan context effects but still have a favorable native-born population structure. Writ large, the net result will be a weaker relationship between people and place effects.

For the foreign born, the covariance term trends dramatically in the other direction, increasing by more than 200 percent between 2000 and 2007–2009, and becomes the second largest component overall, surpassing the variance in demographic structure effects. By the time of the recession, places with the most favorable metro contexts for poverty reduction have immigrant populations with the most favorable demographic characteristics. Perhaps this is because the foreign born who are least likely to be poor have made spatial adjustments to local labor market conditions. The flip side is that immigrants with the least favorable characteristics for poverty avoidance have become more likely to live in places with poor economic conditions. This implies a double disadvantage for immigrants who remain in these places.

NEW DESTINATIONS AND TRENDS IN NATIONAL POVERTY

Finally, we explore the effects of changing demographic characteristics and, most important for this chapter, the shift of immigrant settlement to new destinations on the national poverty rate. This extends the logic and method of the earlier counterfactual experiment to account not only for changes in the percentage foreign

TABLE 5.5   /   Counterfactual Change in Overall U.S. Poverty Rate

	National Poverty Rate	Percentage Point Difference Since 2000
2000 Actual	11.72	
2007–2009 Actual	12.88	1.16
2007–2009 (2000: FB%)	12.77	1.06
2007–2009 (2000: FB%, Geography)	12.75	1.04
2007–2009 (2000: FB%, Geography, FB Characteristics)	12.77	1.05
2007–2009 (2000: FB%, Geography, FB and NB Characteristics)	12.91	1.19

Source: Authors' compilation based on U.S. Census Bureau (2003, 2010).
Note: All numbers in percentages.

born in the country but also for the diffusion of immigrants to places where poverty rates differ from those in traditional gateways, and the changing characteristics of foreign- and native-born populations in the 2000s. This counterfactual uses household rather than person data for the same reasons as the decomposition technique—the need to subdivide the population into subcategories at risk for poverty is most effectively cued on characteristics of the householder. This renders alternative estimates of poverty rates than for individuals but the differences between native- and foreign-born rates and their trends over time are very similar.

Table 5.5 reports the 2000 and 2007–2009 national poverty rates calculated using householders rather than individuals. These rates are lower than for individuals by about 1.2 percentage points but the magnitude of the increase over this period is almost identical to that registered with person data. The shaded cells report what the U.S. poverty rate would have been under various conditions. The shaded cells in row three report the household version of the simple national counterfactual discussed previously. Under this condition—the same foreign-born percentage of the population in 2007–2009 as in 2000—overall poverty would have increased by 1.06 percentage points compared to the actual increase of 1.16 points—a small difference. The next row allocates the foreign-born population to its 2000 geography in addition to rolling back the foreign-born percentage of the population to the same date. Without diffusion in the 2000s, and with no relative growth in the foreign-born population over this time, the increase in overall poverty would have been 1.04 points. In other words, immigrant settlement diffusion to new destinations in the 2000s accounts for a very small fraction of the increase in overall poverty above that accounted for by the changing relative size of the foreign-born population.

The final two rows account for changing immigrant and native-born household characteristics. Essentially, whether we only roll back immigrant characteristics to what they were in 2000 (row five) or roll back both immigrant and native-born characteristics to their 2000 distributions (row six)—the effect on national poverty rates is minimal. In both instances, the counterfactual increase would have been almost identical to the actual increase, just over 1 percentage point. Thus, changes in immigrant or native-born characteristics appear to explain very little of the observed trends. The bottom line is that trends in immigration in the 2000s, including locational changes, appear to have had little effect on changes in aggregate poverty levels.

DISCUSSION

Trends in immigrant poverty in the 2000s differ from those for natives. As native-born poverty rates increased during this decade, driving up overall poverty rates, immigrant poverty rates declined nationally and in many—but not all—subnational locations too. Consequently, the immigrant share of the poor population dropped in many parts of the country, and the share held by natives increased. This happened despite growth in the size of the foreign-born population. This suggests that immigrants were less hard hit by the recession than the U.S.-born although, as noted in chapter 11 of this volume, it may also reflect migration selectivity and household organization responses to the crisis on the part of immigrants.

New destination areas such as emerging and pre-emerging gateways and rural and small metropolitan areas in the South buck this trend. They have a rising fraction of immigrants in their poverty populations, partly because foreign-born poverty rates rose slightly in these locations and partly because immigrant populations—which tend to be poorer than natives—grew faster than native-born populations did. Notably, traditional gateways, where most immigrants continue to live, experienced drops in foreign-born poverty, measured by both rate and poverty population share. Overall, despite the growth of the foreign-born population and settlement in new destinations, immigration trends account for a small fraction of the increase in overall poverty in the 2000s. Increases in native-born poverty rates, nationally and subnationally, drive growth in overall poverty.

In terms of the geography of these trends, we found that some new destination areas had lower immigrant poverty rates than some traditional gateways in 2000, a result that largely accords with previous findings (Crowley, Lichter, and Qian 2006). Emerging gateways, for example, had lower immigrant poverty rates in 2000 than continuous and post–World War II gateways did. Additionally, all three new destination gateway types (emerging, re-emerging, pre-emerging) had lower immigrant poverty rates than in post–World War II gateways. We also confirmed that new destination rural and small metropolitan areas (for example, in the South) have very high rates of immigrant poverty (that is, above rates in traditional large metropolitan gateways).

The 2000s reversed some of these differences. The poverty rate advantage for immigrants in the three new destination gateway types relative to the traditional types narrowed or vanished depending on the comparison locations. The decomposition analysis reveals that in 2000, the three new destination gateway types were all places in which immigrants regardless of demographic characteristics were at lower risk for being poor than in traditional gateways. Thus immigrants were better off—at least in terms of the lower odds of being poor—in these new destination metropolitan areas than in old destinations. Thus, at that time, diffusion of immigrants to these new destinations made sense from an immigrant perspective.

This place advantage, however, eroded partially or completely by 2007–2009, depending on the new destination gateway type. This attenuation of favorable place effects, especially when it occurred in tandem with unfavorable immigrant demographic characteristics (for example, in pre-emerging gateways) is a recipe for increased immigrant poverty. More generally, the relation between people and place effects for immigrants strengthened over the 2000s. New destination locations that had favorable metropolitan contexts but immigrant populations prone to being poor lost their place advantage. This is worrisome because the better performance of immigrants in these emerging gateway metropolitan areas in 2000 may have reflected housing boom driven conditions. It also suggests that immigrants in these places will find it harder to leave the ranks of the poor now that their economies have deteriorated.

Our analysis tracked immigrant and native-born poverty rates from the start of the last decade into the depths of the Great Recession. The effects of that profound economic downturn will reverberate for years, perhaps even decades. Overall poverty tracks closely with unemployment (Isaacs 2011) and, unless we see significant employment growth, poverty rates will likely remain higher than they were a decade or so ago.

A slow recovery will add pressure for immigration reform, which range from a new guest worker program or something far more comprehensive involving dismantling the "family reunification" components of present policy perhaps toward a points system, after Canada's, that favors immigrants with skills. With immigration reform currently gridlocked at the federal level, however, local governments are trying their own hand at legislation. Additionally, although local policy responses to immigration ranges from welcoming to hostile, places with high rates of foreign-born growth and places in the South have shown the greatest tendency to enact exclusionary policies (see chapter 10, this volume; Walker and Leitner 2011). Many of these locales are what we have been calling new immigrant destinations.

This local hostility varies from raw nativism to a concern that current immigration policy represents an unfunded local mandate. Chapter 11 in this volume discusses how 1990s welfare reform has given states facing such political pressures the option to bar immigrants from poverty alleviation and other social programs. Regardless of these program exclusions, many new destinations lack the resources to provide adequate schooling to the children of immigrant newcomers. Local services may already be strained by the recession and the addition of new student-age community members place an added burden on educational services. Schools in these places have suddenly found themselves needing more teachers and aides adept in language remediation but are financially unable to hire additional personnel. A fear, of course, is that children already in or near poverty will grow up with skills and language disadvantages that reduce their chances of socioeconomic success. The addition of welfare bars and a more general local intolerance of new-comers will only serve to further marginalize populations already struggling to provide for themselves and their children.

National Science Foundation grants BCS-0961167 and BCS-0961232 provided funding for the research reported in this paper. Partial support also came from a Eunice Kennedy Shriver National Institute of Child Health and Human Development research infrastructure grant, 5R24HD042828, and training grant, 5T32HD007543, awarded to the Center for Studies in Demography and Ecology at the University of Washington.

NOTES

1. They report exceptions to this trend, however; rural areas in new destination regions recorded relatively high poverty of poverty.
2. Throughout the chapter, the data sources for the poverty calculations and all other variables are the 2000 PUMS from the 2000 decennial census and the 2007–2009 three-year PUMS from the American Community Survey, unless otherwise indicated. We opt for the three-year sample because we wanted a greater sample size for our subgroup metropolitan scale analysis. Our use of the three year sample means that our estimates of poverty are lower than others in this column who use a one-year ACS sample, such as Card and Raphael (chapter 1) and Peri (chapter 2) who use the 2009 single-year ACS.
3. The counterfactual poverty rate is calculated as follows: $p_c = S_i f_{it} q_{it+1}$ where f_{it} is the fraction of the population in category i (native born, foreign born) in t ime t (2000) and q_{it+1} is the poverty rate for persons in the same categories at time $t+1$ (2007–2009). This experiment assumes that growing immigrant populations do not affect native-born poverty rates through increased labor market competition. Steven Raphael and Eugene Smolensky (2009) and Peri (chapter 2, this volume) report that such competition effects on native-born poverty rates are negligible.
4. These county poverty rates come from the 2008 U.S. Census Small Area Income and Poverty Estimates and are available at the Census Bureau website, "State and County Estimates for 2008": see http://www.census.gov/did/www/saipe/data/statecounty/data/2008.html (accessed March 24, 2013).
5. These traditional gateways are New York, Los Angeles, Chicago, San Francisco, Boston, Miami, Houston, and San Diego—that is, continuous and post–World War II gateways as defined by Singer (2004). We define these gateways to include both their principal core and surrounding metropolitan areas. The percentages in this paragraph are calculated from the 2000 census and the 2009 American Community Survey.
6. To test whether the categorical variables in figures 5.3 and figure 5.4 adequately capture variations in household poverty, we estimated a series of negative binomial regressions in which the dependent variable is the count of poor households in the cells of a contin-

gency table. The native-born model is estimated using 144 cells (a four-way table: four categories of race times four age cohorts times three education levels times three family types); the foreign-born model is estimated using 288 cells in a five-way table (same categories as for the native-born subdivided by the binary duration of residence category). Models that include all main effects and the two-way interaction of education with other main effects fit the data for both native- and foreign-born households in both 2000 and 2007–2009 (that is, no significant difference from observations measured by both Deviance and Pearson's c^2 goodness-of-fit statistics). Thus we are confident that a partial interaction of the variables we have selected is sufficient to capture the demographic drivers of subnational variation in native- and foreign-born household poverty rates.

7. We only show the three main components of the variance decomposition on this figure. We do not show the remaining three components — all involving the interaction effect (the last term in equation (2)) — because they are very small.

REFERENCES

Borjas, George J. 1990. *Friends or Strangers*. New York: Basic Books.

———. 1999. *Heaven's Door*. Princeton, N.J.: Princeton University Press.

Boyd, Monica. 1989. "Family and Personal Networks in International Migration: Recent Developments and New Agendas." *International Migration Review* 23(3): 638–70.

Card, David, and Ethan Lewis. 2005. "The Diffusion of Mexican Immigrants in the 1990s: Explanations and Impacts." National Bureau of Economic Research Working Paper No. 11552.

Cooke, Thomas, and Sarah Marchant. 2006. "The Changing Intrametropolitan Location of High-Poverty Neighbourhoods in the U.S., 1990–2000." *Urban Studies* 43(11): 1971–89.

Crowley, Martha, Daniel T. Lichter, and Zhenchao Qian. 2006. "Beyond Gateway Cities: Economic Restructuring and Poverty Among Mexican Immigrant Families and Children." *Family Relations* 55(3): 345–60.

Ellis, Mark, and Jamie Goodwin-White. 2006. "1.5 Generation Internal Migration in the US: Dispersion from States of Immigration?" *International Migration Review* 40(4): 899–926.

Glasmeier, Amy, Ron Martin, Peter Tyler, and Danny Dorling. 2008. "Editorial: Poverty and Place in the UK and the USA." *Cambridge Journal of Regions, Economy and Society* 1(1): 1–16.

Iceland, John. 2006. *Poverty in America: A Handbook*, 2nd ed. Berkeley: University of California Press.

Isaacs, Julia B. 2011. "Child Poverty During the Great Recession: Predicting State Child Poverty Rates for 2010." *IRP* discussion paper no. 1389-11. Madison, Wisc.: Institute for Research on Poverty. Available at: http://www.irp.wisc.edu/publications/dps/pdfs/dp138911.pdf (accessed June 3, 2013).

Jargowsky, Paul A. 1997. *Poverty and Place: Ghettos, Barrios, and the American City*. New York: Russell Sage Foundation.

Jones, Richard C., ed. 2008. *Immigrants Outside Megalopolis: Ethnic Transformation in the Heartland*. Lanham, Md.: Lexington Books.

Kandel, William, Jamila Henderson, Heather Koball, and Randy Capps. 2011. "Moving Up in Rural America: Economic Attainment of Nonmetro Latino Immigrants." *Rural Sociology* 76(1): 101–28.

Kneebone, Elizabeth, and Alan Berube. 2008. *Reversal of Fortune: A New Look at Concentrated Poverty in the 2000s*. Washington, D.C.: The Brookings Institution.

Kodras, Janet E. 1997. "The Changing Map of American Poverty in an Era of Economic Restructuring and Political Realignment." *Economic Geography* 73(1): 67–93.

Lawson, Victoria, Lucy Jarosz, and Anne Bonds. 2010. "Articulations of Place, Poverty, and Race: Dumping Grounds and Unseen Grounds in the Rural American Northwest." *Annals of the Association of American Geographers* 100(3): 655–77.

Leach, Mark A., and Frank D. Bean. 2008. "The Structure and Dynamics of Mexican Migration to New Destinations in the United States." In *New Faces in New Places: The Changing Geography of American Immigration,* edited by Douglas S. Massey. New York: Russell Sage Foundation.

Li, Wei. 2009. *Ethnoburb: The New Ethnic Community in Urban America*. Honolulu: University of Hawaii Press.

Lichter, Daniel T., and Martha L. Crowley. 2002. "Poverty in America: Beyond Welfare Reform." *Population Bulletin* 57(2): 3–36.

Light, Ivan. 2006. *Deflecting Immigration: Networks, Markets, and Regulation in Los Angeles*. New York: Russell Sage Foundation.

Marrow, Helen B. 2011. *New Destination Dreaming: Immigration, Race, and Legal Status in the Rural American South*. Palo Alto, Calif.: Stanford University Press.

Massey, Douglas S. 1990. "Social Structure, Household Strategies, and the Cumulative Causation of Migration." *Population Index* 56(1): 3–26.

Massey, Douglas S. 2008. *New Faces in New Places: The Changing Geography of American Immigration*. New York: Russell Sage Foundation.

Massey, Douglas S., and Chiara Capoferro. 2008. "The Geographic Diversification of American Immigration." In *New Faces in New Places: The Changing Geography of American Immigration,* edited by Douglas S. Massey. New York: Russell Sage Foundation.

Odland, John, and Mark Ellis. 1998. "Variations in the Labour Force Experience of Women Across large Metropolitan Areas in the United States." *Regional Studies* 32(4): 333–47.

Raphael, Steven, and Eugene Smolensky. 2009. "Immigration and Poverty in the United States." *American Economic Review* 99(2): 41–44.

Singer, Audrey. 2004. "The Rise of New Immigrant Gateways." Washington, D.C.: Brookings Institution.

Singer, Audrey, Susan W. Hardwick, and Caroline Brettell, eds. 2008. *Twenty-First Century Gateways: Immigrant Incorporation in Suburban America.*, D.C.: Brookings Institution Press.

U.S. Census Bureau. 2003. 2000 Census of Population and Housing, 5% Use Microdata Sample.

——— . 2010. 2007–2009 American Community Survey, Public Use Microdata Sample.

Waldinger, Roger D., and Michael I. Lichter. 2003. *How the Other Half Works: Immigration and the Social Organization of Labor*. Berkeley: University of California Press.

Walker, Kyle E., and Helga Leitner. 2011. "The Variegated Landscape of Local Immigration Policies in the United States." *Urban Geography* 32 (2): 1–23.

Zúñiga, Victor, and Rubén Hernández-León. 2006. *New Destinations: Mexican Immigration in the United States*. New York: Russell Sage Foundation.

Part II

Intergenerational Mobility Within Immigrant Communities

The effect of immigration on U.S. poverty rates may extend well into the future through the offspring of recent immigrants. Of particular relevance is the degree to which these children experience socioeconomic mobility through educational attainment and occupational choices and outcomes. The three chapters in this section are devoted to understanding this process. Chapter 6 provides an empirical analysis of cross-generational educational mobility within immigrant households, how the degree of mobility differs by country of origin, and the degree to which the educational attainment outcomes of immigrant parents constrain or enhance the comparable outcomes for their children. Chapter 7 looks within the black box and uses qualitative interviews to assess the cultural differences and alternative dominant cognitive frames within national-origin groups that govern educational attainment and socioeconomic mobility. Finally, chapter 8 focuses specifically on unauthorized immigrants who arrived in the United States as small children.

Chapter 6

Intergenerational Mobility

Renee Reichl Luthra and Roger Waldinger

Immigration has long been a major source of economic and demographic growth in the United States. It has also long been a source of inequality. The last great wave of migration, at the turn of the previous century, brought large numbers of relatively lower skilled immigrants to the United States, diversifying the labor market, increasing rates of poverty, and creating an ethnically defined stratification system that endured for several generations (Lieberson and Waters 1988). The 1965 Immigration and Nationality Act, which eliminated nationality-based quotas, has once again opened the United States to a new wave of immigration from Asia, Africa, and the Americas. Bringing increased diversity in formal schooling and ethnic origin, a central source of concern is the impact of this immigration on inequality in the United States.

On one hand, the United States has offered most of these new arrivals a chance to improve their earnings (Clemens, Montenegro, and Pritchett 2008) and better their material conditions relative to their sending countries. On the other hand, the foreign born in the United States are more likely to be poorly educated and poorly paid relative to the receiving country, and to have higher poverty rates than the native population. In the long run, however, the fate of immigrants may not be the central issue when assessing the impact of migration on inequality. Rather, it is the direction and degree of intergenerational mobility—the links between immigrant parents and their children—that will define the impact of immigration on the future of ethnic stratification in the United States.

The question of intergenerational mobility has placed the children of immigrants, also known as the second generation, in the research spotlight. Two central questions guide much of this research. The first is a matter of direction: Which children of immigrants will improve upon, reproduce, or "decline" from the socioeconomic status of their immigrant parents? Second, what can explain the variation in mobility patterns observed between the children of immigrants of different origins and the children of native-born Americans?

In this chapter, we address these questions by examining the transmission of poverty and educational and labor market outcomes from immigrants to their children. Drawing on recent debates surrounding immigrant assimilation in the United States, we formulate a series of competing hypotheses about the direction of intergenerational mobility as well as the degree of transmission by origin group. We then test these hypotheses, first comparing nationally representative age-adjusted poverty rates, educational attainment, and labor market outcomes of immigrants and their descendants to the children of native-born whites, blacks, and Hispanics. We examine these trends more closely with metropolitan level data from the Immigration and Intergenerational Mobility in Metropolitan Los Angeles (IIMMLA). This data allows the measurement of intergenerational educational and occupational mobility by including individual level measures of parental outcomes during the adult respondent's childhood. We frame these findings within the assimilation debate on the U.S. second generation that has burgeoned in the past two decades.

THEORETICAL PERSPECTIVES

In this section, we review current perspectives on immigrant intergenerational mobility.

Assimilation Reformulated

Two competing reformulations of traditional assimilation theory frame the majority of current research on the second generation. Neo-assimilation theory modifies and updates the traditional assimilation perspective, arguing that in their desire to improve their material conditions, immigrants and their descendants will adopt the linguistic, educational, and residential characteristics that make them more like the native born (Alba and Nee 2003). In so doing, the educational and occupational distributions of the native-born descendants of immigrants should come to resemble those of the native population. Although not all immigrants will advance at the same rate, the decline in individual and institutional discrimination, combined with an increase in opportunity as the baby-boomer generation retires, should provide ample opportunity for intergenerational mobility into an increasingly multi-ethnic "mainstream" (Alba 2008).

In contrast, segmented assimilation theory predicts variation within the second generation, both in the direction of intergenerational mobility and its degree. Its central contribution is the identification of three discrete paths for the children of immigrants: the traditional straight line assimilation pattern of parallel acculturation and socioeconomic mobility toward the middle class; "ethnic mobility" of delayed acculturation combined with socioeconomic mobility; and the more novel prediction, "downward mobility" as the fate of the more disadvantaged immigrant groups (Portes and Zhou 1993; Portes and Rumbaut 2001). Only the children of middle-class immigrants can expect both streamlined acculturation and upward mobility into the middle-class mainstream. Those immigrants with less human and financial capital must rely instead on ethnic capital: in their contribution to this volume, Lee and Zhou reveal how resources specific to the Chinese and Vietnamese communities in Los Angeles, such as extracurricular tutoring in ethnic neighborhoods and the "Asian yellow pages" that provide information and rankings of local schools, enable even those Vietnamese with very low levels of schooling to help their children to become high academic achievers. In contrast, the children of less fortunate immigrant groups—those both poor in ethnic and traditional forms of capital—are seen as twice disadvantaged compared to their historical predecessors, by their appearance as visible minorities as well as by a restructured hourglass economy which offers fewer footholds in the climb from lower to middle class. Without the protection of a strong and diverse ethnic community, the children of these immigrant groups are expected to be immobile, stagnating in the low socioeconomic position of their immigrant parents, and reproducing their higher levels of poverty.

Working-Class Hypothesis: Receiving Country Starting Points

The emergence of these two theories has generated much empirical research as well as some further refinements. Through a series of empirical papers, many focusing on the experiences of Mexican immigrants and their descendants, we and our colleagues have argued for a middle ground between the neo- and segmented assimilation models (Luthra and Waldinger 2010; Perlmann and Waldinger 1997; Waldinger 2007; Waldinger and Feliciano 2004). The core argument in much of this work is that the children of disadvantaged immigrant groups such as Mexican Americans will not experience downward mobility, as forecasted by segmented assimilation theory, nor the convergence with the mainstream expected by neo-assimilation, but rather a pluralist or working-class mobility characterized by slow progress that varies across different dimensions of life. For instance, labor market research with the Current Population Survey (CPS) reveals near convergence in the wages of similarly skilled Mexican Americans and native whites but continued variance in employment arrangements, in particular in terms of fringe benefits (Waldinger, Lim, and Cort 2007) and employment sector (Luthra and Waldinger 2010). Recent work by Susan Brown and Frank Bean have found similar evidence of "delayed" incorporation in terms of spatial mobility (Brown 2007) as well as in education (Bean et al. 2011). These authors expect, and indeed have shown, that downward intergenerational mobility or even stagnation are unlikely outcomes for the children of Mexican immigrants, if only because their starting position is so low (Bean and Stevens 2003; Blau and Kahn 2007; Kasinitz 2008). Yet in contrast to neo-assimilation theory, the working-class hypothesis predicts that the interaction of a low socioeconomic starting point, combined with a higher proportion of foreign born with undocumented status (Bean, Brown, and Rumbaut 2006; Bean et al. 2011), will delay the convergence of native whites and Central American immigrants and their descendants.

Like segmented assimilation theory, the working-class hypothesis both emphasizes the high political and socioeconomic hurdles to upward mobility that immigrants face at the individual level, and focuses on the aggregate effects of national group membership. In addition to the individual handicap of low parental education or undocumented status, the lack of socioeconomic diversity among Mexican immigrants further affects mobility beyond the individual level, exerting an independent impact via the "ethnic capital" available to the group as a whole (Borjas 1992). Specifically, the average traits of the Mexican immigrant population—its low levels of education, the prevalence of undocumented status. concentration in unskilled work—is likely to impede the upward mobility of the second generation, depriving them of connections, information, and role models that would facilitate advancement. Gonzales's contribution to this volume, for instance, reveals the dampening effect of undocumented status on upward mobility among the 1.5 generation, leaving even U.S. college graduates without any possibility for higher skilled jobs.

Selection: Sending Country Starting Points

Whereas the working class hypothesis takes the relative position of the foreign born in the receiving country as its point of departure, a parallel strand of research looks to the relative position of the immigrants in the sending country as an important determinant of the outcomes of the second generation (Feliciano 2005a). The argument here is that the higher the socioeconomic standing of immigrants relative to their sending country, the better their children will perform, even controlling for their starting point in the United States. Although immigrant selection receives considerable attention in the economics of migration, it receives far less notice in most of the sociological literature. However, recent work on second-generation performance in the United States (Feliciano 2005a, 2006) as well as in Europe (Heath, Rothon, and Kilpi 2008; Levels, Dronkers, and Kraaykamp 2008; Luthra 2010) have brought the selectivity of the first generation to bear on the outcomes of the second generation. This research argues that insofar as most immigrants arrive with higher than average levels of schooling (Chiquiar and Hanson 2005; Feliciano 2005b), health (Akresh and Frank 2008), or generally unobserved characteristics such as ambition (Chiswick 1999) than the average resident of their native country, assuming equal distributions of the relative mobility characteristics across countries, we should expect higher mobility among the children of immigrants than among the children of the native born. In this way, the sending country selection hypothesis dovetails with both neo-assimilation theory and the working-class hypothesis: all expect upward mobility among most groups.

However, the selection hypothesis also straightforwardly yields implications regarding the degree of mobility to be expected. Whereas neo-assimilation theory is relatively quiet on the mechanisms behind differential mobility patterns across groups, and the working-class hypothesis focuses on the slower achievement of the poorest groups, the selection hypothesis expects variation in mobility patterns to follow the degree of selection from the home country. It is very likely that immigrants who have higher than average education levels or health than nonmigrants in their home countries will pass along these advantages to their children, even if they are relatively disadvantaged in the receiving country. The result will be higher rates of upward mobility among more positively selected groups.

Measuring Mobility and Hypotheses

In this chapter, following previous work on intergenerational mobility (Borjas 1992; Card, DiNardo, and Estes 2000; Solon 1999), we measure the strength of the connection between the educational or occupational status of the immigrant parents and the outcomes of their children using the following model:

$$\hat{Y} = \beta_0 + \beta_1 x,$$

where $\hat{Y}$ is the level of education or occupational status of child (adjusted for age) and x is the level of education or occupational status of his or her parent during his childhood. The larger the size of coefficient β_1, the higher the degree of intergenerational transmission, and the closer the outcomes of the child reproduce the outcomes of the parent. Smaller coefficients β_1 denote greater mobility and regression to the mean level of education or occupational prestige of the child's generation.

The goal of this chapter is to describe and account for variation in intergenerational transmission, β_1. National-origin differences in intergenerational mobility can therefore be indicated by a model that allows the relationship between parent and child to differ across groups, such as:

$$\hat{Y} = \beta_0 + \beta_1 x + \beta_2 g + \beta_3 (x * g),$$

where $\beta_2 g$ is a categorical variable for group membership and $\beta_3 (x * g)$ is an interaction term for parental education or occupation and group membership. National-origin groups with larger β_3 have less intergenerational mobility. Group-level differences in the size of coefficient β_2 affect the intercept and can be interpreted as the main effect of group membership. Higher intercepts indicate better educational or occupational outcomes for the second generation net of differences in parental educational or occupational outcomes. Differences in intercepts can be attributed to a range of unmeasured group-level effects, ranging from the average financial resources of the origin group to its general cultural or religious practices and beliefs.

Overall ethnic differences in second-generation outcomes are therefore a combination of the strength of the parent to child transmission as well as the main effect of ethnic origin. It is important to discuss both. For instance, one second-generation

FIGURE 6.1 / Assimilation Perspectives, Segmented

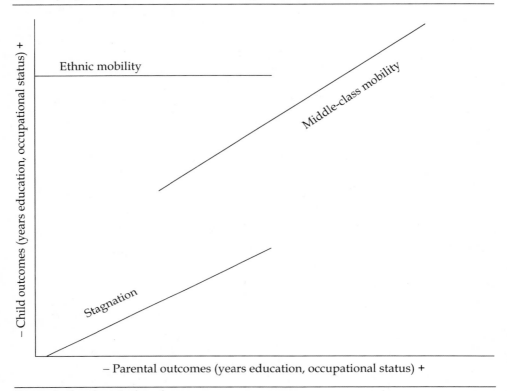

Source: Authors' original work.

group may obtain only high prestige, professional jobs, regardless of parental background, thanks to a high degree of ethnic capital. Another group may be clustered uniformly in low prestige laboring occupations, again regardless of parental background, due to a lack of legal status. Both of these groups would have the same β_3, but the key to their very different social position would be found in the main effect β_2, which would be high in the case of the former and low in the case of the latter.

To account for these two components of intergenerational change, slope, and intercept, we draw from the literature review. These hypotheses are also represented graphically in figures 6.1 through 6.4.

Segmented assimilation

- Intercepts: Advantaged groups will maintain their advantage, and disadvantaged groups without a positive context of reception will maintain their disadvantage. Intercepts for these groups will reflect the starting place of first gen-

FIGURE 6.2   /   Assimilation Perspectives, Neo-Assimilation

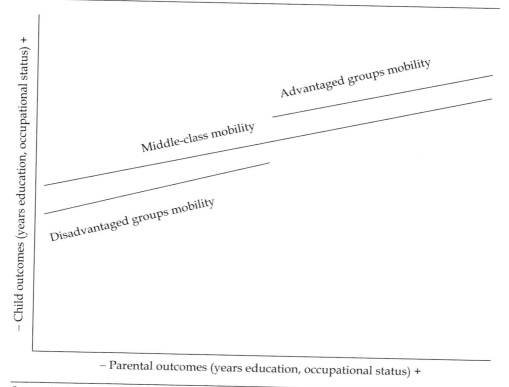

Source: Authors' original work.

eration, without much movement up or down. Only those disadvantaged groups with a positive context of reception (such as Cubans or Vietnamese) will have intercepts higher than their parents' starting points.

- Slopes: slopes will approach 1 for negatively received groups and for advantaged groups, who are expected to reproduce their class position. Slopes will approach 0 for disadvantaged groups with a positive context of reception, who will improve upon their parents' position.

Neo-assimilation

- Intercepts: Neo-assimilation theory predicts convergence toward the receiving country mean. Intercepts will reflect the starting place of parents, but be much more compressed around the receiving country mean. This means that intercepts for the children of disadvantaged migrant groups, such as Mexicans, will be higher than those of their parents, whereas those children of advantaged migrants will be lower.

FIGURE 6.3 / Working-Class Perspective

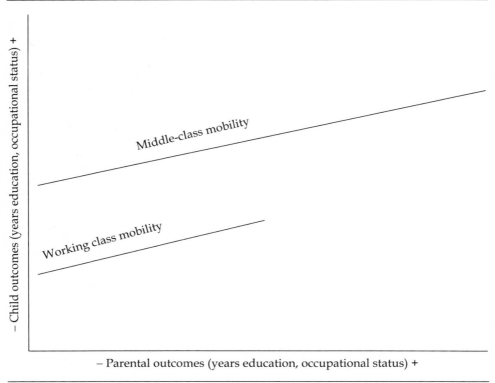

Source: Authors' original work.

- Slopes: Slopes will be moderate for the children of immigrants, and the rate of intergenerational transmission will be similar across groups.

Working Class

- Intercepts: legal difficulties and very low (socioeconomic status) SES will result in lower intercepts for the children of working-class immigrants than for advantaged immigrants and native whites but still higher than their parents.
- Slopes: Slopes will be moderate for the children of immigrants, but due to negative main effects for undocumented and low SES immigrants this will still result in working-class incorporation.

Immigrant Selection Perspective

- Intercepts: The immigrant selection perspective predicts very high intercepts for the children of positively selected groups, with lower intercepts for less positively and negatively selected groups.

FIGURE 6.4 / Selectivity Perspective

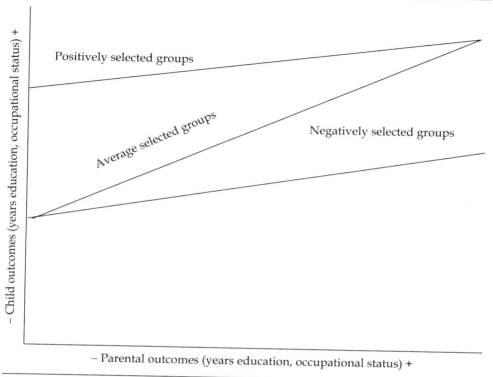

Source: Authors'original work.

- Slopes: Positively and negatively selected immigrants will have fairly shallow slopes, because due to unobserved heterogeneity (selection) parental educational and occupational outcomes are less efficient indicators for the relevant unobserved characteristics in predicting performance in children. Groups that are not strongly negatively or positively selected will have steeper slopes that are more similar to the native population.

DATA

This chapter relies on three data sources. To obtain measures of the current adult children of immigrants, we rely on the 2006, 2008, and 2010 March Current Population Survey, a large nationally representative survey (King et al. 2010). By combining several survey years, these surveys allow the identification of sufficient numbers of 1.5- and second-generation origin groups and provide detailed education and occupational information as well as poverty indicators. The next survey is the IPUMS 1% Metropolitan Sample of the 1980 Census (Ruggles et al. 2010), which we use to examine the characteristics of the foreign born most likely to be parents of the current 1.5- and second-generation adult population. This data allows us to make intergenerational comparisons between the outcomes of today's second generation (between 2006 and 2010) and their foreign-born parents during their childhood (in 1980). The final survey, the Immigration and Intergenerational Mobility in Metropolitan Los Angeles survey, is a metropolitan level data set designed for the study of second-generation mobility (Rumbaut et al. 2008), and thus is uniquely suited for the aims of this chapter.

Current Population Survey

The CPS is a nationally representative sample of approximately 50,000 households, excluding persons in the armed forces and institutionalized living quarters. The survey is conducted monthly, and the March files contain the most extensive information on a variety of poverty indicators: individual and household earnings, employment information, and educational background. Although the survey size is much smaller than the U.S. Census, unlike the census, the CPS inquires after the place of birth of the respondent's parents, allowing the identification of the adult second generation who have left their parents' households. Moreover, although the data lacks the variables necessary to directly measure intergenerational mobility, as in the IIMMLA data set, it does provide a nationally representative overview of each of the immigrant origin groups under consideration here. This data will be used to provide national context and a broader age range to compare to the IIMMLA findings.

IPUMS 1% Metropolitan Sample 1980 Census

The Integrated Public Use Microdata Series (IPUMS) sample is a 1 in 100 random sample of the U.S. population, and thus contains sufficiently large sample sizes of the foreign born to differentiate many national origins. Unfortunately this data cannot be used to identify the native-born children of immigrants, as noted earlier. We use this data to estimate the characteristics of foreign-born adults most likely to be the parents of the second generation between 2006 and 2010. We note, however, that these estimates are only approximations and include many foreign-born adults who are not parents, whose children remained in the country of origin, or who may have returned to their country of origin and taken their children with them.

IIMMLA

The IIMMLA is a telephone survey of young adults, age twenty through thirty-nine, that consists of 4,655 interviews in the Los Angeles metropolitan area—Los

Angeles, Orange, Ventura, Riverside, and San Bernardino counties. The sample has quotas for second- and 1.5-generation groups—Mexicans, Vietnamese, Filipinos, Koreans, Chinese, and Central Americans from Guatemala and El Salvador—and includes three native-parentage comparison groups comprised of third- and later-generation Mexican Americans, non-Hispanic whites, and blacks. IIMMLA is designed to study the second generation and contains multiple measures of parental background and socioeconomic outcomes in young adulthood, as well as current and former legal status.

IIMMLA is a cross-sectional survey, containing numerous retrospective questions that allow us to reconstruct parental characteristics from when the respondents were children. We therefore expect some recall error. IIMMLA also involved targeted random sampling, via the telephone, of selected populations within a predefined geographical region. Due to the well-noted income and age bias arising from telephone surveys, as well as selection by omitting second-generation youth who dispersed from immigrant enclaves away from Los Angeles, we note that the IIMMLA may not be fully representative of all second-generation youth born and raised in Los Angeles.[1] Furthermore, because the second generation is still a young population, IIMMLA sampled young adults ages twenty through thirty-nine, excluding the older second generation. We further limit our sample to adults age twenty-three and older to reduce the number of respondents still in school but still maintain adequate sample size. To correct for missing data in parental occupational and educational status, we use multiple imputation with chained equations (M=30) using the Stata ice command and mi estimation procedures (Royston 2009).

ANALYSIS

To provide a first glance of the relationship between immigration and economic disadvantage, we compare poverty rates, education, and occupation for a nationally representative sample of first-, second-, and 1.5-generation members, acknowledging that this cross-sectional snapshot does not allow us to directly link parents to children.

Descriptive Statistics with the CPS and Census

In tables 6.1 through 6.3, we report the poverty rates, educational attainment, and occupational status of nine immigrant origin groups (first, 1.5, and second generation) as well as third-generation whites, blacks, and Hispanics. Individuals who migrated to the United States at age thirteen or older are recorded as first generation, those who migrated before age thirteen are recorded as 1.5 generation, and the children of at least one foreign-born parent are defined as second generation. The first and 1.5 generation are assigned their country of birth as their national origin. For the second generation, their origins are assigned according to the country of birth of the foreign-born parent; where a child has two foreign-born parents of different origins, the father's origin is used. All statistics reported are restricted to adults age twenty-five and older, and adjusted for the different age distributions of these populations. The results reported are the weighted average of the age-specific rates with the overall second generation population (between 2006 and 2010) as the standard population.

Starting Points: Sending and Receiving Country   Before examining intergenerational comparisons, we review aspects of the socioeconomic standing of different foreign-born groups in the United States, both relative to the third-generation native population as well as to the average resident of the sending country. Table 6.1 displays the age-adjusted poverty rates, educational attainment, and average occupational status scores for the children of native-born non-Hispanic whites, blacks, and Hispanic Americans, and the foreign born of eight origin groups. For comparison, we include the characteristics of the current adult foreign born as well as the adult foreign born in 1980, whom are more likely to be the parents of today's 1.5- and second-generation adults.

In addition, we also include the net difference index (ND) score for the foreign-born groups. This measure uses UNESCO (United Nations Educational, Scientific and Cultural Organization) and census data to calculate a summary measure of the level of educational selectivity of immigrants to the United States relative to nonmigrants in the sending country of similar age. For example, an index of 0.35 indicates that an immigrant's educational attainment will exceed that of a nonmigrant from the same country 35 percent more often than a nonmigrant's education will exceed that of an immigrant from that country (Lieberson 1980, quoted in Feliciano 2005, 849). If the number of immigrants exceeding nonmigrants in educational attainment equals the number of nonmigrants exceeding immigrants in education, the value of the index will be zero. Thus, the higher the index, the more educated the immigrants are relative to the nonmigrant population in their home country. If immigrants are more often less educated than nonmigrants, that is, there is negative selection, the value of the index will be negative.[2]

Table 6.1 shows great variation in both receiving and sending country starting points. The greatest number of immigrants hail from Mexico: approximately 25 percent of the U.S. foreign-born population. Of the nine nationalities highlighted in the table, Mexicans are also the least educated, the most concentrated in jobs of low quality, and the most likely to be in poverty: about 25 percent of the Mexican first generation were in poverty in both 1980 and currently, versus only 8 percent of third-generation whites in 2006 through 2010. Salvadoran immigrants share similarly low educational attainment and occupational status, although their poverty rates are lower, due in part to their smaller family size. Persons born in Puerto Rico and living on the mainland displayed even higher poverty rates than the Mexican foreign born in 1980, although their position has improved slightly in more recent years. They also enjoy both average education and occupation that are

TABLE 6.1 / Sending and Receiving Starting Points

	Percentage in Poverty	Less than High School	College or More	Mean Occupational Status Score	Net Difference Index: Educational Selectivity
Whites 3+ generation	.077	.073	.336	49.1	
Blacks 3+ generation	.207	.159	.185	44.4	
Hispanics 3+ generation	.143	.202	.159	45.5	
Foreign-born U.S. population, 2006–2010					
Western Hemisphere					
Caribbean	.179	.230	.202	41.2	.650
Cuban	.189	.214	.191	42.5	.399
Mexican	.256	.637	.053	35.7	.208
Puerto Rican	.236	.304	.172	43.5	-.064
Salvadoran	.157	.563	.076	36.2	.350
Asia					
Chinese	.149	.133	.580	55.4	.671
Filipino	.055	.059	.532	49.8	.597
Korean	.174	.053	.578	40.6	.525
Vietnamese	.102	.237	.247	48.1	.595
Foreign-born U.S. population, 1980					
Western Hemisphere					
Caribbean	.182	.437	.101	39.5	
Cuban	.136	.367	.175	44.3	
Mexican	.235	.782	.034	36.5	
Puerto Rican	.299	.655	.045	39.1	
Salvadoran	.196	.557	.078	36.9	
Asia					
Chinese	.127	.310	.372	46.9	
Filipino	.080	.227	.431	46.5	
Korean	.123	.269	.313	43.4	
Vietnamese	.307	.409	.122	41.0	

Source: Authors' calculations based on the U.S. 1% Census (1980) and the March Current Population Surveys (2006, 2008, 2010).
Note: Weighted percentages from the U.S. Bureau of the Census 1% Census (1980) and the March current population surveys (2006, 2008, and 2011). Age adjusted with composite second generation (2006–2010) as standard population. The 1.5 generation is defined as foreign born who immigrated before secondary school (younger than thirteen). The second generation are children born in the United States to at least one foreign-born parent. Where national origins of the mother and father differ, the national origin of the father is used. Poverty is defined as the official poverty status of the individual's household according to the definition of poverty originally developed by the Social Security Administration in 1964, later modified by federal interagency committees in 1969 and 1980. High school completion includes GED. College completion includes a bachelor's degree or higher. Occupational status scores are created from ISCO-88 occupation codes into the International Socio-Economic Index Scores (Ganzeboom and Treiman 1996). Net Difference Score from Feliciano (2005).

higher than those of the Mexican immigrants and also possess birthright U.S. citizenship.

For the most part, nationalities falling at the higher end of the spectrum originate in the Eastern Hemisphere. The Filipinos appear to be the most advantaged, showing higher rates of high school and college completion and lower rates of poverty than all other groups, native whites included, and mean occupational scores outdistanced only by the Chinese. On average, the latter are employed in jobs of high quality, but their poverty rates and educational indicators point to significant within group variation, a pattern that holds for the other Asian groups. Thus, although displaying bifurcated educational attainment and twice the poverty rates of native whites, the Chinese stand out with the highest occupational status in both 1980 and today. Koreans have high levels of educational attainment, exceeding the white average, and yet higher levels of poverty and occupational scores below those of whites and immigrants from Cuba, who typically arrive with lower levels of schooling. Their position has also worsened relatively across time, and they currently have higher poverty rates and lower occupational prestige scores in 2006 through 2010 than they did in 1980, despite an improved educational profile. By contrast, the Vietnamese foreign born have a much more positive socioeconomic profile today than in 1980, their poverty rates in 2006 through 2010 at 10 percent versus the high rate of 31 percent in 1980. Although their education levels continue to fall well behind that of the other Asian nationalities in 2006 through 2010, their poverty rates are relatively low and job quality relatively high, perhaps reflecting the advantages associated with their initial status as refugees and the benefits associated with that status. For both the Chinese and Vietnamese, within group variation is probably related to internal ethnic differences and a diversity of points of origin: the Sino-Vietnamese may enjoy advantages not possessed by ethnic Vietnamese, and the stream of highly educated migrants from China is accompanied by a significant number of workers and former peasants, many arriving without legal status.

Despite these complications, an Eastern-Western Hemisphere cleavage emerges, as does a rough hierarchy on each side of the divide. The fairly uniformly advantaged Filipinos stand at the top, followed by the more heterogeneous Chinese and Vietnamese. Although the Vietnamese start off as the most disadvantaged Asian origin group, their position changes significantly by the 2006 to 2010 period. Finally, Koreans appear disadvantaged in the labor market, and their relative position worsens between 1980 and more recent years. Among immigrants from the Western Hemisphere, Caribbeans and Cubans are the most advantaged, though worse off than most of the Asian groups more recently, followed by Puerto Ricans and Salvadorans and then Mexicans. According to the expectations of the working-class hypothesis, we should expect to see the lowest second-generation outcomes among the Latin American–origin groups, as they are the most disadvantaged in terms of education and occupation, and are also the most likely to arrive with undocumented status.

A look at the net difference index scores yields a roughly similar picture. The

Western-Eastern Hemisphere distinction again appears, showing higher levels of educational selectivity observed among immigrants from the Eastern Hemisphere. With index scores twice as high, all Asian groups are much more positively selected than their Western counterparts, with the exception of Caribbeans. Despite their somewhat average educational and occupational characteristics relative to other immigrants in the United States, Puerto Ricans are the only negatively selected group. The expectations of the selectivity hypothesis therefore generally align with those of the working-class hypothesis, in that slower upward mobility is expected among the Latin American groups; however, the selectivity hypothesis suggests that we should expect greater than average upward mobility among the Caribbean and Chinese immigrants.

As a first evaluation of how well the sending and receiving starting points correspond to the mobility we observe, we turn to descriptions of poverty, education, and occupation among the 1.5- and second-generation descendants of these foreign-born groups.

Poverty   In table 6.2, we examine the changes in poverty rates from the first generation in 1980 to the 1.5 and second generation in the 2006 to 2010 period. This table shows that the children of immigrants of all nationalities, both U.S.-raised and even more so U.S.-born, are far less likely to experience poverty than those born abroad. Thus Mexican immigrants who arrived in the United States as children, before enrollment in secondary school (the 1.5 generation) are 32 percent less likely to be in poverty than those who migrate later in life; for this population, poverty rates are similar to the overall Hispanic third generation and 5 percentage points lower than the poverty rates of third-generation blacks. Even though a large percentage of the U.S.-born children of Mexican immigrants grew up in poverty, they are as adults age twenty-five and older less than half as likely as the first generation to be in poverty, and show lower rates of poverty than both blacks and Hispanics of the third generation and beyond.

This pattern of intergenerational improvement is found for essentially every immigrant group observed: all display a steep decline in poverty from the first to the second generation. Moreover, in contrast to Mexican Americans, the native-born children of all Eastern Hemisphere groups report poverty rates that are lower than or indistinguishable from third-generation whites. This cross-sectional data does not directly link parents with children and may be affected by return migration and differential fertility bias among the foreign born in 1980. Still, little evidence of downward mobility appears. These data show that, rather than joining a disadvantaged minority class, every group approaches or converges with the native white norm within one generation. Moreover, the variation of poverty rates across immigrant groups drops by more than half from the first to the second generation (from 0.08 to 0.037), pointing toward the type of convergent outcomes expected by neo-assimilation theory. That many of these second-generation adults grew up in poor households, among which heads often lacked legal status for a significant time, makes this shift across generations still more remarkable.

TABLE 6.2 / Age-Adjusted Poverty Rates

	1980	2006–2010	
Whites 3+ generation	.084	.077	
Blacks 3+ generation	.252	.207	
Hispanics 3+ generation	.170	.143	

	Generation		
	1st	1.5	2nd
Western Hemisphere			
Caribbean	.182	.071	.133
Cuban	.136	.055	.069
Mexican	.235	.159	.116
Puerto Rican	.299	.202	.154
Salvadoran	.196	.081	.122
Asia			
Chinese	.127	.041	.065
Filipino	.080	.037	.067
Korean	.123	.075	.081
Vietnamese	.307	.067	.048
Standard deviation	.080	.056	.037

Source: Authors' calculations based on the U.S. 1% Census (1980) and the March Current Population Surveys (2006, 2008, 2010).
Note: Weighted percentages from the U.S. 1% Census (1980) and the March current population surveys 2006, 2008, and 2010. Age adjusted with composite second generation (2006–2010) as standard population. The 1.5 generation is defined as foreign born who immigrated before secondary school (younger than thirteen). The second generation are children born in the United States to at least one foreign-born parent. Where national origins of the mother and father differ, the national origin of the father is used. Poverty is defined as the official poverty status of the individual's household according to the definition of poverty originally developed by the Social Security Administration in 1964, later modified by federal interagency committees in 1969 and 1980.

Educational Attainment Table 6.3 displays the percentage of each group at the lowest and highest ends of the educational spectrum. Observing rates of high school noncompletion, on the one hand, and college completion on the other, we see that in most cases the second generation outperforms the first generation. Although comparing the foreign- to the U.S.-born demonstrates that rates of high school completion increase in every case, the contrast in college completion among the foreign and U.S. born is less consistent. Moreover, the pattern of change from one generation to the next varies, both across groups and depending on the benchmark.

Not surprisingly, offspring in the least skilled groups show the largest gains relative to their immigrant parents. For example, among the Mexican second generation, the percentage of those with less than a high school degree drops by more than two-thirds, and the level of college completion rises by more than four. The

TABLE 6.3 / High School and College Completion

	1980		2006–2010	
	Less than High School	College or More	Less than High School	College or More
Whites 3+ generation	.240	.200	.073	.336
Blacks 3+ generation	.441	.089	.159	.185
Hispanics 3+ generation	.475	.080	.202	.159

	Generation					
	1st		1.5		2nd	
	Less than High School	College or More	Less than High School	College or More	Less than High School	College or More
Western Hemisphere						
Caribbean	.437	.101	.217	.328	.069	.395
Cuban	.367	.175	.210	.269	.132	.384
Mexican	.782	.034	.406	.093	.239	.156
Puerto Rican	.655	.045	.274	.108	.165	.169
Salvadoran	.557	.078	.478	.164	.172	.264
Asia						
Chinese	.310	.372	.192	.552	.043	.669
Filipino	.227	.431	.142	.389	.048	.426
Korean	.269	.313	.178	.481	.114	.508
Vietnamese	.409	.122	.281	.363	.186	.426
Standard deviation	.185	.149	.111	.161	.067	.163

Source: Authors' calculations based on the U.S. 1% Census (1980) and the March Current Population Surveys (2006, 2008, 2010).
Note: Weighted percentages from the U.S. 1% Census (1980) and the March current population surveys (2006, 2008, and 2010). Age adjusted with composite second generation (2006–2010) as standard population. The 1.5 generation is defined as foreign born who immigrated before secondary school (younger than thirteen). The second generation are children born in the United States to at least one foreign-born parent. Where national origins of the mother and father differ, the national origin of the father is used. High school completion includes GED. College completion includes a bachelor's degree or higher.

gains for Salvadorans are similar; among the Vietnamese, the most disadvantaged of the Asian groups, the U.S. born are two and a half times more likely to have completed college than those born abroad. For comparison, although native high school completion also increased dramatically from 1980 to the 2006 to 2010 period, the native-born college completion rates increases pale in comparison with the large gains made by the children of Western Hemisphere and Vietnamese immigrants.

Other Eastern Hemisphere immigrants display somewhat more modest success: the Chinese and Korean intergenerational comparisons show gains more in line with native whites; among the Filipinos, college completion rates are indistinguishable between the first generation and the second. This kind of convergence toward the receiving country mean, disadvantaged immigrant groups improving and advantaged groups maintaining or falling in their relative educational position, is largely in line with traditional assimilation theory.

Despite this convergence, large differences between the second generation and native whites remain, underscoring the enduring legacy of a low receiving country starting point at the time of arrival. Thus, significant improvement from first to second generation still leaves Mexican immigrant offspring well below the levels for the white native born. Although the greatest gap involves college completion, rates of high school completion show that Mexicans are well short of catch-up on this count as well.

On the other hand, one also notices the importance of sending country selectivity, particularly in college completion rates. Despite a first-generation educational and occupational profile nearly as disadvantaged as that of the Mexicans and Puerto Ricans, the children of more positively selected Salvadoran immigrants attain higher education than their counterparts do. The influence of source country selectivity is also consistent with the pattern among the Caribbean and Chinese second generation, who make greater strides in college education relative to the first generation than Filipinos and Koreans, among whom there is evidence of maintenance or even regression toward the mean from the very high education levels of their immigrant parents. The findings of nearly universal improvement from first to second generation align well with neo-assimilation theory, as does the decreasing variation in college noncompletion rates among immigrant groups with each generation. Yet the continued lower college and high school completion rates of the Latin American groups support the working-class hypothesis, and levels of variation in upward mobility between Asian and Latin American groups attest to the importance of sending country selectivity.

Occupational Attainment Further evidence of catch-up appears when the focus turns to occupational attainment (see table 6.4). In the first generation, only the Chinese and Filipinos have international socioeconomic index (ISEI) scores at or above the white mean. In the second generation, by contrast, only Salvadorans, Mexicans, and Puerto Ricans have scores below the white mean. Moreover, every group improves in occupational status from one generation to the next.

TABLE 6.4 / Mean Occupational Status Scores

Native Group	1980	2006–2010	
White	45.9	49.1	
Black	40.3	44.4	
Hispanic	41.8	45.5	

	Generation		
	1st	1.5	2nd
Western Hemisphere			
Caribbean	39.5	50.1	51.1
Cuban	44.3	50.6	53.8
Mexican	36.5	42.1	45.0
Puerto Rican	39.1	44.2	46.4
Salvadoran	36.9	44.0	47.5
Asia			
Chinese	46.9	52.4	56.6
Filipino	46.5	53.3	55.1
Korean	43.4	47.4	54.1
Vietnamese	41.0	51.1	52.1
Standard deviation	3.900	4.063	4.126

Source: Authors' calculations based on the U.S. 1% Census (1980) and the March Current Population Surveys (2006, 2008, 2010).
Note: Weighted means from the U.S. 1% Census (1980) and the March current population surveys (2006, 2008, and 2010). Age adjusted with composite second generation (2006–2010) as standard population. The 1.5 generation is defined as foreign born who immigrated before secondary school (younger than thirteen). The second generation are children born in the United States to at least one foreign-born parent. Where national origins of the mother and father differ, the national origin of the father is used. Occupational status scores are created from ISCO-88 occupation codes into the International Socio-Economic Index Scores (Ganzeboom and Treiman 1996).

We also note considerable variation in occupational assimilation trajectories. As would be expected from their education profiles, the Mexican and Salvadoran second generation make large gains relative to the first generation. The change in ISEI scores from first to second generations is roughly equivalent to a shift from a semi-skilled factory worker to a factory supervisor, making the intergenerational contrast quite similar to the earlier experience of Poles or Italians (Perlmann 2005). Although occupational upgrading of this sort is a significant improvement, the occupational status of these second-generation groups continues to lag behind the status of third-generation whites.

As noted, all of the other second-generation groups enjoy ISEI scores that match or exceed the native white benchmark. Every group, with the exception of Puerto Ricans, experiences at least a 9 point increase in their average score. Given that the Korean second generation does not quite achieve the educational attainment of the first generation, their higher ISEI scores suggest that they are largely free of the problems—most notably, lack of U.S.-appropriate skills and credentials—that stand in the way of the Korean foreign born.

These patterns of change in occupational status again provide no evidence of the stagnation or decline expected by segmented assimilation, but the intergenerational changes among Salvadorans and Mexicans seem to bear out the working-class incorporation hypothesis. Moreover, differences in the degree of upward mobility in this indicator is generally low: each group makes large and similar gains from the first to second generation, such that the ethnic inequality declines between all immigrant groups and native whites but the differences between different immigrant nationalities persists across generations.

In sum, our review of these three indicators points toward nearly universal upward mobility, as expected by assimilation theories, albeit at different rates for different groups, as suggested both by the working-class and selectivity hypotheses. Because the CPS does not allow us to directly compare children with parents, these indicators are impressionistic; still, there is little evidence of any substantial downward mobility. The low educational attainment and occupational status of the children of Mexican and Salvadoran immigrants does give pause, however, before we can discard a related concern of substantial second-generation disadvantage. Although Salvadorans and Mexicans avoid the higher rates of poverty experienced by older native minority groups, their higher than average rates of high school noncompletion and lower occupational attainment may indicate significant hardship, roughly comparable to that of third-generation blacks and Hispanics.

Intergenerational Mobility with IIMMLA

To more directly assess both the mechanisms behind the variation in outcomes observed and whether a significant minority of the second generation are experiencing downward mobility, we now turn to the IIMMLA data, focusing on the relationship between parents' and child's educational and occupational attainment.

Educational attainment is measured as the respondent's years of education at the time of survey. Respondents reported both the number of years they and their parents attended any school (grades in grammar and high school and years of study at postsecondary institutions), which were translated into years of education. Both mother's and father's education are used in all analyses.

Occupational attainment of father and respondent is measured as the primary occupation, recoded from census codes into Treiman's occupational prestige scores. We use father's occupation because approximately a third of our respondents reported that their mothers did not work. Parental occupational attainment is only gathered for the second generation; this analysis therefore omits the native comparison samples. Second-generation respondents who have never worked, or who reported that their father did not work or who could not answer questions about their father (N=215, or 6 percent of the second-generation sample) were not imputed for these variables and are omitted. We emphasize again that nearly half of our sample is still enrolled in school, as well as beginning their careers, and so these estimates are likely lower than what the respondent's *eventual* occupational attainment will be.[3]

We measure *generation* status much like the CPS: the first generation are those who arrived at ages thirteen and older, the 1.5 generation those who arrived before the age of thirteen, the second generation those born in the United States to two foreign-born parents, and the 2.5 generation those who have one U.S.-born parent.

Legal status is a central explanatory variable in the working-class hypothesis and an important part of the context of reception within segmented assimilation theory. IIMMLA contains a host of questions surrounding the present legal status and status on arrival of immigrant parents as well as the 1.5-generation respondents in the sample. Through the process of elimination, the answers to these questions can be combined to create a four-category indicator of legal status: children of immigrants who have had citizenship since birth, naturalized citizens, those respondents who currently have a green card or are applying for U.S. citizenship, and a residual category of other statuses. This small residual group contains first- and 1.5-generation youth who arrived under a variety of original statuses (student, refugee, temporary worker) as well as young adults who are undocumented.

Origins are again assigned as the country of birth for foreign-born respondents; for the second generation, we report the nativity of the foreign-born parent, where these disagree, the father's country of origin is used. Due to differences in the data available in IIMMLA and CPS, we substitute third-generation Hispanics with third-generation Mexicans in the Los Angeles region as a comparison group, and restrict analysis to a smaller subset of national origins: Mexican, Salvadoran, Chinese, Filipino, Vietnamese, and Korean.

As to *controls*, all analyses are conducted for men and women separately. Age is also included as a control in all analyses.

In the *analysis*, respondent's years of education and occupational prestige are regressed on mother and father's education and father's occupational prestige. The MI suite in Stata 11 is used to analyze the thirty multiply imputed IIMMLA datasets.

Descriptive Statistics

Descriptive statistics for the IMMLA dataset is found in table 6.5. The educational and occupational characteristics in this sample are roughly similar to those observed in the nationally representative CPS data. All of the Eastern Hemisphere second-generation groups in IIMMLA have more education than the native comparison groups, and the variation in education among second-generation respondents is lower than that for their immigrant parents. Mexican and Salvadoran second-generation respondents have similar educational attainment as third-generation Mexican Americans, and nearly two years less education on average

TABLE 6.5 / Descriptive Statistics, Los Angeles 2004

	Whites 3+	Blacks 3+	Mexicans 3+	Mexico	Salvador	China	Philippines	Korea	Vietnam
Respondent's years education	14.8	13.7	13.4	13.1	13.5	16.3	15.2	16.0	15.7
Father's years education	14.4	13.0	12.3	8.1	10.2	14.8	15.0	15.0	13.1
Mother's years education	13.9	13.3	12.0	8.1	9.6	13.0	15.0	13.8	10.9
Respondent's occupational prestige				43.2	43.9	53.3	48.6	52.3	50.5
Father's occupational prestige				36.5	36.6	48.3	49.9	47.7	43.5
Generation status									
1st: arrived age thirteen+				.093	.092	.121	.049	.091	.119
1.5: arrived before thirteen				.307	.466	.450	.468	.606	.687
2nd: born in United States				.457	.411	.375	.405	.266	.187
2.5: one U.S.-born parent				.187	.031	.054	.078	.037	.008
Legal status									
Birthright citizen				.644	.442	.429	.482	.303	.194
Naturalized citizen				.176	.288	.532	.444	.583	.742
Permanent resident				.112	.221	.032	.067	.098	.060
Other				.067	.049	.007	.007	.014	.004

Source: Authors' calculations based on the Immigration and Intergenerational Mobility in Metropolitan Los Angeles (2004).

Note: Men and women, age twenty-two to thirty-nine. IIMMLA Multiple Imputed Data (M=30), mean and proportion estimates using Stata mi estimation commands. The first generation is defined as foreign born who immigrated at age thirteen or older. The 1.5 generation defined as foreign born who immigrated before secondary school (younger than thirteen). The second generation are children born in the United States to two foreign-born parents, 2.5 generation defined as those with one foreign born, one native-born parent. Where foreign national origins of the mother and father differ, the national origin of the father is used. Occupational status scores are created from ISCO-88 occupation codes into the International Socio-Economic Index Scores (Ganzeboom and Treiman 1996).

than native whites. Information on parental occupational prestige is available only for the children of immigrants, but the ranking is consistent with education, Mexican and Salvadoran immigrant parents displaying occupations nearly 10 points lower than their Chinese, Filipino, and Korean counterparts, two-thirds of a standard deviation lower on the occupational prestige scale. Occupational inequality among the second generation, though compressed, remains, Eastern Hemisphere respondents reporting higher prestige jobs than Western Hemisphere respondents.

National-origin groups also show compositional differences in generational and legal status. Time of arrival is important. For instance, whereas 80 percent of Vietnamese respondents were born abroad, fewer than 50 percent of Mexican respondents were. Mexican-origin respondents are also more likely than other groups to have a U.S.-born parent, likely attributable to the longer duration of Mexican migration to the United States and thus enhanced prospects for within-ethnic marriages to the native born. Mexican and Salvadoran respondents stand out as the only groups with a non-negligible proportion who are not citizens or green card holders. All other groups are much more likely to be naturalized citizens.

Educational Mobility

Table 6.6 presents coefficients regressing fathers' and mothers' educational attainment on the educational attainment of the respondent. Men and women are modeled separately. Immediately apparent is that the relationship between parental education and respondent education is more consistent and stronger for the native born than for any immigrant group. Each additional year of mother's education is associated with approximately a 0.2 to 0.3 increase in respondent's education for native black and white men and women, whereas mother's education has essentially no relationship with respondent's education for Korean, Chinese, and Vietnamese second-generation men and women, as well as Salvadoran men. Where a relationship exists, it is much weaker, only passing 0.2 for Filipino and Salvadoran women. Father's education is less consistently statistically significant, though it does exert an independent effect for third-generation and second-generation Mexican, Filipino, and Korean men, as well as native white and second-generation Chinese and Mexican women. In general, variation in the intergenerational transmission of educational attainment is high, and mobility for all immigrant origin groups is higher than that for native whites, and to a lesser extent native blacks and Mexicans as well.

The intercepts display a similar level of variation: Western Hemisphere respondents, along with Filipinos and the native born, have much lower intercepts than the children of Chinese, Korean, and Vietnamese immigrants. The relationship between average parental education and respondent's education for each group is plotted in figures 6.5 and 6.6, which provide a clearer picture of each group's respective intercepts and slopes. As expected by neo-assimilation theory, and already observed in the CPS, every immigrant group except Filipinos displays con-

TABLE 6.6 / Parental Education and Completed Schooling, Los Angeles 2004

	Men			Women		
	Father's Education	Mother's Education	Intercept	Father's Education	Mother's Education	Intercept
Whites 3+ generation	.039	.320	7.757	.146	.318	7.974
SE	.062	.074		.067	.073	
Blacks 3+ generation	.101	.206	7.810	.095	.190	9.511
SE	.063	.084		.059	.062	
Mexican 3+ Generation	.212	.160	6.764	.137	.224	8.716
SE	.079	.073		.081	.074	
Mexico	.092	.089	9.842	.080	.126	10.890
SE	.033	.035		.031	.031	
Salvadoran	.022	.045	11.166	.045	.215	10.643
SE	.059	.066		.082	.070	
Chinese	.076	.053	12.717	.135	-.013	14.010
SE	.067	.066		.059	.063	
Filipino	.160	.197	8.088	.113	.232	9.652
SE	.079	.093		.083	.077	
Korean	.124	.009	12.149	.074	.042	13.927
SE	.068	.081		.074	.082	
Vietnamese	.019	.083	12.703	.069	-.006	14.378
SE	.068	.061		.075	.052	

Source: Authors' calculations based on the Immigration and Intergenerational Mobility in Metropolitan Los Angeles (2004).
Note: Men and women, age twenty-two to thirty-nine. IIMMLA Multiple Imputed Data (M=30), effects and standard errors computed using Stata mi estimation commands. Dependent variable is respondent's years of schooling. Models include controls for respondent's age.

vergence in their intercepts: the second generation intercepts are closer to the mean years of education of fourteen years than the mean outcomes among the foreign born. Three different integration pathways are clearly visible. Chinese, Vietnamese, and Korean respondents form one pattern—high intercepts and flat slopes. As expected by the segmented assimilation and selectivity perspectives, these highly selected groups perform well regardless of parental educational background.

The next identifiable pattern includes Mexican and Salvadoran respondents, and is what we would expect from the working-class hypothesis: they do not reproduce the low levels of education of their parents, as evidenced by their higher intercepts than both native-born groups and their parents, yet they share with Eastern Hemisphere respondents a flatter slope than native groups. This combination of flat slope and lower intercept, however, means that their attainment is lower than other groups among the children of higher educated parents. The end story is consistent with the working-class hypothesis: strong improvement over parents, but continued disadvantage relative to other groups.

FIGURE 6.5 / Parental and Respondent Education, Men

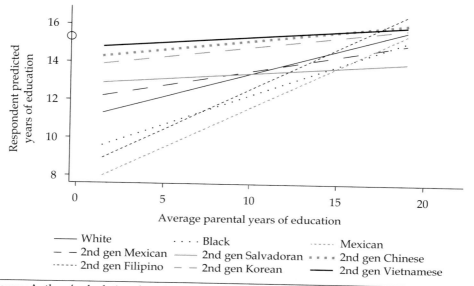

Source: Authors' calculations based on the Immigration and Intergenerational Mobility in Metropolitan Los Angeles (2004).

FIGURE 6.6 / Parental and Respondent Education, Women

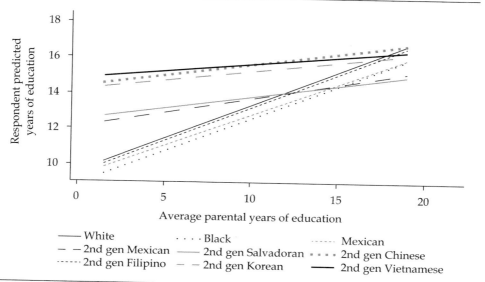

Source: Authors' calculations based on the Immigration and Intergenerational Mobility in Metropolitan Los Angeles (2004).

Finally, both Filipinos and native groups show a steep slope and high class re-production, yet Filipinos are disadvantaged relative to native whites in terms of their intercepts, Filipino men in particular, though their steeper slopes mean that they outperform whites with higher parental education levels. The Filipino inte-gration path is distinct from other Eastern Hemisphere immigrants, though gener-ally advantaged over Western Hemisphere immigrants.

In sum, all groups are converging across generations, as evidenced by the lower variability in educational outcomes among the second generation than among the first. Korean, Chinese, and Vietnamese respondents display intergenerational mo-bility patterns consistent with the selectivity hypothesis, Salvadorans and Mexi-cans consistent with the working-class hypothesis, and Filipinos most closely mir-roring the middle-class mobility process expected by segmented assimilation. No group shows stagnation—every group has intercepts on par with or above the mean education levels of the most disadvantaged foreign-born groups, Salvador-ans and Mexicans.

We now turn to two of the central explanatory variables in the segmented as-similation and working-class hypothesis: legal status and parental occupation. Table 6.7 shows the relationship between these variables and years education, re-stricting analysis to the children of immigrants and including controls for immi-grant origins and parental education. The Mexican second generation is now the omitted category. The first columns for men and women also control for genera-tional status, the second includes occupational prestige of the father, and the third controls for legal status and father's occupational prestige, but generation is omit-ted because it is perfectly correlated with legal status.

Generational status collectively is significant only for women, and the 1.5 and second generation report higher educational attainment than foreign-born women who arrived after the age of thirteen. This advantage for the U.S. born is significant only for the children of two foreign-born parents, however; the 2.5 generation does not report higher educational attainment than those who were foreign born, net of parental education.

As expected by the working-class hypothesis, regardless of their education and legal status, the children of immigrant men in working-class occupations are lower achievers. The effect is modest, a standard deviation increase (15 points) in father's occupational status is associated with a 0.17 increase in years of education, and this effect is significant for male respondents only. The effect of legal status is much more pronounced: men with only a green card report three-quarters of a year less schooling than their birthright citizen counterparts, and women with a green card have over a year less schooling, net of parental education and father's occupational prestige. Both respondents with legal statuses other than green card and those who are undocumented report less schooling, men slightly less than one year and women more than two.

Our estimates for the effect of legal status may be overestimated because of un-measured characteristics that both preclude naturalization and affect educational attainment. Unfortunately, we cannot estimate the degree of bias here, but the dif-ference between those with and without citizenship appears to be both strong and independent of two major confounders, namely parental education and occupa-

TABLE 6.7 / Generation, Prestige, and Status, and Completed Schooling, Los Angeles 2004

	Years Completed Schooling: Men			Years Completed Schooling: Women		
	Model 1	Model 2	Model 3	Model 1	Model 2	Model 3
Generation (1st generation omitted)						
1.5 generation	.402	.455		.699	.714	
SE	-.241	-.241		-.239	-.241	
2nd generation	.472	.508		1.104	1.114	
SE	-.250	-.250		-.248	-.250	
2.5 generation	.496	.540		.499	.499	
SE	-.295	-.295		-.287	-.288	
Father's occupational prestige		.013	.011		.005	.005
SE		-.005	-.005		-.005	-.005
Legal status (birth citizens omitted)						
Naturalized citizens			.156			.036
SE			-.141			-.137
Green card / applying for citizenship			-.746			-1.181
SE			-.210			-.213
Other status			-.833			-2.443
SE			-.367			-.407
Parental education, country of origin fixed effects, and interactions	X	X	X	X	X	X

Source: Authors' calculations based on the Immigration and Intergenerational Mobility in Metropolitan Los Angeles (2004).
Note: Men and women, age twenty-two to thirty-nine. IIMMLA Multiple Imputed Data (M=30), marginal effects and standard errors computed using Stata mi estimation commands. Dependent variable is respondent's years of schooling. Models include controls for respondent's age, country of origin, mother's education, father's education, and interaction terms between parental education and country of origin.

tional status. In contrast, there is no difference between naturalized and birthright citizens, and that between those with a green card and those with temporary status is also insignificant for both men and women at the 0.05 level. It is important to remember from the descriptive statistics that the majority of noncitizen respondents in this sample are of Mexican origin; however, the negative association between noncitizen status and educational attainment remains strong and significant even if Mexican-origin respondents are omitted from the analysis.

As expected by both segmented assimilation and the working-class perspectives, a lack of citizenship and working-class employment in the first generation delays the academic performance of the second generation. The majority of noncitizens are Mexican and Salvadoran, and thus legal disadvantage has the most substantive application to these groups. However, controlling for compositional differences in legal status and parental occupational prestige does little to account for the difference in educational attainment between Eastern and Western Hemisphere respondents. The main effect (not shown) of Chinese, Korean, and Vietnamese origins on educational attainment—relative to Mexican origins—remains large and generally unaltered when we include father's occupational prestige and legal status in the model. Even after controlling for these differences, these Eastern Hemisphere groups continue to have approximately three years more education than their Mexican counterparts.

Occupational Status

Intergenerational transmission processes among the children of immigrants has been shown to differ across socioeconomic indicators (Waldinger and Feliciano 2004). Next, we turn to the relationship between father and respondent's occupational prestige. Because IIMMLA did not gather occupational information for the native comparison groups, this analysis is restricted to the children of immigrants. The slopes and intercepts for the relationship between national origins, father's prestige, and respondent's prestige are found in table 6.8.

We first see that the relationship between father and respondents' occupation is essentially nonexistent, especially for women. Only Korean women, and Vietnamese and Filipino men, display a significant relationship between father and respondent's occupational status. The strongest relationship observed, for Vietnamese men, is that one standard deviation in father's occupational prestige score (15 points) is associated with slightly more than one-quarter of a standard deviation in respondent's occupational prestige (3.6 points). Origin differences in intergenerational transmission differ by gender—among women, the strongest intergenerational transmission is among Koreans, whereas for men, the strongest relationships between father and son are reported for Vietnamese and Filipinos. Because of the young age of this sample, the relationships observed with this data are tentative at best; it is well known that intergenerational occupational and income relationships observed among recent labor market entrants is lower than for older men (Solon 2002). Still, despite the young age of the sample, we can already observe large differences in the main effects of national origins, as reflected in the intercepts. Most notably, we see that Chinese and Korean men, and all Eastern Hemisphere women, have higher intercepts than the other origin groups.

Plotted expected values provide a useful overview of these relationships. Figures 6.7 and 6.8 plot the relationship between father and respondent's occupational prestige. Looking first at men, we see again three transmission patterns, though the origin group constellations differ slightly from those we observed with educational transmission. At the top, we see the children of positively selected Korean and Chinese immigrants have minimal slopes and high intercepts. Mexican and Salvadoran men show working-class mobility at the bottom, with fairly modest slopes and low intercepts. In the middle, displaying mainstream or middle-class mobility patterns, are Filipino and Vietnamese men, with low intercepts but sharper slopes that allow them to overtake men from other origins at higher ends of the distribution of father's prestige. Patterns among women are similar, though not identical. Again, as anticipated by the selectivity hypothesis,

TABLE 6.8   /   Occupational Prestige, Los Angeles 2004

	Men		Women	
	Father's Prestige	Intercept	Father's Prestige	Intercept
Mexican	.104	37.7	.009	44.5
SE	.068		.065	
Salvadoran	.116	37.9	.084	42.8
SE	.112		.131	
Chinese	.041	51.0	.099	48.9
SE	.074		.068	
Filipino	.195	38.0	.064	46.2
SE	.087		.073	
Korean	.011	50.2	.140	47.1
SE	.082		.074	
Vietnamese	.241	39.4	.008	50.8
SE	.103		.082	

Source: Authors' calculations based on the Immigration and Intergenerational Mobility in Metro-politan Los Angeles (2004).
Note: Men and women age twenty-two to thirty-nine with at least one foreign-born parent. IIM-MLA Multiple Imputed Data (M=30), marginal effects and standard errors computed using Stata mi estimation commands. Dependent variable is the occupational prestige of respondent's pri-mary occupation, father's occupational prestige derived from respondent's report of father's oc-cupation during respondent's childhood. Models include controls for respondent's age.

Korean and Chinese women have high intercepts and shallow slopes, though steeper than men's. Mexican and Salvadoran women have shallow or flat slopes, and low intercepts. Vietnamese women display flatter slopes, with higher inter-cepts than Vietnamese men, breaking away from the Filipino pattern.

In sum, intergenerational transmission in occupational prestige is similar to educational transmission: intercepts for all groups are higher than the average oc-cupational prestige scores of the most disadvantaged foreign-born groups, Mexi-can and Salvadorans. They are also somewhat less varied than the average occu-pational prestige scores of their immigrant parents. Korean, Chinese, and to a lesser extent Vietnamese respondents display a highly advantaged, select or ethnic mobility pattern of high intercepts and flat slopes. Salvadoran and Mexican re-spondents display flat slopes and low intercepts, a working-class or less-selective transmission pattern. Finally, Filipinos display a more mainstream or middle-class incorporation pattern of stronger intergenerational transmission, at least for men.

We next turn to the effect of generation, parental education, and legal status on second generation occupational prestige. The results of these models are found in table 6.9. Generational status is collectively insignificant at the 0.05 level for women. For men, 1.5-generation respondents who arrived before the age of thir-teen or were born in the United States have higher occupational prestige than first-generation respondents, but this association is primarily accounted for by the

FIGURE 6.7 / Occupational Prestige, Men

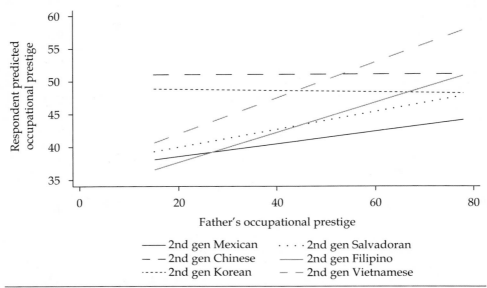

Source: Authors' calculations based on the Immigration and Intergenerational Mobility in Metropolitan Los Angeles (2004).

FIGURE 6.8 / Occupational Prestige, Women

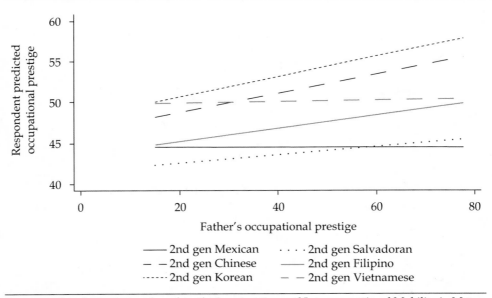

Source: Authors' calculations based on the Immigration and Intergenerational Mobility in Metropolitan Los Angeles (2004).

TABLE 6.9 / Generation, Education, and Status, and Occupational Prestige, Los Angeles 2004

	Men			Women		
	Model 1	Model 2	Model 3	Model 1	Model 2	Model 3
Generation (1st generation omitted)						
1.5 generation	4.015	3.450		-1.849	-1.966	
SE	-1.580	-1.572		-1.428	-1.426	
2nd generation	3.206	1.897		-.927	-1.246	
SE	-1.604	-1.615		-1.459	-1.467	
2.5 generation	3.908	2.106		-1.974	-2.549	
SE	-1.890	-1.892		-1.667	-1.689	
Mother's education		.235	.223		.063	.005
SE		-.133	-.133		-.113	-.112
Father's education		.377	.355		.203	.187
SE		-.135	-.134		-.114	-.113
Legal status (birth citizens omitted)						
Naturalized citizens			2.925			1.024
SE			-.886			-.784
Green card / applying for citizenship			-2.630			-2.796
SE			-1.344			-1.252
Other status			-6.664			-8.149
			-2.391			-2.487
Father's occupational prestige, country of origin fixed effects, and interactions	X	X	X	X	X	X

Source: Authors' calculations based on the Immigration and Intergenerational Mobility in Metropolitan Los Angeles (2004).
Note: IIMMLA Multiple Imputed Data (M=30), marginal effects and standard errors computed using Stata mi estimation commands. Dependent variable is occupational prestige of respondent's primary occupation. Models include controls for respondent's age, country of origin, father's occupational prestige, and interaction terms between parental education and country of origin.

higher education of the parents of the 1.5 and second generation. Father's education is significantly associated with occupation for both men and women, but only very modestly: each year of father's education is associated with only one-fifth to one-third of one point on the occupational prestige scale. Ignoring possible issues of endogeneity mentioned, legal status appears to be the most important variable in predicting occupational prestige: those most likely to be undocumented ("other" status) are in occupations 7 and 8 points lower on the occupational prestige scale than birthright citizen men and women, respectively, net of parental occupation and education. Because Mexican and Salvadoran respondents make up the majority of those without citizenship, legal status accounts for some of their occupational disadvantage.

CONCLUSION

The contemporary second generation is beginning to transform the United States as the offspring of the "new immigrants" from elsewhere in the Americas and from Asia move through schools and enter the labor market. As this population has grown, the related research has burgeoned. The questions of whether these immigrant offspring will move ahead and why some groups might progress at differing rates have sparked considerable debate.

Debate over this issue began on a note of inflected pessimism, because scholars have underscored the ways in which the circumstances of contemporary migration, combined with the low skills of many migrants, are likely to throw up obstacles to second-generation progress. Many immigrants are converging on low-skill, poorly paid, stigmatized jobs and encountering a negative reception, the most salient feature of which has been unauthorized status. The low-skilled foreign born in particular are adversely affected by labor market trends — most notably the shift from a manufacturing to service-based economy, increasing the earnings premium placed on higher education (Goldin and Katz 2007). Given these hurdles, researchers have wondered whether the U.S.-born descendants of today's immigrants can surmount the difficult conditions that they encounter (Portes and Zhou 1993; Portes and Rumbaut 2001). Hypothesizing segmented assimilation, these scholars forecast a future of lasting inequality, in which the immigrant offspring of working-class, racialized migrants—Mexicans, Central Americans, Caribbeans, and others—will stagnate or possibly even fall below the positions occupied by their working-class parents (Portes and Fernández-Kelly 2008).

Confronting this challenge head on, Alba and Nee's recent effort to update assimilation theory for the twenty-first century — *Remaking the American Mainstream* (2003) — contends that the forces propelling advancement for immigrants of all skill levels remain strong. On the one hand are significant similarities in the characteristics and labor market placement of immigrants in the current and past eras of mass migration. Whether past or present, whether from Italy or Mexico, peasant migrants and their descendants are expected to follow a similar path of upward mobility in the labor market. On the other hand, conditions affecting all immigrants, regardless of skill level, have changed in one crucial respect: unlike the last era of mass migration, labor markets are now structured in such a way as to diminish discrimination. This shift facilitates movement into the economic mainstream, "that part of society within which ethnic and racial origins have at most minor impacts on life chances" (Alba and Nee 2003, 12) and where good jobs—of the same quality as those accessed by Italian, Polish, and other children of the last mass migration—can still be found.

If the predictions of the segmented assimilation model are accurate, we would expect the high poverty rates and disadvantaged educational and occupational profiles of the foreign born to prevail among their U.S.-born children and grandchildren; Alba and Nee's revised assimilation model suggests the opposite. As we have shown in this chapter, neither perspective provides an adequate account of today's reality. On the one hand, little evidence suggests that the offspring of the least skilled immigrants are prevented from moving ahead, let alone from falling behind their parents. At the aggregate level, all indicators point to second-generation progress, whether the focus is trained on poverty, education, or occupation. Analysis of intergenerational changes at the individual level underscores those conclusions: whether occupational or educational, intergenerational transmission is lower among the children of immigrants than the children of the native born, a generalization that holds for all groups. Even among the most disadvantaged groups, among whom a parental experience of undocumented status is common, upward mobility for the offspring of low-skilled immigrants prevails.

On the other hand, comparisons across groups show variations in mobility trajectories not anticipated by either of the two most influential approaches. Thus, although the children of unskilled Mexican or Salvadoran immigrants are not stagnating at the bottom, contrary to the expectations of segmented assimilation, among more advantaged Mexican or Salvadoran parents the successful transmission of their resources seems problematic, contrary to the expectations of the standard assimilation approach. This pattern of low intergenerational transmission combined with low intercepts, a pattern of upward movement from the bottom with impediments from the middle on is instead more compatible with our hypothesis of working-class incorporation. Underscoring the ways in which the circumstances of migration are likely to slow advancement for the children of working-class immigrants, the working-class hypothesis is borne out by the analysis of intergenerational mobility, where we see that acquisition of U.S. citizenship and higher parental occupational status exercise positive effects on second-generation mobility.

However, our own approach only goes so far, failing to illuminate the full range of variation among the increasingly diverse population of immigrant offspring, a problem shared by the standard assimilation approach, which forecasts upward movement without generating expectations regarding differences in rates or patterns. As we have noted, disparities in attainment and mobility often fall along an Eastern-Western Hemisphere divide, Eastern Hemisphere immigrants entering with more advantages and then experiencing greater success in transmitting those resources from parents to children. Yet that generalization also requires further complication, given significant differences within both the Eastern and the Western Hemisphere streams. Furthermore, some of the seemingly more advantaged groups, most notably the Filipinos, do not seem to enjoy the uniformly high performance of the other groups of the Eastern Hemisphere, displaying intergenerational transmission patterns that more closely mirror the native born—a middle-class or mainstream rather than selective or ethnic mobility integration pattern. As we suggest, these intergroup disparities may reflect differences in at-origin selectivity. Thus, the most successful group of immigrant offspring—enjoying the most consistently high education and occupational status—are the Chinese, who are also a highly selective migration stream.

In the end, explaining the full range of interethnic variation may exceed the capacity of any of the prevailing approaches. The number of groups is small; each is affected by unique historical experiences, at least to some degree; and each is also characterized by a certain degree of at-origin heterogeneity, though that too is highly variable. Perhaps the greatest value added is through further close analysis of the children of Mexican immigrants, at once the overwhelmingly largest group of immigrant offspring, the one among whom undocumented status is most prevalent, and therefore the one most likely to be affected by the increasingly adverse conditions to which undocumented immigrants are exposed. It is the experience of this population that will largely determine the future of the new second generation and the degree to which today's immigrant offspring capture the American dream to which their parents have surely aspired.

NOTES

1. In a similar survey, the Children of Immigrants Longitudinal Survey (CILS), approximately 20 percent of second-generation youth surveyed in early adolescence had moved out of their childhood city of residence by their mid-twenties. These respondents had higher educational attainment than those who remained.
2. Cynthia Feliciano (2005), following Stanley Lieberson (1980), calculated the net difference index along all points of the education distribution, as the measure of selectivity. The net difference index is calculated based on the percentage of immigrants with the same attainment as nonmigrants, the percentage of immigrants with more education than nonmigrants, and the percentage of immigrants with less education than nonmigrants.
3. Restricting the sample to age twenty-five and older does not substantively alter the results.

REFERENCES

Akresh, Ilana R., and Reanne Frank. 2008. "Health Selection Among New Immigrants." *American Journal of Public Health* 98(11): 2058–64.

Alba, Richard D. 2008. "Why We Still Need a Theory of Mainstream Assimilation." *Migration und Integration: Kölner Zeitschrift für Soziologie und Sozialpyschologie Sonderheft* 48(1): 37–56.

Alba, Richard D., and Victor Nee. 2003. *Remaking the American Mainstream: Assimilation and Contemporary Immigration.* Cambridge, Mass.: Harvard University Press.

Bean, Frank D., and Gillian Stevens. 2003. *America's Newcomers and the Dynamics of Diversity.* New York: Russell Sage Foundation.

Bean, Frank D., Susan K. Brown, and Ruben G. Rumbaut. 2006. "Mexican Immigrant Political and Economic Incorporation." *Perspectives on Politics* 4(2): 309–13.

Bean, Frank D., Mark A. Leach, Susan K. Brown, James D. Bachmeier, and John R. Hipp. 2011. "The Educational Legacy of Unauthorized Migration: Comparisons Across U.S.-Immigrant Groups in How Parents' Status Affects Their Offspring." *International Migration Review* 45(2): 348–85.

Blau, Francine D., and Lawrence M. Kahn. 2007. "Gender and Assimilation Among Mexican Americans." In *Mexican Immigration,* edited by George J. Borjas. Chicago: University of Chicago and National Bureau of Economic Research.

Borjas, George J. 1992. "Ethnic Capital and Intergenerational Mobility." *Quarterly Journal of Economics* 107(1): 123–50.

Brown, Susan K. 2007. "Delayed Spatial Assimilation: Multigenerational Incorporation of the Mexican-Origin Population in Los Angeles." *City & Community* 6(3): 193–209.

Card, David, John DiNardo, and Eugena Estes. 2000. "The More Things Change: Immigrants and the Children of Immigrants in the 1940s, the 1970s, and the 1990s." *NBER Chapters* no. 6057. Cambridge, Mass.: National Bureau of Economic Research.

Chiquiar, Daniel, and Gordon H. Hanson. 2005. "International Migration, Self-Selection, and the Distribution of Wages: Evidence from Mexico and the United States." *Journal of Political Economy* 113(2): 239–81.

Chiswick, Barry R. 1999. "Are Immigrants Favorably Self-Selected?" *The American Economic Review* 89(2): 181–185.

Clemens, Michael A., Claudio E. Montenegro, and Lant Pritchett. 2008. "The Place Premium: Wage Differences for Identical Workers Across the U.S. Border." *Policy Research* working paper no. 4671. Washington, D.C.: The World Bank.

Feliciano, Cynthia. 2005a. "Does Selective Migration Matter? Explaining Ethnic Disparities in Educational Attainment Among Immigrants' Children." *International Migration Review* 39(4): 841–71.

———. 2005b. "Educational Selectivity in U.S. Immigration: How Do Immigrants Compare to Those Left Behind?" *Demography* 42(1): 131–52.

———. 2006. "Beyond the Family: The Influence of Premigration Group Status on the Educational Expectations of Immigrants' Children." *Sociology of Education* 79(4): 281–303.

Ganzeboom, Harry B. G., and Donald J. Treiman. 1996. "Internationally Comparable Measures of Occupational Status for the 1988 International Standard Classification of Occupations." *Social Science Research* 25: 201–39.

Goldin, Claudia, and Lawrence F. Katz. 2007. "Long-Run Changes in the U.S. Wage Structure: Narrowing, Widening, Polarizing." *NBER* working paper no. 13568. Cambridge, Mass.: National Bureau of Economic Research.

Heath, Anthony F., Catherine Rothon, and Elina Kilpi. 2008. "The Second Generation in Western Europe: Education, Unemployment, and Occupational Attainment." *Annual Review of Sociology* 34(August 2008): 211–35.

Kasinitz, Philip. 2008. *Inheriting the City: The Children of Immigrants Come of Age*. Cambridge, Mass.: Harvard University Press.

King, Miriam, Steven Ruggles, J. Trent Alexander, Sarah Flood, Katie Genadek, Matthew B. Schroeder, Brandon Trampe, and Rebecca Vick. 2010. "Integrated Public Use Microdata Series, Current Population Survey: Version 3.0. [Machine-readable database]." Minneapolis: University of Minnesota.

Levels, Mark, Jaap Dronkers, and Gerbert Kraaykamp. 2008. "Immigrant Children's Educational Achievement in Western Countries: Origin, Destination, and Community Effects on Mathematical Performance." *American Sociological Review* 73(5): 835–53.

Lieberson, Stanley. 1980. *A Piece of the Pie: Blacks and White Immigrants Since 1880*. Berkeley: University of California Press.

Lieberson, Stanley, and Mary C. Waters. 1988. *From Many Strands: Ethnic and Racial Groups In Contemporary America*. New York: Russell Sage Foundation.

Luthra, Renee Reichl. 2010. "Intergenerational Returns to Migration? Comparing Educational Performance on Both Sides of the German Border." *ISER* working paper 2010-34. Colchester, Essex: Institute for Social and Economic Research.

——. 2013. "Explaining Ethnic Inequality in the German Labor Market: Labor Market Institutions, Context of Reception, and Boundaries." *European Sociological Review*. doi:10.1093/esr/jcs081

Luthra, Renee Reichl, and Roger Waldinger. 2010. "Into the Mainstream? Labor Market Outcomes of Mexican-Origin Workers." *International Migration Review* 44(4): 830–68.

Perlmann, Joel. 2005. *Italians Then, Mexicans Now: Immigrant Origins and Second-Generation Progress, 1890–2000*. New York: Russell Sage Foundation.

Perlmann, Joel, and Roger Waldinger. 1997. "Second Generation Decline? Children of Immigrants, Past and Present a Reconsideration." *International Migration Review* 31(4): 893–922.

Portes, Alejandro, and Patricia Fernández-Kelly. 2008. "No Margin for Error: Educational and Occupational Achievement Among Disadvantaged Children of Immigrants." *Annals of the American Academy of Political and Social Science* 620(2008): 12–36.

Portes, Alejandro, and Rubén G. Rumbaut. 2001. *Legacies: The Story of the Immigrant Second Generation*. Berkeley: University of California Press / New York: Russell Sage Foundation.

Portes, Alejandro, and Min Zhou. 1993. "The New Second Generation: Segmented Assimilation and Its Variants." *Annals of the American Academy of Political and Social Science* 530(1993): 74–96.

Royston, Patrick. 2009. "Multiple Imputation of Missing Values: Further Update of ice, with an Emphasis on Categorical Variables." *The Stata Journal* 7(4): 455–64.

Ruggles, Steven, J. Trent Alexander, Katie Genadek, Ronald Goeken, Matthew B. Schroeder, and Matthew Sobek. 2010. "Integrated Public Use Microdata Series Version 5.0 [Machine-readable database]." Minneapolis: University of Minnesota.

Rumbaut, Rubén G., Frank D. Bean, Leo R. Chávez, Jennifer Lee, Susan K. Brown, Louis DeSipio, and Min Zhou. 2008. "Immigration and Intergenerational Mobility in Metropolitan Los Angeles (IIMMLA), 2004." Inter-University Consortium for Political and Social Research (ICPSR) [distributor].

Solon, Gary. 1999. "Intergenerational Mobility in the Labor Market." In *Handbook of Labor Economics*, vol. 3, chap. 29, edited by Orley C. Ashenfelter and David Card. Philadelphia, Pa.: Elsevier.

———. 2002. "Cross-Country Differences in Intergenerational Earnings Mobility." *Journal of Economic Perspectives* 16(1): 59–66.

Waldinger, Roger. 2007. "Did Manufacturing Matter? The Experience of Yesterday's Second Generation: A Reassessment." *International Migration Review* 41(1): 3–39.

Waldinger, Roger, and Cynthia Feliciano. 2004. "Will the New Second Generation Experience 'Downward Assimilation'? Segmented Assimilation Re-Assessed." *Ethnic and Racial Studies* 27(2): 376–402.

Waldinger, Roger, Nelson Lim, and David Cort. 2007. "Bad Jobs, Good Jobs, No Jobs? The Employment Experience of the Mexican American Second Generation." *Journal of Ethnic and Migration Studies* 33(1): 1–35.

Chapter 7

Frames of Achievement and Opportunity Horizons

Jennifer Lee and Min Zhou

In the status attainment model, family socioeconomic status (SES) — measured by parental education, occupation, income, and wealth — is the most significant variable in determining an individual's mobility outcomes (Blau and Duncan 1967; Duncan, Featherman, and Duncan 1972). Prior research in immigration has relied on this model to explain intergenerational mobility, poverty, and inequality. The children of immigrants born to parents with low human and economic capital exhibit poorer educational and occupational outcomes than their second-generation counterparts whose parents are more highly educated and more highly selected (Feliciano 2005; Kasinitz et al. 2009; see also chapters 5, 6, and 8, this volume). However, empirical evidence reveals an anomaly. Some second-generation Chinese and Vietnamese have immigrant parents who arrive to the United States with less than an elementary school education, no English-language skills, and little financial capital, yet graduate as high school valedictorians, gain admission into elite universities, and pursue graduate degrees. How do we explain the mobility patterns of these second-generation Asians, especially when they defy traditional status attainment models?

Most vexing are the patterns of academic achievement among second-generation Asians; research has shown that even when controlling for familial background, ethnicity remains significant, and being Chinese, Korean, or Vietnamese gives immigrant children an advantage in educational attainment, whereas being Mexican or Dominican results in a distinct disadvantage (Fuligni 1997; Itzigsohn 2009; Kao 1995; Kao and Tienda 1998; Kasinitz et al. 2009; Lopez 2003; Louie 2004; Luckingham 1994; Portes and Hao 2004; Steinberg 1996; Telles and Ortiz 2008; Zhou and Bankston 1998). Ethnicity matters, but largely missing from the immigration and inequality research is exactly how it matters.

In this chapter, we draw on classic sociological concepts such as frames, reference groups, and role models to illustrate how ethnicity and culture can operate as "ethnic capital" for the children of immigrants, particularly for those who lack parental human capital and hail from poor socioeconomic backgrounds. As George Borjas explains, "the skills of the next generation depend not only on what parents do but also on 'ethnic capital,' or the characteristics of the ethnic environment where children are raised" (2006, 65). We address three research questions. First, how do immigrant parents and their children frame academic success? Second, where do these frames come from? Third, how do frames influence academic achievement and mobility outcomes?

We find that frames are formed by the selectivity of immigration, which affects the reference group by which immigrants and their children measure their progress. These frames are supported by resources that are created and available within ethnic communities, and reinforced by an immigrant group's reception by the host society. More concretely, the high selectivity of Asian immigration creates a strict frame of academic achievement among 1.5- and second-generation Chinese and Vietnamese, which is supported by the accessibility of ethnic and panethnic resources; these resources help poor and working-class coethnics override their low socioeconomic background. By contrast, the low selectivity of Mexican immigration and the dearth of comparable ethnic resources limit the frame of achievement for the 1.5 and second generation. The children of Mexican immigrants may attain intergenerational mobility, but they remain at a competitive disadvantage with respect to their second-generation Chinese and Vietnamese peers. The analyses are based on 140 in-depth interviews with 1.5- and second-generation Chinese, Vietnamese, and Mexican adults randomly drawn from the survey of Immigration and Intergenerational Mobility in Metropolitan Los Angeles (IIMMLA).[1]

RECONSIDERING CULTURE, IMMIGRATION, AND INEQUALITY

For decades, sociologists had retreated from examining the relationship between culture and inequality, due, in large part, to the backlash and stigma that resulted from "the culture of poverty model" advanced by Oscar Lewis (1966). But a new generation of scholars has emerged and placed culture at the forefront of the poverty and inequality research. Departing from the generation of the past, this cadre of scholars rejects the definition of culture as a core set of values, norms, behavioral standards, and worldviews which, once formed, is self-perpetuating and immune to structural changes (Lewis 1966; Sowell 1981).

This new generation of researchers conceives of culture as meanings, beliefs, models, and frames that individuals adopt to interpret and make sense of their life experiences. In addition to refining the definition of culture, scholars use analytical concepts such as frames, narratives, schemas, repertoires, and cultural capital to aptly measure its effects. Defining and measuring culture through a more refined lens, researchers have illustrated its role in determining outcomes ranging from educational attainment, employment, community involvement, political participation, welfare receipt, to teenage pregnancy (Binder et al. 2008; Carter 2005;

Fernández-Kelly 2008; Harding 2007; Lareau 2003; Polletta 2006; Skrentny 2008; Small 2004; Small, Harding, and Lamont 2010; Smith 2007; Snow et al. 1986; Vaisey 2010; Van Hook and Bean 2009; Young 2010).

Frames

In the vast literature in the field of culture, we found the concept of frames particularly useful in understanding the mobility outcomes among members of the new second generation. Erving Goffman (1974) conceived of a frame as a lens through which we observe, interpret, and analyze our social life. Most plainly, frames are ways of understanding how the world works, and by understanding the different frames that members of different ethnic groups employ in their decision-making process, we may begin to understand the inter-group variations in attitudes and behavior. Frames, however, are not culturally intrinsic, nor do they cause particular behavior; rather, they make certain patterns of behavior possible or likely by delineating horizons of possibilities (Small, Harding, and Lamont 2010). For example, in his study of a Latino housing project in Boston, Mario Small (2004) used the concept of frames to understand the variation in community participation among its residents. He found that the frames through which the Latino residents viewed the neighborhood, rather than how much the residents valued community involvement in itself, affected participation. Residents who framed the community as a beautiful neighborhood to be preserved were more likely to participate than those who viewed the neighborhood as a ghetto that they wished to escape.

In addition, in a study of African American men in poverty, Alford Young (2010) employed the concept of frames to examine mean-making processes. He found that while most African American men adhered to the same general contours in defining "a good job" (such as salary, benefits, opportunities for promotion, personal growth, and respect), their frames differed in the degree with which the men emphasized particular features of a social reality or lived experience. Differences in the framing of situations, Young found, affected the men's orientation toward work and their employment outcomes.

Applying the concept of frames to immigration research sheds new light in understanding interethnic differences in second-generation educational achievement. We find that though immigrant parents and their children value education, the frame through which they define a *good education* differs across ethnic groups. For example, some members of the second generation frame it as graduating from high school, attending a local community college, and earning an occupational certificate that allows them to work as lab technicians or dental assistants. Others frame it as graduating as the high school valedictorian, getting into a highly competitive university, and then going to law or medical school in order to work in a high-status profession. In other words, it is not that some second-generation groups value education more than others, but rather, they construct remarkably different notions of what a good education and academic success mean depending on the frame that is accessible to them, and that which they adopt.

Ethnic Resources

Having certain values is a necessary, although not sufficient, condition to enact a frame; to do so requires support and reinforcement mechanisms. This is where ethnicity comes in. Because of the selectivity of immigration, newcomers arrive in the United States with different levels of group SES, and the children of immigrants from highly selected groups have a competitive advantage over others. Their ability to access ethnic resources—which are often created by middle-class members of the first generation—helps them to achieve mobility in spite of low parental human capital and poor socioeconomic status in three critical ways.

First, immigrants and their children, especially those from poor and working-class backgrounds, benefit from tangible resources that the ethnic economy provides—such as jobs, housing, and opportunities for self-employment for immigrant adults, and after-school tutoring, supplementary educational programs, and college preparation classes for children (Zhou 2009). Second, coethnics also benefit from intangible resources that are accessible through ethnic networks and through participation in the ethnic community. Through these networks, ethnic group members acquire relevant information needed to facilitate their children's educational attainment (Lee 2012b; Zhou and Bankston 1998; Zhou and Cho 2010). For example, information about high school rankings, neighborhoods with strong school districts, Advanced Placement (AP) classes, tutoring, and the college admissions process are often disseminated through ethnic channels—both formally through ethnic newspapers and media, and informally through kin and coethnic friendship circles—thereby making the information available across class lines. Third, the sizable presence of a strong middle-class and visible examples of successful coethnics provide role models and mobility prototypes for coethnics to emulate, and also lay out mobility pathways to follow (Borjas 2006; Fernández-Kelly 2008; Hyman and Singer 1968; Merton 1949; Zuckerman 1988; Zhou and Cho 2010). Hence, high-achieving coethnics and panethnics—rather than middle-class whites—become the reference group by which second-generation Asians measure their progress; consequently, they adopt a frame for achievement that expands their opportunity horizons in ways that defy traditional status attainment models.

DATA AND METHODS

The data include 140 face-to-face, life-history interviews with 1.5- and second-generation Mexican, Chinese, and Vietnamese randomly drawn from the Immigration and Intergenerational Mobility in Metropolitan Los Angeles survey—a telephone survey of 4,800 randomly selected 1.5- and second-generation respondents between the ages of twenty and forty in the Los Angeles metropolitan area. Because IIMMLA includes respondents from five counties (Los Angeles, Orange, San Bernardino, Riverside, and Ventura), the respondents are drawn from geographically, socioeconomically, and racially and ethnically diverse neighborhoods in the Los Angeles metropolitan area.

Lasting between one and a half and two hours, the in-depth interviews provide rich detail about the respondents' life histories by focusing on the contexts under which the respondents made choices about their educational and occupational trajectories—data that we were unable to glean from the IIMMLA survey. The interviews covered a wide array of topics related to mobility ranging from educational and employment decisions, school and work experiences, familial obligations, neighborhood and community resources, in-group and out-group perceptions, and racial-ethnic identification.

Because the study focused on how the respondents frame success, we inquired about how they defined "a good education," "doing well in school," "a good job," and "success" more generally. Their answers provided insight into the frame that the respondents adopted when measuring success, how their frame affected the decisions they made about their educational and occupational pathways, and which reference group they turned to when assessing their academic and occupational achievements. Combined with descriptive analyses of the IIMMLA survey data, the in-depth interviews provided the specific context within which respondents make decisions about their educational and occupational pursuits, which also helped to explain the divergent mobility patterns among the 1.5- and second-generation Mexicans on the one hand and the Chinese and Vietnamese on the other.

The Los Angeles metropolitan area is a strategic research site to study the 1.5 and second generation because 62 percent of the area's residents are immigrants or the children of immigrants. Among the various ethnic groups in the IIMMLA survey, we choose to compare 1.5- and second-generation Chinese, Vietnamese, and Mexicans because certain similarities and differences across mobility measures allow us to study the effects of ethnicity. We include Mexicans because they are by far the largest immigrant group in Los Angeles and the country: more than 5 million people of Mexican origin live in the Los Angeles metropolitan area, accounting for 32 percent of the area's residents; nationally, Mexicans make up more than 30 percent of all immigrants to the United States. Their sheer size—combined with their disadvantaged socioeconomic position and the unauthorized legal status of many newcomers—often makes Mexicans and their children the focus of public policy debates in immigration (Bean and Stevens 2003; Lee and Bean 2010; Massey, Durand, and Malone 2002; Telles and Ortiz 2008).

We include the Vietnamese because they are the largest non-European refugee group in the United States and concentrate predominantly in the Los Angeles metropolitan area (Zhou and Bankston 1998). Moreover, the Vietnamese provide a useful comparison with the Mexicans because while the two groups differ with respect to citizenship and immigration status, both have relatively low socioeconomic backgrounds on arrival to the United States compared with native-born whites and blacks (Bloemraad 2006).

We include Chinese in the study because they are the largest Asian ethnic group in the country, accounting for nearly 23 percent of the Asian population. The Chinese are also the largest Asian ethnic group in the Los Angeles region and have a migration history that dates back longer than most other national-origin groups. Moreover, Chinese immigrants in Los Angeles are diverse with respect to socio-economic background, even among those who hail from mainland China alone; they include low-skilled urban workers and uneducated rural peasants whose profiles are similar to those of low-skilled Mexicans and Vietnamese, as well as educated professionals who arrive with higher levels of education than native-born whites. Finally, along with other East Asian ethnic groups, such as Japanese and Koreans, Chinese have been touted by the U.S. host society as a "model minority," whose success is often attributed to their "superior" cultural values, work ethic, entrepreneurial spirit, and strong family cohesion (Kao 1995; Lee 2002, 2012a; Lee and Zhou 2004). Thus, comparing three diverse 1.5- and second-generation national origin groups is a unique opportunity to examine how immigrant selectivity and ethnicity affect the frames of academic achievement to produce diverse educational outcomes.

SECOND-GENERATION CHINESE, VIETNAMESE, AND MEXICANS AT A GLANCE

Descriptive analyses from the IIMMLA survey data reveal discernible patterns of difference among LA's 1.5- and second-generation Chinese, Vietnamese, and Mexicans. We also include third-plus-generation Mexicans, non-Hispanic blacks, and non-Hispanic whites for reference. Table 7.1 provides a glimpse of some demographic and family characteristics, revealing several notable patterns. First, Vietnamese are relatively young compared to Chinese and Mexicans; their median age is twenty-five years, versus twenty-seven for Chinese and twenty-eight for Mexicans. They also have a higher percentage of 1.5 generation in their population, which, along with their young age, reflects the relative recency of Vietnamese immigration to the United States.

Second, Chinese immigrant parents exhibit much higher levels of human and financial capital than the other groups; they are more highly educated, more likely to be English-proficient, and more likely to own a home—resources that translate into intergenerational advantages for their children. More than 60 percent of Chinese immigrant fathers and more than 40 percent of Chinese immigrant mothers have a bachelor's degree, which exceeds the educational attainment of native-born blacks and whites, and reflects the high selectivity of Chinese immigration.

By comparison, Mexican immigrants display the lowest levels of education of the groups. Nearly 60 percent of Mexican immigrant fathers and mothers have not graduated from high school, consequently placing their children at a relative disadvantage from the starting gate. The Vietnamese immigrants fall in between the

Chinese and Mexicans, but evince lower levels of educational attainment than native-born whites and blacks, especially Vietnamese mothers, more than 30 percent of whom have not graduated from high school.

Third, both 1.5- and second-generation Chinese and Vietnamese were more likely to grow up in two-parent, married households than their Mexicans counterparts. This is salient because previous research has shown that children who grow up in single-parent homes are less likely to finish high school and attend college, less likely to find and maintain a steady job, and more likely to become teenage mothers (McLanahan and Bumpass 1988; McLanahan and Sandefur 1994). This line of research also helps to elucidate, in part, the divergent patterns of teenage childbearing among 1.5- and second-generation Mexicans on the one hand, and the Chinese and Vietnamese on the other. As table 7.2 shows, 30 percent of Mexican females have given birth during their teenage years, compared with only 8 percent of Vietnamese, and none of Chinese (Rumbaut 2008). Patterns of teenage childbearing are significant in that research has shown that this is directly linked to poorer educational outcomes (McLanahan 1985).

Table 7.2 illustrates other cross-sectional outcomes in educational attainment and labor market status among the three groups. As predicted by the status attainment model, the 1.5- and second-generation Chinese outpace both the Vietnamese and the Mexicans on educational and socioeconomic measures, reflecting the intergenerational transmission of parental advantage. Nearly two-thirds (64 percent) of 1.5- and second-generation Chinese have earned a bachelor's degree, and of this group, more than one-fifth have attained a graduate degree (22 percent), figures that exceed the educational attainment of native-born whites. Moreover, none of 1.5- and second-generation Chinese have dropped out of high school, and 18 percent hold a professional occupation.

Although the 1.5- and second-generation Mexicans have the lowest levels of education of the groups, what gets lost in cross-sectional comparisons is the remarkable intergenerational mobility they have made. Close to 60 percent of Mexican immigrant mothers and fathers did not graduate from high school, but this drops to 14 percent in one generation. Moreover, more than 17 percent of 1.5- and second-generation Mexicans have a bachelor's degree, more than double that of Mexican immigrant fathers and triple that of Mexican immigrant mothers. Although the adult children of Mexican immigrants have the least education of the 1.5- and second-generation groups, they have attained the most intergenerational mobility.

Most striking, however, is the educational attainment of the 1.5- and second-generation Vietnamese, who within one generation surpass native-born blacks and whites, despite their immigrant parents' lower education than both native-born groups. Nearly half (49 percent) of the adult children of Vietnamese immigrants have attained a bachelor's degree, and of this group, 11 percent have earned a graduate degree. Moreover, 14 percent hold a professional occupation.[2] The young median age of the 1.5- and second-generation Vietnamese (twenty-five) is also important given that some of respondents had not completed their education at the time of the survey; some were in still in college or graduate school, and oth-

TABLE 7.1 / Selected Characteristics of Los Angeles' New Second Generation

Characteristics	1.5 and Second Generation			Third-Plus Generation		
	Chinese	Vietnamese	Mexican	Mexican	Black	White
Female	43.5	49.9	49.7	52.0	53.7	50.6
Median age	27.0	25.0	28.0	29.0	31.0	30.0
Citizenship status						
Citizen by birth	45.3	29.4	65.6	100.0	100.0	100.0
Citizen through naturalization	49.8	64.3	15.1	–	–	–
Permanent resident	4.4	6.1	11.8	–	–	–
Undocumented status	0.5	0.2	7.5	–	–	–
Parental SES						
Father with no English proficiency	7.0	7.9	15.2	–	–	–
Mother with no English proficiency	7.8	12.0	19.1	–	–	–
Father with no high school diploma	7.5	15.6	54.5	17.2	10.9	3.5
Mother with no high school diploma	12.2	30.5	58.0	22.4	9.0	4.4
Father with a bachelor's degree or more	61.3	31.9	7.3	14.7	35.0	46.5
Mother with a bachelor's degree or more	42.3	16.1	5.3	11.3	28.0	36.3
Parent ever been undocumented	1.0	0.6	10.4	–	–	–
Parent owning a home	86.5	58.8	62.8	73.1	67.5	89.2
Family situation						
Both parents married	85.5	83.6	72.0	53.8	43.3	51.9
Grew up living with both parents	85.6	83.1	72.2	62.2	45.4	64.8
Total	400	401	844	400	401	402

Source: Authors' compilation based on Immigration and Intergenerational Mobility in Metropolitan Los Angeles.

TABLE 7.2 / Divergent Outcomes of Los Angeles' New Second Generation

Outcomes	1.5 and Second Generation			Third-Plus Generation		
	Chinese	Vietnamese	Mexican	Mexican	Black	White
Education						
No high school diploma	0.0	1.0	13.8	9.5	6.7	3.7
High school diploma	4.5	6.7	32.7	30.3	24.2	17.7
Some college	32.4	44.1	35.9	41.4	45.1	32.5
Bachelor's degree	41.5	37.7	12.6	14.5	18.8	31.8
Graduate degrees	21.6	10.5	5.0	4.3	5.2	14.3
Labor market status*						
Professional occupations	17.9	14.0	3.6	5.9	4.6	9.6
Earnings						
$20,000 or less	43.6	53.3	76.7	70.4	73.7	60.2
$20,001 to $50,000	48.4	39.0	22.5	28.3	24.7	33.9
Over $50,000	8.0	7.7	0.8	1.3	1.7	5.9
Family situation						
Married	26.0	24.4	39.5	41.0	25.9	44.6
Mean age when first child was born	30.2	27.5	22.0	22.7	22.3	25.4
Having children at teen age	0.0	2.2	12.5	12.8	12.0	2.9
Incarceration	1.8	3.2	9.8	15.0	19.3	10.6
Total	400	401	844	400	401	402

Source: Authors' compilation based on Immigration and Intergenerational Mobility in Metropolitan Los Angeles.

ers were about to enter graduate programs, indicating that the percentage who earn bachelor's and graduate degrees will climb higher than 49 percent and 11 percent, respectively, in the near future.

That the educational outcomes of the 1.5- and second-generation Vietnamese surpass those of native-born whites and blacks in one generation, and move in the direction of the 1.5- and second-generation Chinese suggests that race, ethnicity, and culture may affect educational outcomes in unforeseen ways.

FRAMES OF ACHIEVEMENT

We now turn to the in-depth, life history interviews of our respondents to illustrate how ethnicity affects opportunity horizons and educational attainment. We focus on the frames that different ethnic groups adopt, how these frames are supported and enacted within their ethnic groups, and how they influence mobility outcomes.

Second-Generation Chinese and Vietnamese: "A is for Average, and B is an Asian Fail"

Applying the concept of frames to our research, we find that while our respondents uniformly value education, the frames through which 1.5- and second-generation Chinese and Vietnamese define "a good education" differed starkly from their Mexican counterparts. For Chinese and Vietnamese respondents, high school was mandatory, college was an obligation, and only after earning an advanced degree does one deserve kudos. For example, Caroline, a thirty-five-year-old second-generation Chinese woman who works in the film industry noted that her mother, who holds a bachelor's degree, believes that it is ludicrous that graduating from high school is cause for celebration among Americans, as she described her mother's educational expectations for her children:

> The idea of graduating from high school for my mother was not a great congratulatory day. I was happy, but you know what? My mother was very blunt, she said, "This is a good day, but it's not that special."
>
> She said to me that a lot of Westerners in American society value high school. She finds it absurd that graduating from high school is made into a big deal because you should graduate high school; everyone should. It's not necessarily a privilege; it's an obligation. You must go to high school, and you must finish. It's a further obligation that you go to college and get a bachelor's degree. Thereafter, if you get a Ph.D. or a master's, that's the big thing; that's the icing on the cake with a cherry on top, and that's what she values.

Not only was college an expectation for the 1.5- and second-generation Chinese and Vietnamese, but both groups also adopted a similar frame for what "doing well in school" means; it entails getting straight As, graduating as valedictorian or salutatorian, getting into one of the top University of California (UC) schools or an Ivy League one, and then going to graduate school in order to enter one of the "four professions": doctor, lawyer, pharmacist, or engineer. So exacting is the frame for doing well in school that Asian respondents described the value of grades on an Asian scale as "A is for average, and B is an Asian fail," and others clarified that the stakes have risen so that an A minus is now an Asian fail. So popular is this perception that the television series *Glee* recently aired an episode titled "Asian F" to reflect the shock of a student's Chinese parents when their son received an A minus in one of his classes. For the Chinese and Vietnamese respondents, the obvious yet narrow path to academic success involves excelling in high school by getting excellent grades in order to get into an elite university, and then pursuing a graduate degree in order to land a high-status, professional job.

Most remarkable was the consistency with which the Chinese and Vietnamese respondents recounted this frame, regardless of parental education, occupation, and migration history. Second-generation Vietnamese whose parents migrated as refugees with only a fourth-grade education, who do not speak English, and who work in ethnic restaurants were just as likely to recount this frame as second-generation Chinese whose parents have advanced degrees and work as doctors and engineers. For example, when we asked Maryann, a twenty-four-year-old second-generation Vietnamese woman who grew up in the housing projects in downtown Los Angeles how she defines success, she said, "getting into one of the top schools," which, by her account, included UCLA, Berkeley, Yale, Harvard, Princeton, and Stanford, and then working in one of the "top professions" as a "doctor or lawyer." When we asked Maryann how she learned about the top schools and top professions, she answered, "Other parents, like their friends who have kids. We know a few families who have kids who have gone to Yale, and they're doctors now, and they're doing really well for themselves."

Maryann's parents have only a sixth-grade education, work in Chinatown's garment factories, speak limited English, and live in Los Angeles housing projects surrounded by Mexican immigrant neighbors who are similarly disadvantaged. Yet despite this, she readily recounted a frame for academic success that mirrored that of her middle-class coethnic and Chinese peers. Low parental human capital did not stunt Maryann's opportunity horizon, nor did it truncate her educational expectations.

Although Maryann did not graduate from any of the "top schools" she listed, she did graduate from a California State (Cal State) university and is now a substitute teacher while she works toward earning her master's in education. Despite the extraordinary mobility that she has made within one generation, she feels that she departed from the traditional Asian frame of success because she earned only a 3.5 grade point average (GPA) and not from a University of California school. By Maryann's account, her GPA "wasn't great," and she describes herself as "an average person" who was "never really focused on school," especially compared with her twin sister, who earned top billing as the high school valedictorian and graduated from UC Berkeley.

Maryann was not unique among the Chinese and Vietnamese respondents who described themselves as average and not as motivated because they felt that they did not fit the exacting frame for academic success. Those who graduated with GPAs of 3.5 and 3.6 consistently pointed to coethnics and panethnic peers whose GPAs exceed 4.0, and earned admission to elite public and private universities. So exacting is the frame for academic success that even among those whose GPAs exceeded 4.0 felt that they were not as academically successful as they and their parents would have liked. For example, Hannah is a twenty-five-year-old second-generation Vietnamese woman who graduated third in her high school class with a GPA of 4.21, was voted most likely to succeed by her peers, and earned admission to the University of California—Los Angeles and Berkeley. Despite Hannah's stellar accomplishments, when we asked whether she and her parents were proud of her academic achievement in high school, she casually replied, "It would have been better if I was first or second."

Doing Well in School Is "the Asian Thing"

So ingrained is the frame for academic success among 1.5- and second-generation Vietnamese and Chinese that doing well in school is labeled as "the Asian thing" by Asian and non-Asian students alike. In fact, when we asked our respondents whether they felt that doing well in school was "acting white," none of them had ever heard of this, and none agreed with the association (Carter 2005). Debra, a 1.5-generation Chinese woman explained it this way:

> Doing well in school is the Asian thing. You just see a lot more Asians being valedictorians, being top ten, never getting in trouble with the teachers, and entering into the good UC's and the Ivy League schools. And I even heard jokes from my best friend, this Caucasian girl, she liked hanging around with Asians because she knew that Asians were good students. The ones I that I hung around with ended up at Harvard, Stanford, Cal.

Rebecca, a twenty-six-year-old second-generation Vietnamese who just graduated from law school, echoed Debra's sentiments and explained that doing well in school was not framed as acting white; on the contrary, the white students in her high school were known as the jocks, cheerleaders, and partiers who were not concerned with doing well in school, as she described:

> The white people were associated with being the jocks, the cheerleaders; they didn't care about academics. The Asians—we weren't the pretty blondes, we didn't do the cheerleading—we focused more on our classes. For example, if you looked at all the AP students, they were predominantly Asian, and I think the whites were considered the partiers and the ones that went out and did the whole jock thing.

Furthermore, when we asked Rebecca whether doing well in school was considered "uncool" in any way, she said flatly, "No, I didn't feel that way. If anything, it was a thing to have on your side." Hence, not only is "doing well in school" coded as the Asian thing, it has no association whatsoever with whiteness, anti-blackness, or one's cool factor. In a racially and ethnically diverse context like Los Angeles, the frame for academic achievement has moved beyond the black-white binary to reflect the new racial-ethnic diversity, and in the process, Asians have become the new reference group for academic excellence. The coding of academic excellence as an Asian thing is not unique to Los Angeles; Tomás Jiménez and Adam Horowitz (forthcoming) reach a similar conclusion in Silicon Valley, California, where the influx of highly skilled immigrants from east and south Asia have redefined the meaning and association of academic achievement and whiteness.

Second-Generation Mexicans: "My mom never said to me to, 'get an A.' She said, 'Do Your Best . . .'"

The 1.5- and second-generation Mexicans explained that they and their parents strongly value education, but their frame of academic achievement and doing well in school differed starkly from that adopted by their Chinese and Vietnamese counterparts. Most notably, the frame is less exacting, and entails finishing high school, possibly going to college (regardless of which college), and having some type of career. Unlike the Chinese and Vietnamese respondents, the 1.5- and second-generation Mexicans who aspired to go to college generally limited their scope to public colleges in the Los Angeles area, and often, to local community colleges in their neighborhood. Few made choices beyond their opportunity horizon to the top schools, to which many of the Chinese and Vietnamese respondents aspired.

Most of the Mexican respondents did not make status distinctions among colleges, and few understood the differences between community colleges, California State schools, University of California schools, and elite private institutions. When they distinguished among the college tiers, they generally pointed to the fact that the UCs were more expensive than the Cal State schools or the local community colleges, but most did not understand why college tuition varied among the public colleges, and importantly, they did they realize how college rankings and prestige affect labor market prospects and outcomes. Their immigrant parents knew even less, and had little or no understanding of the requirements needed for admission into the various types of colleges, which explains, in part, why the frame for academic success among Mexican immigrants and their children was relatively broad.

For instance, Danielle is a thirty-four-year-old 1.5-generation Mexican who earned a bachelor's and master's in education from a Cal State school, and now works as a kindergarten teacher. She is one of the most highly educated among the Mexican respondents we interviewed, and while she acknowledged that her parents have always wanted her to go to college, they never specified what type of college, as Danielle explained, "It didn't matter, and they didn't really know which college is better or which college you should go to. I don't think it really mattered as long as I was going to college."

In part, the Mexican respondents and their parents did not distinguish among the different college tiers because their understanding of the academic requirements and the selection process by which students are admitted to colleges was minimal or nonexistent. Many of the Mexican respondents did not know that the SAT exams were required for admission into the UC system, and therefore never took them during high school. Unable to guide their children, the Mexican immigrant parents trusted that the teachers and guidance counselors would impart the knowledge to their children. However, this was often not the case because most of the Mexican respondents were not placed in the AP or Honors tracks in high school or in "zero period," sessions when teachers disseminate information about college and place college in the opportunity horizon for high school students.

The achievement frame was also gendered among 1.5- and second-generation Mexicans, and entailed personal components that involved departing from behavior that they felt was the norm among their siblings and coethnic peers. For the women, it meant not getting pregnant in high school like their sisters, cousins, and friends; for the men, it meant not getting involved in gangs or landing in jail. For example, Nadia, a twenty-eight-year-old second-generation Mexican woman who is working toward her master's in education, noted with enormous pride that she has conquered many firsts in her family: to have not gotten pregnant as a teenager, to have finished high school, and to have graduated from college:

> I think I've already done some difference in the cycle of my family; going to college pretty much broke that cycle. I didn't get pregnant at sixteen like my mom did, or my aunts, or my grandmother did. I kept going with school. So I pretty much broke that cycle. I don't want it repeated with my sister. I'm twenty-eight years old, and I don't have any kids; I'm not married and I'm still trying to finish what's most important to me, which is my education.

Not only is Nadia the first in her family to go to college, she is also working toward her master's degree in education, despite that her parents cannot understand the point of staying in school after having earned her bachelor's degree. When we asked Nadia about her parents' expectations, she explained that, while her parents wanted her to do well in high school and go to college, they never concretely specified what this meant or provided the steps to achieve these goals. Comparing her parents with those of her Chinese friend's parents, Nadia noticed a clear difference in the way both sets of parents conveyed their educational expectations of their children; her friend's Chinese parents held higher and more exacting standards, and Nadia pondered whether the differences may be cultural:

> I don't know if that has something to do with the culture, but I had a friend who is Chinese, and she had strict parents. You had to get an A; it's kind of hard to explain. My Mom never said to me to, "get an A." She said, "do your best," you know? Sometimes my Dad, once in a while, he would say, "finish school, go to college," but he wouldn't get into much detail.

Other Mexican respondents noted that their parents wanted them to finish high school, but held no educational expectations beyond that. For example, Julia is a forty-year-old second-generation Mexican female who attended community college but never completed the requirements to earn her associate's degree. She was raised by a single mother who earned a living as a migrant worker, and would often work in the fields with her mother after school and on weekends. Julia now works as a correctional officer, and when we asked about her mother's educational aspirations for her and her siblings, she was candid:

> Our Mexican culture doesn't really value education. We're here for the money and the quick dollar, and education is like something that's not seen for them, or they didn't have it so they didn't feel it was important. As long as you make ends meet with whatever. It was weird because now that I grew up and I have kids, I want them to go to school. But back then it wasn't like that. Our parents were like just go to school and finish the day, and they didn't talk about college. There was no money for college so why talk about it?

Although Julia attributes her parents' views about education and their lack of interest in college to Mexican culture" she also casually but insightfully adds that "there was no money for college," which led her and her parents believe that college was beyond her opportunity horizon.

ENACTING THE FRAMES AND EXPANDING OPPORTUNITY HORIZONS

Simply adopting an achievement frame in itself is not enough to usher a particular outcome. In other words, adopting a frame that makes college a non-negotiable does not mean that one will go to college and graduate with a degree. For frames to be effective, they need individual and institutional support as well as reinforcement mechanisms.

The Chinese Yellow Book and Ethnic Supplemental Education

Chinese and Vietnamese immigrant parents support and reinforce the strict frame for academic success by drawing on tangible and intangible resources from both public sources and ethnic communities. For example, they select to live in neighborhoods based on the strength of the public school district, demand that their children be placed in the Honors and Advanced Placement tracks in high school, and provide supplemental education and tutoring (mostly through ethnic institutions) to ensure that they do. Furthermore, parents consistently point to coethnic role models to show that academic success is realistic and attainable for their children.

Consider Christopher, a twenty-seven-year-old second-generation Vietnamese whose refugee parents have only a fourth-grade education, yet graduated from the University of Texas with a degree in computer science. Christopher now works as a financial analyst for a management consulting firm and earns an annual salary of $70,000, which is more than his parents' combined earnings. Despite his parents' poor human capital, Christopher benefited from having slightly older, high-achieving cousins who served as his academic role models whose paths he could emulate. In addition, at the advice of their friends, Christopher's parents (who live in a low-income, predominantly Vietnamese immigrant community in Westminster) transferred legal guardianship of their son to one of their coethnic friends so that he could attend a more competitive public high school in an affluent neighborhood in Orange County. Not only did the transfer offer Christopher a stronger education, it also shielded him from his potential involvement in Vietnamese gangs, which was a serious concern in his parents' neighborhood. Hence, Christopher's parents tapped into their ethnic networks to learn how they could provide Christopher a better education in spite of their socioeconomic disadvantage. With the support of their more privileged coethnics, they were able to enact an achievement frame that shielded Christopher from the possibility of stagnant or downward mobility.

Like Christopher, Jason—a twenty-five-year-old second-generation Chinese—grew up in a working-class neighborhood in Long Beach. As soon as his parents could afford to do so, they moved their family to a modest home in Cerritos, which they selected because they learned from *The Chinese Yellow Book*, which publishes the area's ethnic businesses as well as the rankings of southern California's public high schools and nation's top colleges, that Cerritos High School "ranks in the teens." When Jason initially moved to Cerritos and took the junior high school admissions exam, he was placed in the school's regular track rather than the AP academic track. Dismayed and concerned, Jason's parents promptly enrolled their son into an after-school Chinese academy, which they learned about from *The Chinese Yellow Book*. When Jason took the exam for high school, he was placed in the AP track. His parents' efforts, along with Jason's hard work, paid off; he graduated in the top 10 percent of his high school and was admitted into all of the UC campuses to which he applied. Although his parents wanted him to go to Berkeley, he chose UCLA because it was closer to home. Moreover, because he was able to apply his high school AP credits to college, he graduated from UCLA in three years, and is now attending a UC law school.

The Chinese Yellow Book is a 2,500-page, 3.5-inch thick telephone directory that lists the area's ethnic business and rankings of the area's high schools and the nation's top colleges. Advertisements for supplemental education—including tutoring, SAT prep courses, and taking classes ahead of schedule—are offered in a range of prices and are prominent in the Chinese, Korean, and Vietnamese yellow books as well as in ethnic newspapers. These forms of ethnic media are one of the ways in which information passes along ethnic channels and is freely available to coethnics across class lines.

Supplemental education was not unique to Jason's experience. For many of the Chinese and Vietnamese respondents, supplemental education was such an integral part of their adolescence that they hardly characterized it as supplemental; rather, it was an insurance policy so that Chinese and Vietnamese children would excel in their classes during the regular academic year. For example, Hannah, the twenty-five-year-old second-generation Vietnamese woman who graduated third in her class with a 4.21 GPA, noted that her summers were reserved for summer school and tutoring:

> Summertime, besides going to summer school every single year, we also did tutoring classes to get ahead. I believe it was my junior year summer, I was taking classes at Golden West [Community College] for calculus or something like that. And then younger than that, like in junior high and stuff, we were taking a class ahead, like math classes. Like, if we were going to take geometry, then we were doing it in the summertime already, or algebra in the summertime, the summer before. In the Asian community, I think everyone does tutoring.

When we asked Hannah whether she felt the tutoring and extra classes helped her academic achievement, she answered, "Oh yeah, definitely!" Hannah's parents' insistence on supplemental education for their three children has paid off: she is currently applying to pharmacy school; her sister is currently enrolled in pharmacy school; and her brother is in medical school. Because supplementary education in Asian ethnic communities is available in a wide price range (and some is free), poor and working-class coethnics are able to access these resources, just like their middle-class counterparts.

Homophilous Peer Networks

The frame is also reinforced through friendship and peer networks that often fall along ethnic and panethnic lines. These networks are more ethnically and panethnically homophilous than one would expect based on the racial-ethnic diversity in Los Angeles because the segregation within its public high schools and the academic tracking within them. Based on our respondents' experiences, most of the students in the AP and Honors classes were Asian, making interethnic friendships between Mexicans and Asians unlikely. However, ethnic and panethnic friendships that crossed class lines were not uncommon among 1.5- and second-generation Chinese and Vietnamese, and served as an additional ethnic resource for those whose parents lack human capital.

Cindy, a thirty-two-year-old 1.5-generation Chinese woman, is a prime example. Cindy came to the United States at the age of three with her parents, neither of whom had graduated from high school. Her father completed the sixth grade in Hong Kong, and her mother the eighth grade. Neither parent speaks English, which has relegated them to low-wage service-sector jobs; her father has always worked in ethnic restaurants and her mother cleans houses. While neither was able to give her advice about high school or college, Cindy said that she "always knew" that she would go to college, and was fortunate enough to have the help of her high school friends who provided information about college admissions and pushed her to excel.

When we asked the ethnic backgrounds of her closest friends in high school, Cindy answered, "All Asian. Chinese, Vietnamese, Taiwanese." When we asked how her friends affected her academic performance in school, and she replied, "I think we just pushed each other to the other same level. You don't want to do poorly because your friend was doing better than you, so, you know, you just kept up." She then elaborated: "Well, in high school, they took up all the AP classes, they took zero period, and they went to all the UCs, and you just knew. You spend four years with the same people you kind of know who's smart and who isn't."

For Cindy and other Chinese and Vietnamese respondents, high-achieving co-ethnic and panethnic role models were an essential component of their academic success; they set the standard for academic achievement, and also charted a viable pathway to achieve it.

Cindy's parents' limited financial resources circumscribed her college choices and constrained her from choosing a college that would have necessitated that she move out of her parents' house, but it did not alter her frame for academic success. Cindy chose to attend a Cal State school, which was both a cheaper option than a UC school and made it possible for her to live at home and save money. By making these choices, Cindy did not have to work during college, which freed her of the burden of balancing school and work, which in turn enabled her to graduate in four years. She now works as a claims adjuster for an insurance company and earns $65,000 annually — far more than her parents' salaries combined.

Public Resources: Teachers, Counselors, and Coaches

Chinese and Vietnamese respondents benefited from tangible and intangible ethnic resources, but Mexican respondents did not have these resources at their disposal. None of the respondents mentioned that they had ever had any supplementary schooling such as tutoring or SAT prep courses, and those who learned about the college admissions process acquired this information through school zero periods or from college outreach programs. Others pointed to a particular teacher, guidance counselor, or coach who had encouraged them to apply for college and helped them with their applications. Without the benefit of tangible and intangible ethnic resources, Mexican students had to rely on publicly available resources, which were pivotal in determining the exceptional academic outcomes of the highest-achieving among the Mexican respondents, as Camilla's case illustrates.

Camilla — a twenty-seven-year-old second-generation Mexican woman who earned her bachelor's and master's from the University of Southern California (USC) — is a prime example of how a counselor can intervene and change a student's achievement frame, thereby placing college within the realm of one's opportunity horizon. Camilla's parents arrived from Mexico as unauthorized migrants and worked in LA's garment factories. Although Camilla's parents wanted her and her twin sister to go to college, they had no way to help them achieve this goal, so when the twins graduated from high school, they enrolled in the local community college. While there, they met a counselor who "went above and be-yond" by providing step-by-step instructions about gaining admission into a four-year university, which paid off when Camilla was accepted to USC, and her twin sister to Berkeley, as she explained:

> When I was applying to schools, I really had no idea what it was about because we didn't have models with friends or family. I didn't know what units were, and I really didn't know what college was. To me, it just sounded like an extension of high school to get a degree, a better degree, but I really didn't know the difference. At first, it was really confusing.
>
> Luckily at the community college, we met a counselor who went above and be-yond in helping us and to explain. The counselor, she was African American, and was really encouraging, and she really went above and beyond for those students. She really kind of walked me through the whole steps and taught me what a credit unit was all about and what I needed, how many units and credits and classes I needed to keep moving forward, and to choose my own classes. At the time, I didn't know how to do that.

Camilla's counselor went a step further. When she and her sister were accepted at USC and Berkeley, her parents were opposed to their moving out of the house to go to college; they did not understand why the girls needed to leave when local colleges were available. To help persuade her parents, Camilla's guidance coun-selor visited them to explain the benefits of allowing their daughters to leave home and attend these prestigious universities. When we asked Camilla why her par-ents were initially opposed to the idea, she explained that they had two reasons. First, "it was part of the culture" that Mexican daughters are not supposed to leave home until they are married. Second, her parents felt they had no way to protect their daughters should something happen to them.

Camilla's parents' reservations and fears are not unique. The Mexican respon-dents who gained admission to college often stay local and live at home, for sev-eral reasons. Some respondents and their parents did not understand the status differences among colleges. Some parents insisted on protecting their unmarried daughters, which meant that the daughters stayed at home. Finally, some of the Mexican respondents were economically constrained and unable to move away because they had to provide financial assistance to their parents' household as soon as they graduated from high school (Turley 2009; Vallejo and Lee 2009). Hence, it is not that Mexican immigrant parents do not value education; they want their children to do well in school and go to college, but they lack both the class and ethnic resources that enable them to enact a frame for academic success.

In Camilla's case, however, the intervention of a counselor legitimated the move from her parents' household to the USC dorms. Camilla's educational attainment is extraordinary given her parents' low level of education, previously unauthor-ized status, and the lack of ethnic resources. Her counselor was pivotal in paving her educational path, but most of her coethnics were not as fortunate, and, further-more, many lack visible role models to which they may turn as mobility prototypes. Lacking the ethnic capital and resources that are readily accessible to Chinese and Vietnamese parents and students, Mexicans must trust and rely on the only resources that are available to them: publicly available resources, which are already spread thin and dwindling in this economic environment.

DISCUSSION AND CONCLUSIONS

We began this chapter with a vexing question: how do some second-generation ethnic groups exhibit academic outcomes that defy traditional status attainment models? For example, some Chinese and many Vietnamese immigrants arrive in the United States with less than a high school education, few labor market skills, and little command of the English language, yet their children graduate at the top of their high school classes, gain admission into the competitive University of California system, and then pursue graduate degrees.

Although status attainment models cannot explain these outcomes, sociologists have largely refrained from considering the roles of culture and ethnicity. The absence of a strong sociological voice has left the door wide open for racial-ethnic and cultural stereotypes to emerge and persist, including "illegal," "poverty-stricken" Mexicans, and "model minority" Asians. To rectify this theoretical and empirical shortcoming, we draw on the classic sociological concepts of frames, reference groups, and role models to examine how ethnicity and culture operate as ethnic capital to influence the frames of achievement and expand opportunity horizons. The availability of ethnic capital reduces the risk of stagnant or downward mobility for the children of immigrants, particularly for those who lack parental human capital and hail from poor socioeconomic backgrounds.

Based on 140 in-depth interviews with a randomly drawn sample of adult children of Chinese, Vietnamese, and Mexican immigrants in Los Angeles, we find that 1.5- and second-generation Chinese and Vietnamese share a similar frame of achievement that differs from that of their Mexican counterparts. Regardless of parental socioeconomic background and migration history, the 1.5- and second-generation Chinese and Vietnamese respondents recounted a sharply focused frame for achievement that entails getting straight As in high school, graduating from an elite university, and pursuing an advanced degree. The frame reflects a particular mobility strategy in which academic success becomes the pragmatic goal in itself because Chinese and Vietnamese immigrant parents perceive education as the only sure path to mobility—a perception they have imparted to their children. The high selectivity of Asian immigration translates into a strong middle class within ethnic communities, who not only set the frame for achievement, but also create the necessary, supplemental resources to achieve it. But this is not the case for Mexicans, whose middle-class presence is not as large or as visible, and is overshadowed by their more economically disadvantaged coethnics. The children of Mexican immigrants do not benefit from ethnic capital as do their Asian ethnic counterparts.

What is unique in the Chinese, Vietnamese, and other Asian ethnic communities is their ethnic system of supplementary education—one they have developed in parallel to that in non-Asian, middle-class communities. This elaborate system—which is absent in other racial-ethnic minority enclaves—offers a diversity of services with a wide price range, some of which are freely available (Zhou and Cho 2010). These services are available to coethnic and panethnic group members, regardless of class status, so that poor and working-class Chinese and Vietnamese are privy to them, just like their middle-class and affluent counterparts.

The heterogeneity within ethnic communities also offers the opportunity for poor and working-class coethnics to look to middle-class counterparts as mobility prototypes whose educational pathways they can emulate, and as the reference group by which they measure their progress. So rather than turning to native-born whites, coethnics (and in some cases, panethnics) become the reference group by Chinese and Vietnamese chart their educational and mobility pathways and measure their academic success (Lee 2012b; Zhou and Lee 2007; Zhou et al. 2008). The accessibility of tangible and intangible ethnic resources explain why the educational outcomes of the 1.5- and second-generation Vietnamese—whose parents arrive with less education than both native-born whites and blacks—are more similar to the Chinese than to Mexicans or native-born whites or blacks.

Furthermore, despite their low levels of human and economic capital, Vietnamese immigrants have two distinct advantages over their Mexican counterparts. First, as political refugees, they are eligible for government benefits that help supplement their household incomes and their communities, thereby providing additional support to build ethnic institutions (Bloemraad 2006; Zhou and Bankston 1998). These benefits are denied to Mexican immigrants, most of whom arrive as labor migrants, and many who enter the United States as unauthorized migrants who remain ineligible for any government benefits (Bean and Stevens 2003; Massey, Durand, and Malone 2002; Telles and Ortiz 2008). Second, as Asian Americans, they benefit from the positive stereotypes associated with their racial status, which enables them to shed the stigma associated with destitute refugees who take advantage of the government's generous welfare system. Moreover, because the U.S. host society has elevated expectations of them, the children of Vietnamese immigrants raise their frame of achievement and perform in a manner in which they confirm the positive stereotype (Lee 2012a).

The 1.5- and second-generation Chinese, Vietnamese, and Mexican respondents framed academic success as an Asian thing, but the mechanisms by which these students achieve success are by no means exclusive to Asians (Karabel 2005; Lareau 2003; Steinberg 1981). A look back shows that second- and later-generation Jews had high academic and occupational outcomes that parallel those of 1.5- and second-generation Chinese and Vietnamese, which Stephen Steinberg (1981) has attributed to the immigrant selectivity of Jewish immigrants from Europe. Unlike Italian and Irish immigrants who arrived to the United States from rural, peasant backgrounds, Jewish immigrants migrated from urban areas and many hailed from the merchant class. The pre-migration skills of the earlier wave of Jewish immigrants fit into America's booming industrial economy, and many chose self-employment as the route to upward mobility (Lee 2002; Steinberg 1981). Subsequent waves of Jewish immigrants and their children benefited from the ethnic capital that the earlier waves created, including educational and occupational opportunities reserved for coethnics (Waldinger 1996).

While immigrants and their children rely on coethnic and panethnic resources, wealthy, native-born Americans can turn to class resources to help their children attain exceptional academic outcomes. For example, parents whose children attend New York's elite private high schools spend several hundred dollars an hour on tutors for the SAT exams and specific subjects, which can amount to as much as $35,000 a year—nearly the equivalent of one year's tuition.[3] However, unlike their Asian counterparts, these parents are less likely to admit doing so, not only because the practice is frowned upon by the schools, but also because they do not wish to convey the image that their children need extra help. The openness with which Asian parents admit to supplementing their children's education with tutors and after-school programs compared to the reticence among non-Asian parents explains why the practice is framed along racial-ethnic rather than class lines.

The group that loses out in the academic race to get ahead is the children of Mexican immigrants, who are not only hampered by the low SES in their families but also the lack the ethnic resources and capital to compensate. Unable to turn to their immigrant parents for support and lacking ethnic resources, they rely on the only resources available: those publicly available in their schools and through nonprofit institutions such as zero periods, guidance counselors, and college outreach programs. But these institutional resources are already spread thin and dwindling even further in the current economic climate. They are barely enough to offer modest educational support for the children of Mexican immigrants, much less foster a rigorous educational environment to counteract their poor class background.

Family and group SES continue to operate as the most important set of structural factors that determine the mobility outcomes of immigrants and their children, but we find that external support—in the form of public policy, civil society, or ethnic communities—is essential to lift immigrant families out of poverty and to circumvent stagnant intergenerational mobility. Immigrant groups who are highly selected are better equipped to provide the external support within their ethnic communities, but those who are not as highly selected do not have that option. That the children of Mexican immigrants make such impressive intergenerational gains attests to their perseverance in their quest to get ahead. Because they rely exclusively on publicly available resources to attain mobility requires that we invest more in these resources to ensure that future generations are able to do the same.

The authors wish to thank the Russell Sage Foundation for generously supporting the research on which this chapter is based (grant nos. 88–06–04 and 88–08–18). For critical comments and helpful suggestions, we thank Aixa Cintrón-Vélez (our program officer at the Russell Sage Foundation), the anonymous reviewers, and the participants at the National Poverty Center's conference on "Immigration, Poverty, and Socioeconomic Inequality," especially Taeku Lee, Steven Raphael, and David Card. For invaluable research assistance, we thank Jody Agius Vallejo, Rosaura Tafoya-Estrada, Leisy Abrego, James Bany, and Kris Noam-Zuidervaart.

NOTES

1. IIMMLA is a multi-investigator study that examines patterns of intra- and intergenerational mobility among the adult children of immigrants in the greater Los Angeles metropolitan area. It includes a telephone survey of 4,800 randomly selected respondents in five counties of metropolitan Los Angeles (Los Angeles, Orange, San Bernardino, Riverside and Ventura), targeting 1.5 and second-generation adults between the ages of twenty and forty.
2. We examined these measures based on the 2000 U.S. Census data for the Los Angeles region and found similar trends regarding intergroup differences.
3. Jenny Anderson, "Push for A's at Private Schools Is Keeping Costly Tutors Busy," *New York Times*, June 7, 2011.

REFERENCES

Bean, Frank D., and Gillian Stevens. 2003. *America's Newcomers and the Dynamics of Diversity*. New York: Russell Sage Foundation.

Binder, Amy, Mary Blair-Loy, John Evans, Kwai Ng, and Michael Schudson. 2008. "Introduction: The Diversity of Culture." *The Annals of the American Academy of Political and Social Science* 619(1): 6–14.

Blau, Peter, and Otis Dudley Duncan. 1967. *American Occupational Structure*. New York: John Wiley & Sons.

Bloemraad, Irene. 2006. *Becoming a Citizen: Incorporating Immigrants and Refugees in the United States and Canada*. Berkeley: University of California Press.

Borjas, George G. 2006. "Making It in America: Social Mobility in the Immigrant Population." *The Future of Children* 16(2): 55–71.

Carter, Prudence L. 2005. *Keepin' It Real: School Success Beyond Black and White*. New York: Oxford University Press.

Duncan, Otis Dudley, David L. Featherman, and Beverly Duncan. 1972. *Socioeconomic Background and Achievement*. New York: Seminar Press.

Feliciano, Cynthia. 2005. "Does Selective Migration Matter? Explaining Ethnic Disparities in Educational Attainment among Immigrants' Children." *International Migration Review* 39(4): 841–71.

Fernández-Kelly, Patricia. 2008. "The Back Pocket Map: Social Class and Cultural Capital as Transferable Assets in the Advancement of Second-Generation Immigrants." *The Annals of the American Academy of Political and Social Science* 620(1): 116–37.

Fuligni, Andrew J. 1997. "The Academic Achievement of Adolescents from Immigrant

Families: The Roles of Family Background, Attitudes and Behavior." *Child Development* 68(2): 351–63.

Goffman, Erving. 1974. *Frame Analysis.* Cambridge, Mass.: Harvard University Press.

Harding, David J. 2007. "Cultural Context, Sexual Behavior, and Romantic Relationships in Disadvantaged Neighborhoods." *American Sociological Review* 72(3): 341–64.

Hyman, Herbert H., and Eleanor Singer, eds. 1968. *Readings in Reference Group Theory and Research.* New York: Free Press.

Itzigsohn, José. 2009. *Encountering American Fault Lines: Race, Class, and the Dominican Experience in Providence.* New York: Russell Sage Foundation.

Jiménez, Tomás, and Adam Louis Horowitz. Forthcoming. "When White Is Just Alright: How Immigrants Redefine Achievement and Reconfigure the Ethnoracial Hierarchy." *American Sociological Review.*

Kao, Grace. 1995. "Asian Americans as Model Minorities? A Look at Their Academic Performance." *American Journal of Education* 103(2): 121–59.

Kao, Grace, and Marta Tienda. 1998. "Educational Aspirations of Minority Youth." *American Journal of Education* 106(3): 349–84.

Karabel, Jerome. 2005. *The Chosen.* New York: Houghton Mifflin.

Kasinitz, Philip, John H. Mollenkopf, Mary C. Waters, and Jennifer Holdaway. 2009. *Inheriting the City.* New York: Russell Sage Foundation.

Lareau, Annette. 2003. *Unequal Childhoods.* Berkeley: University of California Press.

Lee, Jennifer. 2012a. "Asian American Exceptionalism and Stereotype Promise." *The Society Pages,* May 4, 2012. http://thesocietypages.org/papers/asian-american-exceptionalism-and-stereotype-promise (accessed June 11, 2013).

———. 2012b. "Tiger Kids and the Success Frame." *The Society Pages,* April 18, 2012. http://thesocietypages.org/papers/tiger-kids-and-the-success-frame (accessed June 11, 2013).

———. 2002. *Civility in the City: Blacks, Jews, and Koreans in Urban America.* Cambridge, Mass.: Harvard University Press.

Lee, Jennifer, and Frank D. Bean. 2010. *The Diversity Paradox: Immigration and the Color Line in Twenty-First Century America.* New York: Russell Sage Foundation.

Lee, Jennifer, and Min Zhou, eds. 2004. *Asian American Youth: Culture, Identity, and Ethnicity.* New York: Routledge.

Lewis, Oscar. 1966. *La Vida: A Puerto Rican Family in the Culture of Poverty – San Juan and New York.* New York: Random House.

Lopez, Nancy. 2003. *Hopeful Girls, Troubled Boys: Race and Gender Disparity in Urban Education.* New York: Routledge.

Louie, Vivian. 2004. *Compelled to Excel: Immigration, Education, and Opportunity among Chinese Americans.* Palo Alto, Calif.: Stanford University Press.

Luckingham, Bradford. 1994. *Minorities in Phoenix: A Profile of Mexican American, Chinese American, and African American Communities, 1860–1992.* Tempe: Arizona State University Press.

Massey, Douglas, Jorge Durand, and Nolan J. Malone. 2002. *Beyond Smoke and Mirrors: Mexican Immigration in an Era of Economic Integration.* New York: Russell Sage Foundation.

McLanahan, Sara. 1985. "Family Structure and the Reproduction of Poverty." *American Journal of Sociology* 90(4): 873–901.

McLanahan, Sara, and Larry Bumpass. 1988. "Intergenerational Consequences of Family Disruption." *American Journal of Sociology* 94(1): 130–52.

McLanahan, Sara, and Gary Sandefur. 1994. *Growing Up With a Single Parent*. Cambridge, Mass.: Harvard University Press.

Merton, Robert K. 1949. "Patterns of Influence: Local and Cosmopolitan Influentials." In *Social Theory and Social Structure*. New York: Free Press.

Polletta, Francesca. 2006. *It Was Like a Fever: Storytelling in Protest and Politics*. Chicago: University of Chicago Press.

Portes, Alejandro, and Lingxin Hao. 2004. "The Schooling of Children of Immigrants." *Proceedings of the National Academy of Sciences* 101(33): 11920–27.

Rumbaut, Rubén G. 2008. "The Coming of the Second Generation: Immigrants and Ethnic Mobility in Southern California." *The Annals of the American Academy of Political and Social Science* 620(November): 196–236.

Skrentny, John D. 2008. "Culture and Race/Ethnicity: Bolder, Deeper and Broader." *The Annals of the American Academy of Political and Social Science* 619(1): 59–77.

Small, Mario L. 2004. *Villa Victoria: The Transformations of Social Capital in a Boston Barrio*. Chicago: University of Chicago Press.

Small, Mario L., David J. Harding, and Michèle Lamont. 2010. "Reconsidering Culture and Poverty." *The Annals of the American Academy of Political and Social Science* 629(1): 6–27.

Smith, Sandra S. 2007. *Lone Pursuit: Distrust and Defensive Individualism Among the Black Poor*. New York: Russell Sage Foundation.

Snow, David A., E. Burke Rochford Jr., Steven K. Worden, and Robert D. Benford. 1986. "Frame Alignment Processes, Micromobilization, and Movement Participation." *American Sociological Review* 51(4): 464–81.

Sowell, Thomas. 1981. *Ethnic America: A History*. New York: Basic Books.

Steinberg, Laurence. 1996. "Ethnicity and Adolescent Achievement." *American Educator* 20(2): 28–48.

Steinberg, Stephen. 1981. *The Ethnic Myth: Race, Ethnicity, and Class in America*. Boston, Mass.: Beacon.

Telles, Edward E., and Vilma Ortiz. 2008. *Generations of Exclusion: Mexican Americans, Assimilation, and Race*. New York: Russell Sage Foundation.

Turley, Ruth N. López. 2009. "College Proximity: Mapping Access to Opportunity." *Sociology of Education* 82(1): 126–46.

Vaisey, Stephen. 2010. "What People Want: Rethinking Poverty, Culture, and Educational Attainment." *The Annals of the American Academy of Political and Social Science* 629(1): 75–101.

Vallejo, Jody Agius, and Jennifer Lee. 2009. "Brown Picket Fences: The Immigrant Narrative and 'Giving Back' Among the Mexican-Origin Middle Class." *Ethnicities* 9(1): 5–31.

Van Hook, Jennifer, and Frank D. Bean. 2009. "Explaining Mexican-Immigrant Welfare Behaviors: The Importance of Employment-Related Cultural Repertoires." *American Sociological Review* 74(3): 423–44.

Waldinger, Roger. 1996. *Still the Promised City? African Americans and New Immigrants in Postindustrial New York*. Cambridge, Mass.: Harvard University Press.

Young, Alford A. 2010. "New Life for an Old Concept: Frame Analysis and the Reinvigoration of Studies in Culture and Poverty." *The Annals of the American Academy of Political and Social Science* 629(1): 53–74.

Zhou, Min. 2009. "How Neighborhoods Matter for Immigrant Children: The Formation of Educational Resources in Chinatown, Koreatown, and Pico Union, Los Angeles." *Journal of Ethnic and Migration Studies* 35(7): 1153–79.

Zhou, Min, and Carl L. Bankston III. 1998. *Growing Up American: How Vietnamese Children Adapt to Life in the United States.* New York: Russell Sage Foundation.

Zhou, Min, and Myungduk Cho. 2010. "Noneconomic Effects of Ethnic Entrepreneurship: Evidence from Chinatown and Koreatown in Los Angeles, USA." *Thunderbird International Business Review* 52(2): 83–96.

Zhou, Min, and Jennifer Lee. 2007. "Becoming Ethnic or Becoming American? Reflecting on the Divergent Pathways to Social Mobility and Assimilation Among the New Second Generation" *Du Bois Review* 4(1): 1–17.

Zhou, Min, Jennifer Lee, Jody Agius Vallejo, Rosaura Tafoya-Estrada, and Yang Sao Xiong. 2008. "Success Attained, Deterred, and Denied: Divergent Pathways to Social Mobility among the New Second Generation in Los Angeles." *The Annals of the American Academy of Political and Social Science* 620(1): 37–61.

Zuckerman, Harriet. 1988. "The Role of the Role Model: The Other Side of a Sociological Coinage." In *Surveying Social Life*, edited by Hubert J. O'Gorman. Middletown, Conn.: Wesleyan University Press.

Chapter 8

Reassessing Human Capital and Intergenerational Mobility

Roberto G. Gonzales

This chapter examines the adult experiences of undocumented immigrants who migrate as children and must navigate legal and economic limitations (for expanded versions of some of the arguments presented here, see Gonzales 2010a, 2011). Empirically, I draw from 150 life history interviews and four and a half years of fieldwork with 1.5-generation young adults of Mexican origin living in the Los Angeles Metropolitan area. In doing so, I focus attention on the ways family poverty and the limitations of unauthorized residency status constrain choices and, in turn, shape expectations and aspirations. My analysis compares the experiences of two groups of differently achieving young adults I call *college-goers* and *early-exiters*. The college-goers make up the top strata of their communities. During their school years, support from teachers and other adults, coupled with their internalization of the notion that their hard work will garner them success, helped them to maintain positive attitudes about their futures and achieve academic success. Their educational trajectories stand in stark contrast to the early-exiters, a group composed of young adults who left the school system at or before their high school graduation. Instead of daily lives spent with high achieving peers and in pursuit of advanced degrees, their concerns quickly shifted to more immediate needs, such as keeping jobs and meeting mounting expenses.

Gabriel

Gabriel has experienced more than his share of life's setbacks.[1] At twenty-eight, he confronts the everyday difficulties of low-wage work and legal limitations. He works with Mexican and Vietnamese immigrants in a factory, assembling car parts. Although he makes only $8 an hour—hardly enough to meet his personal expenses and the $350 a month he provides to his mother—he tells me that this is the first full-time job he has ever held for more than three months.

When I met him in 2003, he was living his life with little hope to join mainstream society. A series of blocked opportunities had left him frustrated and deflated. He had started taking classes at a community college a year prior, but stopped going because he could not afford tuition, fees, and books. To make matters worse, he was fired from his job when his employer received a No-Match letter from the Social Security Administration (SSA), indicating that the Social Security number he was using did not match SSA records. Gabriel does not have a valid state-issued identification card. He is not a citizen of the United States. He is not authorized to legally work in the United States. The termination put him and his family in a bind and unable to come up with enough money to cover the rent. Feeling like a burden to his mother, Gabriel decided to find a place of his own.

Gabriel has been in the United States since he was six years old. After finalizing a divorce in Mexico, his mother packed up what little she had and told her children they were going to Disneyland. As a single mother of three her first years in the United States were marred with hardship and struggle. Undocumented, with less than a third grade education, and without other family members in the United States, Gabriel's mother struggled to make ends meet. A series of close calls with immigration agents left her scared and further isolated her and the kids. She began working as an at-home babysitter and has done so for more than twenty years. In addition to her meager wages, she has no co-workers and few friends to whom to look for support. Because she works from home, she has few opportunities to become integrated into the community. She also has no foreseeable path to legalization. These limiting circumstances undoubtedly have consequences for her children.

Gabriel has the cumulative disadvantages of undocumented status. With only a high school degree and a handful of community college credits, he has spent much of his years since high school toiling in low-wage jobs and avoiding being caught. His world is narrowly circumscribed by his legal limitations and lack of good options. He has not been in school on a full-time basis for more than ten years. Without the safety net of school, he must struggle in the world of low-wage work, and be ready to leave his job at a moment's notice. He cannot afford to be out of work very long, as he is responsible for both his own bills and a substantial portion of his mother's expenses.

Nimo

Those who meet Nimo are often surprised by his high level of optimism. Although he comes from the same neighborhood and went to the same high school as Gabriel, his outlook diverges greatly. At twenty-five, he looks young for his age. His black hair sets off his brown skin. His frail stature and small, soft hands tell you that he has not worked a day of hard labor in his life. Yet his wide smile conceals a life of poverty and limitation. He lives with his mother and sister in a low-income, densely segregated Mexican immigrant community in southern California. Together they share a room in his aunt's two-bedroom apartment. His father died when he was very young. Since then, his mother has raised him and his younger sister in the United States by herself. Nimo's aunt does not ask for much in rent, in part because she knows her sister can barely make ends meet with the meager wages she earns piecemeal as a seamstress, and in part because she is also paid rent from a former coworker who uses a closet space as a bedroom. Although cramped in the tiny 850 square feet apartment, the seven members get along very well.

Nimo does not drive. To get around he takes public transportation. Most destinations in his daily routine require at least one transfer and a lot of patience. He is in his final year at a California State University, his commute to school, round trip, eats up nearly five hours of his day.[2]

Nimo's family left Mexico City when he was six years old, joining the hundreds of thousands of Mexican families migrating each year during the late 1980s and 1990s in search of a better life (Passel 2006). Like many other undocumented immigrants, his mother worked hard to make ends meet.[3] She moved from one factory job to another until she settled into seamstress work. Although her wages were not high, she learned quickly that she could make a little more if she took work home. Over the years, she developed arthritis in her hands and a nagging toothache from the stress. Raising two children on her own was difficult, however, and she needed the security of steady work. She hoped for a change in her circumstances and prayed that by the time her children grew up there would be more opportunities for them. Meanwhile, Nimo's immigration status did not present too many barriers for him while in school. With the assistance of supportive teachers and community mentors, he excelled in academics and participated in a broad range of school- and community-based activities. Although he was ineligible for crucially needed federal and state financial aid, he was persuaded to first enroll in community college then transfer to a four-year institution.[4]

Given Nimo's economic and legal profile, most people would not be surprised to find a bitter and worn-down young man with little hope for the future. Instead, he plans diligently, exploring his options for graduate study and internships. "Nothing stands in my way," he told me one day as we walked through his university campus. "I don't think giving up is an issue . . . I kind of want to start doing internships before [working] because then you have practice in the field, and then when you go on the real job, you are familiar with it. You need to learn how to plan for things."

Nimo's positive school experiences have allowed him to maintain a sense of optimism, despite his inability to legally work. His entire tuition has been covered by a mentor he met in high school, who has also committed to funding his graduate studies. His mother does not ask for financial assistance, so he has worked only minimally throughout college. And although his bus commute is extremely time consuming, he uses the time to, as he says, "read and think." Without the various barriers of financing college, supporting his family, and having to work and drive, he is able to concentrate on school and maintain high aspirations for the future.

Nimo is one of the more than 2.1 million undocumented young people who have lived in the United States since childhood (Batalova and McHugh 2010).

While the Supreme Court guarantees their rights to K-12 schooling (Olivas 2007),[5] their undocumented status limits their ability to participate in most adult pursuits. Nimo's circumstances represent wasted talent. His education has prepared him to join other college graduates starting careers. His positive attitude and high aspirations would be assets in the workforce. These unique qualities make him an obvious candidate for proposals aimed at legalizing high achieving immigrant youngsters.[6] He has even been interviewed by local and national media as someone who would benefit from such legislation. For now, however, he must wait.

Both of these young men have seen friends and family members move forward, weigh options, and begin careers—all the while, they are left immobile. They belong to a relatively recent, sizeable, and vulnerable population of which very little is known. Undocumented immigrants like them, who begin their U.S. life as children, make up nearly 20 percent of the total undocumented population (Batalova and McHugh 2010). Much of what is known about these young men and women comes from journalistic accounts of high school valedictorians and class presidents struggling to gain entry into postsecondary institutions. Over the last several years, the scholarly community has made great strides in examining how family poverty and undocumented status frame their lives and constrict their trajectories. Yet we still know very little about how they are faring in their adult lives. Almost half of this population has reached adulthood and, because of state-level legislation aimed at widening access to postsecondary education, increasing numbers have earned two- and four-year degrees. However, legal exclusions are, perhaps, even more consequential in adulthood.

The comparative focus of this study provides a great deal of insight into such phenomena of educational and economic incorporation, school stratification, and immigration status. Although these findings complicate contemporary arguments about immigrant intergenerational progress and longstanding assessments of human capital as the driver for social and economic mobility, they also identify mechanisms that shape important opportunities and experiences of success.

EDUCATIONAL ATTAINMENT IN THE TWENTY-FIRST CENTURY

Contemporary immigration scholarship suggests that long-held expectations of a linear generational process of economic incorporation are being challenged by the experiences of today's immigrants and their children (Gans 1992; Portes and Zhou 1993; Portes and Rumbaut 2006). Much of current theorizing has built on what was once a singular focus on human capital, toward broader conceptualizations that more fully incorporate a constellation of various contexts of reception (Portes 1981; Portes and Bach 1985; Portes and Rumbaut 2006). By focusing on the interplay between human-level variables—human capital, social capital, and cultural capital—and structural contexts, they stress that multiple factors channel today's immigrants and their children into different segments of society (Portes and Rumbaut 2001, 2006; Portes and Zhou 1993). Drawing attention to the varied experiences

of today's immigrants, many have questioned the chances of subsequent generations to do as well as previous waves, due to increasing fault lines of inequality
along race and ethnicity, poor public schools, and differential access to today's
labor market (Gans 1992; Portes and Rumbaut 2006, 2001; Portes and Zhou 1993;
Rumbaut 2008, 2005, 1997; Zhou 1997).

Nevertheless, a central focus on human capital continues to drive most studies
of stratification. Indeed, most immigration scholars agree that the accumulation of
education, job training, and experience is key to upward assimilation (Zhou 1997).
Studies on the children of immigrants have highlighted the importance of parental
human capital (Kao and Tienda 1995; Portes and Rumbaut 2001), school peer influence (Portes and Zhou 1993; Portes and MacLeod 1996), and community and
neighborhood (Zhou 2008; Zhou and Bankston 1998), but the link between school
outcomes and future success has been a central thread throughout much of the
literature (Kasinitz et al. 2008; Portes and Rumbaut 2001, 2006; Waters 1999; Zhou
and Bankston 1998; Suarez-Orozco and Suarez-Orozco 1995; Suarez-Orozco,
Suarez-Orozco, and Todorova 2008). These observations come when educational
attainment has become critical to the social mobility of today's children of immigrants. Given the changes in the U.S. economy and the structure of the labor
market, today's ticket to social and economic mobility is unquestionably a college
degree. To be sure, a small portion of young people with modest levels of education manage to find skilled blue-collar jobs. Most, however, will need a college
degree to effectively compete for jobs that offer decent wages, benefits, job security, and the possibility of advancement.

Although educational attainment is critical to success, the opportunity structure
is not experienced uniformly. Research suggests that children from poor and minority families have greater difficulties attaining significant levels of education
because of historic disadvantage (Alba and Nee 2003; Portes and Rumbaut 2001;
Telles and Ortiz 2008). Disadvantaged students are particularly harmed by stratification mechanisms in schools, namely, curriculum tracking and highly differentiated curriculum within the tracks (Oakes 1985; Lucas and Berends 2002). To be
sure, decisions regarding student placement are influenced by scarce resources
and partial information, and sometimes personal prejudices and beliefs, but such
decisions are highly consequential. Particularly in large urban schools, which are
typically characterized by high ratios of teachers and counselors to students and a
lack of adequate time and resources to be distributed among the entire student
body, school placement—by virtue of program of study, classes, teachers, and
peer group—determines students' access to valuable resources (Gibson, Gándara,
and Peterson-Koyama 2004). What is and is not provided to students has a strong
bearing on future educational and occupational paths.

Indeed students from disadvantaged groups face difficulty within the school
system. However, they do not experience it uniformly. Research shows that even
in majority-minority schools, systems of stratification provide both disadvantages
and benefits for minority students (Conchas 2001; Conchas and Clark 2002; Gan-
dara 1995; Mehan et al. 1996). Sociologist Gilberto Conchas (2001), for example,
argues that schools structure failure and success. Although volumes of studies

suggest that poor and minority students often suffer the negative consequences of tracking, Conchas finds that a portion of these students get tracked for success.

As the attainment of advanced degrees has a strong bearing on future success, what happens in high school has become increasingly consequential to those pursuits. However, the field of play is much more complicated for undocumented immigrant students. Because of Supreme Court ruling in Plyler v. Doe (1982), undocumented children have a constitutionally guaranteed right to a K-12 education. They can also attend postsecondary institutions in most states, and can receive some form of tuition assistance in some. However, as adults they cannot legally put that education to use in the job market. They are also excluded from many aspects of the polity. These young people are particularly vulnerable and have arguably greater needs than their documented peers. Legal and financial constraints create added layers of need in navigating the successful completion of high school and the transition to postsecondary schooling. Restriction from financial aid makes such guidance all the more important. To be without such assistance can mean the difference between a seamless transition from high school to college or an early entry to the low-skilled labor market.

STUDYING UNDOCUMENTED YOUNG ADULTS IN LOS ANGELES

Until very recently it has been difficult to study undocumented youth and young adults because their numbers were prohibitively small. Studying hard to reach populations is often challenging, in general, but locating, gaining access, and building trust and rapport with individuals from these populations involves added layers of difficulty, time, and cost. Moreover, studying children often does not provide enough insight into their futures as adults and to the ways in which legal barriers shape daily lives and, in turn, alter trajectories over time.

To gain a deep understanding of lives of undocumented immigrants who migrate as children, we must go beyond traditional methods. Indeed, a deeper understanding of these young men and women requires a familiarity with their lives, barriers, pathways, aspirations and disappointments. Such depth of knowledge can only be achieved by gaining a glimpse into their world, putting in significant time, gaining access, and building trust and rapport. Because of their circumstances, it is extremely difficult to apply a random sampling frame. Moreover, the total number of cases to be observed or interviewed is likely to be substantially smaller than in a conventional sample survey, regardless of the sampling procedure used. Also, problems of attrition that characterize most longitudinal research efforts pose added problems with already small and potentially uncooperative samples of respondents. According to Nancy Foner, although this approach has its downside, a systematic, qualitative study of a small number of people over time produces up-close, in-depth knowledge of individuals that large-scale surveys often miss or, in some cases, get wrong (2003, 26–27).

Therefore, the methodological decisions made in conducting this study reflect my attempts to gain rapport and, thus, a better informed picture of the ways in which undocumented status shapes daily life and adult trajectories. Data collection for this study involved nearly four and a half years of field work during the periods of 2003 to 2007 and 2008 to 2009 in the Los Angeles metropolitan area.[7] I spent long stretches of time in the field and made numerous contacts with people. I recruited respondents from various settings, including continuation schools, community organizations, college campuses, and churches. I accompanied respondents throughout their school and work days, volunteered at local schools and organizations, and sat in on numerous community meetings. I built on the initial group of respondents by using snowball sampling to identify subsequent respondents.

In addition, I conducted individual in-depth life history interviews with 150 1.5-generation Mexican-origin young adults between the ages of twenty and thirty-four. All respondents spent much of their childhood, adolescence, and adulthood in undocumented residency status. With the exception of eight Central Americans, who were either Guatemalan or Salvadoran, all were born in Mexico. In addition to sampling interviewees by national origin, I also designed the sampling process to include relatively equal numbers of males (seventy-one) and females (seventy-nine) and equal numbers of individuals who dropped out of or completed high school (seventy-three) and those who attended at least two years of college (seventy-seven). While the number of undocumented college-goers in California (and the United States) is much smaller than those pursuing postsecondary education, I wanted to oversample high achievers to gain deeper insight into the mechanisms that promote successful trajectories. Of the seventy-seven college respondents, nine had advanced degrees at the time of the interview, twenty-two had earned bachelor's degrees, twenty-six were enrolled in four-year universities, and twenty were enrolled in or had attended community college. The majority attended a California public college or university. Of the seventy-three respondents who exited school at or before high school graduation, thirty-one had not earned a high school degree at the time of last contact, and forty-two held high school diplomas or their equivalent (as a result of graduating with their original high school class or later obtaining their degree).

Although relying on self-reporting to understand earlier aspects of their lives is not ideal, given the circumstances, it was the best way to put together the various pieces of life narratives to better understand the influence of immigration status, educational attainment, and work opportunities on their adolescent and adult trajectories. The questions I asked respondents broadly captured their school experiences, relationships, work histories, and general experiences of being unauthorized. Questions also addressed respondents' pasts and their present lives as well as future expectations and aspirations. Interviews ranged in length from one hour and forty minutes to three hours and twenty minutes. In analyzing interview transcripts, I used open coding techniques. I placed conceptual labels on responses that described discrete events, experiences, and feelings reported in the interviews; analyzed each interview across all questions to identify meta-themes; and examined responses for common meta-themes across all interviews.

I chose the five-county Los Angeles metropolitan area because of its large numbers of undocumented residents. California is home to almost 2.5 million unauthorized immigrants, nearly 25 percent of the national total. It has an even larger share of the unauthorized students, between 25 and 40 percent at all grade levels (Batalova and McHugh 2010; Passel 2003). Although many recent immigrants have dispersed to new destination states in the South and the Midwest (Marrow 2009; Massey 2008; Singer 2004; Zúñiga and Hernández-León 2005), California still has the largest undocumented immigrant population in the country. The numbers of undocumented immigrants from countries outside Latin America have risen slightly since 2000, but those from Mexico continue to account for the majority. In fact, no other sending country constitutes even a double-digit share of the total (Passel and Cohn 2009).

A PORTRAIT OF DIFFERENTLY ACHIEVING YOUNG ADULTS

Given the structure of today's labor market, returns on education over the last two to three decades have increased sharply. To compete for good jobs, an advanced degree is a must. Nevertheless, a significant segment of the adult U.S. population has only a high school diploma. To be sure, this group is rapidly falling behind. Nonetheless, contemporary research on this very population is at best scant, in that much of what we know today has been generated by studying high achievers.

Today's researchers have a good sense of the populations at risk of falling behind. We also know about family- and community-level risk factors for educational and economic stagnation. The profile of undocumented immigrant families, however, provides a picture of ongoing disadvantage that has long-lasting effects. Indeed, because of parental economic and legal limitations, undocumented immigrant children face challenges above and beyond those of their native-born and documented counterparts. Additionally, their immigration status constraints pose serious barriers, particularly in late adolescence and adulthood.

Due to parental constraints, undocumented immigrant youth face notable barriers growing up (Yoshikawa 2011). Parents in these families are often in low-paying, unstable jobs for long periods. As a result, the children are much more likely to be poor, live in crowded housing, lack health care, and be in households where families have trouble paying the rent and affording food (Capps et al. 2005). Indeed, the average income of families with at least one undocumented parent is 40 percent lower than that of either native-born families or legal immigrant families (Passel 2006), and almost two-thirds of undocumented children under eighteen are low income (Batalova and McHugh 2010). Furthermore, being undocumented also both increases the likelihood that families will lack health insurance and lowers their chances of accessing bank accounts and other financial services (Fortuny, Capps, and Passel 2007). Due to fear of deportation, such families are also less likely to apply for food stamp benefits or go into a government agency to apply for their children's health care benefits, even though their children may be eligible (Yoshikawa 2011). In the longer term, undocumented status keeps families in the shadows, avoiding many of the very institutions that have traditionally benefited immigrant families (Menjívar and Abrego 2009). Research shows that such indicators of disadvantage have particularly strong effects when experienced in early childhood (Yoshikawa 2011; Duncan, Ziol-Guest, and Kalil 2010). Some evidence also suggests that parental immigration status hampers the educational attainment of children (Bean et al. 2011). In 2008, 31 percent of all children of immigrants in K-12 public schools in the United States, or almost one in fourteen children in public school had at least one undocumented immigrant parent (Passel and Cohn 2009). When one thinks of the scope of the problem, such disadvantage translates into large proportions of our nation's student population growing up significantly behind the starting line.

As undocumented youth grow older, options decrease as family responsibilities increase. Respondents for this study contributed a monthly average of $285 to their parents. Males contributed almost $400 a month, some more than $1,000, and females a little under $200. In contrast, only ten in nearly 150 reported receiving any monthly support from parents. Contrary to contemporary research findings that most young adults are relying more on their parents to support them as they go to college, marry, and buy homes, many undocumented youngsters do not experience such advantages. In fact, many are struggling to balance their own financial needs with ongoing family contributions.

The combination of scarce family resources and federal exclusion from financial aid makes the path to higher education steep for undocumented high school students. Estimates reveal that as few as 5 to 10 percent of all undocumented high school graduates ever reach postsecondary institutions (Passel 2003), and the vast majority attend community colleges (Flores 2010). Among eighteen- to twenty-four-year-olds, more than 40 percent do not complete high school, and only 49 percent of high school graduates go to college. Within this age group, those who arrive in the United States before the age of fourteen fare slightly better: 72 percent finish high school, 61 percent of whom go on to college. But these figures are still much lower than the numbers for U.S.-born residents (Passel and Cohn 2009). Although it is difficult to ascertain accurate estimates of undocumented students in various public and private postsecondary systems, data from the University of California system indicate that though undocumented Latino students make up a much larger proportion statewide than their undocumented Asian counterparts, the numbers of students from these two groups who benefit from the state's Assembly Bill 540 is roughly equal, suggesting disproportionate avenues of access. Research suggests that state laws allowing undocumented students to pay resident tuition have increased the number of high school graduates matriculating to college over the past decade (Flores 2010). Nonetheless, steep financial barriers prohibit many undocumented immigrant students from enrolling in college.

The educational success of a small, but significant portion of undocumented young adults demonstrates that although the general outlook for them is bleak, it is tempered by variance. To understand their divergent experiences, we must assess two parallel processes: the forces against which they push against as they make critical transitions through adolescence and young adulthood, and the ways in which the educational system mediates those critical transitions.

As undocumented youth begin to make critical adolescent and adult transitions, they approach their legal limitations. Because late adolescence and early adulthood entail losing the legally protected status of K-12 students, and the entrance into roles that require legal status as the basis for participation, they experience a movement from experiences of belonging to exclusion, from a de facto legal status to an illegal one (see Gonzales 2011). In the process, they must "learn to be illegal," a transformation that involves almost completely retooling daily routines, survival skills, aspirations, and social patterns. This transition has profound implications for identity formation, friendship patterns, aspirations and expectations, and social and economic mobility.

These processes do not happen uniformly. Education is a great mediator, particularly at the late adolescent and early adult transitions. Undocumented youngsters enter these transitions at different levels of education and with differential sources of support. Whereas some have the necessary grades and important relationships with teachers and other adults who can assist them in the college process, others lack the proper school standing to make the transition to postsecondary schooling. As a result, those with better educational preparation are able to move seamlessly from high school to college, thus preserving the legal buffer of school, whereas others make more difficult transitions to work and the difficulties of undocumented adult life.

Indeed, the opportunities afforded to college-goers and the difficulties experienced by the early-exiters stem, in large part, from the availability of such school resources. On their college campuses, they enjoyed a safe space to pursue higher education, and maintain and enlarge networks of upwardly mobile peers and campus-based mentors. These relationships provided support, guidance, and the opportunities to be integrated into a positive and legally permissible environment. Their friendship networks were ethnically and economically diverse, affording them important opportunities to broaden their worldview and envision successful lives. The pursuit of a college education also allowed college-goers to build valuable human capital in the form of knowledge, advanced degrees, and skills that would allow them to be competitive in high-skilled occupations if their immigration status no longer presented a barrier to the workforce. Their time in school also limited their interaction with unauthorized pursuits and encounters with law enforcement.

For early-exiters, entry into adulthood was marked by the pressures of earning enough to meet their basic needs and help out their families. The world of low-wage clandestine work was a major environment change from their years in school. Because their job options are limited, they settled uncomfortably into low-wage, often physically exhausting jobs. They were limited to occupations that paid cash or required minimal inspection of official right-to-work documents, such as low-end service sector work, light manufacturing, construction, and private business such as landscaping, housekeeping, and cleaning. These industries employ a disproportionate number of undocumented workers. Most do not offer benefits, opportunities to advance, or job security. Their co-workers are often adult migrants who speak minimal English and have little education. They found very little in common. Social time was dramatically reduced by long hours at work, the starting of families and an increased distance from childhood friends.

SCHOOLS STRUCTURE EARLY OUTCOMES

Why do some undocumented immigrant students do well in school when educational trajectories intersect with seemingly insurmountable social, legal, and financial barriers? The school experiences of undocumented immigrant students provide useful findings for scholars and policymakers alike. As such, issues affecting their postsecondary matriculation and subsequent academic or career pursuits are important clues to the larger puzzle of what it takes for them to lead healthy lives in early adulthood.

Because of the low levels of education that characterize labor migrants, an overwhelming majority of undocumented immigrant students outpace their parents' education, often in middle school. Also, because of long hours at work and low levels of education and English fluency, parents are at a distinct disadvantage and often unable to provide academic support. As a result, these young people are often without family assistance with school and guidance from which to make decisions about life after high school. To be sure, nearly all those interviewed indicated that their parents encouraged them to do well in school. Nevertheless, they felt as though they needed to go outside of the home for assistance.

Accessing School Resources

College-goers and early-exiters have similar family, community, and school profiles. But in assessing their divergent trajectories school experiences stand out as an important mediator in their divergent trajectories. In particular, those who excelled in school benefited from positive school environments that fostered learning and the development of school-based social capital, and were shielded from the broader problems that plagued many public schools. Smaller learning environments fostered the development of relationships with teachers and adults who could leverage resources needed to advance to institutions of higher learning. By school officials actively working to incorporate students into the culture of the school, and illuminate the various pathways to postsecondary education, these young people were provided additional opportunities for achieving educational success.

College-goers spoke very favorably about their high school experiences. Carolina explained: "Being in AP sets a different atmosphere. The teachers set the tone for you." College-going respondents enjoyed visits to university campuses, ongoing support from school counselors, and assistance with college applications. They also described the benefits of having friends that pushed them to do well in school.

As research suggests, the positive peer support has several benefits. With good modeling, peers support, teach, and compete with each other in ways that enhance their intellectual development and advance their academic pursuits. Peer groups also enhanced respondents' social capital, as they maximized resources by sharing information with each other. JD explained her peer support system:

It was a group of people helping. My friend Amanda, whenever she would get one piece of information or she heard something, she'd let me know. Or we would help each other. There was someone from a different university coming in to talk. We would sign up and get information and give it each other.

Undocumented students encounter additional barriers to the already formidable ones low-income students confront in trying to finish high school and advance to postsecondary institutions. Their exclusions from federal financial aid and the legal work force dramatically limit their options after high school. Because school is one of the few legally permissible avenues, making a seamless transition from high school to college is critical, because it allows them a productive path and keeps them from activities that place them on the wrong side of the law. Additionally, the college campus shelters undocumented students from run-ins with law enforcement or immigration officials.

To make these difficult transitions to postsecondary schooling, undocumented immigrant students must not only take the right courses and show the ability to navigate the college application process, both of which are difficult for many low-income youth. They must also find ways other than traditional financial aid to secure adequate funding for tuition and fees. This is no easy task. Undocumented status arouses the always-present fear of punishment by immigration authorities or by peer stigmatization. As a result, many undocumented youngsters do not disclose the details of their unauthorized status to school personnel for fear of negative repercussions.

Because college-goers enjoyed trusting relationships with teachers and counselors, many of them felt comfortable talking openly about their immigration status. Luis, who later graduated from a university in northern California, described these school benefits.

I had help from counselors, from teachers, from the principal. They were helpful; they were my mentors. Any help that I needed in terms of questions on writing my personal statement or college applications . . . those were the people that I would always go to. I'm sure I would not have gone to college if they hadn't been there for me.

Teachers helped respondents explore college options, often teaching themselves as they went along. When Aldo was on the verge of dropping out, his AP (Advanced Placement) history teacher intervened. Aldo's earning power was needed by his economically challenged family. Feeling the burden of family needs and not seeing a way out of his situation, Aldo had decided to leave school in order to earn money. His AP history teacher pleaded with him to reconsider his decision. Aldo explained his family's circumstances and added that "school probably was not going to be useful anyway" as he could not get a good job even if he went to college. His teacher mobilized other teachers and started a fund to provide him extra money through the remainder of his senior year.

On the Wrong Side of the Tracking

The experiences of early-exiters stand in direct contrast to their college-going counterparts. Most of them reported feeling disconnected at school, not having significant relationships with teachers. Many felt as though they were negatively labeled, left to fall through the cracks, and shut out of many important services. Like the college-goers, they attended overcrowded schools in very large school districts, where the ratios of students to counselors were nearly 1,000 to 1.[8] But in contrast to the small classes and specialized attention described by the college-goers, many early-exiters sat in classrooms with student-teacher ratios as high as 40 to 1. Many of them did not ever meet with counselors. When I asked them about relationships with teachers and counselors, many early-exiters could not name even one.

Sergio, who discovered the consequences of his unauthorized status his sophomore year, acted out his frustrations at school. He had been saving money for his first car by helping his father mow lawns when he realized that he did not have a social security number and, as a result, could not drive. I asked him why he did not try to talk with someone at school:

> I had problems with teachers. I didn't like them and they did not like me. I didn't like people telling me what to do, but at the same time, I felt bad. I just felt like nobody there cared about me. I was a troublemaker, and that's all they wanted to see. Nobody knew me.

Structurally, Sergio did not have many options. Labeled a troublemaker, he failed to receive anything other than negative attention. School personnel did not uncover his problems because they did not take the time to get to know him. He was reluctant to seek help because he did not have any trusting relationships to draw on. In contrast to the students who believed they were "college material" and whose teachers dissuaded them from dropping out of high school, Sergio's status as a troublemaker underscores the influence of the school stratification system. His problems with his immigration status were never uncovered.

Karina, on the other hand, maintained a B average in school but was quiet and did not garner the attention of her teachers. None of her friends knew of her undocumented status. When it came time to apply to college, she had no assistance and was reluctant to ask for it because she did not want to disclose her immigration status. Unaware of legislation in California that would have allowed her to qualify for residency tuition, Karina settled for a community college, taking classes on a part-time basis:

I didn't know anything about AB 540 so the reason I didn't go to university, well first of all was because I was lacking the money so even if I were . . . well maybe if I knew the information I could have gotten a scholarship or something. But I didn't know anything. I didn't even know we had AB 540 so I thought I was going to pay like twenty thousand so I was like "no way I was going to pay that." So that's why I didn't go. Nobody told me anything. I don't know if my counselors knew, but they never told me anything.

In their large, under-resourced, high schools early-exiters found themselves on the wrong side of the stratification system and, as a consequence, without critical resources. Perhaps most importantly, they did not have the opportunities to develop trusting relationships with adults to guide them through what was probably the most important and daunting transition in their lives. Ultimately, this had negative effects, channeling them into worlds of low-wage work and daily contact with their legal limitations and the constant threat of apprehension and deportation.

WHEN THE SAFETY NET OF SCHOOL DISAPPEARS

Whereas transitioning out of high school is marked with stigma, fear, difficulty, and frustration, the transition from high school to the world of work and uncertainly can be harrowing. Without the legal and psychological protections of school, this important turning point into the harsh condition of illegality leaves most undocumented youngsters with few options. Undocumented adolescents are unprepared when the important protections of school and childhood disappear. This transition marks their entry into the adult world, where they must take care of themselves and help support their families.

Urban poverty inquiry over the last decade has introduced two important urban populations as worthy of investigation: the working poor and young adults. Contemporary studies of the working poor (Shipler 2004; Ehrenreich 2002; Romero 2002; Newman 1999) have brought to the fore the problems confronting millions of working Americans. Katherine Newman (1999), for example, identifies the working poor as an important, yet invisible, population to urban poverty scholarship. According to Newman, we know very little about the working poor even though they are a growing and significant portion of the population. This important research demonstrates that contemporary poverty is not limited to joblessness. Rather, millions of men and women both work and live in poverty.

Contemporary scholarship is making up some ground in understanding more about young, working-poor adults in urban America, but much less is known about their undocumented counterparts who face life after high school in poverty and illegality. Most find themselves struggling to find their niche in a labor market in which they do not fully fit. Their English-language proficiency and levels of education could place them in a higher skilled category relative to their parents, but their undocumented status limits their mobility. Consequently, their expectations clash not only with labor market realities, but also with those of their employers, who become accustomed to the attitudes and work ethic of first generation low-skilled immigrants (Waldinger 1996). As such, undocumented young people may be at a greater risk for experiencing downward assimilation, not wanting to accept their position within society and the labor market, but with few options (Portes and Rumbaut 2006; Gans 1992).

Early Transitions to Work and Uncertainty

Leo Chavez (1998) describes the process of "learning to live as an 'illegal alien'" as a constant fear of deportation, feelings of confinement, and a heightened awareness of their status as outsiders. This type of on-the-job education is a developed set of survival skills that keep undocumented immigrants safe and help them make ends meet. Their undocumented children, however, do not undergo much of this process until later in their lives. As Eric, from Riverside, explained,

> I had grown up thinking I was going to have a better life. I saw my older (American born) cousins get good jobs. I mean, they're not lawyers or anything like that, but they're not in restaurants or mowing lawns. I thought, yeah, when I graduate from school, I can make some good money, maybe even go to college.

For many early-exiters, "learning to be 'illegal'" involved an even steeper learning curve from that undergone by their parents early in the migration process. Without legal immigration status and strong networks of support, early-exiters experienced life after high school to be rife with difficulty. Economic circumstances, family need, and a lack of other options forced them to make difficult choices about working and driving illegally. Employment options were as narrowly circumscribed as those of their parents.

Janet, who has been employed by various maid services, told me she cried every day after work for the first two months:

> I can't believe this is my life. When I was in school I never thought I'd be doing this. I mean, I was never an honors student, but I thought I would have a lot better job. It's really hard, you know. I make beds, I clean toilets. The sad thing is when I get paid. I work this hard, for nothing.

Undocumented status required early-exiters to quickly integrate a new set of skills into their everyday lives. While financial need forced them into the workforce, a lack of experience placed them at a disadvantage in the low-wage job sector, where they became part of the same job pool as their parents and other migrant workers with much less education but more work experience. Many described difficulty finding jobs. Others failed to stay on at jobs after noticeably falling behind other workers.

Early-exiters also recounted difficulty negotiating precarious situations because their undocumented status forced them to confront experiences for which K-12 schooling did not prepare them. Pedro found himself in legal trouble when, after completing a day job, he tried to cash his check at the local currency exchange. A teller called Pedro's employer to verify its legitimacy, and he denied writing the check and called the police. When the police arrived, they found multiple sets of identification in Pedro's possession and took him to jail for identity fraud. This incident awoke Pedro to the reality that his inexperience with undocumented life could have grave consequences, including arrest and even deportation.

Early Exits from College

Among undocumented immigrant students nationally, the combination of scarce family resources and the exclusion from federal and state financial aid extremely limits postsecondary goals. Undocumented immigrant high school graduates in California are eligible to attend public universities at in-state tuition rates, but family finances usually curb their ability to participate in higher education. As a result, the vast majority of them attend community college.

Because of the mismatch of the costs of college and available funds, many respondents experienced postsecondary schooling as a discontinuous, nonlinear process. As a result, many entered only to drop out shortly after. Several respondents found themselves struggling to balance regular college attendance with increasing needs to work. When I met Eloy he was twenty-five and had been taking community college classes on and off for more than five years.

> I feel like I'm running in place. I'm at the same place I was when I was twenty. I just can't get ahead. It's stressful. I've done all of this, and I still don't have my [associate's] degree. To be honest, I don't think I'm going to reach my goal. I mean, I'm not in school now and it's getting to be, like I am starting to think it's not going to matter anyway.

Others continued to persist despite considerable barriers. Cory, in her eighth year at the University of California has enrolled one quarter at a time, working full time the remainder of the year to pay for tuition and living expenses. She told me that she would like to do more, "but I've got to accept what I can do and make the best of that." Still others have been forced to take leaves of absence to save for subsequent school terms or to pay off school debt. Grace, whom I met during her freshman year, found that with tuition increases each year, she was unable to keep up with her payments. During her junior year, after accumulating a significant debt, she left school for two quarters in order to pay off the debt and reenroll.

Faced with family responsibilities to work, inconsistent availability of scholarships, debt, and long commutes (particularly in California), most respondents did not fully benefit from the college experience. Many made long bus commutes from home to their campuses (some upwards of two-plus hours each way) and lamented that, as a result, they did not have time to meet their professors during office hours or to take part in on-campus study groups. Janelle, who attends a California State school, conveyed her frustration of not being able to access important forms of school support: "Look, there's only so much on campus that I'm eligible for. Everything requires U.S. citizenship. So, I'm really limited by my situation."

Taken together the cumulative disadvantages of undocumented status—the inability to receive financial aid, exclusion from important federally funded sources of support, and restriction from any form of work study—tremendously limits on-campus options for financial, social and academic support. Coupled with low family income, high family need, and the inability to engage in most means towards earning money, respondents found the road through higher education to be an increasingly narrow pathway. Many did not make it. For many who did, their experiences show them struggling to keep pace.

A New Glass Ceiling

At some point during their adult lives, doors stop opening altogether. Whether because of blocked opportunities within the labor market or the end of educational opportunities, a time comes when undocumented young adults run out of options. Without a change in immigration status they must eventually confront the full limitations of exclusion. These experiences contradict all these young people have been taught in school, that education earned through their hard work will mean something. Instead of joining friends and peers in jobs that match their educational preparation, they must try their luck in the clandestine low-wage labor market—a daunting task considering their relative lack of preparation and experience. The cognitive dissonance can be debilitating. At the time of they interviews, nine respondents held advance degrees and an additional twenty-two had graduated from four-year institutions. None is in a job that reflects his or her educational achievement.

As the experiences of college-goers poignantly illustrate, at some point in early adulthood once-divergent trajectories converge. Whether because of barriers to the completion of college or barriers to the legal workforce after college, college-going young adults join their early-exiter peers in the low-wage labor market in jobs they once shunned. For decades, research has touted the importance of human capital. For undocumented young adults with college degrees, such an accumulation of education, experience, and degrees has little consequence to their everyday lives. Instead, they must toil in low-wage jobs, stay carefully hidden, and become lumped into a broader pool of undocumented workers.

Irene, for example, graduated from a university in southern California in 2010 with a major in film studies. At the time of her interview, she was contemplating her next step, working at a cafe owned by a close friend, and anxious to continue her pursuit of film. She found, however, that the cost of renting the needed equipment was prohibitive. Faced with limited choices, she had moved home with her parents in Boyle Heights, where she had little room in the small two-bedroom apartment she shared with nine family members.

Similarly, Enrique, who holds a master's degree in public health, has been out of school for nearly four years. Although he had initially pursued unpaid opportunities that matched his educational preparation, financial need caused him to look for work that would provide a paycheck. Over the last three years, thanks to referrals from family and friends, he has held a string of low-wage jobs in restaurants, construction, and landscaping. None of these jobs promises stability, decent wages, or benefits. Any one of them he could have started in high school.

Esperanza's experience characterizes that of many other undocumented college graduates I interviewed. Now five years out of college, she must conceal her education, her perfect English, and all the lessons a university education has given her in order to fit in at her various low-wage jobs. She explains that she feels out of place, but has little choice other than to survive: "Thinking about it makes me feel so stupid . . . Because they ask me, 'Que estas haciendo aqui?' [What are you doing here?] You can speak English. You graduated from high school.'"

DISCUSSIONS AND CONCLUSIONS

Since leaving the field in 2010, several developments have shaped educational and occupational access for undocumented immigrant students. Although the Development, Relief, and Education for Alien Minors (DREAM) Act failed to pass the Senate in 2010, in the summer of 2012, President Obama announced a change in his administration's immigration policy that would provide deferred action and work permits to an estimated 1.4 to 1.7 million young undocumented immigrants who have lived in the United States since childhood. In California, Governor Jerry Brown signed into law Assembly Bills 130 and 131 (two parts of the California DREAM Act), granting undocumented immigrant students access to state financial aid at public universities and community colleges. It is too soon to tell the kind of impact these changes will have on young people in the long term. But with more support for postsecondary education and the ability to pursue paid internships, work study positions on college campuses, and jobs that match their educational preparations and credentials, a select group of undocumented youngsters may be able to more substantially support themselves and their families, and feel encouraged to achieve more education. Nevertheless, a larger group of undocumented immigrant youngsters may still find itself ineligible for these benefits.

With or without these new forms of widened access, the urgent needs for legalization remain unaddressed, and the problems undocumented immigrant young people confront on a daily basis persist. Research suggests that this sizeable and vulnerable subset of the immigrant population is at risk of becoming a disenfranchised underclass, cut off from the very means through which to lift itself out of poverty. Their tenuous situation stems from a confluence of contradictory laws that allow them to legally attend school and thus attain an education, but deny them the opportunities to put that education to work. This not only limits them, it also denies the country the opportunity to benefit from their participation.

Indeed, legalization lifts the biggest barrier these young people confront because it allows them to legally participate in a world in which they know very well. Providing viable pathways to legalization can help to move these young people out of poverty, integrate them into adult society, and give them opportunities to compete for financial aid and jobs. Indeed, tens of thousands of undocumented young adults could benefit right away, and hundreds of thousands of others might be motivated to stay in school.

When given an opportunity to regularize their status, undocumented immigrants have experienced substantial upward mobility. For instance, undocumented immigrants who received legal status under the 1986 Immigration Reform and Control Act have moved on to significantly better jobs over time (Kossoudji and Cobb-Clark 2000; Powers, Kraly, and Seltzer 2004) and increased their wages by roughly 15 percent within five years (Smith, Kramer, and Singer 1996). Given the opportunity to receive additional education and training and move into better paying jobs, legalized immigrants pay more in taxes and have more money to spend and invest.

It is therefore likely that if currently undocumented youth were granted legal status, they would not only improve their circumstances, but make greater contributions to the U.S. economy. In fact, the economic benefits derived from obtaining legal status would likely be even greater for them because they could immediately fill job shortages in needed high- and semi-skilled job sectors (Cheeseman-Day and Newburger 2002). However, until then, their educational attainment matters very little to their present adult pursuits.

NOTES

1. All names in this chapter are pseudonyms. To protect identities I have also modified specific details about families, schools, places of work, and in some cases neighborhoods.

2. The California public postsecondary system has three tiers: the University of California campuses, the California State University campuses, and the California Community Colleges. To further protect identities, I list only the general system and not individual campuses (for example, University of California rather than University of California, Riverside).

3. I use the terms *undocumented* and *unauthorized* interchangeably when referring to the young adults in my study. I lean more toward *undocumented* because this most accurately describes how the young adults characterize their circumstances in both English and Spanish. However, when referring to processes that shape their experiences and the state of being in the world, I incorporate the term used by social scientists, *illegality*. This concept provides a greater degree of analytical purchase and requires further explanation.

4. Undocumented immigrants are excluded from receipt of federal financial aid. This in-

cludes Pell Grants and subsidized student loans. They are also ineligible for state financial aid in most states.

5. Plyler v. Doe, 457 U.S. 202 (1982), was a case in which the Supreme Court of the United States struck down a state statute denying funding for education undocumented immigrants and simultaneously struck down a municipal school district's attempt to undocumented immigrant students an annual $1,000 tuition fee for each illegal immigrant student to compensate for the lost state funding (http://en.wikipedia.org/wiki/Plyler _v._Doe).

6. The Development, Relief, and Education for Alien Minors (DREAM) Act, first introduced in Congress in 2001, is proposed legislation that would provide a path to legalization for eligible unauthorized youth and young adults. The DREAM Act would authorize cancellation of removal and adjustment of status for undocumented children if they satisfy the following conditions: entered the United States before age sixteen; have been continuously present in the country for five years before the bill was enacted; have obtained a high school diploma or its equivalent; and demonstrated good moral character.

7. The Los Angeles Metropolitan Area is made up of five counties: Los Angeles, Ventura, Riverside, San Bernardino, and Orange.

8. Although California has made important strides in reducing class size raising academic standards, increasing accountability, and improving teacher preparation, it continues to lag behind the rest of the country in counseling services. The ratio of students per counselor in the state averages 945 to 1, compared with the national average of 477 to 1, ranking California last in the nation. See California Department of Education, "Research on School Counseling Effectiveness." Available at: http://www.cde.ca.gov/ls/ cg/rh/counseffective.asp (accessed March 19, 2013).

REFERENCES

Alba, Richard, and Victor Nee. 2003. *Remaking the American Mainstream: Assimilation and Contemporary Immigration.* Cambridge, Mass.: Harvard University Press.

Batalova, Jeanne, and Margie McHugh. 2010. "DREAM vs. Reality: An Analysis of Potential DREAM Act Beneficiaries." *Insight* (July 2010): 1–23.

Bean, Frank, D., Mark A. Leach, Susan K. Brown, James D. Bachmeier, and John R. Hipp. 2011. "The Educational Legacy of Unauthorized Migration: Comparisons Across U.S. Immigrant Groups in How Parent's Status Affects Their Offspring." *International Migration Review* 45(2): 348–85.

Capps, Randolph, Rosa Maria Castañeda, Ajay Chaudry, and Robert Santos. 2007. *Paying the Price: The Impact of Immigration Raids on America's Children.* Washington, D.C.: The Urban Institute.

Capps, Randy, Michael Fix, Jason Ost, Jane Reardon-Anderson, and Jeffrey S. Passel. 2005. "The Health and Well-Being of Young Children of Immigrants." Washington, D.C.: The Urban Institute.

Chavez, Leo R. 1998. *Shadowed Lives: Undocumented Immigrants in American Society*. Fort Worth, Tex.: Harcourt Brace.

Cheeseman-Day, Jennifer, and Eric C. Newburger. 2002. *The Big Pay Off: Educational Attainment & Synthetic Estimates of Work Life Earnings*. Washington, D.C.: U.S. Census Bureau.

Conchas, Gilberto Q. 2001. "Structuring Failure and Success: Understanding the Variability in Latino School Engagement. *Harvard Educational Review* 71(3), 475–504.

Conchas, Gilberto Q., and Patricia A. Clark. 2002. "Career Academies and Urban Minority Schooling: Forging Optimism Despite Limited Opportunity." *Journal of Education for Students Placed at Risk* 7(3), 287–311.

Duncan, Greg J., Kathleen Ziol-Guest, and Ariel Kalil. 2010. "Early Childhood Poverty and Adult Attainment, Behavior, and Health." *Child Development* 81(1): 292–311.

Ehrenreich, Barbara. 2002. *Nickled and Dimed: On (Not) Getting by in America*. New York: Henry Holt.

Flores, Stella M. 2010. "State 'Dream Acts': The Effect of In-State Resident Tuition Policies on the College Enrollment of Undocumented Latino Students in the United States." *The Review of Higher Education* 33(2): 239–28.

Foner, Nancy. 2003. *American Arrivals: Anthropology Engages the New Immigration*. Santa Fe, N.M.: School of American Research Press.

Fortuny, Karina, Randolph Capps, and Jeffrey Passel. 2007. "The Characteristics of Unauthorized Immigrants in California, Los Angeles County, and the United States." Washington, D.C.: Urban Institute.

Gándara, Patricia. 1995. *Over the Ivy Walls: The Educational Mobility of Low-Income Chicanos*. Albany: State University of New York Press.

Gans, Herbert J. 1992. "Second-Generation Decline: Scenarios for the Economic and Ethnic Futures of the Post-1965 American Immigrants." *Ethnic and Racial Studies* 15(2): 173–92.

Ganzeboom, Harry B.G., and Donald J. Treiman. 1996. "Internationally Comparable Measures of Occupational Status for the 1988 International Standard Classification of Occupations." *Social Science Research* 25: 201–39.

Gibson, Margaret A., Patricia Gándara, and Jill Peterson-Koyama. 2004. *School Connections: U.S. Mexican Youth, Peers, and School Achievement*. New York: Teachers College Press.

Gonzales, Roberto G. 2010a. "On the Wrong Side of the Tracks: The Consequences of School Stratification Systems for Unauthorized Mexican Students." *Peabody Journal of Education* 85(4): 469–85.

———. 2010b. "More than Just Access: Undocumented Students Navigating the Post-Secondary Terrain." *Journal of College Admissions* 206(Winter): 48–52.

———. 2011. "Learning to be Illegal: Undocumented Youth and Shifting Legal Contexts in the Transition to Adulthood." *American Sociological Review* 76(4): 602–19.

Kao, Grace, and Marta Tienda. 1995. "Optimism and Achievement: The Educational Performance of Immigrant Youth." *Social Science Quarterly*. 76: 1–19.

Kasinitz, Philip, John H. Mollenkopf, Mary C. Waters, and Jennifer Holdaway. 2008. *Inheriting the City: The Children of Immigrants Come of Age*. Cambridge, Mass.: Harvard University Press.

Kossoudji, Sherrie A., and Deborah A. Cobb-Clark. 2000. "URCA's Impact on the Occupational Concentration and Mobility of Newly-Legalized Mexican Men." *Journal of Population Economics* 13(1): 81–98.

Lucas, Samuel R., and Mark Berends. 2002. "Sociodemographic Diversity, Correlated Achievement, and *de facto* Tracking. *Sociology of Education* 75(2): 328–48.

Marrow, Helen B. 2009. "Immigrant Bureaucratic Incorporation: The Dual Roles of Professional Missions and Government Policies." *American Sociological Review*, 74(5): 756–76.

Massey, Douglas S. 2008. *New Faces in New Places: The New Geography of American Immigration.* New York: Russell Sage Foundation.

Mehan, Hugh, Irene Villanueva, Lea Hubbard, and Angela Lintz. 1996. *Constructing School Success: The Consequences of Untracking Low-Achieving Students.* New York: Cambridge University Press.

Menjívar, Cecilia, and Leisy Abrego. 2009. "Parents and Children Across Borders: Legal Instability and Intergenerational Relations in Guatemalan and Salvadoran Families." In *Across Generations: Immigrant Families in America*, edited by Nancy Foner. New York: New York University Press.

Newman, Katherine. 1999. *No Shame in My Game: The Working Poor in the Inner City.* New York: Russell Sage Foundation.

Oakes, Jeannie. 1985. *Keeping Track: How Schools Structure Inequality.* New Haven, Conn.: Yale University Press.

Olivas, Michael A. 2007. "Immigration—Related State and Local Ordinances: Preemption, Prejudice, and the Proper Role for Enforcement." *University of Chicago Legal Forum* 2007:27–56.

Passel, Jeffrey S. 2003. *Further Demographic Information Relating to the DREAM Act.* Washington, D.C.: The Urban Institute.

———. 2006. "The Size and Characteristics of the Unauthorized Migrant Population in the U.S.: Estimates based on the March 2005 Current Population Survey." Washington, D.C.: Pew Hispanic Center.

Passel, Jeffrey S, and D'Vera Cohn. 2009. "A Portrait of Unauthorized Immigrants in the United States." Washington, D.C.: Pew Hispanic Center. Available at: http://pewhispanic.org/files/reports/107.pdf (accessed May 27, 2013).

Portes, Alejandro. 1981. "Modes of Structural Incorporation and Present Theories of Labor Immigration." In *Global Trends in Migration: Theory and Research on International Population Movements*, edited by M. M. Kritz. New York, N.Y.: Center for Migration Studies.

Portes, Alejandro, and Robert Bach. 1985. *Latin Journey: Cuban and Mexican Immigrants in the United States.* Berkeley: University of California Press.

Portes, Alejandro, and Dag MacLeod. 1996. "Educational Progress of Children of Immigrants: The Roles of Class, Ethnicity, and School Context." *Sociology of Education* 69: 255–75.

Portes, Alejandro, and Rubén G. Rumbaut. 2006. *Immigrant America: A Portrait,* 3rd ed. Berkeley: University of California Press.

Portes, Alejandro, and Min Zhou. 1993. "The New Second Generation: Segmented Assimilation and Its Variants." *The Annals of the American Academy of Political and Social Science* 530(1): 74–96.

Powers, Mary G., Ellen Percy Kraly, and William Seltzer. 2004. "IRCA: Lessons of the Last U.S. Legalization Program." *Migration Information Source* July. Available at: http://www.migrationpolicy.org/pubs/PolicyBrief_No3_Aug05.pdf (accessed May 27, 2013).

Romero, Mary. 2002. *Maid in the USA.* New York: Routledge.

Settersten, Richard A., Jr., Frank F. Furstenberg, and Rubén G. Rumbaut. 2005. *On the Frontier of Adulthood: Theory, Research, and Public Policy.* Chicago: University of Chicago Press.

Shipler, David K. 2004. *The Working Poor: Invisible in America.* New York: Alfred A. Knopf.

Singer, Audrey. 2004. "The Rise of New Immigrant Gateways." Washington, D.C.: The Brookings Institution. Available at: http://www.brookings.edu/urban/pubs/20040301_gateways.pdf (accessed May 27, 2013).

Smith, Robert Courtney. 2008. "Horatio Alger Lives in Brooklyn: Extrafamily Support, Intrafamily Dynamics, and Socially Neutral Operating Identities in Exceptional Mobility Among Children of Mexican Immigrants." *The Annals of the American Academy of Political and Social Science* 620(12): 270–90.

Smith, Shirley, Roger G. Kramer, and Audrey Singer. 1996. *Effects of the Immigration Reform and Control Act: Characteristics and Labor Market Behavior of the Legalized Population Five Years Following Legalization.* Washington, D.C.: Bureau of International Labor Affairs, U.S. Department of Labor.

Suárez-Orozco, Carola, and Marcelo Suárez-Orozco. 1995. *Transformations: Migration, Family Life, and Achievement Motivation among Latino Adolescents.* Stanford, Calif.: Stanford University Press.

Suárez-Orozco, Carola, Marcelo M. Suárez-Orozco, and Irina Todorova. 2008. *Learning a New Land: Immigrant Students in American Society.* Cambridge, Mass.: Harvard University Press.

Telles, Edward E., and Vilma Ortiz. 2008. *Generations of Exclusion: Mexican Americans, Assimilation, and Race.* New York: Russell Sage Foundation Press.

Waldinger, Roger. 1996. *Still the Promised City? African Americans and New Immigrants in Postindustrial New York.* Cambridge, Mass.: Harvard University Press.

Waters, Mary C. 1999. *Black Identities: West Indian Immigrant Dreams and American Realities.* New York: Russell Sage Foundation Press.

Yoshikawa, Hirokazu. 2011. *Immigrants Raising Citizens: Undocumented Parents and Their Young Children.* New York: Russell Sage Foundation.

Zhou, Min. 1997. "Segmented Assimilation: Issues, Controversies, and Recent Research on the New Second Generation." *International Migration Review* 4: 825–58.

———. 2008. "The Ethnic System of Supplementary Education: Non-profit and For-profit Institutions in Los Angeles' Chinese Immigrant Community." In *Toward Positive Youth Development: Transforming Schools and Community Programs*, edited by B. Shinn and H. Yoshikawa. New York: Oxford University Press.

Zhou, Min, and Carl L. Bankston III. 1998. *Growing Up American: How Vietnamese Children Adapt to Life in the United States.* New York: Russell Sage Foundation Press.

Zúñiga, Victor, and Ruben Hernández-León, eds. 2005. *New Destinations: Mexican Immigration in the United States.* New York: Russell Sage Foundation.

Part III

Public Policy and Poverty Among the Foreign Born

The material well-being of the various immigrant communities in the United States are touched in various ways by policies passed and implemented at the federal and state levels. In addition to the impacts of changes in immigration policy, border enforcement, and internal enforcement of labor laws, policies regarding eligibility for antipoverty programs as well as political participation likely impact immigrant earnings and by extensions poverty rates. The four chapters in this section are devoted to studying the role of such policies. Chapter 9 takes a long view of American immigration policy and assesses the role of changes over the past half century in generating a Latin underclass. Chapter 10 looks specifically at the effects of recent state efforts to limit the employment opportunities available to undocumented immigrants on the employment outcomes of those most likely to be unauthorized. Chapter 11 provides a thorough analysis of how the foreign-born population interacts with the U.S. social safety net. Finally, chapter 12 assesses the degree to which the effective disenfranchisement of noncitizens impacts redistributive politics.

Chapter 9

Immigration Enforcement as a Race-Making Institution

Douglas S. Massey

With a population of 50.5 million in 2010, Latinos are the largest minority group in the United States, 16.3 percent of the population, versus the African American 12.6 percent. Mexicans alone numbered 31.8 million that year, some 10.3 percent of the U.S. population (Ennis, Ríos-Vargas, and Albert 2011). Although fertility will play a large role in population growth moving forward, through 2008 the main source of Latino increase was immigration (Pew Hispanic Center 2011). From 1970 to 2010, the percentage of Latino foreign born rose from 29 percent to 39 percent and national origins shifted (Acosta and de la Cruz 2011). Whereas in 1970 Mexicans made up just 60 percent and Central Americans only 3 percent of all Latinos, by 2010 the former accounted for 63 percent and the latter 8 percent. South Americans, meanwhile, grew from 3 percent to 6 percent as Latinos of Caribbean origin fell from 25 percent to around 15 percent (Ennis, Ríos-Vargas, and Albert 2011).

This shift in origins and nativity was accompanied by a revolutionary shift in legal status. Whereas Latino immigrants from the Caribbean are overwhelmingly either legal residents or U.S. citizens, 58 percent of all Mexican immigrants in 2010 were unauthorized, compared with 57 percent of those born in El Salvador, 71 percent of those from Guatemala, and 77 percent of those from Honduras. Even considering everyone of Mexican, Salvadoran, Guatemalan, and Honduran origin, the unauthorized proportions were 21 percent, 38 percent, 50 percent, and 51 percent, respectively, in 2010 (Massey and Pren 2012a). Illegality has thus become a fundamental condition of life for sizeable shares of Mexicans and Central Americans living in the United States.

As Latinos grew in number and visibility in the United States after 1965, they were subject to a systematic process of racialization—a dedicated campaign of psychological framing and social boundary construction intended to position them as a stigmatized out-group in American social cognition (Lee and Fiske 2006;

Massey 2009, 2011). In the media, they were demonized as a grave threat to the American culture, society, and the economy (Santa Ana 2002; Chavez 2008). In the legal realm, they were systematically excluded from rights, privileges, and protections extended to other Americans (Legomsky 2000; Zolberg 2006; Newton 2008). In the domain of public policy, they were subject to increasingly harsh and repressive enforcement actions that drove them ever further underground (Massey, Durand, and Pren 2009; Massey 2013). The net effect was to place Latinos in a uniquely tenuous and vulnerable position that pushed them steadily downward the socioeconomic hierarchy (Massey 2007; Massey and Pren 2012a).

Although the racialization of Latinos goes back to 1848, when the Treaty of Guadalupe Hidalgo brought some fifty thousand Mexicans into the United States, the contemporary era of racial formation can be traced back to the 1960s, when the United States adopted a new set of immigration policies that made it difficult for Mexicans and other Latin Americans to enter the country legally (Massey and Pren 2012a). Although the number of Latino arrivals changed little in subsequent years, their composition after 1965 shifted dramatically from documented to undocumented (Massey, Durand, and Pren 2009). The rise of mass undocumented migration offered political entrepreneurs a tempting opportunity to mobilize anti-immigrant sentiment for their own purposes by framing Latinos as "illegal" "lawbreakers" and thus inherently dangerous, threatening, and inimical to American values.

Between 1965 and 2000 a new "Latino threat narrative" came to dominate public debate and media coverage of Latinos in the United States (Chavez 2001, 2008) and U.S. policymakers responded by launching what Jeffrey Rosen called in a 1995 *New Republic* article a "war on immigrants" ("The War on Immigrants: Why the Courts Can't Save Us," January 30). This so-called war involved an unprecedented militarization of the Mexico-U.S. border, a massive expansion of the immigrant detention system, and a return to mass deportations for the first time since the 1930s (Massey and Sánchez 2010). Government repression accelerated markedly after September 11, 2001, as the war on immigrants was increasingly conflated with the war on terror (Massey and Sánchez 2010; Massey and Pren 2012b). By 2010, America's immigration enforcement apparatus had become a central race-making institution for Latinos, on a par with the criminal justice system for African Americans.

MANUFACTURING ILLEGALITY

Latin American migration to the United States is nothing new, of course. Except for a short gap during the Great Depression, Mexicans have been migrating to the United States in significant numbers since early in the twentieth century (Cardoso 1980; Massey, Durand, and Malone 2002). After 1945, they were joined by successive waves of immigrants from other Latin American nations, first from Puerto Rico, then Cuba and the Dominican Republic, followed in the 1980s by those from Central and South America (Bean and Tienda 1987; Bergad and Klein 2010). Apart from Mexicans, these successive waves came in response to political and economic interventions within the region by the United States, beginning with Operation Bootstrap in Puerto Rico and continuing with Cold War operations in Cuba and the Dominican Republic, the Contra War in Central America, and the application of structural adjustment policies throughout South America under the neoliberal economic regime of "the Washington Consensus" (Massey, Sánchez, and Behrman 2006; Riosmena 2010).

Before 1965, it was relatively easy for Latin Americans to enter the United States legally because no numerical limits had been placed on immigrants from the Western Hemisphere. Mexico, in particular, also benefitted from a generous bilateral guest worker agreement known as the Bracero Program that in its twenty-two-year history brought nearly five million Mexican workers into the United States on temporary work visas (Massey, Durand, and Malone 2002; Calavita 1992). During the late 1950s, legal Mexican immigration averaged around fifty thousand persons per year, Bracero migration around 450,000 annually, and other nations in Latin America upward of ten thousand. Undocumented migration, meanwhile, was virtually nonexistent (Massey, Durand, and Malone 2002; Massey and Pren 2012a). In 1960, for example, apprehensions at the Mexico-U.S. border numbered only thirty thousand, and deportations from within the United States only seven thousand.

During the late 1950s and early 1960s, the total annual inflow of migrants from Mexico alone fluctuated around half a million per year, all legally. At the end of 1964, however, the United States unilaterally terminated the Bracero Program over Mexican protests; in the following year, Congress passed amendments to the Immigration and Nationality Act that placed the first cap — 120,000 — on immigration from the Western Hemisphere. Additional amendments enacted in 1976 put each country in the hemisphere under an annual quota of just twenty thousand immigrant visas (Zolberg 2006).

The effects of these new restrictions were particularly dramatic for Mexico. Whereas in 1956, 65,000 Mexicans entered the United States in documented status and another 445,000 as guest workers, by 1976 the guest worker program was long gone and legal immigration was capped at 20,000 per year. Although immediate relatives of U.S. citizens were exempted from the numerical cap, the total number of migrants entering from Mexico was down 86 percent from its peak in the late 1950s. Despite the curtailment of avenues for legal entry, however, the demand for Mexican workers did not change and Mexicans continued to flow to the jobs they had traditionally held (Massey, Durand, and Malone 2002; Massey and Pren 2012a).

The inevitable result of curtailing opportunities for legal entry from Mexico was a sharp rise in undocumented migration. Figure 9.1 shows Mexican migration to the United States in three legal categories: documented (permanent resident aliens), temporary (Braceros and other legal temporary workers), and undocumented (those crossing the border or working without authorization). Data on documented and temporary migrants come from the U.S. Office of Immigration Statistics (2012) whereas data on undocumented migration comes from study estimates (Massey, Durand, and Pren 2009). In this study, the authors calculated prob-

FIGURE 9.1 / Mexican Migration to the United States

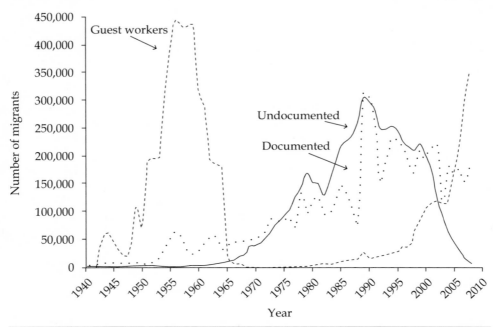

Source: Author's compilation of data from the Office of Immigration Statistics, U.S. Department of Homeland Security and predecessor agencies.

abilities of undocumented entry and exit using data from the Mexican Migration Project and then applied these to population counts taken from the Mexican census to compute annual net undocumented migration between Mexico and the United States.

As can be seen, when the Bracero Program ended in 1965 and dramatically reduced opportunities for migration in legal status, both documented and especially undocumented migration from Mexico began to increase. Net undocumented entries rose from near zero in the early 1960s to peak at around 300,000 per year in 1990. Documented migration also rose from around 50,000 per year in the early 1960s to fluctuate between 100,000 and 150,000 during the late 1970s and early 1980s as legal immigrants circumvented the country caps by naturalizing, thus rendering their spouses, minor children, and parents exempt from numerical limitation. In addition, Congress in 1986 authorized and amnesty for undocumented residents and enacted a special legalization for agricultural workers that caused another surge of adjustments to permanent resident status and ultimately citizenship in subsequent years.

Owing to U.S. policy shifts between the early 1960s and the early 1980s, therefore, Mexican immigration was transformed from an overwhelmingly legal to a substantially illegal flow. According to the data shown in figure 9.1, among Mexicans arriving from 1955 to 1965, 87 percent were legal temporary workers, 12 percent were legal permanent residents, and only 1 percent were undocumented. Among those arriving from 1985 to 1995, however, 55 percent were undocumented, 41 percent were legal residents, and 4 percent were temporary workers. In other words, the composition of the Mexican inflow shifted dramatically after 1965, even though its size had not changed very much. Except for a brief surge in 1990 attributable to the legalization programs, total in-migration from Mexico has fluctuated around 500,000 persons before and after 1965.

The other major surge in undocumented migration from Latin America came during the 1980s with the U.S. Contra Intervention in Nicaragua and the broader prosecution of the Cold War within Central America. Research clearly indicates that outflows from Central America during the 1980s were driven by the U.S.-sponsored Contra intervention (Lundquist and Massey 2005) as well as the violence and the economic dislocations it produced (Stanley 1987; Jones 1989; Funkhouser 1992; Morrison and May 1994; Alvarado and Massey 2010). Owing to the restrictions imposed in 1965, however, refugees from Central America could enter the United States legally by only a few avenues. Not surprisingly, most ended up coming as undocumented migrants, either moving through Mexico to cross the border without authorization of entering as tourists and overstaying their visas.

Although emigrants from Guatemala, El Salvador, Honduras, and Nicaragua left for the same underlying reasons, those from Nicaragua were treated very differently by U.S. authorities. Whereas the Nicaraguan Adjustment and Central American Relief Act offered an easy pathway to legal status for Nicaraguans, it grudgingly offered only temporary protected status to other Central Americans. Whereas Nicaraguans had the good fortune of fleeing a left-wing regime at odds with the United States, those from Guatemala, El Salvador, and Honduras had the bad luck to come from nations dominated by right-wing regimes allied with the United States. As a result, although most Central Americans were at some point undocumented, Nicaraguans were able to adjust to documented status whereas other Central Americans ended up languishing in temporary protected status until it was finally revoked with end of the Cold War, pushing them into undocumented status.

Once again, U.S. policies had manufactured a large population of undocumented migrants. After Mexico, which accounted for an estimated 62 percent of undocumented migrants present in the United States as of January 1, 2010, the next largest contributors were El Salvador (6 percent), Guatemala (5 percent), and Honduras (3 percent) (Hoefer, Rytina, and Baker 2010). All told, three-quarters of all undocumented migrants come from Mexico or Central America, and no other nation makes up more than 2 percent of the total. When most Americans visualize an "illegal immigrant," they see a Mexican and, if not a Mexican in particular, certainly a Latino (Lee and Fiske 2006). Adding Latino migrants from the Caribbean, South America, and Panama, we find that Latin Americans make up more than 80 percent of the total unauthorized population. It is doubtful, of course, whether the average Anglo American can distinguish between a Mexican, Salvadoran, a Dominican, or a Colombian and many simply get categorized as Mexican, which has become the default Latino identity in the American mind (Lee and Fiske 2006).

RISE OF THE LATINO THREAT NARRATIVE

Throughout U.S. history, immigrants have periodically served as scapegoats for America's problems, being blamed for joblessness, low wages, and high social spending while being framed as threats to national security owing to their supposed moral deficits, suspect ideologies, and subversive intentions (Higham 1955; Zolberg 2006; Schrag 2010). Anti-immigrant hostility rises during periods of economic dislocation, ideological conflict, and political uncertainty (Massey 1999; Meyers 2004). The 1970s and 1980s were such a period, as the long postwar economic boom faltered, the New Deal Coalition unraveled, and the Cold War reached its apex. After a brief respite during the 1990s, when the economy rebounded and the Cold War receded, the conditions for popular xenophobia returned with a vengeance with the bursting of the stock market bubble in 2000, the terrorist attacks in 2001, and the collapse of the economy in 2008 (Massey and Sánchez 2010).

Under these circumstances, anti-immigrant hostility is only to be expected. Since 1965, however, portrayals of Latin American immigrants as a threat to American society have been greatly facilitated by the fact that a rising share of Latino immigrants are present in the country illegally and thus readily framed as lawbreakers, criminals, and terrorists. The growing predominance of undocumented migrants among Latin Americans has contributed to the rise of what Leo Chavez (2008) has called the "Latino threat narrative." Among national magazine covers on immigration he examined between 1965 and 2000, two-thirds portrayed immigration as threatening or alarming, and the frequency of these depictions steadily rose over time, going from a relative share of just 18 percent in the 1970s to 45 percent in the 1990s (Chavez 2001).

At first the most popular alarmist metaphors were marine, picturing immigration as a "rising tide" or "tidal wave" that was "flooding" the United States and threatening to "drown" its culture and "inundate" its society. During the 1980s, however, marine imagery gave way to martial metaphors (Chavez 2001) as the Mexico-U.S. border was framed as a "battleground" that was "under attack" from "alien invaders" (Dunn 1996; Rotella 1998). Border Patrol Officers became "defenders" who, though "outgunned," valiantly fought to "hold the line" against attacking "hoards" who launched "Banzai charges" along a beleaguered "front" (Andreas 2000). Latinos within the United States became a "ticking time bomb" waiting to "explode" and destroy the American way of life (Santa Ana 2002).

The Latino threat narrative gained particular traction in the 1980s when President Reagan labeled undocumented migration a "threat to national security," noting that terrorists and subversives were just" two days driving time from the nearest border crossing" and referring to foreigners in the United States as a "fifth column" who would "feed on the anger and frustration of recent Central and South American immigrants" (Massey, Durand, and Malone 2002, 87). Thereafter war metaphors became the standard trope in describing Latin American immigrants (Chavez 2008).

Lou Dobbs (2006), for example, has portrayed the "invasion of illegal aliens" as part of a broader "war on the middle class." Patrick Buchanan (2006) framed it as part of an "Aztlan Plot" hatched by Mexicans to recapture lands lost in 1848, stating that "if we do not get control of our borders and stop this greatest invasion in history, I see the dissolution of the U.S. and the loss of the American southwest" (*Time*, August 28, 6). Harvard professor Samuel Huntington warned Americans of the impending "Hispanic challenge" that would occur because "the persistent inflow of Hispanic immigrants threatens to divide the United States into two peoples, two cultures, and two languages. Unlike past immigrant groups, Mexicans and other Latinos have not assimilated into mainstream U.S. culture. . . . The United States ignores this challenge at its peril" (2004, 1).

Efforts by politicians, academicians, and pundits to portray Latin Americans as a threat to American society made considerable headway with the public. According to polls conducted by the Pew Charitable Trusts, as late as 2000 just 38 percent of Americans agreed that "immigrants today are a burden on our country because they take our jobs, housing, and health care." Five years later, the percentage had risen to 44 percent and as the drumbeat of anti-immigrant rhetoric reached a crescendo in 2006 it became a majority viewpoint at 52 percent. The percentage of Americans rating immigration as a moderately big or very large national problem rose from 69 percent in 2002 to 74 percent in 2006, by which time nearly half of all Americans, 48 percent, agreed that "newcomers from other countries threaten traditional American values and customs" and 54 percent said that Americans needed to be "protected against foreign influence" (see Kohut and Suro 2006).

More tangible evidence of the shift in attitudes is the sharp increase in anti-Latino hate crimes, which had been declining before 9/11. According to U.S. Justice Department statistics, the number of anti-Hispanic hate crimes increased 24 percent from 2002 to 2007 and the number of victims by 30 percent (Federal Bureau of Investigation 2009). By 2008, random killings of Latinos had become common in headlines throughout the country; and according one news story, attacks on immigrants had become "such an established pastime that the youths . . . had a casual and derogatory term for it, 'beaner hopping.' One of the blithely youths told the authorities, 'I don't go out doing this very often, maybe once a week'" (Anne Barnard "Seeing a Pattern of Hate in Attacks on Immigrants on Long Island," *New York Times*, January 8, 2009, p. A1).

Immigrants clearly perceive the rising hostility against them. By 2006, 70 percent of Latino immigrants had come to view anti-Hispanic discrimination as a major problem in the United States, 68 percent worried about being deported themselves, and 35 percent knew someone who had been deported (Kohut and Suru 2006). Half of all Latino immigrants interviewed in 2010 felt that Americans were less accepting of immigrants than they had been five years earlier (Lopez, Morin, and Taylor 2010). Whereas only 47 percent of Latinos saw discrimination against them as a major problem in American society in 2002, by 2010 the share had risen to 61 percent, and another 24 percent viewed it as at least a minor problem, bringing the total seeing discrimination as problematic to 85 percent (Lopez, Morin, and Taylor 2010).

DECLARING THE WAR ON IMMIGRANTS

Although the wave of anti–immigrant hysteria picked up new momentum after September 11, the shift toward more restrictive immigration policies can be traced back to 1965 when, as already noted, the United States began to close off avenues for legal entry from Latin America. Since then, each surge in anti-immigrant propaganda within the media has coincided with the introduction or enactment of more restrictive immigration policies. This association has been demonstrated by a count of the frequency with which articles in leading newspapers — the *New York Times, Wall Street Journal, Los Angeles Times,* and *Washington Post* — made references to undocumented or Mexican migration as a "crisis," "flood," or "invasion" during the years from 1965 through 2009 (Massey and Pren 2012b).

These framings of immigration increased steadily from 1965 to 1979 (Massey and Pren 2012b). After peaking in 1980, the frequency of negative framings thereafter fluctuated, each peak coinciding with the passage of another piece of restrictive immigration legislation or the launching of a new repressive border operation. In 1980, Congress removed refugees from the immigration preference system and capped the total number of refugees at 70,000 per year while reducing the world ceiling to just 270,000 visas. The level of anti-immigrant propaganda dropped for a short time thereafter but rose again to peak again in 1986, when Congress passed the Immigration Reform and Control Act (IRCA), which funded a new expansion of the Border Patrol, authorized the president to declare "immigration emergencies" and assume special powers, and criminalized the hiring of undocumented migrants (Massey, Durand, and Malone 2002).

With these measures in place, media references to invasions, floods, and crises fell once again through 1992, by which time it became clear to everyone that the restrictive measures authorized by IRCA were not slowing illegal migration and that the undocumented population was once again growing rapidly. Alarmist depictions once again rose in the media and peaked in 1994 when voters in California passed Proposition 187, the Save Our State Initiative, which framed undocumented migrants as criminals, freeloaders, and predators; compelled state and local officials to turn them in to federal authorities; and banned them from receiving public services (Jacobson 2008). The same year, federal authorities responded to the surge in anti-immigrant sentiment in California by launching Operation Gatekeeper in San Diego — an all-out militarization of the border with Tijuana designed to stop the flow of undocumented migrants through what had been the busiest sector of the two-thousand-mile frontier (Rotella 1998; Andreas 2000; Massey, Durand, and Malone 2002).

The resulting upsurge in border apprehensions only underscored the continuing reality of undocumented migration, however, and did not placate public opinion. In 1996, Congress responded to the continued anti-immigration agitation by passing three major pieces of restrictive legislation. The Illegal Immigration Reform and Immigrant Responsibility Act authorized the hiring of thousands of additional Border Patrol agents and the construction of more walls and fences to bring the militarization of the border to new heights (Massey, Durand, and Malone 2002). It also permitted the removal of aliens from ports of entry without judicial hearing, declared undocumented migrants ineligible for federally subsidized benefits, and in an effort to restrict family migration further, required sponsors of legal immigrants to provide affidavits of support that demonstrated a household income at least 125 percent of the federal poverty line (see chapter 12, this volume). The new law also contained a provision known as 287(g) that authorized local agencies to assist in federal immigration enforcement (Newton 2008).

At the same time, the Personal Responsibility and Work Opportunity Reconciliation Act of 1996 extended the portrayal of undocumented migrants as greedy freeloaders to legal immigrants and placed new restrictions on the access of legal permanent residents to public services, barring them from receiving food stamps, Supplemental Security Income, and other means tested benefits for five years after admission (see chapter 11, this volume). Finally, the Antiterrorism and Effective Death Penalty Act formalized the equation of immigrants with terrorists and lawbreakers by declaring any alien who had ever committed a crime, no matter how long ago, to be subject to immediate deportation (Newton 2008; Massey 2011).

The Antiterrorism Act also gave the federal government broad new police powers for the "expedited exclusion" of any alien who had ever crossed the border without documents, no matter what his or her current legal status (Legomsky 2000, 1616). Given that the majority of legal immigrants to the United States from Latin America first entered as undocumented migrants (Massey and Malone 2003), this new provision instantly rendered millions of legal immigrants—and the vast majority of Mexican resident aliens—as deportable for past infractions. It also granted the State Department authority to designate any organization as terrorist, thereby making all members of groups so designated immediately excludable. It also narrowed the grounds for asylum and added alien smuggling to the list of crimes covered by the RICO (Racketeer Influenced Corrupt Organizations) statute, severely limiting the possibilities for judicial review of deportations (Zolberg 2006).

The most recent surge in anti-immigrant sentiment came in response to the terrorist attacks of September 11, when on October 26, 2001, Congress passed, without significant debate, the USA PATRIOT Act, which granted executive authorities even more powers to deport, without hearings or presentation of evidence, all aliens—legal or illegal, temporary or permanent—that the attorney general had "reason to believe" might commit, further, or facilitate acts of terrorism. For the first time since the Alien and Sedition Act of 1798, Congress authorized the arrest, imprisonment, and deportation noncitizens on the orders of the Attorney General without judicial review (Zolberg 2006).

As anti-immigrant hysteria continued to rise, however, and was increasingly conflated with the war on terror, in 2005 the U.S. House of Representatives passed HR 4437, the Border Protection, Antiterrorism, and Illegal Immigration Control Act of 2005, authored by Representative James Sensenbrenner of Wisconsin. Although it did not clear the Senate, the latter bill would have constructed seven hundred miles of additional fencing along the border, required local law enforcement officials to turn undocumented migrants over to federal authorities for deportation, and declared virtually any immigration violation to be a felony, thus preventing migrants even from applying for legalization for ten years.

None of these repressive federal initiatives was enough to placate the hysteria cultivated by the Latino threat narrative, and after 2005 an unprecedented surge in anti-immigrant measures was enacted at the state and local levels (Hopkins 2010). According to the National Council of State Legislatures (2009), some two hundred bills on immigration were introduced and thirty-eight laws enacted in 2005; by 2007, immigration-related legislation had tripled to 1,562 bills introduced and 240 laws were passed. Sarah Bohn and Magnus Lofstrom (chapter 10, this volume) show that one such law passed in Arizona reduced the likelihood of wage and salary employment among likely undocumented migrants while increasing their rate of self-employment, and in so doing contributed to a rise in Latino poverty. At present, nearly half of all states have signed cooperative agreements with the federal government under the 287(g) provision to assist in the arrest, incarceration, and deportation of immigrants (Massey and Sánchez 2010).

PROSECUTING THE WAR ON IMMIGRANTS

In sum, over the past several decades, the repressive power of the state has increasingly been directed against immigrants, documented as well as undocumented. Although the escalation of anti-immigrant repression is apparent at the state and local levels, it is most clearly reflected in federal statistics. Figure 9.2 shows trends in the budget of the U.S. Border Patrol, the number of Border Patrol Agents, and the number of deportations from the United States (U.S. Office of Immigration Statistics 2012). Each series has been divided by its value in 1986 to indicate the factor by which the enforcement effort has increased since then.

Although U.S. enforcement actions begin to rise after the passage of IRCA in 1986, the pace of change accelerated markedly during the 1990s and then rose exponentially after 2001. By 2010, the Border Patrol budget stood at twenty-four times its 1986 level, the number of deportations had risen sixteen times, and the number of Border Patrol Agents had grown by a factor of six. These massive increases in the enforcement effort occurred despite the fact that the rate of undocumented migration had actually been declining since 1990 and, in fact, plummeted after 2001 to reach levels near zero by 2008 (see figure 9.1). In a very real way, the United States increasingly looks like a police state to immigrants, whatever their documentation. It is as if the militarized border program of 1953–1954 (Operation Wetback) has been made permanent and the mass deportation campaigns of 1929–1934 have been institutionalized at more than three times their earlier size.

FIGURE 9.2 / Immigration Enforcement Relative to Levels

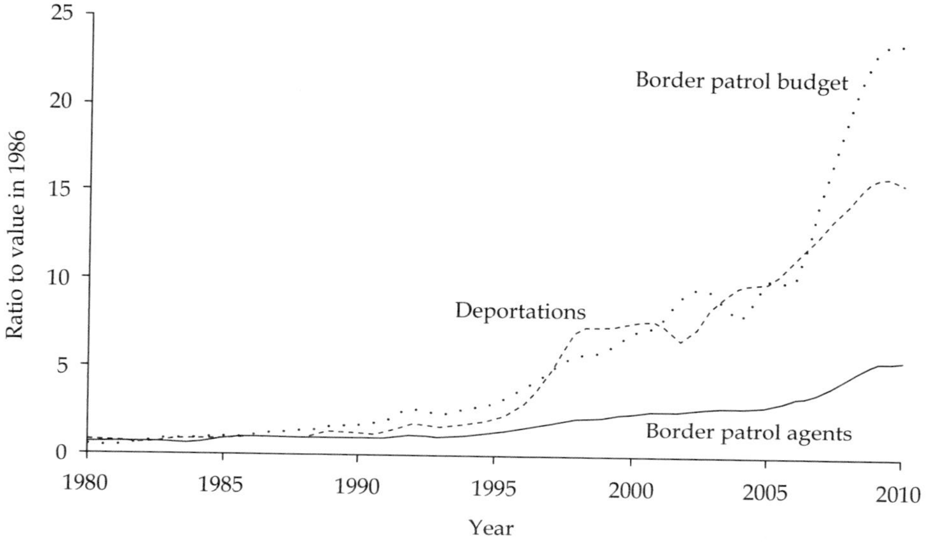

Source: Author's compilation of data from the Office of Immigration Statistics, U.S. Department of Homeland Security and predecessor agencies.

BUILDING A NEW UNDERCLASS

Paradoxically, the effect of increased immigration enforcement was actually to *increase* the net inflow of undocumented migrants and to spread them more widely throughout the nation (Massey, Durand, and Malone 2002; Massey 2008; Massey, Rugh, and Pren 2010). Once they had experienced the costs and risks of undocumented border crossing, migrants declined to repeat the experience and remained north of the border rather than returning home, bringing about a pronounced decline in levels of out-migration (Redburn, Reuter, and Majmundar 2011). With the full-scale militarization of the border in San Diego and the erection of a steel wall from the Pacific Ocean to the peaks of the Sierra Madre, immigrants were diverted from California toward new crossing points along the border with Arizona and to new destinations throughout the United States (see the chapter 5, this volume). Mexican migration was thus transformed from a largely circular movement of male workers going to three states into a settled population of families living in fifty states (Massey, Durand, and Pren 2009). By 2010, more Latinos were living in undocumented status in more places than at any point in American history (Massey 2011; Massey and Pren 2012a).

As a result of U.S. actions over the past several decades, never before have so many U.S. residents lacked basic legal protections. Undocumented migrants currently constitute 33 percent of all foreigners present in the United States, more than 40 percent of those from Latin America, and large majorities of those from Mexico and Central America. Furthermore, because undocumented migrants generally live in households that include family members who are documented, the share people touched by illegal migration is actually much larger. According to estimates by Jeffrey Passel (2006), about 25 percent of all persons living in households that contain undocumented migrants are themselves U.S. citizens.

Recent survey data illustrate the degree to which the fates of immigrant and native Latinos are interconnected. In 2008, 35 percent of native-born Latinos said they worried about deportation some or a lot, presumably not because they were personally at risk of deportation but because they were worried about the potential deportation of a friend or relative (Lopez and Minushkin 2008). By 2010, this share had risen to 52 percent, whereas among the foreign born the figure stood at 68 percent. Even among Latino immigrants who were U.S. citizens, 58 percent said they worried about deportation some or a lot; the figure rose to 71 percent among legal residents and 84 percent among noncitizens who were not legal residents (Lopez, Morin, and Taylor 2010). Among the latter two groups, 40 percent and 45 percent, respectively, said they knew someone who had been deported. As of 2007, 53 percent of native-born Latinos said that the immigration debate had made life difficult for them, compared with 72 percent of those born abroad (Pew Hispanic Center 2007).

By 2008, Latinos had become much more pessimistic about life in the United States, 63 percent of foreign-born Hispanics and 30 percent of natives saying that the situation for Hispanics had deteriorated over the previous year. Regardless of birthplace, the vast majority of Hispanics disapproved of workplace raids, 76 percent; the criminal prosecution of employers who hired undocumented migrants, 70 percent; and the arrest and deportation of the migrants, 73 percent (Lopez and Minushkin 2008). Only 46 percent of all Hispanics were confident that the police would treat them fairly; just 49 percent said they expected fair treatment in the courts (Lopez and Livingston 2009).

Net undocumented migration appears now to have dropped to zero not because of U.S. enforcement efforts, but instead because of a collapsed U.S. economy, declining population growth in Mexico, and generally favorable economic conditions throughout Latin America (Wasem 2011; Redburn, Reuter, and Majmundar 2011). In the past decade, however, the falling number of undocumented migrants has been offset by a rising number of temporary workers. With little fanfare or public awareness, mass guest worker recruitment has returned to the United States, bringing annual entries up to levels last seen in the 1950 (Massey and Pren 2012b). Although only a tiny fraction of Mexicans who entered the United States in 2010 were unauthorized, most who entered with documents nonetheless did not have full labor rights. Of the 655,767 legal entries from Mexico for work or residence that year, only 139,000 (21 percent) had permanent resident visas that conferred labor rights in the United States (U.S. Office of Immigration Statistics 2012). The overwhelming majority arrived with a temporary visa that tied them to a specific employer, offered little or no job mobility, and conferred severely constrained labor rights.

FIGURE 9.3 / Median Personal Income, Males

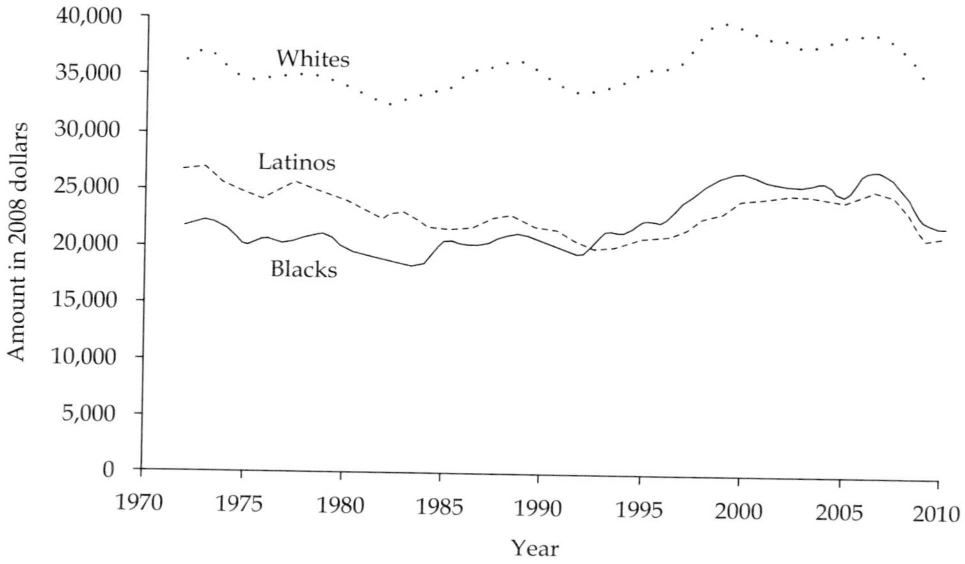

Source: Author's compilation of data from the U.S. Census Bureau.

Over the past several decades, U.S. immigration and border policies have thus increased the number of Latinos in vulnerable positions, dramatically increased the level of official repression directed against them, and provided new incentives for employers to discriminate and exploit those with undocumented or marginally legal status. With more people occupying ever more vulnerable and exploitable positions in the U.S. labor market, the socioeconomic status of Latinos generally declined over the past several decades. After 1990, after holding an intermediate position between blacks and whites in the American status hierarchy, Latinos increasingly joined African Americans at the bottom to make up a new American underclass (Massey 2007). In the absence of meaningful immigration reform and a curtailment of repression against immigrants, this population can only be expected to see its problems proliferate and multiply.

Figure 9.3 illustrates the decline in Latino socioeconomic status with trends in median personal income earned by white, black, and Latino males from 1972 through 2010 (in constant dollars). Obviously, white men earned substantially more income than black and Latino workers throughout the period, but whereas Latinos clearly occupied a middle position during the early 1970s, their intermediate status began to erode during the 1980s; after a crossover in 1992, Latino males supplanted black males at the bottom and have remained there ever since.

These figures, of course, do not control for human capital and other characteristics of white, black, and Latino workers; and some have argued that the deteriora-

FIGURE 9.4 / Median Personal Income, Females

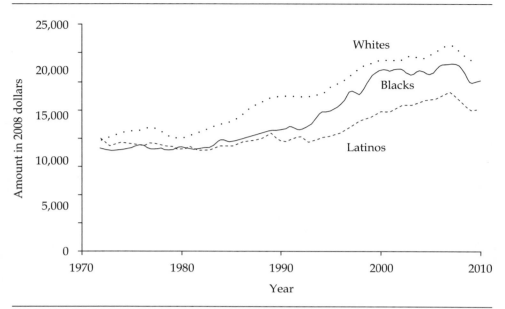

Source: Author's compilation of data from the U.S. Census Bureau.

tion in the relative economic standing of Latinos reflects the declining quality of successive immigrant cohorts, especially for Mexicans (Borjas 1995, 1999; see also chapter 3, this volume). In their analysis of Mexican male wages from 1950 through 2008, however, Douglas Massey and Julia Gelatt (2010) show that on observable traits such as education and experience the average quality of immigrant cohorts steadily improved over time, both absolutely and relative to native white workers. Although it is possible that unobservable indicators of quality deteriorated, this is unlikely because one would then have to argue that observable and unobservable indicators of productivity were negatively correlated. Massey and Gelatt suggest that what changed over time was not so much the characteristics of immigrants, as how various forms of human capital were rewarded in the U.S. labor market. Their analysis documented declining rates of earnings return to English-language ability, U.S. experience, education, skill, and age, beginning in the 1990s and accelerating after 2000. The share of variance in male wages explained by background characteristics fell from 0.28 in 1950 to 0.11 in 2007, indicating a significantly weaker connection between human capital inputs and wage outputs.

In a counterfactual analysis, Massey and Gelatt (2010) also estimated that if background characteristics had been rewarded at the same rate as in 1980, male Mexican wages would have risen by 10 percent, whereas if means had been held to their 1980 values, wages would have declined by 4 percent. That male immigrants wages declined occurred despite and not because human capital levels were rising, and this came about because the rewards to human capital were si-

FIGURE 9.5   /   Poverty Rate, Families

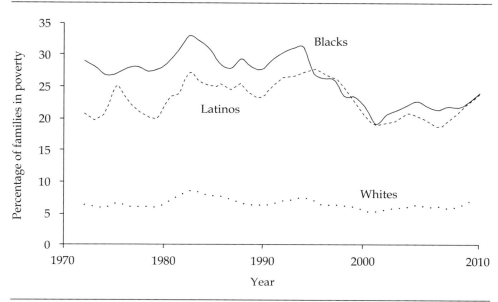

Source: Author's compilation of data from the U.S. Census Bureau.

multaneously falling. Although Massey and Gelatt did not consider female wages, figure 9.4 reveals that the earnings of Latinas have deteriorated even more dramatically than among their male counterparts.

In the early 1970s, all women earned relatively low incomes—both absolutely and compared with men. Things began to change in 1980, however, when the incomes of white women began to rise steadily, going from a little over $12,000 that year to peak at almost $23,000 in 2007. Although the upturn for black women trailed that of white women, beginning around 1985 their incomes also began to rise and this increase accelerated during the 1990s to narrow the black-white gap substantially, with black female income peaking at almost $21,000 in 2007. In contrast, the income of Latinas remained flat until 1993 and then rose at a slower rate than either white or black women, so that by 2010 the Latina-white gap was wider than it had ever been. Whereas white and Latina women earned roughly the same incomes in 1972, by 2010 Latinas earned 25 percent less than whites.

The shifting fortunes of Latinos and African Americans in U.S. labor markets are clearly reflected in U.S. poverty statistics. Figure 9.5 shows trends in the poverty rate for white, black, and Latino families from 1972 to 2010. Once again, Latinos occupied a middle position until 1994, when black and Latino poverty rates converged. From then until 2000, black and Latino families shared the same poverty trajectory. In 2000, black poverty rates began to rise above those of Latinos until 2008. The onset of the Great Recession brought them back together at around 24 percent in 2010, some 3.4 times greater than the 7 percent among white families.

In sum, the foreign data clearly suggest that something happened over the course of the 1990s to undermine earnings among Latinos living in the United States. Using data from the Mexican Migration Project, Kirsten Gentsch and Massey (2011) confirmed a clear break in the labor market status of Mexican immigrant workers before and after the mid-1990s. This showed that the wage and occupational returns to various forms of human capital declined after harsher immigration and enforcement policies were steadily imposed. A growing proportion of the migrant work force came to lack labor rights, either for a lack of documentation or because they held temporary visas. In a follow-up study, the authors showed that controlling for individual characteristics helped explain the decline in the wages somewhat, but did not eliminate the downward trend, which only was explained fully when the percentage of undocumented Mexican immigrants was added to the model (Massey and Gentsch 2012). As the share of Mexican immigrants without authorization steadily rose, the competitive position of Mexican workers deteriorated and earnings fell in real terms.

The deterioration in the labor market position of Hispanics relative to blacks was accompanied by a similar reversal of fortune in U.S. housing markets. In 1989, Hispanics were 19 percent less likely than blacks to experience adverse treatment in America's rental housing markets. In 2000, they were 8 percent more likely suffer discrimination. In addition, although the incidence of discriminatory treatment fell for both groups in the sales market, the decline for Hispanics was much smaller. As a result, whereas blacks in 1989 were twice as likely as Hispanics to experience discrimination in home sales, by 2000 Hispanics were 18 percent more likely than blacks to experience it (Turner et al. 2002). Consistent with these data, in their audit of rental housing in the San Francisco Bay area, Thomas Purnell, William Isardi, and John Baugh (1999) documented extensive "linguistic profiling" that excluded speakers of Chicano English from access to housing. In addition, several state and local initiatives have sought to mandate discrimination on the basis of legal status by forbidding real estate agents from renting or selling homes to those present without authorization (Hopkins 2010).

Figure 9.6 shows trends in the residential segregation of Latinos living in 287 U.S. metropolitan areas with consistent metropolitan boundaries between 1970 and 2010 (from Massey and Rugh 2012). Segregation is measured both in terms of residential dissimilarity—the relative percentage of Latinos and non-Hispanic whites who would have to exchange census tracts to achieve an even distribution—and spatial isolation—the percentage of Latinos living in the tract inhabited by the average Latino. As can be seen, Latino-white dissimilarity increased slightly between 1970 and 2010 by 6.5 percent. At the same time, Latino spatial isolation rose by a remarkable 74 percent in response to rapid population increases in the context of slowly rising segregation. In contrast, over the same period black-white dissimilarity fell by 23 percent and black isolation fell by 33 percent (Massey and Rugh 2012). As a result by 2010 the average Latino lived in a neighborhood that was 46.5 percent Latino while the average African American lived in a neighborhood that was 45.3 percent black, making Latinos the most spatially isolated group in metropolitan America for the very first time.

FIGURE 9.6 / Latino Residential Segregation, 287 Metropolitan Areas

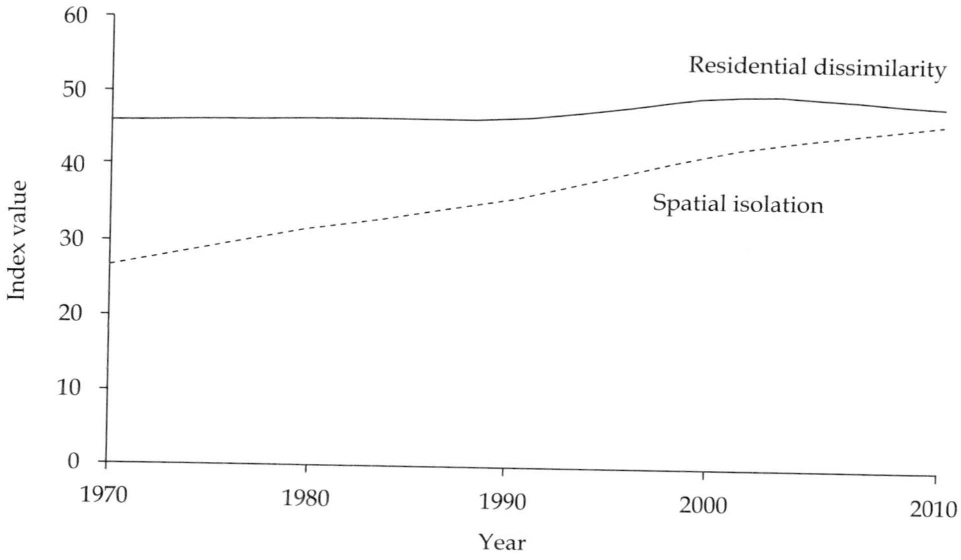

Source: Author's compilation of data from the U.S. Census Bureau.

The growing segregation and isolation of Latinos in the United States contributes strongly to their vulnerability to exogenous economic shocks (see chapter 4, in this volume). First, any shock that increases poverty and disadvantage among members of a segregated group will increase the spatial concentration of poverty and disadvantage that group experiences (Massey and Denton 1993; Massey and Fischer 2000; Quillian 2012). In addition, residential segregation is a powerful predictor of the number and rate of foreclosures experienced during the housing bust of 2008, in that segregated minority neighborhoods were explicitly targeted for predatory lending during the housing boom (Rugh and Massey 2010). As a result, groups that were more segregated residentially experienced greater risk to their wealth when the housing bust caused home values to deflate rapidly after 2007. Indeed, Latinos were doubly disadvantaged, not only by their relatively high residential segregation, but also by their regional concentration areas hardest hit by the housing crisis, such as California, Florida, Nevada, and Arizona.

The effect of the crisis on Latino wealth is indicated in figure 9.7, which shows trends in median net wealth for black and Latino households. Historically, both groups have been characterized by low levels of wealth, which before 2000 averaged between just $6,000 and $10,000, compared with a range of $70,000 to $80,000 for white households (not shown). Beginning in 2001, the net wealth of Latino and black households began to rise as the housing boom began to reach into their neighborhoods; both groups were targeted for extensive subprime mortgage lend-

FIGURE 9.7 / Median Net Household Wealth

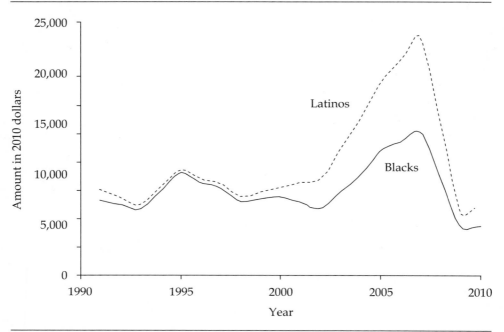

Source: Author's compilation of data from the U.S. Census Bureau.

ing. Given that Latinos were disproportionately living in states affected by the boom, their net wealth rose faster and higher than blacks, peaking at $24,000 in 2007; the peak for blacks was only $14,000. With the collapse of housing prices, however, both groups ended up much at the same place, with a net worth of just $6,000 for Latinos and $5,000 for blacks by 2009. Latinos, however, saw the greatest decline in net wealth of any major group—a drop of 73 percent between peak and trough.

IMMIGRATION REFORM AS SOCIAL JUSTICE

Over the past four decades, the immigration enforcement system of the United States has become increasingly important a major race-making institution in much the same way that the criminal justice system did for African Americans over the same period. Arrests and incarcerations increased dramatically, as did apprehensions and deportations. At the same time, relevant agency budgets also increased dramatically. The immigrant detention system is now the fastest growing component of America's prison industrial complex. In 2011, for example, some 429,000 immigrants were incarcerated and awaiting trial or deportation,

FIGURE 9.8 / Latinos and Blacks Incarcerated in State and Federal Prisons

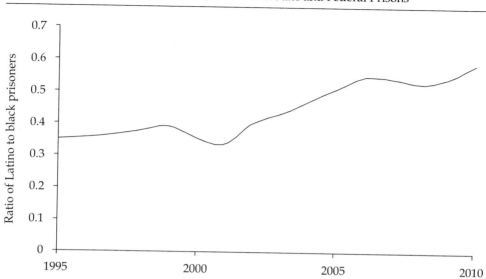

Source: Author's compilation of data from the U.S. Bureau of Justice Statistics.

397,000 were expelled from the United States, and 328,000 were apprehended at the Mexico-U.S. border (American Civil Liberties Union 2012; U.S. Office of Immigration Statistics 2012). Figure 9.8 reveals that the number incarcerated among Latinos is rapidly rising relative to African Americans. Whereas the ratio of Latino to black prisoners in state and federal penal institutions averaged between 0.34 and 0.39, after 2001 it rose steadily, to peak at around 0.59 in 2010. At this rate of change, Latinos will surpass African Americans as the largest prison population within two decades.

Whereas the prison industrial complex created among African Americans a large population of current and ex-felons who suffer a variety of forms of exclusion and discrimination (Pager 2007; Pettit 2012), it has among Latinos generated a population of marginalized, repressed, and eminently exploitable undocumented migrants as well as of felons. Despite all their well-documented disadvantages, however, black felons at least retain basic social and economic rights as American citizens, whereas undocumented migrants under current circumstances have virtually no rights. They are subject to arrest, incarceration without representation, and summary deportation without trial or benefit of counsel. Even documented migrants may now be arrested, detailed, and deported on the say-so of low-level Justice Department officials; they have been declared by Congress to be deportable ex post facto for crimes they committed earlier (see Legomsky 2000).

The situation is especially dire for Mexicans, the nation's largest immigrant group and the second largest minority after African Americans. At present, nearly 60 percent of all persons born in Mexico are the United States illegally; among legal Mexican-born residents, two-thirds first entered the United States without documents, thus rendering them legally deportable under current law (Massey and Malone 2003). These figures imply that nearly a quarter (23 percent) of all Mexican immigrants in the United States are undocumented, and that another 8 percent are formerly undocumented, putting roughly 33 percent of all Mexican Americans at serious risk of deportation.

The consequences of this massive illegality and marginality have only begun to be explored, but represent a compelling agenda future research. Key issues of importance to the current and future welfare of Latinos in general and Mexicans in particular include the effect on earnings and occupational mobility of being undocumented; the effect on earnings and occupational mobility of being formerly undocumented; the effects on the health and education of citizen children of having undocumented parents; and the long-term social and economic consequences of being formerly undocumented or growing up in a family that includes undocumented members.

Given the clear magnitude of the immigration enforcement system's effect on the status and welfare of Latinos in the United States, current proposals for immigration reform carry implications that extend well beyond immigrant assimilation. For years, critics of immigration reform have demanded that U.S. authorities gain "control" of the Mexico-U.S. border before considering broader reforms. According to current estimates, that goal has been achieved. Net undocumented migration has dropped to zero and the total size of the undocumented population has stabilized. The time has come, therefore, to consider the three principal proposals put forward to achieve comprehensive immigration reform: increasing the size of the annual quota for immigration from Mexico, creating a new guest worker program, and creating a path to legalization for those already here.

In practice, the first two goals have already been realized. Although quota limits remain in place and certainly deserve to be expanded, Latin American immigrants have increasingly taken matters into their own hands by naturalizing to U.S. citizenship. In doing so, they acquire the right to sponsor the entry of spouses, minor children, and parents without numerical limitation, and that to petition for the entry of brothers and sisters through the quota system itself. This shift has been especially noticeable among Mexicans, who historically have exhibited one of the lowest rates of naturalization among all immigrant groups.

Given rising pressures and penalties placed on legal resident aliens and the increasing difficulty of securing the entry of relatives through the preference system, legal Mexican immigrants have flocked toward U.S. citizenship in record numbers. From 1970 through 1985, Mexican naturalization averaged just 8,900 persons per year. After the passage of IRCA and the escalation of enforcement beginning in 1986, the average increased to 29,000 per year through 1995. After reductions in the options for family migration imposed on legal residents in 1990 and the new penalties on noncitizens enacted in 1996, the number of naturalizations surged to 125,000 per year from 1996 to 2010: 255,000 in 1996, 208,000 in 1998, and 232,000 in

2008. As a result, whereas just 24 percent of all Mexicans entered outside of numerical limitations as citizen relatives in 1995, 59 percent did so by 2010.

Thus the principal piece of unfinished business in immigration reform is the legalization of the roughly 11 million undocumented migrants still present in the United States (Passel, Cohen, and Gonzalez-Barrera 2012). Until the burden of illegality is lifted from their shoulders, they will remain vulnerable and exploitable with almost no possibility of upward mobility. Among those out of status, somewhere around 3 million entered the country as minors, typically as infants or young children in the company of their parents. These people did not make the decision to violate U.S. immigration laws and should not be held responsibilities for their parents' choices. In the absence of a criminal record or other disqualifying circumstances, these undocumented migrants should be offered an immediate and unconditional amnesty and be allowed to proceed with their lives in the only country most of them know.

Of those who entered undocumented status as adults, some portion only came recently and do not seek long-term residence in the United States, only intermittent short-term access to the U.S. labor market on acceptable legal terms. The recent expansion of guest worker migration has made temporary visas available to such people, and many appear to have taken up the offer as the estimated size of the undocumented population dropped from 11.6 million to 10.8 million between 2008 and 2009 (Hoeffer, Rytina, and Baker 2009, 2010). Interestingly, the estimated number of undocumented Mexicans dropped by 380,000 as 361,000 guest workers entered on temporary visas, suggesting that as legal avenues for entry are opened illegal migration will correspondingly drop.

For immigrants with deeper roots and longer durations of residence in the United States, however, the only humane and realistic option is to create a pathway to legal permanent residence. Longer-term immigrants would be offered temporary legalization that would give them the right to live and work in the United States for five years, during which time they would be able to accumulate points toward some threshold required for adjustment to permanent residence. These points would be awarded for time spent in the United States, payment of taxes, having U.S.-citizen children, learning English, studying civics, holding a job, owning a home, or whatever other socially desirable behaviors might be appropriate. Once the minimum threshold was achieved, migrants would pay a fine as restitution for violating immigration law, and then, having paid their debt to society, be allowed to get on with their lives as legal permanent residents of the United States, with the option to become citizens after the usual five years in permanent resident status.

REFERENCES

Acosta, Yesenia D., and G. Patricia de la Cruz. 2011. *The Foreign Born From Latin America and the Caribbean: 2010.* American Community Survey Briefs. Washington: U.S. Census Bureau.

Alvarado, Steven E., and Douglas S. Massey. 2010. "In Search of Peace: Structural Adjustment, Violence, and International Migration." *Annals of the American Academy of Political and Social Science* 630(1): 294–321.

American Civil Liberties Union. 2012. "Immigration Detention." *ACLU.org*, Available at: http://www.aclu.org/immigrants-rights/detention (accessed November 12, 2012).

Andreas, Peter. 2000. *Border Games: Policing the US-Mexico Divide*. Ithaca, N.Y.: Cornell University Press.

Bean, Frank D., and Marta Tienda. 1987. *The Hispanic Population of the United States*. New York: Russell Sage Foundation.

Bergad, Laird W., and Herbert S. Klein. 2010. *Hispanics in the United States: A Demographic, Social, and Economic History, 1980–2005*. New York: Cambridge University Press.

Borjas, George J. 1995. "Assimilation and Changes in Cohort Quality Revisited: What Happened to Immigrant Earnings in the 1980s?" *Journal of Labor Economics* 13(2): 201–45.

———. 1999. *Heaven's Door: Immigration Policy and the American Economy*. Princeton, N.J.: Princeton University Press.

Buchanan, Patrick J. 2006. *State of Emergency: The Third World Invasion and Conquest of America*. New York: Thomas Dunne Books.

Calavita, Kitty. 1992. *Inside the State: The Bracero Program, Immigration, and the INS*. New York: Routledge.

Cardoso, Lawrence. 1980. *Mexican Emigration to the United States 1897–1931*. Tucson: University of Arizona Press.

Chavez, Leo R. 2001. *Covering Immigration: Population Images and the Politics of the Nation*. Berkeley: University of California Press.

———. 2008. *The Latino Threat: Constructing Immigrants, Citizens, and the Nation*. Palo Alto, Calif.: Stanford University Press.

Dobbs, Lou. 2006. *War on the Middle Class: How the Government, Big Business, and Special Interest Groups Are Waging War on the American Dream and How to Fight Back*. New York: Viking.

Dunn, Timothy J. 1996. *The Militarization of the U.S.-Mexico Border, 1978–1992: Low-Intensity Conflict Doctrine Comes Home*. Austin: University of Texas, Center for Mexican American Studies.

Ennis, Sharon R., Merarys Ríos-Vargas, and Nora G. Albert. 2011. "The Hispanic Population: 2010." Washington: U.S. Census Bureau.

Federal Bureau of Investigation. 2009. *Hate Crime Statistics*. Washington, D.C.: Federal Bureau of Investigation. Available at: http://www.fbi.gov/ucr/ucr.htm#hate (accessed December 12, 2012).

Funkhouser, Edward. 1992. "Migration from Nicaragua: Some Recent Evidence." *World Development* 20(8): 1209–18.

Gentsch, Kirsten, and Douglas S. Massey. 2011. "Labor Market Outcomes for Legal Mexican Immigrants under the New Regime of Immigration Enforcement." *Social Science Quarterly* 92(3): 875–93.

Higham, John. 1955. *Strangers in the Land: Patterns of American Nativism, 1860–1925*. New Brunswick, N.J.: Rutgers University Press.

Hoeffer, Michael, Nancy Rytina, and Bryan C. Baker. 2009. *Estimates of the Unauthorized Im-*

migrant Population Residing in the United States: January 2008. Washington: U.S. Department of Homeland Security, Office of Immigration Statistics.

———. 2010. *Estimates of the Unauthorized Immigrant Population Residing in the United States: January 2009.* Washington: U.S. Department of Homeland Security, Office of Immigration Statistics.

Hopkins, Daniel J. 2010. "Politicized Places: Explaining Where and When Immigrants Provoke Local Opposition." *American Political Science Review* 104(1): 40–60.

Huntington, Samuel P. 2004, March 1. "The Hispanic Challenge." *Foreign Policy*, p. 1. Available at: http://www.foreignpolicy.com/articles/2004/03/01/the_hispanic_challenge (accessed June 11, 2013).

Jacobson, Robin Dale. 2008. *The New Nativism: Proposition 187 and the Debate Over Immigration.* Minneapolis: University of Minnesota Press.

Jones, Richard C. 1989. "Causes of Salvadoran Migration to the United States." *The Geographical Review* 79(2): 183–94.

Kohut, Andrew, and Roberto Suro. 2006. *America's Immigration Quandary: No Consensus on Immigration Problem or Proposed Fixes.* Washington, D.C.: Pew Research Center for the People and the Press and Pew Hispanic Center.

Lee, Tiane L., and Susan T. Fiske. 2006. "Not an Outgroup, Not Yet an Ingroup: Immigrants in the Stereotype Content Model." *International Journal of Intercultural Relations* 30(6): 751–68.

Legomsky, Stephen H. 2000. "Fear and Loathing in Congress and the Courts: Immigration and Judicial Review." *Texas Law Review* 78(2000): 1612–20.

Lopez, Mark Hugo, and Gretchen Livingston. 2009. "Hispanics and the Criminal Justice System: Low Confidence, High Exposure." Washington, D.C.: Pew Hispanic Center.

Lopez, Mark Hugo, and Susan Minushkin. 2008. "2008 National Survey of Latinos: Hispanics See Their Situation in U.S. as Deteriorating; Oppose Key Immigration Enforcement Measures." Washington, D.C.: Pew Hispanic Center.

Lopez, Mark Hugo, Rich Morin, and Paul Taylor. 2010. "Illegal Immigration Backlash Worries, Divides Latinos." Washington, D.C.: Pew Hispanic Center.

Lundquist, Jennifer H., and Douglas S. Massey. 2005. "The Contra War and Nicaraguan Migration to the United States." *Journal of Latin American Studies* 37(1): 29–53.

Massey, Douglas S. 1999. "International Migration at the Dawn of the Twenty-First Century: The Role of the State." *Population and Development Review* 25(2): 303–23.

———. 2007. *Categorically Unequal: The American Stratification System.* New York: Russell Sage Foundation.

———. 2008. *New Faces in New Places: The Changing Geography of American Immigration.* New York: Russell Sage Foundation.

———. 2009. "Racial Formation in Theory and Practice: The Case of Mexicans in the United States." *Race and Social Problems* 1(1): 12–26.

———. 2011. "Epilogue: The Past and Future of Mexico-U.S. Migration." In *Beyond la Frontera: The History of Mexico-U.S. Migration,* edited by Mark Overmyer-Velázquez. New York: Oxford University Press.

———. 2013. "The Racialization of Latinos in the United States." In *The Oxford Handbook on Ethnicity, Crime, and Immigration,* edited by Michael Tonry and Sandra Bucerius. New York: Oxford University Press.

Massey, Douglas S., and Nancy A. Denton. 1993. *American Apartheid: Segregation and the Making of the Underclass*. Cambridge, Mass.: Harvard University Press.

Massey, Douglas S., and Mary J. Fischer. 2000. "How Segregation Concentrates Poverty." *Ethnic and Racial Studies* 23(4): 670–91.

Massey, Douglas S., and Julia Gelatt. 2010. "What Happened to the Wages of Mexican Immigrants? Trends and Interpretations." *Latino Studies* 8(Autumn): 328–54.

Massey, Douglas S., and Kirsten Gentsch. 2012. "Undocumented Migration and the Wages of Mexican Immigrants." Unpublished paper.

Massey, Douglas S., and Nolan J. Malone. 2003. "Pathways to Legalization." *Population Research and Policy Review* 21(6): 473–504.

Massey, Douglas S., and Karen A. Pren. 2012a. "Unintended Consequences of US Immigration Policy: Explaining the Post-1965 Surge from Latin America." *Population and Development Review* 38(1): 1–29.

——— . 2012b. "Origins of the New Latino Underclass." *Race and Social Problems* 4(1): 5–17.

Massey, Douglas S., and Jacob S. Rugh. 2012. "Stalled Integration or End of the Segregated Century? U.S. Racial Segregation over Four Decades." Unpublished paper.

Massey, Douglas S., and Magaly Sánchez R. 2010. *Brokered Boundaries: Creating Immigrant Identity in Anti-Immigrant Times*. New York: Russell Sage Foundation.

Massey, Douglas S., Jorge Durand, and Nolan J. Malone. 2002. *Beyond Smoke and Mirrors: Mexican Immigration in an Age of Economic Integration*. New York: Russell Sage Foundation.

Massey, Douglas S., Jorge Durand, and Karen A. Pren. 2009. "Nuevos Escenarios de la Migración México-Estados Unidos: Las Consecuencias de la Guerra Antiinmigrante." *Papeles de Población* 15(61): 101–28.

Massey, Douglas S., Jacob S. Rugh, and Karen A. Pren. 2010. "The Geography of Undocumented Mexican Migration." *Mexican Studies/Estudios Mexicanos* 26(1): 120–52.

Massey, Douglas S., Magaly Sánchez R, and Jere R. Behrman. 2006. *Chronicle of a Myth Foretold: The Washington Consensus in Latin America*. Thousand Oaks, Calif.: Sage Publications.

Meyers, Eytan. 2004. *International Immigration Policy: A Theoretical and Comparative Analysis*. London: Palgrave Macmillan.

Morrison, Andrew R., and Rachel A. May. 1994. "Escape from Terror: Violence and Migration in Post-Revolutionary Guatemala." *Latin American Research Review* 29(1): 111–32.

National Council of State Legislatures. 2009. *Immigrant Policy Project: 2009 Immigration-Related Bills and Resolutions*. Washington, D.C.: National Council of State Legislatures. Available at: http://www.ncsl.org/documents/immig/2009ImmigFinalApril222009.pdf (accessed June 24, 2009).

Newton, Lina. 2008. *Illegal, Alien, or Immigrant: The Politics of Immigration Reform*. New York: New York University Press.

Pager, Devah. 2007. *Marked: Race, Crime, and Finding Work in an Era of Mass Incarceration*. Chicago: University of Chicago Press.

Passel, Jeffrey. 2006. "The Size and Characteristics of the Unauthorized Migrant Population in the U.S.: Estimates Based on the March 2005 Current Population Survey." Washington, D.C.: Pew Hispanic Center.

Passel, Jeffrey S., D'Vera Cohen, and Ana Gonzalez-Barrera. 2012. "Net Migration from Mexico Falls to Zero—and Perhaps Less." Washington, D.C.: Pew Hispanic Center.

Pettit, Becky. 2012. *Invisible Men: Mass Incarceration and the Myth of Black Progress.* New York: Russell Sage Foundation.

Pew Hispanic Center. 2007. "The 2007 National Survey of Latinos: As Illegal Immigration Issue Heats Up, Hispanics Feel a Chill." Washington, D.C.: Pew Hispanic Center.

——— . 2011. "The Mexican-American Boom: Births Overtake Immigration." Washington, D.C.: Pew Hispanic Center.

Purnell, Thomas, William Idsardi, and John Baugh. 1999. "Perceptual and Phonetic Experiments on American English Dialect Identification." *Journal of Language and Social Psychology* 18(1): 10–30.

Quillian, Lincoln. 2012. "Segregation and Poverty Concentration: The Role of Three Segregations." *American Sociological Review* 77(3): 354–79.

Redburn, Steve, Peter Reuter, and Malay Majmundar. 2011. *Budgeting for Immigration Enforcement: A Path to Better Performance.* Washington, D.C.: National Academies Press.

Riosmena, Fernando. 2010. "Playing Favorites: The Legal Auspices of Latin American Migration to the United States." In *Continental Divides: International Migration in the Americas,* edited by Katharine Donato, John Hiskey, Jorge Durand, and Douglas S. Massey. Thousand Oaks, Calif.: Sage Publications.

Rotella, Sebastian. 1998. *Twilight on the Line: Underworlds and Politics at the U.S.-Mexico Border.* New York: W. W. Norton.

Rugh, Jacob S., and Douglas S. Massey. 2010. "Racial Segregation and the American Foreclosure Crisis." *American Sociological Review* 75(5): 629–51.

Santa Ana, Otto. 2002. *Brown Tide Rising: Metaphors of Latinos in Contemporary American Public Discourse.* Austin: University of Texas Press.

Schrag, Peter. 2010. *Not Fit for Our Society: Immigration and Nativism in America.* Berkeley: University of California Press.

Stanley, William D. 1987. "Economic Migrants or Refugees from Violence? A Time-Series Analysis of Salvadoran Migration to the United States." *Latin American Research Review* 22(1): 132–54.

Turner, Margery A., Stephen L. Ross, George C. Galster, and John Yinger. 2002. *Discrimination in Metropolitan Housing Markets: National Results from Phase I.* Washington: U.S. Department of Housing and Urban Development.

U.S. Office of Immigration Statistics. 2012. *The 2011 Yearbook of Immigration Statistics.* Washington: U.S. Office of Immigration Statistics. Available at: http://www.dhs.gov/files/statistics/publications/yearbook.shtm (accessed March 15, 2013).

Wasem, Ruth E. 2011. "Unauthorized Aliens Residing in the United States: Estimates Since 1986." *CRS* Report for Congress no. RL33874. Washington, D.C.: Congressional Research Service.

Zolberg, Aristide R. 2006. *A Nation by Design: Immigration Policy in the Fashioning of America.* New York: Russell Sage Foundation.

Chapter 10

Employment Effects of State Legislation

Sarah Bohn and Magnus Lofstrom

Three United States is home to a large and growing number of unauthorized
immigrants. The most recent estimates indicate that this population increased from about 3 million in the late 1980s to around 11 million in 2009
(Passel and Cohn 2010). The legal immigrant population has also grown substantially over this time, as described in chapter 1 and throughout this volume, but the
unauthorized immigrant population has grown at an even higher rate. Not surprisingly, the size and growth of the unauthorized population has not gone un-
noticed and is the source of much controversy surrounding immigration policy.
Reflected in both the recent efforts to reform the country's immigration policy and
the last major immigration reform, the 1986 Immigration Reform and Control Act
(IRCA), policymakers recognize that employment is the primary draw for most
unauthorized immigrants. Instituting employer sanctions for hiring unauthorized
immigrants was a key component of IRCA. However, the sanctions were little
enforced and the lure of jobs and higher wages continue to attract numerous immigrants in spite of lacking legal rights to work in the United States.

Despite several attempts at immigration reform, Congress has not been able to
pass either comprehensive or piecemeal immigration legislation addressing illegal
immigration. Reform efforts failed in 2006 and 2007, and its failure to pass the
(Development, Relief, and Education for Alien Minors) DREAM Act in 2010 is one
such example of congressional gridlock on immigration. In the absence of federal
legislative action, states have increasingly taken it upon themselves to address the
issue of illegal immigration. This trend is evident by the increase from thirty-eight
immigration-related pieces of legislation passed by states in 2005 to 346 in 2010.
Although these bills cover a wide range of issues, many — 118 laws in thirty-seven
states between 2005 and 2010 — directly target the employment opportunities of
unauthorized immigrants.

Arizona is leading the charge against illegal immigration.[1] Years before passing
the highly publicized and controversial Senate bill 1070 (SB 1070) in April 2010,
Arizona introduced legislation targeting employers hiring unauthorized immi-

grants.[2] The Legal Arizona Worker Act (LAWA) was passed in July 2007 and implemented in January 2008. Although the law includes state-imposed employer sanctions against firms knowingly hiring unauthorized workers—business licenses suspension and possible revocation for repeat offenders—the arguably most important feature is the requirement that all employers use the federal E-Verify online work authorization system for all new hires. A number of states—Utah, South Carolina, Mississippi, and Oklahoma—have since implemented similar mandates. Other states have proposed or discussed similar measures. Arizona is an important test case for understanding the impacts of state legislation on employment of unauthorized immigrants. The possibility of other states following Arizona's example is even more likely given the May 2011 U.S. Supreme Court decision upholding the legality of LAWA.

Very little is known about the impacts of these laws, but previous research shows that LAWA induced sizeable responses among the unauthorized population. The population of noncitizen Hispanic immigrants in Arizona—a high proportion of whom are unauthorized immigrants—fell by roughly 92,000 (roughly 17 percent) due to LAWA, for example (Bohn, Lofstrom, and Raphael 2011). This shift came about through a combination of out-migration from Arizona to other states and abroad as well as a slowing of the inflow of new unauthorized immigrants to the state.

The intent of policies like LAWA is to limit unauthorized workers' economic opportunities as a way to deter further illegal immigration and as such are likely to increase poverty among an already marginalized population. Hence, in this chapter we take an additional step to address the important question of how those unauthorized immigrants who chose to stay in—or chose to come to—Arizona are affected by LAWA. Specifically, we analyze LAWA's impact on labor market opportunities of unauthorized workers in Arizona. We assess whether the legislation reduced their employment opportunities in formal employment (the wage and salary sector). We also look for evidence of an unintended consequence of the policy: whether LAWA pushed workers into informal employment, and, if so, what the likely consequences are for these workers and their families. An increase in informal employment is clearly not the objective of the policy because the shift may be associated with lower income tax revenues due to both lower earnings and fewer workers contributing to the tax system. For workers pushed into informal employment, the effects are likely to be fewer benefits, lower wages, and potential for worsened working conditions. To estimate any shifts into informal employment, we obtain estimates of LAWA's impact on the self-employment rate in Arizona.

STATE-LEVEL IMMIGRATION LEGISLATION

The increased efforts by states to address employment of unauthorized immigrants—an issue historically in the federal domain—represent an important shift in national immigration policy. State laws vary greatly in their restrictiveness and in the implementation related to employment of unauthorized immigrants. Most of the comprehensive laws mandate use of E-Verify.

E-Verify

E-Verify is an online system created and managed by the federal government to provide information to employers about whether an individual is authorized to work in the United States. E-Verify is intended to verify workers' Form I-9 information against Social Security Administration (SSA) and Citizenship and Immigration Services (USCIS) databases. E-Verify completes two verification tasks: authentication of identity and verification of work authorization. The system functions for all workers, citizens and noncitizens, and is intended for authorizing new hires only. Employers are not permitted to use E-Verify to check authorization of individuals until they have been hired and submit an I-9.

The federal government does not require employers to use E-Verify, except for firms with certain federal government contracts (administrative order instituted September 8, 2009). E-Verify provides quick results if identity and work authorization are confirmed—which, according to Westat (2009), occurs about 95 percent of the time. When confirmation is not granted, referred to as tentative nonconfirmation (TNC), the employee may appeal. While a TNC is being contested, employers are not allowed to dismiss the worker solely on the basis of the record. If an employee fails to or is unable to correct his or her TNC, employers are required to terminate the employee after a relatively short period.

The main problems with E-Verify are delays in correcting tentative nonconfirmations, erroneous confirmations, and insufficient capacity as more employers enroll. Intensive refinement of the system in recent years has led to a decline in E-Verify error rates. For authorized workers, the accuracy rate of E-Verify is at least 99 percent, and unlikely to get much better. For unauthorized workers, the error rate may be as high as 54 percent (Westat 2009). The costs—primarily time and energy—of correcting errors fall on the new hires as well as on local U.S. Department of Homeland Security (DHS) and SSA offices where individuals must go to correct errors. Verification can be circumvented by employers' avoiding using the system, identity theft, or applicants' falsifying documents. Federal law and current state law therefore supplement verification tools with enforcement.

The results of E-Verify at this time are not reported to any agency responsible for immigration enforcement. That is, even if a new hire is found to be unauthorized, these results are not transmitted to DHS or Immigration and Customs Enforcement (ICE) for investigation, detainment, or deportation of the individual.

Existing State Laws

Colorado was the first state to pass legislation intended to reduce the hiring of unauthorized workers. Colorado's law requires any person or entity entering a public contract with the state on or after August 2006 to certify that it has verified the legal status of all new hires using the E-Verify program. Similar laws or executive orders were enacted in Georgia in 2007, Rhode Island and Minnesota in 2008, and Missouri and Utah in 2009. South Carolina, Utah, and Mississippi have passed legislation that phases in E-Verify use over time according to business size. In South Carolina, employers of all sizes were required to use E-Verify by July 2010. In Mississippi, all employers are legislated to be phased in by July 2011. The penalties for hiring unauthorized workers are stringent under the Mississippi law, and include loss of public contracts and suspension of business licenses. Utah's mandate covers all employers with fifteen or more employees as of July 2010. Oklahoma is a special case. The first phase of its legislation was scheduled to go into effect in November 2007, but a court challenge has held up implementation. To date, Oklahoma has yet to implement the provisions of its bill.

The 2007 Legal Arizona Workers' Act

Arizona's Legal Arizona Workers' Act—signed into law in July 2007 and effective January 1, 2008—imposes sanctions on employers who knowingly hire unauthorized immigrants: a business license suspension for the first offense and license revocation for a second. LAWA is unique among recent state legislation on the employment of unauthorized immigrants in that it covers all firms, not just public agencies or those with state government contracts. It also mandates that all employers located in the state use E-Verify. Its broad range makes LAWA a good example of state legislation that mimics recent federal reform proposals. Arizona is also the only place where all employers have been required to use E-Verify for enough time to allow for a reliable empirical evaluation.

Although the legislation has faced a number of legal challenges, it has been upheld by the federal district and appellate courts. The challenges to LAWA focus on the right of states to legislate on immigration enforcement. The U.S. Supreme Court heard arguments in the case, Chamber of Commerce et al. v. Whiting, in December 2010 and ruled in favor of the legislation in May 2011. The clearing of the constitutionality hurdle may spur additional interest in passing such laws.

We expect that LAWA's impacts to date largely stem from a deterrent or compliance effect prompted by the E-Verify mandate rather than from employer sanctioning. Despite the sanctions established in LAWA, few have been assessed to date. Through April 2010, more than two full years following LAWA's enactment, only three prosecutions had been pursued, all in a single county (Maricopa). Few sanctions may reflect the lack of resources in the county attorney offices responsible for investigating claims. Few sanctions may also reflect high compliance among employers. Indeed, statistics from the E-Verify system indicate growth in number of firms enrolled in Arizona: from 300 in March 2007 to 38,000 in January 2010 (Westat 2009; Arizona Attorney General 2010). Arizona firm enrollment represents roughly one-third of all firms enrolled nationwide. Further, estimates suggest that roughly 700,000 new hires made between October 2008 and September 2009 were run through E-Verify in Arizona (*Arizona Republic*, July 28, 2010). This correlates to roughly 50 percent of all new hires in the state.

EFFECT OF STATE IMMIGRATION LEGISLATION ON STATE LABOR MARKETS

The intention of Arizona's LAWA is to deter the hiring of unauthorized immigrant workers by making it more expensive for employers to do so and simultaneously making Arizona less attractive to both existing and potential future unauthorized immigrants. A motivation behind such legislation is to improve labor market opportunities for those legally eligible to work in the United States. Whether such legislation is effective in this regard depends in large part on the degree to which authorized and unauthorized workers compete with one another in the labor market. As Giovanni Peri and Ethan Lewis show in chapters 2 and 3 of this volume, immigrants have little overall effect on natives in the labor market in large part because they are not closely substitutable. These findings suggest that LAWA is most likely to improve labor market outcomes for authorized workers most closely substitutable for unauthorized workers. Hence the labor market effects of LAWA are likely to vary by skill, nativity, ethnicity, gender, and the interaction of these dimensions.

To the extent that employers can distinguish unauthorized workers from documented workers, state laws punishing employers who hire the unauthorized can be modeled as increasing the relative costs of hiring unauthorized workers. Standard labor demand theory predicts that this would induce two reinforcing effects on the demand for unauthorized immigrants and two offsetting effects on demand for other workers. Regarding the targeted workers, higher costs of hiring unauthorized workers should induce both employer substitution toward other workers and a general reduction in employment associated with the higher compliance costs (such as additional verification requirements and the penalty if caught). These effects should unambiguously reduce demand for unauthorized workers, lowering employment levels and perhaps average wages.

However, theory does not yield an unambiguous prediction for other groups of workers. To the extent that authorized immigrants and specific groups of the native born are easily substitutable in production for unauthorized immigrants, employer substitution will boost labor demand for such workers and ultimately affect their average employment and earnings. However, the size of this substitution effect will be smallest for those who are the least like the unauthorized. In fact, certain labor groups are likely to be complementary in production with unauthorized labor, implying that regardless of the scale of production in the economy, an increase in the cost of hiring unauthorized workers would actually harm these natives.

For all authorized workers, even those who are close substitutes for the unauthorized, higher compliance costs may result in a reduction in the overall scale of an organization's activities. Hence, offsetting substitution and scale effects do not permit prediction of the impact of these laws on documented immigrants and the native born. Theory does suggest, however, that, with perfect information on legal status, those authorized workers most similar in skill to the unauthorized stand to gain the most.

When employers cannot easily distinguish the documented from the unauthorized, the potential impacts of such state legislation are complicated by the likelihood that employers form probabilistic assessments of the legal status of specific applicants and then act on those assessments. Specifically, if they cannot be certain who is and who is not authorized, employers may infer legal status through such visible signals as ethnicity, accent, or surname.

Even an accurate verification system, however, may lead some employers to avoid hiring individuals from these groups given that authorization through E-Verify is not checked until after the individual has been hired. In the event of an accurate nonconfirmation of work authorization, the new hire has a period in which to correct the finding through DHS or SSA (this is the new hire's responsibility and not the employer's). During this period, the employer cannot fire the employee except for issues unrelated to work authorization status. The employer may then lose productivity of the new hire during the waiting period and incur additional hiring costs. In Arizona, Hispanic or foreign-born applicants, in particular those with less education, are most likely to be negatively affected by this potential employer behavior.

Last, LAWA's E-Verify mandate applies to all employers and for all new employees. However, it includes only licensed business in the definition of employers. LAWA also specifically excludes independent contractors from the definition of an employee. Thus, one way to avoid use of E-Verify is to enter into an independent contractor arrangement rather than formal wage-salary employment. It is possible that workers would maintain the same work activities and employer but shift the relationship from being a wage worker to a contractor, for example. It is hence important to also study whether LAWA induced unauthorized immigrants who remained in Arizona to rely on self-employment, or informal employment, to a greater extent as a consequence of LAWA, and how this affected their and their families' economic well-being. What informal or self-employment would mean for unauthorized workers in Arizona varies widely. Beyond independent contracting, other common examples of self-employment among unauthorized workers may also include, for example, day laborers and micro-entrepreneurs, work typically associated with the informal labor market.

A shift toward work in the informal sector is of greatest concern for the targeted population—unauthorized immigrants. Unauthorized immigrants who choose to live in Arizona are likely to have more limited opportunities for employment, particularly in the formal sector. Informal work has economic consequences for workers—specifically, lower earnings and potential exploitation—as well as for the economy more broadly—lower tax revenue. The Congressional Budget Office, in assessing the cost of E-Verify, estimates that a U.S.-wide mandate would decrease revenue $17.3 billion over nine years as a result of unauthorized workers shifting to being paid outside the tax system (Congressional Budget Office 2008).

Because LAWA applies only to Arizona, workers have the option of migrating elsewhere, where obtaining a job in the formal sector is easier. However, the more states that enact employment enforcement legislation, the fewer the options for unauthorized immigrants, and thus the larger the potential growth in informal employment. This concern is particularly salient when employment enforcement laws are enacted piecemeal on a state-by-state basis and without reform to the other aspects of immigration policy. We discuss these issues in more detail in the following section.

DATA AND EMPIRICAL STRATEGY

To assess the employment effects of LAWA, we follow the approach of Sarah Bohn, Magnus Lofstrom, and Steven Raphael (2011), which solely examined overall population outcomes. We analyze data from all monthly Current Population Survey (CPS) data sets collected between January 1998 and December 2009. These data provide details on the employment of individuals in each state as well as information on race-ethnicity, education, age, and other demographic characteristics including immigration status (native-U.S. born or foreign-born naturalized citizen, or not a citizen). Our analysis primarily focuses on the impacts on the population targeted by LAWA: unauthorized immigrants. Ideally, we would like to directly examine outcomes of unauthorized workers in Arizona. But neither these CPS data nor any suitable available other data allow for precise identification of individual unauthorized immigrants.[3] Nonetheless, among certain population groups that we can identify in the data, the likelihood of being unauthorized is substantially elevated. In particular, by definition there should be no unauthorized immigrants among those who report being either naturalized immigrant or U.S. born. Further, unauthorized immigrants are more likely to be men, of working age of Hispanic origin, and have fewer years of formal education (Passel and Cohn 2010).

Thus, for our analysis, we examine outcomes for the following demographic groups that have varying proportions of unauthorized immigrants:

- foreign-born noncitizen Hispanics
- foreign-born naturalized citizen Hispanics
- native-born Hispanics
- native-born non-Hispanic whites

We estimate that in Arizona upward of 80 to 90 percent of the first group, foreign-born noncitizen Hispanics, are unauthorized.[4] The second group, assuming no reporting error, should include no unauthorized immigrants. The last two groups, both native-born, should also by definition include no unauthorized immigrants. Given that unauthorized immigrants are more likely to be men and have less education, much of the focus is on men with high school degrees or less.

To obtain large enough samples of these relatively small demographic groups, we combine monthly CPS files within years and estimate employment outcomes on an annual basis, from 1998 to 2009. The CPS data, nor any other comprehensive data source, do not yet allow for robust analysis of wages through 2009. The CPS data, though relatively current, do not have large enough samples in our narrowly defined demographic groups. Larger samples are available in the American Community Survey (ACS), but currently these data only report wages through 2008. We therefore focus on examining employment rather than wages. We estimate impacts on two primary and mutually exclusive outcomes: employment in wage and salary work and self-employment.

To identify the causal impact of LAWA on employment outcomes in Arizona, we use the synthetic control approach of Alberto Abadie, Alexis Diamond, and Jens Hainmueller (2010). Key to the identification strategy is charting the appropriate counterfactual path for Arizona in absence of LAWA. A number of approaches are possible. One is to select states that share similar population and economic characteristics and trends as Arizona, for example, the states bordering Arizona—a traditional difference-in-difference approach. Another would be to use a data-driven search for comparison states based on pre-LAWA population and employment characteristics and trends (the synthetic control method of Abadie et al. 2010). We use both, but focus on the latter, because it is arguably the most reliable and essentially incorporates the first strategy. It allows the data to tell us which states best match Arizona's pre-LAWA experience. We also implement the alternative strategy of using only neighboring areas—Nevada, New Mexico, Utah, and inland California. This approach, which relies on ACS data, generates results similar to those presented in the chapter and are available on request.

The synthetic control method allows for robust analysis in the single policy change—single state context. We summarize the methodology for charting a counterfactual post-LAWA path for Arizona. The idea is to generate a comparison group from a convex combination of states in a large donor pool. Let the index $j = (0, 1, \ldots, J)$ denote states. The value $j = 0$ corresponds to Arizona and $j = (1, \ldots, J)$ correspond to each of the other J states that are candidate contributors to the control group (that is, the donor pool). Define F_0 as a 9×1 vector with elements equal to the group-specific employment outcome in Arizona in years 1998 through 2006, our pre-intervention period. Similarly, define the $9 \times J$ matrix F_1 as the collection of comparable time series for each of the J states in the donor pool, each column corresponding to a separate state-level time series from 1998 through 2006.

The synthetic control method identifies a convex combination of the J states in the donor pool that best approximates the pre-intervention time series for the treated state. Define the $J \times 1$ weighting vector $W = (w_1, w_2, \ldots, w_J)'$ such that $\Sigma_{j=1} w_j = 1$, and $w_j \geq 0$ for $j = (1, \ldots, J)$. The product $F_1 W$ then gives a weighted average of the pre-intervention time series for all states omitting Arizona, with the difference between Arizona and this average given by $F_0 - F_1 W$. The synthetic control method essentially chooses a value for the weighting vector, W, that yields a synthetic comparison group—an average of some subset of donor states—that best approximates the pre-intervention path for Arizona. Specifically, the weighting vector is chosen by solving the constrained quadratic minimization problem:

$$W^* = \text{arg}_w\min(F_0 - F_1W)' V(F_0 - F_1W) \tag{1}$$

s.t.

$$W'i = 1, w_j \geq 0, j = (1, \ldots J)$$

where V is a 9×9, diagonal positive-definite matrix with diagonal elements providing the relative weights for the contribution of the square of the elements in the vector $F_0 - F_1W$ to the objective function being minimized.

Once an optimal weighting vector W^* is chosen, both the pre-intervention path as well as the post-intervention values for the dependent variable in "synthetic Arizona" can be tabulated by calculating the corresponding weighted average for each year using the donor states with positive weights. The post-intervention values for the synthetic control group serve as our counterfactual outcomes for Arizona.

Our principal estimate of the impacts of LAWA on employment outcomes uses the synthetic control group to calculate a simple difference-in-differences estimate. Specifically, define $Outcome^{AZ}_{pre}$ as the average value of the outcome of interest for Arizona for the pre-intervention period 1998 through 2006 and $Outcome^{AZ}_{post}$ as the corresponding average for the two post-treatment years 2008 and 2009. Define the similar averages $Outcome^{AZ}_{pre}$ and $Outcome^{AZ}_{post}$ for the synthetic control group. Our difference-in-differences estimate subtracts the pre-intervention difference between the averages for Arizona and synthetic Arizona from the comparable post-intervention difference, or

$$DD_{AZ} = (Outcome^{AZ}_{post} - Outcome^{synth}_{post}) - (Outcome^{AZ}_{pre} - Outcome^{synth}_{pre}) \tag{2}$$

To formally test the significance of any observed relative decline in Arizona's foreign-born population, we apply the permutation test suggested by Abadie and his colleagues (2010) to the difference-in-difference estimator displaced in equation (2).[5] Specifically, for each state in the donor pool, we identify synthetic comparison groups based on the solution to the quadratic minimization problem in equation (1). We then estimate the difference-in-difference in equation (2) for each state as if these states had passed the equivalent of a LAWA with comparable timing. The distribution of these placebo difference-in-difference estimates then provides the equivalent of a sampling distribution for the estimate DD_{AZ}. Specifically, if the cumulative density function of the complete set of DD estimates is given by $F(.)$, the p-value from a one-tailed test of the hypothesis that $DD_{AZ} < 0$ is given by $F(DD_{AZ})$.

To interpret DD_{AZ} as a causal estimate of LAWA's employment effects, we must make the case that LAWA is an exogenous shock to the labor market. For example, if high unemployment among the foreign born and the attendant problems led

Arizona to enact legislation to discourage future migration to the state, inference on DD_{AZ} would be compromised. In fact, LAWA was debated and passed during a period of economic growth but was enacted at a time of declining labor market conditions. A number of facts suggest that the passage and enactment of LAWA was not driven by employment conditions in the state at the time but instead reflected Arizona's perceived long-term problem of unauthorized immigration, also experienced by other states. To start, LAWA represents the ultimate manifestation of a fairly lengthy legislative debate that crossed multiple legislation sessions. Moreover, uncertainty was considerable as to whether LAWA would be enacted on January 1, 2008. Federal lawsuits challenging the constitutionality of LAWA were brought by an alliance of civil rights advocates, business interests, and immigrant rights groups. The challenge was dismissed, but not until early December. Anecdotal evidence suggests that those likely to be affected by actual implementation followed the court challenge and were conditioning their responses on the ultimate legal outcome (see *Arizona Republic*, October 8, 2007).

A further challenge to causal interpretation of DD_{AZ} is potential coincident timing of other changes in Arizona's labor market that could work in the same direction as LAWA. Although LAWA has the potential to affect the labor market, a number of other forces also drive labor market conditions. We argue that, under the synthetic control approach, unless the timing of these other forces was exactly coincident with that of LAWA, our estimates represent the causal relationship between LAWA and Arizona's employment outcomes. This argument hinges on the ability of the synthetic control method to match Arizona's pre-LAWA trends with those of other states and to determine whether Arizona's pre-post changes stand out from the placebo estimates for all other states. We show in the following section that both of these conditions are satisfied. Given that, we need only address the two major factors coincident with LAWA that could invalidate the claim of causality.

First, we are concerned about the potential coincidence of federal immigration enforcement increases with the enactment of LAWA. We have reviewed DHS data and found nothing to suggest that federal enforcement increases at the border or in internal investigations happened differently in Arizona than in other border states or at exactly the same time as LAWA. The Arizona Border Control Initiative, which built up infrastructure on Arizona's border with Mexico predated LAWA by a few years. Further, our review of DHS arrest and apprehension data suggests that a similar percentage of all border apprehensions occurred in the Tucson sector, about 42 percent, following LAWA and the number of arrests resulting from ICE investigations actually fell (Office of Immigration Statistics 2010).

Second, the Great Recession occurred at approximately the same time as the enactment of LAWA. Evidence indicates that the recession reduced the inflow of new immigrants to the United States and to Arizona. Our empirical approach comparing trends in Arizona with other states already accounts for any changes that affect the country as a whole or the selected comparison states. However, one of the industries hit hardest, construction, is a leading employers of unauthorized immigrants. Furthermore, construction is one of the biggest industries in Ari-

FIGURE 10.1 / Annual Employment Growth

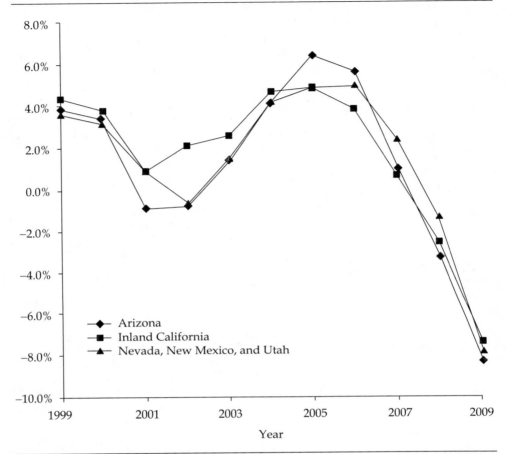

Source: Authors' compilation based on Quarterly Census of Employment and Wages (QCEW).

zona—close to 11 percent of total private employment in 2006—and thus declines in the state's economy can have a significant impact. Thus, it is important in our evaluation strategy to ensure that we do not attribute changes in population to LAWA if they were in fact driven by the decline in construction and real estate in Arizona specifically. To validate our empirical approach, we assess official statistics on employment trends in Arizona and neighboring states during the recession, based on the Quarterly Census of Employment and Wages (QCEW) data.

The recent recession caused a clear reduction in Arizona's workforce. Figure 10.1 shows strong employment growth from 2003 to 2006 and a noticeable slow down in 2007. This was followed by 3 and 8 percent decreases in 2008 and 2009, respectively. Figure 10.1 also shows that the negative employment effects of the recession on employment were not any stronger in Arizona than in neighboring

FIGURE 10.2 / Annual Employment Growth in Construction

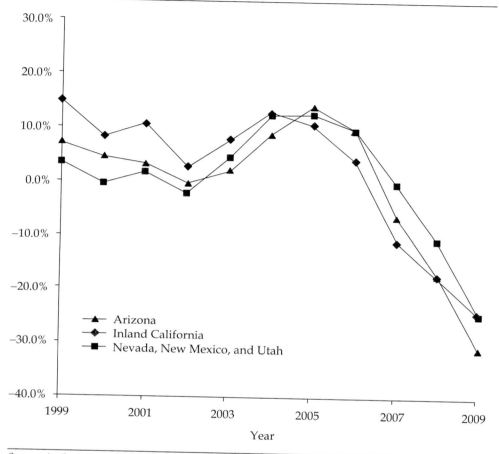

Source: Authors' compilation Based on Quarterly Census of Employment and Wages (QCEW).

areas, including inland California (an area that shares many of the characteristics and trends of Arizona, and therefore used in our empirical analysis). Last, an application of the synthetic cohort method to employment growth fails to reveal a LAWA effect in Arizona.

Importantly, the recession was precipitated by a housing crisis, which brought new housing construction to a near standstill. That many unauthorized immigrants are, or perhaps more accurately were, employed in the construction sector means that they may have been particularly affected by the recession. However, a look at construction employment data reveals no evidence that Arizona's construction industry fared much differently in the recession than its neighboring areas (figure 10.2).

Overall, the QCEW data indicate that though Arizona's labor market was strongly affected by the recession, those of other states were as well, including its neighbors. The similarity in trends indicates that our empirical strategy is appropriate for identifying causality despite the recent recession.

EMPIRICAL RESULTS: EMPLOYMENT EFFECTS OF LAWA?

We begin our analysis of whether LAWA affected employment opportunities of illegal immigrants in Arizona by examining employment rates, defined here as the ratio of persons employed in the wage and salary sector. As discussed, for those workers who remained in Arizona following LAWA, a variety of employment effects is plausible. To the extent that firms are hiring and are in compliance with LAWA, unauthorized immigrants are less likely to find employment. The legislation has potential spillover effects on other workers, in both positive and negative directions.

The data indicate that noncitizen Hispanics in Arizona experienced a particularly large post-LAWA drop in employment. Figure 10.3 shows that before the passing of LAWA in 2007, the employment rate of noncitizen Hispanics in wage and salary work was relatively stable at around 60 to 63 percent: lower than non-Hispanic whites but similar to native and naturalized Hispanics. The data, however, show a different pattern in the post-LAWA period. The employment rate of noncitizen Hispanics in particular drops sharply in 2008, and by 2009 they have substantially lower employment rates than the other groups.

Because we want to focus on individuals who are likely to work, we next restrict our sample to men age sixteen to sixty. Furthermore, although we estimate outcomes for all groups, we pay particular attention to the one with the highest proportion of unauthorized workers: the less educated, that is, a high school diploma or less.

To probe the employment changes further, we apply the synthetic control approach and use the comparison states, which mimic Arizona's 1998 to 2006 employment trend. In this exercise, we omit from the donor pool four states with broadly applied restrictions on the employment of unauthorized immigrants—Mississippi, Rhode Island, South Carolina, and Utah—even though the timing of their legislation postdates LAWA.[6] In addition, in identifying synthetic control states for placebo tests on each of the other states in the donor pool, we omit Arizona. Because unauthorized immigrants in Arizona experience some of the sharpest drops in employment following LAWA, omitting Arizona from the donor pool for estimating the placebo intervention effects should impart a negative bias. This specification choice should make it more difficult for us to find a significant effect.

The states receiving positive weights in the synthetic control for Arizona vary depending on the outcome variable and the subgroup analyzed. For example, for the wage and salary employment rate analysis among noncitizen Hispanics with a high school diploma or less, six states were assigned positive weights but two combined for more than 90 percent of the weight—California at 0.845 and New

FIGURE 10.3 / Wage-Salary Employment Rates, Groups

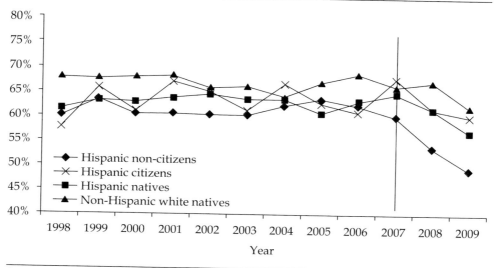

Year

Source: Authors' compilation based on monthly Current Population Survey.

Mexico at 0.077. For the same group in our analysis of the self-employment rate, nine states received positive weights — Massachusetts at 0.42, Florida at 0.143, and Tennessee at 0.141 having the largest.

LAWA Effects on Formal Employment

Figure 10.4 shows that before LAWA, the wage and salary employment rates of noncitizen Hispanics matched those of noncitizens in the synthetic Arizona quite well. Average pre-intervention differences between Arizona and the synthetic control groups are near zero for each outcome, with quite small root mean squared errors. Hence, the synthetic control approach passes the first hurdle — succeeds in obtaining of convex combination of states that match Arizona's pre-LAWA trend. Beginning in 2007, we observe a divergent pattern. In the two post-LAWA years, we observe the noncitizen Hispanic employment rate is between 11 and 12 percentage points lower than in the comparison states.

Average differences between Arizona and the synthetic control are calculated in the pre-LAWA period (1998–2006) and post-LAWA period (2008–2009). These and the difference-in-difference estimate, DD_{AZ}, are presented in table 10.1 (third row). Following LAWA, the employment rate of noncitizen Hispanic men with lower levels of educational attainment fell slightly more than 11 percentage points relative to the synthetic control. To obtain a *p*-value on DD_{AZ} as well its nonparametric rank, we replicate the synthetic control method on each state in the donor pool and obtain a distribution of difference-in-difference estimates.

FIGURE 10.4 / Wage-Salary Employment Rates, Hispanic Noncitizen Men with High School or Less

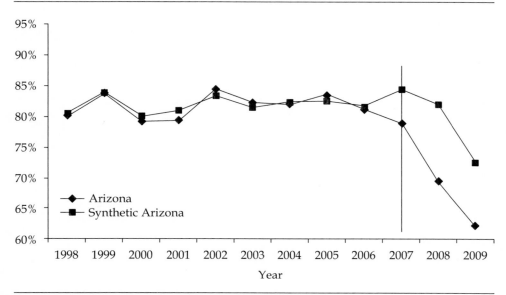

Source: Authors' compilation based on monthly Current Population Survey.
Note: Synthetic Arizona consists of the following states (with weights in parentheses): California (0.845), New Mexico (0.077), Indiana (0.04), Nebraska (0 .024), District of Columbia (0.011), and Washington (0.003).

The set of difference-in-difference point estimates, DD, is used to calculate the p-value and rank of DD_{AZ}. These statistics are given in the last two columns of table 10.1 (see also figure 10.5).[7] We find that the difference-in-difference estimate for Arizona stands out as a clear outlier in the distribution of placebo estimates. The 11.4 point decline is the largest among all states and is a statistically significant decline. Using the size of the noncitizen Hispanic population and workforce in Arizona in 2006 as the base, about 531,000 and 308,000 respectively, our estimates suggest that LAWA caused a drop in wage and salary employment of roughly 56,000 noncitizen Hispanic workers.

The first panel of table 10.1 reveals that wage and salary employment declines among likely unauthorized workers in Arizona comes from the less educated and males. This is driven, of course, by the fact that most unauthorized immigrants in the state are in these two subgroups. Note, however that we do not detect any statistically significant declines in wage and salary employment among likely unauthorized women due to LAWA.

The next three panels of table 10.1 show a lack of evidence for impacts of LAWA on the competing groups of workers we examine. No declines or improvements in wage and salary employment for less-skilled naturalized Hispanics, native-born

TABLE 10.1 / Estimated Impact of LAWA, Wage–Salary Employment

	Pre-Average Difference Relative to Synthetic Cohort	Post-Average Difference Relative to Synthetic Cohort	Change, Post Minus Pre (Difference-In-Difference Estimate)	Rank, Difference-In-Difference Estimate	P-value From One-Tailed Test, $P(|\Delta| < |\Delta AZ|)$
Hispanic noncitizens					
All	-0.0033	-0.1081	-0.1048	43/45	0.067
High school or less	-0.0036	-0.0660	-0.0623	34/40	0.175
High school or less, men	-0.0009	-0.1151	-0.1142	40/40	0.025
High school or less, women	-0.0138	-0.0294	-0.0156	24/40	0.425
Hispanic citizens					
All	-0.0061	-0.0074	-0.0013	22/44	0.523
High school or less	-0.0104	0.0273	0.0377	21/35	0.429
High school or less, men	-0.0129	-0.0755	-0.0626	28/38	0.289
High school or less, women	-0.0042	0.0945	0.0987	22/35	0.400
Hispanic natives					
All	0.0002	0.0229	0.0227	23/45	0.511
High school or less	0.0009	0.0513	0.0504	24/45	0.489
High school or less, men	-0.0001	0.0106	0.0107	23/45	0.511
high school or less, women	-0.0027	0.0054	0.0080	21/44	0.455
Non-Hispanic white natives					
All	-0.0006	-0.0032	-0.0027	23/45	0.511
High school or less	0.0002	-0.0154	-0.0156	33/45	0.289
High school or less, men	0.0022	-0.0335	-0.0357	37/45	0.200
High school or less, women	0.0002	0.0142	0.0139	36/45	0.222

Source: Authors' compilation based on 1998–2009 monthly Current Population Survey.

FIGURE 10.5 / Difference in Wage-Salary Employment Rates Relative to the Synthetic Control Group, Hispanic Noncitizen Men with High School or Less

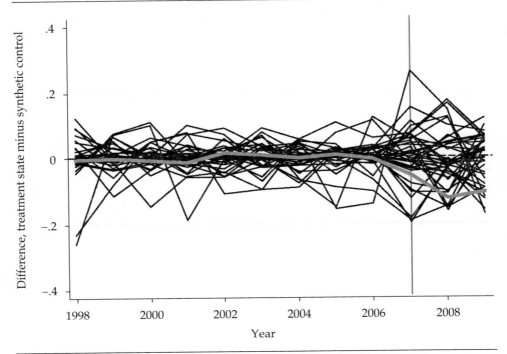

Source: Authors' compilation based on monthly Current Population Survey.
Note: Arizona displayed with thick gray line.

Hispanics, or native-born whites are statistically significant. The full set of wage and salary employment results suggests that LAWA achieved its goal of reducing the employment of unauthorized immigrants in Arizona. No evidence, however, indicates success toward the secondary goal of such legislation—to improve the employment opportunities for competing workers.

LAWA Effects on Self-Employment

Wage and salary employment tells only part of the story. LAWA's E-Verify mandate includes only licensed businesses within its employer definition and specifically excludes independent contractors from its definition of an employee.[8] Thus, one way to avoid E-Verify is to enter into independent contractor arrangements rather than formal wage and salary employment. Using self-employment as a proxy to potentially capture this effect, we next assess the impact of LAWA on

FIGURE 10.6 / Self-Employment Rates, Hispanic Noncitizen Men with High School or Less

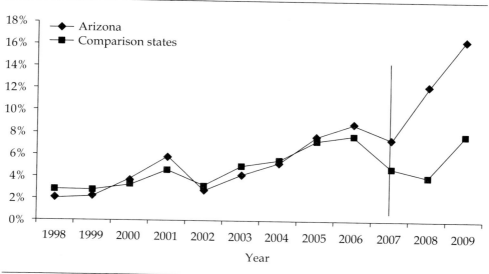

Source: Authors' compilation based on monthly Current Population Survey.
Note: Synthetic Arizona consists of the following states (with weights in parentheses): Washington (0.32), Massachusetts (0.243), Alaska (0.143), California (0.108), Iowa (0.082), Louisiana (0.076), Ohio (0.023) and Texas (0.005).

self-employment among the likely unauthorized workers in Arizona and their substitutes.

The synthetic cohort results strongly suggest that Arizona's legislation substantially increased self-employment among noncitizen Hispanic immigrants. Figure 10.6 indicates that the self-employment rate among Hispanic noncitizen men was on the rise before LAWA in both Arizona and the comparison states. However, the rise between 2007 and 2009 is substantially greater in Arizona. The estimate of the magnitude of LAWA's self-employment effect is about 8 percentage points, roughly double the self-employment rate. Table 10.2 presents the point estimates of difference in pre- and post-LAWA for Arizona relative to the synthetic control. The difference-in-difference estimate suggests that the self-employment rate for likely unauthorized men in Arizona rose 8.3 percentage points higher relative to the synthetic control group.

Conducting the same placebo test on the set of self-employment rate outcomes yields similar conclusions. For likely unauthorized less-skilled men, the rise in self-employment rate is a clear outlier among all states, as shown in figure 10.7. The 8.3 percentage point relative increase ranks second-largest among states and is statistically significant at the 5 percent level (see table 10.2). Calculating from the

TABLE 10.2 / Estimated Impact of LAWA, Self-Employment

	Pre-Average Difference Relative to Synthetic Cohort	Post-Average Difference Relative to Synthetic Cohort	Change, Post Minus Pre (Difference-In-Difference Estimate)	Rank, Difference-In-Difference Estimate	P-value From One-Tailed Test, $P(|\Delta| < |\Delta AZ|)$
Hispanic noncitizens					
All	0.0002	0.0423	0.0421	41/45	0.111
High school or less	0.0000	0.0305	0.0305	32/40	0.225
High school or less, men	0.0002	0.0836	0.0834	39/40	0.050
High school or less, women	0.0004	0.0012	0.0008	21/40	0.500
Hispanic Citizens					
All	0.0002	0.0200	0.0198	34/44	0.250
High school or less	0.0005	0.0235	0.0230	22/35	0.400
High school or less, men	0.0057	0.0849	0.0792	32/38	0.184
High school or less, women	-0.0001	-0.0327	-0.0326	23/35	0.371
Hispanic Natives					
All	-0.0001	-0.0072	-0.0072	32/45	0.311
High school or less	-0.0001	-0.0094	-0.0093	29/45	0.378
High school or less, men	0.0001	0.0002	0.0001	25/45	0.467
High school or less, women	-0.0006	-0.0088	-0.0082	25/44	0.477
Non-Hispanic White Natives					
All	-0.0001	-0.0075	-0.0074	38/45	0.178
High school or less	-0.0003	-0.0117	-0.0115	41/45	0.111
High school or less, men	-0.0009	-0.0072	-0.0063	34/45	0.267
High school or less, women	-0.0004	-0.0067	-0.0063	31/45	0.333

Source: Authors' compilation based on 1998–2009 monthly Current Population Survey.

FIGURE 10.7 / Difference in Self-Employment Rates Relative to the Synthetic Control Group, Hispanic Noncitizen Men with High School or Less, All States

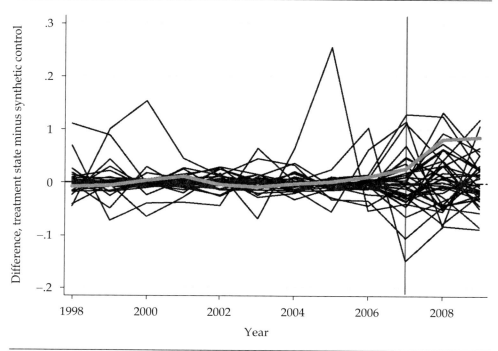

Source: Authors' compilation based on monthly Current Population Survey.
Note: Arizona displayed with thick gray line.

base of 308,000 workers in 2006 yields an increase of approximately 25,000 self-employed Hispanic noncitizens due to LAWA. For men and women of other ethnic and nativity groups, there is no evidence of statistically significant change in the self-employment rate due to LAWA.

In sum, these results suggest that among unauthorized men in Arizona, wage and salary employment opportunities became quite limited as a result of LAWA, and many opted to shift their efforts to self-employment. These effects are concentrated among the group of less-skilled and likely unauthorized men. We find no convincing evidence of spillover effects to competing low-skilled groups.

Not only did the unauthorized population of decline by roughly 90,000 (Bohn, Lofstrom, and Raphael 2011), the unauthorized workers who chose to live in Arizona following LAWA saw sizeable changes in employment opportunities. LAWA caused a decline of more than 50,000 unauthorized workers in wage and salary jobs. This drop appears not to have had deleterious consequences—or observable benefits—for competing workers. The unintended consequence of declining employment opportunities for unauthorized workers, however, is a sizeable shift—about 25,000 people—into self-employment.

These findings raise the concern of a move into underground economies as an unintended consequence of legislation aimed at reducing the employment of unauthorized immigrant workers. In the following section, we take the next step to look at what this shift into self-employment means for the economic well-being of unauthorized immigrants.

Robustness Checks of Employments Effects

We next explore the robustness of the estimated impacts of LAWA on formal and self-employment. We focus on the group of with the highest proportion of unauthorized workers: noncitizen Hispanic men with no schooling beyond high school. This is the only group for which we obtain strong evidence of an impact of the legislation on employment.

We begin by exploring the sensitivity of whether the year of the passage of legislation, 2007, is defined as a pre- or post-LAWA year. In all the estimates we have presented thus far, we define the post-period as calendar years 2008 and 2009 because LAWA was implemented on January 1, 2008. Furthermore, we have not matched the treatment to the synthetic controls with 2007 values and instead have omitted this year from our post-treatment period. Arguably, because the legislation was not in effect in 2007 and hence no hires were subject to the E-Verify mandate, this year should be included as a pre-LAWA year. The results when this is implemented, shown in the second rows in each of the panels in table 10.3, reveal that it has no real impact on the estimated effects of LAWA on either the wage-salary or self-employment rates (for ease of comparison, we repeat the corresponding table 10.1 and 10.2 results as the top row of each panel). On the other hand, one might contend that 2007 should be included as a post-treatment year because the legislation was passed mid-2007 and changes may have taken place in anticipation. We do find somewhat smaller effects (by about 2 percentage points) when 2007 is defined as a treatment year, shown in the third row of each table 10.3 panel. The rank test of this robustness check puts the estimated impacts in the upper tail of the placebo estimates. These estimates no longer stand out as the most extreme, however, because both outcomes of the Arizona difference-in-difference estimates are thirty-eighth in magnitude out of forty states. We do not think it is appropriate to define 2007 as a treatment year because the anticipatory effects should plausibly be small: the mandatory use of E-Verify did not begin until January 2008, whether the law would go into effect at that time was uncertain, and the enhanced verification requirement does not apply retroactively Although the estimates are not particularly sensitive to how 2007 is handled, our preferred approach is to match only on the 1998 to 2006 period and to omit 2007 in the difference-in-difference calculations.

Our estimates may have been partially influenced by employment outcomes in the states making up "synthetic Arizona," which may in turn have been influenced by the influx of immigrants from Arizona. This could be a particularly important source of bias if migrants were to leave Arizona for neighboring states such as

Table 10.3 / Sensitivity of Estimated Impact of LAWA, Hispanic Noncitizen Men with High School or Less

	Pre-Average Difference Relative to Synthetic Cohort	Post-Average Difference Relative to Synthetic Cohort	Change, Post Minus Pre (Difference-In-Difference Estimate)	Rank, Difference-In-Difference Estimate	P-value From One-Tailed Test, P($|\Delta| < |\Delta AZ|$)
Wage-salary employment					
Exclude 2007 (Row 3, table 10.1)	-0.0009	-0.1151	-0.1142	40/40	0.025
Include 2007 as a pre-period	-0.0010	-0.1032	-0.1021	40/40	0.025
Include 2007 as a post-period	-0.0009	-0.0954	-0.0944	38/40	0.075
Excluding states bordering Arizona	-0.0009	-0.1151	-0.1142	37/37	0.027
Falsification test, 2004 as treatment year	-0.0005	0.0311	0.0316	27/40	0.350
Estimates based on employment generated state weights, matched on subsample:					
Noncitizen Hispanic men with high school or less[a]	-0.0136	-0.1185	-0.1049	N/A	N/A
Self-Employment					
Exclude 2007	0.0002	0.0836	0.0834	39/40	0.050
Include 2007 as a pre-period	0.0003	0.0796	0.0793	39/40	0.050
Include 2007 as a post-period	0.0011	0.0645	0.0634	38/40	0.075
Excluding states bordering Arizona	0.0002	0.0836	0.0834	36/37	0.054
Falsification test, 2004 as treatment year	0.0018	0.0435	0.0417	34/40	0.175
Estimates based on employment generated state weights, matched on sub-sample:					
Noncitizen Hispanic men with high school or less[a]	0.0108	0.0799	0.0691	N/A	N/A

Source: Authors' compilation based on 1998–2009 monthly Current Population Survey.
[a]States receiving nonzero weights (weight): California (0.771), New Mexico (0.121), Washington (0.098), Louisiana (0.007), and Indiana (0.003).

New Mexico and California, because both these states contribute disproportionately to the synthetic control group for many of the employment outcomes we analyze, and are also plausibly the most likely destination states for such migrants. To explore this possibility, we estimate our models restricting the donor pool to states that do not neighbor Arizona, results shown in the fourth rows of each table 10.3 panel. Both the estimated magnitudes and statistical significance are remarkably similar to those including neighboring states in the donor pool. This strongly suggests that our preferred estimates of LAWA's employment effects are not due to migration responses that alter employment outcomes in the neighboring states.

Migration could still bias our estimates, however, if it yields a compositional change in the targeted population that remains in Arizona following LAWA. In particular, we are concerned with skill characteristics that drive the employment outcomes we measure. To address this concern, we examine observable skill characteristics of the immigrant population in Arizona before and after LAWA and immigrants who left Arizona after LAWA was enacted. Because of small sample sizes in the CPS, for this exercise we use the American Community Survey for 2005 through 2010 and identify Hispanic noncitizen immigrants. (Finer subgroups are identifiable but sample sizes among migrants are unreliably small.) We identify immigrants who left Arizona for another state in the post-LAWA period, 2008–2009.[9] Because the ACS inquires about migration in the year before the survey, for this "leaver" group, we observe outcomes and characteristics as of 2009–2010, which is not the same as the post-LAWA period used throughout this chapter. Thus, for comparison we provide statistics on the Arizona immigrant population in 2009–2010 and 2008–2009.

As shown in table 10.4, compared with those in Arizona, Hispanic noncitizens who left were slightly younger, more likely male and more likely to be a recent immigrant, consistent with typical migration patterns. There appears to be little compositional shift across these groups in terms of education, birthplace (Mexico), or marital status. Leavers are more likely to be proficient in English, which may suggest higher underlying skill. However, for those working, if there are differences in skill, they are not reflected in income differentials at the median. Employment outcomes are affected both by LAWA, as we argue, and potentially by compositional changes in the immigrant population.[10] However, we provide them here to show that Hispanic noncitizens who left Arizona were less likely to be employed, more likely unemployed, and much less likely to be self-employed than those in Arizona. Overall, but recognizing the limitations in the comparisons, the data do not indicate that those who left Arizona had more favorable labor-market relevant characteristics. Also, given sample size constraints, we view these results overall as suggestive that if anything a compositional change due to migration out of Arizona would bias us against finding an effect of LAWA.

We also explored a falsification test in which we imposed a treatment in a pre-LAWA year. The selected year needs to provide enough pre-treatment years to reliably identify appropriate synthetic control groups and allow for pre-LAWA time that is clearly not influenced by the legislation (and hence can serve as the fake treatment period). We chose 2004 because it matches the criteria and stood

TABLE 10.4 / Descriptive Statistics, Hispanic Noncitizens Residing in Arizona Before and/or After LAWA

	Pre-LAWA		Post-LAWA	
	2005–2006	2008–2009	2009–2010	
Group	AZ	AZ	AZ	Leavers
Average:				
Age	33.7	35.5	36.4	32.6
High school dropout	0.50	0.52	0.49	0.48
High school or less	0.85	0.84	0.82	0.84
Female	0.43	0.44	0.46	0.41
Married	0.58	0.53	0.55	0.54
Born in Mexico	0.94	0.94	0.93	0.92
Recent immigrant (<10 years)	0.57	0.45	0.39	0.41
Limited English proficiency	0.64	0.60	0.57	0.42
Employed	0.67	0.62	0.58	0.44
Unemployed	0.07	0.10	0.14	0.22
Self-employed	0.07	0.09	0.09	0.02
For employed persons, median:				
Total personal income	18,000	20,000	19,200	20,000
Income from wage and salary	17,000	18,300	18,000	20,000
Total family income	31,200	34,000	30,900	25,000
N	6,353	6,001	5,839	136

Source: Authors' compilation based on 2005–2010 American Community Survey.
Note: Restricted to age sixteen through sixty-five. Leavers are defined by current residence in any state other than Arizona and reporting lived in Arizona one year before survey. All other columns include all Hispanic noncitizens in Arizona.

out in terms of employment outcomes, especially in construction employment (as figure 10.2 indicates). The results, shown in row five of each panel in table 10.3, fail to convincingly identify any noticeable effects in Arizona.

Last, we explore the sensitivity of the results stemming from the synthetic control method, which — to obtain the most appropriate counterfactual for Arizona — generates different state weights across the outcomes and subgroups analyzed. That is, the composition of the synthetic control group varies with each outcomes and subgroup. Our approach here is to match on the total employment rate (both wage-salary and self-employment) for noncitizen Hispanic men with high school or less. This will generate a set of state weights that we then apply equally to the wage-salary and self-employment rate time series. Repeating this exercise for all donor states is cumbersome at best, and hence we do not have placebo estimates to compare the difference-in-difference estimates with. Our discussion instead focuses on the magnitudes of the estimated effects, shown in the bottom rows of each table 10.3 panel. Not surprisingly, given that we do not use the combination of state weights yielded by the constrained minimization problem for the specific outcome and group at hand, the pre-LAWA differences between Arizona and the synthetic comparison groups are somewhat greater than those in the top row of each panel. However, the post-LAWA differences are quite similar in magnitude to those obtained when the matching is done based on the specific outcome in question. As a result, the estimated difference-in-differences are about 1 percentage point smaller, suggesting only a small sensitivity to using a more uniform set of state weights based on overall employment.

Overall, the sensitivity analyses point toward robustness of our main results that LAWA severely limited formal employment opportunities for unauthorized immigrants, and that as a result many opted for more informal employment, as measured by the increase in self-employment.

EFFECT OF SELF-EMPLOYMENT SHIFT

A specific concern about a rise in self-employment is an associated growth in the underground labor market, also known as informal, shadow, under-the-table, or off-the-books employment. Although clearly not all self-employment is underground work and not all underground work is recorded as self-employment, overlap between the two is substantial. Both self-employment and informal employment raise concerns about economic consequences for workers and increased potential for exploitation. Furthermore, growth in self- and underground employment reduces the government's ability to generate revenue through taxation. We first examine the literature on what informal employment likely means for unauthorized workers following LAWA, given that our data cannot inform this important question. We then assess what the broader but overlapping arena of self-employment means from available data.

What Is Informal Employment?

Informal work is difficult both to define and to measure, given that by nature underground work arrangements aim to avoid detection (Schneider and Enste 2000). Informal work is most simply described as that which exists outside the legal boundaries set by local, state, or federal government (Feige 1990; Flaming, Haydamack, and Joassart 2005). Informal work is thus not directly reported in official records or surveys. However, in our data, those who report self-employment are more likely to be in informal work arrangements than those who report wage and salary work, all else being equal. In fact, some studies use self-employment as a proxy for informal labor (Flaming, Haydamack, and Joassart 2005; De Soto 1989).

Our focus on unauthorized immigrants—or, in our data, noncitizen Hispanic men—elevates the concern about a shift toward informal labor. Researchers have noted the ties between immigrants and informal work, explained by lack of documentation to work in the formal labor market; the incidence of underground economic activity in ethnic enclaves; and overrepresentation of immigrants in industries with a higher probability of underground activity (Bohn and Owens 2012; Marcelli, Pastor, and Joassart 1999; Light 2006). For this reason, some researchers have used the concentration of unauthorized workers in an industry as a proxy for the informality of work (Marcelli, Pastor, and Joassart 1999).

Given that our population of interest—unauthorized workers—and an outcome of interest—self-employment—are both separately used in the literature as proxies for informal work, the unexpected rise in self-employment due to LAWA is inextricably tied to a likely rise in underground labor. What this means for unauthorized immigrants is better understood by looking to the literature on informal work. We draw from studies that detail the outcomes for informally employed immigrants in various cities.

Informal employment is linked in the public mind to day labor—especially immigrant day laborers—in large part because this type of informal employment is most noticeable. The most comprehensive study on day labor—the National Day Labor Survey (NDLS)—finds that a vast majority (79 percent) of day labor jobs are informal (Valenzuela et al. 2006). They represent a small fraction of informal employment, however. Using the NDLS for California only, one study finds that day labor accounts for only 3 percent of the undocumented workforce and only 0.2 percent of the total workforce (Gonzalez 2007). This same study, though, finds that Latino immigrants working as day laborers earn more than 50 percent less per week than the average Latino immigrant and are less likely to find employment. As expected, the NDLS indicates that the top five occupations for day laborers are construction worker, gardener and landscaper, painter, roofer, and drywall installer.

Construction and landscaping industries are linked to informal employment of immigrants more broadly (Bohn and Owens 2012; Flaming, Haydamack, and Joassart 2005). The study of Los Angeles informal employment by Daniel Flaming and his colleagues estimates that 10 percent of informal employment occurred in construction and 4 percent in landscaping services. A higher proportion of informal work can be attributed to manufacturing (20 percent) and retail trade (15 percent), as well as in private households (9 percent) and accommodation and food services (6 percent). The earnings for these workers are estimated at $16,553 for men and $7,630 for women in 1999, significantly lower than the Los Angeles median at that time of roughly $32,000 for men and $30,000 for women.[11] Informally employed unauthorized immigrants in private households and landscaping earn among the least, roughly around $10,000 annually in 1999.

The relatively low observed earnings for these unauthorized immigrants in informal jobs is of concern for their economic well-being and potential for economic assimilation. Annette Bernhardt, Siobhan McGrath, and James DeFilippis (2007) also identify cases of wage and hour violations on the part of employers in unregulated work arrangements. These violations also likely contribute to lower earnings, and include failure to pay minimum wage, overtime, or tips as well as full or partial nonpayment of wages. In addition, Bernhardt and her colleagues identify a host of other workplace violations that raise concern about workers employed informally. These include health and safety violations, lack of worker compensation coverage, discrimination, retaliation against the right to organize, and forced labor.

Particularly relevant to our analysis of LAWA, Bernhardt and her colleagues (2007) identify abuse of independent contractor status. As noted earlier, independent contractors are excluded from LAWA's E-Verify mandate. Thus one way to avoid detection is for a worker to shift into an independent contractor relationship with the employer. Bernhardt and her colleagues note that because independent contractors are not employees under the law, they are excluded from various wage and worker protections. They document a number of employer strategies to evade legal obligations by reclassifying workers as independent contractors. In their field study in New York City, they find that undocumented immigrants (and particularly recent arrivals) are at greatest risk to the host of workplace violations in informal work arrangements.

To our knowledge, no detailed study focuses on informally employed unauthorized immigrants in Arizona. However, we can learn from the case studies discussed here about the likely consequences for a shift to informal employment among noncitizen Hispanics in Arizona. This shift is likely to be correlated with constricted annual earnings, higher poverty rates, and increased potential for numerous types of workplace violations.

Self-Employment and Unauthorized Immigrants

To learn more about what self-employment means for the economic well-being and poverty of unauthorized immigrants, we generate descriptive statistics from the 2008 and 2009 American Community Survey. The intersection between restricted labor market opportunities and poverty-related outcomes for unauthorized immigrants is particularly important given the evidence Marianne Bitler and Hilary Hoynes on the low participation rates among this group in safety net programs for which they are eligible (see chapter 11, this volume). We restrict our sample to noncitizen and naturalized Hispanic immigrant men with a high school degree or less who reported being employed in the sample period. We do this because it is only among low-skilled noncitizen Hispanics we find statistically significant employment effects. The ACS data provide the detail required for examining the income and poverty-related outcomes of self-employed and probably unauthorized workers, but the sample size and period of analysis is limited. We use these data to describe what self-employment generally means for noncitizen Hispanics. Each survey reports on labor market outcomes for the preceding year; that is, the most recent outcomes we can examine are those pertaining to 2008. Indeed, this is what prevents us from using the ACS data in the empirical analysis of LAWA's effects presented earlier. Furthermore, the sample size of this subgroup in Arizona alone is quite small, so we look at the average outcomes for self-employed noncitizen Hispanics across the United States.

Self-employment among noncitizen Hispanics is concentrated in a handful of industries. Table 10.5 reveals that two industries alone represent two-thirds of the

TABLE 10.5 / Industrial and Occupational Distributions, Low-Skilled Self-Employed Hispanic Noncitizen Men

Top Fifteen Industries	%	Top Fifteen Occupations	%
Construction	46.6	Grounds maintenance workers	14.8
Landscaping services	17.7	Construction laborers	14.2
Automotive repair and maintenance	4.9	Carpenters	7.4
Truck transportation	3.7	Painters, construction, and maintenance	6.5
Restaurants and other food services	3.1	Drivers, sales workers, and truck drivers	4.6
Building services	2.5	Automotive service technicians and mechanics	3.3
Private households, services	1.5	Supervisors-managers, construction	2.6
Crop production	1.1	Supervisors-managers, landscaping	2.6
Taxi and limousine service	0.9	Carpet, floor, and tile installers and finishers	2.3
Independent artists and performing arts	0.9	Managers, all other	2.1
Grocery stores	0.8	Construction managers	2.1
Automobile dealers	0.7	Supervisors-managers, retail sales	2.1
Other direct selling establishments	0.7	Retail salespersons	2.1
Car washes	0.7	Drywall and ceiling tile installers and tapers	2.0
Recyclable material, merchant wholesalers	0.7	Roofers	1.9
All other industries	13.8	All other occupations	29.6

Source: Authors' compilation based on 2008–2009 American Community Survey.

industries of self-employment: construction (46.6 percent) and landscaping services (17.7 percent). Rounding out the top five are automotive repair and maintenance (4.9 percent), truck transportation (3.7 percent), and restaurant and food services (3.1 percent). The industry concentration is consistent with that of the informal sector discussed earlier, and not surprising given the skill background of noncitizen Hispanic men as represented by their reported occupations. Table 10.5 also shows that construction laborers (14.2 percent), carpenters (7.4 percent), and painters (6.5 percent) are three of the top five occupations. The other two are grounds maintenance workers (14.8 percent) and drivers (4.6 percent). Overall, the industry and occupational distributions are those that typify informal employment and the conditions and concerns of this sector plausibly apply to noncitizen Hispanic self-employment.

Table 10.6 reveals only minor differences separate our sample of noncitizen Hispanic men in self-employment and wage and salary employment. Those who report being self-employed are slightly older (38.4 years old in self-employment and 35.5 years old in wage and salary employment) and have been in the United States longer (15.5 and 13.2 years respectively) but are roughly equally likely to be high school graduates (30 and 31 percent), of limited English proficiency (82 and 84 percent) and work roughly the same number of hours per week (39.6 and 40.7

TABLE 10.6 / Descriptive Statistics, Low-Skilled Hispanic Men

	Noncitizens		Naturalized	
	Self-Employed	Wage-Salary	Self-Employed	Wage-Salary
Age	38.4	35.5	46.8	44.2
Years in the U.S.	15.5	13.2	26.5	24.9
High school graduate	0.30	0.31	0.43	0.45
Limited English proficiency	0.82	0.84	0.61	0.63
Married	0.62	0.55	0.81	0.75
Family size	3.77	3.69	3.87	3.96
Number of children	1.30	1.02	1.57	1.44
Number of children younger than 5	0.28	0.27	0.19	0.20
Usual hours work per week	39.56	40.67	43.06	41.73
Mean				
Total personal income	26,000	23,700	41,400	35,500
Total personal earnings	25,600	23,500	39,700	34,500
Total family income	44,600	43,400	65,600	61,200
Total household income	52,700	55,200	69,900	66,300
Median				
Total personal income	18,000	20,000	30,000	30,000
Total personal earnings	18,000	20,000	28,800	30,000
Total family income	30,000	34,400	50,000	52,200
Total household income	39,000	46,000	54,400	57,100
Income percent of poverty threshold	193	205	266	273
Below poverty threshold	0.27	0.18	0.12	0.07
Any health insurance	0.18	0.32	0.43	0.70
Private health insurance	0.12	0.28	0.33	0.64
Public health insurance	0.06	0.05	0.12	0.09
Number of observations	5,466	51,946	2,150	14,929

Source: Authors' compilation based on 2008–2009 American Community Survey.

hours). Household composition shows several differences. The self-employed are more likely to be married (62 and 55 percent) and to have more children (1.30 and 1.02). Overall, the differences are quite small and unlikely to be sources of substantial differences in economic well-being.

A comparison of income and benefits indicate lower economic well-being among the self-employed than among those in formal employment. Although mean annual earnings and income among the self-employed is generally higher (the exception is total household income), the lower median annual earnings reveal that this is driven by a few relatively successful individuals. The low median annual personal income of $18,000 and annual family income of $30,000 of those who report being self-employed are about 10 percent lower than those in formal employment.[12] The self-employed are also substantially more likely to have incomes below the poverty threshold: 27 percent of the self-employed versus 18 percent of those in wage and salary employment. Although only one in three wage and salary noncitizen workers in our sample has health insurance (32 percent), fewer than one in five of the self-employed has health insurance (18 percent).

The ACS data provide a picture of self-employment consistent with that gleaned from the informal employment literature reviewed earlier. This suggests that a rise in self-employment due to LAWA is likely to be driven by a rise in underground employment. The literature and our data description indicate that unauthorized workers in less formal work arrangements are likely to earn less, to be uninsured, and to be in poverty.

CONCLUSIONS

Using the synthetic control approach for assessing the impact of a single policy change in single area, we estimate the impact of the Legal Arizona Workers Act of 2007 on employment in Arizona. Evidence to date implies that LAWA was largely successful in meeting its goal of deterring unauthorized immigration to the state and preventing employment of unauthorized workers. In previous work, we estimate a roughly 17 percent decline in unauthorized population of the state (Bohn, Lofstrom, and Raphael 2010). In this chapter, we find that for the unauthorized workers who chose to live in Arizona following LAWA, there were sizeable shifts in employment opportunities. LAWA caused a decline in the rate of formal employment by about 11 percentage points. This decline appears not to have had deleterious consequences—nor observable benefits—for competing workers.

However, the unintended consequence of the LAWA-induced declining employment opportunities for unauthorized workers was a doubling of the rate of self-employment for unauthorized, less-skilled men, from 8 to 16 percent.

Although an increase in self-employment does not necessarily imply growth in the underground labor market, we find suggestive evidence that for unauthorized workers in Arizona the two are likely to go hand in hand. Our analysis and review of the literature suggests that self-employment for low-skilled noncitizen Hispanic immigrants is associated with constricted earnings, increase in poverty, and a decrease in health insurance coverage.

Furthermore, to the extent that self-employment reflects less formal work arrangements, consequences for the broader economy are potentially deleterious. The self-employed contribute less revenue through taxation. Additionally, the potential for worker exploitation is elevated in less formal work arrangements given the lack of worker protections.

Although Arizona's E-Verify mandate achieved its goal of deterring unauthorized immigration and employment, it also generated unintended consequences on the labor market. The induced shift toward less formal work arrangements for unauthorized immigrants who continued to live in the state after January 1, 2008, likely has negative implications on their economic well-being. Some of the affected workers are likely to migrate elsewhere for better labor market opportunities. However, for unauthorized immigrants unlikely to migrate due to family ties, for example, consequences on economic well-being are substantive and potentially long term. This could extend not just to unauthorized immigrants but also to their native-born children or relatives. Policymakers should into account both the intended and unintended consequences of similar E-Verify mandates.

Corresponding author. Research Fellow, Public Policy Institute of California (PPIC), 500 Washington Street, Suite 600, San Francisco, CA 94111, (415) 291-4454 e-mail: lofstrom@ppic.org. We gratefully acknowledge the support of the Russell Sage Foundation. We also like to thank the editors, Judith Gans, Hans Johnson, Heather Koball, Ethan Lewis, Fernando Lozano, Albert Liu, Jordan Matsudaira, Marie Mora, David Neumark, Pia Orrenius, Jeffrey Passel, Karthick Ramakrishnan, Marc Rosenblum, and participants at the San Francisco Federal Reserve Bank's 2010 Applied Micro Conference, the Population Association of America's 2011, the American Economic Association's 2012 Annual Meeting, the Immigration and Poverty Conference at the University of California (UC) Davis for helpful feedback and seminar participants at UC Irvine, UC Merced and University of Otago.

NOTES

1. Note that two decades earlier, California was the state leading the same charge. The growth in immigration to new destinations relative to traditional ones like California (as detailed in chapter 5, this volume) is one of the trends hypothesized to be driving shifts in the public policy arena.
2. SB 1070 targets unauthorized immigrants directly, as opposed to employers, and criminalizes failure to carry immigration documents and give the police broad power to detain anyone suspected of being in the country illegally. The constitutionality of the law is in question and prior to enactment a federal judge issued an injunction blocking the most controversial provisions, including the one requiring police to check individual's immigration status while enforcing other laws if there was reason to believe the person was in the country illegally.
3. Furthermore, obtaining survey responses from unauthorized immigrants is also a challenge, perhaps increasingly during periods of heightened public debate about immigration issues. The Census Bureau has made concerted efforts over time to refine methods for obtaining representative samples even within hard-to-reach populations like unauthorized. Regardless, undercounting—or miscounting—unauthorized immigrants is unlikely to affect our results unless the characteristics of unauthorized immigrants who respond vary systematically across states. In Bohn, Lofstrom, and Raphael (2011) we do not see evidence of false spikes in the various population ratios corresponding with LAWA in particular.
4. For example, our calculations from census data indicate roughly 517,000 noncitizen Hispanic immigrants resided in Arizona in 2008. For this same year, Jeffrey Passel and

D'Vera Cohn (2009a) estimated approximately 475,000 unauthorized immigrants in the state. Similarly, for our finer definition of likely unauthorized *workers* used in the traditional difference-in-difference approach, based on ACS data, we estimate 229,000 likely unauthorized in Arizona in 2008 whereas Passel and Cohn (2009b) estimate 240,000 unauthorized immigrants in Arizona's labor force in the same year.

5. Thomas Buchmueller, John DiNardo, and Robert Valletta (2009) use a similar permutation test to that described here to test for an impact of Hawaii's employer-mandate to provide health insurance benefits to employees on benefits coverage, health care costs, wages and employment.

6. Moreover, the donor pool of states is further restricted for some of the smaller population subgroups due to the corresponding small CPS sample size.

7. Figure 10.5 graphically displays the raw data needed to conduct the permutation test of the significance of the relative declines in Arizona. Specifically, for each of the forty donor states as well as for Arizona, the figures display the year-by-year difference between the outcome variable for the "treated" state and the outcome variable for the synthetic control. The differences for each of the donor states are displayed with the thin black lines while the differences for Arizona are displayed by the red thick line.

8. Regulations regarding business licensure vary by city and county. At the state level, the Arizona Department of Revenue does not require licensing of businesses that employ withholding-exempt employees only. This includes seasonal workers and domestic help. (Telephone communication with Arizona Department of Revenue, July 13, 2010.)

9. Note that one important group for whom we have no information is those who left Arizona for abroad.

10. In addition, employment opportunities for those remaining in Arizona may be improved due to an outflow of migrants following LAWA. This should bias against finding negative employment effects of the policy.

11. Authors' calculations from the 2000 Census Summary File 3 [machine-readable data files] prepared by the U.S. Census Bureau.

12. The 10 percent self-employment disadvantage is very similar to what we observe in data from the Survey of Income and Program Participation. Using a similarly defined sample of low-skilled noncitizen Hispanic men, we found an unadjusted mean difference in the log of annual earnings of about 9.5 percent. In an OLS regression including controls for factors such as age, experience, education, family composition, geographic location and previous year's labor market status, the self-employment disadvantage was slightly greater, about 14.8 percent.

REFERENCES

Abadie, Alberto, Alexis Diamond, and Jens Hainmueller. 2010. "Synthetic Control Methods for Comparative Case Studies: Estimating the Effect of California's Tobacco Control Program. *Journal of the American Statistical Association* 105(490): 493–505.

Arizona Attorney General. 2010. "Legal AZ Workers Act: For Employers." http://www .azag.gov/legal-az-workers-act/employers (accessed March 24, 2013).

Bernhardt, Annette, Siobhan McGrath, and James DeFilippis. 2007. "Unregulated Work in the Global City: Employment and Labor Law Violations in New York City." New York: Brennan Center for Justice.

Bohn, Sarah, and Emily Owens. 2012. "Immigration and Informal Labor." *Industrial Relations* 51(4): 845–73.

Bohn, Sarah, Magnus Lofstrom, and Steven Raphael. 2011. "Did the 2007 Legal Arizona Workers Act Reduce the State's Unauthorized Immigrant Population?" *IZA* working paper no. 5682. Bonn: Institute for the Study of Labor.

Buchmueller, Thomas C., John DiNardo, and Robert G. Valleta. 2009. "The Effect of An Employer Health Insurance Mandate on Health Insurance Coverage and the Demand for Labor: Evidence from Hawaii." *Federal Reserve Bank* working paper no. 2009-08. San Francisco: Federal Reserve Bank.

Congressional Budget Office (CBO). 2008. Memo from Director Orzag to Committee on the Judiciary, April 4, 2008. Available at: http://www.cbo.gov/sites/default/files/cbofiles/ftpdocs/91xx/doc9100/hr4088ltr.pdf (accessed January 21, 2011).

De Soto, Hernando. 1989. *The Other Path.* New York: Harper & Row.

Feige, Edgar. 1990. "Defining and Estimating Underground and Informal Economies: The New Institutional Economics Approach." *World Development* 18(7): 989–1002.

Flaming, Daniel, Brent Haydamack, and Pascale Joassart. 2005. *Hopeful Workers, Marginal Jobs: LA's Off-the Books Labor Force.* Los Angeles: Economic Roundtable.

Gonzalez, Arturo. 2007. "Day Labor in the Golden State." *California Economic Policy* 3(3): 1–21.

Light, Ivan. 2006. *Deflecting Immigration: Networks, Markets, and Regulation in Los Angeles.* New York: Russell Sage Foundation.

Marcelli, Enrico A., Manuel Pastor Jr., and Pascale M. Joassart. 1999. "Estimating the Effects of Informal Economic Activity: Evidence from Los Angeles County." *Journal of Economic Issues* 33(3): 579–607.

National Conference of State Legislatures. 2006–2010. 2006–2010 State Legislation Related to Immigrations: Enacted and Vetoed. Washington DC.

Office of Immigration Statistics. 2010. "2009 Yearbook of Immigration Statistics." Washington: U.S. Department of Homeland Security.

Passel, Jeffrey, and D'Vera Cohn. 2009a. "A Portrait of Unauthorized Immigrants in the United States." Washington, D.C.: Pew Hispanic Center.

———. 2009b. "Mexican Immigrants: How Many Come? How Many Leave?" Washington, D.C.: Pew Hispanic Center.

———. 2010. "U.S. Unauthorized Immigration Flows Are Down Sharply Since Mid-Decade." Washington, D.C.: Pew Hispanic Center.

Schneider, Friedrich, and Dominik Enste. 2000. "Shadow Economies: Sizes, Causes, and Consequences" *Journal of Economic Literature* 38(1): 77–114.

Valenzuela, Abel, Nik Theodore, Edwin Melendez, and Ana Luz Gonzalez. 2006. "On The Corner: Day Labor in the United States." Los Angeles: UCLA Center for the Study of Urban Poverty.

Westat. 2009. *Findings of the E-Verify Program Evaluation.* Washington: U.S. Department of Homeland Security.

Chapter 11

Immigrants, Welfare Reform, and the U.S. Safety Net

Marianne P. Bitler and Hilary W. Hoynes

Beginning with the Personal Responsibility and Work Opportunity Reconciliation Act (PRWORA) of 1996, many of the central safety net programs in the United States eliminated benefits for legal immigrants, who previously had been eligible on the same terms as citizens. These dramatic cutbacks affected eligibility for numerous government programs: cash welfare assistance for families with children, Aid to Families with Dependent Children (AFDC)/Temporary Assistance for Needy Families (TANF); food stamps, now Supplemental Nutrition Assistance Program (SNAP); Medicaid; State Children's Health Insurance Program (SCHIP); and Supplemental Security Income (SSI). Subsequent federal legislation passed over the next decade reinstated immigrant eligibility for some, but not all, of these programs, leading to a confusing patchwork of eligibility rules varying by immigrant status, arrival year, and program.

A central tenet of welfare reform was the devolution of responsibility to states for designing their TANF programs. One component of this not widely discussed in the context of welfare reform, however, is that the 1996 law also gave states the responsibility to set eligibility rules for many safety net programs for legal immigrants, policy previously solely in the federal realm. In the wake of welfare reform, many states took advantage of this new power and restored access to the safety net for immigrants that had been cut out in the federal welfare reform law. Now, fifteen years after welfare reform, states are legislating immigration policies in wide ranging areas, including law enforcement, identification and driver's licenses, and hiring practices and employment (see Segreto and Morse 2011). Thus, with hindsight it is clear that the 1996 welfare reform ushered in a new period of active state immigration policy and "immigration policy federalism."

The focus in the welfare reform legislation on scaling back the safety net for immigrants was, in some part, a response to concerns that generous public benefits lead to in-migration to the U.S. and interstate flows of immigrants responding to "welfare magnets" (for example, Borjas 1999) although the empirical evidence does not uniformly support this theory (for example, Zavodny 1999; Kaushal 2005; Van Hook and Bean 2009). Further, the scaling back of immigrant access to the safety net was also a response to concerns about higher participation among immigrants than among natives (Borjas 1995) although other studies find lower participation rates (Capps, Fix, and Henderson 2009). Higher rates of participation by immigrants are in part explained by immigrants' lower incomes, and are concentrated among the elderly (Borjas and Hilton 1996; Hu 1998) and refugee populations (Fix and Passel 1994). Notably, noncitizen use of Supplemental Security Income — cash welfare for the aged and disabled — rose by 80 percent between 1990 and 1995 (Social Security Administration 2010).[1]

In this chapter, we comprehensively examine the status of the U.S. safety net for immigrants and their family members. In doing so, we examine the central means tested programs for families with children including TANF, SNAP, SSI, Medicaid, SCHIP, and the Earned Income Tax Credit (EITC) as well as Unemployment Insurance (UI). We begin by documenting the policy changes that affected immigrant eligibility for these programs. Using the annual social and economic supplement to the Current Population Survey for survey years 1995 through 2010 along with administrative data (where available), we analyze trends in program participation, income, and poverty among immigrants and natives. We pay particular attention to the recent period and examine how immigrants and their children are faring in the "Great Recession" with an eye toward revealing how these policy changes have affected the success of the safety net in protecting this population. Although we analyze data before and after welfare reform, our analysis is descriptive. We cannot necessarily claim to identify the causal impacts of reform.

Ours is not the first study to examine the impacts of welfare reform on immigrants. Many studies document a decline in immigrant use of the safety net following passage of PRWORA (for a recent and comprehensive review of the literature, see Fix, Capps, and Kaushal 2009). This reflects the direct effect of limiting eligibility to groups of previously covered immigrants. Some results, however, indicate that the relative decline in immigrant participation is in part due to a differential response to the strong labor market of the late 1990s related to immigrant's being located in different states and having lower skill levels than natives (Lofstrom and Bean 2002; Haider et al. 2004). In addition, many papers argue that there has been a "chilling effect" (Fix and Passell 1999) of the policy change, leading to reductions in program participation for groups and programs even where there was no change in program eligibility. A growing literature examine impacts of these policy changes on outcomes including naturalization (Van Hook 2003), employment (Kaestner and Kaushal 2005; Lofstrom and Bean 2002), food insecurity (Borjas 2004), health insurance (Borjas 2003; Kaushal and Kaestner 2005), birth outcomes (Joyce et al. 2001), poverty status (Borjas 2011), and location (Kaushal 2005).

Given this literature, our study makes three contributions. First, we update the descriptive evidence on program participation among immigrants and natives using data through 2009. Second, we explore how the composition of income differs between lower-income immigrants and natives before and after welfare reform. Third, we examine trends in poverty and extreme poverty with a focus on the differences in the recent Great Recession. We focus on poverty in families and households with children. Also in this volume, chapters 4 and 5 present some complementary analysis of poverty for all immigrant and native households and families.

Our analysis yields several interesting and important findings for families with children. First, we show that immigrants generally participate in the safety net at lower rates than natives once we restrict ourselves to comparisons within the set of lower-income families.[2] This is true for almost all programs we consider and is true both before and after welfare reform. Second, the national trends in safety net participation are broadly consistent with the finding of reduced immigrant access to the safety net since welfare reform. Similarly, our results show that immigrants rely more on earnings as a source of income (than do natives) and the degree of reliance has increased in the wake of welfare reform. Finally, using variation in state labor market conditions, we find that child poverty rates for immigrant-headed households have risen with unemployment in the Great Recession at rates far exceeding the rise for children in native-headed households. That is, a given increase in unemployment causes a larger increase in poverty for children in immigrant-headed compared to native-headed households. In addition, the safety net has acted to dampen the effect of both the 2001 and the 2008 recessions for children of the native born but not for children of immigrants.

U.S. SAFETY NET PROGRAMS, IMMIGRANTS, AND POLICY CHANGES

In this chapter, we focus on the means-tested safety net for families with children. Our definition of *safety net* programs encompasses programs that ensure against short-term or long-term negative shocks to income. By *means-tested* programs, we mean those limited to households, families, and individuals with low income, and sometimes low assets. Using this definition, table 11.1 presents an overview of the central safety net programs for families with children, split by cash versus noncash transfers. The two primary programs for low-income families include cash welfare (previously AFDC, now TANF) and food assistance (previously the Food Stamp Program, now SNAP). Food Stamps is by far the larger program of the two, especially since welfare reform: in 2009, for example, 15 million families (or single individuals) received food stamps, at a cost of $50 billion (2009 dollars), whereas fewer than 2 million received cash welfare, at a cost of $9 billion. Food stamps are also more universally available, all types of families being eligible. The Earned Income Tax Credit provides tax-based aid for low-income working families with children. In 2008, the most recent year for which data are available, 25 million families received the EITC at a cost of $51 billion (2008 dollars).[3] Supplemental Security Income is another cash program, primarily serving poor elderly and disabled adults, but also disabled children in poor families. Finally, although not

TABLE 11.1 / Expenditures and Participation in Cash or Near-Cash Safety Net Programs

	Number of Recipients (thousands)	Total Benefit Payments (millions of 2009$)	Average Monthly Benefit (2009$)	Estimated Number of Children Removed from Poverty (millions, in 2011)
Cash or near cash means tested programs				
Temporary Assistance for Needy Families	1,796	$9,324	$397	0.4
Food Stamp Program	15,232	$50,360	$276	2.1
Federal Earned Income Tax Credit	24,757	$50,669	$171	4.7
Supplemental Security Income, non-Disabled	6,407	$41,023	$517	0.6
Noncash means tested programs				
Medicaid, Children (2007)	27,527	$53,716	n/a	n/a
Medicaid, All (2007)	56,821	$276,246	n/a	n/a
National School Lunch Program, Free and Reduced Price (2009)	19,446	$7,563	n/a	0.7
School Breakfast Program, Free and Reduced Price (2009)	9,068	$2,498	n/a	n/a
Other short-term income replacement programs				
Unemployment Compensation, Total	5,757	$131,420	n/a	1.0

Source: Authors' compilation based on the following: For TANF, Food Stamps, the child nutrition programs, and Unemployment Compensation program data sources, see the appendix; EITC data are from the Tax Policy Center (2010); SSI data are from Social Security Administration (2010); poverty data are from Short (2012).

Note: Data for all programs refer to calendar year 2009 and are in 2009 dollars except the EITC, which refers to 2008 (and amounts are in 2008 dollars), TANF and the child nutrition programs (National School Lunch Program and School Breakfast Program), which are for fiscal year 2009 (year ending September 30, 2009), and Medicaid which refers to 2007 (and amounts are in 2007 dollars). SSI includes federal and state supplement payments and participation and the EITC includes the total tax cost (not just refundable portion).

means tested, unemployment compensation is obviously a critical element of the safety net and the central income replacement program in recessions. The program differs from the programs mentioned because it is a social insurance program, determined by work history, and not conditioned on current income. In 2009, on average, about 6 million persons per week received some form of unemployment compensation at a cost of nearly $131 billion dollars (2009 dollars).

The average monthly payment per recipient family in 2009 was $397 for cash welfare and $276 for food stamps. Earned Income Tax Credit payments in 2008 averaged $2,046 per year, or $171 per month. In the final column of table 11.1, we report results on the estimated number of children these programs lifted out of poverty in 2011. This is based on the new supplemental poverty measure, first released in November 2011, which expands the official poverty definition by first including in family resources the cash value of in-kind transfers as well as using a post-tax measure of income. The official poverty measure uses pre-tax income and omits in-kind transfers from income. These results, based on Kathleen Short (2012), show that the EITC and food stamps are the largest antipoverty programs for children, having removed 4.7 and 2.1, respectively, million from poverty. This is followed by unemployment insurance, which removed 1 million children from poverty; SSI, which removed 0.6 million; and TANF, which removed 0.4 million.

Beyond these cash or near-cash programs, important in-kind programs are also part of the safety net for low-income families. Medicaid and the State Children's Health Insurance Program both provide health insurance to low-income children, Medicaid provides it to families. In 2007, Medicaid served 27.5 million children at a cost of 53.7 billion dollars (2009 dollars).[4] The National School Lunch Program provides free and reduced price meals for nearly 20 million children under 185 percent of the federal poverty level every day at the cost of $7.5 billion, and subsidizes hot lunches for another 11 million paying students. The school breakfast program provides around 9 million students each day meals at a cost of about $2.5 billion. Although not shown in table 11.1, we consider other in-kind safety net benefits such as public housing and rental vouchers and Low-Income Energy Assistance Program (LIHEAP).[5] The recent Census Bureau study on the new supplemental poverty measure (details discussed in the following section) calculates the reduction in the new supplemental measure from including many of these in-kind programs in resources. Here, the EITC causes the largest reduction in the supplemental poverty measure, bringing the 2010 child poverty rate from 22.4 percent to 18.2 percent. SNAP also leads to a relatively large reduction from 21.2 percent to 18.2 percent. Smaller reductions occur for housing subsidies, the school lunch program, and LIHEAP (Short 2011).

Eligibility Rules and Benefits

Before outlining the changes in immigrant eligibility after welfare reform, we review the eligibility and benefit rules for the main safety net programs. Cash welfare for low-income families started with AFDC, a program created by the Social Security Act of 1935. The program was jointly funded by the state and federal governments, with a higher federal matching rate for expenditures made by lower income states. States had the authority to set benefit levels; federal rules dictated most of the remaining eligibility and benefit rules. A family was eligible if it satisfied income and asset tests and assistance was primarily limited to single women with children. The benefits were structured in a manner typical for income support programs: if a family had no income, it received the maximum benefit or "guarantee." As earnings or allowable income increased, the benefit was reduced by the benefit reduction rate, leading to an implicit tax rate on earned income.

Historically, this rate has varied between 67 percent and 100 percent, providing strong disincentives for work (Moffitt 1983). Due to high benefit reduction rates and relatively low maximum benefits, AFDC transferred income to families substantially below the poverty line. For example, before welfare reform under AFDC, the median state provided benefits to families with income up to 68 percent of poverty and the median state's benefit level for a family of three was about 36 percent of the 1996 poverty guideline (U.S. Congress 1996).

Welfare reform began in the early 1990s, when many states were granted waivers to modify their AFDC programs from existing federal rules. About half of the states implemented some sort of welfare waiver between 1992 and 1995. This was followed by federal welfare reform with passage of the Personal Responsibility and Work Opportunity Act in 1996, replacing AFDC with TANF. The key elements of state waivers and TANF legislation include work requirements, lifetime time limits on the duration of welfare receipt, financial sanctions for failing to adhere to work requirements or other rules, and enhanced earnings disregards. These changes were designed to facilitate the transition from welfare to work and to reduce dependence on cash welfare. States have considerable discretion in setting TANF policies, but by federal law, programs must include work requirements and lifetime limits of five or fewer years (for more information about reform, see Bitler and Hoynes 2010; Grogger and Karoly 2005).

Food stamps–SNAP is also a means-tested program whereby eligible families and individuals must satisfy income and asset tests; benefits are also assigned using maximum benefits and tax rates on earned income. The similarities with AFDC-TANF end there. First, food stamps is a federal program with all funding, except for 50 percent of administrative costs, provided by the federal government. Second, unlike virtually all cash programs in the United States, food stamp eligibility is not limited to certain targeted groups such as families with children, aged, and the disabled.[6] Third, the benefit reduction rate is relatively low (30 percent) and the income eligibility threshold is relatively high (130 percent of the poverty guideline). The lower benefit reduction rate means that the food stamp program serves not only the nonworking poor (those receiving cash welfare) but also the working poor. Using benefits dispersed on debit cards (which replaced paper vouchers) recipients are allowed to use their benefits to buy a wide array of food items (although not prepared foods), yet the behavioral response of food expenditures to food stamps is similar to the response to cash (Fraker et al. 1992; Ohls et al. 1992; Hoynes and Schanzenbach 2009). After welfare reform, food stamps is the key U.S. safety net program, and the only one that is both universal (based almost exclusively on economic need) and has a fully funded entitlement. Caseloads and benefits adjust automatically with increased eligibility for the program (recessions) and costs are uncapped.

The EITC is a federal tax credit for low-income working families; more than half the states have supplemental EITC credits. The EITC is primarily available to families with children, though a small credit is available for childless tax filers. The credit is a function of earnings and number of children and, due to a relative low phase-out rate of about 20 percent, extends relatively high in the income distribution. For example, in 2011 the maximum credit was $3,094 ($5,112) and eligibility extended to earnings of $36,052 ($40,964) for families with one child (two or more children).

The other safety net programs—public housing and vouchers-rent subsidies, free and reduced price school lunch and breakfast, SSI, Medicaid, WIC (Women, Infants, and Children Special Nutrition Program), and LIHEAP—are income- and in some cases asset-tested and targeted. For example, SSI is available only to disabled adults and children, whereas school lunch and breakfasts are available only for school-age children.

Immigrants and the Safety Net

Before welfare reform, a "bright line" distinguished between legal immigrants and unauthorized residents in determining eligibility for safety net programs.[7] Legal immigrants—lawful permanent residents (LPRs)—were eligible for most safety net programs on the same terms as citizens. Unauthorized immigrants were not. Those in the country legally but temporarily, such as residents on student visas, were also generally ineligible for these programs. There were exceptions: unauthorized immigrants maintained eligibility for free and reduced price School Lunch and Breakfast, WIC, emergency Medicaid, and state-funded emergency programs. In addition, refugees and asylum seekers also sometimes faced different rules than others. For the tax-based safety net, EITC recipients are required to have valid social security numbers; so again LPRs are eligible and unauthorized immigrants are not.[8]

The landscape for authorized immigrant eligibility for the safety net changed dramatically with passage of PRWORA and the Illegal Immigration Reform and Immigrant Responsibility Act (IIRIRA). New bright lines separated eligibility for LPRs versus naturalized citizens and for LPRs in the country before PRWORA (pre-enactment immigrants) versus those entering the country after PRWORA (post-enactment immigrants). Further, these new rules affected not only eligibility for TANF (the main subject of the PRWORA legislation) but also eligibility for SSI, food stamps, Medicaid, and, when it was introduced in 1997, the State Children's Health Insurance Program.

The PRWORA and IIRIRA policy changes are summarized in table 11.2. For each of the main safety net programs, we document eligibility for pre- and post-enactment immigrants, and within those groups for qualified immigrants—LPRs, refugees, asylum seekers, and certain battered spouses and children—and for exempted immigrants among the qualified who faced, in some cases, more lenient eligibility requirements (refugee and asylum seekers, those with forty quarters of work in the United States, and military). Not included in table 11.2 are unqualified immigrants—that is, all other immigrants, including the unauthorized, and those with permission to remain in the United States but without legal permanent resident status—who before and after welfare reform are ineligible for the programs.

As noted, before welfare reform, citizens and LPRs were treated identically in

(Text continues on p. 326)

TABLE 11.2 / Federal Laws Regarding Immigrant Eligibility for Federal Safety Net Programs

	Prior to PRWORA	August 22, 1996 Illegal Immigration Reform and Immigrant Responsibility Act (IIRIRA)[a] Personal Responsibility and Work Opportunity Reconciliation Act (PRWORA)[b]
TANF		
Pre-enactment immigrants		
Qualified immigrants	Eligible	Eligible; State option to bar
Exempted groups		
40 quarters of work	Eligible	Eligible
Military	Eligible	Eligible
Refugees/asylees	Eligible	Eligible for first 5 yrs; State option after
Post-enactment immigrants		
Qualified immigrants	Eligible	Barred for first 5 yrs; State option after
Exempted groups		
40 quarters of work	Eligible	Barred for first 5 yrs; State option after
Military	Eligible	Eligible
Refugees/asylees	Eligible	Eligible for first 5 yrs; State option after
Medicaid		
Pre-enactment immigrants		
Qualified immigrants	Eligible	Eligible; State option to bar
Exempted groups		
40 quarters of work	Eligible	Eligible
Military	Eligible	Eligible
Refugees/asylees	Eligible	Eligible for first 5 yrs; State option after
Post-enactment immigrants		
Qualified immigrants	Eligible	Barred for first 5 yrs; State option after
Exempted groups		
40 quarters of work	Eligible	Barred for first 5 yrs; State option after
Military	Eligible	Eligible
Refugees/asylees	Eligible	Eligible for first 5 yrs; State option after
SCHIP		
Pre-enactment immigrants		
Qualified immigrants		
Exempted groups		
40 quarters of work		
Military		
Refugees/asylees		
Post-enactment immigrants		
Qualified immigrants		
Exempted groups		
40 quarters of work		
Military		
Refugees/asylees		

1997 Balanced Budget Act[c]	1998 Agriculture, Research Extension and Education Reform Act[d]	2002 Farm Security and Rural Investment Act[e]	2009 Children's Health Insurance Program Reauthorization Act[f]
Eligible for first 7 yrs; State option after			
			Eligible; State option to bar
Eligible for first 7 yrs; State option after			
[SCHIP enacted in 1997] Eligible			
Eligible			
Eligible			
Eligible			
Barred for first 5 yrs			
			Eligible; State option to bar
Eligible			
Eligible			

(*Table continues on p. 324*)

TABLE 11.2 / (*Continued*)

	Prior to PRWORA	August 22, 1996 Illegal Immigration Reform and Immigrant Responsibility Act (IIRIRA)[a] Personal Responsibility and Work Opportunity Reconciliation Act (PRWORA)[b]
Food Stamps		
Pre-enactment immigrants		
Qualified immigrants	Eligible	Ineligible
Exempted groups		
40 quarters of work	Eligible	Eligible
Military	Eligible	Eligible
Refugees/asylees	Eligible	Eligible for first 5 yrs
Post-enactment immigrants		
Qualified immigrants	Eligible	Ineligible
Exempted groups		
40 quarters of work	Eligible	Barred for first 5 yrs
Military	Eligible	Eligible
Refugees/asylees	Eligible	Eligible for first 5 yrs
SSI		
Pre-enactment immigrants		
Qualified immigrants	Eligible	Ineligible
Exempted groups		
40 quarters of work	Eligible	Eligible
Military	Eligible	Eligible
Refugees/asylees	Eligible	Eligible for first 5 yrs
Post-enactment immigrants		
Qualified immigrants	Eligible	Ineligible
Exempted groups		
40 quarters of work	Eligible	Barred for first 5 yrs
Military	Eligible	Eligible
Refugees/asylees	Eligible	Eligible for first 5 yrs

Source: Authors' compilation.
Note: Table refers to eligibility for programs under Federal law for qualified immigrants, see text for more details. Rules under SCHIP apply to standalone SCHIP programs. SCHIP programs offered through Medicaid operate under Medicaid rules.
[a]Legislation can be found in http://www.nacua.org/documents/iirira.pdf (accessed May 23, 2013).
[b]Legislation can be found in Section 400-451 of http://www.fns.usda.gov/snap/rules/Legislation/pdfs/PL_104-193.pdf (accessed May 23, 2013).

1997 Balanced Budget Act[c]	1998 Agriculture, Research Extension and Education Reform Act[d]	2002 Farm Security and Rural Investment Act[e]	2009 Children's Health Insurance Program Reauthorization Act[f]
	Eligibility restored if as of 8/22/96 are children, disabled, blind, elderly		
	Eligible for first 7 yrs		
		Eligibility restored to children, disabled; rest barred first 5 yrs	
	Eligible for first 7 yrs		
Eligibility extended to SSI recip as of 8/22/96 and those legally residing in US on 8/22/96			
Eligible for first 7 yrs			
Eligible for first 7 yrs			

[c]Legislation can be found in Sections 5301-5308 and 5561-5574 of http://www.gpo.gov/fdsys/pkg/BILLS-105hr2015enr/pdf/BILLS-105hr2015enr.pdf (accessed May 23, 2013).
[d]Legislation can be found in Section 501-510 in http://www.csrees.usda.gov/about/offices/legis/pdfs/areera98.pdf (accessed May 23, 2013).
[e]Legislation can be found in Section 4401 of: http://www.ers.usda.gov/publications/ap-administrative-publication/ap-022.aspx#.UaoyFUAccl8 (accessed May 23, 2013).
[f]Legislation can be found in Section 214 of: http://frwebgate.access.gpo.gov/cgi-bin/getdoc.cgi?dbname=111_cong_public_laws&docid=f:publ003.111 (accessed May 23, 2013).

terms of eligibility for these safety net programs; thus, in the first column of table 11.2 all groups are identified as eligible. Following welfare reform, as shown in column 2, federal law extended eligibility for TANF and Medicaid to pre-enactment immigrants, and post-enactment immigrants were barred until they had been in the United States for five years.[9] The eligibility changes were even more severe for food stamps and SSI—for those programs qualified nonexempt pre- and post-enactment immigrants were barred from receiving benefits until they had accumulated ten years of work history.[10]

Eligibility was unchanged for school lunch and breakfast, where access is dictated by court decision for school-based programs (Wasem 2010) and the EITC. Notably, U.S.-born children of immigrants, who make up the great majority of children in immigrant-headed families, are citizens and remain eligible for all programs.

In addition to these new rules, PRWORA essentially devolved responsibilities governing immigrants' rights for public benefits to the states. As a result, states gained the authority to deny benefits to qualified immigrants. This is indicated in table 11.2 by "state option to bar." States also gained the authority to grant eligibility to immigrants made ineligible by the federal welfare reform law. Interestingly, PRWORA and IIRIRA seemed to have set in motion a movement whereby states are increasingly involved in immigration policies, a realm historically governed by federal policies. As of 2011, states are not only passing laws concerning immigrant access to public benefits, but also passing laws regarding hiring and access to employment, driver's licenses, higher education, and so on. Sarah Bohn and Magnus Lofstrom evaluate the effects of one such policy, Arizona's efforts to ban the unauthorized from working, in chapter 10 of this volume.

In the decade following welfare reform, subsequent law reinstated eligibility for some groups and some programs. These legislative changes are also documented in table 11.2. For example, the 1997 Balanced Budget Act reinstated benefits for pre-enactment immigrants for SSI. A 1998 agriculture bill restored food stamp eligibility to pre-enactment LPR children, disabled persons, the blind, and the elderly. Later, the 2002 Farm Bill restored food stamp eligibility to all LPR children and disabled persons, regardless of their time resident in United States. It also restored food stamp eligibility to LPR adults in the country for five or more years. In 2009, the SCHIP reauthorization bill lifted the five-year bar on participation for post-enactment immigrants for Medicaid and SCHIP for children and pregnant women.

The PRWORA legislation affects only federal funding for safety net programs. Consequently, in the face of the withdrawal of federal support for some LPRs, many states chose to maintain coverage for legal immigrants with state-funded replacement coverage, known as *fill in* programs. Additionally, with the new authority given to them by PRWORA, some states further reduced eligibility for pre-enactment immigrants, who were still eligible under the federal law. We document these state policies for TANF, Medicaid, SCHIP, SSI, and Food Stamps in tables 11.A1 through 11.A5. In those tables, an X indicates that a state, in a given year, provides benefits for the specified immigrant group. Here we simply document these program changes and descriptively assess immigrants before and after welfare reform. We leave to future work the analysis of the role played by the policies enacted by the states.[11]

Given all these changes, each affecting various groups and programs differently, it would not be surprising if there was and is considerable confusion about immigrant eligibility for safety net programs. Many studies have documented so-called chilling effects—that is, a reduction in utilization for programs in the absence of a change in eligibility (for a review, see Fix, Capps, and Kaushal 2009).

DATA, SAMPLE, AND DEFINITIONS

Our analysis uses data from the 1995 to 2010 Annual Social and Economic Supplement (ASEC) to the Current Population Survey, administered to most households in March. The ASEC is an annual survey that collects labor market, income, and program participation information for the previous calendar year, as well as demographic information from the time of the survey. The sample size is approximately 150,000 persons or 57,000 households per year. Our sample uses the 1995 through 2010 Current Population Survey (CPS), corresponding to 1994 through 2009 calendar year outcomes. We could not use a longer pre-welfare period because the CPS begins reporting information on immigrant status only in the 1994 survey year. However, because of problems with the weights for immigrants and data on country of origin in the 1994 survey year, we begin our analysis with 1995.[12] For all analyses, we limit the sample to include only those households with children under age eighteen.

We use the CPS to construct two groups: *natives*—who we define as those born in the United States, Puerto Rico, or outlying areas, or born outside the United States but with at least one parent being an American citizen—and *immigrants*—who we define as any foreign-born individual. Our immigrant group therefore consists of naturalized citizens, LPRs, refugees, temporary legal or illegal foreign-born residents, and unauthorized immigrants. We pool these groups because of changes in naturalization (Van Hook 2003) and the inflow of unauthorized immigrants during this period. We also use the question "When did you come to the United States to stay" to assign individuals to pre- and post-enactment groups and whether they are subject to the five-year bar.[13]

We assign all outcomes including safety net program participation and poverty at the household level. Household characteristics, including immigration status, are assigned using the values of the head of household. We also provide analyses of children using their immigrant status along with that of the head of household. That allows us to distinguish between citizen children of an immigrant head and noncitizen children of an immigrant head.[14]

The safety net programs we measure in the CPS include ADFC/TANF, food stamps, Medicaid, SCHIP (after it became law), SSI, school lunch, LIHEAP, and housing benefits (public housing and Section 8 rental subsidies).[15] SCHIP allowed states to offer Medicaid coverage to a higher income group of children or provide a separate program for these children. In our analysis, we pool Medicaid with SCHIP when they are asked about separately. In addition, the CPS provides imputed data for the cash value of some programs (public housing, Medicaid, and Medicare) and for taxes owed and tax credits (for example, the EITC or child tax credits) that households could obtain, based on their family structure.

Official poverty status in the United States is determined by comparing total pre-tax family cash income to poverty thresholds, which vary by family size, number of children, and presence of elderly persons. In 2009, the poverty threshold for a family of four—two adults, two children—was roughly $22,000. We use household income to assign poverty status, comparing income with the appropriate household poverty threshold. To address some of the many criticisms of the official poverty measure (for example, Citro and Michael 1995), we also use an alternative poverty measure in which income is measured after tax and after transfer, using the imputed values for taxes and transfers described earlier.[16]

In our results, we compare outcomes for households headed by natives and immigrants before and after welfare reform. We do not make any claim that this identifies the causal impact of welfare reform. We assert instead that it provides important descriptive evidence on immigrant well-being compared with natives. To illustrate the challenge to causal identification, we present in table 11.3 the means for demographics, employment, and income for households with children headed by natives (column 1) and immigrants (column 2) from the ASEC for calendar year 2009. The table makes it clear that immigrants are significantly more disadvantaged than natives are: less education, less earnings, less health insurance coverage, and less income as well as larger household sizes. At the same time, immigrant household heads are more likely to be married. To avoid having our comparisons confuse these differences with policy effects, we limit our sample whenever possible to households with income below 200 percent of poverty.[17] The characteristics for immigrant- and native-headed households in this lower income sample are provided in columns 3 and 4, and show somewhat more similarity between the groups. Even in the lower income sample, immigrants are less educated and have larger households than natives, but they also have higher earnings and household income and are more likely to be married and have more male household members than native households under 200 percent of poverty. The proportions of immigrants and natives below the poverty line show that the incomes are quite similar once we condition on being in this lower income sample. Interestingly, the means at the bottom of the table show that almost 90 percent of immigrant-headed households include a native-born child. In contrast, few native-headed households include anyone foreign born.

RESULTS: THE SAFETY NET

We begin with our sample of all children using the 1995–2010 CPS. Program participation is measured at the household level and refers to the prior calendar year,

TABLE 11.3 / Characteristics of Households with Children, by Immigrant Status of Head of Household

Characteristics of household	All Households		Households < 200% Poverty	
	Natives	Immigrants	Natives	Immigrants
Characteristics of household head (at survey)				
Mean age	40.1	40.5	37.5	39.2
Male	0.467	0.524	0.327	0.470
White, non-Hispanic	0.715	0.140	0.550	0.082
Black, non-Hispanic	0.156	0.092	0.268	0.095
Hispanic	0.098	0.544	0.149	0.696
Less than high school	0.089	0.319	0.199	0.476
High school	0.285	0.241	0.389	0.281
More than high school	0.625	0.440	0.412	0.242
Never married	0.154	0.111	0.303	0.159
Married	0.661	0.758	0.410	0.687
Female unmarried family	0.226	0.153	0.435	0.216
Employed	0.725	0.716	0.522	0.611
Not in labor force	0.192	0.201	0.338	0.277
Any health insurance	0.847	0.648	0.691	0.479
Characteristics of the household				
Number of children	1.8	2.0	2.1	2.2
Any elderly	0.05	0.07	0.05	0.06
Number of persons	3.9	4.4	4.0	4.5
Own home	0.679	0.515	0.403	0.336
Household earnings	$74,210	$61,938	$17,894	$22,913
Household income	$81,615	$66,423	$23,639	$25,854
Less than 50% FPL	0.058	0.081	0.180	0.161
Less than 100% FPL	0.139	0.222	0.433	0.440
Less then 150% FPL	0.230	0.376	0.715	0.746
Greater than 200% FPL	0.678	0.496	0.000	0.000
Any foreign born	0.058	1.000	0.055	1.000
Any adult born citizen	1.000	0.248	1.000	0.193
Any child born citizen	0.996	0.877	0.998	0.873
Any child foreign born	0.008	0.226	0.004	0.263

Source: Authors' calculations based on 2010 CPS Annual Social and Economic Supplement data for households with at least one child.
Note: Demographics and living arrangements refer to the time of the survey (February, March, or April 2010) and income and program receipt refer to calendar year 2009. Statistics are weighted.

thus the data cover calendar years 1994 through 2009. We begin by stratifying children using the immigration status of the head of household, splitting the sample into households headed by natives (born a citizen) and immigrants (foreign born). Figure 11.1 presents the proportion of children with any household safety

FIGURE 11.1 / Household Safety Net Participation Rates, Children by Immigrant Status of Head, Any Safety Net

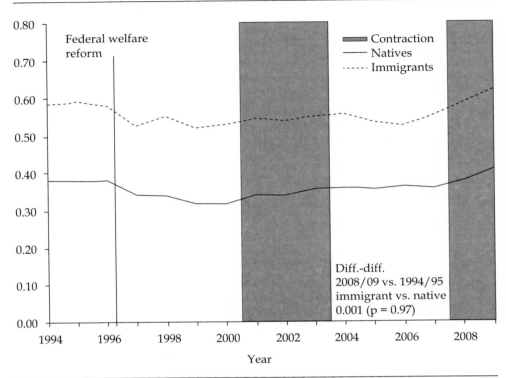

Source: Authors' calculations based on 1995–2010 Current Population Survey and Annual Social and Economic Supplement data.
Note: Sample includes children under eighteen and program participation is measured at the household level. Any safety net program participation means someone in the household participated in public assistance, food stamps, Medicaid, free or reduced price school lunch, SSI, public housing or received a rental subsidy from the government, or energy assistance. Shaded areas refer to annual periods of labor market contraction. Native household heads are those who were born in the United States or Puerto Rico or outlying areas or who were born abroad to U.S. parents, immigrant heads are other foreign born. See text for details.

net participation. This measure includes cash welfare (AFDC-TANF, general assistance), food stamps, Medicaid or SCHIP, SSI, public housing, subsidized housing, school lunch, and energy assistance. Shaded regions are periods of labor market contractions.[18] We mark federal welfare reform in 1996 with a vertical line. The figure shows higher use of the safety net overall for immigrants compared with natives. Both groups show a reduction in safety net use post welfare reform and are trending similarly. Figure 11.2 presents two key elements of the cash or near cash safety net, cash welfare (solid line and dashed line) and food stamp benefits

FIGURE 11.2 / Household Safety Net Participation Rates, Children by Immigrant Status of Head, Public Assistance and Food Stamps

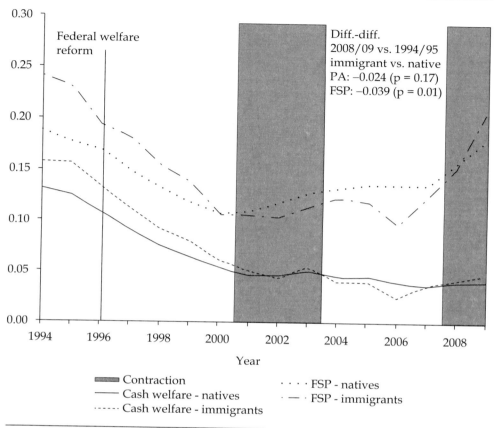

Source: Authors' calculations based on 1995–2010 Current Population Survey and Annual Social and Economic Supplement data.

Note: Sample includes children under eighteen and program participation is measured at the household level. Any safety net program participation means someone in the household partici- pated in public assistance, food stamps, Medicaid, free or reduced price school lunch, SSI, public housing or received a rental subsidy from the government, or energy assistance. Shaded areas refer to annual periods of labor market contraction. Native household heads are those who were born in the United States or Puerto Rico or outlying areas or who were born abroad to U.S. par- ents, immigrant heads are other foreign born. See text for details.

(dotted line and dashed/dotted line). Before welfare reform, immigrants (dashed line) participated at higher levels compared with natives (solid line). The gap narrows, however, and by the end of the 1990s immigrants and natives have quite similar participation rates.

As a descriptive summary measure of the impact of welfare reform on figures 11.1 and 11.2, we provide the mean difference-in-difference estimate of program participation for immigrants versus natives, using 1994–1995 as the before welfare reform period and 2008–2009 as the after. These calculations show that food stamp participation declined by 3.9 percentage points for immigrants relative to natives (p-value 0.01) and public assistance participation declined by a (statistically insignificant) 2.4 percentage points relative to natives. The broader measure of "any safety net participation" did not change for immigrants relative to natives after reform.

As shown in table 11.3, immigrants have, on average, lower incomes than natives. Thus the differences across groups in figures 11.1 and 11.2 may reflect in part different levels of disadvantage. Figures 11.3 through 11.8 present program participation for children living in households under 200 percent of poverty: any safety net participation, cash welfare, food stamps, Medicaid-SCHIP,[19] school lunch, and SSI. The graphs are similar to figures 11.1 and 11.2 except now we split the child sample into three groups: child living with a native household head,[20] native child living with an immigrant head, and immigrant child living with an immigrant head. This allows us to explore outcomes for native children in mixed-status households whose eligibility for these programs did not change over this period.

Several findings are apparent from these graphs. First, immigrants generally participate in the safety net at lower rates than natives do. This is true for the entire period for cash welfare (figure 11.4), food stamps (figure 11.5) and SSI (figure 11.8), and is true both before and after welfare reform. Children who are themselves immigrants are less likely to participate in Medicaid-SCHIP across the entire period as well, and native children of immigrant parents about as likely as children of native parents. The main exception is the school lunch program (figure 11.7), in which immigrants have consistently participated at higher rates than natives. Overall, our measure of any safety net participation (figure 11.3) is higher for immigrants than for natives, driven primarily by this higher participation in the school lunch program. Immigrant children in immigrant-headed households consistently participate in each of the programs or in the any safety net measure at the lowest levels among the three groups.[21]

Second, these national trends in safety net participation are broadly consistent with the finding of reduced immigrant access to the safety net after welfare reform. To explore this more concretely, we present the difference-in-difference estimates of the change in safety net participation for immigrants versus natives in 2008–2009 compared with 1994–1995. These simply take the change in participation for immigrants and subtract the change in participation for natives; and we show this estimate for each panel. The results show that immigrant food stamp participation since reform has declined by 5.7 percentage points relative to natives

(Text continues on p. 339)

FIGURE 11.3 / Household Safety Net Participation, Rates in Households with Income Less than 200 Percent Poverty, Children by Own and Head's Immigrant Status, Any Safety Net

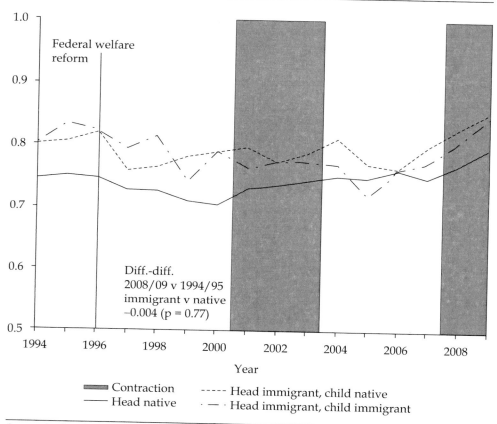

Source: Authors' calculations based on 1995–2010 Current Population Survey and Annual Social and Economic Supplement data.

Note: Sample includes children under eighteen with household income below 200 percent poverty, Program participation is measured at the household level. Any safety net program participation means someone in the household participated in public assistance, food stamps, Medicaid, free or reduced price school lunch, SSI, public housing or received a rental subsidy from the government, or energy assistance. Shaded areas refer to annual periods of labor market contraction. Native household heads are those who were born in the United States or Puerto Rico or outlying areas or who were born abroad to U.S. parents, immigrant heads are other foreign born. Children's immigration status defined in same way. Figures are weighted. Shaded areas refer to annual periods of labor market contraction. See text for details.

FIGURE 11.4 / Household Safety Net Participation, Rates in Households with Income Less than 200 Percent Poverty, Children by Own and Head's Immigrant Status, AFDC-TANF

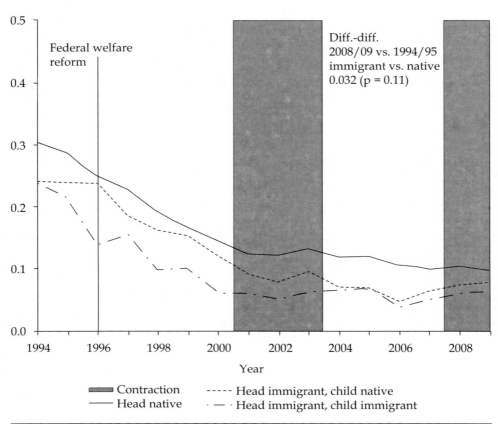

Source: Authors' calculations from 1995–2010 Current Population Survey Annual and Social Economic Supplement data.

Note: Sample includes children under eighteen with household income below 200 percent poverty, Program participation is measured at the household level. Any safety net program participation means someone in the household participated in public assistance, food stamps, Medicaid, free or reduced price school lunch, SSI, public housing or received a rental subsidy from the government, or energy assistance. Shaded areas refer to annual periods of labor market contraction. Native household heads are those who were born in the United States or Puerto Rico or outlying areas or who were born abroad to U.S. parents, immigrant heads are other foreign born. Children's immigration status defined in same way. Figures are weighted. Shaded areas refer to annual periods of labor market contraction. See text for details.

FIGURE 11.5 / Household Safety Net Participation, Rates in Households with Income Less than 200 Percent Poverty, Children by Own and Head's Immigrant Status, Food Stamps

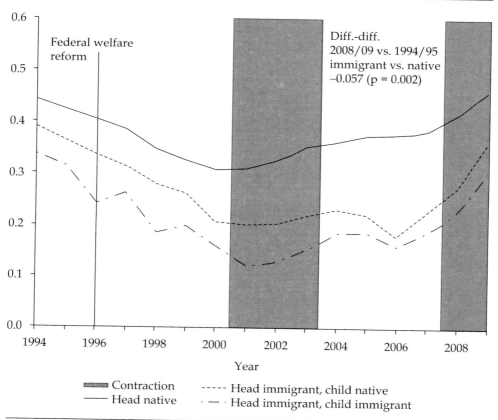

Source: Authors' calculations from 1995–2010 Current Population Survey Annual and Social Economic Supplement data.
Note: Sample includes children under eighteen with household income below 200 percent poverty, Program participation is measured at the household level. Any safety net program participation means someone in the household participated in public assistance, food stamps, Medicaid, free or reduced price school lunch, SSI, public housing or received a rental subsidy from the government, or energy assistance. Shaded areas refer to annual periods of labor market contraction. Native household heads are those who were born in the United States or Puerto Rico or outlying areas or who were born abroad to U.S. parents, immigrant heads are other foreign born. Children's immigration status defined in same way. Figures are weighted. Shaded areas refer to annual periods of labor market contraction. See text for details.

FIGURE 11.6 / Household Safety Net Participation, Rates in Households with Income
Less than 200 Percent Poverty, Children by Own and Head's Immigrant
Status, Medicaid-SCHIP

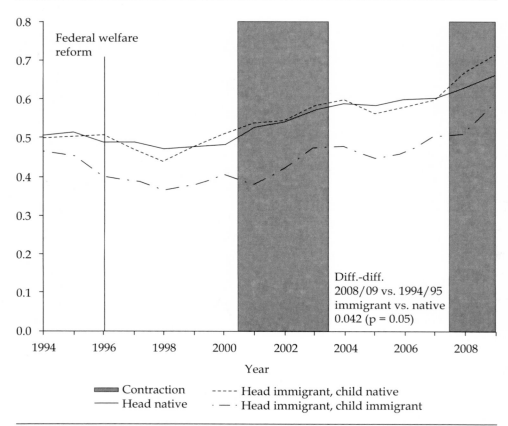

Source: Authors' calculations from 1995–2010 Current Population Survey Annual and Social Economic Supplement data.
Note: Sample includes children under eighteen with household income below 200 percent poverty, Program participation is measured at the household level. Any safety net program participation means someone in the household participated in public assistance, food stamps, Medicaid, free or reduced price school lunch, SSI, public housing or received a rental subsidy from the
government, or energy assistance. Shaded areas refer to annual periods of labor market contraction. Native household heads are those who were born in the United States or Puerto Rico or
outlying areas or who were born abroad to U.S. parents, immigrant heads are other foreign born.
Children's immigration status defined in same way. Figures are weighted. Shaded areas refer to
annual periods of labor market contraction. See text for details.

FIGURE 11.7 / Household Safety Net Participation, Rates in Households with Income Less than 200 Percent Poverty, Children by Own and Head's Immigrant Status, School Lunch

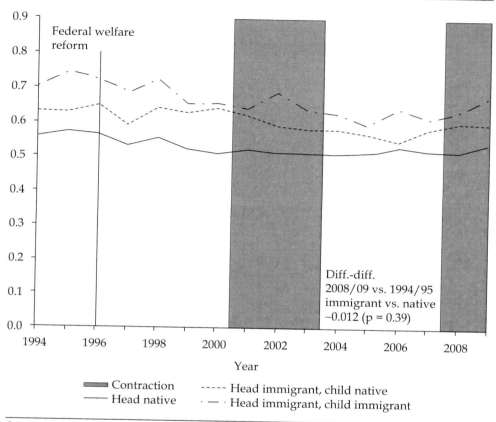

Federal welfare reform

Diff.-diff.
2008/09 vs. 1994/95
immigrant vs. native
−0.012 (p = 0.39)

Year

Contraction
Head native
----- Head immigrant, child native
· — · Head immigrant, child immigrant

Source: Authors' calculations from 1995–2010 Current Population Survey Annual and Social Economic Supplement data.

Note: Sample includes children under eighteen with household income below 200 percent poverty, Program participation is measured at the household level. Any safety net program participation means someone in the household participated in public assistance, food stamps, Medicaid, free or reduced price school lunch, SSI, public housing or received a rental subsidy from the government, or energy assistance. Shaded areas refer to annual periods of labor market contraction. Native household heads are those who were born in the United States or Puerto Rico or outlying areas or who were born abroad to U.S. parents, immigrant heads are other foreign born. Children's immigration status defined in same way. Figures are weighted. Shaded areas refer to annual periods of labor market contraction. See text for details.

FIGURE 11.8 / Household Safety Net Participation, Rates in Households with Income Less than 200 Percent Poverty, Children by Own and Head's Immigrant Status, SSI

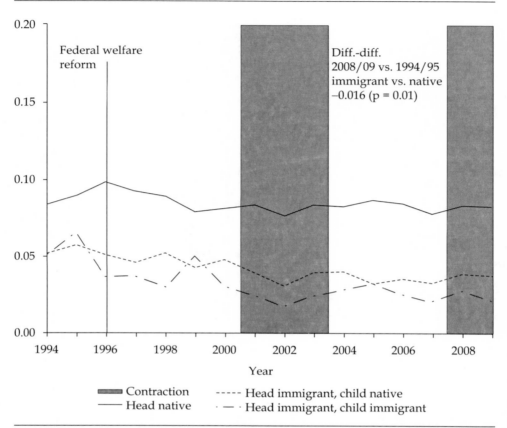

Source: Authors' calculations from 1995–2010 Current Population Survey Annual and Social Economic Supplement data.

Note: Sample includes children under eighteen with household income below 200 percent poverty, Program participation is measured at the household level. Any safety net program participation means someone in the household participated in public assistance, food stamps, Medicaid, free or reduced price school lunch, SSI, public housing or received a rental subsidy from the government, or energy assistance. Shaded areas refer to annual periods of labor market contraction. Native household heads are those who were born in the United States or Puerto Rico or outlying areas or who were born abroad to U.S. parents, immigrant heads are other foreign born. Children's immigration status defined in same way. Figures are weighted. Shaded areas refer to annual periods of labor market contraction. See text for details.

FIGURE 11.9 / Percent Distribution of Children in Households, with Income Less than 200 Percent Poverty, by Own and Head's Immigrant Status

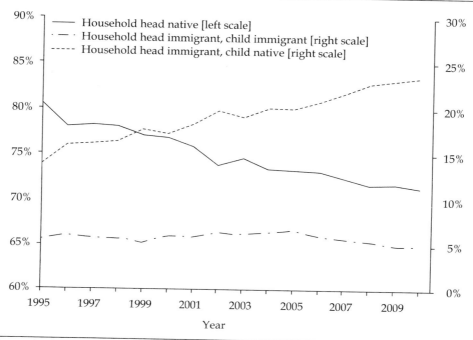

Source: Authors' calculations based on 1995–2010 Current Population Survey Annual Social and Economic Supplement data.
Note: Sample includes children under eighteen in households with income less than 200 percent of poverty. Native household heads are those who were born in the United States or Puerto Rico or outlying areas or who were born abroad to U.S. parents, immigrant heads are other foreign born. Children's immigration status defined in same way. Figures are weighted. See text for details.

(*p*-value 0.002) and immigrant SSI participation has declined by 1.6 percentage points relative to natives (*p*-value 0.01). School lunch participation also declined by 1.2 percentage points for immigrants relative to natives, but the differences are not statistically significant. Medicaid-SCHIP is the main exception, with an increase of 4.2 percentage points for immigrants relative to natives (*p*-value 0.05). Interestingly, for participation in Medicaid-SCHIP, children in native-headed households and native children in mixed-status households have almost identical levels and trends in participation, which may reflect SCHIP's outreach efforts aimed at immigrant families (Aizer 2003, 2007).

Overall, given the greater severity of the restrictions on access to food stamps and SSI (versus TANF and Medicaid-SCHIP), we would expect to see larger relative declines for immigrants since reform for use of those programs. Similarly, we would expect the smallest changes in participation for school lunch, given that welfare reform did not affect eligibility for this program. The results are broadly consistent these predictions.

Of course, it is possible that other factors that may be changing over this period that may affect the native-immigrant comparisons. Thus we are cautious about drawing strong conclusions from this analysis of the results in figures 11.1 through 11.8. As an illustration of the general issues at play here, figure 11.9 presents the trends in the percent distribution of children in households with income less than 200 percent of official poverty for our three immigration-status groups. Overtime, native children in immigrant-headed households are a increasing share of the sample (13.9 percent in 1995 to 23.5 percent in 2010) and children in native-headed households are declining (80.5 percent in 1995 to 71.5 percent in 2010). The share of children under 200 percent of poverty who are immigrant children in immigrant-headed households also declined from 5.6 percent to 5.0 percent.

Recall that the post-reform immigrant eligibility rules differentiate between pre- and post-enactment immigrants and between those who have been in the United States for at least five years and those fewer than five years.[22] Recent immigrants are least likely to be eligible since reform, and longer-term residents more likely, but still not necessarily at the levels they were before the Personal Responsibility and Work Opportunity Reconciliation Act (PRWORA). Given this, in table 11.4 we explore further the impact of the policy changes by examining safety net participation separately for immigrants arriving within the past five years to those who arrived more than five years ago. In particular, we identify participation for five groups. In our pre-reform years (1994 and 1995), we calculate safety net participation for recent immigrants (head arrived five or fewer years ago) and other immigrants (head arrived six or more years ago). In our post-reform years (2008–2009), we break down the six-or-more group into those with heads who arrived before enactment of PRWORA and those who arrived after.[23] At the bottom of the table, we present two before and after reform differences, in each case comparing individuals in different years-in-U.S. group (five or fewer years, six or more) who arrived before enactment to a group arriving after. The data are largely consistent with these expectations. Recently arrived immigrants have larger reductions in use of public assistance and food stamps and substantially smaller increases in use of Medicaid-SCHIP than less-recently arrived immigrants do. For example, receipt of public assistance (food stamps) declined by 21.4 (6.4) percentage points for children in households headed by immigrants who arrived five or fewer years ago, versus 14.9 (3.7) percentage points for children in households headed by immigrants who arrived six or more years ago. School lunch and SSI show the opposite pattern in relative changes in use, with larger decreases for those arriving longer ago. Again, Medicaid looks quite different.

In addition to tabulating the CPS data, we use the available administrative data to further explore trends in program participation. In figure 11.10, we present the percent of SSI participants who were noncitizens for 1980 through 2009. We plot this separately for all recipients, aged recipients, and disabled or blind recipients. We are focused on households with children. That said, SSI is not a very heavily used safety net program in our population of interest. This is clear in figure 11.8,

TABLE 11.4 / Household Safety Net Participation Rates, for Immigrant-Headed Households with Children with Income Less than 200 Percent of Poverty

		N	Any Safety Net	Public Assistance	Food Stamps	Medicaid-SCHIP	School Lunch	SSI
Pre-reform (1994–1995)								
Arrived six+ years ago, pre-enactment	(1)	6294	0.811	0.221	0.353	0.474	0.680	0.058
Arrived ≤ five years ago, pre-enactment	(2)	1648	0.792	0.287	0.394	0.553	0.569	0.049
Post-reform (2008–2009)								
Arrived six+ years ago, pre-enactment	(3)	6898	0.837	0.076	0.301	0.672	0.634	0.048
Arrived six+ years ago, post-enactment	(4)	3669	0.843	0.072	0.316	0.676	0.601	0.022
Arrived ≤ five years ago, post-enactment	(5)	1875	0.836	0.073	0.330	0.645	0.532	0.018
Post-reform–Pre-reform								
Arrived six+ years ago	(4)–(1)		0.032	−0.149	−0.037	0.202	−0.079	−0.036
Arrived ≤ five years ago	(5)–(2)		0.044	−0.214	−0.064	0.092	−0.036	−0.031

Source: Authors' calculations based on 1995, 1995, and 2010 CPS Annual Social and Economic Supplement data.

Note: Sample includes households with children under eighteen with heads born not a U.S. citizen and living in households with income under 200 percent of poverty and program participation is measured at the household level. Any safety net program participation means someone in the household participated in public assistance (AFDC-TANF or GA), food stamps, Medicaid-SCHIP, free or reduced price school lunch, SSI, public housing or received a rental subsidy from the government, or energy assistance. Arrival cohort is assigned using when the household head came to the United States to stay. See text for details about coding of time of arrival.

which shows that SSI participation rates never rise above 10 percent and are mostly below 5 percent of children in immigrant households. Given the small share of elderly persons in our sample of households with children (table 11.3), the SSI disabled caseload is the most relevant for our purposes. This said, figure 11.10 shows a dramatic decline in noncitizen SSI participation following federal welfare reform, with little recovery through 2009. Potentially more relevant is the AFDC-TANF child-only caseload. This consists of administrative cases without an adult participant, the largest group of which being when the child is a citizen but the parent is not (Blank 2001; DHHS 2008). As such, child-only caseloads may be a useful proxy for program participation among native children in mixed-status households. Figure 11.11 presents the administrative data on the child-only caseload per thousand persons for fiscal years 1995 through 2008. The child-only caseload declines sharply and dramatically following welfare reform. It then steadily and slowly increases, but never returns to its pre-reform level. Ruth Wasem (2010) reports trends in the noncitizen fraction of food stamp participation based on Food Stamp Quality Con-

FIGURE 11.10 / Noncitizens as Percentage of all SSI Recipients

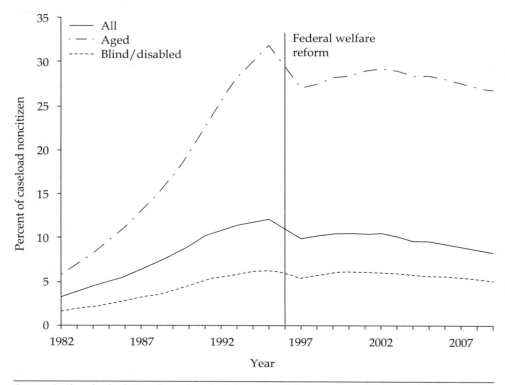

Source: Authors' calculations based on Social Security Administration (2010), table 29.

trol data. That data show a similar pattern, a sharp decline in the noncitizen share in 1997 with little recovery since then. Overall, 7.1 percent of the food stamp caseload consisted of noncitizens in 1989; in 2009 only 3.8 percent did.

RESULTS: INCOME AND POVERTY

Having established the basic facts on program participation, we move on to analyze immigrant well-being before and after welfare reform. In particular, we quantify the importance of safety net programs by exploring the sources of household income and how they have changed over time. We also examine child poverty and extreme poverty for immigrants and natives.

We begin by presenting the share of the quantity household cash income plus food stamps contributed by each source for households with children in extreme poverty (below 50 percent of official poverty). We compare these sources of income for a year before reform (1994) and a year after reform (2009). Ideally, we

FIGURE 11.11 / Child-Only Caseload in AFDC-TANF, per 1,000 Population

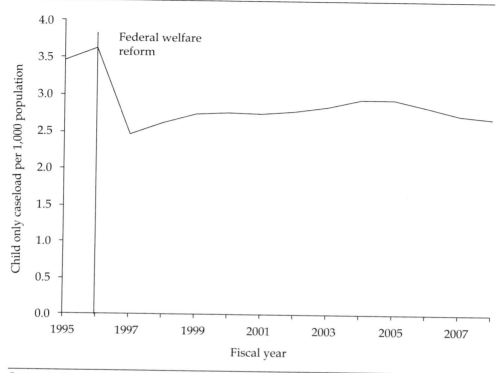

Source: Authors' calculations based on United States Department of Health and Human Services 1995–2008.

would have compared data for two similar points in the business cycle, but data limitations prohibit this. In 2009, U.S. unemployment was 9.3 percent, the peak in the annual rate for the Great Recession. The early 1990s recession level of unemployment peaked at 7.5 percent in 1992 and by 1994 was down to 6.1 percent. We present a graph for households headed by natives (figure 11.12) and households headed by immigrants (figure 11.13). We show shares for some important income sources for lower income households: Earnings, cash welfare, food stamps, SSI, unemployment compensation (pooled with workers compensation and veterans payments), and child support combined with alimony.

The most striking feature of figures 11.12 and 11.13 is that households headed by low-income immigrants rely much more heavily on earnings than native-headed households do. In 2009, among households with children in extreme poverty, almost 50 percent of income comes from earnings for immigrant-headed households versus less than 30 percent for native-headed ones. This difference was present before reform but has grown since. Second, the figures clearly show the declining role of cash welfare as a countercyclical income source for the poor

FIGURE 11.12 / Share of Income, by Source, for Households with Children Below 50 Percent Official Poverty, 1994 and 2009, Native-Headed Households

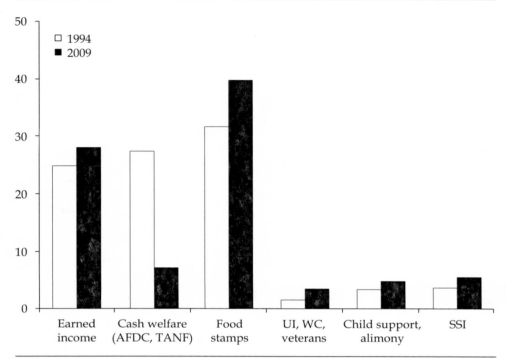

Source: Authors' calculations based on 1995 and 2010 Current Population Survey Annual and Social Economic Supplement data.

Note: Sample includes households with children in which income is below 50 percent of official poverty, poverty is assigned at the household level. Total income includes the value of food stamps. Native household heads are those who were born in the United States or Puerto Rico or outlying areas or who were born abroad to U.S. parents, immigrant heads are other foreign born. Categories of income do not sum to 1, some income categories are omitted. Figures are weighted.

and the increasing role played by food stamps and earnings for both immigrants and natives. The other categories of income presented are less important sources for this group. That said, the share of income from SSI is increasing over this period for natives and decreasing for immigrants (the opposite pattern holds for child support and alimony).

Figures 11.14 through 11.17 present the same information for samples of households with children below 100 percent of poverty (figures 11.14 and 11.15) and below 200 percent poverty (Figures 11.16 and 11.17). Although the magnitudes change, the basic findings are similar: immigrants tend to rely more on earnings and that has increased over time; cash welfare is now much less important than it was; food stamps are much more important. Notably, in 2009, earnings represent 70 percent (80 percent) of total income (cash income plus food stamps) for immi-

FIGURE 11.13 / Share of Income, by Source, for Households with Children Below 50 Percent Official Poverty, 1994 and 2009, Immigrant-Headed Households

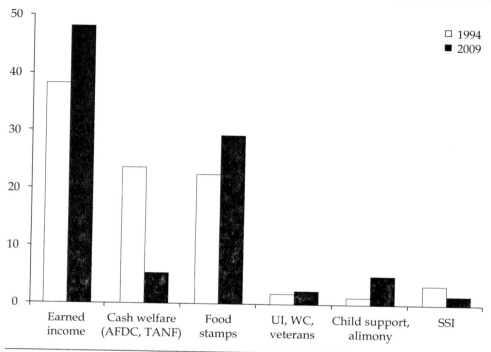

Source: Authors' calculations based on 1995 and 2010 Current Population Survey Annual and Social Economic Supplement data.
Note: Sample includes households with children in which income is below 50 percent of official poverty, poverty is assigned at the household level. Total income includes the value of food stamps. Native household heads are those who were born in the United States or Puerto Rico or outlying areas or who were born abroad to U.S. parent(s), immigrant heads are other foreign born. Categories of income do not sum to 1, some income categories are omitted. Figures are weighted.

grant households below poverty (below 200 percent poverty). For natives, earnings are 45 percent for those below poverty and just over 60 percent for those below 200 percent of poverty.[24]

One reason the results may differ for immigrants and natives may be the immigrants' more disadvantaged status even within a given poverty sample. To address this, we examined similar graphs in which we reweighted the native group to match the income distribution of immigrants (based on 25 percent bins of the income-to-poverty distribution).[25] This made little difference in the results, which perhaps is not surprising given the similarity in the income distribution in the two groups once we condition on being below 200 percent of poverty (see table 11.3). In addition, it is well known that, beginning in the 1990s, immigrant populations

FIGURE 11.14 / Share of Income, by Source, for Households with Children Below
Official Poverty, 1994 and 2009, Native-Headed Households

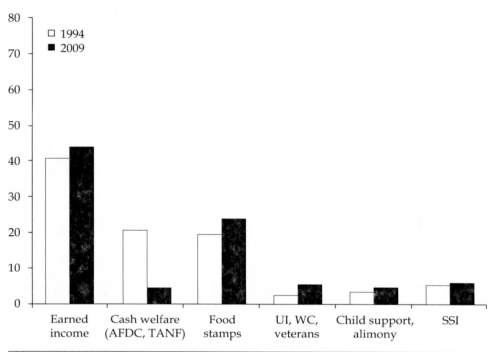

Source: Authors' calculations based on 1995 and 2010 Current Population Survey Annual and Social Economic Supplement data.
Note: Sample includes households with children in which income is below 100 percent of official poverty, poverty is assigned at the household level. Total income includes the value of food stamps. Native household heads are those who were born in the United States or Puerto Rico or outlying areas or who were born abroad to U.S. parents, immigrant heads are other foreign born. Categories of income do not sum to 1, some income categories are omitted. Figures are weighted.

grew significantly beyond the traditional immigrant destination states (for example, Massey 2008).[26] Much of the growth has been in areas where the safety net is less generous, such as the southeast. To address this, we reweighted the immigrant groups in 1994 and 2009 to represent their state population shares in 1990.[27] This too made little difference to the results, which may reflect that though the growth rate increased in new destination areas, the overall population of immigrants is still dominated by their shares in traditional destination states.[28]

What is the result of all these changes to the safety net? One important measure is the incidence of poverty, and how it compares between immigrants and natives. In the remainder of our analysis, we present new evidence on trends in child poverty for immigrants versus natives.[29] We return to our three groups analyzed ear-

FIGURE 11.15 / Share of Income, by Source, for Households with Children Below Official Poverty, 1994 and 2009, Immigrant-Headed Households

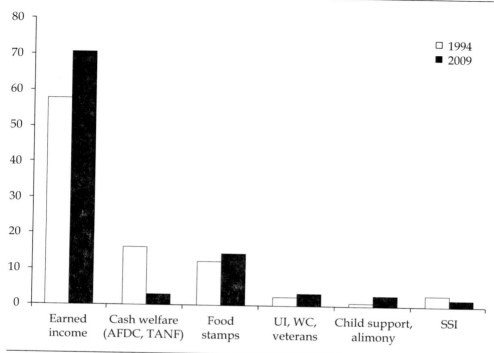

Source: Authors' calculations based on 1995 and 2010 Current Population Survey Annual and Social Economic Supplement data.
Note: Sample includes households with children in which income is below 100 percent of official poverty, poverty is assigned at the household level. Total income includes the value of food stamps. Native household heads are those who were born in the United States or Puerto Rico or outlying areas or who were born abroad to U.S. parent(s), immigrant heads are other foreign born. Categories of income do not sum to 1, some income categories are omitted. Figures are weighted.

lier: native children living in households headed by natives, immigrant children living with immigrant heads, and native children living with immigrant heads. Figure 11.18 presents the percentage of children living in extreme poverty for 1994 through 2009, using the official poverty measure. Figure 11.19 presents those living in poverty for the same period. Overall, poverty rates for children in immigrant households exceed those of their counterparts in native households. This is true before and after welfare reform. Interestingly, during the 1990s, the gap between extreme poverty rates for native children living in mixed-status households and for those in native households narrowed substantially. All of these series illustrate the countercyclical nature of poverty, and improvements during this pe-

FIGURE 11.16 / Share of Income, by Source, for Households with Children Below 200
Percent Official Poverty, 1994 and 2009, Native-Headed Households

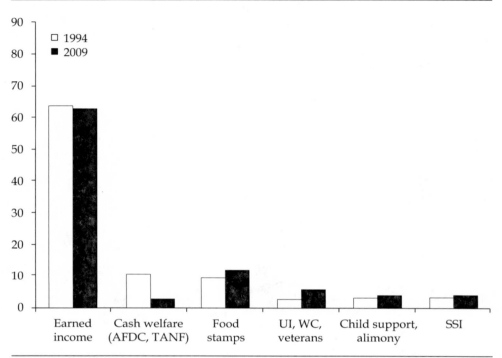

Source: Authors' calculations based on 1995 and 2010 Current Population Survey Annual and
Social Economic Supplement data.
Note: Sample includes households with children in which income is below 200 percent of official
poverty, poverty is assigned at the household level. Total income includes the value of food
stamps. Native household heads are those who were born in the United States or Puerto Rico or
outlying areas or who were born abroad to U.S. parents, immigrant heads are other foreign born.
Categories of income do not sum to 1, some income categories are omitted. Figures are weighted.

riod were especially apparent in the long economic expansion of the 1990s. However, it is striking that child poverty among immigrant-headed households has
increased more in the current recession compared with natives.

Many concerns have been raised about the ability of the official poverty measure
to capture resources households have. In particular, the official poverty measure
uses pre-tax income — which does not include the EITC, child tax credits, and the
effects of the tax system — and does not count in-kind transfers such as food stamps
in the measure of household income.[30] To address this concern, and to explore
more the role of the safety net in the wake of welfare reform, we present in figure
11.20 the percentage of children living below poverty using our alternative income

FIGURE 11.17 / Share of Income, by Source, for Households with Children Below 200 Percent Official Poverty, 1994 and 2009, Immigrant-Headed Households

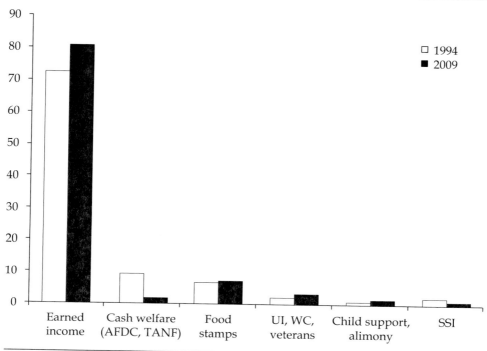

Source: Authors' calculations based on 1995 and 2010 Current Population Survey Annual and Social Economic Supplement data.
Note: Sample includes households with children in which income is below 200 percent of official poverty, poverty is assigned at the household level. Total income includes the value of food stamps. Native household heads are those who were born in the United States or Puerto Rico or outlying areas or who were born abroad to U.S. parents, immigrant heads are other foreign born. Categories of income do not sum to 1, some income categories are omitted. Figures are weighted.

measure. We construct alternative income by adding to money income the cash value of food stamps, school lunch, energy assistance, and housing subsidies and then subtracting payroll taxes, and net federal and state taxes (including the EITC and child tax credits). Poverty rates are lower using alternative income, and appear to be slightly less countercyclical, as we would expect if the safety net is insuring families against short-term income losses. Interestingly, alternative poverty actually declines for children in immigrant-headed households in 2009, which is surprising given that the unemployment rate rose between 2008 and 2009. It appears that the large increase in food stamp participation in these households at the end of the period (figure 11.5) may explain part of this difference.

FIGURE 11.18 / Child Poverty Rates, by Immigrant Status of Child and Head of Household, Below 50 Percent Official Poverty

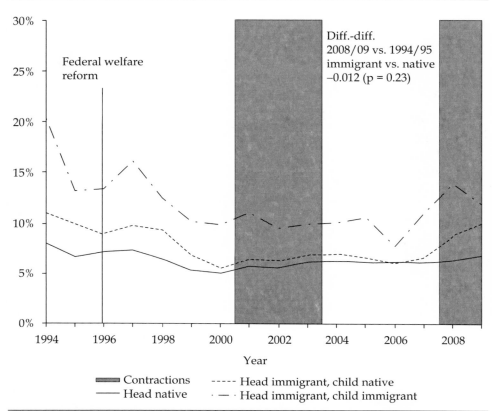

Source: Authors' calculations based on 1995–2010 Current Population Survey Annual and Social Economic Supplement data.
Note: Sample includes children and poverty is assigned at the household level. Official poverty uses total household income and household size and the official census poverty thresholds; alternative poverty uses total cash income plus the EITC and child tax credits and other transfers minus FICA and state and local taxes. Native household heads are those who were born in the United States or Puerto Rico or outlying areas or who were born abroad to U.S. parents, immigrant heads are other foreign born. Children's immigration status assigned analogously. Figures are weighted. Shaded areas refer to annual periods of labor market contraction. See text for details.

The difference-in-difference estimates show that poverty rates declined for children in immigrant-headed households, compared with natives, after welfare reform (2008–2009) relative to before reform (1994–1995). This result is unexpected but may be explained by a change in the composition of immigrant children (see figure 11.9). That is, although the time series plot in figures 11.18 through 11.20 shows that a rise in poverty for immigrant children beginning in 2007, the

FIGURE 11.19 / Child Poverty Rates, by Immigrant Status of Child and Head of Household, Below 100 Percent Official Poverty

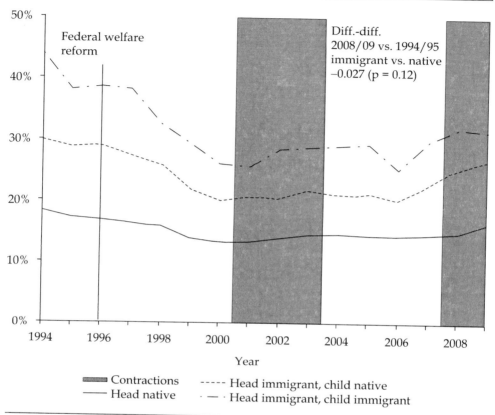

Source: Authors' calculations based on 1995–2010 Current Population Survey Annual and Social Economic Supplement data.

Note: Sample includes children and poverty is assigned at the household level. Official poverty uses total household income and household size and the official census poverty thresholds; alternative poverty uses total cash income plus the EITC and child tax credits and other transfers minus FICA and state and local taxes. Native household heads are those who were born in the United States or Puerto Rico or outlying areas or who were born abroad to U.S. parents, immigrant heads are other foreign born. Children's immigration status assigned analogously. Figures are weighted. Shaded areas refer to annual periods of labor market contraction. See text for details.

difference-in-difference reflects the decrease in immigrant poverty between 1994 and 1999.

To further explore the role of welfare reform, we present mean poverty rates for immigrant groups in table 11.5 adopting the same groups we presented in table 11.4 (before and after welfare reform, five years or fewer and six years or more since arrival, and pre-and post-enactment arrival). Again, at the bottom of the

FIGURE 11.20 / Child Poverty Rates, by Immigrant Status of Child and Head of Household, Below 100 Percent Alternative Poverty

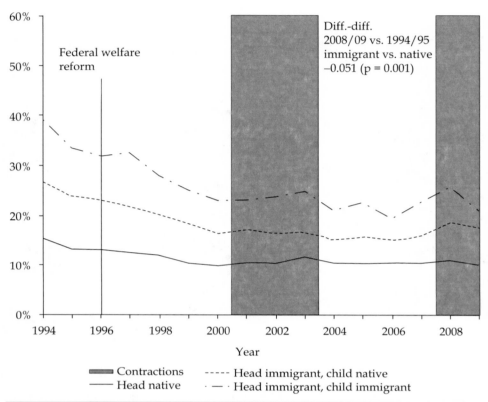

Federal welfare reform

Diff.-diff.
2008/09 vs. 1994/95
immigrant vs. native
−0.051 (p = 0.001)

Year

▬▬ Contractions   ----- Head immigrant, child native
──── Head native   · — · Head immigrant, child immigrant

Source: Authors' calculations based on 1995–2010 Current Population Survey Annual and Social Economic Supplement data.

Note: Sample includes children and poverty is assigned at the household level. Official poverty uses total household income and household size and the official census poverty thresholds; alternative poverty uses total cash income plus the EITC and child tax credits and other transfers minus FICA and state and local taxes. Native household heads are those who were born in the United States or Puerto Rico or outlying areas or who were born abroad to U.S. parents, immigrant heads are other foreign born. Children's immigration status assigned analogously. Figures are weighted. Shaded areas refer to annual periods of labor market contraction. See text for details.

table we present the two before and after reform comparisons. We find increases or no change in most poverty measures for immigrants who came at least six years ago, but surprisingly, we find decreases in poverty for those who arrived five or fewer years ago. This is puzzling, given the expectation that these recent immigrants are the least likely since reform to have access to the safety net. Several ex-

TABLE 11.5 / Poverty Rates for Immigrant-Headed Households with Children

		N	Below 50% Poverty	Below 100% Poverty	Below 50% Alternative Poverty	Below 100% Alternative Poverty
Pre-reform (1994–1995)						
Arrived six+ years ago, pre-enactment	(1)	10245	0.103	0.296	0.044	0.256
Arrived ≤ five years ago, pre-enactment	(2)	2301	0.187	0.425	0.124	0.372
Post-reform (2008–2009)						
Arrived six+ years ago, pre-enactment	(3)	13377	0.082	0.229	0.045	0.155
Arrived six+ years ago, post-enactment	(4)	5979	0.109	0.319	0.057	0.218
Arrived ≤ five years ago, post-enactment	(5)	2982	0.153	0.359	0.079	0.277
Post-reform–Pre-reform						
Arrived six+ years ago	(4)–(1)		0.006	0.023	0.013	-0.038
Arrived ≤ five years ago	(5)–(2)		-0.034	-0.066	-0.045	-0.095

Source: Authors' calculations based on 1995, 1995, and 2010 CPS Annual Social and Economic Supplement data.
Note: Sample includes households with children under eighteen with heads born not a U.S. citizen and program participation is measured at the household level. Extreme poverty and official poverty calculated using official CPS poverty thresholds and income sources and household size; alternative poverty calculated using official CPS poverty thresholds and household size, and using household income measured as CPS cash income minus FICA and state and local taxes plus the EITC and relevant child tax credits plus cash transfers. Arrival cohort is assigned using when the household head came to the United States to stay. See text for details about coding of time of arrival.

planations are possible. First, it is possible that the recession has led to reduced return migration (say, from Mexico) or increased outflows, and that those who leave or don't return are negatively selected. Michael Rendall, Peter Brownell, and Sarah Kups (2011) suggest a possible decline in return migration from the United States to Mexico in the Great Recession. Jennifer Van Hook and Weiwei Zhang (2011) show that having children is negatively correlated with emigration. A second explanation is that immigrant households are doubling up in response to the Great Recession, and that this is most common for those with the least amount of access to the safety net, those who arrived within the last five years. Rakesh Kochhar and D'Vera Cohn (2011) use the American Community Survey data, finding that living in multigenerational households is more common in 2009 than 2007 as a share of households, and that some part of this might reflect doubling up in response to the Great Recession. A third possibility is that the CPS is simply missing more unauthorized immigrants who are reluctant to participate given recent leg-

FIGURE 11.21 / Change in Unemployment Rate and Child Poverty, 2007–2009, by State, Below 50 Percent Poverty, Native Heads

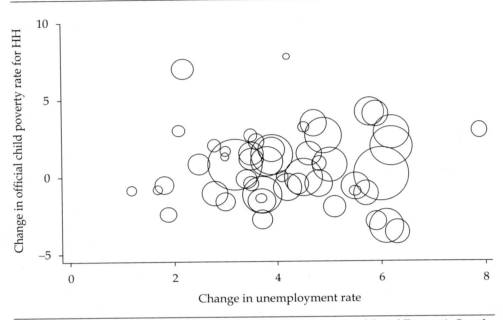

Source: Authors' calculations based on 2008 and 2010 CPS Annual and Social Economic Supplement Data.
Note: Scatterplots of state data where each point is the change in unemployment rate and poverty for a state between the peak and through of the contraction (2007–2009). Sample includes children and poverty is assigned at the household level. Official poverty uses total household income and household size and the official Census poverty thresholds; alternative poverty uses total cash income plus the EITC and child tax credits and other transfers minus FICA and state and local taxes. Native household heads are those who were born in the United States or Puerto Rico or outlying areas or who were born abroad to U.S. parents, immigrant heads are other foreign born. See text for details.

islation that is restrictive toward the unauthorized, though this seems unlikely to drive our findings for citizen children of immigrants.

Given the severity of the Great Recession, during which the unemployment rate has risen from 4.6 in 2007 to 9.3 in 2009, it is of interest to explore more fully the well-being of immigrants and natives in the current period. In particular, we take advantage of the substantial geographic variation in the severity of the recession and plot the change in state unemployment rates against the change in the state child poverty rate between 2007 and 2009. (Chapter 5 of this volume presents a complementary analysis of the effects of metro area's contributions to the variance of poverty.) We present the results for native-headed and immigrant-headed households in a series of scatter plots. Figures 11.21 and 11.22 show extreme child

FIGURE 11.22 / Change in Unemployment Rate and Child Poverty, 2007–2009, by State, Below 50 Percent Poverty, Immigrant Heads

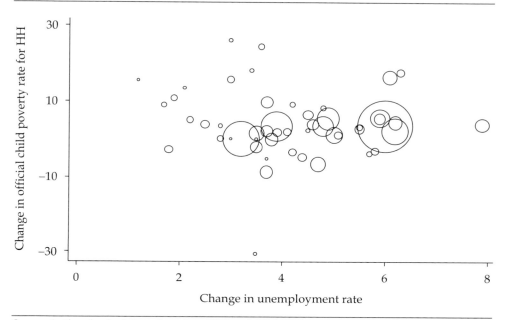

Source: Authors' calculations based on 2008 and 2010 CPS Annual and Social Economic Supplement Data.

Note: Scatterplots of state data where each point is the change in unemployment rate and poverty for a state between the peak and through of the contraction (2007–2009). Sample includes children and poverty is assigned at the household level. Official poverty uses total household income and household size and the official Census poverty thresholds; alternative poverty uses total cash income plus the EITC and child tax credits and other transfers minus FICA and state and local taxes. Native household heads are those who were born in the United States or Puerto Rico or outlying areas or who were born abroad to U.S. parents, immigrant heads are other foreign born. See text for details.

poverty, Figures 11.23 and 11.24 show official child poverty. Figures 11.25 and 11.26 show child alternative poverty. In each graph, the x-axis is the change in unemployment rates by state between 2007 and 2009. On the y-axis is the change in state child poverty rates over the same period. The size of each state-group's population is represented by the size of the circle representing the data point. These figures show that variation is considerable across states in the magnitude of the Great Recession: between 2007 and 2009, state changes in the unemployment rate ranged from about 1.2 percentage points in North Dakota to 7.9 in Nevada. We leverage this variation to explore how the Great Recession affects child poverty in immigrant and native families.

Several findings are apparent from these figures. First, they reveal an upward

FIGURE 11.23 / Change in Unemployment Rate and Child Poverty, 2007–2009, by State, Below 100 Percent Poverty, Native Heads

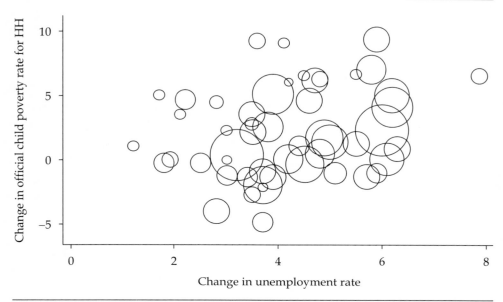

Source: Authors' calculations based on 2008 and 2010 CPS Annual and Social Economic Supplement Data.

Note: Scatterplots of state data where each point is the change in unemployment rate and poverty for a state between the peak and through of the contraction (2007–2009). Sample includes children and poverty is assigned at the household level. Official poverty uses total household income and household size and the official Census poverty thresholds; alternative poverty uses total cash income plus the EITC and child tax credits and other transfers minus FICA and state and local taxes. Native household heads are those who were born in the United States or Puerto Rico or outlying areas or who were born abroad to U.S. parents, immigrant heads are other foreign born. See text for details.

sloping tendency, showing the strong positive correlation between the severity of the recession and the increase in official child poverty. Second, the poverty rate changes are everywhere higher for children in immigrant-headed households, implying that this recession led to larger increases in poverty for that group (note the different y-axis scales for immigrant and native groups). Third, the scatterplots have steeper slopes for children in immigrant-headed households, suggesting that a given increase in unemployment leads to larger increases in poverty for immigrants compared to natives.

To explore this more fully, table 11.6 presents estimates of the correlation between changes in state unemployment rates and child poverty (for example, the implied best-fit slope of the data in the scatterplots). Specifically, we regress the change in state poverty rates on the change in state unemployment rates and a constant. The regression is weighted using the population in each state-group cell.

FIGURE 11.24 / Change in Unemployment Rate and Child Poverty, 2007–2009, by State, Below 100 Percent Poverty, Immigrant Heads

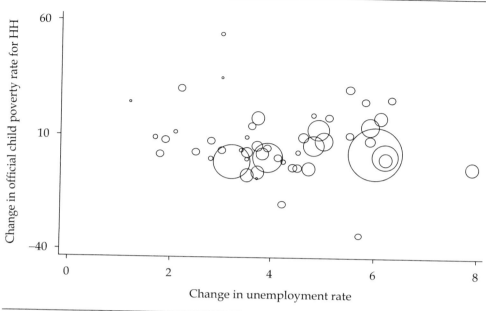

Source: Authors' calculations based on 2008 and 2010 CPS Annual and Social Economic Supplement Data.

Note: Scatterplots of state data where each point is the change in unemployment rate and poverty for a state between the peak and through of the contraction (2007–2009). Sample includes children and poverty is assigned at the household level. Official poverty uses total household income and household size and the official Census poverty thresholds; alternative poverty uses total cash income plus the EITC and child tax credits and other transfers minus FICA and state and local taxes. Native household heads are those who were born in the United States or Puerto Rico or outlying areas or who were born abroad to U.S. parents, immigrant heads are other foreign born. See text for details.

An advantage of this approach over the time series approach is that it allows for a common time trend that may confound the simple time series. The first panel of the table presents the estimates for the data in figures 11.21 through 11.26 — children in immigrant- and native-headed households. The first number, for example, shows that a 1 percentage point increase in the unemployment rate leads to a 0.82 percentage point increase in the official poverty rate for children in native-headed households versus a 0.92 percentage point increase for immigrants. We present similar figures for alternative poverty and extreme poverty. Although few of the coefficients are statistically significant, the results from this first panel of table 11.6 show that immigrant child poverty rates increase more with unemployment than those of native children; that is, the estimates in the second row are everywhere higher than those in the first row. Second, the safety net provides less protection

FIGURE 11.25 / Change in Unemployment Rate and Child Poverty, 2007–2009, by State, Below 100 Percent Alternative Poverty, Native Heads

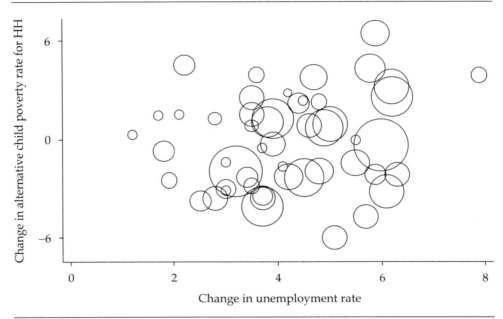

Source: Authors' calculations based on 2008 and 2010 CPS Annual and Social Economic Supplement Data.
Note: Scatterplots of state data where each point is the change in unemployment rate and poverty for a state between the peak and through of the contraction (2007–2009). Sample includes children and poverty is assigned at the household level. Official poverty uses total household income and household size and the official Census poverty thresholds; alternative poverty uses total cash income plus the EITC and child tax credits and other transfers minus FICA and state and local taxes. Native household heads are those who were born in the United States or Puerto Rico or outlying areas or who were born abroad to U.S. parents, immigrant heads are other foreign born. See text for details.

for immigrant children than for native children: a 1 percentage point increase in the unemployment rate increases alternative poverty by 0.59 for natives (down from 0.82 for official poverty), whereas immigrant poverty increases by 1.5 percentage points (up from 0.92 for official poverty). This is consistent with lower safety net participation for immigrants since reform.[31]

We explore this further by presenting similar estimates for non-native children with Mexican heads versus non-Mexican non-native heads (panel 2), naturalized heads versus noncitizen heads (panel 3), and noncitizen Hispanic heads versus noncitizen non-Hispanic heads (panel 4). In each panel, the second row represents the group (for example, Mexican, noncitizen, Hispanic noncitizen) more likely to be affected by the changes in eligibility due to welfare reform. The results are strik-

FIGURE 11.26 / Change in Unemployment Rate and Child Poverty, 2007–2009, by State, Below 100 Percent Poverty, Immigrant Heads

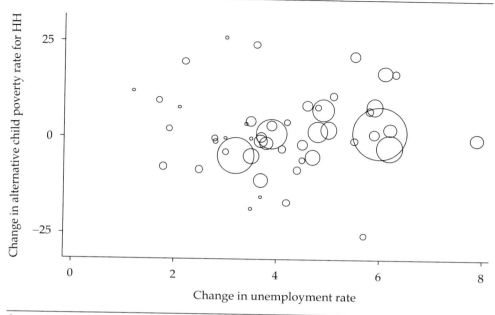

Source: Authors' calculations based on 2008 and 2010 CPS Annual and Social Economic Supplement Data.

Note: Scatterplots of state data where each point is the change in unemployment rate and poverty for a state between the peak and through of the contraction (2007–2009). Sample includes children and poverty is assigned at the household level. Official poverty uses total household income and household size and the official Census poverty thresholds; alternative poverty uses total cash income plus the EITC and child tax credits and other transfers minus FICA and state and local taxes. Native household heads are those who were born in the United States or Puerto Rico or outlying areas or who were born abroad to U.S. parents, immigrant heads are other foreign born. See text for details.

ing, though not always very precisely estimated. In each panel, the more affected group shows a far larger increase in child poverty and far less protection from the safety net. For example, a 1 percentage point increase in the unemployment rate leads to a 0.89 percentage point increase in official poverty for children in households headed by the Mexican born versus a 0.34 percentage point increase for those in households headed by other foreign born. Using alternative poverty, the gap grows to 2.69 for Mexican-born heads compared to 0.17 for other foreign-born heads. In each panel, the group more affected by welfare reform (second in panel) shows a larger sensitivity of alternative poverty to increases in the unemployment rate. All four coefficients for the effect of unemployment on poverty for the noncitizen heads are statistically significant.

TABLE 11.6 / Impact of State Unemployment Rates on State Child Poverty Rates, 2007–2009

	Below 100% Poverty	Below 100% Aternative Poverty	Below 50% Poverty	Below 50% Alternative Poverty
Sample: All children				
Native head	0.82**	0.59**	0.04	0.17
	(0.31)	(0.29)	(0.22)	(0.17)
Non-native head	0.92	1.50**	0.82*	0.76
	(0.83)	(0.63)	(0.47)	(0.46)
Sample: All children with non-native heads				
Non-Mexican head	0.34	0.17	0.31	0.16
	(1.03)	(0.80)	(0.60)	(0.47)
Mexican head	0.89	2.69**	1.38	1.32*
	(1.22)	(1.11)	(0.83)	(0.76)
Sample: All children with non-native heads				
Naturalized head	−0.42	0.74	0.36	0.15
	(1.15)	(0.96)	(0.74)	(0.66)
Noncitizen head	2.54**	2.46**	1.43**	1.28**
	(1.06)	(0.94)	(0.68)	(0.57)
Sample: All children with noncitizen heads				
Non-Hispanic head	0.79	−0.80	1.59	1.56
	(1.76)	(1.37)	(1.15)	(1.01)
Hispanic head	2.44**	3.18***	1.29	1.14
	(1.05)	(1.14)	(0.84)	(0.76)

Source: Authors' calculations.
Note: Each cell in the table presents the estimate of a regression of change in state child poverty rates on change in state unemployment rate for 2007–2009. Estimates are weighted using the population in the cell. Sample includes children and poverty is assigned at the household level. Official poverty uses total household income and household size and the official Census poverty thresholds; alternative poverty uses total cash income plus the EITC and child tax credits and other transfers minus FICA and state and local taxes. Native household heads are those who were born in the United States or Puerto Rico or outlying areas or who were born abroad to U.S. parent(s), immigrant heads are other foreign born. See text for details.
*p < 0.10; **p < 0.05; ***p < 0.01

CONCLUSIONS

The 1996 federal welfare reform legislation has ushered in a new era for the safety net in the United States. As is well known, welfare reform replaced AFDC with TANF, introducing lifetime limits on participation and stringent work requirements. Some fifteen years later, welfare caseloads have decreased dramatically and TANF provides minimal countercyclical aid. But, less known is that not only did PRWORA "change welfare as we know it," it also changed immigration policy as we know it. PRWORA severely curtailed access to TANF, as well as to other key safety net programs such as food stamps and SSI access, for legal immigrants who previously had been treated the same as natives. Notably, the policy essentially devolved immigration policy to states, which are now engaged in many aspects of immigration policy around hiring and employment, driver's licenses, and others that had previously been in the federal realm.

In this chapter, we comprehensively examine program participation and poverty for immigrants with respect to natives in the era since welfare reform. We update the existing literature by focusing on children, updating the analysis through 2009, and paying particular attention to the well-being of children using official and alternative poverty measures.

We find that participation in the safety net declined for immigrants, and that the declines were largest for food stamps and SSI (the programs with the most severe restrictions for immigrants). Medicaid-SCHIP participation actually increased for immigrants compared to natives which may reflect important outreach efforts of those programs to minority groups. We find that among low-income households with children, immigrant households rely more heavily on earnings and less on the safety net, and these differences have grown since welfare reform. Using variation across states in the magnitude of the Great Recession, our results show that labor market contractions have led to larger increases in poverty rates for children in immigrant-headed households than in native-headed households. Our results also show that the safety net acts to dampen the effects of the economic downturn on child poverty for native-headed households but offers measurably less protection for immigrant-headed households.

Chapter prepared for the project "Immigration, Poverty, and Socioeconomic Inequality," organized by the National Poverty Center and the Russell Sage Foundation. We thank David Card, Steve Raphael, Laura Hill, Magnus Lofstrom, Sheldon Danziger, Cybelle Fox, Madeline Zavodny, Pia Orrenius, Frank Bean, and Signe-Mary McKernan, and other preconference participants and book chapter authors for helpful suggestions and Matthew Larsen for excellent research assistance. Bitler worked on this chapter while visiting the Federal Reserve Bank of San Francisco. The views in this chapter are solely the responsibility of the authors and should not be interpreted as reflecting the views of the Federal Reserve Bank of San Francisco or the Board of Governors of the Federal Reserve System.

APPENDIX: DATA AND SOURCES

Contractions and expansions: We identified annual periods of contractions as the range of years from lowest to highest annual unemployment and the expansions as the range of years from highest to lowest annual unemployment rates that are near the beginning and end points of the various NBER recessions (National Bureau of Economic Research 2012). The contraction periods are 2000–2003 (NBER recession: 3/2001–11/2001), and 2007–2009 (NBER recession 12/2007–6/2009). The expansion periods are 1992–2000 and 2003–2007. The end period of 2009 for the most recent contraction may end up not being the peak annual unemployment period, but is the last year for which the bulk of our data are available.

AFDC/TANF administrative data on caseloads and expenditures: TANF caseloads and expenditures are from the Office of Family Assistance, TANF Data and Reports, http://www.acf.hhs.gov/programs/ofa/programs/tanf/data-reports (accessed March 22, 2013). TANF total expenditures includes all expenditures (maintenance of effort from the state and federal sources, including separate state programs, combined federal and state expenditures on assistance, nonassistance, and both together, "Table F—Combined Spending of Federal and State Funds Expended in FY 2009"). Federal stimulus American Recovery and Reinvestment Act (ARRA) is included in the 2009 data. The average monthly TANF benefit is the average family benefit for 2006, inflated to be in 2009 real dollars. See DHHS, Office of Family Assistance, *Eight Annual Report to Congress,* June 1, 2009, http://www.acf.hhs.gov/programs/ofa/resource/eighth-annual-report-to-congress (accessed March 22, 2013). All AFDC and TANF data are for the fiscal year (year ending September 30).

Food Stamp administrative data on caseloads and expenditures: Caseload and expenditures come from unpublished U.S. Department of Agriculture (USDA) data generously provided by Katie Fitzpatrick and John Kirlin, of the Economic Research Service, USDA.

Reduced Price School Lunch and Breakfast caseloads and expenditures: These figures can be found in table 4 (recipients, lunch), table 6 (costs, lunch), table 8 (recipients, breakfast), and table 10 (costs, breakfast) at the USDA Food and Nutrition Service, Data and Statistics, http://www.fns.usda.gov/fns/key_data/march-2010.pdf. Recipients are average daily (accessed March 22, 2012).

Unemployment Insurance administrative data on caseloads and expenditures: Data for calendar years come from unpublished data provided by the Office of the Chief Economist at the Department of Labor. The average benefit is the weekly average benefit amount for 2009, quarter 4, from "Unemployment Insurance Data Summary," http://workforcesecurity.doleta.gov/unemploy/content/data_stats/datasum09/DataSum_2009_4.pdf (accessed March 22, 2013).

Deflator: The CPI-U is from the "Economic Report of the President," U.S. Government Printing Office, http://www.gpo.gov/fdsys/browse/collection.action?collectionCode=ERP (accessed March 22, 2013).

TABLE 11.A1 / Immigrant Eligibility, State TANF

	State Option to Bar but State Chooses Not to		State Fill-in Programs, Post-Enactment Immigrants During Five-Year Bar											
	Pre-Enactment Immigrants	Post-Enactment Immigrants, Post Five-Year	1997	1998	1999	2000	2001	2002	2003	2004	2005	2006	2007	2008
Alabama	X	X												
Alaska	X	X												
Arizona	X	X												
Arkansas	X	X												
California	X	X		X	X	X	X	X	X	X	X	X	X	X
Colorado	X	X												
Connecticut	X	X	X^a	X^a	X^a	X^a	X^a	X^a						
Delaware	X	X			X^a	X^a	X^a	X^a	X	X	X	X	X	X
District of Columbia	X	X												
Florida	X	X												
Georgia	X	X		X	X	X	X	X	X	X	X			
Hawaii	X	X		X	X	X	X	X	X	X	X	X	X	X
Idaho	X	X		X	X	X	X	X	X	X	X	X	X	X
Illinois	X	X												
Indiana	X	X												
Iowa		X												
Kansas		X												
Kentucky		X												
Louisiana		X												

TABLE 11.A1 / (Continued)

	State Option to Bar but State Chooses Not to		State Fill-in Programs, Post-Enactment Immigrants During Five-Year Bar											
	Pre-Enactment Immigrants	Post-Enactment Immigrants, Post Five-Year	1997	1998	1999	2000	2001	2002	2003	2004	2005	2006	2007	2008
Maine	X	X	X	X	X	X	X	X	X	X	X	X	X	X
Maryland	X	X	X[a]	X	X	X	X	X	X	X	X	X	X	X
Massachusetts	X	X	X[a]	X[a]	X[a]	X[a]	X[a]	X[a]						
Michigan	X	X												
Minnesota	X	X												
Mississippi														
Missouri	X	X		X	X	X	X	X	X					
Montana	X	X												
Nebraska	X	X		X	X	X	X	X	X	X	X	X	X	X
Nevada	X	X												
New Hampshire	X	X												
New Jersey	X	X												
New Mexico	X	X		X	X	X	X	X	X	X	X	X	X	X
New York	X	X		X	X	X	X	X	X	X	X	X	X	X
North Carolina	X	X												
North Dakota	X	X												
Ohio	X	X												
Oklahoma	X	X												

Oregon	X	X	X	X	X	X	X	X	X	X	X	X
Pennsylvania	X	X	X	X	X	X	X	X	X	X	X	X
Rhode Island	X	X	X	X	X	X	X	X	X	X	X	X
South Carolina	X			X	X	X	X	X	X	X		
South Dakota	X											
Tennessee	X	X	X	X	X	X	X	X	X			
Texas	X											
Utah	X	X	X	X	X	X	X	X	X	X	X	X
Vermont	X	X	X	X	X	X	X	X	X	X	X	X
Virginia	X	X										
Washington	X		X	X	X	X	X	X	X	X	X	X
West Virginia	X											
Wisconsin	X	X	X	X	X	X	X	X	X	X	X	X
Wyoming	X	X	X	X	X	X	X	X	X	X	X	X

Source: Authors' compilation based on Welfare Rules Database (http://anfdata.urban.org/wrd/WRDWelcome.cfm) cross-checked with Wendy Zimmerman and Karen Tumlin (1999) and the National Immigration Law Center (2002) and (2004).

Note: An "X" indicates that the state covers Legal Permanent Residents (LPRs) in that year without any caveats and the state has implemented TANF. Prior to TANF implementation, AFDC rules dictate eligibility. Certain subgroups of immigrants may be covered in unmarked states (see source data for details). State policies electing whether to bar immigrants (first two columns) rarely changed over time; "X" indicates covered as of TANF implementation. Exceptions include Idaho and North Dakota (both began coverage for post-enactment, post-five-year bar group in 2004) and Montana (coverage for pre-enactment group discontinued in 2002; coverage for post-enactment, post-five-year bar discontinued in 2002 and reinstated in 2009). The coverage indicator is consistent across sources except for the following cases: for pre-enactment immigrants: Alabama in 1998; Mississippi in 1998, 2002, and 2004; and Montana in 2002 and 2004. For post-enactment post, five-year bar: Alabama, Florida, Idaho, Louisiana, Ohio, and Utah in 1998; Arkansas, Montana, and South Carolina in 2002 and 2003; North Dakota in 2004. For post-enactment, during five-year bar: Hawaii, New Mexico, and New York in 1998 and Georgia 2004. In these cases the cross checked sources indicate opposite coverage of what is listed.

[a]Immigrants only eligible after they have resided in this state for six months.

TABLE 11.A2 / Immigrant Eligibility, State Medicaid

	Pre-Enactment	State Option to Bar				State Fill-in Programs, Post-Enactment Immigrants During Five-Year Bar				
		Post-Enactment, Post Five-Year Bar								
		1998	2002	2005	2008	1998	2002	2005	2006	2007
Alabama	X		a	a	a					
Alaska	X	X	X	X	X					
Arizona	X		X	X	X					
Arkansas	X	X	X	X	X					
California	X	X	X	X	X	X	X	X	X	X
Colorado	X	X	X	X	X					
Connecticut	X	X	X	X	X	X	X	X	X	X
Delaware	X	X	X	X	X	X	X	X	X	X
District of Columbia	X		X	X	X				X	X
Florida	X	X	X	X	X					
Georgia	X	X	X	X	X					
Hawaii	X	X	X	X	X	X	X^b	X^b	$X^{b,c}$	$X^{b,c}$
Idaho	X			X	X					
Illinois	X	X	X	X	X	$X^{b,c}$	X^d	X^d	X^d	X^b
Indiana	X		a	X	X					
Iowa	X	X	X	X	X					
Kansas	X	X	X	X	X					
Kentucky	X	X	X	X	X					
Louisiana	X	X	X	X	X					
Maine	X	X	X	X	X	X	X	X	X	X
Maryland	X	X	X	X	X	$X^{b,c}$	$X^{b,c}$	X	X^c	$X^{b,c}$
Massachusetts	X	X	X	X	X	X	X	X^e	X^e	X^e
Michigan	X	X	X	X	X		X^c			
Minnesota	X	X	X	X	X	X	X	X	X	X
Mississippi	X		a	a	a					
Missouri	X	X	X	X	X					
Montana	X	X	X	X	X					X^b
Nebraska	X	X	X	X	X	X	X	X	X	X
Nevada	X	X	X	X	X					
New Hampshire	X	X	X	X	X					
New Jersey	X	X	X	X	X			X	X	X^f	X^f
New Mexico	X		X	X	X					
New York	X	X	X	X	X			X	X	X	X
North Carolina	X	X	X	X	X					
North Dakota	X	X	a	a	a					
Ohio	X		a	a	a					
Oklahoma	X		X	X	X					
Oregon	X		X	X	X					
Pennsylvania	X	X	X	X	X	X^g	X	X	X	X
Rhode Island	X	X	X	X	X	$X^{b,c}$	$X^{b,c}$	$X^{b,c}$	X^b	X^b
South Carolina	X		X	X	X					
South Dakota	X		X	X	X					

TABLE 11.A2 / (Continued)

| | | State Option to Bar | | | | State Fill-in Programs, Post-Enactment Immigrants During Five-Year Bar | | | | |
| | Pre-Enactment | Post-Enactment, Post Five-Year Bar | | | | | | | | |
		1998	2002	2005	2008	1998	2002	2005	2006	2007
Tennessee	X	X	X	X	X					
Texas	X		a	a	a		X[b]	X[b]	X[b]	X[b]
Utah	X	X	X	X	X					
Vermont	X	X	X	X	X					
Virginia	X		a	a	a					
Washington	X		X	X	X	X[g]	X[b,c]	X[h]	X[h]	X[h]
West Virginia	X		X	X	X					
Wisconsin	X	X	X	X	X					
Wyoming	a		a	a	a					

Source: Authors' compilation based on Wendy Zimmerman, Karen Tumlin, and Jason Ost (1999) for 1998 and National Immigration Law Center for 2002, 2005, 2006, 2007, and 2008.

Note: An "X" indicates that the state covers Legal Permanent Residents (LPRs) in that year (see footnotes for major exceptions). Certain subgroups of immigrants may be covered in unmarked states (see source data for details). In 1998 a blank for post-enactment, post- five-year bar can mean the state has not implemented this policy yet.

[a]Only to LPRs with forty quarters of work and the veteran and "refugee" categories.
[b]Available for children.
[c]Available for pregnant women.
[d]Only available to children, pregnant women, or disabled immigrants.
[e]Seniors and disabled eligible up to 100 percent FPL; children up to 200 percent FPL. All children are eligible for preventative care.
[f]Children and parents are eligible. Beginning in 2007, limited funds for prenatal care are available for up to 200 percent of the federal poverty line.
[g]Must be a resident for six months (Pennsylvania) or one year (Washington) before eligibility begins.
[h]Seniors and disabled immigrants receiving cash assistance are eligible. Prenatal care is available. Children are covered up to 100 percent of the FPL, however total allowances are capped.

TABLE 11.A3 / Immigrant Eligibility, State SCHIP

	State Fill-in Programs, Post-Enactment Immigrants During Five-Year Bar				
	2002	2004	2005	2006	2007
Alabama					
Alaska					
Arizona					
Arkansas					
California	X	X	X	X	X
Colorado					
Connecticut	X	X	X	X	X
Delaware					
District of Columbia	X	X	X	X	X
Florida	X	X	X[a]	X[a]	X[a]
Georgia					
Hawaii	X	X	X	X	X
Idaho					
Illinois	X	X	X	X	X
Indiana	X				
Iowa					
Kansas					
Kentucky					
Louisiana					
Maine	X	X	X	X	X
Maryland	X	X			X
Massachusetts	X	X	X	X	X
Michigan					
Minnesota	X	X	X	X	X
Mississippi					
Missouri					
Montana					
Nebraska	X	X	X	X	X
Nevada					
New Hampshire					
New Jersey	X	X	X	X	X
New Mexico					
New York	X	X	X	X	X
North Carolina					
North Dakota					
Ohio					
Oklahoma					
Oregon					
Pennsylvania	X	X	X	X	X
Rhode Island	X	X	X	X	X
South Carolina					
South Dakota					
Tennessee					

TABLE 11.A3 / (*Continued*)

	State Fill-in Programs, Post-Enactment Immigrants During Five-Year Bar				
	2002	2004	2005	2006	2007
Texas	X	X	X	X	X
Utah					
Vermont					
Virginia					
Washington	X	X	X	X	X
West Virginia					
Wisconsin					
Wyoming					

Source: Authors' compilation based on the National Immigration Law Center for 2002, 2005, 2006, and 2007 and Shawn Fremstad and Laure Cox (2004) for 2004.

Note: Policies listed for SCHIP plans via Medicaid, separate state program, or a combination of the two. An "X" indicates that the state covers Legal Permanent Residents (LPRs) in that year (see note for major exceptions). Sources include the National Immigration Law Center for 2002, 2005, 2006, and 2007 and Shawn Fremstad and Laure Cox (2004) for 2004. Certain subgroups of immigrants may be covered in unmarked states (see source data for details).

[a]*Funding* is capped such that everyone is covered who was covered as of July 1, 2000. However, anyone applying afterwards was put on a waiting list. A second freeze and removal of the waiting list was done in July 2003.

TABLE 11.A4 / Immigrant Eligibility, State SSI

	State Fill-in Programs, Post-Enactment Immigrants			
	1998	2002	2005	2006
Alabama				
Alaska				
Arizona				
Arkansas				
California		X	X	X
Colorado				
Connecticut				
Delaware				
District of Columbia				
Florida				
Georgia				
Hawaii		X	X	X
Idaho				
Illinois[a]				
Indiana				
Iowa				
Kansas				
Kentucky				
Louisiana				
Maine	X	X	X	X
Maryland				
Massachusetts				
Michigan				
Minnesota				
Mississippi				
Missouri				
Montana				
Nebraska		X	X	X
Nevada				
New Hampshire	X[b]	X[b]	X[b]	X[b]
New Jersey				
New Mexico				
New York				
North Carolina				
North Dakota				
Ohio				
Oklahoma				
Oregon	X			
Pennsylvania				
Rhode Island				
South Carolina				
South Dakota				
Tennessee				
Texas				
Utah				

TABLE 11.A4 / (Continued)

	State Fill-in Programs, Post-Enactment Immigrants			
	1998	2002	2005	2006
Vermont				
Virginia				
Washington				
West Virginia				
Wisconsin				
Wyoming				

Source: Authors' compilation based on Wendy Zimmerman and Karen Tumlin (1999) for 1998, and the National Immigration Law Center for 2002, 2005, and 2006.

Note: An "X" indicates that the state covers Legal Permanent Residents (LPRs) in that year (see footnotes for major exceptions). Following the Balanced Budget Act of 1997, all immigrants receiving SSI prior to 1996 as well as those who entered before 1996 and would become eligible, were eligible for SSI.

aIllinois is recorded immigrants was also covering pre-enactment immigrants who are sixty-five or older, and are determined ineligible because they do not have a disability in 2002, 2005, and 2006 and covering refugees past their seven-year quota in 2005 and 2006.

bFunds only available after the individual exceeds the five-year bar.

TABLE 11.A5 / Immigrant Eligibility, State Food Stamps

	State Fill-in Programs, Pre-Enactment Immigrants				State Fill-in Programs, Post-Enactment Immigrants									
	1998	2001	2002	2003	1998	2001	2002	2003	2004	2005	2006	2007	2008	2009
Alabama														
Alaska														
Arizona														
Arkansas														
California	X	X	X	X	X	X	X	X	X	X	X	X	X	X
Colorado														
Connecticut	X	X	X	X	X	X	X[a]	X	X	X	X	X	X	X
Delaware														
District of Columbia														
Florida	X[b]													
Georgia														
Hawaii														
Idaho														
Illinois	X	X[c]	X[c]											
Indiana														
Iowa														
Kansas														
Kentucky														
Louisiana														
Maine	X	X	X	X	X	X	X	X	X	X	X	X	X	X
Maryland					X[d1]	X[d]	X[d]	X[d]						
Massachusetts	X	X	X[a]		X	X	X[a]							
Michigan														
Minnesota	X	X	X	X	X	X	X	X	X	X	X	X	X	X
Mississippi														
Missouri	X[e]													
Montana														
Nebraska	X	X	X	X	X	X	X	X	X	X	X	X	X	X
Nevada														
New Hampshire												X		
New Jersey	X	X[f]	X[f]											
New Mexico														
New York	X[d]	X[g]	X[g]											
North Carolina														
North Dakota														
Ohio	X[e]	X[h]	X[h]											
Oklahoma														
Oregon														
Pennsylvania														
Rhode Island	X	X[i]	X[i]											
South Carolina														

TABLE 11.A5 / (Continued)

	State Fill-in Programs, Pre-Enactment Immigrants				State Fill-in Programs, Post-Enactment Immigrants									
	1998	2001	2002	2003	1998	2001	2002	2003	2004	2005	2006	2007	2008	2009
South Dakota														
Tennessee														
Texas	X[e]	X[j]	X[j]											
Utah														
Vermont														
Virginia														
Washington	X	X	X	X	X	X	X	X	X	X	X	X	X	X
West Virginia														
Wisconsin	X	X	X	X	X	X	X	X	X	X	X	X	X	X
Wyoming														

Source: Authors' compilation based on Wendy Zimmerman and Karen Tumlin (1999) for 1998, Schwartz (2001) for 2001, National Immigrant Law Center for 2002, and the USDA's "Food Stamp Program State Options Report" for 2003–2009.

Note: An "X" indicates that the state covers legal permanent residents (LPRs) in that year (see footnotes for major exceptions). In 1998 the Agriculture Research, Extension, and Education Reform Act restored eligibility for pre-enactment immigrants receiving payments or assistance for blindness or disability, those who were sixty-five or older on August 22, 1996, and pre-enactment minors. The 2002 Farm Bill gave eligibility for Post-Enactment immigrants who have lived in the United States for five years, and for all immigrant children and disabled individuals. Effective October 1 , 2002, "qualified" immigrants receiving disability-related assistance will be eligible. Effective April 1, 2003, "qualified" immigrants who have lived in the United States for five or more years as a "qualified" immigrant will be eligible. Effective October 1, 2003, "qualified" immigrant children will be eligible, regardless of their date of entry.
[a]Qualified immigrants in Massachusetts in 2002 and immigrants entering after April 1, 1998, in Connecticut in 2002 must meet a six-month residency requirement.
[b]Only children, elderly, and disabled are covered.
[c]Only available to those age sixty to sixty-four (without a disability) or parents residing with children who are eligible for federal food stamps.
[d]Only available to children younger than eighteen.
[e]Only available to former food stamp recipients.
[f]Only eligible if the immigrant is sixty-five or older; a legal guardian living with dependent children under eighteen; mentally or physically incapacitated; receiving GA benefits and considered unemployable. Must apply for citizenship within sixty days of being certified for food stamps.
[g]Only eligible between the ages of sixty and sixty-eight. Must live in the same county as on August 22, 1996.
[h]Only eligible if between sixty-five and sixty-eight, are eligible for SSI, have been in the United States for five years, and are Ohio residents as of August 22, 1996.
[i]Must be residents of Rhode Island before August 22, 1996.
[j]Only eligible if turned sixty-five after August 22, 1996, but before March 1, 1998, and have received food stamps anytime from September 1996 to August 1997.

NOTES

1. This discussion of the political context for the immigrant policy changes is based on Ronald Haskins (2009).
2. Because immigrant families are less advantaged than the native born, and most safety net programs condition on being low income, a comparison of participation rates in the full population is not apples to apples.
3. A small EITC is available for childless individuals.
4. SCHIP was created in 1997 to provide insurance coverage for low- to moderate-income children, that is, those in families with incomes just above states' Medicaid eligibility threshold. Some states have SCHIPs that are expansions of their Medicaid programs for children, and others have stand-alone programs.
5. Another element of the safety net is Supplemental Nutrition Program for Women, Infants, and Children (WIC), which provides food packages and nutritional counseling to income-eligible pregnant and post-partum women and children up to age five. Some states also provide general assistance to low-income individuals or have state-specific supplements to the EITC or SSI.
6. Since PWRORA was enacted, the only general limitation on eligibility is for able-bodied adults without dependents, who were limited in how many months of food stamps they could get in a given time period. These restrictions for some adults have been lifted in many states during the Great Recession.
7. Douglas Massey presents the history of U.S. policy toward Latino immigrants, with a focus on policy changes related to legal status (chapter 9, this volume).
8. Unauthorized immigrants can file and pay taxes using an individual taxpayer identification number (ITIN). They are not, however, eligible to receive the EITC.
9. As documented in table 11.2, refugees and asylum seekers and those in the military face different rules. Given they are a relatively small share of total qualified immigrants, we do not discuss these rules in the text.
10. The 1996 IIRIRA also changed rules for those who sponsor legal immigrants arriving or becoming LPRs, requiring that sponsors' income be treated as available to the immigrants when assessing eligibility for needs-based assistance costs.
11. A growing literature uses this state-year policy variation in access to the safety net to estimate the impact of reforms on safety net participation (Borjas 2003; Kaushal and Kaestner 2005; Royer 2005; Watson 2010; Borjas 2011), food insecurity (Borjas 2004; Ratcliffe, McKernan, and Zhang 2011), and location choice (Kaushal 2005).
12. Our decision to exclude 1994 survey year CPS data comes from communication with various immigration scholars. Dianne Schmidley and Gregory Robinson (1998) discuss some of these issues, noting potential issues with comparability for 1994 and 1995. Various papers include the 1995 data (for example, Borjas 2004) although sometimes with special adjusted weights created by Jeffrey Passel. In general, it is desirable to include 1995 data as it increases our pre-PRWORA sample (income is measured for the 1994 year). Findings are generally robust to omitting the 1995 survey year (1994 calendar year) measures.
13. Those born outside the United States are asked when they came to the United States to

stay. Responses pool the most recent year with the most recent two to three years (and the first three months of the current year). Before this, two-year periods of arrival are pooled. Consequently, we can consistently defined a variable that is 1 if the immigrant arrived at least four years and four months ago and at most six years and three months ago for even years, and at least five years and four months and at most seven years and three months for odd years. Because this question asks when you came to the United States to stay, research suggests this may not correspond to either the first or last U.S. trip (Redstone and Massey 2004). For individuals born in Puerto Rico or other territories or born abroad of U.S. parents, we set this variable to 0. We can identify for most years whether individuals came to the United States before August 1996 or after. We cannot do so consistently for 1997, and therefore do not define it for survey year 1997.

14. We choose to analyze households because use of some of the safety net programs (food stamps, school lunch, LIHEAP, public housing, and Section 8 rental subsidies) are reported only at the household level. This approach also takes into account income or resource sharing that may occur in households containing multiple families.

15. Note that the CPS questions about cash assistance typically ask about receipt of money from federal, state, or local sources. So, technically, the measure of AFDC-TANF also includes state programs such as general assistance or emergency assistance. These programs are thought to be quite small relative to TANF-AFDC. Similarly, the questions about public housing and SSI mention state, federal and other assistance, suggesting that state add-on SSI and non–federally funded public housing will be captured.

16. In November 2011, the Census Bureau released a report introducing the new Supplemental Poverty Measure, or SPM (Short 2011). The plan is to maintain the official poverty measure but to also release estimates of the SPM each year. Our "alternative income measure" comes from working definitions adopted by the Census Bureau in 1999. It is quite similar to the income concept used in the SPM in that it is net of federal taxes and adds valuation for many in-kind benefits. In particular, we define alternative income by adding to money income the cash value of food stamps, school lunch, and housing subsidies and then subtract payroll taxes, and net federal and state taxes (including the EITC). Our approach is similar to some of the experimental poverty measures tabulated annually at the Census Bureau as in Joe Dalaker (2005). In addition, however, the SPM alters the thresholds used to define poverty by incorporating various expenses and allowing for geographic differences. The overall impact is to increase poverty slightly, from 15.3 to 16.0 among all persons in 2010. Unfortunately, at this time it is not possible to create a consistent series for the SPM over our period of interest.

17. Here we use official poverty because alternative poverty includes many programs for which immigrants are not eligible in some or all years.

18. We use an approach we used in an earlier study (Bitler and Hoynes 2010) to construct annual periods of contraction using the official monthly NBER recession dating combined with examination of the national peaks and troughs in the unemployment rate (for details, see appendix).

19. SCHIP legislation is passed in 1997 and the CPS begins measuring participation in 2000. For all years, we combine Medicaid and SCHIP.

20. Almost all children living with native household heads are themselves natives.

21. Of course, to the extent that states or localities implement new programs that are not

reported in the CPS or increase their spending targeted to the immigrants losing access to benefits, these declines in safety net participation may be slightly overstated. We found no evidence of any substantive such programs in the most recent Great Recession period.

22. We focus here more on entry within the last five years or further back because we have so few pre-PRWORA observations due to the limited years that the CPS includes immigrant status.

23. Unfortunately, given the data restrictions discussed in footnote 13 we cannot do this comparison systematically. First, for some key post-reform years, it is impossible to uniquely classify individuals as pre- and post-enactment (for example, 1997 observations cannot cleanly be assigned as before or after 1996 arrival). Second, the policies are changing frequently across states and over time in a way that complicates a simple differences-in-differences analysis. Because policies at the state and federal level change considerably in the period post-PWRORA but before 2002, it is hard to assign these observations to a consistent treatment or control group. By 2008–2009, however, policies have settled out for the federal government and across states, and it is clear what policies apply across immigrant statuses.

24. On average, for households under 200 percent of poverty, the components we show make up 81 percent of total household income (including food stamps). The three largest remaining categories (pooling 2009 and 1994) are Social Security payments (pools OASI and DI): 5.1 percent, asset income (includes rents, dividends, and interest income): 3.5 percent, and retirement income: 2.8 percent.

25. To do this, we summarized the shares within each bins, and then allocated the native shares according to the relative shares of immigrants in each bin.

26. Mark Ellis, Richard Wright, and Matthew Townley present both poverty trends and decompositions of contributors to poverty at the MSA level by type of destination, separating effects for traditional gateway destinations and new destinations (chapter 5, this volume).

27. We did this by using the IPUMS 1990 census (Ruggles et al. 2008) 1 percent micro data and calculating the share of households with children within each state that were immigrant or native headed. We used these weights to summarize the state-by-year-by native/non-native head weighted percentages for each group.

28. Results for the two reweighting procedures are available on request.

29. Related to this, chapter 13 in this volume presents evidence about the relative well-being of immigrants and natives in Western Europe.

30. Other differences between our measure and the new supplemental measure are discussed in footnote 16.

31. Note that these results lead to different conclusions about the relative well-being of immigrants post reform compared to the trends in poverty in figure 11.20—the time series trends show gains in poverty for immigrants versus natives since welfare reform. Using state variation in the cycle, with the ability to control for secular time trends, leads us to the opposite conclusion.

REFERENCES

Aizer, Anna. 2003. "Low Take-Up in Medicaid: Does Outreach Matter and for Whom?" *American Economic Review* 93(2): 238–41.

———. 2007. "Public Health Insurance, Program Take-up and Child Health." *Review of Economics and Statistics* 89(3): 400–15.

Bitler, Marianne and Hilary Hoynes. 2010. "The State of the Safety Net in the Post-Welfare Reform Era." *Brookings Papers on Economic Activity* 2010 (Fall): 71–127.

Blank, Rebecca. 2001. "What Causes Public Assistance Caseloads to Grow?" *Journal of Human Resources* 36(1): 85–118.

Borjas, George. 1995. "Immigration and Welfare, 1970–1990." *Research in Labor Economics* 14 (April): 251–80.

———. 1999. "Immigration and Welfare Magnets." *Journal of Labor Economics* 17(4): 607–37.

———. 2003. "Welfare Reform, Labor Supply and Health Insurance in the Immigrant Population." *Journal of Health Economics* 22(6): 933–58.

———. 2004. "Food Insecurity and Public Assistance." *Journal of Public Economics* 88(7–8): 1421–43.

———. 2011. "Poverty and Program Participation Among Immigrant Children." *The Future of Children* 21(1): 247–66.

Borjas, George, and Lynette Hilton. 1996. "Immigration and the Welfare State: Immigrant Participation in Means-Tested Entitlement Programs." *Quarterly Journal of Economics* 1996 (May): 575–604.

Capps, Randy, Michael E. Fix, and Everett Henderson. 2009. "Trends in Immigrants' Use of Public Assistance after Welfare Reform." In *Immigrants and Welfare*, edited by Michael E. Fix. New York: Russell Sage Foundation.

Citro, Constance, and Robert Michael, eds. 1995. *Measuring Poverty: A New Approach.* Washington, D.C.: National Academy Press.

Dalaker, Joe. 2005. "Alternative Poverty Estimates in the United States." *Current Population Report* P60–227. Washington, D.C.: U.S. Census Bureau.

Fix, Michael E., and Jeffrey S. Passel. 1999. *Trends in Noncitizens' and Citizens' Use of Public Benefits Following Welfare Reform: 1994–1997.* Washington, D.C.: The Urban Institute.

———. 1994. *Immigration and Immigrants: Setting the Record Straight.* Washington, D.C.: The Urban Institute.

Fix, Michael E., Randy Capps, and Neeraj Kaushal. 2009. "Immigrants and Welfare: Overview." In *Immigrants and Welfare*, edited by Michael E. Fix. New York: Russell Sage Foundation.

Fraker, Thomas M., Alberto P. Martini, James C. Ohls, Michael Ponza, and Elizabeth A. Quinn. 1992. *The Evaluation of the Alabama Food Stamp Cash-Out Demonstration*, vol. 1, *Recipient Impacts*. Princeton, N.J.: Mathematica Policy Research.

Fremstad, Shawn, and Laure Cox. 2004. "Covering New Americans: A Review of Federal and States Policies Related to Immigrants' Eligibility and Access to Publicly Funded Health Insurance." Washington, DC: Kaiser Commission on Medicaid and the Uninsured.

Grogger, Jeffrey, and Lynn Karoly. 2005. *Welfare Reform: Effects of a Decade of Change*. Cambridge, Mass.: Harvard University Press.

Haider, Steven J., Robert F. Schoeni, Yuhua Bao, and Caroline Danielson .2004. "Immigrants, Welfare Reform, and the Economy." *Journal of Policy Analysis and Management* 23(4): 745–64.

Haskins, Ron. 2009. "Limiting Welfare Benefits for Noncitizens: Emergence of Compromises." In *Immigrants and Welfare*, edited by Michael E. Fix. New York: Russell Sage Foundation.

Hoynes, Hilary, and Diane Whitmore Schanzenbach. 2009. "Consumption Reponses to In-Kind Transfers: Evidence from the Introduction of the Food Stamp Program." *American Economic Journal: Applied Economics* 1(4): 109–39.

Hu, Wei-Yin. 1998. "Elderly Immigrants on Welfare." *Journal of Human Resources* 33(3): 711–41.

Joyce, Ted, Tamar Bauer, Howard Minkoff, and Robert Kaestner. 2001. "Welfare Reform and the Perinatal Health and Health Care Use of Latino Women in California, New York City, and Texas." *American Journal of Public Health* 91(11): 1857–64.

Kaestner, Robert, and Neeraj Kaushal. 2005. "Immigrant and Native Responses to Welfare Reform." *Journal of Population Economics* 18(1): 69–92.

Kaushal, Neeraj. 2005. "New Immigrants' Location Choices: Magnets Without Welfare." *Journal of Labor Economics* 23(1): 59–80.

Kaushal, Neeraj, and Robert Kaestner. 2005. "Welfare Reform and Health Insurance of Immigrants." *Health Services Research* 40(3): 697–722.

Kochhar, Rakesh, and D'Vera Cohn. 2011. "Fighting Poverty in a Tough Economy, Americans Move in with Their Relatives." Washington, D.C.: Pew Research Center.

Lofstrom, Magnus, and Frank D. Bean. 2002. "Assessing Immigrant Policy Options: Labor Market Conditions and Post-Reform Declines in Welfare Receipt Among Immigrants." *Demography* 39(4): 617–37.

Massey, Douglas. 2008. *New Faces in New Places: The Changing Geography of American Immigration*. New York: Russell Sage Foundation.

Moffitt, Robert. 1983. "An Economic Model of Welfare Stigma." *American Economic Review* 73(5): 1023–35.

National Immigration Law Center. 2002. *Guide to Immigrant Eligibility for Federal Benefits*, 4th ed. Los Angeles: National Immigration Law Center.

National Bureau of Economic Research (NBER). 2012. "U.S. Business Cycle Expansions and Contractions." Available at: http://www.nber.org/cycles/cyclesmain.html (accessed August 14, 2010).

Ohls, James C., Thomas M. Fraker, Alberto P. Martini, and Michael Ponza. 1992. *The Effects of Cash-Out on Food Use by Food Stamp Program Participants in San Diego*. Alexandria, Va.: U.S. Department of Agriculture, Food and Nutrition Service, Office of Analysis and Evaluation.

Ratcliffe, Caroline, Signe-Mary Mckernan, and Sisi Zhang. 2011. "How Much Does the Supplemental Nutrition Assistance Program Reduce Food Insecurity?" *American Journal of Agricultural Economics* 93(4): 1082–98.

Redstone, Ilana, and Douglas Massey. 2004. "Coming to Stay: An Analysis of the U.S. Census Question on Immigrants' Year of Arrival." *Demography* 41(4): 721–38.

Rendall, Michael S., Peter Brownell, and Sarah Kups. 2011. "Declining Return Migration from the United States to Mexico in the Late-2000s Recession: A Research Note." *Demography* 48(3): 1049–58.

Royer, Heather. 2005. "The Response to a Loss in Medicaid Eligibility: Pregnant Immigrant Mothers in the Wake of Welfare Reform." Mimeo.

Ruggles, Steven, Matthew Sobek, Trent Alexander, Catherine A. Fitch, Ronald Goeken, Patricia Kelly Hall, Miriam King, and Chad Ronnander. 2008. Integrated Public Use Microdata Series: Version 4.0 [Machine-readable database]. Minneapolis: Minnesota Population Center.

Schwartz, Sonya. 2001. "Immigrant Access to Food Stamps: Overcoming Barriers to Participation." *Clearinghouse Review: Journal of Poverty, Law, and Policy* (September-October): 260–75.

Schmidley, A. Dianne, and J. Gregory Robinson. 1998. "How Well Does the Current Population Survey Measure the Foreign Born Population in the United States?" *Population Division* working paper 22. Washington: U.S. Bureau of the Census,

Segreto, Joy, and Ann Morse. 2011. "2011 Immigration-Related Laws and Resolutions in the States (January-June)." Denver, Colo.: National Conference of State Legislatures. Available at: http://www.ncsl.org/default.aspx?TabId=23362 (accessed March 20, 2013).

Short, Kathleen. 2011. "The Research Supplemental Poverty Measure: 2010." *Current Population Reports* P60–241. Washington: U.S. Census Bureau. Available at: http://www.census.gov/hhes/povmeas/methodology/supplemental/research/Short_Research SPM2010.pdf (accessed May 23, 2013).

Short, Kathleen. 2012. "The Research Supplemental Poverty Measure: 2011." *Current Population Reports* P60–244. Washington: U.S. Census Bureau.

Social Security Administration. 2010. *SSI Annual Statistical Report 2009*. Released Sept 2010.

Tax Policy Center. 2010. "Tax Facts on Historical EITC." Washington, D.C.: Urban Institute and Brookings Institution. http://www.taxpolicycenter.org/taxfacts/displayafact.cfm?Docid=37 (accessed March 20, 2013).

U.S. Congress. House of Representatives. 1996. *Background Material and Data on Programs Within the Jurisdiction of the House Committee on Ways and Means*. Green Book. Washington, D.C.: Government Printing Office.

U.S. Department of Agriculture. 2003. "Food Stamp Program State Options Report," 3rd ed. Washington: U.S. Department of Agriculture, Food and Nutrition Service.

———. 2004. "Food Stamp Program State Options Report," 4th ed. Washington: U.S. Department of Agriculture, Food and Nutrition Service.

———. 2005. "Food Stamp Program State Options Report," 5th ed. Washington: U.S. Department of Agriculture, Food and Nutrition Service.

———. 2006. "Food Stamp Program State Options Report," 6th ed. Washington: U.S. Department of Agriculture, Food and Nutrition Service.

———. 2007. "Food Stamp Program State Options Report," 7th ed. Washington: U.S. Department of Agriculture, Food and Nutrition Service.

———. 2008. "Food Stamp Program State Options Report," 8th ed. Washington: U.S. Department of Agriculture, Food and Nutrition Service.

U.S. Department of Health and Human Services (DHHS). 2008. *Temporary Assistance for Needy Families Program (TANF): Eighth Annual Report to Congress*. Washington, D.C.: U.S.

Department of Health and Human Services, Administration for Children and Families, Office of Family Assistance.

U.S. Department of Health and Human Services, Office of Family Assistance, TANF Caseload Data, 1995–2008. Available at: archive.acf.hhs.gov/programs/ofa/data-reports/caseload/caseload_recent.html (accessed May 23, 2013).

U.S. Department of Labor. 2009. "Unemployment Insurance Data Summary, 4th Quarter 2009." Available at: http://workforecesecurity.doleta.gov/unemploy/content/data_stats/datasum09/DataSum_2009_4.pdf (accessed August 14, 2010).

Van Hook, Jennifer. 2003. "Welfare Reform Chilling Effects on Noncitizens: Changes in Noncitizen Recipiency or Shifts in Citizenship Status?" *Social Science Quarterly* 84(3): 613–31.

Van Hook, Jennifer, and Frank Bean. 2009 "Immigrant Welfare Receipt: Implication for Immigrant Settlement and Integration." In *The Impact of Welfare Reform on America's Newcomers,* edited by Michael Fox. New York: Russell Sage Foundation.

Van Hook, Jennifer, and Weiwei Zhang. 2011. "Who Stays? Who Goes? Selective Emigration Among the Foreign-Born." *Population Research and Policy Review* 30(1): 1–24.

Wasem, Ruth Ellen. 2010. "Noncitizen Eligibility for Federal Public Assistance: Policy Overview and Trends." *CRS Report for Congress* RL33809. Washington, D.C.: Congressional Research Service.

Watson, Tara. 2010. "Inside The Refrigerator: Immigration Enforcement and Chilling Effects In Medicaid Participation." *NBER* working paper 16278. Cambridge, Mass.: National Bureau of Economic Research.

Zavodny, Madeline. 1999. "Determinants of Recent Immigrants' Locational Choices." *International Migration Review* 33(4): 1014–30.

Zimmerman, Wendy, and Karen Tumlin. 1999. "Patchwork Policies: State Assistance for Immigrants Under Welfare Reform." Occasional paper no. 24. Washington, D.C.: The Urban Institute.

Zimmerman, Wendy, Karen C. Tumlin, and Jason Ost. 1999. "State Snapshots of Public Benefits for Immigrants: A Supplemental Report to 'Patchwork Policies.'" Occasional paper no. 24 supplemental report. Washington, D.C.: Urban Institute.

Chapter 12

Immigration and Redistributive Social Policy

Cybelle Fox, Irene Bloemraad, and Christel Kesler

The pervasiveness of contemporary immigration and the historic image of the United States as a nation of immigrants make it hard to remember that in 1965 almost 95 percent of the U.S. population was native born (Gibson and Lennon 1999). Immigration was a negligible issue, and few could imagine the diversity we see today. Indeed, in signing the Immigration and Nationality Act of 1965, President Lyndon B. Johnson proclaimed, "This bill . . . is not a revolutionary bill. It does not affect the lives of millions. It will not reshape the structure of our daily lives."[1] Johnson could not have been more wrong. The removal of racially restrictive national-origin quotas and their replacement by a set of preference categories based on family ties, economic contribution and flight from persecution opened the doors to mass migration. By 2011, more than 40 million people, or 13 percent of the country's residents, were born outside the United States. In California, the most "immigrant" state in the nation, more than one in four people were foreign-born.

The dramatic changes in immigration since 1965 have overlapped with other significant transformations in U.S. society. About a decade or so after Johnson signed the Immigration and Nationality Act, the United States started on a trajectory of growing inequality between the richest and poorest residents, one that continues to the present day (Piketty and Saez 2003; McCarty, Poole, and Rosenthal 2006). Rising inequality, however, has not been offset by more generous welfare spending for poor people. Over this period, the politics of welfare retrenchment steadily gained ground. In 1996, President Clinton, fulfilling his pledge to "end welfare as we know it," signed the Personal Responsibility and Work Opportunity Reconciliation Act (PRWORA).[2] As a result, the number of welfare recipients plummeted from an all time high of 14.2 million in 1994 to 3.8 million by 2008 (Danziger 2010, 528).

Some observers suggest that these phenomena may be linked. Immigration scholars and advocates, for example, point out that among its provisions, PRWORA included an entire section affecting noncitizens, in many cases eliminating their eligibility altogether.[3] More broadly, in their detailed look at economic inequality and political polarization, Nolan McCarty, Keith Poole, and Howard Rosenthal have argued that the "movement to the right, away from redistribution, has been facilitated by immigration. . . . Because noncitizens are ineligible to vote, less pressure to redistribute comes from the bottom of the income distribution" (2006, 13). Others suggest a more diffuse mechanism: as societies diversify due to immigration, feelings of solidarity and mutual obligations fade and, with it, social trust and a political commitment to redistribution (Goodhart 2004a, 2004b; Putnam 2007). Has the dramatic rise in immigration affected redistribution in the United States? This chapter investigates that question by examining variation in U.S. state spending on low-income individuals over time.

We examine some of the reasons that two seemingly separate phenomena — rising immigration and changing social redistribution — might be causally related. Although the subject has been touched on by a handful of scholars, and at times debated by political observers, we know of no study in the United States that systematically lays out distinct theoretical accounts for why these phenomena might be linked. We analyze empirical trends, first through a descriptive profile of patterns at the national level followed by a detailed statistical analysis across U.S. states and over time. Do states with more immigration provide fewer resources to low income residents than states with less immigration? Have states that experienced larger increases in their immigrant population seen more cuts or slower growth in social spending than states with smaller increases in the proportion of immigrants? Our empirical results underscore the enduring significance of racial dynamics in understanding patterns of social spending in the United States. But they also reveal some surprising findings, including evidence that challenges a simple story that growing immigration generates a backlash against redistribution.

WHY MIGHT IMMIGRATION AFFECT REDISTRIBUTIVE SOCIAL SPENDING?

We focus on three possible mechanisms by which immigration might influence redistributive social spending: noncitizen disenfranchisement, racial or immigrant threat, and racial fractionalization. An understanding and appreciation for the distinctions between these models are important not only for careful empirical analysis, but also because the posited mechanisms suggest quite different policy responses for those concerned about redistributive social policy in the United States.

Noncitizen Disenfranchisement

Immigration may hinder redistribution because, with very few exceptions, noncitizens cannot participate in elections. Although the U.S naturalization process is quite open compared to that of many countries, citizenship acquisition is relatively low: fewer than 45 percent of the foreign born were naturalized citizens in 2011. This is in part due to the substantial undocumented population; an estimated 11 million people, about 28 percent of all foreign-born individuals, live as unauthorized residents (Hoefer, Rytina, and Baker 2011; Passel and Cohn 2011). But even among those legally eligible, many do not acquire citizenship, in part because fees have risen precipitously over the last fifteen years and institutional support for naturalization is limited (Bloemraad 2006). The proportion of noncitizens in U.S. states varies significantly, from less than 1 percent in places such as Montana and West Virginia, to 10 percent or more: 15 percent in California, 12 percent in Nevada, 11 percent in Texas, and 10 percent in New York, and New Jersey (for state data, see table 12.A1). Nationally, 7 percent of the population did not hold U.S. citizenship in 2011. The presence of a large group of people excluded from the political system raises important questions about democratic legitimacy. It could also lead to public policies at odds with those that would have been passed if noncitizens had electoral voice (Citrin and Highton 2002).

Potential policy effects depend, however, on whether noncitizens have interests or preferences distinct from those of citizens who participate in elections. Noncitizens might prefer social spending more than U.S. voters because of favorable attitudes to redistribution that they bring from their homelands (Roh 2008), due to sympathy with newly arriving, poorer compatriots, or because of their personal socioeconomic situation. In regards to the latter, in 2009, the median income of noncitizen households was just $39,983 versus $51,919 for native-born households; this income also supported, on average, more people in noncitizen households. Surveys of the general U.S. population typically find greater support for social welfare spending among those with less income (AuClaire 1984; Hasenfeld and Rafferty 1989). If the relationship between socioeconomic condition and support for redistribution is equally applicable to the noncitizen population, we would expect noncitizens to back such policies more than citizens. Indeed, McCarty, Poole, and Rosenthal (2006) conclude that the rise in the number of noncitizens is a crucial explanation for why rising inequality has not translated into more political pressure for redistribution. Noncitizens are disproportionately poor and disenfranchised while citizens, who tend to be richer, vote for policies that benefit themselves.

The disenfranchisement hypothesis rests on three key assumptions: that noncitizens do, in fact, have different policy preferences for redistribution; that, if given the vote, noncitizens would cast a ballot; and that the newly enfranchised could affect policy by voting in support of redistributive social policies. Because virtually no academic analyses of the immigrant disenfranchisement hypothesis have been undertaken, we consider the potential validity of each assumption.

First, scholars know little about the actual policy preferences of noncitizens. Surveys tapping political preferences often restrict their sample to citizens or likely voters. In general opinion polls, interviewers rarely collect data on respondents' citizenship status or birthplace. Even when they do, the sample of noncitizens is usually too small to generate accurate inferences to the entire population of noncitizens.[4]

To get a sense of noncitizens' policy preferences on social spending, we leverage

TABLE 12.1 / Attitudes Toward Taxes and Spending, California Residents, 2010–2012

	Noncitizens	Naturalized Citizens	U.S.-Born Citizens	Registered Voters	Likely Voters
Would you pay higher taxes to maintain health and human services?[a]					
Yes	71.9	52.5	51.5	50.5	48.0
No	26.0	45.2	45.7	46.9	49.6
Don't know	2.1	2.4	2.8	2.6	2.4
Total[c]	100.0	100.1	100.0	100.0	100.0
N	1,119	1,789	8,965	10,063	7,911
Would you support or oppose spending cuts to health and human services?[b]					
Support	21.3	33.6	36.5	38.1	39.8
Oppose	77.1	63.3	60.0	58.4	56.2
Don't know	1.7	3.1	3.5	3.6	4.1
Total[c]	100.1	100.0	100.0	100.1	100.1
N	527	860	4,551	5,136	4,100

Source: Authors' compilation based on pooled Public Policy Institute of California Statewide Surveys, January and May, 2010–2012 (Public Policy Institute of California 2013).
[a]The survey question was "What if the state said it needed more money just to maintain current funding for health and human services? Would you be willing to pay higher taxes for this purpose, or not?" The question in May 2012 differed slightly, asking, "Would you be willing to pay higher taxes for health and human services, or not?" All questions were preceded by the statement, "Tax increases could be used to help reduce the state budget deficit."
[b]The survey question was "Spending cuts could be used to help reduce the state budget deficit. . . . How about cutting spending on health and human services? Do you support or oppose this proposal?"
[c]Percentages are calculated using survey weights and do not always equal 100 due to rounding. The number of survey respondents reported is the unweighted sample.

the Public Policy Institute of California's (PPIC) Statewide Survey, a poll that seeks to reflect the views of all adult Californians, regardless of nativity or citizenship.[5] Two questions are particularly germane: whether the respondent would be willing to pay higher taxes to maintain health and human services in California, and whether the respondent supported or opposed spending cuts to health and human services. Table 12.1 shows differences of opinion—some of which are substantial— between various groups of Californians. Noncitizens are by far the most supportive of using tax dollars to maintain program funding, 72 percent, and the most likely to oppose spending cuts, 77 percent. Support for taxpayer-funded health and human services diminishes as we move from naturalized citizens to U.S.-born citizens, and even further when we consider only those who report being registered voters. Strikingly, those who are likely voters—people who have voted regularly in the past—are the least likely to favor tax increases to maintain funding, 48 percent, and they are the least likely to oppose spending cuts, 56 percent, relative to the other groups. This suggests a wide gulf in policy preferences, at least on this issue, between noncitizens and those citizens most likely to vote in California.

But are these attitudinal differences large enough to affect the outcome of redistributive policy battles? A second assumption of the disenfranchisement hypothesis is that, were they given the right to vote, noncitizens would use the power of the ballot box. Some evidence indicates that naturalized black and Latino citizens report voting more than their U.S.-born counterparts (Ramakrishnan and Espenshade 2001; Ramakrishnan 2005).[6] However, those who naturalize are a self-selected group, in terms of both interests and resources. For example, naturalized immigrants might seek citizenship because they are more interested in politics than the average person. We also know that characteristics that influence voting, such as higher education, also facilitate and help predict the acquisition of citizenship. Among the general population, those with less education and less income are also less likely to vote. This suggests that even if the United States were to allow noncitizen suffrage tomorrow, it is not clear how many current noncitizens would avail themselves of the opportunity.[7]

Finally, even if we assume that noncitizens have distinct policy preferences and that they would exercise formal political voice if permitted, the disenfranchisement hypothesis assumes that their participation would be consequential. Is this likely?

One context where it might matter is in places that permit direct democracy through initiatives and referenda. In these cases, noncitizen voting might tip the scales in favor of greater redistribution, at least in states with large noncitizen populations. California, which has more noncitizens than any other state, is well known for its use of initiatives and referenda: voters regularly make decisions on everything from property taxes to use of the death penalty. The survey data from table 12.1 suggest that, if we consider likely voters with a clear opinion, a slight majority, 50.8 percent, would oppose tax increases to maintain health and human services.[8] However, if all California residents, including noncitizens, could vote, a ballot initiative in favor of higher taxes to fund health and human services would pass with 52.8 percent of all votes cast.[9] That is, noncitizens could change the trajectory of redistribution in a state, choosing taxes over social spending cuts.[10]

On the other hand, only a minority of states allows initiatives on statutory matters, and most redistributive questions are settled through the legislature. A second and more common way that voters affect policy outcomes is to back parties or people they hope will represent their views in the legislature (Brooks and Manza 2007). Yet some political scientists have shown that elected officials pay relatively little attention to the views of their poorer constituents (Gilens 2005; Bartels 2008; Hacker and Pierson 2010). For example, based on his analysis of more than 1,900 proposed policy changes and actual policy adoption, Martin Gilens argues that "when Americans with different income levels differ in their policy preferences, actual policy outcomes strongly reflect the preferences of the most affluent but bear virtually no relationship to the preferences of poor and middle income Americans" (2005, 778). Put another way, even if noncitizens were much more likely to support redistribution and had the opportunity to vote on this basis, this research suggests that their views would not count for much.

Noncitizens also tend to live in political districts already held by Democrats—the party most associated with redistributive social spending. Considering the twenty congressional districts with the highest foreign-born populations in 2009, ranging from Florida's 21st district (55.5 percent) to California's 38th district (37.3 percent), we find that seventeen of the twenty are held by Democrats. The three Republican representatives all come from the Miami area, and none are conservative ideologues, at least relative to other members of their party. If we consider the ten California congressional districts with the highest incidence of noncitizen disenfranchisement among residents, ranging from the 31st district in the Los Angeles area (35 percent) to the 39th district (about 20 percent), we find a similar story. All ten districts are held by Democrats, and in all but one of these, the Democratic candidate won handily over the challenger in the 2010 elections.[11] This suggests that naturalized immigrants and U.S.-born co-ethnics might, in part, be providing political voice to noncitizens. Of course, partisan outcomes in other elections—be it in other places, or for state or local elections—might change if noncitizens could vote. Also, noncitizens could help elect Democrats who more strongly favor redistribution, all else equal. Nevertheless, it is certainly not the case that extending the vote to noncitizens would redraw, overnight, the partisan map of the United States.

In sum, the possible effect of noncitizen disenfranchisement on redistributive social spending is not straightforward. One the one hand, noncitizens appear to support redistribution more than citizens and, on the aggregate, could benefit more from redistributive social spending given lower incomes and higher poverty rates. In direct democracy systems with significant numbers of noncitizens, they could conceivably swing specific redistributive votes. On the other hand, suffrage rights do not automatically translate into voter turnout, and evidence exists that elected officials pay little attention to the views of their poorer constituents.

Group Threat

Noncitizen disenfranchisement is not the only way immigration may influence redistribution. The pioneering work of V. O. Key (1949) and Hubert Blalock (1967) suggests immigration and redistribution might be linked through the dynamics of group threat. A group threat model argues that dominant group support for and actual spending on social welfare policies will decrease as the proportion of the subordinate group increases due to a feeling of threat—social, economic, cultural, or political—among the dominant group. Threatened majority group members then use the ballot box to voice their anxiety, supporting candidates that oppose generous social welfare programs.

The threat model was originally developed to understand relations between blacks and whites, but it can be extended to other U.S. racial minorities. The growth in immigration over the last four decades has had a profound impact on the racial and ethnic composition of the United States. In 1965, Latinos and Asians combined made up scarcely more than 2 percent of the U.S. population; by 2010, their share had increased to almost 24 percent (Humes, Jones, and Ramirez 2011, 4). It is possible that American citizens, especially those in the white majority, feel threatened by the rapidly changing racial and ethnic composition of American society and express this fear through decreasing support for redistribution.

Previous research has found some evidence that states or cities with more Latinos spend less on social welfare (Preuhs 2007; Fox 2010), have less generous benefit levels (Hero and Preuhs 2007; Preuhs 2007; Fellowes and Rowe 2004) and are more likely to adopt punitive social welfare programs (Gais and Weaver 2002; Soss et al. 2001; Fox 2012). Not all studies, however, find such an effect, and most do not find consistent effects across all measured outcomes (Fellows and Rowe 2004; Gais and Weaver 2002; Soss et al. 2001). With respect to Asian populations, to our knowledge, no studies find a negative relationship between the size or share of the Asian population and social welfare spending, but the threat hypothesis would suggest that this is a possibility.[12] Southeast Asians, many who came to the United States as refugees, have been stereotyped as welfare dependent, and in the run-up to welfare reform in 1996, elderly Chinese immigrants were accused of migrating to the United States with the sole purpose of receiving Supplemental Security Income benefits (Fujiwara 2008; Reese 2005, 184). Using the National Election Study, Jack Citrin and his colleagues (1997) found that respondents who had cooler feelings toward Asians (and Latinos) tended to support delays of one year in the provision of benefits to immigrants.

We can also imagine a group threat story centered on migrants as foreigners, rather than on racial minorities. Immigrants' cultures, religions, languages, and perceived un-American habits may generate feelings of threat, as could the sense that foreigners are invading the country, undermining the social, economic, political, and cultural fabric of the United States (for example, Huntington 2004). Indeed, Leo Chavez's (2001) study of popular magazine covers shows recurring images of borders or coastlines under siege by waves of newcomers, visual representations that certainly convey threat for some Americans.

The limited empirical evidence evaluating an immigrant threat effect is mixed. In a study of city spending on public and private relief on the eve of the Great Depression, Cybelle Fox (2010) finds that cities with more European immigrants spent more on relief than cities with more native-born whites. In the contemporary period, Daniel Hopkins argues that hostile political reactions to immigrants are more likely in communities that undergo sudden influxes of immigrants, but only "when salient national rhetoric reinforces the threat" (2010, 40). Hopkins's measures of "politicized reactions" tap anti-immigrant sentiment more than attitudes toward redistribution, so it remains an open question whether immigrant threat is a separate and consequential process for social spending beyond existing models of racial threat.[13]

Fractionalization

Fractionalization models consider how the overall level of diversity or heterogeneity in a community might affect welfare spending and public goods (Alesina and Glaeser 2004). These models do not rely on a sense of particular threat by one group vis-à-vis another. Instead, it is alleged that diversity "fractures" group cohesion and can reduce social spending through a series of mechanisms undermining class consciousness (Gitlin 1995), social solidarity (Carens 1988; Miller 1995), or levels of trust and generosity (Putnam 2007), all factors that are presumed necessary for the development and preservation of a generous welfare state. Importantly, the fracturing effects of diversity even undermine ties among people of the same background such that everyone in heterogeneous communities ends up "hunkering down," in Robert Putnam's terminology (2007, 149).

A capacious fractionalization approach defines diversity to include any socially significant difference, whether due to race, ethnicity, culture, language, religion, or national origin. This makes the argument particularly relevant for communities experiencing rapid changes due to immigration (Banting and Kymlicka 2006; Crepaz 2008; Putnam 2007; Soroka, Johnston, and Banting 2006). The empirical evidence for a specific immigrant effect is, however, contested. Although Putnam suggests that, "In the short to medium run . . . immigration and ethnic diversity challenge social solidarity" (2007, 138), he relies on measures of ethno-racial fractionalization rather than ones specific to immigration. Indeed, U.S. research examining the effects of fractionalization finds the strongest and most consistent effects for racial and ethnic fractionalization (Alesina and La Ferrara 2002; Hero 2003). In contrast, a cross-national study that used twenty-six immigrant-related diversity measures finds no evidence that higher immigration correlates with reduced generalized trust (Hooghe et al. 2009), a finding replicated by Maurice Gesthuizen and his colleagues (2009). The presumption is that higher trust correlates with more generous social policy. Given, in the U.S. context, the significance of *racial* fractionalization on measures of trust and redistribution, we focus on it.

EVALUATING WHETHER IMMIGRATION MATTERS FOR REDISTRIBUTION: THE NATIONAL CONTEXT

All three sets of arguments we outline—noncitizen disenfranchisement, group threat, and fractionalization—suggest that as the immigrant population in the United States increased after 1965, these demographic changes drove down, or slowed down, government spending on social benefits. Can we find empirical evidence to support these hypotheses? We first examine national trends, focusing on income assistance programs that target low-income individuals.

Income maintenance programs in the United States are funded by a complicated and ever shifting mix of federal and state dollars. Some income maintenance programs come in the form of cash assistance for needy individuals. These include Temporary Assistance to Needy Families (TANF), formerly Aid to Families with Dependent Children (AFDC); Supplemental Security Income (SSI); and General Assistance. Other programs offer nutritional assistance, including the Supplemental Nutrition Assistance Program (SNAP), formerly Food Stamps, and Women, Infants, and Children (WIC). Assistance programs also include those providing credits through the tax system, principally the Earned Income Tax Credit (EITC) and the Child Tax Credit.[14] Some of these programs are funded and administered by the federal government, such as EITC; some are administered by states with both federal and state funding, such as AFDC-TANF; and others are financed and administered solely by state and local governments, such as General Assistance. In addition, states may choose to use state funds to supplement federal programs, such as SSI and EITC (for an extended discussion of the social safety net, see chapter 11, this volume).

It is important to consider trends in participation in all of these programs, rather than only focus on a single program like AFDC-TANF, a traditional focus of welfare studies. First, scholars who suggest that there might be a trade-off between immigration and redistribution conceive of redistribution in broad terms; they worry that total social support for the poor will decrease in response to greater diversity. Second, the more holistic approach is necessary because all these programs target those in need, and because people move between the different programs (Schmidt 2004). For example, to reduce state welfare costs, states have long made concerted efforts to move their AFDC-TANF recipients onto the SSI rolls because SSI benefits are both more generous and federally funded. AFDC-TANF families also have large financial incentives to move a family member onto SSI if they can qualify. In 2008, a single mother with two children living in Texas would have qualified for only $244 a month in TANF benefits. But if one of those children transferred onto the federal SSI program, the total family benefit would have increase to $848 (Wiseman 2010). If we only focused on AFDC-TANF, we would not be able to capture individuals who transfer from AFDC-TANF to SSI or General Assistance. We would also fail to capture those who left AFDC-TANF to work but who continue to receive food stamps or began receiving EITC. From the perspective of poor and low-income families, all of these transfers provide redistributive benefits.

Considering all of these programs, we find limited evidence for a negative relationship between immigration and income maintenance programs. Figure 12.1 tracks the total number of participants in these various income-transfer programs since 1965, when the Immigration and Nationality Act reopened the doors to mass migration. The AFDC-TANF trend line seems most consistent with a story about welfare retrenchment in the face of increased immigration: after participation in AFDC increased during the Great Society period of policy expansion, which started in 1964, it then stabilized after the 1972 presidential election and Nixon's shift to the right on welfare issues, only to decline precipitously after the 1996 welfare reforms replaced AFDC with TANF. Beyond AFDC-TANF, however, we see considerable expansion in the SNAP and EITC programs, a gradual but sustained expansion of the WIC program, and a more modest expansion of the SSI program.

In addition to individual participation, we can also examine how income transfers per poor person have changed over this period. We use data from the U.S. Department of Commerce's Bureau of Economic Analysis (BEA), which estimates federal and state government transfers received by people who live and work in each state. The BEA divides their data into four categories: family assistance (AFDC-TANF); SSI; SNAP; and "Other," which includes EITC, Child Tax Credits,

Figure 12.1 / Recipients of Income Maintenance Programs

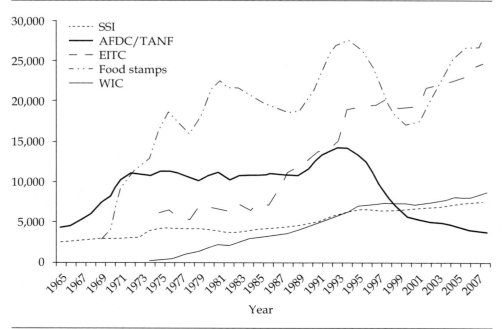

Source: Adapted from Scholz, Moffit, and Cowan (2008) (see also the note below).
Note: Figures in thousands. Most of the data for the period from 1970–2005 are adapted from Scholz et al. (2008). Where possible, we extended the figure backward and forward with data from the USDA; the 1969, 1972, and 2011 U.S. Statistical Abstract; and the Tax Policy Center. In some instances, there are slight discrepancies in measurement between Scholz et al. and the data points we added. Where the discrepancies were large, we did not extend the graph. Prior to 1972, SSI data included recipients of Old Age Assistance, Aid to the Blind, and Aid to the Permanently and Totally Disabled.

General Assistance, Energy Assistance, Refugee Assistance, and foster care payments.[15]

Figure 12.2 plots total income maintenance transfers per poor person from 1965 to 2008 (in constant 2008 dollars) against the foreign-born share of the population.[16] As the foreign-born share grew from 5 percent to more than 12 percent over the four decades, per poor person transfers for all income maintenance programs, combined, also increased. In figure 12.3, we disaggregate the total-transfer measure into its component parts. Here we can see that much of the increase in total transfers came from "other social spending," reflecting the significant expansion of the EITC program over this period. SSI and SNAP transfers grew much more modestly, while family assistance transfers declined significantly over time, providing a similar story to that of program participation numbers in Figure 12.1. Clearly no simple story supports an immigration–social spending trade-off.

Income transfer spending per poor person is a function of eligibility rules, take-

FIGURE 12.2 / Social Spending and the Foreign Born

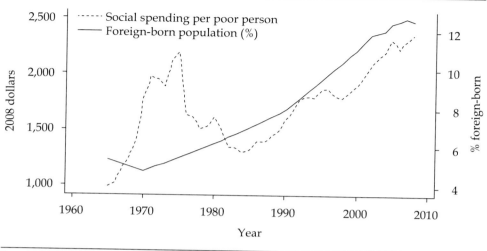

Source: Authors' compilation based on Bureau of Economic Analysis (2011), Ruggles et al. (2010), and King et al. (2010).

FIGURE 12.3 / Disaggregated Social Spending and the Foreign Born

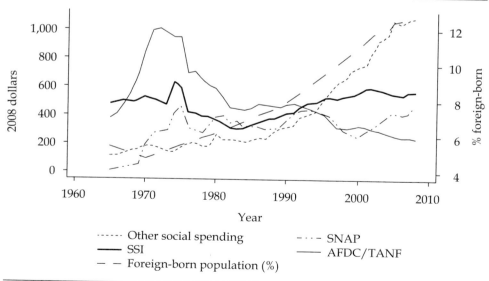

Source: Authors' compilation based on Bureau of Economic Analysis (2011), Ruggles et al. (2010), and King et al. (2010).

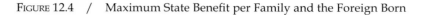

FIGURE 12.4   /   Maximum State Benefit per Family and the Foreign Born

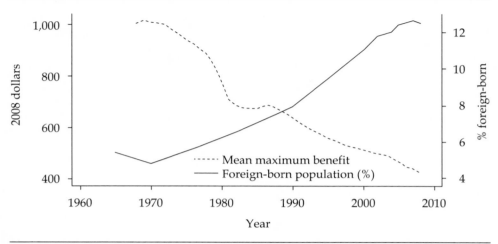

Source: Authors' compilation based on Hoynes (2011), Urban Institute (2011), and Ruggles et al. (2010).

up rates, and benefit levels. Figure 12.4 homes in on this last component: changes in the maximum state AFDC-TANF benefit for a family of three, averaged across all states for each year in the time series.[17] We clearly see that the real value of such benefits has declined precipitously over time as the proportion of the immigrant population has increased; the relationship is consistent with the argument of a trade-off between immigration and welfare generosity.

In sum, social spending as a whole has increased during this period of rising immigration, but AFDC-TANF benefits — whether measured as the number of recipients, the dollar amount spent per poor person, or maximum benefit levels — have clearly declined. The two opposing trends — increases in total redistributive spending, but decreases in welfare spending — indicate no simple relationship between redistribution policy and immigration. Of course, it is possible that total social spending might have increased even more had there been little or no immigration. Alternatively, the overall increase in spending could suggest a positive relationship between immigration and redistribution, at least in some areas. Significantly, although growth in the population of poor immigrants might increase total social spending (given a larger pool of recipients), our measures of spending per poor person suggest that, even net of demographic growth, governments in the United States have been, on average, providing more financial resources per poor resident. We cannot tell, however, from this simple set of national trend lines whether the correlations between the growing proportion of foreign-born residents and redistributive social spending might be spurious, driven by other factors that have changed over time. To get some purchase on this, we increase our effective sample size by turning to interstate differences in spending.

EVALUATING WHETHER IMMIGRATION MATTERS FOR REDISTRIBUTION: DIFFERENCES BETWEEN STATES

Shifting our attention to the states allows us to take advantage of the fact that states have different levels of immigration and different rates at which their immigrant population changes. For example, Massachusetts has more foreign-born residents than Georgia (14 percent and 9 percent, respectively), but Georgia's immigrant population has grown much faster, increasing 8.5 percentage points over the last four decades versus only 4 points in Massachusetts (see table 12.A1). By comparing states, we can see whether total transfers are lower in states that have a large immigrant population, like Massachusetts, but also whether they grow more slowly in states that have had big increases in their immigrant populations, like Georgia.

To do this, we created a time series dataset for fifty states from 1965 through 2008.[18] This gives us more than 2,000 data points, allowing us to test various theories about the relationship (if any) between immigration and redistribution. We start in 1965 because of data availability and because this is the year President Johnson signed the Immigration and Nationality Act, opening the door to contemporary migration. We include data on social spending, benefit maximums, poverty, states' fiscal capacity, unemployment, and demographics drawn from various sources: the Bureau of Economic Analysis, the U.S. Census and American Community Surveys, the Current Population Survey, and secondary sources.

Our first set of analyses focuses on two dependent variables related to actual social spending. One is a measure of family assistance transfers (AFDC-TANF), per capita, in constant 2008 dollars. This is a common focus in U.S. welfare studies. Family assistance was also the only income maintenance program to show a decline in spending over time. Finally, family assistance is funded by both state and federal moneys, whereas many of the other programs we examine are funded largely by federal transfers. As a result, if there is a trade-off between immigration and redistributive spending working through states' political decision-making, it may lie primarily in family assistance.

Our second indicator is a measure of combined federal and state income maintenance transfers per capita in constant 2008 dollars.[19] This measure captures the relationship between immigration and total redistributive spending as experienced by state residents on the ground. This is important because funding sources for income maintenance programs have shifted significantly over time. In 1965, states played a much larger role relative to the federal government in funding income maintenance programs than they do today, a shift that has been accelerating since the 1990s (Moffit 2007). Indeed, as states pulled back on AFDC-TANF funding, the federal government expanded eligibility and spending on EITC, helping fill part of the void left by state cuts. TANF and EITC are not perfect substitutes, however, and many poor families have struggled to find or keep work in the aftermath of welfare reform, rendering it difficult to take advantage of EITC and generating substantial hardship (Danziger 2010). Nevertheless, because we are interested in whether total redistribution declines for the poor in the face of growing immigration, we contend that analysts must consider this more holistic measure as well.

Indeed, changing rules regarding the eligibility of immigrants for social benefits further justifies attention to combined state and federal spending. Between 1972 and 1996, states were prohibited from establishing eligibility restrictions for welfare programs that targeted legal immigrants. Most unauthorized migrants were barred from using income maintenance programs during this period, but most legal immigrants were treated the same as U.S. citizens. Under the 1996 welfare reform act, however, significant eligibility restrictions were legislated, which barred some legal immigrants' access to income maintenance; restrictions did, however, vary by program area, as outlined in the previous chapter. Most legal immigrants who entered the United States after PRWORA was enacted were denied TANF, SSI, and food stamps, but most legal immigrants remain eligible for the EITC, and all immigrants—regardless of status—remain eligible for WIC.

Things become even more complex when we consider that after 1996, states were permitted to pass more stringent immigrant TANF restrictions than the federal government, but they could also choose to use their state funds to cover immigrants barred by federal law. State responses consequently ran the gamut from those that choose to deny more categories of immigrants than required by federal law, to those that created replacement programs to cover many legal immigrants barred from federal programs. Many states fell between these extremes. More confusing still, since the 1996 reforms, the federal and state governments continue to amend their laws—sometimes yearly—to broaden or restrict immigrant eligibility (Zimmerman and Tumlin 1999; Tumlin, Zimmerman, and Ost 1999).[20] Given all of these changes, it is not surprising that chapter 11 finds that immigrant participation in social welfare programs decreased after 1996. Some observers argue that this may be because some noncitizens were no longer eligible, because of confusing rules, or due to a "chilling effect" that made eligible noncitizens reluctant to apply for benefits (Fix and Passel 2002; Watson 2010). Total transfers may have decreased when immigrants were dropped from assistance, but it is also possible that immigrants switched to state or federal programs with fewer restrictions.[21] Dropping out of, or moving between, benefit programs likely varies over time and between states due to local legislation, bureaucratic procedures, and varying administrative support for poor residents. These variations further underscore the need for a holistic analysis of spending. If the federal government fills in when a state pulls back on social welfare spending, because immigrants shift from TANF to SSI or EITC, for example, we expect to find no relationship between immigration and actual redistribution—an important possibility to consider. On the other hand, if there is no substitution between state and federal funding, we expect a weaker relationship between immigration and total redistribution than if we used a measure over which states have more control. In addition, if state fiscal capacity, more than need, determines state social welfare spending, it is possible that states replaced the immigrants dropped from assistance programs with native-born residents on waiting lists, resulting in no net change in total spending. By focusing on both state and federal transfers, we hope to capture the net result of all of these complicated dynamics.

In addition to our two social spending measures, we also investigate two specific policy choices over which states have significant control: AFDC-TANF benefit levels and immigrants' access to social welfare benefits. The first additional dependent variable, AFDC-TANF benefit maximums, taps generosity in redistribution for those deemed eligible. Some states may, for example, restrict benefits to a small group through restrictive rules or high bureaucratic hurdles—actions likely reflected in lower total AFDC-TANF spending—but they might be relatively generous to those who qualify. For this measure, we focus on the maximum benefit for a family of three.

The possible trade-off between generous benefits and restricted eligibility raises another pathway to welfare state retrenchment: welfare chauvinism, through which governments do not necessarily modify overall spending but do restrict those receiving benefits. Indeed, various scholars point to a relationship between immigration and welfare restrictions targeted at immigrants (Alvarez and Butterfield 2000; Lee, Ottati, and Hussain 2001; Citrin et al. 1997). As the earlier discussion makes clear, states had to decide whether to use their funds to cover noncitizens barred from receiving federal funds after 1996. Our last dependent variable is consequently a measure of state immigrant welfare generosity developed by Rodney Hero and Robert Preuhs (2007). The scale, which runs from –1.11 (the least generous) to 1.67 (the most generous), captures whether a state provided welfare benefits to immigrants in eight specific domains in 1998, ranging from Medicaid funding for nonemergency care for some undocumented immigrants, to providing legal noncitizen immigrants with TANF during the federally imposed five-year bar on immigrant eligibility.[22]

Modeling the Theorized Determinants of Social Spending

As we have outlined, immigration might affect redistribution for a number of reasons, each with different causal mechanisms that drive how these two phenomena might be related. To examine the *noncitizen disenfranchisement* hypothesis, we include a variable that measures the fraction of the voting age population that is noncitizen, controlling for the fraction of the voting age population that is naturalized.[23] For all our statistical models, we lag our key independent variables to the most recent election, because these theories operate through the political process.[24]

To examine the *immigrant threat* hypotheses, we include a variable capturing the foreign-born proportion of the state population. This measure presumes that foreignness, in general, will drive political reactions over redistributive social policy. However, as noted earlier, most contemporary immigrants are nonwhite, so we also consider the possibility of a *racial threat* model, which we measure with variables capturing the proportion of the state population that is Asian or Latino.[25] Because not all racial and ethnic groups are necessarily equally threatening to whites, we consider these proportions independently.

According to a *fractionalization* model, states that are more homogeneous should spend the most on redistribution. This theory presumes that all diversity has the same effect on redistribution, for the same reasons, and through the same means. Studies in this tradition typically compute diversity with a Herfindahl index to measure the probability that two randomly selected individuals from a given population belong to different groups (Alesina, Baqir, and Easterly 1999). Unlike group threat, this theory assumes that the presence or absence of any specific group is irrelevant, that only the mix of different groups matters. Thus, states that are 30 percent Asian and 70 percent white should redistribute as much as those that are 30 percent white and 70 percent Latino. We create a Herfindahl index that includes six ethno-racial groups: whites, blacks, Latinos, Asians, American Indians, and "other." All else equal, we expect that the higher the racial fractionalization, the less redistribution.

Because noncitizen disenfranchisement, group threat, and fractionalization are all meant to capture different aspects of immigration, we would expect these measures to be highly correlated with one another. Table 12.2 provides a correlation matrix of these variables. Given the long-standing ethno-racial diversity of the United States, correlations between proportion Asian, proportion Latino, fractionalization and our disenfranchisement variables, though high, do not raise inordinate concern. In contrast, the two measures meant to capture noncitizen disenfranchisement (proportion noncitizens and proportion naturalized immigrants) are highly correlated (0.83). In our models, we consequently include our explanatory variables first separately, and then jointly, to be more certain that our results are not spurious. The correlation between our measure of immigrant threat (proportion foreign born) and our measure of noncitizen disenfranchisement is also high, at over 0.9. We therefore cannot test these theories against each other in the same model.

Controls

When we test whether group threat, fractionalization, or noncitizen disenfranchisement influences redistribution, we want to make sure that differences in state fiscal capacity, need, and basic demographics are not skewing or driving our results. For example, we might expect more redistribution in states with greater fiscal capacity given that they should have more resources to be able to meet the needs of their poorest residents. We therefore control for state *personal income per capita* (Gais, Dadayan, Bae, and Kwan 2009).[26] We exclude transfer income from these personal income figures because we worry that it is too closely related to our dependent variables.[27]

TABLE 12.2 / Correlation Matrix of Main Independent Variables

	Proportion Asian	Proportion Latino	Fractionalization	Proportion Foreign Born	Proportion Non-citizens VAP	Proportion Naturalized VAP
Proportion Asian	1.000					
Proportion Latino	0.4941	1.000				
Fractionalization	0.4866	0.6323	1.000			
Proportion foreign born	0.8067	0.6163	0.4801	1.000		
Proportion noncitizens, VAP	0.8630	0.6877	0.5740	0.9637	1.000	
Proportion naturalized, VAP	0.6636	0.4690	0.3100	0.9352	0.8258	1.000

Source: Authors' compilation.
Note: Figures include only the lower forty-eight states. VAP = voting age population.

Alternatively, we might expect more spending on redistribution in states with higher levels of need among the state's residents. Because some programs target unemployed families in poverty (for example, AFDC-TANF), whereas others target the working poor (for example, EITC), and some cover both groups (for example, SNAP), we control for two measures of need: the *pre-transfer poverty rate* and the *unemployment rate*.[28] The age structure of the population might also play a role in social spending. Many income maintenance programs target children, so we include a control for the fraction of the state population that is *under eighteen*. Likewise, SSI benefits are designed in part to supplement the incomes of poor elderly individuals, so we include a control for the fraction of the state population that is *sixty-five and over*.

Numerous studies have demonstrated a negative correlation between *percent black* and white support for redistribution or actual spending on redistributive programs (Alesina, Glaeser, and Sacerdote 2001; Brown 1995; Howard 1999; Moller 2002; Orr 1976; Wright 1976; Fox 2004, 2010). Scholars also document a positive correlation between percent black and the punitive character of state welfare programs (Fellowes and Rowe 2004; Fording 2003; Gais and Weaver 2002; Soss et al. 2001; Schram et al. 2009). Given that we want to identify the potential effects of immigration, net of long-standing black-white dynamics, we control for percentage black.[29]

Finally, we include a control for total national social spending (in models with total state social spending as the dependent variable) or total national AFDC-TANF spending (in models with state AFDC-TANF spending or maximum benefit levels as the dependent variable). We include it because we want to control for unmeasured, nationally constant but historically fluctuating factors (economic, political, and so on) that could affect spending and generosity.[30]

Unlike many other studies (for example, Barrilleaux, Holbrook, and Langer 2002; Gais, Dadayan, Bae, and Kwan 2009), we do not control for ideological or partisan political differences across states or over time. Our reasoning is that such political mechanisms act as mediators in the theories we consider and are thus integral to them. For example, rising racial fractionalization might lead voters to become more conservative and elect more Republicans, who then decrease social spending. In this case, ideology and partisanship are not exogenous determinants of social spending, so we leave them out of the model.

DOES IMMIGRATION MATTER FOR REDISTRIBUTION? MODEL RESULTS

To investigate the possible links between immigration and redistribution, we use regression models with either fixed effects or random effects for states. We calculate and present robust standard errors, clustered by state, for all models. Our fixed-effects models allow us to see how changes in immigration over time, within states, are related to income transfers in those states. Our random effects models capture both between- and within-state effects, allowing us to see how variation in levels of immigration across states, as well as changes in immigration over time within states, influence income transfers. Given that the results are broadly similar across both types of models, we present only the fixed-effect results because we believe that it is a stronger test of our hypotheses and because these models require fewer assumptions about the structure of error terms.[31]

Because we have no exogenous variation in the three theoretical mechanism variables that might permit identification of their effects on government benefits, we must be cautious in our interpretation of the results. Our modeling strategy does not allow us to definitively infer causation. Nonetheless, our results suggest patterns of association that shed important empirical light on the hypotheses we presented earlier. Given the dearth of research on this topic, we believe these analyses provide a valuable starting point for additional research.

Explaining Total Income Transfers

We start with the model of total per capita income transfers. Table 12.3 includes results for separate tests of the noncitizen disenfranchisement, immigrant threat, racial threat, and racial fractionalization hypotheses. Strikingly, neither the noncitizen disenfranchisement nor the immigrant threat hypothesis are supported, quite the opposite. We find, if anything, positive effects of both noncitizen and naturalized citizen measures on total per capita income transfers, and a significant positive relationship for the proportion of the population that is foreign born.[32] We also find little to no support for the racial threat and racial fractionalization models, though the signs of the relevant coefficients are in some cases in the negative direction suggested by our hypotheses. Thus, the more fractionalization or the larger the proportion of Asians, the less redistribution there is, in line with racial fractionalization and racial threat arguments; the coefficients in these models are, however, statistically insignificant.[33] In contrast, we find, if anything, a positive (but insignificant) relationship between the share of Latinos in the population and redistribution.

In table 12.4, we pit these theories against one another where we are able to do so. When combined, all the immigration variables—proportion noncitizen, naturalized citizen, and foreign born—remain positive and generally significant in explaining total income maintenance spending per capita, so hypotheses about immigrant disenfranchisement and immigrant threat receive no support. In contrast, a clearer race story emerges compared to the simpler models of table 12.3. In all of the combined models, proportion Asian, proportion Latino, and racial fractionalization become negative and significantly correlated with total income maintenance transfer, per capita. If there is a trade-off between immigration and redistribution, it appears to be more about the changes in the racial composition brought on by immigration than due to the effects of migration and the foreign-born population, per se.

TABLE 12.3 / Total Income Maintenance Transfer Models, 1965–2008

	Noncitizen Disenfranchisement	Immigrant Threat	Racial Threat	Racial Fractionalization
National social spending	0.903***	0.923***	0.939***	0.967***
Poverty rate	-90.777	-91.157	-71.955	-53.414
Personal income	-0.004**	-0.005***	-0.003	-0.002
Proportion unemployed	15.771	70.600	121.196	118.704
Proportion over sixty-five	57.693	48.367	276.775	314.645
Proportion under eighteen	-647.765**	-605.964*	-353.631	-272.963
Proportion black	-619.200	-612.759	-412.357	-653.633
Proportion noncitizen, VAP	317.269			
Proportion naturalized, VAP	704.644			
Proportion foreign born		586.496***		
Proportion Asian			-886.824	
Proportion Latino			461.252	
Racial fractionalization				-5.869
Constant	318.640*	306.307*	142.956	121.746

Source: Authors' compilation.
Note: Fixed-effects models. Spending and income per capita, 2008 dollars. VAP = voting age population.
*$p < 0.10$, **$p < 0.05$, ***$p < 0.01$

TABLE 12.4 / Total Income Maintenance Transfer Models, Comparative, 1965–2008

	Noncitizen Disenfranchisement vs. Racial Threat	Noncitizen Disenfranchisement vs. Fractionalization	Racial Threat vs. Immigrant Threat	Fractionalization vs. Immigrant Threat
National social spending	0.892***	0.930***	0.946***	0.955***
Poverty rate	-8.495	-57.324	28.228	-36.634
Personal income	-0.003*	-0.003*	-0.003*	-0.003*
Proportion unemployed	-33.408	1.051	40.025	25.282
Proportion over sixty-five	124.614	-22.240	71.264	-66.122
Proportion under eighteen	-611.995**	-633.162**	-549.687*	-623.401**
Proportion black	-374.257	-143.365	-272.750	-73.896
Proportion noncitizen, VAP	2,030.071***	1,017.030**		
Proportion naturalized, VAP	1,189.524**	499.835		
Proportion Asian	-2,465.378***		-2,504.313***	
Proportion Latino	-740.529*		-707.997*	
Racial fractionalization		-350.777**		-365.176**
Proportion foreign born			2,094.938***	1,056.114***
Constant	230.560	310.127*	169.223	287.805

Source: Authors' compilation.
Note: Fixed-effect models. Spending and income per capita, 2008 dollars. VAP = voting age population.
*$p < 0.10$, **$p < 0.05$, ***$p < 0.01$

Explaining Family Assistance Transfers

Next, we model spending on family assistance transfers, moving from a broad-based redistribution measure to a much more targeted one. The total income transfer model aimed to capture the totality of redistribution benefits paid from federal or state government coffers that might be available to poor residents; this measure narrows down to a prominent state-controlled welfare benefit. Unlike the total income transfers model, we start this model in 1973, just after Nixon's re-election and his rightward shift on welfare policy. As we saw in figure 12.1, the family assistance program expanded considerably from 1965 to 1972. Eligibility for AFDC expanded in response to several Supreme Court decisions, the demands of the civil rights and welfare rights movements, and growing urban unrest (Quadagno 1994; Piven and Cloward 1971, 1977). This was a distinct political moment in the history of the U.S. welfare state, and the models that best describe welfare spending throughout much of American history simply break down here.

In table 12.5, we consider each model independently and find results for AFDC-TANF spending to be quite similar to those for total income transfers. That is, the proportion noncitizen and foreign born continue to have a surprising positive relationship with per capita spending, albeit a small and statistically insignificant one. These results contradict the disenfranchisement and immigrant threat hypotheses. Conversely, we also find that higher racial fractionalization and a larger share of Asians is associated with less AFDC-TANF spending per capita, though

TABLE 12.5 / AFDC-TANF Spending Models, 1973–2008

	Noncitizen Disenfran- chisement	Immigrant Threat	Racial Threat	Racial Fractional- ization
National social spending	0.594***	0.589***	0.650***	0.527***
Poverty rate	−80.421***	−77.044**	−41.504	−67.495**
Personal income	−0.002*	−0.002*	0.000	−0.001
Proportion unemployed	205.176**	204.916**	241.137**	218.399**
Proportion over sixty-five	196.928	210.146	327.780	268.750
Proportion under eighteen	−92.579	−101.456	10.290	−16.177
Proportion black	−731.653***	−733.687***	−350.614	−727.874**
Proportion noncitizen, VAP	220.156			
Proportion naturalized, VAP	−96.493			
Proportion foreign born		107.056		
Proportion Asian			−1,681.787***	
Proportion Latino			458.092***	
Racial fractionalization				−17.750
Constant	141.997*	137.076	−2.909	109.537

Source: Authors' compilation.
Note: Fixed-effect models. Spending and income per capita, 2008 dollars. VAP = voting age population.
*p < 0.01, **p < 0.05, ***p < 0.01

TABLE 12.6 / AFDC-TANF Spending Models, Comparative, 1973–2008

	Noncitizen Disen-franchisement vs. Racial Threat	Noncitizen Disenfranchise-ment vs. Fractionalization	Racial Threat vs. Immigrant Threat	Fractionaliza-tion vs. Immigrant Threat
National social spending	0.704***	0.535***	0.706***	0.553***
Poverty rate	−22.101	−69.873**	−24.926	−68.921**
Personal income	0.000	−0.001	0.000	−0.001
Proportion unemployed	231.283**	212.648**	229.392**	208.311**
Proportion over sixty-five	327.980	191.153	336.558	208.430
Proportion under eighteen	−113.443	−67.169	−100.263	−98.316
Proportion black	−379.050*	−567.963**	−397.591**	−626.153**
Proportion noncitizen, VAP	927.771**	456.036		
Proportion naturalized, VAP	503.391	−159.777		
Proportion Asian	−2,315.617***		−2,303.207***	
Proportion Latino	−93.869		−14.407	
Racial fractionalization		−128.187		−84.775
Proportion foreign born			859.597**	210.810
Constant	15.700	145.628*	8.849	139.352

Source: Authors' compilation.
Note: Fixed-effect models. Spending and income per capita, 2008 dollars. VAP = voting age population.
*$p < 0.10$, **$p < 0.05$, ***$p < 0.01$

the factionalization coefficient fails to achieve statistical significance.[34] A larger Latino share is, in contrast, positively and significantly associated with per capita AFDC-TANF transfers.

In table 12.6, we again pit pairs of theories against one another. The findings are largely consistent with the emerging story: negative but insignificant coefficients for racial fractionalization and proportion Latino once controlling for immigrant variables, negative and significant coefficients for proportion Asian, and largely positive coefficients for the various immigrant-related measures, a number of which are statistically significant. Thus, holding constant changing racial demographics, a larger foreign-born population or noncitizen population (net of the naturalized citizen population) is associated with increased spending on family assistance transfers.

Explaining AFDC-TANF Benefit Levels

We shift now to models that predict the maximum AFDC-TANF benefit level for a family of three across states and over time. This is a simpler outcome than the

TABLE 12.7 / Maximum AFDC-TANF Models, 1968–2008

	Noncitizen Disenfranchisement	Immigrant Threat	Racial Threat	Racial Fractionalization
National social spending	0.957***	1.234***	1.077***	0.660**
Poverty rate	−750.531***	−859.960***	−690.890***	−553.024***
Personal income	−0.013***	−0.015***	−0.008**	−0.001
Proportion unemployed	−1,048.064***	−912.713**	−674.384*	−485.324
Proportion over sixty-five	−232.895	−291.315	382.784	315.084
Proportion under eighteen	1,599.532**	1,659.211**	2,332.939***	2,407.062***
Proportion black	−2,492.898	−2,636.293	−2,083.541	−909.264
Proportion noncitizen, VAP	−1,955.730			
Proportion naturalized, VAP	3,122.905*			
Proportion foreign born		227.209		
Proportion Asian			−3,555.975*	
Proportion Latino			122.655	
Racial fractionalization				−1,308.582***
Constant	915.333**	975.159**	483.799	523.283

Source: Authors' compilation.
Note: Fixed-effect models. Spending and income per capita, 2008 dollars. VAP = voting age population.
*p < 0.10, **p < 0.05, ***p < 0.01

previous two, because it does not include the complex dynamics of benefit take-up, that is, who learns about and is deemed eligible for government assistance. Because figure 12.4 does not show the same dramatic rise in AFDC benefit levels before 1973 as in AFDC spending levels (see figures 12.1 and 12.3), our analysis includes all years for which we have data (1968 to 2008).

Perhaps surprisingly, given that this analysis sidesteps issues of benefit take-up and eligibility restrictions, our results are not dramatically different than in the spending models. Table 12.7 presents a test of each hypothesis separately. Unlike previous results, we do find that as the proportion of noncitizens in a state's population grows (net of the proportion of naturalized immigrants), AFDC-TANF benefit generosity appears to decline, but the association is statistically insignificant. Conversely, as naturalized immigrants make up a larger proportion of the voting age population in a state, maximum benefit levels increase, and this effect is marginally significant. In the immigrant threat model, as in prior models, we see a positive but insignificant effect of immigrant population size. For racial fractionalization and proportion Asian, we find the same negative, significant relationship and slightly positive but insignificant results for proportion Latino.

We test whether these results hold up when examining multiple theories simultaneously. The findings, reported in table 12.8, show that disenfranchisement results change direction once we consider race: net of racial composition and fractionalization measures, the higher a state's proportion of immigrants and even

TABLE 12.8 / Maximum AFDC-TANF Benefit Models, Comparative, 1968–2008

	Noncitizen Disenfran-chisement vs. Racial Threat	Noncitizen Disenfran-chisement vs. Fractionali-zation	Racial Threat vs. Immigrant Threat	Fractionali-zation vs. Immigrant Threat
National social spending	0.807***	0.583**	1.433***	0.858***
Poverty rate	-440.751***	-524.692***	-416.015**	-517.673***
Personal income	-0.009**	-0.004	-0.007*	-0.003
Proportion unemployed	-1,161.597***	-888.294***	-1,099.620***	-883.811***
Proportion over sixty-five	59.982	-592.602	-259.451	-789.292
Proportion under eighteen	1,778.527***	1,509.098***	1,514.329**	1,331.673**
Proportion black	-1,869.172	831.025	-1,737.741	979.713
Proportion noncitizen, VAP	4,487.089***	2,813.003***		
Proportion naturalized, VAP	4,987.320***	2,042.061		
Proportion Asian	-8,110.224***		-9,052.977***	
Proportion Latino	-3,167.644***		-3,760.216***	
Racial fractionalization		-2,461.637***		-2,512.258***
Proportion foreign born			7,169.028***	3,437.550***
Constant	623.254	985.029***	583.741	987.851***

Source: Authors' compilation.
Note: Fixed-effect models. Spending and income per capita, 2008 dollars. VAP = voting age population.
*$p < 0.10$, **$p < 0.05$, ***$p < 0.01$

noncitizen immigrants, the higher the maximum benefit level. Thus the disenfran-chisement and immigrant threat hypotheses continue to find no support: a higher proportion of immigrants, including noncitizens, is associated with higher benefit levels. Conversely, racial diversity, either measured through a fractionalization score or by proportion Asian or Latino in the state population, has a statistically significant negative relationship with benefit levels for a family of three when we include disenfranchisement or immigrant threat variables.

Explaining Immigrant Welfare Generosity

Finally, we consider an outcome variable most directly tied to immigration: a state's welfare generosity toward immigrants in 1998. Because we have only one year of data and a continuous dependent variable, we run an ordinary least squares regression and use all fifty states. The results, in table 12.9, show—not surprisingly, given limited cases—that few of the coefficients reach statistical significance, although the direction of the estimated effects are in line with a racial threat or fractionalization explanation of changes in redistribution. For the immi-grant variables, the direction of the relationship is similar to the simple models predicting maximum AFDC-TANF spending for a family of three: the proportion

TABLE 12.9 / Immigrant Welfare Generosity Models, 1998

	Immigrant Threat	Racial Threat	Racial Fractionali-zation	Noncitizen Disenfran-chisement
Poverty rate	−4.093	−3.362	−3.025	−3.731
Personal income	0.000**	0.000***	0.000***	0.000**
Proportion unemployed	25.108*	26.825*	32.307**	23.066
Proportion over sixty-five	12.857	12.894	12.896	12.165
Proportion under eighteen	0.737	2.229	4.145	1.289
Proportion black	−0.1491	−1.549		−1.461
Proportion foreign born	0.146			
Proportion Asian		0.027		
Proportion Latino		−0.689		
Racial fractionalization			−1.123	
Proportion noncitizen, VAP				−2.459
Proportion naturalized, VAP				3.757
Constant	−5.151	−6.049	−7.149*	−5.174

Source: Authors' compilation.
Note: Spending and income per capita, 2008 dollars. VAP = voting-age population.
*$p < 0.10$, **$p < 0.05$, *** $p < 0.01$

of foreign-born residents shows a positive correlation, as does the proportion of naturalized citizens in the voting age population, but the relationship with the proportion of noncitizens is negative. In the AFDC-TANF benefits model, this partial support for a disenfranchisement hypothesis disappeared when we included race variables, but here we cannot do a similar test given only fifty cases. The bottom line, based on the statistical insignificance of the coefficients, is consistent with the results of previous studies (Hero and Preuhs 2006, 2007). Specifically, no strong evidence exists for noncitizen disenfranchisement, threat, or fractionalization in explaining whether a state will be more or less generous toward immigrants right after federal rules regarding social welfare changed in 1996.

LESSONS FROM STATE MODELS AND CONCLUDING THOUGHTS

The American welfare state is a complex institution, encompassing numerous programs that redistribute money to the poor and working poor, with various levels of generosity and with distinct rules for eligibility. Because of this system, we have considered numerous measures of social redistribution to examine the extent to which rising numbers of immigrants might affect redistribution policy.

In the end, our results suggest that race—an enduring challenge for the U.S. welfare state and at the center of redistributive politics for so long—continues to be a key determinant of social redistribution. This is the case whether we consider the historic — and still significant — dynamic of black-white race relations or the growing proportion and complexity of ethno-racial diversity generated by immigration. In virtually all of our models, the proportion of black residents in a state had a negative relationship with redistributive outcomes, as we would expect based on extensive scholarship in this area. We add to these analyses by considering additional racial minority groups and racial fractionalization. The latter is negatively associated with total income transfers and family assistance transfers per capita, as well as maximum AFDC-TANF spending levels. The proportion of Asians in a state is also negatively associated with total income transfers, family assistance transfers per capita, and benefit levels. This effect is not particularly robust, however, and must be treated with caution given the small Asian population, relative to other groups, and their concentration in a handful of states.[35]

Conversely, our results support neither the noncitizen disenfranchisement nor the immigrant threat hypotheses. The proportion of foreign-born residents in a state's population, in particular, shows a consistent, positive relationship with our diverse measures of social redistribution. Tests for an immigrant disenfranchisement hypothesis also find little support. In the few cases where the proportion of noncitizens in the voting age population is negatively associated with an outcome, such effects wash away — indeed, become positive — when we control for racial threat or racial fractionalization. Although counterintuitive in the context of immigrant backlash stories, our findings are consistent with other empirical research that argues that race has long been more important than immigration in the politics of redistribution (Fox 2010, 2012).

In this context, the results for a "Latino threat" dynamic are particularly revealing. In each stand-alone test of a racial threat model, regardless of the redistribution measure, we find either no significant relationship or a positive relationship between the proportion of Latinos in a state and our outcome measures, suggesting that benefit levels and spending on redistribution per capita increase as the Latino population of a state increases. However, this relationship seems to be due to the fact that the proportion of Latinos and the proportion of immigrants are highly, but not perfectly, correlated. When we include measures for the proportion of foreign-born state residents or variables related to noncitizenship simultaneously with the proportion of Latinos, the Latino threat measure changes directions, becoming negative and usually statistically significant across our outcomes. At the same time, we find that most immigrant-related measures are positively associated with more generous spending and benefits. These results suggest that any perceived negative "immigrant" effect on redistribution in the United States is not truly about foreign-born individuals, but instead likely related to threat and fractionalization dynamics linked to the Latino (and Asian) population, whether foreign born or native born.

The positive relationship between foreign-born residents and redistribution is in many ways surprising, especially given that few of the foreign born in the United

States have acquired citizenship and can, if they choose, use the ballot box to affect social welfare policy. Of course, it is possible that our null findings are simply a measurement issue. The proportion of noncitizens and naturalized immigrants in the voting age population is highly correlated. This makes it hard to estimate the effects jointly. But the consistency of our findings suggests some real, substantive dynamic.[36]

In speculating about mechanisms that could explain a positive relationship between immigration and redistribution, net of the negative effects of race, we should remember that the voting booth is not the only way individuals can exercise political muscle (see, for example, Voss and Bloemraad 2011). In California, immigrants and their advocates engaged in grassroots activism to restore immigrant benefits after 1996, joining protests, holding sit-ins, testifying at public hearings, and writing letters to elected representatives. The high-profile suicides of some elderly immigrants cut from the welfare rolls also spurred sympathetic individuals to join the movement. In response, California legislators developed a Cash Assistance Program for Immigrants (CAPI) for the elderly and disabled who had been cut from SSI in the wake of welfare reform (Reese and Ramirez 2003; Fujiwara 2008). Some scholars argue that aggregate welfare state spending typically increases—at least in the short term—in response to these sorts of protest activities (Piven and Cloward 1971). A social movements approach reminds us that immigrants—even noncitizens—have political agency.

If we consider the formal political system, it is also possible that the U.S.-born adult children of noncitizens, who automatically acquire U.S. citizenship at birth, are voting on their parents' behalf. With the rise in the immigrant population comes an increase in the second generation, the U.S.-born children of immigrants. As more and more of this group come of age, they might play an increasingly determinative role in elections, as some have argued was the case in the 2012 elections. In a similar fashion, co-ethnic citizens, either naturalized or with long roots in the country, might mitigate the worst disenfranchisement effects or advocate for the interests of low-income noncitizens within the political system. For example, between 1984 and 2010, the number of Latino state legislators increased from 106 to 245, the majority of whom were U.S. born; Robert Preuhs argues that, at least in some places, "Latino descriptive representation does influence welfare policy, primarily by offsetting the degree to which larger Latino populations are met with lower levels of welfare provision" (2007, 277).[37] In California, the rising share of Latino legislators has been identified as one factor that led California to restore immigrant access to welfare after the 1996 reforms (Brown 2013; Reese and Ramirez 2003). As we discussed earlier, many of the congressional districts with the largest share of noncitizens are held by Democratic lawmakers who tend to be more supportive of redistribution than their Republican rivals.

More generally, the most immigrant-dense areas of the United States might already have built up institutional, social, and political structures that can lobby for and protect immigrants from pressures to reduce redistributive spending. Because immigration flows are strongly affected by social networks—new immigrants tend to settle in places where earlier immigrants have landed — the institutional structures put in place a century ago to provide benefits to European immigrants, in particular, might still have some historical reach into the present (Fox 2010, 2012). In these places, native-born citizens might also hold stronger pro-immigrant attitudes than Americans in other parts of the country. As new immigrant flows move into areas with little experience of migration, notably to the U.S. South, it will be fascinating to see whether newcomers push these states to be more generous in their redistributive efforts. If not, it would underscore that the effect of immigration depends heavily on a state's historic experience with immigration.

In the end, we are left with a somewhat puzzling and troubling portrait of changes to social redistribution over the past forty-five years. We know that retrenchment in some areas has been significant, although, as we show, there has also been expansion in others, notably in programs like EITC. We might well expect that where there has been retrenchment, the rapid and significant rise in immigration could be a cause: Americans might fear foreign newcomers, though these newcomers usually have few political tools to advocate for more generous social benefits. Yet our analysis instead suggests that race, not migration, is at the heart of restrictive policies and spending. In line with a long and troubled racial history in the United States, neither citizenship nor U.S. birth matters as much as being a racial minority when it comes to predicting less generous redistribution efforts.

Immigration scholars and advocates frequently point to the 1996 welfare reform act as a key piece in a shift toward more anti-immigrant policies. They underscore how the legislation targeted immigrants, in particular, by drawing a much starker line between citizens and noncitizens, including legal permanent residents. Yet immigrants were far from the only ones affected; the changes to welfare reform hit poor minority communities particularly hard. In signing PRWORA, President Clinton declared, "I am proud to have signed this legislation," but he took pains to bemoan two aspects of the law: cuts to food stamps and the provisions affecting legal immigrants. Claiming that he was "deeply disappointed that this legislation would deny Federal assistance to legal immigrants and their children," he vowed to work with Congress "in a bipartisan effort to correct the provisions of this legislation that go too far and have nothing to do with welfare reform" (Clinton 1996). In ensuing years, Congress did indeed roll back some of the immigrant restrictions; it did little, however, to alleviate the lot of U.S. citizens affected by the law, many of minority backgrounds — a dynamic fully consistent with our empirical results. It remains to be seen whether current and future immigrants — who are overwhelmingly people of color — will assist in expanding the American welfare state, or instead get caught in race-based attacks on redistributive social policy.

TABLE 12.A1 / Proportion of Foreign-Born or Noncitizen U.S. and State Population, 1965–2008

	Foreign Born 1965	Foreign Born 2008	Percentage Point Change in Foreign Born 1965–2008	Noncitizen Residents, 2008
United States	5.1	12.4	7.3	7.1
Alabama	0.6	2.8	2.2	2.2
Alaska	3.4	6.2	2.8	3.3
Arizona	5.2	14.4	9.2	9.5
Arkansas	0.6	3.8	3.2	2.9
California	8.9	26.8	17.9	14.6
Colorado	3.6	10.2	6.6	6.5
Connecticut	10.1	13.2	3.1	7.1
Delaware	2.9	7.9	5.0	4.8
Florida	6.9	18.6	11.7	9.7
Georgia	0.9	9.4	8.5	6.1
Hawaii	10.8	17.6	6.8	7.3
Idaho	2.2	5.8	3.6	4.2
Illinois	6.4	13.9	7.5	7.4
Indiana	1.9	4.0	2.1	2.8
Iowa	1.8	3.8	2.0	2.5
Kansas	1.6	6.1	4.5	4.2
Kentucky	0.7	2.7	2.0	2.0
Louisiana	1.1	3.0	1.9	1.9
Maine	5.6	3.1	-2.5	1.5
Maryland	3.4	12.6	9.2	7.0
Massachusetts	10.1	14.4	4.3	7.3
Michigan	6.1	5.8	-0.3	3.2
Minnesota	3.6	6.8	3.2	3.8
Mississippi	0.4	2.0	1.6	1.4
Missouri	1.7	3.6	1.9	2.0
Montana	3.9	2.1	-1.8	0.9
Nebraska	2.4	6.0	3.6	4.1
Nevada	4.8	19.1	14.3	11.6
New Hampshire	6.5	4.9	-1.6	2.5
New Jersey	10.0	20.0	10.0	10.1
New Mexico	2.5	9.3	6.8	6.4
New York	14.1	21.7	7.6	10.2
North Carolina	0.7	7.0	6.3	4.9
North Dakota	4.3	2.2	-2.1	1.5
Ohio	3.6	3.8	0.2	1.9
Oklahoma	0.9	5.0	4.1	3.4
Oregon	3.7	9.6	5.9	6.1
Pennsylvania	4.6	5.3	0.7	2.7
Rhode Island	9.2	12.5	3.3	6.6
South Carolina	0.7	4.3	3.6	3.0
South Dakota	2.3	1.9	-0.4	1.6

TABLE 12.A1 / (Continued)

	Foreign Born 1965	Foreign Born 2008	Percentage Point Change in Foreign Born 1965–2008	Noncitizen Residents, 2008
Tennessee	0.6	4.0	3.4	2.7
Texas	3.3	16.0	12.7	10.9
Utah	3.5	8.2	4.7	5.2
Vermont	5.6	3.9	-1.7	1.4
Virginia	1.7	10.2	8.5	5.6
Washington	6.0	12.3	6.3	6.7
West Virginia	1.2	1.3	0.1	0.7
Wisconsin	3.9	4.5	0.6	2.6
Wyoming	2.9	2.4	-0.5	2.0

Source: Authors' compilation. 1965 figures from 1960 and 1970 U.S. decennial census statistics; 2008 figures from the American Community Survey.

TABLE 12.A2 / Districts with Highest Proportion of Foreign-Born Residents, 2009–2011

Congressional District	Percent Foreign-Born	Representative	Party	Ideology (according to Govtrack.us)	Represents District Since
FL District 21	55.5	Diaz-Balart	R	rank and file Republican	2011
FL District 18	51.9	Ros-Lehtinen	R	moderate Republican leader	1989
CA District 31	51.4	Becerra	D	rank and file Democrat	2003
CA District 47	48.1	Sanchez	D	rank and file Democrat	2003
NY District 5	47.1	Ackerman	D	rank and file Democrat	1993
FL District 25	45.3	Rivera	R	centrist Republican follower	2011
CA District 34	44.5	Roybal-Allard	D	rank and file Democrat	2003
NY District 6	43.3	Meeks	D	rank and file Democrat	1997
CA District 29	43.2	Schiff	D	moderate Democratic leader	2003
CA District 28	42.3	Berman	D	moderate Democratic leader	2003
CA District 32	41.8	Chu	D	rank and file Democrat	2009
NY District 9	40.4	Weiner	D	rank and file Democrat	1999
NJ District 13	39.9	Sires	D	rank and file Democrat	2006
NY District 12	39.8	Velazquez	D	moderate Democratic follower	1993
NY District 7	39.4	Crowley	D	moderate Democrat leader	1999
NY District 11	38.9	Clarke	D	far-left Democrat	2007
CA District 27	37.9	Sherman	D	rank and file Democrat	2003
CA District 13	37.6	Stark	D	far-left Democrat	1993
CA District 16	37.4	Lofgren	D	moderate Democratic leader	1995
CA District 38	37.3	Napolitano	D	rank and file Democrat	2003

Source: Authors' compilation based on Public Policy Institute of California (2013), U.S. Census Bureau (2012), and Govtrack (2012).

NOTES

1. "President Lyndon B. Johnson's Remarks at the Signing of the Immigration Bill, Liberty Island, New York, October 3, 1965," Lyndon B. Johnson Library and Museum, http://www.lbjlib.utexas.edu/johnson/archives.hom/speeches.hom/651003.asp (accessed June 15, 2011).

2. In accepting his party's nomination as presidential candidate in 1992, Bill Clinton vowed to the Democratic National Convention to "end welfare as we know it." For text and audio of the speech, see William Jefferson Clinton, "Democratic Presidential Nomination Acceptance Speech," *American Rhetoric*, July 16, 1992, http://www.americanrhetoric.com/speeches/wjclinton1992dnc.htm (accessed March 19, 2013).

3. Title IV's heading made its purpose clear: "Restricting Welfare and Public Benefits for Aliens,"110 Stat. 2105, Public Law 104-193 (for the text, see http://www.gpo.gov/fdsys/pkg/PLAW-104publ193/html/PLAW-104publ193.htm).

4. Indeed, there are good reasons to believe that noncitizens would be undersampled in such surveys due to language barriers or higher than normal refusal rates, especially among unauthorized immigrants.

5. The PPIC Statewide Survey is a random digit dialing poll of all landlines and cell phones with a California exchange. We pool six surveys, from the months of January and May in 2010, 2011 and 2012. Each survey had about 2,000 respondents. All surveys were conducted in English and Spanish, and a few also included translations in some Asian languages. For more on methodology, see *Public Policy Institute of California*, "Survey Methodology," http://www.ppic.org/content/other/SurveyMethodology.pdf accessed March 19, 2013).

6. In contrast, the highest rate of reported voting among whites is found in the second generation (the children of immigrants), and among Asian Americans in the third and later generations.

7. Studies of European countries that permit noncitizen suffrage generally find that noncitizens vote at lower rates than both naturalized citizens and native-born citizens (see, for example, Groenendijk 2008).

8. This calculation is based on the weighted number of likely voters who clearly expressed an opinion: 3,047 respondents who oppose higher taxes and 2,951 who would pay higher taxes to maintain health and human services.

9. This is based on the (admittedly heroic) assumption that these residents would turn out to vote in such numbers that their ballots constituted the same proportion of all ballots cast as the percentage of noncitizens in the general population (15 percent), and that the remainder of the voters reflected the opinion of "likely voters" with individuals responding "don't know" taken out of the calculation.

10. In November 2012, a majority of California voters, 55.2 percent, approved Proposition 30, which increased the state sales tax and income tax on those earning over $250,000 to pay for K-12 schools and community colleges. It is doubtful that these results would have been replicated if tax increases had been directed to social benefits. In the PPIC survey data, although a slight majority of likely voters opposed tax hikes to maintain health and human services, almost two-thirds (64 percent) claimed that they would

support tax increases to maintain K-12 public education, suggesting greater support for education than redistribution.

11. Table 12.A2 lists the most "immigrant" congressional districts.

12. Our limited knowledge stems in part from the fact that many studies exclude Asians from their models, even when they focus on race effects (see, for example, Hero and Preuhs 2007; Fellowes and Rowe 2004; Gais and Weaver 2002).

13. Daniel Hopkins looks at whether respondents feel that immigration should be increased or decreased, and whether they agree that immigrants are getting too demanding in their push for rights (2010, 46, 52).

14. This list of means-tested programs funded by state and federal dollars is certainly not exhaustive. We have excluded from our analysis health insurance programs (for example, Medicaid and State Children's Health Insurance Programs); housing aid (for example, Public Housing and Section 8); Head Start and child care assistance; and school-based nutrition programs (school breakfast and school lunch).

15. These data can be found at http://www.bea.gov/regional/spi/default.cfm?selTable =SA35andselSeries=ancillary. They exclude administrative costs (for a description of the data and methods used to calculate transfers, see Bureau of Economic Analysis 1999).

16. Our measure of poverty is calculated prior to taxes and transfers and is constructed from Current Population Survey income microdata (King et al. 2010). Figures for 1965 through 1967 are extrapolated and for a few smaller states, figures through 1976 are for multistate regions rather than individual states. Following other poverty scholars (for example, Rainwater and Smeeding 2003), we calculate household market income using information about wages, salaries, and business and farm income. We then use a cut-off variable available in the CPS to determine whether this market income is above or below the official poverty line, given the household's size and composition. Though poverty is by a household's income, the poverty rate is calculated at the individual level for each state.

17. We thank Hilary Hoynes for sharing her dataset on maximum AFDC-TANF benefits from 1968 to 2007. The original sources of these data include unpublished tables from the Department of Health and Human Services (1968–1979) and the University of Kentucky Poverty Center (1980–). We add 2008 data from the Urban Institute (see http://anfdata.urban.org/wrd/maps.cfm, table IIA.4). We choose to focus on figures that pertain to a family of three, because of their consistent availability over time and so that our analysis is in line with that of other similar analyses (for example, Hero and Preuhs 2003). The mean maximums in figure 12.4 are calculated by averaging the state maximums across all states.

18. Our database covers all fifty states, but we exclude Hawaii and Alaska from our statistical models. Hawaii is a significant outlier for a key variable of interest, the proportion of the state's population that is Asian, and for some key independent variables, information is missing for Hawaii and Alaska in earlier years.

19. This includes AFDC-TANF, SSI, SNAP, General Assistance, WIC, EITC, Child Tax Credits, Energy Assistance, Foster Care payments, and Refugee Assistance.

20. The National Immigration Law Center provides updates of state and federal changes in immigrant eligibility for various programs (see "Guide to Immigrant Eligibility for

Federal Programs," October 2012, http://www.nilc.org/pubs/Guide_update.htm, accessed March 24, 2013).

21. It is not clear how many immigrants do so. In theory, immigrants cut from TANF who find work might qualify for EITC, which had no restrictions on legal immigrants. But one study found that among low income families surveyed, 73 percent of native-born U.S. citizens had heard of the EITC, and 50 percent had received it. But among the non-citizens, only 22 percent had heard of the program and only 9 percent had received it (Phillips 2001).

22. The specific benefits measured were "state-funded TANF during the federally imposed five-year bar on immigrant welfare eligibility; TANF after the federal five-year bar; state general assistance benefits; state-funded food stamps; a substitute program for Supplemental Security Income (SSI); state Medicaid funds during the five-year bar; Medicaid funding for nonemergency care for some undocumented immigrants; state-funded health care programs; and state-funded prenatal care" (Hero and Preuhs 2007, 502).

23. As discussed and elaborated in chapter 11, citizenship status only became tightly tied to social benefits in 1996 with the federal overhaul to welfare policy. Legal permanent residents thereafter arguably had an increased incentive to naturalize, and some state governments and nonprofit social service providers engaged in concerted efforts to help noncitizens acquire citizenship so that they could remain eligible for federal benefits. We thus considered the possibility that after 1996, immigrants may naturalize selectively to receive welfare benefits, resulting in an association between naturalization and spending in the reverse causal direction from what we posit. We conducted a sensitivity analysis for the models discussed below, limited to the years before 1996. Those results are nearly identical to models for all years and are available on request. The similarity of results is consistent with studies that find immigrant naturalization is not a function of punitive policy or simple cost/benefit calculations but rather the "warmth of the welcome" accorded to immigrants (Bloemraad 2006; Van Hook, Brown, and Bean 2006).

24. This means a one-year lag in odd (non-election) years and a two year lag in even (election) years, on the assumption that, because elections are very late in the year, spending in that year is more closely related to the previous election.

25. Because race and Hispanic ethnicity questions are separate in the census and the ACS, we define Latinos as those *of any race* reporting Hispanic ethnicity.

26. State personal income comes from the Commerce Department's Bureau of Economic Analysis (http://www.bea.gov/regional/spi/default.cfm?selTable=summary).

27. In practice, values of the variable with and without transfer data are highly correlated.

28. As noted in the description of figures 12.2 and 12.3, our measure of poverty is calculated prior to taxes and transfers and is constructed from Current Population Survey income microdata. State unemployment figures are drawn from two sources. For 1976 through 2008, they are from official Bureau of Labor Statistics Reports. For 1965 through 1975, we thank Timothy Besley and Anne Case for making available their compilation of figures from the President's Manpower Reports. The unemployment rate and the poverty rate have a correlation of only 0.38.

29. Of course, some of the immigrants who move to the United States self-categorize or are

viewed by others as black, but it is a small proportion of the total: 8 percent of all foreign-born residents. These individuals will be captured in proportional measures of immigrants, naturalized citizens or noncitizens in a state's population.

30. This specification was more parsimonious than a year fixed-effects specification. However, the results are similar if we include year fixed effects instead.

31. Because states vary in so many ways, many of which we are not able to capture with our controls, we prefer the models of change over time within states. Fixed-effects models also require fewer possibly unwarranted assumptions about the correlation of error terms. Results of the random effects models are available on request.

32. The negative relationship between state fiscal capacity and spending that we see throughout our model results has also been noted by other scholars (Gais, Dadayan, and Kwan 2009), who show that spending on cash assistance in high fiscal capacity states has declined rapidly over the last three decades, largely converging with spending in low fiscal capacity states. High fiscal capacity states continued to spend more overall, but they shifted their funds to "social services" rather than income transfers.

33. Our analyses are limited to the forty-eight contiguous United States, but we note that this particular result depends on the exclusion of Hawaii and it is somewhat sensitive to the exclusion of New Jersey. Hawaii has a particularly large Asian population and relatively high social spending. New Jersey's Asian population increased from less than 1 percent in 1965 to more than 7 percent by 2008. New York saw a similar increase but the results are not sensitive to the exclusion of that state.

34. Again, however, the "Asian threat" effect depends on the exclusion of Hawaii in our models.

35. See note 33.

36. Some political actors and academics speculate about a "welfare magnet" effect, whereby immigrants purposefully move to states with more generous social benefits (for example, Borjas 1999a). It is also argued that the material and psychic costs to internal migration are greater for the native born than for immigrants (Borjas 1999b, 116–18). These observers could read our results as consistent with the welfare magnet hypothesis. Although it is possible, we find this conclusion unlikely, especially as a dynamic with a sustained effect across all the decades we analyze. One empirical analysis of recent immigrants' locational choices, prior to welfare reform in 1996, found that the primary determinant of residential location for foreign-born newcomers (other than refugees) was the presence of other settled immigrants, not social benefits (Zavodny 1999), a finding consistent with social network accounts of migration. Others underscore that the logic of the welfare magnet argument would predict differential migration between high-skilled and low-skilled immigrants or high take-up rates of social benefits by immigrants. However, in an analysis that leveraged interstate variation in benefits before and after 1996, Neeraj Kaushal (2005) finds that although there is a modest increase in migration to more generous states after 1996, in many cases the up-tick is more dramatic for higher skilled, married immigrant women rather than low-skilled, unmarried women, the group Kaushal suggests is most at risk for being on welfare. Other analyses find, after 1996, that immigrants and immigrant households were, all else equal, less likely to receive social benefits (Fix and Passel 2002; Van Hook and Bean 2009; chapter 11, this volume), a finding counterintuitive to the argument that immigrants seek out

places with more generous redistribution so that they can benefit from public programs. In considering the effects of welfare reform shortly after its passage, George Borjas predicted, "If magnet effects are indeed a problem, the main immigrant-receiving states will soon be leading the 'race to the bottom' [in welfare generosity], as they attempt to minimize the fiscal burden imposed by the purposive clustering of immigrants in those states that provide the highest benefits" (2009b. 118). This does not seem to have been the case.

37. For more, see "A Profile of Latino Elected Officials in the United States and their Progress Since 1996," NALEO Education Fund, http://www.naleo.org/downloads/Direc Summary2010B.pdf (accessed March 24, 2013).

REFERENCES

Alesina, Alberto, Reza Baqir, and William Easterly. 1999. "Public Goods and Ethnic Divisions." *Quarterly Journal of Economics* 114(4): 1243–84

Alesina, Alberto, and Edward Glaeser. 2004. *Fighting Poverty in the US and Europe: A World of Difference.* Oxford: Oxford University Press.

Alesina, Alberto, and Eliana La Ferrara. 2002. "Who Trusts Others?" *Journal of Public Economics* 85(2): 207–34.

Alesina, Alberto, Edward Glaeser, and Bruce Sacerdote. 2001. "Why Doesn't the United States Have a European-Style Welfare State?" Brookings Papers on Economic Activity. Washington, D.C.: Brookings Institution.

Alvarez, R. Michael, and Tara L. Butterfield. 2000. "The Resurgence of Nativism in California? The Case of Proposition 187 and Illegal Immigration." *Social Science Quarterly* 81(1): 167–79.

AuClaire, Philip Arthur. 1984. "Public Attitudes Toward Social Welfare Expenditures." *Social Work* 29(2): 139–44.

Banting, Keith, and Will Kymlicka, eds. 2006. *Multiculturalism and the Welfare State: Recognition and Redistribution in Contemporary Democracies.* Oxford: Oxford University Press.

Barrilleaux, Charles, Thomas Holbrook, and Laura Langer. 2002. "Electoral Competition, Legislative Balance and American State Welfare Policy." *American Journal of Political Science* 46(2): 415–27.

Bartels, Larry M. 2008. *Unequal Democracy: The Political Economy of the New Gilded Age.* New York and Princeton, N.J.: Russell Sage Foundation and Princeton University Press.

Blalock, Hubert M. 1967. *Toward a Theory of Minority-Group Relations.* New York: John Wiley and Sons.

Bloemraad, Irene. 2006. "Becoming a Citizen in the United States and Canada: Structured Mobilization and Immigrant Political Incorporation." *Social Forces* 85(2): 667–69.

Borjas, George J. 1999a. "Immigration and Welfare Magnets." *Journal of Labor Economics* 17(4): 607–37.

———. 1999b. *Heaven's Door: Immigration Policy and the American Economy.* Princeton, N.J.: Princeton University Press.

Brooks, Clem, and Jeff Manza. 2007. *Why Welfare States Persist: The Importance of Public Opinion in Democracies.* Chicago: University of Chicago Press.

Brown, Hana. 2013. "Race, Legality, and the Social Policy Consequences of Anti-Immigration Mobilization." *American Sociological Review* 78(2): 290–314.

Brown, Robert D. 1995. "Party Cleavages and Welfare Effort in the American States." *American Political Science Review* 89(1): 23–33.

Bureau of Economic Analysis, 1999, "State Personal Income: 1929–1997" (Washington: U.S. Department of Commerce). Available at: http://www.bea.gov/scb/pdf/regional/perinc/meth/spi2997.pdf (accessed March 24, 2013).

Bureau of Economic Analysis, U.S. Department of Commerce [Interactive Data]. Regional Data, Annual State Personal Income and Employment, accessed 2011.

Carens, Joseph H. 1988. "Immigration and the Welfare State." In *Democracy and the Welfare State*, edited by Amy Gutman. Princeton, N.J.: Princeton University Press.

Chavez, Leo R. 2001. *Covering Immigration: Popular Images and the Politics of the Nation*. Berkeley: University of California Press.

Citrin, Jack, and Benjamin Highton. 2002. *How Race, Ethnicity and Immigration Shape the California Electorate*. San Francisco: Public Policy Institute of California.

Citrin, Jack, Donald P. Green, Christopher Muste, and Cara Wong. 1997. "Public Opinion Toward Immigration Reform: The Role of Economic Motivations." *Journal of Politics* 59(3): 858–81.

Clinton, William Jefferson. 1996. "Statement by the President." Press Release, August 22. Washington, D.C.: The White House, Office of the Press Secretary. Available at: http://clinton6.nara.gov/1996/08/1996-08-22-president-statement-on-welfare-reform-bill.html (accessed March 24, 2013).

Crepaz, Markus. 2008. *Trust Beyond Borders: Immigration, The Welfare State, and Identity in Modern Societies*. Ann Arbor: University of Michigan Press.

Danziger, Sandra. 2010. "The Decline of Cash Welfare and Implications for Social Policy and Poverty." *Annual Review of Sociology* 35(2020): 523–45.

Fellowes, Matthew C., and Gretchen Rowe. 2004. "Politics and the New American Welfare States." *American Journal of Political Science* 48(2): 362–73.

Fix, Michael. and Jeffrey Passel. 2002. "The Scope and Impact of Welfare Reform's Immigrant Provisions." Washington, D.C.: The Urban Institute.

Fording, Richard. 2003. "'Laboratories of Democracy' or Symbolic Politics? The Racial Origins of Welfare Reform." In *Race and the Politics of Welfare Reform*, edited by Sanford F. Schram, Joe Soss, and Richard C. Fording. Ann Arbor: University of Michigan Press.

Fox, Cybelle. 2004. "The Changing Color of Welfare? How Whites' Attitudes Towards Latinos Influence Support for Welfare." *American Journal of Sociology* 110(3): 580–625.

———. 2010. "The Three Worlds of Relief: Race, Immigration, and City-Level Spending on Public and Private Outdoor Relief in the United States, 1929." *American Journal of Sociology* 116(2): 453–502.

———. 2012. *Three Worlds of Relief: Race, Immigration, and the American Welfare State from the Progressive Era to the New Deal*. Princeton, N.J.: Princeton University Press.

Fujiwara, Lynn. 2008. *Mothers Without Citizenship: Asian Immigrant Families and the Consequences of Welfare Reform*. Minneapolis: University of Minnesota Press.

Gais, Thomas and R. Kent Weaver. 2002. "State Policy Choices Under Welfare Reform." Policy Brief no. 21. Washington, D.C.: Brookings Institution.

Gais, Thomas, Lucy Dadayan, Suho Bae, and Sung Kyun Kwan. 2009. "The Decline of States

Financing the U.S. Safety Net: Retrenchment in State and Local Social Welfare Spending, 1977–2007." New York: Nelson A Rockefeller Institute of Government.

Gesthuizen, Maurice, Tom van der Meer, and Peer Scheepers. 2009. "Ethnic Diversity and Social Capital in Europe: Tests of Putnam's Thesis in European Countries." *Scandinavian Political Studies* 32(2): 121–42.

Gibson, Campbell, and Emily Lennon. 1999. "Historical Census Statistics on the Foreign-Born Population of the United States: 1850–1990." *U.S. Census Bureau* working paper no. 29. Washington, D.C.: Government Printing Office.

Gilens, Martin. 2005. "Inequality and Democratic Responsiveness." *Public Opinion Quarterly* 69(5): 778–96.

Gitlin, Todd. 1995. *The Twilight of Common Dreams: Why America Is Wracked by Culture Wars.* New York: Metropolitan Books.

Goodhart, David. 2004a. "Too Diverse?" *Prospect Magazine* 95 (February). Available at: http://www.prospectmagazine.co.uk/magazine/too-diverse-david-goodhart-multiculturalism-britain-immigration-globalisation (accessed March 22, 2013).

———. 2004b. "Diversity Divide." *Prospect Magazine* 97 (April). Available at: http://www .prospectmagazine.co.uk/magazine/diversitydivide (accessed March 22, 2013).

Govtrack. 2012. *Members of Congress, Sponsorship Analysis.* Data generated by authors, using http://www.govtrack.us/congress/members/ (accessed June 12, 2012).

Groenendijk, K. 2008. *Local Voting Rights for Non-Nationals in Europe: What We Know and What We Need to Learn.* Washington D.C.: Migration Policy Institute.

Hacker, Jacob S., and Paul Pierson. 2010. *Winner-Take-All Politics: How Washington Made the Rich Richer – and Turned Its Back on the Middle Class.* New York: Simon and Schuster.

Hasenfeld, Yeheskel, and Jane A. Rafferty. 1989. "The Determinants of Public Attitudes Toward the Welfare State." *Social Forces* 67(4): 1027–48.

Hero, Rodney E. 2003. "Social Capital and Racial Inequality in America." *Perspectives on Politics* 1(1): 113–22.

Hero, Rodney, and Robert Preuhs. 2006. "From Civil Rights to Multiculturalism and Welfare for Immigrants: An Egalitarian Tradition Across the American States?" *Du Bois Review: Social Science Research on Race* 3(2): 317–40.

———. 2007. "Immigration and the Evolving American Welfare State: Examining Policies in the U.S. States." *American Journal of Political Science* 51(3): 498–517.

Hoefer, Michael, Nancy Rytina, and Bryan C. Baker. 2011. "Estimates of the Unauthorized Immigrant Population Residing in the United States: January 2010." Washington: U.S. Department of Homeland Security, Office of Immigration Statistics.

Hooghe, Marc, Tim Reeskens, Dietlind Stolle, and Ann Trappers. 2009. "Ethnic Diversity and Generalized Trust in Europe: A Cross-National Multilevel Study." *Comparative Political Studies* 42(2): 198–223.

Hopkins, Daniel J. 2010. "Politicized Places: Explaining Where and When Immigrants Provoke Local Opposition." *American Political Science Review* 104(1):40–60.

Howard, Christopher. 1999. "The American Welfare State, or States?" *Political Research Quarterly* 52(2): 421–42.

Humes, Karen R., Nicholas A. Jones, and Roberto R. Ramirez. 2011. "Overview of Race and Hispanic Origin: 2010." *Census Brief* C2010BR-02. Washington: U.S. Census Bureau. Available at: http://www.census.gov/prod/cen2010/briefs/c2010br-02.pdf.

Huntington, Samuel. 2004. "The Hispanic Challenge."*Foreign Policy* (March/April): 30–45.

Kaushal, Neeraj. 2005. "New Immigrants' Location Choices: Magnets Without Welfare." *Journal of Labor Economics* 23(1): 59–80.

Key, V. O. 1949. *Southern Politics in State and Nation*. Knoxville: University of Tennessee Press.

King, Miriam, Steven Ruggles, J. Trent Alexander, Sarah Flood, Katie Genadek, Mathew B. Schroeder, Brandon Trampe, and Rebecca Vick. 2010. Integrated Public Use Microdata Series, Current Population Survey, Version 3.0. [Machine-readable database]. Minneapolis: University of Minnesota.

Lee, Yueh-Ting, Victor Ottati, and Imtiaz Hussain. 2001. "Attitudes Toward 'Illegal' Immigration into the United States: California Proposition 187." *Hispanic Journal of Behavioral Sciences* 23(4): 430–43.

McCarty, Nolan, Keith T. Poole, and Howard Rosenthal. 2006. *Polarized America: The Dance of Ideology and Unequal Riches*. Cambridge, Mass.: MIT Press.

Miller, David. 1995. *On Nationality*. New York: Oxford University Press.

Moffit, Robert. 2007. "Four Decades of Antipoverty Policy: Past Developments and Future Directions." *Focus* 25(1): 359–44.

Moller, Stephanie. 2002. "Supporting Poor Single Mothers: Gender and Race in the U.S. Welfare State." *Gender and Society* 16(4): 465–84.

Orr, Larry. 1976. "Income Transfers as a Public Good: An Application to AFDC." *The American Economic Review* 66(3): 359–71.

Passel, Jeffrey S., and D'Vera Cohn. 2011. "Unauthorized Immigrant Population: National and State Trends, 2010." Washington, D.C.: Pew Hispanic Center.

Phillips, Katherin Ross. 2001. "Who Knows About the Earned Income Tax Credit." *New Federalism* series no. B-27. Washington, D.C.: The Urban Institute.

Piketty, Thomas, and Emmanuel Saez. 2003. "Income Inequality in the United States, 1913–1998." *Quarterly Journal of Economics* 118(1): 1–39.

Piven, Frances Fox, and Richard Cloward. 1971/1993. *Regulating the Poor: The Functions of Public Welfare*. New York: Vintage Books.

———. 1977/1979. *Poor People's Movements: Why they Succeed, How they Fail*. New York: Vintage Books.

Preuhs, Robert. 2007. "Descriptive Representation as a Mechanism to Mitigate Policy Backlash: Latino Incorporation and Welfare Policy in the American States." *Political Research Quarterly* 60(2): 277–92

Public Policy Institute of California. 2013. *PPIC Statewide Survey.* January and May 2010, 2011, 2012. Available at: http://www.ppic.org/main/series.asp?i=12 (accessed April 11, 2013).

Putnam, Robert D. 2007. "E Pluribus Unum: Diversity and Community in the Twenty-first Century." *Scandinavian Political Studies* 30 (2): 137–74.

Quadagno, Jill. 1994. *The Color of Welfare: How Racism Undermined the War on Poverty*. Oxford: Oxford University Press.

Rainwater, Lee and, Timothy M. Smeeding. 2003. *Poor Kids in a Rich Country: America's Children in Comparative Perspective*. New York: Russell Sage Foundation.

Ramakrishnan, S. Karthick. 2005. *Democracy in Immigrant America: Changing Demographics and Political Participation*. Palo Alto, Calif.: Stanford University Press.

Ramakrishnan, S. Karthick and Thomas J. Espenshade. 2001. "Immigrant Incorporation and Political Participation in the United States." *International Migration Review* 35(3): 870–907.

Reese, Ellen. 2005. *Backlash Against Welfare Mothers: Past and Present*. Berkeley: University of California Press.

Reese, Ellen, and Elvia Ramirez. 2003. "The Politics of Welfare Inclusion: Explaining State-Level Restorations of Legal Immigrants' Welfare Rights." Paper presented at the American Sociological Association. Atlanta (August 16, 2003).

Roh, Jungho. 2008. "Immigrants in the United States and their Political Views on Welfare." Paper presented at the Midwest Political Science Association. Chicago (April 3, 2008).

Ruggles, Steven J., Trent Alexander, Katie Genadek, Ronald Goeken, Matthew B. Schroeder, and Matthew Sobek. 2010. Integrated Public Use Microdata Series, Version 5.0. [Machine-Readable Database]. Minneapolis: University of Minnesota.

Schmidt, Lucie. 2004. "Effects of Welfare Reform on the Supplemental Security Income (SSI) Program." Policy Brief no. 4. Ann Arbor, Mich.: National Poverty Center.

Schram, Sanford F., Joe Soss, Richard C. Fording, and Linda Houser. 2009. "Deciding to Discipline: Race, Choice, and Punishment at the Frontlines of Welfare Reform." *American Sociological Review* 74(3): 398–422.

Soroka, Stuart, Richard Johnston, and Keith Banting. 2006. "Immigration and Redistribution in a Global Era." In *Globalization and Egalitarian Redistribution*, edited by Sam Bowles, Pranab Bardhan, and Michael Wallerstein. Princeton, N.J.: Princeton University Press and Russell Sage Foundation.

Soss, Joe, Sanford F. Schram, Thomas P. Vartanian, and Erin O'Brien. 2001. "Setting the Terms of Relief: Explaining State Policy Choices in the Devolution Revolution." *American Journal of Political Science* 45(2): 378–95.

Tax Policy Center. "Earned Income Tax Credit: Number of Recipients and Amount of Credit, 1975–2010," November 20, 2012. Available at: http://www.taxpolicycenter.org/taxfacts/Content/PDF/eitc_recipients.pdf (accessed May 28, 2013).

Tumlin, Karen, Wendy Zimmerman, and Jason Ost. 1999. *State Snapshots of Public Benefits for Immigrants: A Supplemental Report to "Patchwork Policies."* The Urban Institute, Washington, D.C.

Urban Institute. 2011. Welfare Rules Database [Interactive Data]. Washington, D.C. Available at: http://anfdata.urban.org/wrd/WRDWelcome.cfm (accessed October 15, 2011).

U.S. Census Bureau. 1969. *Statistical Abstract of the United States: 1969*. Washington, DC. Available at: http://www2.census.gov/prod2/statcomp/documents/1969-05.pdf (accessed May 28, 2013).

——— . 1972. *Statistical Abstract of the United States: 1972*. Washington, DC. Available at: http://www2.census.gov/prod2/statcomp/documents/1972-05.pdf (accessed May 28, 2013).

——— . 2011. *Statistical Abstract of the United States: 2011*. Washington, DC. Available at: http://www.census.gov/compendia/statab/2011/tables/11s0561.pdf (accessed May 28, 2013).

——— . 2012. *2010 American Community Survey 1-Year Estimates*. Data generated by authors, using American FactFinder. Available at: http://factfinder2.census.gov (accessed June 12, 2012).

U.S. Department of Agriculture. "Supplemental Nutrition Assistance Program: Average Monthly Participation (Persons)," Data as of May 10, 2013. Available at: http://www.fns.usda.gov/pd/15SNAPpartPP.htm (accessed May 28, 2013).

———. "WIC Program Participation and Costs," Data as of May 10, 2013. Available at: http://www.fns.usda.gov/pd/wisummary.htm (accessed May 28, 2013).

Van Hook, Jennifer, and Frank D. Bean. 2009. "Explaining Mexican-Immigrant Welfare Behaviors: The Importance of Employment-Related Cultural Repertoires." *American Sociological Review* 74(3): 423–44.

Van Hook, Jennifer, Susan K. Brown, and Frank D. Bean. 2006. "For Love or Money? Welfare Reform and Immigrant Naturalization." *Social Forces* 85(2): 643–66.

Voss, Kim, and Irene Bloemraad. 2011. *Rallying for Immigrant Rights: The Fight for Inclusion in 21st Century America*. Berkeley: University of California Press.

Watson, Tara. 2010. "Inside the Refrigerator: Immigration Enforcement and Chilling in Immigrant Medicaid Participation." *NBER* working paper 16278. Cambridge, Mass.: National Bureau of Economic Research.

Wiseman, Michael. 2010. "Supplemental Security Income for the Second Decade." Washington, D.C.: The Urban Institute. Available at: http://www.urban.org/uploadedpdf/412266-supplementalsecurityincome.pdf (accessed May 31, 2011).

Wright, Gerald C. Jr. 1976. "Racism and Welfare Policy in America." *Social Science Quarterly* 57: 718–30.

Zavodny, Madeline. 1999. "Determinants of Recent Immigrants' Locational Choices." *International Migration Review* 33(4): 1014–30.

Zimmerman, Wendy, and Karen Tumlin. 1999. *Patchwork Policies: State Assistance for Immigrants Under Welfare Reform*. Washington, D.C.: The Urban Institute.

Part IV

Immigrants in Europe

The primary focus of this volume is on immigration and poverty in the United States. Increasingly, however, immigration is a concern in other developed countries, including the nations of Europe, which have experienced unprecedented increases in immigrant inflows over the past two decades. Chapter 13 provides an overview of the recent experiences of the foreign born in Western European countries.

Chapter 13

Immigration: The European Experience

Christian Dustmann and Tommaso Frattini

For most European countries, large-scale immigration is a more recent phenomenon than for countries such as Australia, the United States, or Canada. For instance, although Germany and Spain today have foreign-born populations similar to that of the United States in relative terms (14.5 percent and 13 percent of their total populations, respectively), the share of foreign born in West Germany before 1960 and in Spain before the early 1990s was below 1 percent. By contrast, the foreign-born population in the United States was 12.5 percent in 2009, but 13.6 percent in 1900. Immigration to Europe is also heterogeneous: immigrant populations differ in terms of ethnicity, origin, and educational attainment. For instance, more than 70 percent of the foreign born population in Ireland comes from within the EU, but only 21 percent does in the neighboring United Kingdom, where almost one-third of the immigrant population comes from South Asia.

Why are immigrant populations so different across countries? How are the different historical experiences of individual countries reflected in the current composition of immigrants and their labor market integration? We begin with a brief overview of the history of migration to European countries, highlighting differences and similarities across countries.

MIGRATION TO EUROPE: A BRIEF HISTORICAL PERSPECTIVE

The heterogeneity in migrations experienced across countries is enormous after World War II. Some countries saw large immigration, others predominantly emigration, and still others have changed from emigration to immigration. Countries differ also in the type, origin, and composition of their immigrant populations.

Population Movements After World War II

The peace treaties at the end of World War II lay the foundation for the new geopolitical landscape in postwar Europe, giving rise to large population movements into and across Europe. Countries like Germany and Austria were substantially reduced in their national boundaries, and other countries expanded. Further, the beginning of the cold war created a politically and economically divided Europe with separate political structures and economic systems. The postwar period also saw a continuation of decolonization and the withdrawal of the old colonial powers from their former colonies. Strong economic growth in some European countries in the decades between the mid-1950s and the mid-1970s led to large immigration movements from the periphery of Europe into its center, and from countries to which links existed through colonial histories. In addition, the foundation of the European Economic Community in 1957 and its subsequent expansion, establishing an ever-larger common market with free movement of people, goods, and capital affected migration movements. Finally, the collapse of the Soviet empire led to conflicts and refugee movements as a consequence of a worldwide political and economic restructuring, as well as previously suppressed intra-European movements.

Immediate Postwar Period

An immediate consequence of the partitions and political separations following World War II were large intra-European movements due to displacement and forced resettlement. The country most affected was Germany. According to John Salt and Hugh Clout (1976), by 1950 some 7.8 million refugees had found a new home in West Germany and 3.5 million in East Germany. Refugees were largely displaced ethnic German populations from new Eastern bloc countries like Poland, Czechoslovakia, Hungary, and the Soviet Union, or refugees who resettled for political reasons. These movements gradually ebbed away as eastern European countries became increasingly insulated, symbolized by the building of the Berlin wall in 1961.

Economic Expansion and Decolonization

Starting in the early 1950s, European countries experienced a second large migration wave, quite different from the first. This time the movement was one from southern Europe, as well as non-European Mediterranean countries and former colonies, into western and northern Europe. Reasons for these movements were a combination of the tremendous economic expansion, due to reconstruction of the economies of northern European countries, coupled with serious labor shortages, as well as decolonization of former colonial powers. A most significant feature of these migrations was that they drew ethnically diverse populations into European countries that so far had been ethnically homogenous.

Many European colonial powers—such as the United Kingdom, France, Netherlands, Belgium, and Portugal—lost their colonies in the immediate postwar decades. Among the significant events were the independence from Great Britain of India and Pakistan in 1947 and of Ghana in 1957, Congo's from Belgium in 1960, and Algeria's from France in 1962. Population movements from the former colonies to the home countries were initially facilitated by former colonial powers granting rights to citizens of former colonies. Decolonization let Europeans who had settled in former colonies, sometimes for several generations, migrate back after colonial rule had ceased, but it also saw citizens of former colonies moving to Europe, sometimes for political but more often for economic reasons. During this period, the Netherlands received immigrants from Indonesia in the 1950s and from Surinam in early 1970s. The United Kingdom received immigrants from the Caribbean, Asia, and East Africa—some 20,000 Ugandan Asians in 1972 alone as a result of political persecution. After the Algerian war in 1962, France received 1 million Algerians of European origin (McDonald 1965) as well as many Northern African immigrants. It is these populations and their children who were at the root of recent social tensions, for instance in the Netherlands in 2004 and in France in 2005.

These large inflows were initially quite easily absorbed, due to the economic expansion of western and northern Europe, and the accompanying need of their industries for low skilled labor. In fact, immigrants were largely welcomed and immigrations were encouraged. Former colonial powers—such as France and the United Kingdom—drew mainly on their former colonies to satisfy demands for unskilled labor. Other countries—such as Germany, Austria, or the Scandinavian countries—actively recruited workers predominantly from the southern peripheries of Europe, the Mediterranean countries, and Turkey. Recruitment of a migrant unskilled workforce was usually regulated by bilateral agreements. An important feature of these migrations was that they were considered temporary: migrants were expected to return to their home countries after the economic boom had ebbed. In the absence of any contractual or legal arrangements on their temporary status, however, many immigrants settled permanently. By 1973, the total foreign population in Germany alone had grown to 3.9 million, some 9.8 percent of the population.

This second large immigration wave came to a halt with the first oil crisis in 1973, leading to an economic downturn and a sharp increase in unemployment in most western and northern European countries. Nevertheless, immigration did not cease after 1973. Many immigrants settled more permanently and were joined by their families. Migration into northern Europe between 1973 and 1985 was thus predominantly characterized by family reunification.

The period between 1950 and 1973 saw opposite movements in the southern European countries. Southern Europe during the 1950s and 1960s was economically a mirror image of northern Europe, with sluggish economic development and high unemployment. The booming north was a magnet for people, whereas the south was characterized by emigration, and to some extent return migration.

Eastern and central European countries during this period were hidden behind the Iron Curtain. Although they did not participate in the large economic boom experienced in northern Europe, there was substantial difference in economic growth and prosperity, which, in a similar way, led to migration movements mainly for economic reasons.

Fall of the Berlin Wall

The next big population movement was initiated in the late 1980s by liberalized Soviet policy and accelerated by the fall of the Berlin wall in 1989. Initially, liberalization led to large East-West migrations, predominantly of people whose movements were suppressed during the Soviet era. Most significant was the movement of ethnic Germans from Eastern Europe and the former Soviet Union to Germany. In 1990 alone, more than 397,000 ethnic Germans came to Germany from eastern Europe and the former Soviet Union. During the 1990s, this inflow remained high, more than 700,000 entering Germany between 1996 and 2001 (Glitz 2012).

The collapse of Soviet rule in the early 1990s led to a wave of civil conflict and separations that led to large displacements of civil populations. The Balkan wars led to large asylum and refugee migrations. This time, however, migrations were targeting not only northern Europe, but also southern Europe. Southern countries had, partly as a result of their incorporation into the European Union, seen rapid economic development and convergence to northern Europe during the 1980s. Immigration was not limited to former western European countries, however. The fall of the Iron Curtain and the transition of former Soviet Bloc countries to free market economies led to different economic developments in these countries, triggering migration flows from the poorer countries to the richer. During the Balkan wars, countries that either had already large populations from the former Yugoslavia, such as Germany or Austria, and countries that were immediate neighbors, such as Greece, experienced large in-migrations. This wave of immigration ebbed down toward the end of the 1990s, when the conflicts ended.

EU Eastern Enlargement and Beyond

The next wave of movements in Europe was mainly internal, and triggered by the expansion of the European Union toward the former Eastern European countries. European legislation foresees that citizens of countries that join the European Union can freely move across those countries. However, established member states may impose, during a seven-year transition period, limitations to the employment of citizens of new member countries (for details, see Dustmann et al. 2003). After the EU accession of eight central and eastern European countries on

May 1, 2004, the United Kingdom, Sweden, and Ireland allowed citizens of the new accession countries to work in their labor markets immediately, which led to sizeable movements from particularly Poland (the largest of the new accession countries) into these countries. It is estimated that between 2004 and 2008, Poland experienced the net outflow of more than 300,000 citizens, about 1 percent of the total population (see Dustmann, Frattini, and Rosso 2012). Also, enlargement led to movements into other European countries like Italy and Spain. Although new EU citizens were allowed to freely travel to these countries, taking up an employee job was illegal, and led many new accession citizens to engage in illegal work relationships. Further, continuing conflicts around the world, and improved travel and information technologies dramatically increased the pressure on Europe's southern borders, with countries like Italy and Greece receiving large inflows of asylum and illegal immigrants, many arriving by boat on largely uncontrollable sea borders.

Table 13.1 illustrates the magnitude and the composition of immigrant populations in different European countries as of 2007–2009, and contrasts them with the United States.[1]

In many of the countries presented in table 13.1, the stock of immigrants in total population is above 10 percent. Southern European countries and the Nordic countries tend to have the lowest immigrant populations, with the exception of Sweden (15 percent) and Spain (13 percent). Overall, more than 11 percent of the population in European countries are foreign born. This is only 1 percentage point lower than the United States. However, the composition of the immigrant population differs widely between Europe and the United States (see chapter 1, this volume). In the United States, more than 50 percent of the foreign-born population comes from Latin America. In Europe, only 12 percent do. Similarly, one in four immigrants in the United States come from South and East Asia (25 percent). In Europe, only one in ten did (11 percent). Within Europe, heterogeneity is substantial across countries. The colonial heritage and cultural ties are evident in the composition of the immigrant population in Spain, where 47 percent come from Latin America; in France, where 40 percent come from North Africa; Portugal, where 45 percent come from Africa and 21 percent from Latin America; and in the United Kingdom, where 29 percent come from Asia.

The data in table 13.1 are likely to be an underestimate of the total stock of immigrants living in European countries because they do not include undocumented immigrants. Quantifying the size of undocumented migration in Europe is difficult because EU member states do not apply comparable internal apprehension practices, and comparison of country-specific migration-control data is therefore not viable. Estimates of the undocumented populations will therefore have to rely on country-by-country estimates, which are likely to differ in their methodology, timeliness, and reliability. According to recent estimates based on collection and harmonization of estimates from several national sources, the number of immigrants living illegally in the EU-15 countries ranged in 2008 between 1.8 and 3.3 million, or between 0.46 percent and 0.83 percent of the total population (Kovacheva and Vogel 2009). According to these estimates, between 7 percent and 12

TABLE 13.1 / Immigrants as Percentage of Total Population, 2007–2009

	Immigrants in Total Population	Composition of Immigrant Population							
		EU-15	NMS-12	Other Europe	North Africa and Middle East	Other Africa	South and East Asia	North America and Oceania	Latin America
Austria	15.68	17.55	18.7	51.18	3.58	1.2	5.44	1.07	1.29
Belgium	11.76	41.53	6.45	13.83	18.09	10.96	5.48	1.16	2.5
Germany	14.5	25.36	8.38	46.9	7.16	2.33	6.14	2.14	1.6
Denmark	7.98	20.05	5.39	26.27	16.12	4.76	16.75	8.04	2.63
Spain	13.09	13.83	13.76	3.89	15.13	2.86	3.28	0.65	46.6
Finland	2.71	29.86	10.51	33.75	7.16	5.08	8.89	2.73	2.02
France	10.66	27.57	2.99	6.11	40.23	12.08	6.79	1.56	2.67
Greece	7.79	5.85	12.89	61.34	11.98	1.02	4.36	2.21	0.35
Ireland[a]	15.59	40.16	32.66	3.21	1.54	5.71	9.59	5.6	1.53
Italy	7.41	11.37	18.11	26.72	14.03	5.48	11.27	1.81	11.2
Netherlands	10.66	17.39	3.57	16.64	17.22	5.86	17.45	2.51	19.38
Norway	8.69	30.4	5.54	14.16	11.22	7.58	20.99	4.62	5.49
Portugal	6.48	18.51	3.06	8.31	0.23	45.04	1.73	2	21.12
Sweden	15.16	26.33	8.2	21.56	20.45	4.37	10.8	1.55	6.73
United Kingdom	11.34	18.08	13.47	3.56	4.62	16.93	29.05	7.67	6.61
Total	11.27	20.61	10.63	18.91	15.39	8.34	11.25	2.83	12.03
United States	12.50	7.44	3.23	2.57	2.82	3.04	24.75	2.79	53.37

Source: Authors' compilation based on for Europe, EULFS, years 2007, 2008, and 2009; for USA, 2006–2008 American Community Survey 3-Year Estimates, authors' elaboration based on U.S. Census Bureau Table B05006.

Note: Immigrants are defined as *foreign born* in all countries in the first column. In columns 2 through 9, they are defined as *foreign born* in all countries, except for Germany, where they are defined as *foreign nationals*.

[a]Data refer to 2008 and 2009 only.

TABLE 13.2 / Estimates of Undocumented Immigrants, 2009

	As Percent of Total Population		As Percent of Immigrant Population	
	Minimum	Maximum	Minimum	Maximum
Austria	0.22	0.65	2.23	6.55
Belgium[a]	0.82	1.24	9.44	14.16
Denmark[a]	0.02	0.09	0.34	1.69
Finland	0.15	0.23	6.57	9.86
France[a]	0.28	0.63	4.88	10.96
Germany	0.24	0.56	2.70	6.30
Greece	1.53	1.86	19.40	23.50
Ireland[a]	0.68	1.41	6.66	13.78
Italy	0.47	0.77	9.50	15.68
Netherlands[a]	0.38	0.80	9.14	19.21
Norway	0.22	0.68	2.75	8.39
Portugal[a]	0.75	0.94	18.40	22.99
Spain	0.62	0.78	6.08	7.68
Sweden[a]	0.09	0.13	1.63	2.14
United Kingdom	0.68	1.41	11.39	23.58
EU-15[a]	0.46	0.83	6.63	11.87
United States	3.5		28.4	

Source: Authors' compilation based on Vogel and Kolacheva (2009) (European countries) and Hoefer et al. (2010) (United States).
[a]Denotes low-quality estimates.

percent of the total EU-15 immigrant population would be undocumented. In contrast, Michael Hoefer and his colleagues (2010) estimate that 10.8 million unauthorized immigrants, about 28 percent of the total immigrant population, were living in the United States as of January 2009. Based on these estimates, undocumented immigrants are a much larger share of the population in the United States than in Europe. However, the estimates of undocumented immigrants vary largely across EU countries. Table 13.2 reports country-by country estimates of the magnitude of the unauthorized immigrant population in EU-15 countries in 2008; the last row reports for comparison estimates for the United States.

The figures in table 13.2 should be interpreted with caution, given the likely poor quality of estimates for the illegal population of immigrants in the European countries. The estimates suggest that undocumented immigration is close to zero in the Scandinavian countries; the exception is Finland, where legal immigrants are less than 3 percent of the total population (see table 13.1). On the other hand, the undocumented population is estimated to be much larger in southern Europe, except for Spain, and in countries like the Netherlands and the United Kingdom. The upper-bound estimates for Portugal and the United Kingdom point at one in four immigrants being undocumented. Note also that the size of the undocumented population in countries like Italy and Spain fluctuates considerably over time, due to repeated amnesties (see Fasani 2010).

DATA

The study of European immigration is not straightforward due to the scarcity of European-wide datasets. Furthermore, a problem for multinational comparisons is the definition of *immigrants*. In Anglo-Saxon countries, immigrants are people born outside their country of residence. In countries with citizenship based on blood ancestry, however, the term can include people born in the country but who are not citizens (for example, children of Turkish nationals born in Germany). Likewise, people born abroad but whose parents are nationals may not be classified as immigrants, for example, ethnic Germans born in eastern Europe who moved to Germany after 1990. In this chapter, we rely on information on country of birth to define immigrants. However, when we distinguish by areas of origin (including EU or non-EU), we base the classification on nationality for Germany, but use country of birth for other countries.

Our analysis is based on the European Labor Force Survey (EULFS), which is conducted in the twenty-seven member states of the European Union and two countries of the European Free Trade Association (EFTA). It is a large quarterly household sample survey of people age fifteen and older and of persons outside the labor force. The National Statistical Institutes of each member country are responsible for selecting the sample, preparing the questionnaires, conducting the direct interviews among households, and forwarding the results to Eurostat in accordance with the common coding scheme. The data collection started in 1983, though not all countries are included in all years. In spring 2002, the EULFS sample size across the EU was about 1.5 million individuals. The EULFS collects information on respondents' personal circumstances, their household structure and their labor market status during a reference period of one to four weeks immediately before the interview. Personal circumstances include nationality, country of birth, and years of residence in the host country, if applicable. However, the EULFS does not have information on respondents' ethnicity. Additionally, information on household structure is not currently available for Denmark, Finland, Norway, and Sweden. Since 2009, and for that year only, the EULFS provides, for some countries, information on individuals' position in the national distribution of take-home wages. This information is available for Belgium, Germany, Finland, France, and Italy only.[2]

We focus our analysis on fifteen western European countries: fourteen members of the European Union in 1995, plus Norway. To have a large enough sample size, we pool years 2007 through 2009. The primary reason for not considering the new eastern European accession countries is that their experience as immigrant-receiving countries is quite recent and that they have small immigrant populations.

EDUCATION AND LABOR MARKET OUTCOMES

In investigating the labor market performance of immigrants in Europe, we first analyze immigrants' educational achievements, relative to natives, in the countries we consider. The analysis relies on the variable *highest qualification achieved*, which is coded in each country according to the ISCED (International Standard Classification of Education).[3]

Education

In table 13.3, the left columns present the share of natives and immigrants with lower-secondary education (ISCED levels 0–2), and the right columns the share of natives and immigrants with tertiary (ISCED levels 5 and 6) education, for each country.

The numbers show that, on average, immigrants in Europe are slightly less educated than natives: tertiary and lower-secondary education among immigrants is 24 percent and 38 percent; among natives, 26 percent and 32 percent. Further, the correlation between natives' and immigrants' qualifications is positive and statistically significant: 0.7 for tertiary education and 0.6 for lower secondary. These numbers conceal the substantial differences that exist across countries of origin, even within destination country. The last column of table 13.3 presents the (unweighted) standard deviations of the share of lower-secondary educated immigrant from

TABLE 13.3 / Immigration and Education, by Country

	Percent with Lower Secondary Education		Percent with Tertiary Education		Standard Deviation
	Natives	Immigrants	Natives	Immigrants	
Austria	16.33	33.93	17.51	18.07	14.00
Belgium	29.03	42.72	32.8	28.4	15.92
Germany	10.47	37.53	27.02	19.31	15.93
Denmark	23.78	27.10	33.18	33.41	10.11
Spain	50.72	40.60	30.15	24.38	19.70
Finland	19.59	24.54	36.75	31.86	10.65
France	28.38	46.07	27.58	23.98	12.68
Greece	39.25	46.08	22.9	15.69	19.09
Ireland	33.04	18.51	31.32	46.34	10.43
Italy	48.36	45.32	13.62	12.85	13.19
Netherlands	27.18	37.91	31.14	25.91	12.71
Norway	19.90	27.02	34.01	38.51	12.34
Portugal	74.69	52.41	13.01	21.82	14.01
Sweden	15.31	25.18	30.9	31.94	9.19
United Kingdom	30.00	24.28	30.57	33.96	6.79
Total	31.74	38.05	25.83	23.51	15.4

Source: Authors' compilation based on EULFS (2007–2009).
Note: The Standard Deviation column shows the standard deviation of the share of individuals with lower secondary education across different immigrant groups within each country. The sample is restricted to working-age population older than twenty-five, not in full-time education, and not in military service. We define immigrants as *foreign born* in all countries.

TABLE 13.4 / Immigration and Education, by Area of Origin

	Percent with Lower Secondary Education	Percent with Tertiary Education
Natives	31.74	25.83
EU-15	35.08	29.35
NMS-12	23.40	21.03
Other Europe	49.01	14.74
North Africa and near Middle East	50.98	20.52
Other Africa	39.01	27.84
South and East Asia	40.04	26.26
North America and Oceania	14.10	49.55
Latin America	37.19	22.79
All immigrants	38.05	23.51

Source: Authors' compilation based on EULFS (2007–2009).
Note: The sample is restricted to working-age population older than twenty-five, not in full-time education, and not in military service. We define immigrants as *foreign born* in all countries, except for Germany, where they are defined as *foreign nationals*.

different origin groups within each country. It shows that there is considerable heterogeneity in the educational attainment of different immigrant groups within the same destination country (for more detail, see Dustmann and Glitz 2011).

We present differences in educational attainment across countries of origin in table 13.4, where we pool all European countries of destination.

The figures in the table show that North American and Oceanian immigrants are better educated than natives: almost 50 percent of individuals from these groups have a tertiary education, and only 14 percent have less than secondary education. By contrast, non-EU European and North African immigrants appear to have less education than natives, about 50 percent having at most a lower-secondary education. The educational distribution of EU-15 immigrants, on the other hand, is similar to that of natives, though more polarized. Even more dramatic is the polarization of African and Asian immigrants, who display higher tertiary education rates than European natives but also a substantially larger share of less educated individuals.

Employment

Figure 13.1 presents differences in employment probabilities between immigrants and natives across the different countries we consider.

The darker bars report the unconditional immigrant-native difference in employment probabilities (net of year and seasonality effects).[4] The figures show that in most countries immigrants experience a substantial labor market disadvantage. In Spain and Ireland, employment rates of natives and immigrants are not significantly different. In Greece, Italy, and Portugal, however, all three immigration

FIGURE 13.1 / Immigrant-Native Employment Differentials

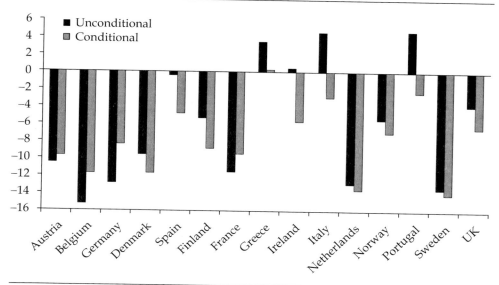

Source: Authors' compilation based on European Labor Force Survey (2007–2009).
Note: The differences in employment probabilities are obtained from regressions of a dummy for employment on a dummy for immigrants. Separate regressions by country.

countries only since the late 1990s, immigrants have a higher probability of employment than natives.

To what extent are these differences due to a different composition of the immigrant and native workforce in terms of age, education (see table 13.3), and gender mix? The lighter bars of figure 13.1 display differences in probability of employment after conditioning on these variables, as well as on the region of residence within a country (for details, see note 4). Clearly, if immigrants and natives lived in the same areas, and were identical in their demographic characteristics, immigrants would still be worse off in most countries. Moreover, conditioning on observable characteristics turns the immigrant-native employment differential negative in Ireland, Italy, and Portugal, and eliminates the positive difference in Greece. Thus, comparing immigrants to natives with the same observable characteristics, and who live in the same geographical areas, shows that immigrants have lower employment probabilities than natives in all countries, except for Greece, where differences disappear.

We have shown that the composition of the immigrant population varies across European countries, and that different origin groups differ, for instance, in their human capital. How do immigrants from different origin regions compare with natives within each of the countries we consider? In table 13.5, we report employment probability differentials where we distinguish between EU and non-EU immigrants, with natives of each country as the reference group.

Immigration, Poverty, and Socioeconomic Inequality

TABLE 13.5 / Immigrant-Native Employment Rate Differentials

	EU	Non-EU	EU	Non-EU	EU	Non-EU
Austria	-0.058**	-0.128**	-0.048**	-0.129**	-0.059**	-0.118**
Belgium	-0.088**	-0.207**	-0.062**	-0.195**	-0.029**	-0.197**
Germany	-0.053**	-0.219**	-0.067**	-0.227**	-0.032**	-0.162**
Denmark	-0.028**	-0.118**	-0.029**	-0.121**	-0.034**	-0.146**
Spain	-0.006	-0.003	-0.008	-0.011*	-0.059**	-0.044**
Finland	0.032*	-0.122**	0.030*	-0.119**	-0.013	-0.150**
France	-0.065**	-0.135**	-0.074**	-0.151**	-0.010	-0.129**
Greece	0.012*	0.040**	0.045**	0.026**	0.003	0.003
Ireland	0.015**	-0.028**	0.013**	-0.027**	-0.035**	-0.130**
Italy	0.042**	0.048**	0.044**	0.010**	-0.027**	-0.032**
Netherlands	-0.053**	-0.149**	-0.043**	-0.147**	-0.061**	-0.156**
Norway	0.019*	-0.100**	0.014	-0.105**	-0.009	-0.108**
Portugal	0.069**	0.041**	0.069**	0.042**	-0.029**	-0.022**
Sweden	-0.090**	-0.158**	-0.094**	-0.167**	-0.079**	-0.174**
United Kingdom	0.037**	-0.073**	0.033**	-0.076**	0.013*	-0.101**
Year and quarter effects	Yes	Yes	Yes	Yes	Yes	Yes
Gender	No	No	Yes	Yes	Yes	Yes
Region effects	No	No	Yes	Yes	Yes	Yes
Age	No	No	No	No	Yes	Yes
Education	No	No	No	No	Yes	Yes

Source: Authors' compilation based on EULFS (2007–2009).
Note: The values are the estimated coefficients of separate regressions by country of a dummy for having a job on dummies for EU and non-EU immigrants. Separate regressions are run for each country. The sample are individuals in working-age population not in military service and not in education or training. We define an individual as in employment if he or she is employed or self-employed. Year and quarter effects: year-quarter interaction dummies. Gender: dummy for female. Age: dummies for five-year age groups. Education: dummies for lower secondary, secondary, and tertiary education.
*p < 0.10, **p < 0.01

Columns 1 and 2 show that in all countries—save Greece, Spain, and Italy—EU immigrants perform better than non-EU immigrants: the difference in EU immigrants' employment rate relative to natives is at least half that of non-EU immigrants. In columns 3 and 4 and 5 and 6, we gradually make immigrants "more similar" to natives. Columns 3 and 4 report the difference in employment probability of EU and non-EU immigrants relative to natives, after controlling for gender composition and regional distribution. The results are only marginally different from those in columns 1 and 2. In columns 5 and 6, we control additionally for differences in age and education between the two populations. This eliminates any difference in the employment probability of natives and EU immigrants in Finland, France, Greece, and Norway. EU immigrants have a higher probability of employment than natives in the United Kingdom, however. In the other countries, the employment gap ranges between 7.9 percentage points in Sweden and 2.7 in Italy in favor of natives. Non-EU immigrants are significantly more disadvantaged in all countries. Even if they had the same characteristics as natives, they would

ᅠ

ᅠ

ᅠᅠ

ᅠ

ᅠ

ᅠ

ᅠᅠ

434 /

still have an employment probability 20 percentage points lower than natives in Belgium, 16 points in Germany, 16 points in the Netherlands, and 17 points in Sweden.

Occupational Distribution

We now consider immigrants' occupational distributions and how these differ between immigrants and natives.

Table 13.6 reports the Duncan dissimilarity index for the distribution of EU (odd columns) and non-EU (even columns) immigrants and natives across occupations (at 1-digit ISCO levels),[5] corrected to account for sampling error (for a similar approach to a different index, see Hellerstein, Neumark, and McInerney 2007; Carrington and Troske 1997). The index can be interpreted as the percentage of immigrants who would be required to change occupation for immigrants and natives to have the same occupational distribution. Therefore, the higher the index, the more dissimilar is the occupational distribution of immigrants and natives.

The first column of table 13.6 presents the overall index for EU immigrants and column 2 the index for non-EU immigrants, both relative to natives. The entries show that in most countries EU immigrants are more similar to natives in their occupational distribution than non-EU immigrants. The exceptions are the two countries with a colonial past, France and the United Kingdom, where non-EU immigrants have an occupational distribution that is closer to that of natives. This may be related to the long experience of extra-European migration to these two countries from their former colonies. As we show, the occupational distribution of immigrants and natives becomes more similar with time spent in the host country.

In general, Nordic and central European countries tend to have a more equal occupational distribution of immigrants and natives, relative to southern European countries. For instance, in Finland, just above 1 percent of EU (13 percent of non-EU) immigrants would have to change jobs to equalize the occupational distribution of immigrants and natives. In the Netherlands, this share is about 5 percent (15 percent), in Italy about 27.5 percent (36 percent), and in Greece about 32 percent (50 percent).

One reason for the differences might simply be the diversity in the composition of the two populations, for example, different education structures. To address this, we divide the population in three education groups based on the International Standard Classification of Education (ISCED) classification, and compute the Duncan dissimilarity index within each group. We report the results in columns 3 through 8. The index tends to be lower for low-education groups, and to increase with the level of education, especially for non-EU immigrants, though there are several exceptions. Columns 9 and 10 report an average of the values of the Duncan index in each education group, weighted by the share of each group in the total population. This gives a measure of occupational dissimilarity conditional on the educational composition of immigrants and natives in each country. The values of columns 9 and 10 are, especially for non-EU immigrants, less than

TABLE 13.6 / Dissimilarity in Occupational Distribution

| | Overall Index | | Index by Educational Level | | | | | | Weighted Average Across Education | |
| | | | Low | | Medium | | High | | | |
	EU	Non-EU	EU	Non-EU	EU	Non-EU	EU	Non-EU	EU	Non-EU
Austria	11.4	34.4	10.2	30.5	11.7	32.9	9.6	19.4	11.1	30.0
Belgium	9.7	18.4	9.5	12.7	7.7	12.8	10.1	16.5	9.0	14.2
Germany	12.2	26.1	12.1	16.1	11.6	19.5	0.1	13.4	8.6	17.4
Denmark	4.1	18.3	1.8	14.5	7.6	18.1	4.1	12.8	5.0	15.5
Spain	17.1	31.4	12.6	21.4	31.9	31.0	20.0	29.7	19.8	26.6
Finland	1.2	13.4	2.1	14.8	6.7	12.0	8.4	19.5	6.6	15.3
France	17.5	12.2	25.0	14.6	8.8	6.7	6.7	13.2	12.0	10.6
Greece	31.9	50.0	32.3	43.9	33.7	45.5	18.5	58.8	29.3	48.4
Ireland	12.1	19.4	9.0	12.7	19.1	20.4	14.8	12.8	15.2	15.8
Italy	27.5	36.2	19.7	19.8	41.7	42.9	19.8	44.5	29.8	34.5
Netherlands	5.4	14.8	8.1	12.9	4.7	9.6	2.0	11.2	4.7	11.0
Norway	10.4	17.2	11.3	9.4	9.0	19.2	9.7	19.6	9.7	17.3
Portugal	8.3	12.2	5.0	15.3	15.2	26.6	6.9	15.6	7.0	17.2
Sweden	4.7	20.8	6.0	19.6	1.8	21.0	8.3	25.8	4.5	22.3
United Kingdom	12.5	9.9	18.7	15.3	18.1	12.2	2.8	4.4	13.1	10.3

Source: Authors' compilation based on EULFS (2007–2009).
Note: The table reports the Duncan dissimilarity index for the occupational distribution of immigrants relative to natives.

FIGURE 13.2 / Occupational Dissimilarity and Years Since Migration, EU Immigrants

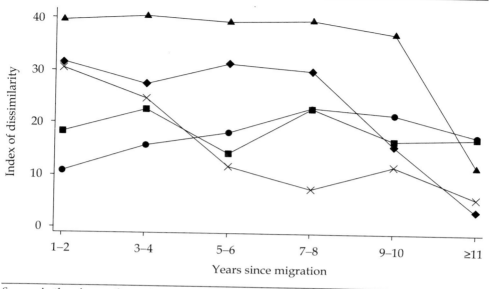

Source: Authors' compilation based on European Labor Force Survey (2007–2009).

those of columns 1 and 2, but the pattern is very similar. This indicates that differences in the educational composition are not the main reason for the differences occupational distribution of immigrants and natives.

How do immigrants assimilate in the host country labor market? Do they become more similar to natives in terms of their occupational distribution as their stay in the country increases? Figures 13.2 and 13.3 suggest that this is indeed the case.

In the figures, we plot the value of the Duncan index versus years of residence in the host country for the five largest EU destination countries: Germany, France, Spain, Italy, and United Kingdom. Figure 13.2 reports the index for EU immigrants, while figure 13.3 displays the index for non-EU immigrants.

In all countries and for both EU and non-EU immigrants, the dissimilarity index decreases with years since migration: the longer the time spent in the host country, the more similar the occupational distribution of immigrants and natives becomes. Interestingly, and especially for non-EU immigrants, the relative ranking of countries remains quite stable over time. Italy has consistently the largest dissimilarity in the occupational distribution of immigrants and natives, save for EU immigrants who have been in the country for more than ten years. Conversely, the United Kingdom, especially for non-EU immigrants, has the highest occupational similarity, although 20 percent of non-EU immigrants who live in the United Kingdom for no more than two years would have to change jobs for their occupational distribution to equalize that of natives. The changes of the index over time could

FIGURE 13.3 / Occupational Dissimilarity and Years Since Migration, Non-EU Immigrants

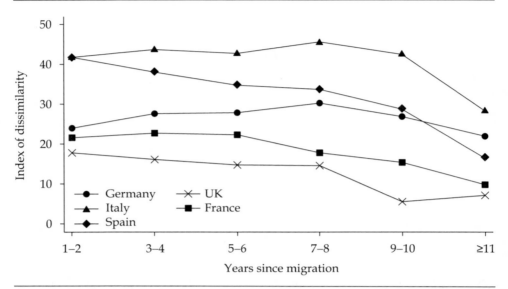

Source: Authors' compilation based on European Labor Force Survey (2007–2009).

also be due to changes in cohort composition, as well as selective emigration. Changes in cohort composition may be particularly relevant in countries such as Spain and Italy, where immigration is a recent phenomenon, and immigrants who were in the country for more than ten years in 2007 through 2009 may differ substantially from later cohorts.

This analysis shows that immigrants and natives are employed in different occupations, but it does not allow establishing whether immigrants are employed in "better" or "worse" occupations than natives.

We now measure the occupational status with the Socio-Economic Index of Occupational Status (ISEI),which captures the attributes of occupations that convert education into income (for a description of the index and its construction, see Ganzeboom, De Graaf, and Treiman 1992). Higher values correspond to occupations that reward education more, and lower values to those with lower returns.

Figure 13.4 shows the differences in the distribution of EU (dashed line) and non-EU (dotted line) immigrants relative to natives across the ISEI scale. If immigrants and natives had the same occupational distribution, then both lines would be horizontal at 0. The figure shows clearly that natives are more concentrated than immigrants in the more skilled (higher indexed) occupations. Within immigrants, non-EU immigrants are more concentrated than EU nationals in less-skilled occupations.

FIGURE 13.4 / Occupational Distribution of Immigrants Relative to Natives

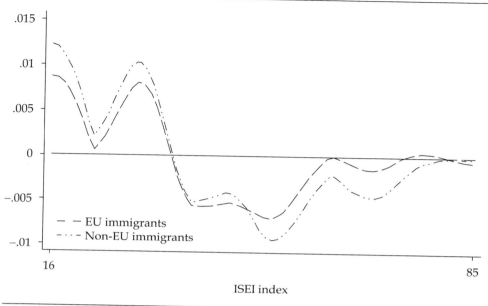

Source: Authors' compilation based on European Labor Force Survey (2007–2009).
Note: The figure reports differences between kernel density estimates of the distribution of immigrants and the distribution of natives across the ISEI scale.

Is this pattern common to all countries? We investigate the cross-country heterogeneity in occupational distributions in table 13.7, where we report the average standard deviation differences in the ISEI index between immigrants and natives in each country.

Columns 1 and 2 report unconditional differences, controlling for year and seasonality only. Non-EU immigrants (column 2) are employed in lower-skill occupations than natives in all countries, except for Ireland and Portugal, where the average value of the index is the same for both extra-EU immigrants and natives. In the United Kingdom, non-EU immigrants are on average employed in slightly higher-skill occupations than natives (7 percent of a standard deviation). The gap between immigrants and natives is highest in southern European countries, except Portugal, between 62 percent and 84 percent of a standard deviation, whereas in Nordic countries the gap is about 35 percent of a standard deviation, and a bit lower in Finland. EU immigrants, conversely, have markedly different performances in different European countries. In Austria, Belgium, Denmark, Finland, Norway, and Portugal, they are employed in more skilled occupations than natives, with an advantage as high as 30 percent of a standard deviation in Portugal. Conversely, in Germany, Spain, France, Greece, Ireland, Italy, and the United Kingdom EU,

TABLE 13.7   /   Immigrant-Native Occupational Differences

	EU	Non-EU	EU	Non-EU	EU	Non-EU
Austria	0.075**	−0.584**	−0.103**	−0.429**	−0.053**	−0.047**
Belgium	0.039**	−0.350**	−0.010	−0.294**	−0.006	−0.082**
Germany	−0.181**	−0.509**	−0.103**	−0.295**	−0.049**	−0.066**
Denmark	0.064*	−0.310**	−0.076**	−0.248**	−0.026**	−0.044**
Spain	−0.405**	−0.620**	−0.445**	−0.492**	−0.082**	−0.081**
Finland	0.073*	−0.199**	0.113**	−0.141**	0.008	−0.038**
France	−0.232**	−0.173**	−0.182**	−0.232**	−0.029**	−0.036**
Greece	−0.525**	−0.845**	−0.477**	−0.591**	−0.112**	−0.121**
Ireland	−0.263**	−0.008	−0.249**	−0.221**	0.001	−0.108**
Italy	−0.603**	−0.779**	−0.595**	−0.634**	−0.114**	−0.125**
Netherlands	0.028	−0.344**	−0.100**	−0.252**	0.007	−0.026**
Norway	0.158**	−0.317**	−0.049*	−0.336**	−0.015	−0.056**
Portugal	0.295**	−0.006	−0.111**	−0.317**	−0.024*	−0.071**
Sweden	0.006	−0.333**	−0.118**	−0.381**	0.010**	−0.036**
United Kingdom	−0.208**	0.069**	−0.237**	−0.115**	−0.039**	−0.030**
Year and quarter effects	Yes	Yes	Yes	Yes	Yes	Yes
Gender	No	No	Yes	Yes	Yes	Yes
Region effects	No	No	Yes	Yes	Yes	Yes
Age	No	No	Yes	Yes	Yes	Yes
Education	No	No	Yes	Yes	Yes	Yes
1-digit occupation	No	No	No	No	Yes	Yes

Source: Authors' compilation based on EULFS (2007–2009).
Note: Table reports the differences (as fractions of a country-specific standard deviation) in Socio-Economic Index (SEI) of immigrant workers relative to native workers. The values are the estimated coefficients of separate regressions by country of the ISEI index (normalized by its standard deviation) on dummies for EU and non-EU immigrants and year-quarter interaction dummies (columns 1–2), and other control variables (columns 3–6). Year and quarter effects: year-quarter interaction dummies. Gender: dummy for female. Region: regional dummies. Age: dummies for five-year age groups. Education: dummies for lower secondary, secondary, and tertiary education. 1-digit occupation: dummies for 1-digit ISCO codes.
$*p < 0.10$, $*p < 0.01$

immigrants are employed in less-skilled occupations than natives. Interestingly, in France and in the United Kingdom, the gap with natives in occupational prestige is higher for EU than for non-EU immigrants.

In columns 3 and 4, we control for differences in gender composition, regional distribution, age structure, and education of immigrants natives. This has important effects for both EU and non-EU immigrants. Once individual characteristics are controlled for, EU immigrants turn out to be employed in less-skilled occupations than natives in all countries, except for Belgium, where there is no significant difference, and Finland, where the occupational advantage of EU immigrants is magnified. Among non-EU immigrants, the difference turns negative also in Portugal and Ireland, where there was no unconditional difference with natives, and in the United Kingdom. Non-EU immigrants in the United Kingdom now display an occupational gap of over 10 percent of a standard deviation relative to British natives.

The previous figures show the distribution of immigrants relative to natives across occupational categories. But how are immigrants allocated to occupational categories within larger occupational groups? This is shown in columns 5 and 6 of table 13.7, where we condition on dummy variables for one-digit ISCO occupations. Thus, the entries in these columns measure the difference in occupational prestige between immigrants and natives within one-digit occupations. Although the gap reduces dramatically in all countries, it is still negative for most countries for EU immigrants, and negative and significant everywhere for non-EU immigrants. Thus, even within broad occupational classes, non-EU immigrants are employed in more unskilled occupations than natives. EU immigrants are more similar to natives: in Ireland and the Netherlands, for example, there are no differences in occupational prestige between natives and EU immigrant within the same occupation group, whereas EU immigrants in Sweden are employed in slightly more skilled jobs within the same occupation group.

IMMIGRANT'S POSITION IN THE EARNINGS DISTRIBUTION

As discussed, no good Europe-wide dataset with reliable wage measures and enough observations to investigate immigrant populations exists. For this section, we therefore use information on individuals' position in the national distribution of monthly take-home pay from main job from the 2009 EULFS. We focus here on Belgium, Germany, Finland, France, and Italy, the only countries where the information is available, and consider all employed individuals with information on position in the distribution of earnings.

Figure 13.5 displays the share of natives, EU, and non-EU immigrants in each decile of the national earnings distribution. If immigrants and natives were equally distributed, the three lines would be flat, and overlap.

Figure 13.5 shows clearly that this is not the case. Non-EU immigrants have on average lower earnings than EU immigrants and natives. About 15 percent of non-EU immigrants are in the bottom decile of the earning distribution, and another 15 percent are in the second decile. Among EU immigrants, 14 percent are in the first decile, and about 13 percent in the second, versus somewhat fewer than 10 percent of natives. The distribution of immigrants across deciles is decreasing, and increasingly fewer immigrants are in higher deciles. However, the decrease is much faster among non-EU immigrants, and the distribution of EU immigrants is relatively flat, at around 9 percent, above the median.

Immigrants, and especially non-EU immigrants, are therefore clearly disadvantaged in terms of income relative to natives, and are overrepresented in the bottom part of the income distribution.

We explore more in detail differences across areas of origin in table 13.8, where

Figure 13.5 / Immigrant and Native Earnings Distribution

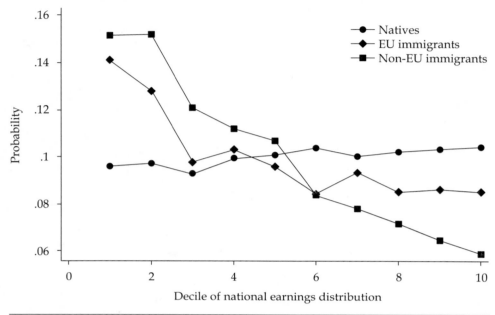

Source: Authors' compilation based on European Labor Force Survey (2009).
Note: The figure reports the share of natives, EU immigrants, and non-EU immigrants in each decile of the national earnings distribution in Belgium, Germany, Finland, France, and Italy pooled.

we report the share of natives and immigrants in each decile of the national earnings distribution, and we distinguish between immigrant groups.

Immigrants from all areas are more likely than natives to be in the bottom deciles of the earnings distribution, except for those from North America and Oceania. Latin American immigrants are most disadvantaged: 21 percent are in the first decile, and another 20 percent in the second decile. Citizens of the new EU member states are also among the most disadvantaged: 19 percent in the bottom decile and 17 percent in the second.

For most origin groups, the distribution over earnings deciles is roughly decreasing. The exceptions are North Americans and Oceanians, for which the distribution is increasing (though not monotonically), and EU-15 immigrants. The latter group has a clearly U-shaped distribution, with higher density at the two tails, and a lower concentration in the central deciles.

In table 13.9, we study the probability of being in the lowest earnings decile across destination countries, and distinguish between EU and non-EU immigrants.

Columns 1 and 2 report differences between EU (column 1) and non-EU (column 2) immigrants in the unconditional probability of being in the bottom decile of the earnings distribution, net of seasonality effects.[6] In all countries, both EU

TABLE 13.8 / Position in National Earnings Distribution

					Decile					
	1	2	3	4	5	6	7	8	9	10
Natives	9.6	9.7	9.3	10.0	10.1	10.4	10.0	10.2	10.4	10.5
EU-15	11.8	10.7	8.2	9.0	8.9	9.2	10.3	10.0	10.8	11.3
NMS-12	18.9	17.3	13.0	13.0	11.1	6.9	7.5	5.5	4.2	2.8
Other Europe	16.1	15.2	10.9	10.7	9.7	9.2	9.4	8.3	6.7	3.8
North Africa and Middle East	12.8	12.7	12.7	11.4	11.9	8.2	7.5	7.2	7.1	8.6
Other Africa	13.7	15.2	15.0	11.4	13.2	8.0	6.6	6.3	5.5	5.1
South and East Asia	17.0	19.7	12.0	13.7	9.0	7.6	6.5	5.3	4.8	4.5
North America and Oceania	7.9	6.9	11.6	10.3	10.6	9.2	6.0	9.9	8.6	19.0
Latin America	20.8	19.8	11.8	9.4	10.4	6.2	5.4	4.7	6.1	5.4

Source: Authors' compilation based on EULFS (2009).
Note: The table reports the percentage of natives and immigrants in each decile of the national earnings distribution in Belgium, Germany, Finland, France, and Italy pooled. We define immigrants as *foreign born* in all countries except for Germany, where they are defined as *foreign nationals*.

TABLE 13.9 / Immigrant-Native Differential Probability of Being in Bottom Earnings Decile

	EU	Non-EU	EU	Non-EU	EU	Non-EU
Belgium	0.035**	0.054**	0.032**	0.048**	0.029**	0.022**
Germany	0.032*	0.065**	0.023*	0.037**	0.016	0.016
Finland	–0.030	0.114**	–0.016	0.126**	–0.020	0.110**
France	0.028**	0.037**	0.029**	0.053**	0.016*	0.032**
Italy	0.093**	0.068**	0.073**	0.067**	0.024**	0.016**
Quarter effects	Yes	Yes	Yes	Yes	Yes	Yes
Gender	No	No	Yes	Yes	Yes	Yes
Region effects	No	No	Yes	Yes	Yes	Yes
Age	No	No	Yes	Yes	Yes	Yes
Education	No	No	Yes	Yes	Yes	Yes
1-digit occupation	No	No	No	No	Yes	Yes

Source: Authors' compilation based on EULFS (2009).
Note: Values are the estimated coefficients of separate regressions by country of a dummy for being in the bottom decile of the earnings distribution on dummies for EU and non-EU immigrants. Separate regressions are run for each country. Quarter effects: quarter dummies. Gender: dummy for female. Age: dummies for five-year age groups. Education: dummies for lower secondary, secondary and tertiary education.
$*p < 0.10, **p < 0.01$

and non-EU immigrants are more likely than natives to be in the bottom decile, except Finland, where there are no differences between natives and EU immigrants. Disadvantage relative to natives is highest for EU immigrants in Italy: their probability of being in the bottom decile is 9 percentage points higher than natives, versus just above 3 points in Belgium and Germany. Italy is also the only country where EU immigrants are worse off than non-EU immigrants, relative to natives. Conversely, in Finland, extra-EU immigrants are more than 11 percentage points more likely than natives and EU immigrants to be at the bottom of the earnings distribution.

In columns 3 and 4, we investigate the extent to which the differences in the probability of being at the bottom of the distribution of earnings are due to differences in immigrants' and natives' characteristics. We report probability differentials after accounting for differences in gender, age, and education, and for the regional distribution of immigrants and natives, which accounts for immigrants' being more likely to settle in the areas with higher wage levels. Conditioning on these characteristics reduces slightly the difference between natives and EU immigrants in Germany and Italy, but has no effect in other countries. For non-EU immigrants, after controlling for all observable characteristics, the probability of being at the bottom of the earnings distribution increases in Finland and France, decreases in Belgium and Germany, and is unaffected in Italy. Finally, in columns 5 and 6, we compare immigrants and natives within the same broad occupation group (1-digit ISCO code). As expected, in most countries controlling for 1-digit occupation makes the probability of being in the bottom decile more similar between immigrants and natives. However, except for Germany, even within the same broad occupation group, immigrants are more likely than natives to be at the bottom of the distribution of earnings.

CHILDREN OF IMMIGRANTS

The economic and social integration of the descendants of immigrants is likely to be one of the key challenges for many European countries over the next several decades. As we show at the beginning of this chapter, many have only a short history of immigration, but the children of immigrants are a sizable and increasing fraction of their populations.

Table 13.10 reports the share of children with immigrant parents over all children under the age of fifteen for all the countries for which we have information on household composition. We distinguish between children of EU and non-EU immigrants, and of mixed couples, where we differentiate between different parental mixes. We also report, for comparison, the share of EU and non-EU immigrants among the adult population (fifteen and older).

In all countries, the descendants of non-EU immigrants account for a larger share of the children population than their parents' share of the adult population. Mean-

TABLE 13.10 / Children in Immigrant Households

| | Children Living in an Immigrant Household | | | | | Percentage of Immigrants in Adult Population | |
| | | | | Mixed | | | |
	EU	Non-EU	EU/ Non-EU	EU/ Native	Non-EU/ Native	EU	Non-EU
Austria	3.16	17.47	0.66	4.47	4.32	5.21	8.36
Belgium	4.09	10.69	0.69	3.78	5.11	5.08	5.49
Germany	1.68	7.97	0.38	2.89	6.05	2.11	3.8
Spain	1.8	8.04	0.21	2.92	3.43	3.39	8.51
France	1.68	10.08	0.28	2.94	6.52	2.89	6.99
Greece	0.93	9.68	0.08	2.16	2.4	1.18	5.4
Ireland	7.73	4.94	0.61	9.86	2.41	8.96	3.3
Italy	1.66	7.81	0.17	2.94	3.91	1.72	4.6
Netherlands	0.84	12.9	0.35	3.11	6.18	1.5	8.14
Portugal	0.68	5.89	0.32	3.24	6.59	0.54	4.02
United Kingdom	2.12	11.03	0.48	2.37	5.06	3.03	7.44
Total	1.86	9.43	0.34	2.95	5.16	2.58	5.96

Source: Authors' compilation based on EULFS (2007–2009).
Note: All numbers are percentages. Children are those under fifteen. EU (non-EU) households are defined as households where the reference person and her or his spouse, if there is a spouse, is an EU (Non-EU) immigrant. Mixed households are households where the reference person and her or his partner have a different immigrant status. We define immigrants as *foreign born* in all countries except for Germany, where they are defined as *foreign nationals*.

while, the proportion of children of EU immigrants in the children population is slightly smaller than that of their parents in the adult population. Across all countries, EU immigrants account for 2.6 percent of the adult population, and their children for 1.9 percent of the population below the age of fifteen. Non-EU immigrants instead account for 6 percent of the adult population, but their children for 9.4 percent of all children. This may suggest a higher fertility of non-EU immigrants, which would shape the ethnic mix of the future. Moreover, almost 8.5 percent of children are from mixed couples, 3 percent having a native and an EU-immigrant parent and more than 5 percent having a native and a non-EU parent. Children of mixed EU and non-EU couples make up only 0.3 percent of all children.

For Belgium, Germany, France, and Italy, we have both information on individuals' position in the national distribution of earnings and information on household structure, and thus can study the extent to which children of immigrants are concentrated in poorest households. The EULFS does not provide information on household income. We therefore define as *low income* those households in which both the reference person and their spouse, if there is a spouse, are in the bottom decile of the earnings distribution. The first column of table 13.11 shows that the share of households that satisfy this criterion is about 5 percent in Belgium, 4 percent in Italy and France, and just over 1 percent in Germany. Column 2 shows that the share of children living in low-income households is slightly lower than the share of households in that category. The remaining columns of table 13.11 report the proportion of children of immigrants or of mixed couples out of all children who live in a low-income household, defined this way.

In all countries, the children of non-EU immigrants are much more likely than the children of natives to belong to a low-income household. For instance, in Italy the children of non-EU immigrants make up fewer than 8 percent of all children, but 20 percent of all children from low-income households. In Belgium, fewer than 11 percent of all children are the descendants of non-EU immigrants, but account for 23 percent of children in low-income households. Similarly, the children of EU immigrants are overrepresented among low-income households in all countries except Germany.[7] The children of EU immigrants in Italy are relatively more likely to be from low-income households: they account for fewer than 2 percent of all children, but 5.5 percent of those from low-income households. On the other hand, the percentage of children of mixed couples in low-income households is lower than the percentage of all children in these households. If belonging to a poor household restricts future opportunities (see, for example, Blanden, Gregg, and Macmillian 2007; Corak 2006; Jäntti et al. 2006; Solon 2002; see also chapters 6 and 7, this volume), then these numbers suggest that the disadvantage of immigrants, particularly from non-EU countries, which we illustrate in the previous sections, may carry over to their children. Research by Christian Dustmann, Tommaso Frattini, and Gianandrea Lanzara (2012) on the educational attainments of the children of immigrants is partly in line with this: they find that gaps in test scores between children of immigrants and children of natives in different countries are strongly related to their parents' achievement. However, their results also show that differences in parental background alone do not account everywhere for the entire immigrant-native achievement gap. In traditional immigration countries, like the

TABLE 13.11 / Households with Both Spouses in Bottom Decile of Earnings Distribution

	House-holds	Children in House-holds with Both Parents in Bottom Decile	Children in Immigrant Households of All Children in Households with Both Parents in Bottom Decile				
			EU	Non-EU	EU/ Non-EU	EU/ Native	Non-EU/ Native
						Mixed	
Belgium	4.88	4.60	6.50	23.01	0.22	2.86	3.39
Germany	1.15	0.80	0	19.19	0	0	5.25
France	4.22	3.35	2.54	19.11	0.08	0.69	5.70
Italy	4.05	3.30	5.55	20.06	0.11	2.01	3.03
Total	2.98	2.53	3.62	19.84	0.10	1.26	4.57

Source: Authors' compilation based on EULFS (2009).
Note: EU (Non-EU) households are defined as households where the reference person and her or his spouse, if there is a spouse, is an EU (Non-EU) immigrant. Mixed households are households where the reference person and her or his partner have a different immigrant status. We define immigrants as *foreign born* in all countries except for Germany, where they are defined as *foreign nationals*.

Anglo-Saxon countries, differences in test score gaps between children of immigrants and children of natives disappear after conditioning on family characteristics. In many European countries, instead, significant differences in test scores between natives and immigrants remain, even after controlling for family characteristics. This suggests that there may be considerable diversity in educational institutions between countries, possibly related to their experience with larger scale immigration.

DISCUSSION AND CONCLUSION

This chapter provides an overview of immigration to Europe, and of the experience of immigrants in the European labor markets. Our brief historical review shows that the different historical circumstances of European countries (like their colonial past) as well as their economic developments, and the demand for labor of their industries in the period after the Second World War, led to different immigration intensities from different origin countries. As a result, different countries in Europe today are home to very dissimilar immigrant populations, in terms of origin, ethnicity, and education. Further, while some countries were home to large immigrant populations already in the 1960s, others experienced large immigration only over the last two decades. Overall, however, large-scale immigration, and in particular immigration from remote parts of the world, is a far more recent phenomenon for any European country, in comparison to the United States.

Across all countries in Europe, immigrants tend to have lower levels of education than natives, with the exception of the United Kingdom. There is a large variation in educational attainments of immigrants according to their origin countries.

Further, immigrants tend to have lower employment probabilities. Similarly, we find that in most countries immigrants hold jobs that are lower ranked in terms of their income potential, even conditional on education. This is particularly the case for non-EU immigrants, who are employed in lower ranked occupations than natives in all countries.

Investigation of the position of immigrants in the overall wage distribution of the receiving countries is—due to data availability—restricted to a subset of countries: Belgium, Germany, Finland, France, and Italy. The picture that emerges is in line with our previous findings: Immigrants are predominantly positioned at the lower parts of the overall wage distributions. Again, we establish large differences according to origin country: although immigrants from the EU-15 countries are fairly similarly distributed across wage distribution deciles to natives, immigrants from non-OECD countries are more likely than natives to be at the bottom of the wage distribution. Consistent with our results on employment probabilities and occupational distribution, differences in education and demographic characteristics between immigrants and natives do not explain these wage differences.

Disadvantage seems to be transferred to the next generation: We show that an over-proportionally large fraction of the children of immigrants, in particular those from non-EU countries, grow up in households that are at the very bottom of the income distribution. About 3 percent of all households consist of parents who are both in the lowest decile of the earnings distribution (or a single parent who is). These households have about 2.5 percent of all children below the age of fifteen. However, 3.6 percent of all children with EU-immigrant background live in such households, and nearly 20 percent of all children with a non-EU-immigrant background. These numbers are quite dramatic, and suggest that disadvantage and poverty affects a substantial fraction of immigrant children.

What conclusions can we draw from this? The picture that emerges for Europe's immigration experience is one of considerable heterogeneity of immigrant populations across the different recipient countries, in terms of ethnicity and country of origin, as well as in terms of education. Across all countries, it seems that immigrants are economically disadvantaged, even if we compare them to natives with the same characteristics. This disadvantage is more pronounced for immigrants from non-EU countries. As we also point out, in comparison with the United States, immigration to Europe is a relatively recent phenomenon. Thus, one reason for the disadvantaged situation of immigrants may be that institutions in European countries have not yet been sufficiently adapted to accommodate foreign born individuals. The large inflows of immigrants into most European countries over recent decades were seldom accompanied by a clear immigration policy or strategies about the long-term integration into economic and social structures. For instance, access to many jobs may require types of social capital that immigrants usually do not have, or access may not be based on meritocratic considerations only. Also, recognition of education and experience acquired in the home countries may be difficult, due to rigid regulations. This might be more of a problem for non-EU immigrants, because EU laws facilitate access of EU immigrants to labor markets of EU member states. On the other hand, in countries like the United States with a long history of large-scale immigration, institutions may have adjusted over the decades and centuries.

To investigate this further is in our view an interesting and exciting research agenda, with important implications for policy. Although this is beyond the scope of this chapter, we would like to conclude with some evidence that is in line with this hypothesis. As we explain, variation across European countries in their exposure to immigration since 1950 is considerable. This allows us to address the question whether the employment gap between immigrants and natives, or the occupational segregation, is larger in countries with a more recent immigration experience. In figures 13.6 through 13.9, we plot the index of occupational dissimilarity between recent immigrants (who have been in the country for at most two years) and natives, and the gap in employment probability gap against the share of foreign born in 2010 over the share of foreign born in 1960, for the European countries in our data set.[8] The latter is an indicator for the length of "exposure" that countries have to foreign-born individuals.

The figures clearly illustrate that both occupational dissimilarity and employment gaps are larger for countries where the ratio of the foreign born in 2010 to 1960 is larger. In particular, a longer exposure to immigration has a greater effect on the labor market assimilation of non-EU immigrants, but does not have an impact on employment probability differential for EU immigrants.

Although these figures are merely suggestive and have to be evaluated with care, they are compatible with the hypothesis that the disadvantage of immigrant populations and their children is partly related to institutions and perhaps the accessibility of labor markets on meritocratic grounds. To explore this further, we plot in figures 13.10 through 13.13 the index of occupational dissimilarity and the employment probability gap for recent immigrants relative to natives against the 2008 OECD index of strictness of employment protection legislation.[9] This index measures the procedures and costs involved in dismissing individuals or groups of workers, or in hiring workers on fixed-term or temporary work agency contracts, and takes values on a six-point scale, with higher values corresponding to stricter regulation.

Figures 13.10 and 13.11 show that recent immigrants in countries with stricter employment protection legislation exhibit an occupational distribution that is more distinct from that of natives, especially for non-EU immigrants. This suggests that in these countries, access to particular occupations is more difficult. However, the gap relative to natives in employment probabilities does not seem to be correlated with the index of employment protection legislation. If anything, it displays a negative correlation with the employment gaps of EU immigrants.

Thus, comparisons of figures 13.6 and 13.7 with 13.10 and 13.11 warn against too simplistic interpretations of one specific feature of host countries' institutions as a reason for immigrants' labor market disadvantage. Nevertheless, we believe that institutions may play an important part in explaining some of the findings presented in this paper. Identifying those that facilitate the assimilation of immigrants is an important area of future research.

FIGURE 13.6 / Historical Immigration and Occupational Dissimilarity, Recent EU Immigrants

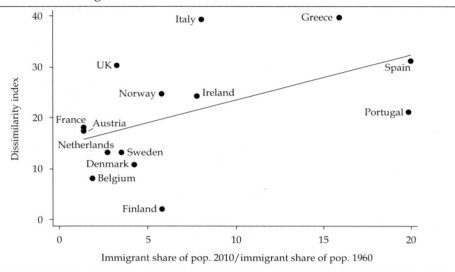

Source: Authors' compilation based on World Bank World Development Indicators and European Labor Force Survey (2007–2009).
Note: We define *recent immigrants* as immigrants who have been in the country for no more than two years.

FIGURE 13.7 / Historical Immigration and Occupational Dissimilarity, Recent Non-EU Immigrants

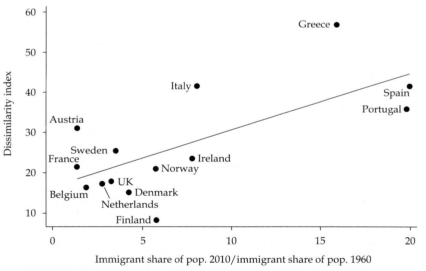

Source: Author's compilation based on World Bank World Development Indicators and European Labor Force Survey (2007–2009).
Note: We define *recent immigrants* as immigrants who have been in the country for no more than two years.

FIGURE 13.8 / Historical Immigration and Employment Probability, Recent EU Immigrants

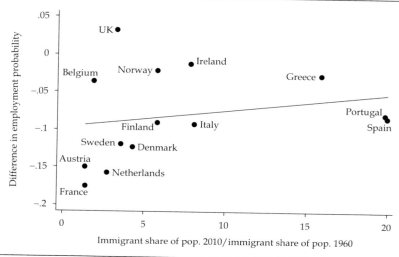

Source: Author's compilation based on World Bank World Development Indicators and European Labor Force Survey (2007–2009).
Note: We define *recent immigrants* as immigrants who have been in the country for no more than two years. Gaps in employment probabilities are relative to natives, and conditional on age, education, region, and gender.

FIGURE 13.9 / Historical Immigration and Employment Probability, Recent Non-EU Immigrants

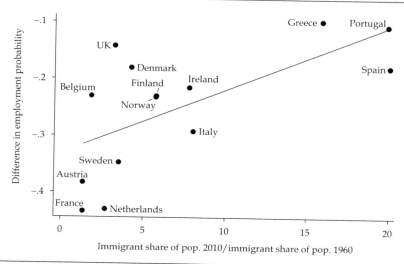

Source: Author's compilation based on World Bank World Development Indicators and European Labor Force Survey (2007–2009).
Note: We define *recent immigrants* as immigrants who have been in the country for no more than two years. Gaps in employment probabilities are relative to natives, and conditional on age, education, region, and gender.

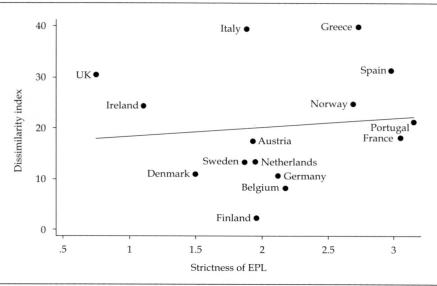

Source: Authors' compilation based on OECD Indicators of Employment Protection and European Labor Force Survey (2007–2009).
Note: We define *recent immigrants* as immigrants who have been in the country for no more than two years.

FIGURE 13.11 / Employment Protection Legislation and Occupational Dissimilarity, Recent Non-EU Immigrants

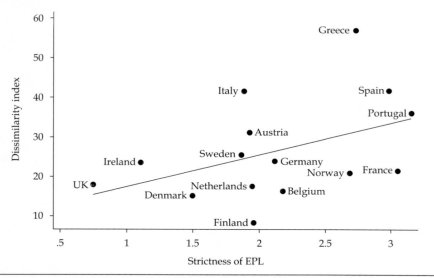

Source: Authors' compilation based on OECD Indicators of Employment Protection and European Labor Force Survey (2007–2009).
Note: We define *recent immigrants* as immigrants who have been in the country for no more than two years.

FIGURE 13.12 / Employment Protection Legislation and Employment Probability, Recent EU Immigrants

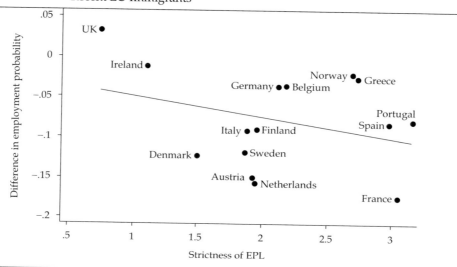

Source: Authors' compilation based on OECD Indicators of Employment Protection and European Labor Force Survey (2007–2009).
Note: We define *recent immigrants* as immigrants who have been in the country for no more than two years. Gaps in employment probabilities are relative to natives, and conditional on age, education, region, and gender.

FIGURE 13.13 / Employment Protection Legislation and Employment Probability, Recent Non-EU Immigrants

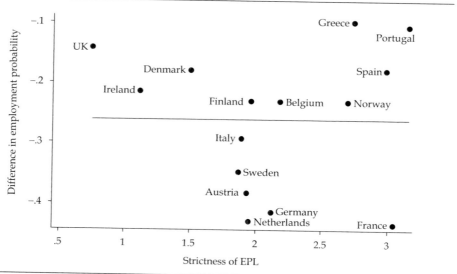

Source: Authors' compilation based on OECD Indicators of Employment Protection and European Labor Force Survey (2007–2009).
Note: We define *recent immigrants* as immigrants who have been in the country for no more than two years. Gaps in employment pro

Acknowledgments—We would like to thank David Card, Enrico Moretti, and Steve Raphael for their constructive comments and suggestions on earlier versions of this paper. We also benefitted of the feedbacks from participants to the National Poverty Center (NPC) Immigration, Poverty, and Socioeconomic Inequality Pre-Conference and Conference in Ann Arbor and Berkeley, respectively. We acknowledge support by the National Poverty Center at the University of Michigan, the Russell Sage Foundation and the Norface programme on migration.

NOTES

1. EU-15 countries: Austria, Belgium, Denmark, Finland, France, Germany, Greece, Ireland, Italy, Luxembourg, Netherlands, Portugal, Spain, Sweden, and United Kingdom; NMS-12 countries (new member states): Bulgaria, the Czech Republic, Estonia, Cyprus, Latvia, Lithuania, Hungary, Malta; Poland, Romania, Slovenia, and Slovakia.

2. The current (2010) EULFS release contains the income decile variable for Greece, Portugal, and the United Kingdom as well, but in these countries there are relevant coding errors, so we exclude them from our analysis.

3. This classification may be problematic for two reasons. A first general problem is that ISCED may not reflect adequately the educational system of all countries, and can therefore lead to difficulties in cross-country comparisons. A second problem, specific to immigration, relates to the fact that foreign qualifications have to be first translated into a country-specific qualification, and then each country's qualification is recoded according to ISCED.

4. *Unconditional* differences in employment probabilities between immigrants and natives are obtained as coefficients on a foreign-born dummy in a regression of a dummy for employment on the foreign-born dummy and year-quarter interaction dummies. *Conditional* differences are obtained from the same regression augmented with a gender dummy, regional dummies, dummies for five-year age brackets, and dummies for lower-secondary, secondary, and tertiary education. We run separate regressions by country, and compute heteroscedasticity-robust standard errors.

5. International Standard Classification of Occupations.

6. The unconditional differences in the probability of being in the bottom decile of the distribution of earnings between immigrants and natives are obtained as coefficients on EU and non-EU-immigrant dummies in a regression of a dummy for being in the bottom decile of the national earnings distribution on the foreign-born dummies and quarter dummies. "Conditional" differences are obtained from the same regression augmented with a gender dummy, regional dummies, dummies for five-year age brackets, dummies for lower-secondary, secondary, and tertiary education, and dummies for 1-digit ISCO codes. We run separate regressions by country, and compute heteroscedasticity-robust standard errors.

7. Note, however, that the sample of children from low-income households in Germany is very small.

8. Data are from the World Bank World Development Indicators. Historical immigration figures are not available for Germany.

9. Similarly, Joshua Angrist and Adriana Kugler (2003) and Francesco D'Amuri and Giovanni Peri (2011) argue that the cross-country differences in the impact of immigration on the labor market outcomes of natives across Europe might be due to differences in the flexibility of national labor markets.

REFERENCES

Angrist, Joshua D., and Adriana Kugler. 2003. "Protective or Counter-Productive? Labor Market Institutions and the Effect of Immigration on EU Natives." *The Economic Journal* 113(488): F302–31.

Blanden, Jo, Paul Gregg, and Lindsey Macmillan. 2007. "Accounting for Intergenerational Income Persistence: Noncognitive Skills, Ability and Education." *The Economic Journal* 117:C43–60.

Carrington, William J., and Kenneth R. Troske. 1997. "On Measuring Segregation in Samples with Small Units." *Journal of Business and Economic Statistics* 15(4): 402–9.

Corak, Miles. 2006. *Research on Economic Inequality*, vol. 13, *Dynamics of Inequality and Poverty*. Bingley, West Yorkshire: Emerald Group.

D'Amuri, Francesco, and Giovanni Peri. 2011. "Immigration, Jobs and Labor Market Institutions: Evidence from Europe." *NBER* working paper 17139. Cambridge, Mass.: National Bureau of Economic Research.

Dustmann, Christian, and Albrecht Glitz. 2011. "Migration and Education." In *Handbook of the Economics of Education*, vol. IV, edited by Eric A. Hanushek, Stephen Machin, and Ludger Woessmann. Waltham, Mass.: Elsevier.

Dustmann, Christian, Tommaso Frattini, and Gianandrea Lanzara. 2012. "Educational Achievement of Second-Generation Immigrants: An International Comparison." *Economic Policy* 27(69): 143–85.

Dustmann, Christian, Tommaso Frattini, and Anna Rosso. 2012. "The Effect of Emigration from Poland on Polish Wages." *CReAM* discussion paper no. 29/12. London: Centre for Research and Analysis of Migration.

Dustmann, Christian, Maria Casanova, Ian Preston, Michael Fertig, and Christoph M. Schmidt. 2003. "The Impact of EU Enlargement on Migration Flows." Home Office Online Report 25/03. London: Home Office, Immigration and Nationality Directorate of the UK.

Fasani, Francesco. 2010. "The Quest for 'La Dolce Vita' Undocumented Migration in Italy." In *Irregular Migration in Europe: Myths and Realities*, edited by Anna Triandafyllidou. London: Ashgate.

Ganzeboom, Harry B. G., De Graaf, Paul M., and Donald J. Treiman (1992). "A Standard International Socio-Economic Index of Occupational Status." *Social Science Research* 21(1): 1–56.

Glitz, Albrecht. 2012. "The Labor Market Impact of Immigration: A Quasi-Experiment Exploiting Immigrant Location Rules in Germany." *Journal of Labor Economics* 30(1): 175–213.

Hellerstein, Judith, David Neumark, and Melissa McInerney. 2007. "Changes in Workplace Segregation in the United States Between 1990 and 2000: Evidence from Matched

Employer-Employee Data." *NBER* working paper 13080. Cambridge, Mass.: National Bureau for Economic Research.

Hoefer, Michael, Nancy Rytina, and Bryan C. Baker. 2010. "Estimates of the Unauthorized Immigrant Population Residing in the United States: January 2009." Washington: U.S. Department of Homeland Security, Office of Immigration Statistics, Policy Directorate.

Jäntti, Markus, Brent Bratsberg, Knut Røed, Oddbjørn Raaum, Robin A. Naylor, Eva Osterbacka, Anders Bjorklund, and Tor Eriksson. 2006. "American Exceptionalism in a New Light: A Comparison of Intergenerational Earnings Mobility in the Nordic Countries, the United Kingdom and the United States." *IZA* discussion paper 1938. Bonn: Institute for the Study of Labor.

Kovacheva, Vesela, and Dita Vogel. 2009. "The Size of the Irregular Foreign Resident Population in the European Union in 2002, 2005 and 2008: Aggregated Estimates." *Database on Irregular Migration* working paper no. 4. Hamburg: Hamburg Institute of International Economics.

McDonald, James R. 1965. "The Repatriation of French Algerians, 1962–63." *International Migration* 3(3): 146–57.

Salt, John, and Hugh Clout, eds. 1976. *Migration in Post-War Europe: Geographical Essays.* London: Oxford University Press.

Solon, Gary. 2002. "Cross-Country Differences in Intergenerational Earnings Mobility." *Journal of Economic Perspectives* 16(3): 59–66.

Vogel, Dita, and Vesela Kovacheva. 2009. Calculation table of EU estimate 2008, last change 30 September 2009, Annex 3 to Kovacheva and Vogel (2009).

Index

Index

blacks (*cont.*)
personal income, **269, 270**; occupational attainment, **187, 190, 214**; population share and redistributive social spending, 398; poverty rate, **150, 151, 184, 271**; socioeconomic status, **181**; wealth, **274**. *See also* African Americans; African immigrants
Blalock, Hubert, 386
Bleakley, Hoyt, 65, 68
Bloemraad, Irene, 23, 381
Bohn, Sarah, 20–21, 266, 282, 288, 312*n*3, 326
border enforcement, 139, 258, 259, 264–67, 291
Border Protection, Antiterrorism, and Illegal Immigration Control Act (2005), 266
Borjas, George, 33, 58*n*3, 207, 415*n*36
Bracero Program, 259, 260
Brown, Jerry, 249
Brown, Susan, 171
Brownell, Peter, 353
Buchanan, Patrick, 263
Buchmueller, Thomas, 313*n*5
Bureau of Economic Analysis (BEA), 389–90, **391,** 393, 413*n*26
Bureau of Labor Statistics, 413*n*28
business licenses, 283, 285, 287, 298

California: ballot initiatives and referenda, 385; Cash Assistance Program for Immigrants, 407; foreign-born population, 381; high school counseling services, 251*n*8; immigrant settlement, 139; immigrant welfare access, 407; immigration rates, 37, 38; noncitizen population, 383; poverty effects of immigration, **46–47**; tax and spending attitudes, **384**; undocumented immigrants, 239, 240, 249, 264, 312*n*1
Cambodian immigrants: poverty rates, 137
Canadian immigrants, **4**
CAPI (Cash Assistance Program for Immigrants), 407
Card, David, 1, 57*n*1, 88
Caribbean immigrants: definition of, 130*n*7; educational attainment, **185,** 186; occu-

pational attainment, **187**; poverty rate, **4, 6,** 184; segregation levels, **102,** 103, **104, 109, 111, 113, 122,** 125, **126**; and segregation of native-born blacks, 117–19; socioeconomic status, **181,** 182–83
Case, Anne, 413*n*28
Cash Assistance Program for Immigrants (CAPI), 407
cash assistance programs, 317–20, 393, 401–2. *See also* Aid to Families with Dependent Children (AFDC); Supplemental Security Income (SSI); Temporary Assistance for Needy Families (TANF)
census data. *See* U.S. Census
Central American immigrants: immigration waves, 258–59; legal status, 261; poverty rate, **4, 6, 15**; segregation levels, **102, 109, 113**; and segregation of native-born blacks, 117–19. *See also specific countries*
Chamber of Commerce et al. v. Whiting, 285
Chavez, Leo, 246, 262, 387
Chicago, Ill.: Spanish speakers in, 61. *See also* gateway cities
child poverty, 150, 317, 318–19, 346–60
children of immigrants: assimilation, 170–71; definitions, 179–80, 189; demographic and family characteristics, 211–15; educational attainment, 2, 16, **195**; in EU, 445–47, 448; human capital studies, 236; occupational prestige, 197–200; with undocumented parent, 240; with undocumented status, 277; voting, 407. *See also* intergenerational mobility, children of immigrants
Children of Immigrants Longitudinal Survey (CILS), 202*n*1
Children's Health Insurance Program Reauthorization Act (2009), **323**
child support, share of income from, **344, 345, 346, 347, 348, 349**
Chin, Aimee, 65, 68
Chinese immigrants: academic achievement, 171, 215–17, 220–25; demographic and

family characteristics, 211–12, **213**; educational attainment, **185,** 186, **190,** 191, **192, 193,** 194, 195–96, 206, 207, 211–15; in inter-ethnic variation in social mobility study, 211; intergenerational mobility, 202; occupational attainment, 186, **187, 190,** 196, 197, **198, 214**; population, 211; poverty rate, **184**; socioeconomic status, **181,** 182; welfare dependency stereotype, 387
The Chinese Yellow Book, 221
Ciccone, Antonio, 32
CILS (Children of Immigrants Longitudinal Survey), 202*n*1
citizenship status. *See* legal status
Citrin, Jack, 387
class consciousness, 388
Clinton, Bill: welfare reform, 381, 408
Clout, Hugh, 424
coaches, 223–25
coethnics, role in social mobility, 209, 226
Cohn, D'Vera, 313*n*4, 353
cohort analysis, of poverty rates, 13–14. *See also* generation status
Cold War, 262
college education: Asian immigrants, 215–20; by country of origin, 184–86; earnings premium, 200; financial aid, 237, 240, 249; undocumented immigrants, 240, 242–44, 247–50. *See also* educational attainment
Colorado: immigration legislation, 283–84; immigration rates, 37–38; poverty effects of immigration, 45–48
community colleges, 218, 240, 247
Conchas, Gilberto, 236–37
Congressional Budget Office, 287
congressional districts, 385–86, **410**
Connecticut: poverty rates, 138
construction industry, 291–92, 293, 307, 309
continuous gateway cities: defined, 140, **141**; population, **141, 143**; poverty rates, 144–48, 152–54
Contra intervention, 261

Index

emerging gateway cities: defined, 140, **141**; population, **141, 143**; poverty rates, 144–48, 152–54, 156–57, 161

employers: E-Verify use, 283, 284, 285–86, 287, 311–12; wage and hour violations, 307

employment: EU immigrant outcomes, 432–45, 448, 449, **451, 453**; formal employment, 266, 295–98; hours of work, 74–75, **76,** 80, **82**; job instability, 239; self-employment, 287, 298–302, 306, 308–11; in underground economy, 306–8; undocumented immigrants, 241–42, 245–47. *See also* labor market competition; occupational attainment and prestige

employment protection legislation, 449, **452–53**

English-language skills: by age at arrival, 64–65; by education level, 62–63, 66–68; and segregation, 98, 99, 110–11, 119–23, 124, 125–27; by time in U.S., 64–65; and wages, 60, 62, 65–70, 75–79. *See also* labor market competition and English-language skills

entropy index, 100

ethnic enclaves, 99, 123, 209

EULFS (European Labor Force Survey). *See* European Labor Force Survey (EULFS)

European Economic Community, 424

European Free Trade Association (EFTA), 430

European immigrants, in EU, 423–56; children of, 445–47, 448; conclusions, 447–53; data sources, 430; educational outcomes, 430–32, 447; employment outcomes, 432–45, 448; history of, 423–27; institutional shortcomings and labor market disadvantage, 448–53; introduction, 24–25, 421, 423; trends, 427–29; undocumented immigrants, 427–29; vs. U.S. immigration, 448–49

European immigrants, in U.S.: population, 3; poverty rate, **4, 6**; segregation levels, **102**, 103, **104, 109, 111, 113, 122**, 125, **126**; and segregation of

native-born blacks, 117–19; social spending effects, 387

European Labor Force Survey (EULFS): children of immigrants, 445–47; educational attainment, 431–32; employment outcomes, 432–45; generally, 430

E-Verify, 283, 284, 285–86, 287, 311–12

exposure index, 100

family assistance transfers, 317–20, 393, 401–2. *See also* Aid to Families with Dependent Children (AFDC); Temporary Assistance for Needy Families (TANF)

family characteristics, inter-ethnic variation in, 211–15

Farm Security and Rural Investment Act (2002), **323,** 326

Fayetteville, Ariz.: poverty effects of immigration, **49–50**; poverty rates, 38

Feliciano, Cynthia, 202*n*2

Filipino immigrants: educational attainment, **185,** 186, **190,** 191, **192, 193,** 194; intergenerational mobility, 202; occupational attainment, 186, **187, 190,** 196, 197, **198**; poverty rate, **184**; socioeconomic status, **181,** 182

financial aid, 237, 240, 249

financial services, 239

Finland, immigrants in: educational attainment, **431**; employment outcomes, **433, 434**; institutional shortcomings and labor market disadvantage, **450–53**; occupational distribution, **436, 440**; population, **428**; wages and earnings, 441–45

fiscal capacity, of states, 393, 394–95, 396, 414*n*32

fixed effects models, 398–99

Flaming, Daniel, 307

Florida: poverty effects of immigration, **46–47**

Foner, Nancy, 237

food insecurity, 316

Food Stamp Quality Control, 341–42

food stamps: data sources, 362; government spending trends, 317, **318,** 388, 389, 390, **391**; immigrant eligibility, 315, 320, 321, **324–25,** 326,

372–73; immigrant program participation, 332, **335,** 340, 341–42, 361; number of recipients, 317, **318**; poverty reduction, 319; share of income from, **344, 345, 346, 347, 348, 349**; welfare reform impact, 315

foreclosures, 273

foreign-born population statistics: English skills, 63; mean hourly wages, **68**; by metro area, 140–44; poverty rates, **68,** 137, 144–48, **151, 154, 155,** 156–59, 161; in Puerto Rico, 83–84; and social redistribution, 406–7; by state, **409–10**; trends, 1, 3, 99, 257, 423

formal employment, 266, 295–98

former gateway cities: defined, 140, **141–42**; population, **141–42, 143**; poverty rates, 144–48, 152–54

Fort Lauderdale, Fla.: poverty effects of immigration, **49–50**

Fox, Cybelle, 23, 381, 387

fractionalization, 387–88, 396, 399–405, 406

framing, 208–9, 215–25, 264

France, immigrants in: children in immigrant households, **445,** 446–47; educational attainment, **431**; employment outcomes, **433, 434**; institutional shortcomings and labor market disadvantage, **450–53**; low-income households, 446, **447**; occupational distribution, **436, 440**; population, 425, 427, **428, 445**; undocumented immigrants, **429**; wages and earnings, 441–45

Frattini, Tommaso, 24–25, 423, 446

Freeman, Richard, 58*n*3

Fremstad, Shawn, **369**

friendship networks, 222–23

gateway cities: classification of, 140, **141–42**; poverty rate trends, 144–48, 161; poverty rate variation, 148–59; segregation, 107–8, 110, 117–19, 121–23, 127; settlement in, 98, 138–44; Singer's typology, 140. *See also* new immigrant destinations

Gelatt, Julia, 270–71

Index

income, household: composition before and after welfare reform, 317, 342–46; immigrant sponsor requirements, 265; by immigrant status, **329**; low-skilled Hispanic men, **310**; noncitizens, 383; in poverty measure, 328; and segregation, 104–5; undocumented immigrants, 239

income, personal, 269–70, **305**, **310**, 396. *See also* wages and earnings

income maintenance programs, 388–92, 399–400

independent contractors, 287, 298–302, 308–11

index of dissimilarity. *See* dissimilarity index

Indian immigrants, **4, 6**

inequality: education, 235–37; growth in U.S., 381; immigration effects, 169; literature review, 207–8; occupations, 191; and redistributive social spending, 383; segmented assimilation theory, 200

informal employment, 306–8

initiatives and referenda, 385

in-kind transfers, 319

institutional shortcomings and labor market disadvantage, EU, 448–53

instrumental variables technique, 29, **91**, 121, 125

Integrated Public Use Microdata Series (IPUMS), 177–78, 376*n*27

intergenerational mobility, introduction, 13–19, 167

intergenerational mobility, children of immigrants, 169–205; conclusions, 200–202; data sources, 170, 177–79; educational attainment, 173, 184–86, 188, 189–96; introduction, 16, 169–70; measurement of, 173–77; occupational attainment, 173, 186–91, 196–200; poverty rates, 183–84; socioeconomic standing of foreign-born in sending vs. receiving country, 180–83; theoretical considerations, 170–73

intergenerational mobility, inter-ethnic variation in, 206–31; conclusions, 225–27; data sources, 209–10; demo-

graphic and family characteristics, 212–15, **213**; introduction, 17–18, 206–7; methodology, 207–11; social frames, 208–9, 215–25

intergenerational mobility, undocumented 1.5-generation immigrants, 232–53; barriers, 239–42; college education, 240, 242–44, 247–48; conclusions, 249–50; glass ceiling, 248–49; high school resources, 241, 242–45; introduction, 18–19, 232–35; literature review, 235–37; methodology, 237–39; transitions to work or adulthood, 241–42, 245–47

international socioeconomic index (ISEI), 186–89

International Standard Classification of Education (ISCED), 431, 435

interviews, 238

IPUMS (Integrated Public Use Microdata Series), 177–78, 376*n*27

Iranzo, Susana, 33

Ireland, immigrants in: children in immigrant households, **445**; educational attainment, **431**; employment outcomes, **433, 434**; institutional shortcomings and labor market disadvantage, **450–53**; occupational distribution, **436, 440**; population, 427, **428, 445**; undocumented immigrants, **429**

Isardi, William, 272

ISCED (International Standard Classification of Education), 431, 435

ISEI (international socioeconomic index), 186–89

isolation index, 100, 273–74

Italy, immigrants in: children in immigrant households, **445**, 446–47; educational attainment, **431**; employment outcomes, **433, 434**; institutional shortcomings and labor market disadvantage, **450–53**; low-income households, 446, **447**; occupational distribution, **436, 440**; population, 427, **428, 445**; undocumented immigrants, **429**; wages and earnings, 441–45

Japanese immigrants, 211

Jewish immigrants, 226–27

Jiménez, Tomás, 218

job instability, 239

Johnson, Lyndon B., 381

Justice, U.S. Department of, 263

Katz, Larry, 58*n*3

Kaushal, Neeraj, 414*n*36

Kesler, Christel, 23, 381

Key, V. O., 386

King, Miriam, **391**

Kochhar, Rakesh, 353

Kodras, Janet, 138

Korean immigrants: educational attainment, **185**, 186, **190**, 191, **192, 193**, 194, 195–96, 206; occupational attainment, **187, 190**, 196, 197, **198**; poverty rate, **184**; socioeconomic status, **181**, 182

Kovacheva, Vesela, **429**

Kugler, Adriana, 455*n*9

Kups, Sarah, 353

labor market access, 236

labor market competition and English-language skills, 60–97; conclusions, 88–89; data sources, 61, 73–75; English-language skills, 62–65; introduction, 9–11, 60–62; methodology, 70–73, 89–92; poverty implications, 61, 66–69, 87–89; results, 75–87; wages, 60, 62, 65–70, 75–79

labor market competition and native poverty, 29–59; conclusions, 51; immigration and poverty trends, 33–38; introduction, 1, 8–9, 29–32; methodology, 32–33, 52–57; results, 39–51

labor market equilibrium model, 30

landscaping industry, 307, 309

Lang, Kevin, 72

language development, 65

language discrimination, 72

language skills, English. *See* English-language skills

Lanzara, Gianandrea, 446

Las Vegas, Nev.: immigration rates, 38; poverty effects of immigration, **49–50**

Latin American immigrants: definition of, 130*n*7; discrimination against, 263–64; earnings, **443**; educational attainment, **432**; in EU, 427,